The Moneywise Guide
to
NORTH AMERICA

USA   CANADA   MEXICO

By Michael Haag, Anna Crew and Vicki León

★
PRESIDIO

THE MONEYWISE GUIDE TO NORTH AMERICA
17th Edition

© Copyright Michael Haag and Anna Crew
ISBN 0 902743 29 5 (Britain)

Co-published by Travelaid Publishing (Michael Haag Limited),
PO Box 369, London NW3 4ER, England and Presidio Press,
31 Pamaron Way, Novato, CA 94947, USA

Library of Congress Cataloging in Publication Data

von Haag, Michael.
  The moneywise guide to North America.

  1. North America—Description and travel—1981-
—Guide-books. I. Crew, Anna. II. León, Vicki. I. Title.
E41.V66 1983   917′.04538   83–3322
ISBN 0–89141–172–0 (USA)

Cover design: Colin Elgie

Moneywise Series General Editor: Michael Haag

Typeset, printed and bound in Great Britain by The Pitman Press, Lower Bristol Road,
Bath BA2 3BL

CONTENTS

THE UNDISCOVERED CONTINENT

The most amazing thing about North America is that after a spell of travelling you find it so different from what you expected it to be. Everyone thinks he has a good idea of what it is all about. Its technology, politics, media and entertainments daily make their mark the world over. It is the most publicised continent on earth.

But the projected image hides, both from foreigners and North Americans themselves, a largely undiscovered continent. The polyglot of peoples out of which Canada, the United States and Mexico are each differently formed can make Europe, for example, look comparatively homogeneous. Just a ride on the New York City subway is enough to convince anyone of that.

There are huge tracts of magnificent landscapes, unsettled and hardly explored. Forests, glaciers, deserts and jungles; mountains, canyons, prairies and seashores. Orchards in Oregon, farming valleys in Vermont, pre-Columbian Indian settlements, many of them unchanged and still inhabited, in Mexico and Arizona, totem poles in British Columbia, fishing villages in Nova Scotia.

The cities: Los Angeles an exploding star, San Francisco riding on a sea of hills, New York a concrete canyon, Chicago scraping the sky with the longest fingers in the world, Houston a port and rocket centre, New Orleans blowing jazz across the Mississippi, Québec only geographically in the New World, its soul still back across the Atlantic, Mexico City a brilliant mosaic of Spanish and Aztec design.

The variety and complexity are more than a lifetime of sitting in front of a television set will even remotely convey to you. And there is the discovery too of the instant, of even the future, for North America is always reaching ahead and you have to be there, in the running, to get a glimpse of tomorrow.

THE MONEYWISE GUIDE

This is a Guide to most of the usual and many of the unusual places in North America and should prove of service to anyone, but most of all the moneywise traveller. North America can be an expensive continent if you let it. But part of its great variety is the many places to eat and sleep and the many different ways of moving about from which you can choose to suit your pocket, and with the help of this Guide it can be a real bargain. Anyone who is happy about spending more money will easily find a $45 hotel bed and a $15 meal, in which case this Guide is content with showing you the way to the Statue of Liberty or the Grand Canyon. But for people really on a budget, this is also a Guide to thousands of inexpensive places to rest your head and fill your belly *and* to get you to the Grand Canyon on a shoestring.

In separate sections this Guide covers the USA, Canada and Mexico. General introductions precede detailed coverage of each country. Make a point of first reading these background chapters: here you will find general information on each country, facts about visas, currency, health and other things, money-saving tips on eating, accommodation and travel. *Note that much of the information found in the US Background section will be of value for travel to Canada and Mexico.*

Each country is then divided into regions, eg The Midwest, and in the case of the USA and Canada, states and provinces within each region follow *alphabetically*. There is also an Index at the back of the Guide.

Hotel and restaurant listings are the result of the first-hand experience of the Guide's authors and its thousands of readers since the preceding edition. Prices quoted are usually the lowest available. Within the same month at the same hotel, one traveller might spend more on a room than another. This is usually because the rooms were of different standards, but never be afraid to question room rates or even to bargain over them. On the other hand, you should allow for inflation which, so far as travel expenditure is concerned anyway, is still running fairly high in America, Canada and especially Mexico.

Please remember that the maps in this Guide are only intended to give you a rough orientation when first arriving in the city. They are not, nor are they intended to be, fully comprehensive. If staying anywhere for any length of time, buy a good street map, though first see if you can get one free from the local Chamber of Commerce or tourist office.

THE FUTURE OF THIS GUIDE

Quoted comments throughout the Guide are genuine remarks made by travellers over the years. Comments from present readers—the more descriptive the better—will add to the colour and usefulness of the next edition.

For brief comments, and most importantly for correcting or adding information about accommodation, fares and so on, please use the Correction and Addition slips at the back of the Guide. Hotel brochures, local bus schedules, maps and similar tidbits are gratefully received. Also welcome are longer accounts, so feel free to send in letters.

In all cases, please write only on one side of each sheet of paper.

1. BACKGROUND USA

BEFORE YOU GO

Before departing for the United States you must obtain one of seven types of **visa** from the nearest American embassy or consulate.

1. *Visitors (B) Visa.* This allows you to remain in the US for a maximum of six months, the period to be determined on arrival by immigration officials based on how long they think your money will hold out. When you first obtain your visa abroad it may be stamped 'valid indefinitely'. This means it may be used repeatedly; but each stay is limited to the six-month maximum. You may not work on a Visitors Visa.

2. *In Transit (C) Visa.* This allows you to go from A to B via the US and to stay in the US a maximum of 29 days. It can be issued for multiple entries.

3. *Student (F) Visa.* You must pursue a fulltime course of study for one year minimum at a school that is identified and approved in advance. Sometimes you have to post a money bond before entering the US. It allows you to work under certain circumstances.

4. *Temporary Workers (H) Visa.* Issued only if you offer specialised skills or qualifications, and requires a written offer from your prospective employer. It's very difficult to obtain.

5. *Exchange (J) Visa.* Issued only if you are part of an organised Exchange Visitor Programme. It allows you to work subject to certain conditions.

6. *Fiance (K) Visa.* Given for the purpose of marrying a US citizen within 90 days. Unfortunately it doesn't allow you to look for 'Mr/Miss Right' during the first 89; you have to show a petition from the spouse-to-be.

7. *Immigrants Visa.* This is the Big One that lets you remain in the US *ad infinitum*. It's subject to the quota limitations imposed on your country of origin. It also subjects you to the possibility of being conscripted into the US military, an eventuality designed to cool the ardour of many a would-be (male) citizen. It takes a long time to obtain.

Immigration officials ask you the purpose of your visit and how long you plan to stay. Probably you have arrived on a pleasure visit. If your visa permits you to work, say so. If you plan to work yet your visa does not allow it, this is no time to be candid. Lots of underground jobs do exist in casual labour, restaurant work and seasonal or farm work, and require little or no documentation. In answer to the question How long do you plan to stay? note that you need not possess X dollars per day or X amount of money. Rather immigration officials are looking for proof of planning. As a reader of this Guide, you're probably on a budget anyway. Immigration officials want to know how you're going

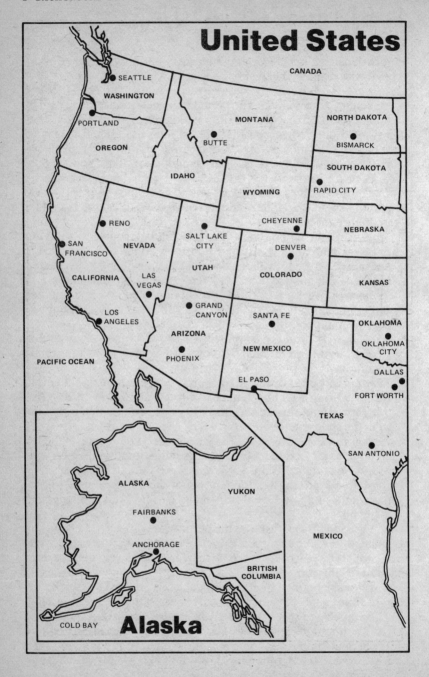

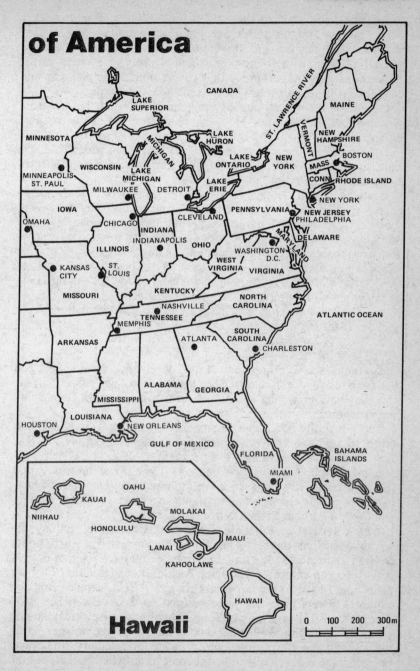

of America

CANADA

LAKE SUPERIOR

LAKE HURON

ST. LAWRENCE RIVER

MAINE

VERMONT

NEW HAMPSHIRE

BOSTON

MINNESOTA

WISCONSIN

MICHIGAN

LAKE ONTARIO

NEW YORK

MASS

CONN RHODE ISLAND

MINNEAPOLIS ST. PAUL

LAKE MICHIGAN

MILWAUKEE

DETROIT

LAKE ERIE

NEW YORK

IOWA

CHICAGO

INDIANA

CLEVELAND

PENNSYLVANIA

NEW JERSEY PHILADELPHIA

OMAHA

INDIANAPOLIS

OHIO

MARYLAND

DELAWARE

ILLINOIS

WASHINGTON D.C.

KANSAS CITY

ST. LOUIS

WEST VIRGINIA

VIRGINIA

MISSOURI

KENTUCKY

NASHVILLE

NORTH CAROLINA

ATLANTIC OCEAN

MEMPHIS

TENNESSEE

ARKANSAS

ATLANTA

SOUTH CAROLINA

CHARLESTON

ALABAMA

GEORGIA

MISSISSIPPI

HOUSTON

LOUISIANA

NEW ORLEANS

GULF OF MEXICO

FLORIDA

BAHAMA ISLANDS

MIAMI

OAHU

KAUAI

NIIHAU

MOLAKAI

HONOLULU

LANAI

MAUI

KAHOOLAWE

HAWAII

Hawaii

0   100   200   300 m

to manage. You need to show them things like your return ticket home; rail, air and bus passes; accommodation reservations; student or senior identification; etc. If you plan to stay in campsites, hostels, guest houses or with friends, tell them. If you have credit cards, show them. Anything to prove that you've done some planning and can make your resources last for the time you wish to stay.

Canadians do not require a visa, and if entering the US from anywhere in the Western Hemisphere do not require a passport either.

Unless you are coming from an infected area, in which case you must have proof of a smallpox vaccination, there are no **health requirements** for entry into the US.

Customs permit foreign residents to bring in one quart (0.946 litres) of alcoholic beverages—liquor, wine or beer (by persons at least 21 years of age), state laws permitting and for personal consumption, 200 cigarettes or 50 cigars or 2 kilos of tobacco or proportionate amounts of each (an additional quantity of 100 cigars may be brought in under your gift exemption), $100 worth of gifts provided you stay at least 72 hours and have not claimed the gift exemption in the previous six months, and your personal effects free of duty.

For further details on visa, health and customs regulations, contact the nearest American embassy or consulate.

GETTING THERE

This Guide is used by readers all over the world, and the best and least expensive way of reaching the United States will vary according to where you're starting out. Check advertisements, ask friends and travel agents.

The possibility of charter flights aside, your budget choice boils down to some sort of scheduled airline flight: economy, APEX, ABC or standby fare, or inclusive package.

Economy fares are pretty expensive; if you're willing to accept a few restrictions you can save a lot of money on other types of fare. (There *are* some cheap economy flights available, eg Metro Airlines and Capitol Airlines to the US from Brussels.)

APEX (Advance Purchase Excursion) tickets are sold by the scheduled airlines themselves and must be purchased at least 21 days before departure. At the time of purchase you must fix your date of departure and return; if you later decide to change either of these dates you'll have to pay a penalty charge. *ABC* (Advance Booking Charter) tickets have the same restrictions as APEX tickets, and despite the word 'charter' you'll probably find yourself travelling on a scheduled airline. The difference is that you have not purchased the ticket from the airline but from an intermediary, the travel operator; the cost is likely to be the same as an APEX ticket, but the operator will throw in a free travelling bag, inflight earphones, or whatever.

Standby fares are the cheapest; you buy the ticket when you like, but space is allocated only on the day of departure. Summer weekends are the most difficult times to get space; midweek departures are usually easier. These tickets are bought directly from the airline, which can advise you of your prospects a day or so before your intended date of departure.

Inclusive packages abound, offering considerable flexibility. Some, however, treat America as a substitute for two weeks on the Costa del Sol—there was never much excuse for fish and chips at Torremolinos when there was all of Spain to see, and there is even less excuse for two weeks of fish and chips in Miami when an entire continent awaits you and is so easy and cheap to explore.

Fly-drive packages including air fare, unlimited mileage car and accommodation vouchers are a good bet, especially if you're travelling as a family or with friends. Prices vary according to size of car, standard of accommodation and the number of people travelling together.

At the same time that you consider how to get to North America, you should be considering how to travel around once there. Certain discounts and travel passes may only be available to non-residents purchasing their tickets abroad; also, when you buy your tickets outside the US you save the sales tax. See the Travel section further on.

CLIMATE

Remember that you are not travelling over a country but across a vast continent and that the climate varies accordingly. Consider that the distance from New York to Miami is equivalent to that from London to Tangier, and that New York and Los Angeles are as distant from each other as London and Baghdad, and you get a good idea of what this can mean.

Indoors, these differences are minimised by central heating and air conditioning, but outside, winters can be very cold in Washington DC and even further south, and summers extremely hot everywhere.

Temperatures approaching 90°F (32°C) day after day, sometimes accompanied by a suffocating humidity, are not unusual in the summer. New York, Washington DC, New Orleans and the Deep South can be particularly unpleasant. As early as September, however, nights can be cool everywhere, and freezing in mountainous areas.

Some generalisations on climatic regions:

New England, the Northeast and Midwest. Cold in the winter, often humid in the summer and as hot as anywhere else in America including Florida and southern California.

The Southwest. Warm to hot throughout the year, and nearly always dry.

The Pacific States. Washington, Oregon and northern California have moderate climates: not too cold in the winter—though often wet, not too hot in the summer. San Francisco is often bathed in summer afternoon fogs. Southern California is warm to hot the year round, and nearly always dry.

The South. Hot in summer, mild in winter though agreeably warm in Florida.

The Mountains. In summer, days are warm but nights can be cold. Very cold throughout the winter.

The Deserts. Very hot and dry throughout the year, but can be cold at night.

What to Take and How to Take It. Take as little as possible, choose clothes for their use in a variety of situations and when you have made your final selection, halve it!

It is always a nuisance to have too much, and anyway you can purchase much of what you need—especially jeans, drip-drys and other casual clothes which tend to be cheaper in North America—during your travels once you are sure you do need it.

Laundromats are often open 24 hours a day. The cost of a wash is usually 75¢; drying machines usually take 25¢—you just keep feeding in the quarters.

Whatever luggage you take, make sure it's easy to handle. Getting on and off buses and trains, even just changing planes, can be an ordeal if your bags are too heavy or too many. The best solution is to take one hold-all, be it a suitcase or a backpack, and then a smaller bag which you can sling from your shoulder. Even when you have to check in your hold-all at the airport or bus station, you can keep all your documents, travellers' cheques and your paperback novel safely and conveniently by your side.

Some tips: at bus stations in particular, make absolutely certain that your bag is going on your bus and that you get a check-in ticket for it. You would be amazed at the number of times bag and body go off in different directions. And if you're a backpacker just arrived in a big city, you can usually leave your pack at one of the museums for free and then skip off to look for a room, or do a little sightseeing unencumbered.

TIME ZONES

The continental US is divided into four time zones, Eastern Standard Time, Central Standard Time, Mountain Standard Time and Pacific Standard Time. Exact zone boundaries are shown on most road maps. Noon EST = 11am CST = 10am MST = 9am PST. Standard time in Hawaii is two hours earlier than PST, ie 9am PST = 7am HST.

City temperatures (in Fahrenheit).

		Jan–Feb	Mar–Apr	May–June	Jul–Aug	Sep–Oct	Nov–Dec
CHICAGO	Low	20°	35°	56°	67°	53°	28°
	High	34	51	74	83	69	42
	Average	27	43	65	75	61	35
DENVER	Low	18	29	58	43	43	22
	High	46	57	88	73	73	50
	Average	32	43	73	58	58	36
HONOLULU	Low	68	69	72	74	73	69
	High	74	75	80	84	83	79
	Average	71	72	76	79	78	74
HOUSTON	Low	48	58	71	75	67	50
	High	64	74	89	93	87	68
	Average	56	66	80	84	77	59
LAS VEGAS	Low	35	47	64	76	61	47
	High	57	73	84	102	87	61
	Average	46	60	79	89	74	54
LOS ANGELES	Low	46	50	57	62	59	49
	High	64	66	71	76	75	69
	Average	55	58	64	69	67	59
MIAMI	Low	59	64	72	75	73	61
	High	77	82	88	89	87	79
	Average	68	73	80	82	80	70
NEW ORLEANS	Low	49	59	71	76	68	52
	High	67	75	87	92	84	68
	Average	58	67	79	84	77	60
NEW YORK	Low	26	38	58	68	54	34
	High	40	54	76	84	72	44
	Average	33	46	67	76	63	39
SAN FRANCISCO	Low	43	46	51	54	52	45
	High	57	64	65	72	72	61
	Average	50	55	58	63	62	53
ST LOUIS	Low	24	38	58	67	52	30
	High	42	60	80	89	76	50
	Average	33	49	69	78	64	40
SEATTLE	Low	24	39	47	54	47	37
	High	46	55	69	76	65	49
	Average	35	47	58	65	56	43
WASHINGTON DC	Low	29	41	61	68	56	35
	High	45	61	79	86	74	51
	Average	37	51	70	77	65	43

Daylight Saving Time occurs widely though not universally throughout the United States; from the end of April to the end of October clocks are put forward one hour. Carefully check air, rail and bus schedules in advance.

THE AMERICAN SITUATION

English Puritans were among the first to establish a successful colonial foothold in what was to become the United States, and they were joined by other northern European Protestants, particularly Germans, Scots and 'Scotch-Irish'. Together they imposed an ethos that was politically individualistic and morally illiberal.

These people were hardly the underdogs of European society; rather they were battling for its mastery. The Reformation in the early 16th century had been a revolution of their making. The 'Scotch-Irish' already had experience of colonising Catholic land in Ulster. Those Puritans who didn't emigrate (and Oliver Cromwell very nearly did) stayed behind and chopped off Charles I's head.

Emigration to the New World was more a feature of their ambition than a symptom of haplessness. Reverses did encourage emigration. Many Germans came to America to escape the ravages of the Thirty Years War, and Puritan emigration flowed most strongly before the success and after the collapse of Cromwell's Protectorate. But by and large theirs was the winning course in Europe and still moreso in America. In America they at once installed themselves as the ascendant majority, a position they retain to this day.

In 1982 the Census Bureau confirmed that an American is more likely to trace his ancestry to German forebears than to any other nationality. The Irish occupy second place, the English third; though when the English, Scots and Welsh are added together, then people of British descent form the largest group in the country. Americans of Scottish descent earn the most money, followed by those of German descent. Five and a half million Americans speak German; its position as the second language to English has only recently been overtaken by Spanish, spoken by 7.7 million.

If the earliest founders of America were already rebelling in their homelands against post-feudal authority, the new world they made in America was an instantly revolutionary environment for the waves of immigrants who followed. Peasant culture had been dominant in Europe for ages; life on the land was usually tightly knit and hedged in with restrictions imposed by law, custom and the pressure of population. A communal and static pattern of existence was the rule. Despite a growing tendency to commercialise land and to trade in real estate, most people had inherited their land rather than bought it. The effect of America on this comparatively changeless pattern was revolutionary. In America the peasant disappeared, and the stable estate or subsistence farm was soon subject to commercial exploitation and market values.

Some were the beneficiaries, some were the victims of this opportunity and exploitation. Eleven percent of the present population are black, coming either directly from Africa or via the West Indies during the days of the slave trade. In the early 19th century the Irish began to flow in, followed by more Germans, and later on large numbers of Mediterranean and eastern European peoples. The many Chinese and Japanese on the West Coast came over around the turn of the century, the Chinese to help construct the railroads, the Japanese as agricultural workers.

The themes of opportunity, exploitation and mobility are basic to the American experience. In America's early development these themes were embodied in the westward moving frontier. The frontier American became nationally minded; he was a firm believer in equality; he was self-reliant and materialistic. But frontiersmen could also be totally lacking in self-discipline, utterly ruthless and always on the lookout for something better in the next territory. The frontier is gone, but the image remains evocative; the Western film is the American morality play.

And still the process continues, though with a change of ethnic complexion. From 1820 to 1960, 82 percent of legal immigrants came from Europe; in the 1970s only 18 percent did so. Instead, immigrants have been pouring in from Puerto Rico (a US possession), Cuba, Ecuador, Haiti, Mexico, the Philippines, India, Korea, Vietnam, Hong Kong and China. During the 1970s 4.3 million legal immigrants, mostly Asians and Latin Americans, entered the United States, compared to 2.5 million in the 1950s and 3.3 million in the 1960s. When an estimate for illegal immigrants is included, total immigration during the 1970s approached 10 million.

Birthrates in Europe, the Soviet Union, Japan and the United States too remain static or decline and population follows suit— except in the United States where population grows by leaps and bounds due to continuing immigration. In Miami, New York and Los Angeles, Spanish has become the second language, yet predictions that Southern California might become overwhelmingly Hispanic are countered now by the large immigration of Koreans, Chinese, Vietnamese and Filipinos. This unrelenting yet changing pattern of immigration means that America is well on its way to becoming the world's first universal nation.

It also means it hardly has the chance to settle down, become mature, get fixed in its ways. The old western frontier may be gone, but America continues to remain a new frontier for further generations of immigrants. It has been said that violence is as American as apple pie; in a society which bulldozes tradition and frantically plants the future anew, there is a lack of communal solidarity, a sense of rootlessness and self-doubt in which violence and crime, along with fads, religious and political frauds and fantasies of escape, superstition and the paranormal flourish. All of it is apple pie, as is the seemingly inexhaustable determination of Americans to put things right, to have that revolutionary idea that the world is still theirs for the making.

MEDIA AND ENTERTAINMENT

Television, and there's lots of it, is stupefying and moronic. The only things worth watching are the old movies or some of the offerings on the public service stations which specialise in BBC reruns condescendingly introduced, often by Alistair Cooke, as being 'for your own good, though we appreciate you are so stupid that we'll have to outline the plot to you beforehand'—or words to that effect. Network television is now being overwhelmed by hundreds of cable and satellite channels which have largely increased the amount of garbage at your fingertips, though proliferation also means catering to special interests, and in amongst the dross you may find your gold. Commercialisation of television has reached saturation point if one accepts that there should be more programming than advertisements; the limit on the number of ads per hour has been lifted, and even public service stations run commercials now.

And there's even more radio, and here the overkill holds promise for in amongst the top-40 musical pop stations there are first-rate classical, jazz, blues, bluegrass, country, R&B, progressive and regional music stations, as well as some solid all-news stations. Radio is also an excellent way of finding out about an area you're visiting or just driving through.

Every city with any claim to consequence will have its theatres and its own orchestra and opera company, with performances often to a very high standard. In this respect, Americans arguably enjoy a greater access to culture than Europeans with their brighter but more centralised cultural traditions.

Hollywood still turns out more films than anywhere else in the world except India, and with the decline of the studios there has been more freelancing, more opportunity for outsiders with new ideas to hit the big screen. In writing, directing and acting, America easily holds its own as one of the four or five great filmmaking nations.

If you're interested in concerts, plays, etc, one easy solution is to look up TICKETRON in the local phone book. They are nationwide agents, but have information on what's on in the particular city you're in—they publish a free monthly list of all events, though take a percentage on any tickets you buy from them.

The *New York Times* is one of the most respected of American newspapers and in content comes closest to being the country's national newspaper. The mammoth Sunday edition of the *Times* should keep you going at least until Tuesday. But generally people prefer those published in their own cities, and of these the *Los Angeles Times* and the *Washington Post* are among the best in the country. The *Wall Street Journal* is a good read for the considerable insight it offers into a great variety of topics both inside and well beyond the world of finance.

Magazines proliferate, covering every interest and point of view. Sample the offerings on hot rods, sex, flying saucers, sport, computers, snowmobiles, collectibles and so on if you want to appreciate the American appetite for every sort of information. Also there are growing numbers of magazines for business women and working mothers, plus large circulation black publications. Some of the best writing is found in *The New Yorker*, *The Atlantic Monthly*—which grew out of the Transcendentalist and anti-slavery movements—*Esquire* and *Playboy*, though the last ministers as much to the senses as to the mind. *Rolling Stone* is the voice of pop, *MS* is for the socially aware ladies who are not yet so socially aware that they read the *Wall Street Journal*, and there's always *Time* and *Newsweek* to read on the toilet.

Last but not least there are the comics, including that whole stable of Marvel heroes (Captain America, Spiderman, The Hulk) who express the variety of American neuroses, or those old standbys from a more innocent, confident age, principally Superman and Scrooge McDuck.

THE GREAT OUTDOORS

One of the most exciting things about North America are the great tracts of unspoilt land. The most superlative examples have usually been specially preserved as National Parks. There are 40 National Parks in the United States, all of which offer the visitor beautiful scenery; everything from fantastic seascapes, deep canyons, spectacular volcanoes, to pure lakes and craggy mountains. Many parks are somewhat off the beaten track and although the roadways in all are excellent, the parks are best seen more slowly on foot, by bicycle, horse, or canoe. Most offer camping facilities (see under Accommodation) and some, cabin or hotel accommodation.

Some parks are free but in general the entrance fee will be $3–$5. Should you intend to use the National Park system extensively, purchase a Golden Eagle Pass, on sale at all parks. The Pass costs $10 and gives you, and anyone accompanying you in a private vehicle, access to all the parks for a year at no further expense. Also, visitors arriving before 7am often get in free.

There are also numerous National Seashores, Monuments and

Forests, and other federally administered preserves as well as some State Parks which should not be overlooked.

Almost all the National Parks are included in this Guide. For more information write directly to the Park, asking for details and brochures. A list of all National Parks in the US follows.

Acadia, Maine.
Arches, Utah.
Badlands, South Dakota.
Big Bend, Texas.
Bryce Canyon, Utah.
Canyonlands, Utah.
Carlsbad Caverns, New Mexico.
Crater Lake, Oregon.
Denali, Alaska.
Everglades, Florida.
Glacier, Montana.
Grand Canyon, Arizona.
Grand Teton, Wyoming.
Great Smoky Mountains.
  Tennessee/North Carolina.
Guadalupe Mountains, Texas.
Haleakala, Island of Maui, Hawaii.
Hawaii Volcanoes, Island of Hawaii,
  Hawaii.
Hot Springs, Arkansas.
Isle Royale, Michigan.
Kings Canyon, California.

Lassen Volcanic, California.
Mammoth Cave, Kentucky.
Mesa Verde, Colorado.
Mount Rainier, Washington.
National Reef, Utah.
North Cascades, Washington.
Olympic, Washington.
Petrified Forest, Arizona.
Platt, Oklahoma.
Redwood, California.
Rocky Mountain, Colorado.
Sequoia, California.
Shenandoah, Virginia.
Theodore Roosevelt, North Dakota.
Virgin Islands, St John,
  Virgin Islands.
Voyageurs, Minnesota.
Wind Cave, South Dakota.
Yellowstone, Wyoming/Montana/
  Idaho.
Yosemite, California.
Zion, Utah.

HEALTH AND WELFARE

There is no free or subsidised national health service in the United States for anyone under retirement age, although Senator Edward Kennedy is pushing for one. For most people, therefore, medical, dental and hospital services have to be paid for and they are expensive. However, the emergency room of any public hospital provides a grudging amount of medical care to anyone who walks in the door, and only charges those who are able to pay, the government reimbursing them for the rest. The 'emergency' doesn't have to be a car crash or the like—it can be a high fever or stomach pains, anything of a reasonably acute nature. Nevertheless, it pays to be insured (ask your travel agent), to get a dental checkup before going, and if you wear glasses or contact lenses to take spares, or at least prescriptions.

MONEY

Dollars and cents are of course the basic units of American money. The back of all dollar bills are green (hence 'greenbacks'), no colour distinctions being made for different denominations. The commonly used coins are: one cent (penny), five cents (nickel), 10 cents (dime), and 25 cents (quarter). 50¢ pieces (half dollars) and silver dollars (not really silver anymore) are gaining in usage, while there has been talk of phasing out the penny—that's inflation for you. A quarter is sometimes called 'two bits', and dollars sometimes 'bucks'.

There is generally no problem in using US dollars in Canada, but this is never possible vice versa.

It's useful always to carry small change for things like exact fare buses, but do not carry large sums of cash. Instead keep the bulk of your money in travellers' cheques which can be purchased both in the US and abroad and should be in dollar denominations. The best known cheques are those of American Express, so you will have the least difficulty cashing these, even in out of the way places. (You can also have your mail sent to American Express offices—ask for a complete list.) Thomas Cook travellers' cheques are also useful, especially as lost ones can be reclaimed at any Hertz Car Rental desk. Dollar denomination cheques can be used like regular money. There's no need to cash them at a bank: use them instead to pay for meals, supermarket purchases or whatever. Ten or 20 dollar cheques are accepted like this almost always and you'll be given change just as though you'd presented the cashier with dollar bills.

Credit cards can be even more valuable than travellers' cheques as they are often used to guarantee room reservations over the phone and are accepted in lieu of a deposit when renting a car—indeed *without* a credit card you may be considered so untrustworthy that not only a deposit but your passport will be held as security too. The major credit cards are Bank Americard and Barclaycard (both VISA cards), American Master Charge and Access (each with the other's symbol on the reverse), Diners Club and American Express. If you hold a bank card (eg VISA), it could well be worthwhile to increase your credit limit for travel puproses—you should ask your bank manager.

Banks. Bank hours are usually 9am–2pm or 3pm Monday to Friday. Many banks stay open until 6pm on Fridays.

If you ever receive a cheque, it is important to cash it in the same area; you'll find it difficult and certainly time-consuming to cash it elsewhere—the American banking system is not as integrated as elsewhere in the world. Some form of identification (eg passport) is necessary when cashing a personal or company cheque.

Tax. There is usually a three to eight percent sales tax on most items over 20¢ and meals over $1. This is never included in the stated price and varies from place to place according to whether you are being charged state or city sales tax. There is also a 'bed tax' in most cities that ranges from five to ten percent on hotel rooms. 'Bed tax' does not generally apply to bed and breakfast places. *Note that unless stated, accommodation rates in this Guide do not include tax.*

ACCOMMODATION

Let's face facts: accommodation in North America is going to absorb at least one-third of your travel money. So how can you keep that figure to a minimum while enjoying your trip to the maximum? Here are eight pointers:

1. *Learn your accommodation options.* You'll constantly hear about the visible and well-advertised options: chain hotels and motels, lodgings close to freeways and tourist attractions, National Park accommodation and the conventional rock-bottom suggestions—YMCAs and youth hostels. But a wealth of inexpensive and almost invisible alternatives exist in North America. Examples: guest and tourist homes; bed and breakfast in private residences; farms and ranches; resorts and retreats; residence clubs, *casas de huespedes* and other pension-style lodgings; free campsites on Indian lands; non-hostel accommodations which honour hostel rates and philosophies; university-associated places to stay, many open to the general public; and self-catering digs, from apartments to rustic cabins to housekeeping/efficiency units in standard hotels/motels. (We will give you lots of specific examples of these choices throughout this edition of the Guide.)

2. *Choose a lodging that also gives you a taste of North America.* Want to stay in a New York City brownstone, a San Francisco painted Victorian, a Maui condo, a solar-heated A-frame near a ski slope? How about spending a few days on a Mississippi River houseboat or riding through Kansas prairies with a covered wagon train? Maybe you'd rather tent-camp in a Sioux teepee, explore a Mennonite farm, go fox-hunting on a Southern plantation, sleep in a goldminer's cabin, gain a few pounds at a Basque boarding-house, beachcomb near a lighthouse hostel or stay in a 400-year-old Mexican mansion. It's all here. And by integrating your sleeping (and sometimes eating) arrangements with an offbeat experience, you'll receive double value. In the process, you'll get acquainted with everyday North Americans from many walks of life.

3. *Rent a room the way you shop for a car.* On or before your arrival, ask a cabbie or bus driver about the current hotel situation. If tourism is down and vacancy rates are up, you'll have added leverage and bargaining power. Use it! Don't be afraid to dicker—hotel/motel rates in the US are extremely fluid and based on what the market will bear. (Unlike Mexico, where they are government regulated.) Rooms within a building are never identical—ask to see the cheapest. It may be small, viewless or noisy. It may also suit your needs very well. If you're willing to share a bath, sleep in a dorm, or take a room without

air-conditioning or TV, *say so*. Most clerks (in the US anyway) will assume you require a private bath and colour TV to sustain life, and won't mention other accommodation.

4. *Use impeccable timing*. Plan ahead to take advantage of special offers and slow times. Do your travelling on weekends so you arrive to catch the midweek (Sunday through Thursday) rates. Alternatively, look for higher-priced hotels at your destination that offer low-cost weekend or 'getaway' packages—often very good value. If you can possibly swing it, travel in May or September: best weather, fewest crowds and significantly lower offseason prices. Another timing tip: the later in the evening it gets, the more likelihood you have of a reduced rate on a room. You may be tired and worried about a place to lay your weary head but remember: the hotel/motel owner is even more worried about filling that room, which goes on costing him money whether empty or full.

5. *Always ask about discounts and special rates*. You'd be amazed at the discount categories that exist in North America. A partial list: senior, student, youth hostel card-holder, bus/train/plane passholder, rental car user, member of Triple-A or other auto club, YMCA/ YWCA member, Sierra Club or other environmental club members, military, family, group, foreign visitor, government employee, airline employee and commercial rate. Incidentally, hotel/motel people sometimes grant 'commercial rates' as a face-saving way to fill rooms, so it pays to flash your company identification or business card and ask for them. Throughout this edition, you'll notice we've indicated specific discount offers where known. 'Being a British student was worth a $2 discount to many motel owners.'

6. *Ask other travellers for accommodation leads*. When travelling in the US most Americans tend to stay with families/friends, at chain motels/hotels, or in campgrounds or RVs. Thus they are often oblivious to the unsung lodging opportunities around them.

7. *Double up. Better yet, triple up*. US lodging (with the exception of hostels, YMCAs and a few hotels/motels that give the lone traveller a break) has a Noah's Ark, two-by-two mentality. Your best bet is to travel with one or more companions. Relish your independence? Then split up and rendezvous with friends every couple of days— you'll still save money. 'Five of us crammed into a $20 double room with owner's consent. Try any motel.'

8. *Learn about local variants and accommodation nomenclature*. Lodging traditions vary around North America. For instance, the best bargains in Hawaii are called hotel apartments—Honolulu is full of them. In Colorado, ski lodges with dorms (ask for 'hiker' or 'skier' rooms) are popular. San Francisco is a mecca for congenial residence clubs, which offer superlative weekly rates for room and board. Parts of the South and New England are full of small guest houses. In

Canada, low-priced B&B digs are called hospitality homes. When you enter an area, ask the Visitors Center or librarians, or look in the phonebook Yellow Pages; if there's a local variant, you should spot it. Second, learn what lodging descriptions really mean. In the US, the cheapest and simplest accommodations are variously described as 'economy', 'budget', 'no frills', 'rustic', 'basic' or 'European-style rooms'. The breakfast portion of bed and breakfast may vary from a continental roll-and-coffee to a full meal; ask. Unlike Europe, many US B&Bs offer (for a modest fee) other meals, transportation, tours and worthwhile goodies from free bike loans to use of libraries, saunas and tennis courts. Beware of lodging descriptions that include the words 'affordable', 'quaint', 'Old World charm' (evidently it costs a fortune to drag charm from the Old World to the New), and 'standard' or 'tourist class' (travel agenteese for mid-price range).

Hotels and motels. Thanks to the great success of the Motel 6 chain, the American travel industry has reluctantly concluded that no-frills lodging is not just a ploy for the pathologically frugal. Thus dozens of budget chain motels have emerged in the last decade. Except for Motel 6, however, they tend to be regional in scope and with prices that vary from unit to unit and season to season. To be fair: many of them offer more for the money (eg pool, larger rooms, tubs, phones, TV, etc). See the Appendix for a list of budget hotel chains in the US.

Budget motels work out cheapest with three or more people. Unfortunately, they are often difficult to reach without a car, but do call to ask about bus connections, if any. As a rule, cheapie motels (chain or non-chain) provide better, cleaner and safer accommodation for the money than do cheap downtown hotels.

Finding a hotel with the ideal mix of low price and reasonable quality is an art. Besides the suggestions in this Guide, you'll do best if you (1) ask the Greyhound/Trailways bus driver and at the terminal; (2) compare notes with other travellers; and (3) check at the Travelers Aid kiosks in transit terminals. It's also wise to leave your luggage in a locker so you can check out your prospects. Ask to see rooms and don't settle for bad-news facilities (eg doors that don't lock or that have signs of forced entry, unclean linen, etc). If you are a woman, we strongly advise you to arrive in big cities during daylight hours. Failing that, the cheapest and safest tactic is to pop your luggage in a locker and spend the night in the ladies' toilet. Most bus station loos have nice large anterooms with chairs, clean floor space, pay phones and a complete dearth of attendants in the wee hours. Don't ask permission to do this, just do it.

A new scheme called Vacation Accommodation Centers has brought together a number of good hotels and other accommodation throughout North America and offers discounts of about 40 percent to

YHA and VAC card holders. Drop in or write to VAC Center, The President Hotel, 234 West 48th Street, New York NY 10036, Tel (212) 582-9760, or VAC Center, Commodore International Hotel, 825 Sutter Street, San Francisco CA 94109, Tel (415) 885-2464, for information and a brochure listing all VAC Centers throughout the US, Canada and Mexico. There is VAC accommodation in Albuquerque, Atlanta, Austin, Boston, Charleston, Death Valley, Denver, Kissimmee, Las Vegas, Los Angeles, Louisville, Memphis, Miami Beach, Nashville, New Orleans, New York City, Orlando, Philadelphia, Phoenix, Portland, Richmond, Salt Lake City, San Francisco, Sioux Falls, St Louis and Washington; in Canada at Montréal, Ottawa and Toronto; and in Mexico at Acapulco.

YMCAs and YWCAs. Most YMCAs that offer lodging are located in the often-cruddy heart of big-city downtowns. Y lodgings have no membership or age restrictions and the use of rec facilities is often free. Two-thirds of them are coed; the rest, men only.

The economics of desperation bring in a mixed clientele; that, coupled with the grimy streets outside and steadily rising prices make the YMCA less and less of a bargain. You will do better with prepaid vouchers (valid at 64 YMCAs in the US and Canada), better still with an AYH card—many Ys give hostel rates. Contact the Y's Way, 356 West 34th Street, New York NY 10001 or call (212) 760-5856 for their brochures.

The women-only YWCAs are concentrated in the Northeast, the Midwest and Texas. They tend to be smaller, more cheerful and better bargains than their YMCA counterparts—if you can get in.

Hostels. AYH-affiliated hostels in the US now number 266 and the number is growing. The situation is bright in the Northeast states and in Ohio, Michigan, Minnesota, Colorado, Arizona, California, Oregon, Washington and Alaska (along the ferry route) but pretty thin elsewhere. There are hostels near Yellowstone and Yosemite, a new one at the Grand Canyon and in expensive cities like Chicago, Houston, New York City, San Francisco, Minneapolis and Miami Beach. Mexico has 20 hostels in Mexico City, Acapulco, Cancun and elsewhere. Canada recently opened hostels in Montréal (summer only) and Toronto.

If you belong to a foreign Youth Hostel Association, you're automatically entitled to use AYH facilities. Annual fees in the US are $14, $7 for seniors, $21 for families. Write AYH, 1332 I Street NW, Washington DC or call toll-free 800-424-9426. It's cheaper if you join in a country other than the US. Many hostels also sell an introductory pass so you can try it on a one-time basis. Other hostels will rent you a bed at a higher, non-member rate.

Pluses of North American hosteling: often in locales of great scenic beauty; a growing number are housed in buildings of historic or architectural interest (from decommissioned lighthouses to adobe haciendas); many offer special activities free or at low cost, from wilderness canoe trips to hot-tubbing. Reader comments show that US hostels are generally more relaxed and friendly than their European counterparts. 'I found youth hostels most convenient places to stay. Full of young people of all nationalities, the hostels were a nucleus of information and I met many travelling partners. Whilst not boasting of exceptional comforts, the hostels generally proved to be very good value and certainly took a lot out of the loneliness of travelling on one's own.'

Drawbacks? Uneven distribution make hiking or biking itineraries impractical, except for certain regions. Remote locales make it tough to use public transit to get to many of them. And hostel curfews and customs can cramp your style, particularly if you plan to do much urban or nighttime sightseeing. This Guide contents itself with mentions of the most popular and logistically critical of the hostels, assuming that those with a deeper interest will already be members and have detailed handbooks. NB: even the handbooks contain out-of-date info; always check locally.

University-associated lodging. Over 230 universities in the US and Canada offer on-campus housing in dorms and residence halls. Points to consider: usually available summer only (exceptions noted in listings); rates vary widely and favour doubles and weekly stays; facilities often heavily booked; campuses can be far from city centres. But it's always worth trying the local student union or campus housing office when in the vicinity. Many of these offerings are open to the general public.

You can also find off-campus residences, fraternity and sorority houses with summer space to rent, all of which tend to be looser, friendlier and cheaper than on-campus options. Fringe benefits: use of kitchen facilities (sometimes) and entree into the thirsty social life of local students, including the infamous TGs or kegger parties.

Camping. Camping provides the cheapest and one of the most enjoyable means of seeing the best parts of North America, the National and State Parks and other preserves. Your choices are almost infinite—free campgrounds in the US alone total over 20,000! State Park camping fees range from zero to $7 and are indicated with the state listings. National Parks (same price range) are given considerable attention in this Guide; for further information, write the National Park Service, US Deptartment of the Interior, Washington DC 20240. Other excellent sources for campgrounds info are the

AAA books, Rand McNally's *Campground and Trailer Guide* (17,000 US and Canada listings) and the tourism offices of each state.

You should be aware that the biggest drawback for the on-foot traveller is access. Ironic as it sounds, you really need a car to get to numerous campgrounds and trailheads to backcountry camping, especially those sites located on National Forest or Bureau of Land Management property. In California, the access problem is alleviated somewhat by CORTEX, a non-profit organisation that provides low-cost charters to wilderness areas and info on regional carriers to parks and other wilderness attractions. Write PO Box 6849, San Francisco CA 94101 for CORTEX information, or call (415) 821-2236 or 864-5821.

Campground facilities vary from fully developed sites with electricity, bunk-equipped cabins and hot showers to primitive sites where you're expected to bury your wastes and pack out your rubbish. Tent campers are advised to avoid RV-oriented campgrounds. They may offer a pool, laundromat, store and other amenities but the noise, asphalt and vehicle fumes sadly dilute the 'wilderness' experience. Although more expensive, private campgrounds can be good: 'We used the KOA campgrounds the whole time—they have the best facilities available. And get a KOA discount card for $2; this allows a 10 percent reduction on cost of campsite.' For the hiking/biking camper, many State Parks offer a few sites designated as 'hiker/biker' for 50¢–$1 per night on a first-come, first-served basis.

In the north, the camping season lasts from mid-May to mid-September or less, depending on weather. In the Rockies and other mountainous areas, temperatures drop dramatically in the evening, making warm clothing vital. In the warm dry Southwest, you probably won't have to put up a tent. At Yellowstone and other northern parks, you may encounter bears who roam the campground for food. These bears are not interested in campers as nourishment and will not harm you as long as you leave them well alone. Do not leave food in the tent, in ice chests, on picnic tables or near your sleeping bag. Lock it in the trunk of your car, or use park-recommended 'bear cables'. Bring along a generous supply of insect repellant and calamine lotion to combat mosquito bites, chigger (a maddening insect that burrows beneath your skin) attacks and poison ivy/poison oak (glossy three-leaved plants).

Popular National and State Parks get very crowded Memorial through Labor Day, making May and September the ideal months for visits. In summer, you may want to book through TICKETRON, the national ticketing service, to ensure a place. To get the best site, try to arrive by 5pm or earlier.

American Indian campgrounds and other Indian-run lodging facilities are a first-rate way to get acquainted with North America's first people. Most sites are located on reservation land which, if you'll remember your history, has traditionally been located about a million miles from nowhere. Although the whites did their best to fob off nothing but marginal lands on the Indians, what they ended up with is often superbly scenic. A car is nearly imperative as you'll find little public transit to and from reservation land. Besides campgrounds, Indian-owned facilities range from simple motels to sumptuous resorts. Some offer traditional dancing, crafts and Indian food. For a detailed and loving look at the Indian nations, read Jamake Highwater's *Indian America* (Fodor). The American Indian Travel Commission, 1100 Connecticut Avenue NW, Washington DC 20034, phone (202) 293-1433 can also give you information.

Bed and breakfast. An old concept in Europe, B&B crossed the Atlantic a few years ago and has now hybridised in several directions. Most visible are the 'too cute to be true' B&B Inns, widely written about and gushed over and punitively expensive in most cases. Least visible but most Moneywise are the private homes in the US, Canada and Mexico which only rent rooms through an agency intermediary. (This is partly for security reasons, partly because of US zoning laws.) Most agencies concentrate on a given city or state; you'll find their names and addresses under the appropriate listing. Their rates run from $15 to $30 single and from $25 to $70 doubles. (NB: higher rates are for incredibly lavish digs.) Booking procedures, type of breakfast, length of stay and other conditions vary from agency to agency. The common denominator is the need to book ahead. If in the US, this can often be handled with a phone call. Only rarely can you breeze into town and get same-day accommodation.

Is the lack of flexibility worth it? Most people think so. Foreign visitors who want to meet locals, see American homes and eat home cooking are particularly enthusiastic. Private home B&Bs are an inexpensive, warm and caring environment for women travellers on their own, too. Bonuses: many B&Bs serve meals other than breakfast and a large number are willing to pick up and deliver guests (sometimes a small fee). Hosts often speak other languages, so make your needs known at booking time. Canadian B&Bs are called hospitality homes. In Mexico, the B&B programme is known as Posada Mexico.

There are at least five B&B umbrella agencies (listed below) which cover a number of states (and countries) and which cater to foreign and US travellers. They can book you into one B&B or work out a whole itinerary of B&Bs for you. Write for details and brochures.

1. B&B International, 151 Ardmore Road, Kensington CA 94707;

call (415) 525-4569. Outstanding host and guest matchups; fees $26 to $60 double, 20 percent less for singles; full breakfast; many homes throughout California, plus Hawaii, Chicago, Boston, New York City, Seattle, Las Vegas and Washington DC.

2. International Spareroom, New Age Travel, 839 Second Street, Suite 3. Encinitas CA 92024. Call (619) 436-9977. Biggest geographic coverage and interesting range of special experience B&Bs (farms, plantations, ranches, etc). In 38 states, Canada and Mexico.

3. Northwest B&B Inc, 7707 SW Locust Street, Portland OR 97223. Call (503) 246-8366. As the name implies, homes in Washington, Oregon, British Columbia, Idaho, Nevada, Arizona and (inexplicably) Florida. Full breakfasts; $15 membership fee (which includes detailed 90-page book of listings); rooms are $14–$25 single, $18–$40 double.

4. B&B League Ltd, 2855 29th Street NW, Washington DC 20008. Phone (202) 232-8718. Recommended primarily for travellers in pairs, since rates are $25–$38 single, $30–$42 double plus $15 annual fee. Continental breakfast. Homes in 30 states.

5. PT International, 1318 SW Troy Street, Portland OR 97219. Phone toll-free 800-547-1463. Highest priced of the lot, worth mentioning because they can be booked through travel agents. Breakfasts usually continental. Singles average $28, doubles $35-up. Homes in 26 states.

Guest houses and tourist homes. Guest or tourist homes are independent B&Bs which may or may not deliver the second B. Most of them are private homes or small family-run places that carry on a homey, homely tradition once widespread in pre-freeway America. In the groundswell of the current B&B fad, many modest guest homes have gone upscale, but a significant number of them maintain low cost and high quality. We've included a clutch of them in our listings. Several guides to guest houses and tourist homes exist, including Rundback's *Guide to Guest Houses* and Coplin's *National Guide to Guest Homes*. It's doubtful, however, that such guides would be of much value to international visitors, who are better served by the B&B umbrella agencies mentioned earlier and the listings in this Guide.

Special experience places. There has been a proliferation of plasticised Wild Wests and Olde Townes selling acres of new crap across the US. Whole villages now turn their energies to the pimping of history and ethnic tradition—*anybody's* tradition. But the ersatz how-it-usta-wuz hasn't entirely driven out the genuine bits and pieces of Americana that remain.

Many of these farms, ranches and outdoor programmes require

you to invest at least a week. Some activities are painstaking recreations of the past (eg covered wagon trips in seven states). Others are activities that are part of a continuing tradition (eg cattle drives, Indian events). You'll see that prices are generally all-inclusive (food, room, activities such as riding); not all of them can be considered cheap, however. So what are they doing in this book? Because they offer a valuable slice of something real, something vanishing, and they allow you to become an active part of the experience rather than a spectator.

Other accommodation possibilities. If you're planning to bicycle around the US, it makes sense to join the League of American Wheelmen, PO Box 988, Dept A, Baltimore MD 21203; call (301) 727-2022. Included in your $15 a year membership is a list of hospitality homes which offer sleeping space (sometimes the floor) for touring cyclists.

Two mutual hospitality exchange programmes also exist. The Globetrotters' Club, BCM/Roving, London WC1N 3XX (postal address only; there is no office) and in the US, Box 9243, North Hollywood CA 91609, has a $10 (£3) membership fee, magazine and directory. Members have the option of choosing to offer hospitality or not. The Traveler's Directory, 6224 Baynton St, Philadelphia PA 19144. An informal, mutual hospitality exchange system listing people worldwide who can stay in each others' homes free of charge when travelling. To be listed, you must complete an application form, giving a brief summary of your interests and what hospitality you can offer. Only those who have listed can obtain a copy of the directory: $10.

FOOD

To eat cheaply and well in America is easy once you realise that menu prices have more to do with restaurant decor and labour costs than with food quality. Plan to get at least some of your meals from non-restaurant sources: supermarkets, open-air farmers markets, truck stops (not Union 76), roadside stands and farms. When possible, avoid higher-priced outlets like 24-hour stores, bus station canteens, street vendors, beach stands, airport restaurants and liquor stores. 'Many supermarkets, especially 7–11s, have microwaves; so a hot stew can be eaten for the price of the can.'

Keep away from endless soft drinks; even at supermarkets, they're 50¢ and up, double that elsewhere. Accompany your dining-out meals with ice water or lower-priced multiple refills like coffee or tea.

Can you eat a good meal in the morning? Then you're wise to start with a big breakfast (best food bargain in the US) and/or to stay in bed and breakfasts, hotels, hostels and other lodgings which include it as part of the price. Not a breakfast eater? Then make lunch your main meal of the day. Always ask about daily specials—usually the tastiest and cheapest choice. (NB: restaurant lunch menus are often identical with dinner ones—except for the price.)

In the evening, plan to eat early (to take advantage of lower-priced 'sunset' or 'Early Bird' specials) or eat in a non-restaurant setting.

Wherever you are, check out the Happy Hour situation. States and cities with liberal liquor laws often honour a daily discount period (usually 4–7pm) with cheap drinks and free food, sometimes a stunning array of it. Fittingly, California is the Happy Hour paradise.

No matter where you are, ethnic restaurants are invariably the cheapest. Chinese, Mexican and Italian can be found in profusion. In larger areas, look for Vietnamese, Greek, German and other specialties. Cafeterias offer cheap if sometimes insipid food; besides downtown, look for them on campuses, around hospitals, in large museums, in department stores and at YMCAs. 'Anyone can eat in university cafeterias—all you want for the price of a burger, fries and soft drink at Mcdonalds.'

Regional and local specialties are usually wonderful, or at the very least a worthwhile cultural experience. As you work your way around the country sample Key lime pie, Virginia ham and redeye gravy, Chicago-style deep-dish pizza, California guacamole dip, Southern grits, Hawaiian poi and roast pig, Wisconsin bratwurst, Maryland crabcakes, Navajo tacos.

In the West, salads and salad bars are generally excellent. Large sandwiches (often with local nomenclature like grinder, submarine, po' boy, blimp, hero, hoagie, etc) on rolls with meatballs, sausage, corned beef, you name it, are available everywhere for a couple of dollars.

Americans are ice cream fanatics and eat it year-round in more flavours and combinations than you've ever dreamed of. Lots of the ice cream parlours will give you free samples until you hit on the one you want most.

As far as franchise places: Tad's Steak Houses in New York, Chicago and San Francisco are recommended. So are the Old Spaghetti Factories, now in 17 cities. But by and large, prices at the big chains (McDonald's, Colonel Sanders, Taco Bell) have risen so greatly and quality has become so uneven that with very little effort you can find a decent little place offering a lunch special for less than a quarter-pounder with fries and a Coke.

Wherever you eat, portions are invariably enormous—you'll soon understand why Americans invented the doggie bag for leftovers! 'Forget doggie bags—nobody objected to our ordering one portion and two plates and sharing—portions still bigger than at home.'

'Nowhere have I found it difficult, and usually I've found it fun, hunting out a place to suit my quite small pocket. I do feel that discovering food, rather than following a map to it, is part of the holiday.'

TRAVEL

The means you choose to travel around North America will depend on your budget, your time, your adventurousness and a number of other factors. Since there are certain discounts available to travellers who buy their tickets outside North America, it is a good idea to give careful consideration to travel plans *before* you go. Also, when you buy your tickets outside the US, you save the eight percent sales tax.

'Canada and the US cater for wheelchairs much better than the UK does. Theatres, museums, pavements, bus stations, even buses are all usually equipped with either lifts or ramps.'

Bus. This is the most popular method of cheap internal travel in America. Two large bus companies, Greyhound and Trailways, have nationwide networks and offer the traveller highly dependable and safe inter-city services. Their terminals provide restaurants, ticket, baggage and parcel services, travel bureaux, restrooms and left-luggage lockers.

Periodic rest stops are made every three to four hours enroute and if you are on a very tight budget you can save by travelling at nights and sleeping on the bus.

Of the two, Greyhound has the greater mileage, with routes extending into Canada and Mexico. Trailways is strongest in the South, the southern part of the Rockies and the South Central states, but they do not offer routes through many other areas, particularly in Canada.

Greyhound and Trailways passes are good for unlimited travel on their route systems, linking more than forty thousand large and small communities in North America. They may also be used on the services of a number of other participating bus lines. With the passes you are free to travel when and where you wish. A Discount Guide may also be obtained; this lists hotels which offer discounts to pass-holders.

Where the route is not covered by Greyhound, you may travel— with their permission—on the Trailways network, or vice versa. This is always worth investigating since the other company's timings and routes may sometimes be preferable. Also, Trailways and Greyhound are now undercutting each other, particularly on popular routes. Always compare prices. Trailways is usually cheaper. The rivalry is not always friendly. Readers have commented that on occasion the two companies refuse to honour each others' passes, and that definite friction exists in certain areas, notably Phoenix, Flagstaff and Las Vegas.

Government deregulation and so price competition between Greyhound and Trailways means that bus pass prices might change; also some of these passes may only be available if purchased outside the US. Unlimited 15-day bus pass $179, 27 days $299, 30 days $325. There's a point-to-point ticket costing $99 and valid between any two destinations in the US, eg New York and San Francisco, permitting you 15 days to cover the *direct distance* and with unlimited stopovers enroute. This is the cheapest way of getting from one coast to the other. Bus passes can be extended at a cost of $10 per day.

Some Tips. Whenever possible, take your bags on to the bus with you, otherwise get a check-in ticket, make sure they are labelled and watch them like a hawk—it is not uncommon for you and your bags to set off in different directions, and without the check-in ticket you may never get them back. 'I never collected my luggage at the bus side, but let it go into the depot until it was convenient for me to collect it, usually just before my next journey. A charge is only made after 72 hours of depot storage.' 'If all lockers are taken, luggage can be stored for up to 24 hours at a cost of 75¢ per piece, in the bus depot luggage store.'

'Bus pass coupons have to be validated each time for further travel. As ticket lines can be very long, it's good to have your ticket stamped for the next journey as soon as you arrive.'

If planning to sleep on the bus, get an inflatable pillow at the station for $1, it can make all the difference to your comfort, though some readers say a sleeping bag is better 'and doesn't puncture'. Malleable wax ear plugs are also a good idea for lighter sleepers. 'Always have a sweatshirt or pullover with you. The one fault drivers have is an imperviousness to cold. Even at 3am on a chill night the air conditioning is set to combat the climate of Alice Springs.'

The bus passes often entitle you to a 10 percent discount at station restaurants (but only if you buy $5 of $10 worth of food coupons), nearby hotels and on various sightseeing tours. It's in fact cheaper to eat away from the stations, but you might not always have the time to do so.

Most bus routes are meant solely to get you from A to B; scenic considerations rarely come into it.

Alternative buses. The late 1960s and early 1970s spawned a new phenonomen, the alternative bus service; its heyday saw companies with colourful names like Purple Goose, Lame Duck, Grey Rabbit and Green Tortoise—all of them operating without licences from the Interstate Commerce Commission, but popular, ramshackle, fun and cheap. Airline and now bus deregulation has made orthodox methods of travel so competitive that many of the alternative bus companies have gone out of business, eg Purple Goose and Lame Duck, while it's rumoured that Grey Rabbit may be on its last legs—maybe even in rabbit heaven by now. Grey Rabbit and Green Tortoise did eventually get licenced, and the latter is still going strong, if not all that quickly.

Green Tortoise makes no effort to get you from coast to coast fast; in fact the journey is more like a tour, wandering for eleven days along a circuitous cross-country route: Boston, New York, a bird sanctuary on Lake Erie, the Indiana Dunes on Lake Michigan, Chicago, through small-town southern Minnesota, camping on the banks of the Missouri, on to the South Dakota Badlands, Wounded Knee, Denver and some whitewater rafting in the Rockies, Bryce Canyon, the north rim of the Grand Canyon, Zion, Las Vegas, Los Angeles, Santa Barbara and a day on the beach, and then San Francisco. These coast-to-coast trips depart weekly and cost around $200. A slightly different route is followed eastbound, in winter the route seeks warmer climes, passing through New Orleans, and there are segments and extensions, eg allowing you to get off at Denver or Chicago, or go up to Washington and Oregon.

Buses accommodate 28 to 44 people and have most of their seats removed and replaced by wooden platforms covered with foam rubber padding. They also have stoves and refrigerators. Often cross-country tours are accompanied by a cook. Passengers can put $5 or so a day into a kitty and get two full meals cooked on the bus but often eaten at some scenic place such as a Louisiana bayou or the banks of the Rio Grande.

Reservations should be made through Green Tortoise, PO Box 24459, San Francisco CA 94124. Or for information phone San Francisco (415) 386-1798, Seattle (206) 324-RIDE, Portland (503) 225-0310, Eugene (503) 344-RIDE, New York (212) 431-3348, or Boston (617) 265-8533.

Car. The car overwhelmingly remains the most popular form of travel and the vast system of super-highways—'monuments to motion'—enable you to cover great distances at high average speeds, despite the nationwide imposition of an idiotic 55mph speed limit. 'The National System of Interstate and Defence Highways is designed for maximum efficiency. For enjoyment, try state and country roads, even for a lengthy trip. The additional time spent will be more than compensated for by the increased intimacy with American culture and scenery.'

Buying a car. For a group of three or four it can be worth while buying a second-hand car. Try to buy and sell privately, utilising the notice boards of universities, and the local press.

Be sure to obtain a 'title' or, in states such as New York, a notarised bill of sale. If stopped by the police, 'proof of ownership' will be required. (In some states it is illegal to drive without this.) Allow for a delay while the title comes through. If you buy from a dealer he can issue temporary licence plates on the spot.

You can have your car checked over at a gas station at a very low cost. If you have to buy new parts get them at one of the nationwide stores like Montgomery Ward or Sears, or from major gas stations like Shell and Mobil. They will give you guarantees and have the advantage of being readily available all over the continent. Garages are efficient and friendly, and if you are from out-of-state, will usually do repairs, however major, on the spot.

Prices of second-hand cars vary very much from place to place and tend to be higher on the West Coast. Prices fall in September when the next year's new cars come on to the market. Leave several days for selling your car and if possible try not to do it in New York.

'Two of us bought a large station wagon for $800 and drove it 12,000 miles in two months. We slept in it often, and sometimes ate in it too. We sold it back to the dealer we bought it from at half-price. Worst problems: two $50 repair bills and finding places to park.'

Insurance. Although insurance cover is not obligatory in every state, you are strongly advised to take out at least third-party cover as insurance claims can be very high and inadequate insurance can lead to financial ruin. Expect to pay at least $250 for your insurance. 'State Farm Insurance, found in all states, offers good service and very good short-term policies.'

Insurance premiums are generally high, particularly for males under 25. Women are considered better risks and their premiums are lower. Premiums are lower if you are resident outside large urban areas. Allow time for your policy to come through.

In states where insurance is compulsory it is necessary to have it before you can register your car.

Licences. All states and provinces of the US and Canada now officially recognise all European licences and those of Japan, Australia and New Zealand among others. However, an International Driving Licence is recommended. Police are more familiar with them and this could save you time and embarrassment (but don't forget to bring your *original* licence too—you may not be able to hire a car or get a drive-away without it). In addition, your own licence can be validated by the AAA office in the USA. Although not a legal requirement, it's a good idea to have it done particularly if your licence is not in English. You won't encounter many multi-lingual patrolmen along the way. You must always have your insurance certificate, car registration certificate and driving licence with you in the car—there is no grace period; you will simply be done for driving without the legally required documents.

Road Tips. Traffic regulations vary from state to state, so familiarise yourself with them in each. The 55mph speed limit is standard, however. For starters, read the *Highway Code of Motoring in the USA* available from the AAA. Many readers recommend buying the Rand McNally *Interstate Road Atlas*, useful even for non-drivers. Maps from gas stations cost around 75¢.

'Most truck drivers have CBs. When driving, follow the example they set. If they adhere to the 55mph limit it means they've picked up the police lurking in the locality. If the truckers exceed the limit it means there are no cops around and it is safe for you to exceed the limit too.'

If you have a breakdown, raising the hood is the recognised distress signal. Also switch on your flashing warning lights.

Never pass a stopped and flashing school bus (they are usually yellow) no matter which side of the road it is on: it is not only against the law, but could easily result in death or injury to young children.

AAA Membership. Benefits: Towing service, $5000 bail if arrested, excellent and free maps and regional guide books, and a comprehensive information and advisory service. For example, the AAA will plan your journey for you, giving the quickest or most scenic routes, and provide detailed maps of the towns you will pass through.

Touring membership costs $40 the first year, $35 thereafter and entitles you to full membership rights. Apply to: AAA, 1712 G. Street NW, Washington DC 20006, or to 750 Third Avenue, New York 10017.

Membership of your own national automobile association entitles you to AAA benefits.

Gasoline. Following the 'fuel crisis' and the sharply rising cost of gas, there's now a worldwide oil glut and gas prices in the US have fallen to about $1.25–$1.50 per gallon, depending in which part of the country you are. (The American gallon is one-fifth smaller than the imperial gallon used in Britain and Canada and is equivalent to 3.8 litres.)

When driving in remote areas, always keep your tank topped up. Gas stations can be few and far between. Keep a reserve supply in a container for emergencies.

Automobile Transporting Companies. Americans change homes more often than any other people, and may live for a few years in New York and then move off to California. When they do move they sometimes put their car (or one of them) into the hands of an automobile transporting company which does no more than find someone like you to drive the car from A to B.

Most movements are from east to west, major starting points being New York, Detroit and Toronto. 'East–west is the easiest route to get; otherwise New York–Florida or New York–Atlanta. The cheapest way to travel bar hitching.' Even on the popular routes you may have to wait a couple of days for a car, particularly in summer.

Conditions regarding age limitation, time schedules, routing, gas and oil expenses, deposit, insurance and medical fitness vary considerably and should always be carefully checked. And another thing: 'The car trunk may be full of the owner's belongings, leaving no room for yours.' A fair example would be for a driver 21 years or over, with character references, to be charged a $50 to $150 deposit, refundable on safe delivery. Three/four people utilising this method could travel from New York to San Francisco for as little as $50 a head in gas and oil.

'You have to take a reasonably direct route, but the time limit (after which you are reported to the FBI) allows a fair amount of sightseeing. I was given nine days for the coast-to-coast trip and made it in six. It's certainly a great way to see America.'

'I drove a new Cadillac with only two thousand miles on the clock. It was air conditioned, everything electric—really unbelievable, and we slept in it at night. Good places to sleep are truck-stops run by Texaco, Union 76, etc. They have 24-hour restaurants and free showers, and the truckers themselves, though rough-looking, are often interesting people to talk to.'

'When asking for your deposit back and before handing the keys over, hold out for cash. American cheques are a bugger to cash.'

The names of companies can be found in the *Yellow Pages* phone directory under 'Automobile and Truck Transporting'. AAACON Auto Transport Inc is one company used by many of our readers in the past, along with Auto Driveaway. A new company that has received favourable reader comment is Dependable. 'Very dependable.' We have listed the addresses of a sampling of automobile transporting companies under the travel headings of many towns and cities around the country.

Car Rentals. The biggest national firms are Hertz, Avis, National, Budget and Dollar. The last two are generally cheaper, but even Hertz can offer some amazing deals. It's important to phone around. Always compare costs per day against costs per mile and other variations, such as unlimited mileage or so many miles free, within the context of your specific needs. Many rental companies offer discount rates to foreign visitors, though sometimes only when bookings are made abroad.

The renter must usually be 21 or over, sometimes over 25. If you don't have a credit card then a hefty cash deposit will be required, and for foreigners a passport may also have to be deposited as security. 'It's very difficult to rent a car without a major credit card, and in many cases it's not possible to leave a deposit.' 'Small companies generally ask drivers to be 25 or over; large companies usually accept drivers from 18 provided they have a major credit card.'

Insurance is not usually included in the cost, or often it's only third-party. It's essential that you take out a full collision waiver (up to $5 per day); the alternative may be a lifetime of paying off someone's massive hospital bills.

Greyhound operates one of the cheapest rental companies, though it concentrates mostly on Florida and California. Alamo generally offers the best deals in Florida. A new phenomenon is companies renting out older cars, eg Rent-a-Wreck, Rent-a-Heap, Rent-a-Junk and Ugly Duckling. But they are not always the cheapest or most flexible, eg in some instances you must stay within a 50- or 100-mile radius of the point of rental. Worth checking out, though.

'Ask a travel agent for good deals; I found them to be in the know.' 'It's a good idea to check with the airline you're travelling on for special arrangements. Sometimes these can only be booked before the flight. For example, on Eastern I was able to rent an unlimited mileage car at one-third the normal daily rate.' 'Don't entertain a firm that charges for mileage and drop-off; there are plenty that don't.' 'If you want unlimited mileage you must usually go to a large company.'

'We found car rental easiest, most convenient and, for groups of three or more, the cheapest way of getting to see National Parks and other areas where transport, other than tours, is minimal.'

Air. The vast distances of the North American continent have resulted in the popularity and relative cheapness of domestic air travel, and since government deregulation there has been a bewildering and ever-changing scramble to offer more for less.

Night flights are cheaper than daytime flights, and family fare schemes mean savings on spouses and children. Standby fares, however, have disappeared. Nevertheless, there can be considerable price competition on certain routes, in particular between New York and Florida, even between majors like Pan Am and Delta.

But the real news in domestic air travel is the rise of small airlines like Peoplexpress, World, Capitol, Republic, NY Air, Pacific Express, Hawaii Express, Texas International, etc, all out to undercut the major carriers.

The situation is incredibly fluid with new and changing bargains almost weekly. When you've decided where and when you want to go, phone around and select the best deal.

Additionally there are two Visit USA bargains available only to non-US residents. The terms and prices may vary from airline to airline, but the principles are the same.

The first offers a discount on all flights on the airline's system though the itinerary must be worked out and paid for prior to departure for the US. Reservations can be made at any time. This scheme may be preferable if you know in advance where you want to go and if you're not stopping at many places.

The second is more like a bus pass: for a fixed all-in price you can cover an unlimited number of miles on the airline's route system within a certain period of time. There may be a few limitations, eg making only two coast-to-coast flights, or being able to make only one stopover at any one city. The validity period is usually about 60 days. This scheme will be preferable if you want to keep your travel arrangements flexible and cover a lot of ground.

Once again, the message is check around to determine which package of price, time limit, route availability, etc, best suits your intentions.

Rail. The railroads played a major role in the history of the United States, but over recent decades declined in service, increased in price, lost money and saw much of their former business go to cars and airlines. Part of the reason for this may have been the great number of competing railways and the inability of the individual companies to undertake the new investment necessary to improve service and efficiency. But then in 1971 AMTRAK was established. All the major lines now operate under the one AMTRAK board, and though the railways remain privately owned, losses on passenger services are made up for by government subsidy.

On long-haul Western routes, outdated equipment has been replaced by new double-decker Superliners, variously fitted up as lounges, dining cars (restaurant upstairs, kitchen below), sleeping cars (with bedrooms) and open-plan coaches. On shorter routes and generally in the East, cylinder-shaped Amcoaches are used, their interiors like luxury airliners.

In the East, frequency, time-keeping and the large number of destinations served permit comparison with European railways. From Chicago westwards it is the trans-Siberian railway that comes to mind. There are only four east-west routes, and only two of these operate daily. Delays are common. But for the traveller that should not matter: the scenery is often spectacular, the service is better than on any railway in the world, you can eat and drink well and inexpensively, and the company is congenial. The Western railways are the last stronghold of graceful travel in America. 'The best way to see a wide variety of scenery. On occasions we felt less worn from 20 hours on a train than four hours on a bus.'

A rundown on some of the more interesting routes:

The Empire Builder runs between Chicago and Seattle via Milwaukee, Minneapolis/St Paul, Fargo in North Dakota, Glacier National Park and Spokane. Majestic scenery. Takes about 46 hours; operates thrice weekly.

The Coast Starlight, between Los Angeles and Seattle, offers superb coastal, forest and mountain scenery. 'Attracts many young people. A highly social train: spontaneous parties and lust.' Takes 33 hours; operates daily.

The San Francisco Zephyr runs between Chicago and Oakland via Omaha, Denver, Cheyenne and Reno—prairies, plains, and best of all the mountains between Reno and Sacramento. Takes 48 hours, operates daily.

The Rio Grande Zephyr is not an AMTRAK train but is instead operated by the Denver and Rio Grande Western Railroad three times a week. The journey, between Denver and Salt Lake City, takes 14 hours, almost all in daylight, and climbs 9000 feet over the Rockies for what is considered the greatest railway ride in America.

Also special are the *Pioneer* between Seattle and Salt Lake City, the *Adirondack* between New York and Montréal, and the crack *Broadway Limited* between New York and Chicago with the finest onboard dining service in the US.

USARAIL passes for unlimited travel are only available outside the US and are not available to US residents. They cost $250 for seven days, $375 for 14 days, $500 for 21 days and $625 for 30 days. There are also family passes where one adult pays full whack while the spouse and any children from 12 to 22 pay half each. Children from 2 to 12 pay even less. The seven-day pass should be considered as no more than a slightly cheaper substitute for a one-way coast-to-coast ticket. That's all you'll have time for, and in fact you'll probably have only enough time in hand to get off the train once or twice enroute. A 14-day pass should be your minimum requirement.

'I travelled 4328 miles on a seven-day pass—in eight days. It's possible to get an extra day or two on a pass as long as you board the train before your pass expires at midnight on your last day. You may ride the train as far as you wish or until the train reaches its destination. For example, I caught the *Southwest Limited* in LA at 7.40pm on the last day. My pass expired at midnight. I could have ridden the train to Chicago, getting there on the second day. As it happens I got off the next morning at Flagstaff. So the pass should not be regarded as just a cheap coast-to-coast ticket. It's possible to go to San Francisco from

New York, stay three nights, go to LA and then catch the train to Chicago all on a seven-day pass with nine days' travel.'

In Britain, tickets, passes and national timetables are available from Thomas Cook. Otherwise, you may send for pass information and a free national timetable to AMTRAK Travel Center, PO Box 311, Addison, Illinois 60101.

Boats. 'If you want to take a longer trip on the Mississippi, you can try to get on a towing boat. But you'll have to work hard. Look in the *Yellow Pages* under "Towing—Marine".'

How about paddling your own canoe? The Appalachian Mountain Club publishes three books of interest to canoeists and kayakers: *AMC River Guide I: Northeastern New England; AMC River Guide II: Central and Southern New England;* and *AMC White Water Handbook for Canoe and Kayak.* They're available by mail from AMC Books, 5 Joy Street, Boston MA 02108.

The Chicagoland Canoe Base Inc, 4019 N Narragansett Avenue, Chicago IL 60634, can provide you with all the information you need on canoes, kayaks, rafts, accessories, rentals, books and maps.

Hitchhiking. Hitchhiking in the United States can vary from state to state, but generally it can be 'superb, simply due to the long rides'.

'A sure way of getting long rides in relative comfort and at speeds in excess of the general 55mph limit is to ask for rides at truck stops. At Union 76 truck stops there will often be hundreds of trucks going to all parts of America. Just ask the drivers in the canteen. By using this method I managed to cover over 1000 miles from Mexico to New Orleans with only two rides'. 'Don't try truck stops unless on your own. Even then, due to new insurance regulations, it's difficult.' 'I had better luck at truck stops at night when drivers like passengers to keep them awake.' 'Truck stop directories can be obtained free at truck stops.' 'Interstate shoulders are good places, but best of all are rest areas on Interstates where you can make personal contact and you can pick and choose a good ride as the unwary driver is making his way from the toilet.'

Hitching is forbidden on freeways and Interstates, so get your rides on the ramps or at service areas. With regard to other roads, the laws vary from state to state, but even when hitching is technically illegal you can usually still get away with it if you are standing on the shoulder or sidewalk, and sometimes even if you are walking with the traffic, regardless of the fact that you might be walking backwards. 'I had no problems except the usual ones. The police are okay, though they may ask to see your identification.' 'Police in New York warned me, "Ten days in jail if we see you again". The next day I was given a ride by a policeman.' And, certainly, being a foreigner helps.

Never carry any dope. Display your national flag. Always carry a sign saying where you want to go. 'We carried two signs: one stating our destination, the other saying PLEASE. Fantastic results.' 'Female hitchhikers should not use destination signs; that way you have a chance to look over the driver before accepting.' Avoid getting off in cities if you don't want to stay there. Ideally, hitch on your own or with a girl; two guys cuts down your chances.

'Warning to female hitchhikers: don't hitch overnight trucks unless willing to satisfy the driver. No malice intended but "payment" is expected. At least that's what I found, and I was hitching with my boyfriend.' 'I often got rides with truckers and found them nice and helpful people. I slept in a cab of a truck three times without having to grant any favours, and I was a female alone. I'm not recommending overnight rides with truckers nor hitching alone for that matter, but I had no bad experiences.'

Holidays, especially Labor Day, are good times to travel as there are millions of cars on the road. If you don't want to thumb, try radio stations or look in the local (especially the freaky) papers. 'For hitching long-distance, or if you're prepared to share the driving, try the ride boards at universities—either advertise yourself or go to see what's offered. I got from Chicago to San Francisco this way in one car.'

'When crossing the US–Canadian border do not say you're a hitchhiker.' 'Beware the heat in the Southwest, ie anywhere between LA and mid-Texas. In this area hitchers should carry a large container of water and some salt tablets. Hitchers have been found dead on the side of the road due to dehydration.' 'People are usually very congenial and offer accommodation and food.' 'I hitched from San Francisco to New York in four and a half days and could have done it in less. I experienced no more hassles than I have in Europe. The Southern states are populated by a different breed of people who are proud to be rebels and consider the Civil War to be still on, but they are still cool for hitching, especially if you are European. By the way, they call you Euro-penises.'

Hitching by air is growing in North America. In our last edition we wrote: 'So try the airports and don't be afraid to ask anyone for a ride'. Sure enough, we got feedback from several readers who went to JFK and tried to hitch a ride on American to San Francisco—and complained to us about their lack of success! So look, dummies, it's like this: the continent is dotted with thousands of *small airfields* located outside most towns from which people fly in *small aircraft* for pleasure or business. Those are the people you ask. 'Difficult across US/Canada border.' 'Air hitching is really difficult but saves so much time it's worth a try.' 'I walked into an air freight company office in

San Francisco and got a free ride back to New York with the overnight packages.'

Bicycle. There's a 4450-mile TransAmerica Trail stretching from Virginia to Oregon, divided into five shorter routes. Five sectional booklets are available, with detailed maps and details of flora, fauna, campsites, eateries, bike shops and gradients enroute. Free leaflet from Bikecentennial, PO Box 8308, Missoula, Montana. Tel: (406) 721-1776. Also, the AYH does bicycle tours; information is available from their headquarters.

A strong bicycle lock is advisable for security when parking in towns, plus a helmet (US drivers are not attuned to looking out for bikes). Bicycles are cheaper in the US than abroad. It's possible to ship a bike around the US with AMTRAK or the bus companies provided it's dismantled and boxed. Bikes can usually be taken free on flights to the US as part of your baggage allowance.

Walking. Yes it is done. Mostly by mad dogs and Englishmen. Like John Lees of Brighton, England, who in 1972 walked from City Hall, Los Angeles, to City Hall, New York, a distance of 2876 miles, in 53 days 12 hours 15 minutes, averaging 53.75 miles per day.

'When asking for directions, remember that most people think you are on wheels. I was directed to one place along a roadway that took me 15 minutes to negotiate in the boiling hot sun, an excursion I could have avoided by cutting—in one-third the time—through a leafy forest. Unfortunately, the guy I asked thought I was a Chevy, so I had to go the long way round.'

A list of more than 25 hiking clubs along the East Coast can be obtained by writing to the Appalachian Trail Conference, Box 236, Harpers Ferry WV 25425. The Conference manages the 2000-mile Maine to Georgia Appalachian Trail in conjunction with the National Park Service. For 50¢ they'll send you information about the trail, membership, etc. Be sure to ask specifically for the list of clubs.

On the West Coast there's the Sierra Club. They can provide information about the Pacific Crest Trail, 2400 miles along the Pacific Coast from Canada to Mexico, plus other walks: 530 Bush Street, San Francisco CA 94108.

Tours. If young and on your own and looking for fun and adventure, check out Trekamerica's camping expeditions: 25 days up the Alaska Highway, for example, or six-week coast to coast journeys, stopping at the most interesting cities, towns and national parks enroute. Expeditions can be purchased with or without air fare to the US; Trekamerica can arrange keyed-in economy, APEX, ABC or standby flights. In Britain, contact Trekamerica, 62 Kenway Road, London

SW5, Tel: 373 5083; in Australia, c/o any branch of the National Australia Bank, Tel: (03) 658-5357 (Melbourne); in New Zealand, c/o Sun Travel, PO Box 4088, Auckland, Tel: 723-003; or through agents throughout Europe and South Africa. In the US they can be contacted c/o Travel Inn, 515 W 42nd Street, New York, (212) 948-2122, and c/o Carmel Hotel, 201 Broadway at 2nd Street, Santa Monica, California, (213) 321-0734. From anywhere else in the US they can be phoned toll-free, 800-221-0596. 'An excellent way to see America if you don't mind camping and long drives. For a girl travelling on her own who didn't want to Greyhound or hitch, it enabled me to see a terrific amount in three weeks at a surprisingly reasonable price. The campgrounds were first class, and I soon made lots of friends.'

Green Tortoise, the alternative bus company, offers what amounts to a tour of the US (see under Buses). For city tours, see under Urban Travel, below.

Urban Travel. City buses and subway systems generally offer good services throughout North America. Usually, a flat fare is used which can make short hops expensive but long rides very reasonable. Many cities have a transfer system allowing you to change from one bus line to another, or even from bus to subway, without paying extra. Stick-ups have meant that bus drivers will not carry any more money than is absolutely necessary, so you must always have the exact fare.

Taxis can be pretty expensive unless shared. The ubiquitous Gray Line company ensures that nearly every city has its bus tour, and some have boat tours as well.

For further details on all forms of urban travel, see under city headings throughout the Guide.

PUBLIC HOLIDAYS
New Year's Day (1 January)
Washington's Birthday (third Monday in February)
Memorial Day (last Monday in May)
Independence Day (4 July)
Labor Day (first Monday in September)
Columbus Day (second Monday in November)
Veterans' Day (11 November)
Thanksgiving (fourth Thursday in November)
Christmas (25 December)

Though many smaller shops and almost all businesses close on public holidays, many of the biggest stores and multiples will make a point of being open—often offering sales. Outside of cities, supermarkets are open during at least part of a public holiday. On days of all primary and general elections all bars are closed. There are numerous other public holidays that are not nationwide, eg Lincoln's Birthday, St Patrick's Day. Jewish New Year brings New York to a standstill.

The summer tourism and recreational season extends from Memorial Day to Labor Day. After Labor Day you can expect some hours or days of opening to be reduced, or some attractions to be closed altogether. The same may apply to related transport services. Unless otherwise specified, times and days of openings in this Guide refer to the summer season. Outside this period, you should phone in advance.

ELECTRICITY
Current is 110–115V, 60 cycles AC. American plugs have two flat pins. Try to get an adaptor before you go.

SHOPPING
Major stores often have long opening hours, eg from 9am or 10am to 9pm or 10pm—on one, several or even all days of the week. Smaller shops in cities are sometimes open all night: you should have no trouble getting a meal or a drink, or shopping for food and other basics, 24 hours a day—though you'll pay more for the privilege.

Large American stores can make their foreign equivalents look like they're suffering from war-time rationing. The variety of goods on offer—and at relatively low prices—is amazing. This is an aspect of what Gerald the Mole in *Tinker, Tailor, Soldier, Spy* called 'the oppression of the masses—institutionalised'. Trotsky observed that Russian soldiers voted for the Revolution with their feet. It would appear that Americans vote cheerfully for 'oppression' with their credit cards.

If coming from abroad you almost certainly won't go wrong in delaying purchase of anything you need until you arrive in the US. Cameras, records, sound equipment, denims, winter wear and of course Western gear are all great buys in the US.

COMMUNICATIONS
Mail. Post offices are infrequent, but since the alternative is a commercial stamp machine which in the spirit of free enterprise sells 18¢ worth of stamps for 25¢, or 39¢ worth for 50¢, it is advisable to stock up at post offices when you can. As of going to press first class letters within the US are 20¢; the air mail rate for post cards to Europe is 28¢, aerogrammes 30¢, air mail letters 40¢.

Mail within the US travels at a snail's pace: allow a week coast to coast, four days for any distance more than around the corner. For guaranteed overnight delivery you have to use Express Mail which has a minimum rate of $8!

It is possible to have mail sent General Delivery (Poste Restante) for collection (also to American Express offices if you use their travellers cheques). The post office will usually keep it for 10 days before returning it to sender.

American post offices deal *only* with mail.

Telegrams. Internal telegrams are sent by Western Union and not from the post office. Telegrams abroad are cheaper by Night Rate. You hand or telephone in your message anytime and ask for second class treatment. But it may take 48 hours before the telegram is delivered.

Telephone. The system is generally highly efficient, except in New York City where, like everything else, it is overloaded. The basic charge from a phone booth was usually 10¢ but is now as likely to be 25¢. Long distance calls are cheap between 5pm and 8am, and at weekends. Between 11pm and 4.30am, seven days a week, three-minute calls can be made anywhere in the US at specially reduced rates not exceeding $1 plus tax.

When calling the operator (0) you put 10¢ (or whatever the local charge is) in the slot. Your money is automatically refunded. In areas considered dangerous, however, and this includes most subway train platforms in New York City, you may call the operator without any money at all, thus saving yourself the trouble of asking your assailant for a dime.

Telephone numbers all over the US have seven digits. All numbers are prefixed by area codes. New York for instance is 212. Use the area code only when dialling another area. A phone number preceded by 800 is a toll-free number—the call costs you nothing.

If making calls from your hotel, remember that it is cheaper to use the phone in the hotel lobby rather than the one in your bedroom. It's always cheaper to dial direct and not through the operator. In most areas local calls are free from private phones. If you make a pay call from a private phone you can get the operator to tell you how much the call cost. A reverse charges call is called a collect call.

Look for pay telephones in drug stores, gas stations, highway rest areas, in transport terminals and along the street.

INFORMATION
A multitude of resources exist in the US both to make your stay more informed and enjoyable and to help you out if you encounter problems. Among the most useful:
1. *Libraries.* One in almost every town, often open late hours and on weekends, libraries and librarians are a traveller's best friend. Besides reference works, atlases, local guidebooks, they offer transit schedules, local and other newspapers, magazines, free community

newspapers, phone books, brochures on helping organisations and are unfailingly kind about answering questions and making phone enquiries for you. They also have toilets, comfy chairs and often a social calendar of free evening events.

2. *Travelers Aid*. Their kiosks are found at bus, train and plane terminals across the country—invaluable for cheap lodging and other suggestions, helpful with free maps and brochures, and solid support if your trip runs into a snag (whether it's a medical, financial or practical problem).

3. *Chambers of Commerce and Visitors Bureaux*. Found almost everywhere, with lots of free materials, maps (although you usually have to purchase the really good maps) and advice. Big-city offices have multilingual staffs, are open longer hours and sometimes weekends. Smaller places are 9am–5pm, Monday to Friday; many have recorded events messages for local activities when they are closed. A major drawback is that they are primarily member organisations; few of them will even recognise much less recommend non-member hotels, restaurants, etc. That means that you won't hear much about low-budget places from them and some bureaux will even try to warn you off such places. Don't buy it.

4. Almost every US community has a *volunteer clearinghouse phone service* designed to answer a variety of needs, from real emergencies to simple orientation. Usually listed in both the white and yellow pages of the phone book, and variously called Hotline, Helpline, Crisis Center, People's Switchboard, Community Switchboard, We Care, or some such. Their well-trained volunteers can steer you to the resources available in the community—free, cheap and not-so-cheap.

5. *Women's Centers and Senior Centers* provide the same kind of clearinghouse info and friendly support on a walk-in basis; you will also find them in nearly every US town and listed in the phone book. The Centers also make excellent places to meet people, and often sponsor a range of free and interesting activities. You might also try the Free Clinics, which still exist in a number of big cities. Many of them operate Hotlines, referral services, crash pad recommendations and other services besides free health care.

6. *Maps*. Besides the free ones from Visitor Centers, State Tourism Offices and so forth, you may be interested in specialty maps, such as Greyhound's excellent 'United States of Greyhound', a monster which shows all of the US and Canadian routes clearly marked, plus major parks and monuments. Free. An organisation called DATO, 1100 Connecticut Avenue NW, Washington DC 20036, publishes a series of maps that show the routes of Lewis and Clark, the pioneer trails such as the Oregon, Santa Fe and Mormon, and Pony Express

routes, allowing you to trace portions of them for yourself. Write for details and prices.

MEETING PEOPLE

Americans are naturally outgoing and hospitable, more so when they detect a foreign accent. Don't be suprised if you are invited to dinner, taken places and shown round the local sights. Staying at a private bed and breakfast is a prime way to mingle with Americans—the services you get and the friendliness you'll receive go far beyond the monetary exchange. State fairs and other such special events—rodeos, clambakes, New England autumn fairs, etc—are an essential slice of the American pie and another way of meeting people informally.

If you want a more organised approach for meeting Americans, we suggest a number of organisations within our listings and also the following (most of which require making advance arrangements):

1. Contact the National Council for International Visitors (NCIV), Meridian House, 1630 Crescent Place NW, Washington DC 20009. Ask for their booklet called *Where to Phone*, a complete rundown of local organisations willing to extend hospitality.
2. Contact Sister Cities International, 1625 I St NW, Suite 424, Washington DC 20006. Over 800 cities in 80 countries around the world are members; write to find out your sister city and what they can do for you when you visit.
3. Enquire at the local Chambers of Commerce and Visitors Bureaux about their 'Visit a local family' programmes, if any. Some of them are very active in this area. A number have volunteer language banks also, if you're having difficulty communicating.
4. Contact the US Travel Service and ask about the Americans at Home programme, US Dept of Commerce, Washington DC 20230. Also offices in Canada, the British Isles, Europe, etc.

DRINKING

Although nationwide Prohibition ended in the US in 1933, you will still find places in which you cannot get a drink at all, or where you cannot stand to drink, or must bring your own bottle—one anomaly after another. This is because each state decides whether it will be 'dry' or 'wet', and sometimes this is left to counties on an optional basis.

American beer (which as a legacy of Prohibition has a low alcohol content) is of the lager variety—Knickerbocker, Schaeffer, Budweiser, Pabst, Rheingold, etc. Bottled beer is always more expensive than draught. America is the home of the cocktail. Spirit concoctions are excellent and a major part of American ingenuity is devoted to thinking up new ones—and extraordinary names for them! Bars never close before midnight, stay open sometimes till 4am, or even 23 hours a day. Try to sample local wines, New York and California turning out the best. Visit a winery in these states too.

The minimum ages for getting a drink in the 50 states are as follows:

Alabama, 19
Alaska, 19
Arizona, 19
Arkansas, 21
California, 21
Colorado, 21 (18 for 3.2 percent beer)
Connecticut, 18
Delaware, 20
District of Columbia 21, (18 for light wine)
Florida, 19
Georgia, 19
Hawaii, 18
Idaho, 19
Illinois, 21
Indiana, 21
Iowa, 19
Kansas, 21 (18 for 3.2 percent beer)
Kentucky, 21
Louisiana, 18
Maine, 20
Maryland, 21 (18 for light wine)
Massachusetts, 20
Michigan, 21
Minnesota, 19
Mississippi, 21 (18 for beer not over 4 percent and light wine)
Missouri, 21

Montana, 19
Nebraska, 20
Nevada, 21
New Hampshire, 20
New Jersey, 19
New Mexico, 21
New York, 19
North Carolina, 21 (18 for light wine)
North Dakota, 21
Ohio, 21 (18 for 3.2 percent beer)
Oklahoma, 21
Oregon, 21
Pennsylvania, 21
Rhode Island, 19
South Carolina, 21 (18 for wine or beer)
South Dakota, 21 (18 for 3.2 percent beer)
Tennessee, 19
Texas, 18
Utah, 21 (Salt Lake City has special drinking codes)
Vermont, 18
Virginia, 21 (18 for beer)
Washington, 21
West Virginia, 18
Wisconsin, 18
Wyoming, 19

TOBACCO
Cigarettes, cigars and pipe tobacco are cheap, cigarettes going for about 80¢ a pack of 20, five big cigars for about the same price. Pipe tobacco is heavily flavoured—imported brands are better and not much more expensive. Unless you learnt to chew tobacco at the same time as you were breast-fed, forget it. Tobacco addicts should stock up on cartons at supermarkets for substantial savings.

DRUGS
You either know what you're doing or you don't. Do not carry drugs across borders or try to get them past airport customs, and don't buy off the streets: too many dealers are either cops or crooks or both.

THE METRIC SYSTEM

The US still uses feet and miles, pounds and gallons, Fahrenheit instead of Centigrade/Celsius, and it appears as though it will for some time to come. The only things that have gone metric are liquor and wine bottles, some gasoline pumps and the National Park Service. A conversion table will be found in the Appendix.

2. USA

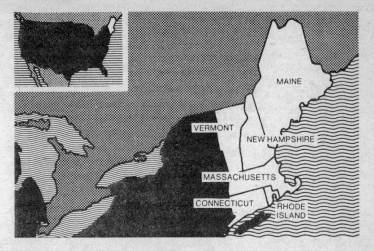

NEW ENGLAND

This was one of the first areas in the New World to be colonised by Europeans, in the persons of the Pilgrim Fathers, and it is the old historical ties, more than any other, which bind these New England states together. Afterwards came successive waves of Irish, Italian, and central European immigrants, all of whom have been assimilated into local society.

To the rest of the United States, a New Englander is a Yankee, and a whole series of myths and legends has grown up around him. The Yankee is well known for canniness, thrift, a taciturn nature and natural suspicion of strangers. The typical white picket fences around the lovely New England homes are pointed out to the newcomer as proof of this last attribute.

Be that as it may, New England is a delightful area to visit, offering the tourist a great variety of scenery from the rugged White Mountains of New Hampshire to the rolling green hills of Vermont, Massachusetts and Connecticut, and the often spectacular coastline, varying in its moods from state to state. In addition there is cosmopolitan Boston, and everywhere in the region revered reminders of early American society.

New England was once known for textiles, shoes and paper. At the time of the Revolution, this was where American machinery was manufactured. The Colt arms factory was here, Eli Whitney developed the cotton gin here. Recently, however, industry has moved away to regions of cheaper labour and New England is now best known for expertise in electronics, advanced technology and education.

The Boston area alone is one of the most remarkable educational complexes in the world. This is in the great tradition of New England which at one time led the nation in politics, culture and industry. New England literature has left its stamp forever on American life and thought.

The seasons are distinct in New England—a long, cold, snowy winter, followed by a short blossom-filled spring, a hot, often humid summer, and best of all for the visitor, a glorious autumn when the leaves turn the hillsides gold, scarlet and amber. The longest continuously marked trail in the world, the Appalachian Trail, begins north of Bangor in Maine and winds more than 2000 miles from Baxter State Park to the mountains of Georgia.

CONNECTICUT

Known as the Constitution or Nutmeg State, Connecticut has historically regarded itself as part of New England, although in reality the area abutting New York State along Long Island Sound has far stronger ties with New York City than it has, say, with Burlington, Vermont, or even with the state capital, Hartford. Many people commute daily to New York from such places as Greenwich, Stamford and Bridgeport, and look to the New York media for their news and entertainment.

Away from the coast, Connecticut is a state of broad rivers, farms, forests, rolling hills and placid colonial villages. In particular, the Litchfield Hills in the northwestern part of the state offer pretty scenery and have several excellent state parks good for camping and walking.

Connecticut is the third smallest state in the Union and one of the most densely populated. Its citizens do not pay state income tax, and were the first to elect a woman governor in her own right.

HARTFORD. The state capital, Hartford is known also as 'the insurance capital of the United States'—the headquarters of 40 insurance companies are located here. With this grey-suited image, Hartford has not been noted for its sparkling social life. But efforts are being made to turn the city into a livelier regional attraction, and the spanking-new Civic Center, a shopping, entertainment and convention complex, should be added to the visitor's list of more antique sights, such as Mark Twain's House, the pre-World War One carousel in Bushnell Park and, in the nearby suburbs of Wethersfield and Farmington, some of the oldest colonial houses in the US.

While here, pick up a copy of the *Hartford Courant*, founded in 1764 and the newspaper with the oldest continuous name and circulation in the nation, possibly in the world.

ACCOMMODATION
Susse Chalet Inn, about 5 mins from downtown, exit 27 off I-91, 525-9306. Pool. $31 double. Hotels downtown are $40–$50 double and up.
YMCA, 160 Jewel St, 522-4183. $17, men and women. Cheap cafe in basement.
YWCA, 135 Broad St, 525-1163. $18 up.

FOOD AND ENTERTAINMENT
Mad Murphy's, Union Place, opp train station. Bar with plenty of atmosphere, live band nightly, draught Heineken, $2 cover.
Brownstone, 124 Asylum St. Good, elegant dining. One for a special night out. Disco in basement.
Last National Bank, 752 Main St. Converted bank vault. Dinner around $8. Phone number is: A-Hold-Up!

OF INTEREST
Old State House, Main St. Formerly a State Capitol, now restored and refurbished back to its 1796 appearance. Also an information centre. Free.
State Capitol, Capitol Ave and Trinity St, exit 46 off I-84. Contains lots of Connecticut historical memorabilia. Free. Tours available Mon–Fri, 9am–3pm.
Bushnell Park, adjacent State Capitol, has a 1914 carousel; you can ride one of its 48 horses or a chariot to the tunes of a Wurlitzer Band Organ for a mere 25¢.
Mark Twain, Harriet Beecher Stowe Houses, Nook Farm, 77 Forest St. M.T. lived here for almost 20 years, publishing his major works from his Victorian-gothic style home, with Mrs Stowe as his next-door neighbour. 10am–4.30pm, summer; 9.30am–4pm winter, closed Mon. Sun 1–4pm. $4 for both houses, or $2.50 for Twain's, $1.75 for Stowe's.
Berenson's Hartford Jai-Alai, 89 Weston St, 525-8611. First jai-alai fronton in northeastern US, top players. Seats $2–$4.
Wadsworth Atheneum, 600 Main St. One of New England's best art collections. Tue–Sun, 11am–5pm. Adults $2, free Thur.

INFORMATION
Traveler's Aid, 179 Allyn St, Suite 211. 522-2247.
Convention and Visitors Bureau, Civic Center Plaza. 728-6789.

TRAVEL
Greyhound is in Church St, Trailways in Union Pl., ditto AMTRAK.

LITCHFIELD HILLS. In the northwestern corner of the state, this is an area of rolling hills, with woods, rivers, streams and lakes. The town of **Litchfield** is noted for its many fine colonial houses. Stroll up Main Street and imagine the fine ladies in their ornate gowns riding out in their carriages. The Litchfield Historical Society contains art and historical exhibits illustrating the town's past, and the town centre itself is a National Historic Site. Harriet Beecher Stowe and Ethan Allen were both born here.

Nearby is **Bantam Lake**, good for water sports including ice yachting in winter, and the **White Memorial Foundation**, a wildlife sanctuary and museum which takes up about half the lake shoreline.

Also nearby is the village of **Washington**, another 'jewel of a colonial village', home to many artists and writers, as well as the American Indian Archaeological Institute, off Route 47. Open daily,

$2. Further west there is **Kent**, and the Sloane-Stanley Museum showing Americana donated by Connecticut artist Eric Sloane.

This is a good area for walking and camping. Two of the nicer state parks, where you can do both, are **Housatonic Meadows** and **Macedonia Brook**, both not far from Kent.

NEW HAVEN. The city grew up around its harbour and Yale University (boola, boola). Although this Ivy League university is one of the best and oldest in the United States, the town has regressed since the 19th century when it was considered one of America's most beautiful cities. Except for the area around The Green, New Haven now looks pretty dismal. On the credit side, however, theatre and music thrive, and there are numerous enjoyable bars, cafes and restaurants patronised by the student population.

Going east along Long Island Sound, you come to New London, from where you can catch a ferry to Long Island. Further still, there's Mystic, enroute to Newport, Rhode Island, and the Massachusetts seacoast.

ACCOMMODATION
Duncan Hotel, 1151 Chapel St, 787-1273. Downtown, right next to Yale, this is the cheapest hotel in town and well-appointed for the price. Colour TV in rooms, Heidelberg Restaurant downstairs (beef and seafood specialties) and use of pool next door. Rooms without bath, $18 single, $25 double. Rooms with bath, $26.50 single, $37 double. Show this Guide for 10% discount.
YMCA, 52 Howe St, 865-3161. $22 single, $19 for AYH members. M & F.
YMCA No. 2, 1435 State St, 497-4822. $18 single, $15 AYH members.

FOOD
Annie's Firehouse Soup Kitchen, 19 Edwards St. Soups, homemade bread, etc. With a real firepole in the middle.
Pepe's. 157 Wooster St. Good pizza. Closed Tue.

OF INTEREST
The Green. Once a wild, swampy forest trodden by Indians, now a shaded park, the Green was the central sector of the original nine town squares laid out in 1638. Despite encroaching modern buildings it still retains much of its original flavour and is flanked on the north side by the impressive, ivy-clad halls of Yale.
Yale University. Highlights include the Old Campus through Phelps Gate off College St, Connecticut Hall (the oldest building), the Art of Architecture Building designed by Paul Rudolph and the Beinecke Rare Book Library. Free guided tours in summer. Weekdays 9.15am, 1.30pm, 3pm. Sun 1.30pm, 3pm. During termtime: Sat 11am, Sun 1.30pm and 3pm.
Yale Art Gallery, Chapel St. The first gallery to be connected with an American university and the home of the Morgan Collection of American Miniatures. Also a good collection of French impressionists. Tue–Sat 10am–5pm, Sun 2–5pm.
Yale Center for British Art, Chapel St. Hogarth, Constable, Turner. More British works than anywhere else outside Britain. Free. Mon–Sat, 10am–5pm, Sun 2–5pm. Free.
Branford Trolley Museum. By bus from Church and Chapel Sts. Admission and ride $2. Details: 467-6927.

Peabody Museum of Natural History, 170 Whitney Ave. Dinosaurs and Conn flora and fauna. Mon–Sat 9am–5pm, Sun 1–5pm. 75¢ adults.

ENTERTAINMENT
Look for current productions at the Long Wharf Theatre (occasional pre-Broadway productions) and the Yale Rep Theatre.
Yale Film Society. 50¢ membership plus small charge per perf. Different film every weekday, 7 and 9pm.

INFORMATION
Maps and guides from the University Information Office, 344 College St, 436-8330.
Traveler's Aid, 1 State St, 624-3136.

TRAVEL
Bus station is at 45 George St.
AMTRAK's *Montrealer* stops at Union Ave.
Connecticut Limousine Service from Sheraton Park Plaza, Temple St. Frequent runs to JFK and La Guardia Airports. $19 each way. 800-922-6161.

NEW LONDON. Off I-95, on the River Thames (pronounced as spelt), this town, once an important whaling port, had the distinction of being burnt to the ground by Benedict Arnold and his cronies in 1781. There are some well-restored houses on Star Street and on Green Street is the Dutch Tavern where Eugene O'Neill would get pissed. 'The best bar in the US; unique atmosphere'.

ACCOMMODATION
The '85' Inn, 85 Vauxhall St, 443-8210. 15 mins walk from downtown. Singles from $20, doubles from $25.
Susse Chalet Motel, West of New London, exit 74 off I-95. 739-6991. Singles $21.20, doubles $25.70. Pool, laundry.
Youth Hostel, 361 Pequot Ave., 443-2811. Reservation necessary.

OF INTEREST
Groton, across the Thames, on Rt 12. The first atomic-powered sub was launched from the US Submarine Base here in 1954. Gray Line does tours if you're not lucky enough to be here on an open day. $5. 449-4779 for info.
Mystic Seaport. Recreated mid-19th century coastal village on Rt 27. Some of the fastest clipper ships were built here—others are currently being built or restored. The last of the wooden whaling ships, the *Charles W. Morgan*, awaits inspection. The cobblestoned streets are lined with restored old houses and lofts. There is also a small planetarium. Open all year except Christmas and New Year. Entrance $8. See also the Mystic Marinelife Aquarium, just off I-95. Whales, sealions, dolphins, seals, etc. Daily 10am–6pm. $5. You can visit Mystic enroute to Newport, Rhode Island.

CONNECTICUT RIVER VALLEY. The lower river valley, where river meets sea, is one of the state's loveliest, most unspoilt and peaceful areas. Once an important seafaring commercial centre, this is now an area for gentle sailing, pottering around the small towns, or watching the wildlife at Selden Neck State Park or out on the salt marshes around Old Lyme.

ACCOMMODATION

Unless you feel like treating yourself to a night at one of the old inns here—The Griswold or the Cooper Beech Inn at Essex, or the Old Lyme Inn or the Bee and Thistle at Old Lyme—at about $45 double, you will have to search out a motel or campground somewhere off I-95.

OF INTEREST

Essex. Main St is lined with white clapboard homes of colonial sea captains. America's first warship, *Oliver Cromwell*, was built here. At the Ivorytown Playhouse Katherine Hepburn 'found out what theatre was all about'.

Essex Steamtrain, off Rt 9. Scenic ride along the banks of the Connecticut River. Daily May–Sept, then Sun until end Oct. $3.95, or for $6.95 you can ride on the Essex Riverboat as well.

Gillette Castle State Park. Across the river from Essex, off Rt 82. Once the estate of actor William Gillette who made his name playing Sherlock Holmes. The castle is built, and furnished, like a Victorian stage-setting. 'Weird.' Daily, 11am–5pm. $1. Reached by the Chester-Hadlyne ferry which has been in service since 1769. The trip across the river costs 75¢.

Old Lyme, Rt 156. Summer artists colony and home of the **Nut Museum**, dedicated to a greater awareness of nuts. $1 plus one nut admission. Wed, Sat, Sun 2–5pm. 434-7636. 'Indescribably bizarre.' A one-time boarding house and centre of the Old Lyme art colony is now the **Florence Griswold Museum**. The bohemian antics of Miss Griswold and her fellow impressionists were considered somewhat shocking by the locals. You can see their work at 96 Lyme St, Tue–Sat 10am–5pm, Sun 1–5pm. $1.

MAINE

More than one hundred years ago, Maine was a comparatively wealthy state—it can be a sadly poor place now—with huge farms, significant ports and fine houses. Since then time has stood still, and this quality, together with just a charming touch of decay, is what makes Maine a great place to get away from it all.

Especially recommended is the drive 'down east' (northeast) along the rocky coastline of the Pine Tree State. On a straight line the coast of Maine is 250 miles long, but the shoreline around all the bays, harbours and peninsulas measures some 2400 miles. Inland are acres of unexplored, moose-filled forests and huge lakes, remote and seldom visited. While in Maine look out for blueberry festivals, clambakes, and lobster picnics. The state annually harvests about 178 million pounds of fish and shellfish, and by far the most valuable part of the catch is lobster. If you enjoy eating lobster, this is undoubtedly the place to do it. You're bound to have potatoes served on the side—Maine produces more spuds than all but three other states.
National Park: Acadia.

PORTLAND. Maine's largest city in a state where cities and towns are few and far between and the gateway to northeast Maine, for it is here that the coast changes from long sections of beach to islands, bays and inlets. Otherwise after an early history of Indian massacres and British burnings and more recent economic decline, Portland is being revitalised and rebuilt, while the attractively preserved Old Port Exchange on the waterfront has a pleasingly 19th century atmosphere.

Travelling north on US 1, you come to Freeport and Camden, or better still, take a ferry to one of the hundreds of islands in Casco Bay, or to the offshore islands of Monhegan and Matinicus. Inland there is vast Sebago Lake for summer swimming, sailing, waterskiing and sunning.

ACCOMMODATION
Susse Chalet Motor Lodge, Brighton Ave, at Maine Turnpike (I-95), exit 8. 774-6101. $21.20 single, $25.70 double.
YMCA, 70 Forest Ave, 773-1736. $16 single. During the summer inevitably full by 8pm.
YWCA, 87 Spring St, 772-1906. $13 per person in a triple, $16 in a double. Free use of pool in the morning. 'A clean, friendly place, very handy for Old Portland.'

FOOD
Horse Feathers, Old Port. Price range $1.50–$7. 'Upscale bar, well bred food and fresh people.'
The Hollow Reed, 334 Fore St. Natural foods and good atmosphere. Omelettes $3 up, full dinners $6 up, lobster expensive.
Carburs, 123 Middle St. '23-page menu of elaborate concoctions from $2 up. I have never eaten so well so cheaply.'

OF INTEREST
Old Port Exchange, on the waterfront. Reconstructed in Victorian style with cobblestone streets, gas lamps, boutiques and restaurants.
Wadsworth-Longfellow House, 487 Congress St. Was the poet's home. Open June through Sept. $1.
Portland Museum of Art, 111 High St.
Old Orchard Beach. Nearby. Nice, but gets very crowded. 'Good for jobs.'
Sabbath Day Lake Shaker Settlement. On Rt 26, 20 miles north. Adults $2.50. May through Sept.
Island trips. Boats leave from Custom House Wharf. 'The harbour is good for meeting people with posh boats: go for a ride around the islands free.'

TRAVEL
Greyhound, St John and Congress Sts, 772-6587.
Trailways, Congress and Portlander Sts, 773-7295.
Ferry to Yarmouth, Nova Scotia, $40 per person one way, $60 per car; 775-5616.

THE MAINE COAST. Taking the coastal route north you hit **Camden**, with Bangor a further 40 miles away. Camden is typical of the small towns and villages dotted up and down the Maine coastline. Picturesquely situated with a busy little harbour, the town has a Cornish-like charm, despite the tourists. Generations of arts have found this coast an inspiration, and although the trash-trend emporia fast encroach, there are still genuine and attractive local craft shops.

If it's not foggy, the observatory atop Mount Battie affords a spectacular view of Camden harbour, the sea and the surrounding hills. It's an enjoyable two-mile hike from the town, with camping available nearby. South of Camden, at **Rockland**, there is the annual Maine Seafood Festival in August.

With a name thought to have been derived from an old hymn tune, **Bangor** is socially about that exciting. The best time to be in Bangor is during the Bangor Fair, held annually during the first week in August and one of the oldest in the country.

Otherwise, by-pass the town and continue on your way to Bar Harbor via the coastal route, or else head inland where thousands of lakes make this a popular area for canoeists. **Moosehead Lake**, 30 miles long and 10 miles wide, is the largest.

BAR HARBOR. A once quiet but now increasingly popular resort on Mount Desert Island, near Acadia National Park, and a good base for the area. Bar Harbor used to be a town of spacious, fashionable summer homes owned by the wealthy, until 1947 when a great fire burnt most of them to the ground.

ACCOMMODATION
Rocky Coast Manor, Mt Desert St, 5 mins walk from town pier, 288-3243. Doubles $26 and up mid-July to end-Aug, otherwise $18 up.
Bass Cottage in the Field, off Main St, downtown, 288-3705. Singles $20 up, doubles $28 up; lower off-season.
Daney Cottage, 18 Hancock St, 288-3856. Baths and showers. $7–$10 per person.
McKay Cottages, 243 Main St, 288-3531. Singles $9–$11, doubles from $18, $4 extra per person. Fridge available for guest use.
YMCA, Mt Desert St, 288-3511, and YWCA, 36 Mt Desert St, cost about the same as cottages.

CAMPING
Army-Navy Surplus Store, 116 Cottage St, 288-3084, sells and rents complete camping gear.

INFORMATION
Chamber of Commerce, Municipal Pier.

TRAVEL
Bar Harbor Bicycle Shop, 141 Cottage St, sells, rents and repairs.
Mopeds of Maine, Main St, rents mopeds, provides maps, guides, picnic baskets.
National Park tours by bus or sailing boat from $5, enquire at Testa's Restaurant, 53 Main St, 288-3327. Eagles, ospreys, seals, etc.
Ferry to Yarmouth, Nova Scotia, $20, plus $40 per car. Phone Canadian National Bluenose Ferry, 288-3395.

ACADIA NATIONAL PARK. Only a stone's throw from Bar Harbor, the park encompasses a magnificent wild, rocky stretch of coast and its hinterland. The granite hills of Acadia sweep down into the Atlantic where the ocean has carved out numerous inlets, cliffs and coves. At every twist and turn of the roads around the coast a new and spectacular view of the sea becomes visible.

For the best view of all, it is an easy walk or drive to the summit of Cadillac Mountain (1530 ft), the highest point. Beneath the 'mountain' spread lakes, cranberry bogs, quiet spruce forests, and the Atlantic itself. The less frequented Isle au Haut, a good place for walking, is also part of Acadia and can be reached by ferry from Stonington on the southern tip of Deer Isle.

The park camping season is from 15 May to 15 October, with a 14-day limit. It's a good place for swimming, fishing, hiking and rock climbing.

ACCOMMODATION
See Bar Harbor for hotels, cottages.
Camping: within the park there are sites at Black Woods and Seawall. Seawall is the nicer of the two and in the summer there are long queues at both. $3 per site. There are also several, more expensive, private sites outside park limits.

INFORMATION
The park Visitors Center is on Rt 3 at Hulls Cove. The rangers give free talks, and a 15-minute film about Isle au Haut is shown on the hour.

THE APPALACHIAN TRAIL. About 100 miles north of Bangor is **Baxter State Park** where Mount Katahdin marks the northern starting point of the Appalachian Trail. This is wild, remote country where moose out-number humans.

Just to the north of Baxter lies the **Allagash Wilderness Waterway**. This is a canoeist's paradise, an area of lakes and rivers preserved in their primitive state to provide white-water and wilderness experience for the modern canoeist.

INFORMATION
Write to the Appalachian Trail Conference, 1916 Sunderland Pl, NW, Washington DC, and to the Appalachian Mountain Club, 5 Joy St, Boston, MA 02108.

MASSACHUSETTS

The Bay State is rivalled only by Virginia in the richness of its history. Massachusetts was the colony where the loudest and most open protests were raised against the British prior to 1777. After the initial skirmishes, the war switched to the other colonies, yet Massachusetts contributed the largest number of troops to the war: 20,000 militia, 67,907 regulars in the Continental Army.

Presidents John Adams, John Quincy Adams and John Kennedy all came from Massachusetts, as did Daniel Webster, while in the field of literature Robert Forst, John Whittier, Emily Dickinson, Louisa Alcott and Henry David Thoreau were either born or came to live here.

Massachusetts takes its name from the Massachuset Indians who occupied the Bay Territory, including Boston, in the early 17th century. An annual Indian pow-wow is still held at Masphee in July.

BOSTON. Boston is a proud Yankee city and seaport thick with reminders of its historic past. Bostonians are fiercely loyal, regarding their city as the hub of New England, and in colonial times of the whole New World. For Boston was the spiritual heart of the Revolution, the birthplace of American commerce and industry, and leader of the new nation in the arts and education. These days, the original WASPs (White Anglo Saxon Protestants) have been joined by successive generations of Blacks, Irish, Poles and Italians, and the city has developed a more cosmopolitan touch.

Boston has a cosier feel to it than most major American cities, and also something of a European flavour. It's compact and therefore a great place to walk (or jog as all the locals do). Within a comparatively small area you can stroll through the old cobbled streets, or on the Common where the colonists grazed their cattle, or down by the harbour or river, or else around such fine examples of modern building as the impressive Government Center. For all its historical associations, Boston is a city of youth and vitality, the city's businesses and amenities catering to the thousands of students at the area's seven major universities. Though accommodation tends to be expensive, there is a considerable variety of inexpensive activities for the visitor.

Music and the arts in general flourish in Boston. At any one time it is possible to sample anything from jazz and folk through to good theatre and modern dance. Sport too has its place, and in summer, when the Boston Red Sox baseball team is battling it out in the race for the American League title, the only real place to be is at Fenway Park, eating hot dogs and guzzling coke, but never on any account cheering for the opposition. In winter the mania transfers itself to football with the New England Patriots, and to ice hockey with the Boston Bruins.

The natural centre for journeys around Massachusetts, Boston is particularly convenient for visits to nearby Cambridge, Concord, Lexington, Saugus, Salem and Gloucester.

ACCOMMODATION

Accommodation in Boston is generally expensive, especially the hotels. We list a few 'cheaper' hotels first, but suggest you consider the guest houses and hostels mentioned further below if you want to keep your accommodation expenditure down to what it would be in most other cities. The Information Center at Boston Common provides a low-cost accommodation list in the $13–$35 range.

Bradford Hotel, 275 Tremont St, 426-1400. Near the Common. All rooms with TV, air conditioning, bath or shower. Cheapest double rooms $52.

Copley Square Hotel, 47 Huntington Ave at Exeter St, 536-9000. Opposite the

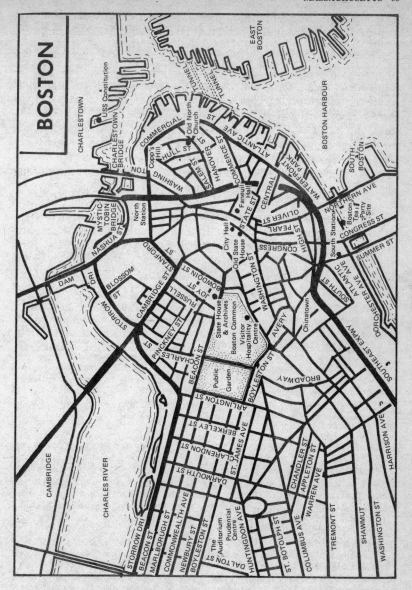

Prudential Center. Most rooms with bath or shower, air conditioning and TV. Singles from $42 up, doubles from $52 up.
Essex Hotel, 695 Atlantic Ave, opposite South Station, downtown. 482-9000. All rooms with bath, TV and radio, some with air conditioning. Singles from $40, doubles from $48. 'Very central and clean.'
Guest houses, hostels, dorms, etc:

Boston University, Office of Summer Housing, 985 Commonwealth Ave, 353-4203. From mid-May to mid-Aug offers singles at $22, doubles at $17 per person.

Garden Hills Dormitories, 164 Marlborough St, 267-0079. From early June to late August offers $10 beds in single or double rooms.

Guest House, 625 Commonwealth Ave, 247-7682. Around $15 per person in double or triple rooms, quads cheaper. 'Nice rooms, TV, shower, with water cooler and free coffee in the hall.'

Mrs Musichuk, 204 Bay State Rd, 267-3042. Singles $13, triples $32, with TV and use of shower. 'Clean and friendly; free tea.' 'Will sleep 4 in 3-bed room.'

YMCA, 316 Huntington Ave, 536-7800. $18 single, $22 double. Limited number of doubles. TV in rooms. Mixed reviews: 'Clean, friendly and safe.' 'Better than most, but the last night I'll ever stay at a YMCA.'

YMCA, United Armed Forces, City Sq, 242-2660. $16 single, or $7.50 with YHA card in room of four. 'Clean.'

YWCA Berkeley Residence Club, 40 Berkeley St, 482-8850. $20 per person, women only.

Boston International Youth Hostel, 12 Hemenway St. Brand new AYH. $7.50 per bed.

For drivers: Susse Chalet Motor Lodges and Inns at Dorchester, Braintree, Cambridge and Newton, singles $21.20 and up, doubles $25.70 and up. Phone toll-free 800-258-1980 for directions, reservations.

FOOD

No-Name Restaurant, 15½ Fisherman's Wharf, near Southeast end of Northern Ave. In old warehouse. Expect queues, Fish meals at $3 up. 'Vibrant atmosphere.'

Regina's Pizzeria, 11½ Thatcher St (yes!), North End. The best, from $3. Open till midnight.

Play It Again Sam, 1314 Commonwealth Ave, Brighton area. Mexican, huge meal for $6. Bars, free shows, movies: $3 per year membership, then free admission.

Friar Tuck's, 2 locations, on State St and on School St. Meal-sized hor d'oeuvres come free between 4 and 8pm with the $1 drink of the night. 'Get there early and eat your fill; ideal way to stretch your budget.'

Haymarket and Quincy Market, nr Government Center, have plenty of good cheap food stalls: Chinese, Italian, Greek, health foods, etc.

OF INTEREST

The Freedom Trail is a walking tour marked out on the streets of downtown Boston beginning in the Park at the Visitors' Center. On it you can visit nearly all Boston's associations with the American Revolution. But the Trail tends to be a little forced and unless you have a passionate interest in American history, forget it. The Trail is clearly marked by a path of red bricks set in the sidewalk. Few visitors to Boston escape it! Also there's a $5 shuttle bus that goes everywhere of historical note; you get on and off and on again when you like—tickets from Boston Common Visitors Center.

There are also bus tours of the Trail. From Copley Sq every hour from 9am to 3pm. Book at Statler Hilton or Sheraton Plaza. Lasts two hours and includes Beacon Hill, Paul Revere's house, USS *Constitution*, Old North Church.

Beacon Hill, especially Louisburg Sq, is Boston's old residential section to which every visitor must make a pilgrimage. Louisa May Alcott, Wm Dean Howels, the Brahmin Literary Set and many other famous Bostonians lived here.

Old State House, corner of Washington and State Sts. Built 1713 as the seat of British colonial government. The Declaration of Independence was read from the East Balcony in 1776. Has an important display of Americana. April–Oct, daily 9.30am–5.30pm; then Mon–Fri 10am–4pm, Sat and Sun 9.30am–5pm.

Faneuil Hall, Merchants Row, Faneuil Hall Sq. The scene of mass meetings during pre-revolutionary period, known as 'the Cradle of Liberty'. Mon–Fri, 9am–5pm, Sat 9am–4pm.

Faneuil Hall Market includes a floor of Faneuil Hall and the adjacent Quincy Market. The whole is a complex of eating places, small shops and produce stands.

Park St Church, Brimstone Corner. Built 1809. Scene of William Lloyd Garrison's first anti-slavery address, also where *America* was first sung, in 1832.

Old North Church, Salem St, near the end of the Freedom Trail. Built 1723. 'Perhaps the most elegant church in the USA.'

Paul Revere House. Revere lived here from 1770 to 1780 and set out from here on the famous ride. Probably the oldest wooden structure in Boston. Built 1670s. 10am–6pm. 75¢.

Boston Common. Boston is the only large American city still to have its common. The Common and Public Gardens are agreeable places for a leisurely stroll, but not at night. Curfew at 9.30pm.

Back Bay. Southwest of the Common. In this area is the first Church of Christ Scientist and the headquarters of the *Christian Science Monitor*, also the **Prudential Center**. The Center is a pleasantly planned complex of shops, restaurants and offices. It costs $2 to go up to the 50th floor for a magnificent view of Boston. Open weekdays. Skywalk open Mon–Thur 9am–11pm, Fri and Sat 9am–midnight, Sun 10am–11pm. Only go on a clear day.

The John Hancock Observatory is the tallest building in Boston. Viewing charge $2.50. 9am–11pm daily, noon 11pm Sun.

Museum of Fine Arts. Fenway and Huntington Ave. One of the finest galleries in America containing many major works. 'Marvellous Egyptian section.' Admission $4, no student reduction, closed Mon. 'Well worth the money; allow at least a whole day.'

Isabella Stewart Gardner Museum, Fenway. A reconstructed Venetian palazzo, originally built as the town house for the gallery's eccentric namesake. Rich in art treasures. Open Tue–Sun 1–5.30pm July and Aug; Tue 1–9.30pm, Wed–Sun 1–5.30pm rest of yr. $1. Concerts Sept–June Tue at 8pm, Thur 4pm, free, and Sun 4pm $1.

To get there take the MBTA bus from Copley Sq along Huntington Ave.

John F Kennedy Library, Columbia Point, overlooking harbour. Striking memorial to JFK, opened in 1979. Kennedy archives and exhibition.

Museum of Science, on the Charles River Dam. $3; $1.50 Fri evenings, plus 75¢ for planetarium. 'Could spend 2 days here and still not see it all.'

Harrison-Gray-Otis Museum, Cambridge St. Simple museum in pleasant house with typical New England fittings $1.

Symphony Hall, Huntington Ave. Free tickets given away at noon for rehearsals the night before debut performances. Home of the Boston Symphony Orchestra and the 'Pops'. In summer the latter play along the Charles River in the open air at **Hatch Memorial Shell**—admission free. 'Take your own picnic and get really laid back.'

Aquarium, Central Wharf, off Atlantic Ave. Admission $5, students $4. 'Excellent! Could spend the whole day there.' Mon–Thur 9am–5pm, Fri 9am–9pm, Sat & Sun 9am–6pm.

The *USS Constitution*, a frigate from the war of 1812, preserved in Boston Navy Yard. Open to the public 9am–5pm, $1.50. Nearby is the **Bunker Hill Monument** commemorating the first set battle of the Revolution. Good views. At the Bunker Hill Pavilion there's a good A/V programme, *The Whites of Their Eyes*, giving the background to the battle with dramatic effects. $1.75, students $1.25.

Boston Teaparty. A replica of a tea ship, *Beaver II*, which sailed the Atlantic in 1973, is moored by the side of the Congress St bridge. Admission to ship and museum $2, students $1.50. 9am–8pm. 'Visitors may throw tea overboard creating their own tea party.' 'A rip-off.'

Harbour Tours. Rowes Wharf, Atlantic Ave. Leaving at 10.15am, 1pm, 2.45pm. $6. Lasts one and a half hours. 'Not worth the money.'

Whale-watching trips, organised by the Aquarium from April through June, $24. 'Terrific experience.'

ENTERTAINMENT

Read *Boston Phoenix* or pick up the *Boston on Stage* monthly newsletter to find out what's on around town. Check the Thur edition of the *Boston Globe* for *Calendar* section on what's on.

Look for free jazz concerts at Copley Sq, lunchtimes in summer.

Spit, 13 Lansdowne St, nr Fenway Park. Punk, new wave, great place for dancing, dress down. Cover varies $3–$5 with the band, often British. Videos.

Metro, 15 Lansdowne St, next door to Spit; Boston's most popular disco, films, videos of yourself dancing. Gay night Sun.

Top of the Hub, bar-drinking and dancing—atop Prudential Center with Boston at your feet. You can get away with paying less than $4.

Pooh's, 464 Commonwealth Ave. 'Some of the finest jazz in Boston.' Cross over to Cambridge for a better, less formal music scene.

Concert Cruise around harbour. Leaves Rowes Wharf, 5.30pm, 6.30pm. $6. Chamber music while you see the harbour.

Tune into WGBH, the city's non-commercial TV channel and reputed to be one of the best in America.

Closest beach is Revere. 'Scruffy but only 60¢ on Blue Line.'

INFORMATION

Visitors Information Center, Boston Common on Tremont St, 338-1976. Pick up the *Boston by Week* pamphlet filled with things to do.

Convention and Tourist Bureau, 900 Boylston St, 536-4100.

Foreign Visitors Center, 15 State St, 262-4830 and 367-9275, for information, guides and interpreters.

Travelers Aid, 294 Stuart St, 542-7286. The best place to go for information on budget accommodation.

Crisis Hotline, 267-9150.

TRAVEL

Public transport, both buses and subways, is operated by the Massachusetts Bay Transit Authority (MBTA). Flat fare 60¢, free transfers. Note that bus and subway services shut down by 1am. For information phone 722-3200. The subway, known as the 'T' (hence T-stations) comprises four intersecting lines, the Blue, Green, Orange and Red. Maps are posted in stations, or you can pick up a free colour-coded map at any station or visitors centre.

Logan Airport is across the bay from downtown: take the Blue Line subway to Airport station from where there's a linking bus to the terminals.

Amtrak passengers will arrive at Back Bay Station, Dartmouth and Buckingham Sts (Green Line subway, Prudential station), or South Station (Red Line), Atlantic Ave. For information at both stations, phone 800-523-5720. Boston and Maine (B&M) trains arrive at North Station, 482-4400, served by Green Line subway. Both B&M and Amtrak serve towns around Boston.

B&M operates a winter ski-train to Massachusetts resorts, $30 inclusive of journey plus boot and ski rental for the day.

Plymouth and Brockton Street Railway Co (a bus service) operates from the Greyhound terminal (773-9400) to Plymouth Hyannis and Provincetown.

Greyhound, 10 St James Ave, 423-5810.

Trailways, South Station (on the Red Line), 742-8800.

Green Tortoise, 586 Green St, Cambridge, 265-8533.

American Auto Transporters, 120 Commonwealth Ave, 262-9590. Drive-away cars,

$150 deposit; they allow 10 days and 3600 miles between Boston and LA for example.
Rides Information Center, 782-7337, or Arrange-a-Ride, Boston University, 353-3641.

SURVIVAL
Masspirg (see Yellow Pages) offers a large number of canvassing jobs, mostly on environmental issues.
Try selling the *Boston Phoenix*, or hot dogs at Red Sox stadium, or the *Boston Globe* by phone, or ice cream from a bicycle.
Filene's Bargain Basement, Washington St. A revered institution with some good buys.
Barnes and Noble Bookstore, Washington St, for great bargains in reading.

CAMBRIDGE. The most famous of the Boston metropolitan area's universities, MIT and Harvard, are in Cambridge. The lifestyle of the concentration of students here sets the pulse for both sides of the Charles River, and Harvard Square is where it all happens. You will be amazed at the diversity of life, entertainment and action to be found in such a small area, and at the frenetic, flamboyant way in which the student and local population conducts its daily business. For a complete change of pace, stroll through Harvard Yard or visit one of the historic houses.

You can take the MBTA to Harvard Square from Boston, but it's better to walk across Harvard Bridge, taking in the cityscapes, and the sailors, windsurfers and rowers on the river below.

ACCOMMODATION
Kirkland Inn, 67 Kirkland St, 547-4600. $44 double.
YMCA, 820 Massachusetts Ave, 876-3860. $16 single, $20 double. Restaurant. Men only.
YWCA, 7 Temple St, 491-6050. $20 single, no dorm accommodation. Women only.

FOOD
Acropolis, 1680 Massachusetts Ave. 'Good, inexpensive Greek, $14 dinner for two, Sun through Thur.'
Chi-chi, Massachusetts Ave, next to the Orson Welles Theatre. 'Inexpensive Mexican food; delicious too.'
Elsie's, Mt Auburn St. A real Harvard institution. Superb, cheap sandwiches. 'Try Freshers Delight.'
The Turtle Cafe, Massachusetts Ave. 'Not cheap but superb Cordon Bleu meals.'
MIT Student Center, Massachusetts Ave. Good value dinner 5–7pm.

OF INTEREST
Harvard University, founded 1636, is the oldest university in North America. Massachusetts Hall (1720) is the oldest building still standing. The University Visitor's Information Center is at 1352 Massachusetts Ave (in the Holyoke Center. *Building Harvard* and *The Story of Harvard* each cost 50¢. There are daily conducted tours at 10am, 11.15am, 2pm, 3.15pm (2pm only after Labor Day); Sun 1.30pm and 3pm. Free.
Walk from Harvard Sq up Brattle St towards **Longfellow's house**, past **Radcliffe**, the women's college. The poet lived here between 1843 and 1882. The house is open to the public and is furnished with Longfellow's furniture and books. In earlier times

George Washington used this house as his HQ. Open daily 9am–4.30pm. 75¢ admission.

Also in the campus area is the **Fogg Art Museum**, Quincy and Broadway; **Le Corbusier's Visual Arts Center; Houghton Museum**, opposite University Chapel housing the Keats collection; the **Peabody Museum of Archaeology and Ethnology**, 11 Divinity Ave, 495-2341, links up with the **Museums of Comparative Zoology, Botany and Mineralogy**, $1.75 for the lot, 'It takes all day to see most of it'. There's a spectacular collection of glass flowers by Theopold and Rudolph Blaschka in the Harvard Botanical Museum. The **Fogg Art Museum** is especially good on things Chinese, but does not open at weekends during the summer.

MIT tours include a look at the lovely chapel designed by Eero Saarinen. Student-conducted tours begin at 10am and 2pm from the Admission Office, Room 3108, Main Building, 77 Massachusetts Ave. Closed weekends. It's probably just as worthwhile to get a map and wander round yourself.

Old Burying Ground, corner of Church and Garden. Graves go back to 1635 and many Revolutionary War heroes and several Harvard presidents are buried here.

Mount Auburn Cemetery on Mt Auburn St contains the graves of Longfellow, James Lowell, Oliver Wendell Holmes and Mary Baker Eddy. This is both a cemetery and a park, with ponds, hills, footpaths, arboretum. 'Quiet relaxing place, great for birdwatching in spring.'

Heritage Trail Walking Tour. The inevitable. Begins Cambridge Common where Washington took command of the Continental Army. Details from City Hall.

ENTERTAINMENT

Watch *Phoenix* for details of concerts and lectures. The active music scene is closely tied to Harvard and MIT and the summer months are therefore quiet.

Cronin's Bar, 114 Mt Auburn St. As seen in the movie *Love Story*.

Jonathan Swifts, Harvard Sq, varied bands nightly, cover from 9pm, happy hour from 4 to 7pm, 2 drinks for the price of one and free food.

The Boathouse, JFK St off Harvard Sq, 'Best Cambridge bar'.

Ryles, 212 Hampshire St, Inman Sq, 876-9330. 'Good jazz, often big names.' Upstairs, cover from 9pm, around $5; downstairs no cover but live music too.

Orson Welles Theatre, 1001 Massachusetts Ave, 868-3600, shows outstanding foreign films and runs an annual horror film festival. $4.50 admission; senior citizens $2.50 Sun–Thur.

There are several inexpensive coffee houses around Harvard Sq and it's worth looking out for pop concerts on Cambridge Common on Sundays.

SHOPPING

Harvard Co-op, Harvard Sq. Bargains, records, books, prints and posters.

LEXINGTON. Lexington shares with Concord the distinction of being the site of the first skirmish in the American Revolution, though when Paul Revere galloped through this 'Birthplace of American Liberty' it was not the depressing and urbanised satellite of Boston that it is today.

Lexington Green, where it all happened two centuries ago (and re-enacted every 19 April). The Green is lined with lovely colonial houses and, on the east side, facing the road by which the British approached, is the famous **Minuteman Statue**. Over in the southwest corner of the green is the **Revolutionary Monument** erected in 1799 to commemorate the 8 minutemen killed here.

Near the Green is **Buckman Tavern**, the oldest of the local hostelries and gathering place for the local minutemen on drill nights.

Hancock-Clarke House, Hancock Street is where Sam Adams and John Hancock were staying when Paul Revere came galloping by to warn them.
Great Meadows Reservation, nr Minuteman National Historical Park. 'Marshland, marvellous for birdwatching.'

INFORMATION
Chamber of Commerce Info Center, nr Buckman Tavern on Mass Ave, has details and literature. Admission to the various historical houses is $1.25, or else you can get a combination ticket at $2.75.

CONCORD. Near Concord's old North Bridge on 19 April 1775, local farmers took aim at advancing British redcoats and 'fired the shot heard round the world'. The British detachment successfully confiscated the rebels' ammunition dump in the village, but suffered 272 casualties before returning to Boston. The bridge is part of the **Minute Man National Historical Park** and a park ranger gives excellent history talks here every hour. Battle re-enactments are staged at the North Bridge, April through October.

This typical and attractive New England village was also the home of the literary Transcendentalist movement. The Emerson house is near the Alcott house on Lexington Road. Thoreau's house is on Main Street and not far away is Walden Pond.

All houses are open to the public until 5pm. There is a museum opposite Emerson's house, $1.25 entry. In season there is an Information Booth near Lexington Road.

TRAVEL
20 miles north of Boston, Concord is served by B&M trains departing from North Station, $2.50 one way.

THE NORTH SHORE. Just north of Boston on US 1 is **Saugus**, founded in 1646 and the birthplace of the American iron industry. The restored ironworks with turning waterwheels, massive hammers and wheezing bellows clanks away at a dollar a peep. Open Tuesday to Sunday, mid-May to mid-October.

Beyond Saugus on US 1 lies **Salem**. At the Witch House here in 1692 the Puritan citizens interrogated their fellows and strung up 19 of them on Gallows Hill. A couple more were crushed to death under heavy stones. Nathaniel Hawthorne worked at the old Customs House, and the House of the Seven Gables made famous in his novel still stands. The house is at 54 Turner Street. Admission is $3 and attractions include secret stairways and hidden compartments.

Chestnut Street is lined with the lovely homes of Salem Clipper captains and owners. The Pioneer Village shows typical homes of the Puritan community, circa 1630, and the *Arabella* is a replica of the ship used to bring these loons across the Atlantic.

On Cape Ann, about 30 miles north of Boston, **Gloucester** was once a major fishing centre. This oldest American seaport retains enough of its salty atmosphere to make it a summer resort and artist colony. Four miles north of Gloucester, off Route 127A, is the typical fishing village of **Rockport**, now full of arty-crafty stores. 'Great for browsing and getting broke.'

On your way north from here to New Hampshire and Maine, there's the small town of **Newburyport** which has 'the most beautiful Y in the USA' in a restored colonial house on Market Street.

PLYMOUTH. Plymouth Rock marks the spot where the Pilgrims landed on 26 December 1620, and established the first English colony north of Virginia. A few 17th-century houses still stand, and on Leyden Street markers indicate where the very first houses stood. The Pilgrims who succumbed to the initial bitter winter are buried on Cole's Hill, and moored by the Rock is *Mayflower II*, a full-size replica of the original.

ACCOMMODATION
Guest houses are the cheapest places to stay here. Try looking in the area behind the Tourist Information Center. Prices start at around $15 single.
Loremar Guest House, 126 Warren Ave, 746-9455. Two miles out of town by the sea. $20, shower, TV.

OF INTEREST
Mayflower II. The replica of the original, built in England and sailed to America in 1957. Admission $2.50 (but see below).
Plimouth Plantation. Replica of original settlement, 3 miles south. $3.50, closes 5pm. It's cheaper if you visit *Mayflower II* and Plimouth Plantation with a combined ticket. 'Both are staffed by American students dressed as Pilgrims and speaking with "English accents".'
Cranberry World, nr *Mayflower II*, free. 'All about cranberries, including free samples; good for a laugh or if it rains.'
Pilgrim Hall Museum, 75 Court St. Personal possessions and records of the Pilgrims. 9.30am–4.30pm. $1.50.

INFORMATION
Plymouth Information Center, North Park just east of US 44 and 3A, 746-3377. Combination ticket to historical attractions available here.

CAPE COD. A 65-mile-long hook jutting out into the Atlantic, the Cape is a narrow string of sand from where, atop a dune, you can gaze over both the ocean and Cape Cod Bay. It's a blustery, chilly spot out of season, but in summer delightfully sunny with a refreshing tang of salt in the air.

Although largely a summer resort, it is still possible to avoid the crowds and escape to deserted sand dunes or down beautiful sandy New England lanes leading to the sea. Achieve this by staying away from Hyannis and the southern coastline below the point where it becomes the Cape Cod National Seashore.

The Hyannis area is the part of the Cape most exploited by tourism and free enterprise, but over in the lower Cape, small towns like

Sandwich, Barnstaple, Catumet and Pocasset remain relatively quiet, even in the high season. After Labor Day of course you can have the whole Cape to yourself. There is plenty of camping near Sandwich where there is also a free public beach.

On the Cape you will come up against numerous private beaches, or public ones which extract heavy parking fees. There's a $1 per car parking fee at the National Seashore Beaches. The Chamber of Commerce booklet *Cape Cod Vacationer* lists all beaches and their status as well as being a mine of other useful information about the area. If you're planning to do a lot of hiking on the Cape, *Hiking Cape Cod* by Witchell and Griswold (East Woods Press) is especially recommended.

Aside from the tourist the Cape's other great source of revenue is the cranberry. Nearly three-quarters of the world's cranberry crop is produced here and in neighbouring Plymouth County.

ACCOMMODATION

Can be expensive, but there are several camping sites and also 3 youth hostels. For more hotel or motel details see under Hyannis or Provincetown, or else consult Yankee Magazine's *Guide to New England* or the *Vacationer*.

Bed and Breakfast, Cape Cod, Box 341, West Hyannisport, (617) 775-2772. Can arrange in-season singles from $26, doubles from $34.

Hostels: at Hyannis (see below), Orleans and Truro, Orleans, Bridge Rd, Eastham, 255-9762. Open 15 May–15 Sept, $6. Truro, N. Pamet Rd, 1½ miles east of Rte 6, 349-3889. Open 15 May–6 Sept, $6. Reservations necessary.

Camping: recommended sites are the Shawne Crowell State Forest at Sandwich and the R C Nickerson State Forest at Brewster, but be warned: 'Campsites are often full right up to Labor Day and you may need to drive right out to North Truro to find a vacancy.'

TRAVEL

Greyhound and Bonanza both run scheduled services from New York, Boston and Providence. Once on the Cape, Cape Cod Bus Lines can get you around.

Bicycle hire: Cove Cycle, Cove Rd, ½ block east of Rte 6A, Orleans. Also try Orleans YH.

Smith's Seashore, Shellers and Eastham. There are several miles of bicycle paths on the National Seashore and by the Cape Cod Canal.

HYANNIS.
The metropolis of the Cape, Hyannis is the main supply centre for the area; shops, schools, hospital, harbour and airport (flights and sailings to Nantucket). Main Street is almost the typical all-American strip; for charm you want the outlying areas like Hyannis Port and Craigville with its excellent beach for swimming.

Very much more upper crust than the other Cape Cod towns, Hyannis is the home of wealthy trendies and is bathed in the aura of the Kennedy family sequestered in Hyannis Port.

ACCOMMODATION

Park Square Village, 156 Main St, 775-5611. 5 minutes from bus station and beach, 10 minutes from ferry. Doubles $35, cheaper after Labor Day. Top floor has dorm facilities and low rates. 'Self-catering villas available or pleasant single and double rooms in large complex; laundry for guests.' 'Excellent situation for the area; a little shabby but clean and very friendly; plenty of rooms so often has vacancies when all else fails.'

Sea Witch Inn, 363 Sea St, 771-4261. Beautiful private home on acre of land; nr beach, short walk to Main St. Rooms, cottage and 2 barn apartments, $12 per person double and up.

Yellowdoor Guest House, 6 Main St, 775-0321. 10 mins from bus station. $8–$15 per person, double. 'Excellent.'

Windrift Motel, 115 Main St, 775-4697. Doubles from $38. Pool.

Hy-Land YH, 465 Falmouth Rd, 775-2970. $5.25 for members, dorm only; family rooms off-season. Open year-round, reservations for July and Aug advisable. 2 miles to ferry and beaches. To get to YH walk 1 mile down Barnstable Rd to Airport Rotary, turn left on Rte 28 North and hostel is ¾ mile on left.

FOOD
Hearth & Kettle, 412 Main St. Open 24 hrs.

ENTERTAINMENT
Craigville Beach. 25¢ per person, or $2 car park. Use Sea St. Beach or go to the nearby free public beach at Falmouth.

INFORMATION
Chamber of Commerce for maps, hotel and job info.
Board of Trade, Baxter and Barnstaple Rds, closer to downtown than Chamber of Commerce.

TRAVEL
During the summer, boats leave daily for Nantucket and Martha's Vineyard. The round trip fare is about $20. Trips round the harbour and to Kennedy compound also available.
U-Pedal-It, 110 Ocean St, 775-1931. All new English bikes, $8 per day.
Cape Cod Bus Lines runs year-round service between Hyannis and Provincetown, (617) 548-0333 for 24-hour info.

PROVINCETOWN. P-town, as it's known locally, is at the very tip of the Cape. The Pilgrim Fathers' first landfall in North America was actually here. They stayed for four or five weeks before moving on to Plymouth. It's a sore point with the town, P-towners believing that they should have the fuss and fame rather than Plymouth. Pilgrim references are therefore much encouraged here.

In summer the town is jampacked with artists, playwrights and craftsmen, and the tourists and hangers-on who come to watch them. It's reputed to be a 90 percent gay community. P-town is an attractive spot with old clapboard houses, narrow streets and miles of sandy beaches. For a special evening's entertainment, take a beach taxi ride over the sand dunes.

ACCOMMODATION
The Cape Codder, 570 Commercial St, 487-0131. Open mid-April to October. 'Private sandy beach, clean comfortable rooms.' Singles from $18, doubles from $26.
Alice Dunham's Guest House, 3 Dyer St, 487-3330. Old sea captain's house. Singles from $18, doubles from $23. 10% discount before 30 May and after Labor Day, and discount when showing this Guide. 'Nicest place in town.'

NANTUCKET. This is where Melville lived when he wrote *Moby Dick*; 'The Little Grey Lady of the Sea', as the island is known. A salty place with cedar shingles, lobsters bought right off the boats, old anchors and whale oil vats, miles of open sand beaches terrific for swimming, surfing, fishing and all-night bonfire parties.

The cobblestoned Main Street and fine colonial homes testify to the past prosperity built on the backs of the hunted whales. Today the money flows in with the flood tide of 'off-islanders' in summer; a crowded place then, but a lot of fun. For the pristine scene come out of season when there's nobody there but the 'on-islanders', many of whom have never seen the mainland.

ACCOMMODATION
The island is generally a very expensive place to stay, and to maintain premium hotel rates any riff-raff caught camping will be fined $50, ie what you would have paid for a bed. But all is not lost:
Flossie's Flop House, 31 India St, $12 per person in a single room, shared room or on the sofa. 'Very entertaining hostess who cares about where you sleep. It's not fancy, but it's a good place and very handy to centre of town. Flossie will put you on the sofa if you're really stuck.'
Other affordables are the White Eagle Hotel, 76 Main St (you must stay more than one night) and the Royal Manor Guest House, Center St, 228-0600.
Star of the Sea YH, Surfside, 3 miles from Nantucket town at the end of Atlantic Ave, 228-0433. Open 1 Apr–31 Oct, $6. During July, Aug and Sept you probably won't get space unless you've reserved far in advance.

FOOD
The Downeyflake, 9 S. Water St. 'Excellent homemade things.'
Captain Tobey's Chowder House, Straight Wharf. 'Good seafood.'

OF INTEREST
Whaling Museum, Broad St. In the 18th and 19th centuries, Nantucket was the best known whaling town in America. You can recapture something of the flavour of those times here.

TRAVEL
During the summer there are daily sailings from Woods Hole to the island. The trip takes 1 hr 40 mins and costs approx $20 round trip. Check times and prices with Hyline, (617) 775-7185, or the Steamship Authority, (617) 771-4000.

MARTHA'S VINEYARD. Named after Martha Gosnold and her wild grapes, this is a quiet and beautiful island. It's also hilly but it's worth the strenuous bike ride to Gay Head at the western tip to watch the setting sun do its light show against the coloured clay cliffs.

Surfing, swimming and sailing are the attractions, though it's going to cost you your tiller arm to hire a boat. Settle instead for a bicycle and peddle around Edgartown, the sailing centre, where you can admire the fine old houses of the whaling captains. Menemsha is a peaceful fishing village where Indian harpooners still make a living by sailing out to spear swordfish. 'The whole island is dry except for

Edgartown and Oaks Bluff. This is worth knowing when you're searching for a drink in Vineyard Haven.'

ACCOMMODATION
Accommodation lists are available from the Chamber of Commerce and tourist information booths across the island.
Guest houses offer reasonable rates; try Wesley House in Oaks Bluff, 'Clean and bright', or Mrs George Baptiste, Vineyard Haven, 693-2923.
West Tisbury YH, 693-2665. Open 1 Apr–30 Nov, $6, reservations essential.
Camping: Webb's Camping Area, Barnes Rd, Oak Bluffs, 693-0233. $12–$15 for 2.
Martha's Vineyard Family Campground, Edgartown Rd, Vineyard Haven, 693-3772. Similar rates.

TRAVEL
See under Hyannis for ferry information.
Anderson's Bike Rentals, $4.50 per day, driving licence as deposit, close to ferry landing.

On Route 6 on the way from the Cape to Providence, Rhode Island, **New Bedford** was once an important whaling port. In the past decade it's undergone massive renovation and has been transformed from a dismal rundown place to a cross between Mystic Seaport and Nantucket. There is a fascinating whaling museum to be visited, as well as several old houses and small craft stores and factories to be seen.

THE BERKSHIRE HILLS. Running north to Vermont and south to Connecticut along the western border of Massachusetts, the Berkshires are gracious, tasteful, subdued, holding on to the values of a bygone age. The towns of Williamstown (famous for its college), Lenox and Stockbridge nestle among the hills, and this is a good area to get off the beaten track and explore the quiet villages, or hike some of the trails around Mount Greylock.

Mount Greylock at 3491 feet is the highest peak in the state. The summit offers splendid views of the Hudson Valley and the Green Mountains of southern Vermont.

The Berkshires are also a cultural centre in summer, the musical and theatrical events being based around Lenox, Lee and Stockbridge. The free *Berkshire Eagle* will keep you abreast of current happenings.

PITTSFIELD. Named after the same Pitt who tagged Pittsburgh, Pennsylvania, this was the birthplace of writer Herman Melville. The Atheneum has a room devoted to his effects, and you can visit his house, Arrowhead, just outside Pittsfield on Holmes Road (442-1793). Nathaniel Hawthorne and Oliver Wendell Holmes also lived or summered around Pittsfield.

Five miles west is **Hancock Shaker Village**, well worth a visit. A religious sect who got nearer my God to Thee by doing an early form of boogalloo, the Shakers had their origins in Manchester, England.

The village, founded in 1790, displays many fine examples of their primitive but beautiful craftsmanship. Alas the Shakers abandoned their village to the tourists in 1960.

ACCOMMODATION
YMCA, 292 North St, 499-7650. All rooms are singles, $15 daily, $46 weekly.
Friendship Tanglewood Inn, 3 miles south of town on Rtes 7 and 20, 442-4000. S32 double up.

TRAVEL
AMTRAK's *Lake Shore Limited*, Boston-Chicago, stops here: 1355 East St.

LENOX. The Tanglewood Music Festival is held here in July and August, with thousands of visitors, outdoor prom style, listening to the Boston Symphony Orchestra. The main shed holds 6000 people, but many prefer to sit out on the lawns with a blanket and picnic. Tickets cost $7 and up; phone (413) 637-1940 for schedules. All kinds of music is performed during the season, and there are many other fringe activities in the area.

ACCOMMODATION
Susse Chalet Motor Lodge, Massachusetts Turnpike, exit 2, on Rtes 7 and 20, 637-3560. $21.20 single, $25.70 double.

Lee is the scene of one of the other main Berkshire festivals, the Jacob's Pillow Dance Festival, held at the Ted Shawn Theater off US 20 east of Lee. This world-famous event frequently attracts the Fonteyns of this world. Tickets cost about $7 up. Also in Lee is the October State Forest, with the Appalachian Trail running through it.

Situated on Route 20 at the junctions of I-86 and Massachusetts Turnpike, **Old Sturbridge**, a preserved and restored early 19th century village, can be visited enroute from Boston (56 miles to the east) and the Berkshires. It's meant to show the visitor life in a rustic Yankee village. Many traditional crafts and trades such as tinsmithing, broom making, or milling are carried on here and demonstrated daily. On less of a grand scale than Williamsburg and perhaps nicer for that. In winter there are old fashioned sleigh rides through the snow, and in summer a toss in the hay. Entrance: $7.

NEW HAMPSHIRE

The Granite State is the only state named after an English county. It is thought by many to be the most visually attractive east of the Mississippi. New Hampshire has a short but sandy Atlantic coastline, several large lakes (the biggest is 72-square-mile Lake Winnipesaukee), the lovely White Mountain range, more than 60 covered wooden bridges and a 90 percent tree cover. Notice the granite walls everywhere. Built by the early settlers to enclose their fields, the walls remain even though most of the fields are forest again. The state is beautiful in summer, spectacularly beautiful during the Fall Foliage Show, and the long, cold, snowy winters make it a popular and fashionable skiing centre.

New Hampshire was the first state to declare its independence and also the first to adopt its own constitution. Nowadays it is regarded as a political barometer, the results of its early primary elections being considered a prophecy of the final outcome in the presidential elections. The inhabitants are mostly genuine Yankees and the state motto 'Live Free or Die' is a reflection of the tough Yankee spirit behind the Revolutionary War.

PORTSMOUTH. Global politics were inaugurated here in 1905 when the treaty ending the Russo-Japanese War was signed under the interested eye of President Theodore Roosevelt. Apart from being a footnote in history, Portsmouth, as New Hampshire's only seaport, has numerous old and well-preserved homes, many of them built by ship captains. Nearby, on New Hampshire's tiny 18-mile coastline, there are numerous fine, sandy beaches, including those at Wallis Sands and Rye Harbor. On Labor Day you can go down to the sea to cheer the Great Bay Day Reggatta.

ACCOMMODATION
Pine Haven Motel, 6½ miles south of town on US 1, 964-8187. Doubles from $30, with bath, free coffee. Open year-round. Nr beaches.

OF INTEREST
Strawberry Banke, 10-acre preservation project in Old South End. This marked the beginning, in 1623, of what later became Portsmouth. Buildings date from 1695 to 1820. Also several exhibits and craft shops. $4.
Old Harbor Area, Bow and Ceres Sts, once the focus of the thriving seaport and now an area of craft shops, eating places, etc.

CONCORD. Capital of New Hampshire, on the Merrimack River, and famous in the 19th century for its Concord coaches, the stagecoaches used throughout the old West. If you're about to tour the state, this is a reasonably central place (and on the main highway for Boston) to start.

About 55 miles to the southwest is 3500 foot Mount Mondanock with a splendid view from the peak of the Northern Appalachians. Take the Greyhound to Jafrey or Troy from where it's five easy walking miles to the summit. Or travelling north there are the lakes of central New Hampshire, and further north still the alpine-like White Mountains.

ACCOMMODATION
New Hampshire Highway Hotel, Ft Eddy Rd, I-93, exit 14, 225-6687. Singles from

$26, doubles from $38. Air conditioning, heated pool, cable TV. Only a few blocks from downtown.

YMCA, 15 North State St, 224-5351. $15 single. Fills early. Men only.

OF INTEREST
State House, Capitol St. The Hall of Flags is worth seeing. Open June–Sept, weekdays 8am–4.30pm, weekends 9am–5pm.
Pierce Manse, Peacock St. Restored home of President Franklin Pierce. 10am–4pm, Mon–Sat. $1.

THE WHITE MOUNTAINS. Dominated by **Mount Washington**, 6288 feet, the highest peak in the northeast where wind velocity has been recorded at 231 miles per hour! Climbing the mountain is quite a feat, but it can be done in summer, and the view is well worth the effort. For the great majority, however, there's a cog railway to the top, with five states and Canada visible on a clear day. It's not cheap though, the three hour round trip costing $16. The auto (toll) road to the summit is equally costly at $8 per car plus $2 for each passenger.

Visit **Franconia Notch** and its 700-foot flume chasm with the **Old Man of the Mountains**, a natural stone profile, rising at the northwest end. **Cannon Mountain** in this area can be conquered by cog railway too.

Cranmore and **Wildcat Mountains** to the southeast of Mount Washington are more sheltered than most, with the best skiing facilities in the White Mountains.

During fine summer weekends, the area attracts crowds of people and anyone seeking a bit of peace and quiet is strongly recommended to search elsewhere. Accommodation and all facilities are expensive.

ACCOMMODATION
Camping is the answer unless you're trail walking. In this case it's worth getting hold of the White Mountain Club leaflet *AMC Huts System*. New Hampshire pioneered the mountain huts system in 1888 and the leaflet gives locations of shelters where meals and accommodation are provided.
Youth Hostel at Twin Mountain, 13 miles north of Franconia Notch, 846-5527, $5.
Camping: several sites at local state parks including Franconia Notch, Crawford Notch, Moose Brook (Gorham) and White Lake (West Ossipee).

LAKE WINNIPESAUKE. Lying just south of the White and Ossipee Mountains, this is New Hampshire's largest body of water and a popular summer spot for visitors. Come here for sunning, swimming and sailing against a backdrop of tree-covered hills. **Center Harbor**, **Wolfboro** and **Meredith** are the main centres for accommodation and sightseeing. There are several campgrounds around the lake.

HANOVER. Fifty-nine miles northwest of Concord and home of the northern-most ivy league college, Dartmouth. Founded in 1769 by one Eleazar Wheelock as an experiment in 'spreading Christian education to the Indians and other youth'. Dartmouth ranks as the nation's ninth oldest college, and has on its campus several lovely old Colonial buildings.

ACCOMMODATION
Chieftain Motel, Rt 10, 2 miles north of Dartmouth College, 643-2550. $30 single, doubles $38 and up. Pool. Open all year.
Occom Inn, N Main St. $10 hostel-type room.
At the college, get information on rooms at fraternity houses, also shelters along the Appalachian Trail.

RHODE ISLAND

A colony founded by Roger Williams who dissented from the Puritan theocracy of Massachusetts, Rhode Island successfully developed by smuggling, slaving and whaling and for a while hesitated to sacrifice its post-Revolutionary War independence by joining the United States. The maritime tradition now survives only at the yacht harbour of Newport, the state having turned to the production of chickens.

Nicknamed Little Rhody, the state is the smallest and most densely populated in the United States.

PROVIDENCE. After being expelled by the Puritan Massachusetts Bay Colony for his liberal beliefs, Roger Williams fled to his friends among the Narragansett Indians in 1636. On land purchased from them, he established the settlement that grew into Providence.

State capital and one of New England's largest cities, Providence is today a modern industrial city and port fiercely proud of its traditions and historic past. Many fine houses and commercial buildings survive from earlier times and these, along with the attractions of ivy league Brown University, are the main points of interest for the casual visitor.

ACCOMMODATION
Susse Chalet Inn, 341 Highland Ave, ½ mile south of I-95, exit 1, 5 miles east of town, 336-7900. $27 single, $31 double, colour TV and FM radio.
In town the cheapest hotel or motel is Wayland Manor, 500 Angel St, 751-7700, $47 double, bath and TV.
YMCA, 160 Broad St, 456-0100, $16 single and up, men and women.
International House, 8 Stimson Ave, 421-7181. For foreign travellers. 'Clean, friendly and cheap.'
Roger Williams College, 255-2280 and 255-2138, offers college rooms to students during the summer at reasonable rates.

FOOD
Panache, 125 N Main St, good quiches and salads.
Silver Top Truck Stop, opp Union Station, sleazy but open all night.
Muldoon's, 250 S Water St, a good Irish pub, sandwiches served.

ENTERTAINMENT
Lupo's Heartbreak Hotel, Washington St, good rock acts.

OF INTEREST

The Arcade, between Westminster and Weybosset Sts, is a Classical Revival style 'Temple of Trade', an early shopping mall dating from 1828.

Beneficient Congregational Church, 300 Weybosset St, dates from 1810 and is one of the earliest examples of Classical Revival in the country. The interior is patterned after New England meetinghouses.

State House, Smith St, with the second largest unsupported marble dome in the world (St Peter's, Rome, is the largest). Inside is the 1663 charter granted by Charles II and a full-length Gilbert Stuart portrait of George Washington.

Across the river on Congdon St is the **Roger Williams National Memorial** with Roger buried at its base. The nearby visitor center at 282 N Main St does a/v shows and tours about the city's founder, who named it in gratitude 'for God's merciful providence unto me in my distress'.

First Baptist Church, 75 N Main St, dates from 1775 and stands where Roger Williams founded the first Baptist church in America in 1638.

Rhode Island School of Design, 224 Benefit St, contains a first-rate **Museum of Art**: 19th C French and modern Latin American painters, 18th C European porcelains and oriental textiles, and classical art. Also the Pendelton House, faithfully furnished replica of an early Providence house. 331-3511. $1.

Providence Athenaeum, 251 Benefit St, a Classical Revival structure chiefly interesting because here Edgar Allen Poe wooed Sarah Helen Whitman, his prototypal *Annabel Lee*.

Brown University, College Hill, has been here since 1770; interesting libraries and exhibitions (eg pre-16th C books, and Renaissance through 20th C paintings in the **Annmary Brown Memorial**). For tours, go to Admissions Office, 863-1000.

College Hill generally is full of early houses, not restored but lived in over the past 200 years or so.

INFORMATION

Providence Preservation Society, 24 Meeting St, 831-7440. Housed in a 1769 school, plenty of info here on historical Providence.

Convention and Visitors Bureau, 10 Dorrance St, 274-1636. 'Very helpful.'

NEWPORT. Thirty miles away from Providence and right on Narragansett Bay, Newport is a lively summer resort and home of the America's Cup races. Although a rival of Boston and New York in colonial times, Newport really came into its own around the turn of the century when the town became the place for millionaires to build their summer 'cottages'. Many of the mansions are now open to the public. Find them close by Newport's fabulous beach and on Bellevue Avenue.

ACCOMMODATION

Hotels here are above average in price.

The Newport County Chamber of Commerce, 10 America's Cup Ave, 847-1600, provides a list including budget and rock-bottom accommodation; guest houses usually offer the best deal.

Queen Ann Inn, 16 Clarke St, 846-5676. Centrally located. $33 double with breakfast. 'Clean, friendly.'

Armed Services YMCA, 50 Washington Sq, 846-3120. $20 single, $14 per person double, YHA members $9. 10 minutes from bus station.

OF INTEREST

The Breakers. Vanderbilt's magnificent mansion, open daily June through October,

$4.50 admission. Also **The Elms**, built for coal magnate E J Berwind, Oliver Belmont's **Belcourt Castle** with 'possibly the world's largest collection of stained glass.' You can buy combination tickets to see 8 mansions in all; it works out cheaper if you can stand the pace.

Hammersmith Farm, on Ocean Dr, was the summer residence of Hugh Auchinloss, step-father of Jacqueline Kennedy Onassis. This was the setting for Jack and Jackie's wedding reception, and was a presidential summer hideaway during the early '60s. Now the only working farm in Newport. $3.50 admission.

Block Island. 9 miles south of the mainland and a peaceful summer resort. There are ferries to the island from Newport and Providence.

TRAVEL
Greyhound serves from NY and Boston, Bonanza from Boston. Also local buses to/from Providence, $1.75. No station, but bus ticket agency at Cote Pharmacy, Broadway.

VERMONT

The Green Mountain State has a quiet rural character. At the time of the creation of the United States the area of Vermont was claimed by New York and New Hampshire, but under the entrepreneurship of Ethan Allen, patriot and profit-minded property man (he and his brothers owned most of the area), it asserted its own independence in the form of a republic, only later, in 1791, acquiescing on its own terms to the Union.

Vermont is famous for maple syrup and the magnificence of its autumn foliage and winter ski trails. The autumn colours are at their best towards the end of September; this is also the time for foliage festivals and get-togethers. March is the time for syrup festivals. If you're in the area then, look out for a sap house and watch the syrup being made. The state has always attracted artists and writers as well as small, experimental schools. It is also one of the few states to ban billboards and to restore the deposit on bottles and cans.

Hikers wanting information or to join up with a group should contact the Green Mountain Club, PO Box 889, Montpelier, VT 05602; Tel: (802) 223-3463. They can put you in touch with their local chapters throughout the state.

BURLINGTON. Vermont's largest city is set on the eastern shores of **Lake Champlain**, the major freshwater lake east of the Great Lakes, and favourite summer playground. Ethan Allen is buried here, in Greenmount Cemetery.

This is a good place from which to visit Fort Ticonderoga on Lake George, New York, or for heading north to Montreal. Or for a tour around Vermont itself: nearby Middlebury, Montpelier and Woodstock in the centre, Bellows Falls and the Green Mountains in the south.

ACCOMMODATION
Bel-Aire Motel, 111 Shelburne St, 1 mile south of town on US 7, 863-3116. Doubles from $26 to $40, air conditioning, cable TV.
Econo Lodge, 1076 Williston Rd, 1¼ miles east on US 2, 863-1125. $32 single, $40 double. Pool, colour TV, air conditioning.
YWCA, 278 Main St, 862-7520. $18 single, some floor space.

OF INTEREST
Robert Hull Fleming Museum, Unit of Vermont, Colchester Ave. Large American-Indian collection. 9am–5pm. Free.
Shelburne Museum, 7 miles south on US 7. This is an outdoor museum of early New England life, $7. 100 acres of Americana. 'Worthwhile if you have a whole day.'
Stowe. A small, pretty town and home of the von Trapp family—the *Sound of Music* bunch. In winter it's a thriving ski resort.

BELLOWS FALLS. Steamtown, USA. There's a 26 mile round trip on an old fashioned steam train operating daily throughout the summer. The ride to Chester is a great way to see the countryside, or in autumn to enjoy the changing foliage in all its brilliance (weekends only, after Labor Day). There's also an extensive collection of locomotives on view, and in the museum, interesting displays pertaining to early railroading. All-inclusive admission, $6.25. From Bellows Falls you go west to the Green Mountains.

ACCOMMODATION
Hetty Green Motel, off Rt 5 exit 6, 463-9879. $28 double. 'Run by Scottish couple, warm welcome, very handy for the museum.'

MIDDLEBURY. This is a small and beautiful New England town, a perfect place to hike from and close to the continuation of the Appalachian Trail. The **Green Mountains**, which extend from Vermont's northern border to the Massachusetts line, are easily accessible to the east of Middlebury. Here you will find rounded wooded hills, green valleys and tiny villages. There are miles and miles of hiking trails, including the Appalachian itself, with overnight shelters and various state parks for camping. One of the nicest state parks is not far from Middlebury, on beautiful **Lake Dunmore**.

Middlebury is the home of the picturesque, stone-built Middlebury College, founded 1800. The town itself is built around a village green and Otter Creek, flowing right through the middle of Middlebury, is one of the few rivers in the Northern Hemisphere to flow north. In wintertime, this is a fine skiing area.

ACCOMMODATION
Middlebury Inn, in centre of village, 388-4961. Singles $22 up, doubles $42. The inn dates from 1808.
St Mary's Church, Middlebury College Campus: 'Ask at the rectory for an inexpensive place to stay the night; they can often help and are very friendly.'

ENTERTAINMENT
The Rosebud Bar, nr cinema off Main St, Frog Hollow, Middlebury. 'Cheap beer

and good food. Specials every night. Popular with Middlebury College and summer camp staff.'
The Alibi, Starr Mill, Frog Hollow, nr Rosebud. 'Movies or bands, occasional cover. Very friendly.'

OF INTEREST
Sheldon Museum. A beautiful old New England home and tavern. Displays include a gun room and nursery. 10am–5pm. $1.
Middlebury College Library has a fine collection of the work of poet Robert Frost.
Frog Hollow Craft Center. Located in a renovated mill by Otter Creek in town centre. Exhibits, local work, classes, workshop, and a festival in July.
Morgan Horse Farm, off Rt 23, 388-2011. Famous Morgan horses bred and trained here. Tours $1.75.
Mt Moosalamoo has 27 historic trails to explore, with breathtaking views of the Adirondacks. It's 1 mile east of Lake Dunmore, 10 miles south of Middlebury. 'On a hot day go to Lana Falls for a refreshing swim in the rock pools.'

TRAVEL
French language students at Middlebury College issue a leaflet about Montréal, *Vous allez à Montréal?*, with info on accommodation, food, entertainment.
Bike rentals from shop next to post office on village green, opp Middlebury Inn.

THE NORTHEAST

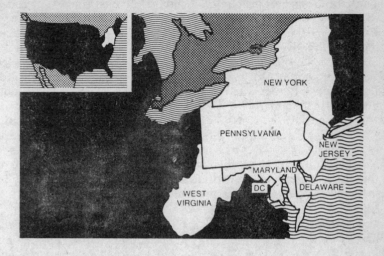

Through the Northeastern region runs most of the 400-mile strip of that megalopolis known as 'Boswash' (Boston to Washington). This rates as the nation's most crowded urban concentration, containing not only the nation's capital, Washington DC, but also the nation's largest city, New York. The region has been called the headquarters for Enterprise America for from the time of the industrial revolution much of the impetus for commercial and industrial expansion has stemmed from these states.

The first railroads west got started here and as long ago as 1752 the forerunner of today's Interstate Highway system, the Cumberland Trail or National Pike, was blazed by Christopher Gist and his Indian friends from Cumberland, Maryland, through the Alleghenies to become the main artery for traders, trappers and settlers heading west.

You would be missing something if during your tour of the Northeast you did not also visit parts of the large tracts of unspoiled countryside within easy reach of the cities. Take your pick from the mountainous Adirondacks in northern New York State, the beautiful coastline of southern Maryland, or the rolling farmlands of western Pennsylvania; and there is greater variety still.

It's also a region rich in historical and cultural associations with a wealth of places to visit and things to do. The climate varies as much as the geography. Winters are very cold and snow can be expected even as far south as Washington, while summers are marked by great heat and humidity.

DELAWARE

The second smallest state in the Union, Delaware is fancifully called the Diamond State because of its value in proportion to its size. Between the Japanese cherry trees overhanging the banks of Wilmington's Brandywine and the Atlantic surf off southerly Fenwick Island lie miles of sandy coastline. Ponds and tidy farms are sprinkled across the wooded backbone of the peninsula which levels out towards the Maryland border where there's even a cypress swamp, the most northerly in the country.

A former slave-holding state, Delaware sided with the North in the Civil War, and ran an 'underground railway', a clandestine escape route from house cellar to house cellar that brought 3000 blacks to Northern freedom. It was then, too, that the Du Ponts, reckoned to be the richest family in the world, made their first multi-millions by manufacturing explosives for the cause.

WILMINGTON. The 'Chemical Capital of the World', being the lucky spot where Eleuthere du Pont decided to build his powder mill in 1802. Wealth, labs, factories and eyesores followed, though downtown renewal has restored the Grand Opera House and there are several other imposing or otherwise interesting historical relics to see before pushing on to Dover, 45 miles due south.

ACCOMMODATION
Kent Manor Hotel, 1051 S Market St, 656-9431. Pool, colour TV, air conditioning, complimentary Continental breakfast. Singles $24, doubles from $30.
Guest House rooms, costing $22 single, $30 double, are available through Roommates, Trolley Square, Suit 17–C, Wilmington. Tel: (302) 475-2826 or 652-5419.
In nearby New Castle (see Of Interest): William Penn Guest House, 206 Delaware St, (302) 328-7736. $28 per room in this 1682 farmhouse in the heart of the historic district.

OF INTEREST
Grand Opera House, built in 1871, with an ornate cast iron facade. It's on the Market St Mall and now houses the Delaware Center for the Performing Arts. Tours Wed 11.30–1.30, free.
Brandywine Park, along the river between Augustine and Market St bridges: playground, zoo and landscaped gardens with 118 Japanese cherry trees. $1 adults, kids over 3 and seniors 50¢.
Holy Trinity (Old Swedes) Church, 606 Church St, the oldest (1698) Protestant church still active in North America. Once severely Swedish Lutheran, now more ornately Episcopalian.
The Rocks, at the foot of 7th St, 1 block south of Church St. A monument marks the site of Fort Christina, built by the Swedish-Dutch expedition which landed here in 1638. Also an 18th C log cabin survives. Free.
Hagley Museum, 3 miles north on Rt 52, then ½ mile east on Rt 141. Tel: 658-2400. Open Tue–Sat 9.30am–4.30pm, Sun 1–5pm, closed Mon. $2.50 admission, students and seniors $2, kids under 14 free. 225-acre complex on the site of the original Du

Pont black powder works, with restored granite buildings amidst wooded hillsides, huge trees, pleasant walks along the Brandywine. Exhibits, demonstrations and museum.

Nemours Mansion and Gardens, 3½ miles northwest on Rockland Rd. 77-room Louis XVI chateau look-alike with all the gear: furniture, tapestries, French gardens, etc., built 1910 by Du Pont bedfellows. 2-hr tours Tue–Sun, $4, under-16s not admitted. Reservations necessary, (302) 573-333.

Winterthur Museum, 6 miles northwest on Rte 52. Once the home of Francis du Pont and now housing 'one of the world's greatest antique collections', with more than 100 period rooms illustrating American decorative arts from the 17th through 19th C. The bulk of the collection is housed in the main museum for which reservations are required; (302) 656-1548. No brats under 12 admitted. Prices vary with season.

Longwood Gardens, yet another Du Pont hangout, formerly the country estate of industrial magnate Pierre S du Pont, 13 miles west of Wilmington at US 1 and Rt 52 nr Kennett Square, PA. Tel: (216) 388-6741. Adults $4, kids 6–14 $1.

New Castle, 6 miles south of Wilmington on Rt 9, is a small town full of the atmosphere and architecture of the colonial and early republic periods. Near Strand and Delaware Sts in 1682 William Pitt first set foot on his vast colonial lands (see Accommodation).

DOVER. One of the oldest state capitals in the nation, Dover was founded in 1683 when William Penn decided to build those amenities of civilised life on the site, a prison and country courthouse. The old section of town is charming, with well-preserved 18th and 19th century houses around the Green surviving from the days when Dover was a favourite coach stop enroute to Philadelphia.

ACCOMMODATION
Best Western-Capitol City Lodge, 246 N Dupont Hwy, 678-0160. Pool, air conditioning, cable TV, coin laundry. Singles from $21, doubles from $24.
Dover Inn, 561 N Dupont Hwy, 678-8900. Pool, air conditioning, cable TV, coin laundry. Singles $29, doubles $29 and up. Special rates for seniors.

OF INTEREST
Old State House, the Green. Built 1792. Fine Georgian architecture, with portraits of Delaware celebrities inside.
Hall of Records. Here you can see the Royal Grant of Charles II and Penn's order to settle the town.
Delaware State Museum, Governor's Ave. Houses a fascinating range of Americana, including Indian artefacts, colonial costumes and an original log cabin built by early Swedish settlers.
John Dickinson Mansion. Home of a Revolutionary notable, 5 miles south on US 113.

THE DELAWARE COAST. Much of the coast follows Delaware Bay out towards the Atlantic and even the southern shore is protected from the open ocean by Fenwick Island. Halfway down the bay is **South Bowers** with its Island Field Archeological Museum and Research Center enclosing the burial ground of a prehistoric 8th century people, the museum depicting their culture and history. **Lewes** (pronounced Lewis) on the Atlantic was first settled by the Dutch, wiped out by the Indians and resettled again; it is now the traditional home of pilots who guide ships up Delaware Bay and is very popular in summer for its beaches. **Rehoboth Beach** further south near Delaware Seashore State Park is also much favoured.

ACCOMMODATION
Lewes: camping at Cape Henlopen State Park on Rt 18, (302) 645-8983.
Rehoboth: camping at Delaware Seashore State Park on Rt 14 at the Indian River inlet, (302) 227-2800.

DISTRICT OF COLUMBIA

Washington, the Federal Capital, is co-extensive with the District of Columbia and lies on the Potomac River between North and South. This was Thomas Jefferson's idea, a seat of government free of regional interest, while Congress entrusted the plan to Frenchman Pierre L'Enfant. When he started work in 1791 Washington was a mosquito-infested swamp, yet L'Enfant envisioned a city to rival the capitals of Europe, at the same time reflecting the bold qualities of the new America.

Washington today has indeed a monumental quality and is a city of broad avenues, magnificent monuments and classical-style buildings, though it is only in recent decades that Washington has truly become the nation's focal point.

John F Kennedy wryly described Washington as a city of 'Northern charm and Southern efficiency'. That was when it was smart to regard the capital as a hick town, but fortunately for the visitor that is no longer quite the full picture. Unchanging is the fact that government is Washington's major business and about 40 percent of the city's workforce is government-employed. The city tends to shut down early as the bureacuratic drones commute back to their outlying homes. But tourism and journalism are now both major industries here and the opening of the Kennedy Center in the 1970s has at last put Washington on the international cultural map. Even once sedate Georgetown, an area of cobblestoned streets and charming 18th and 19th century townhouses, now booms with discos and flutters with art galleries and expensive boutiques lodged in converted slave quarters.

Failing a stake in Georgetown, Foggy Bottom, Chevy Chase or some other ritzy area, many Washingtonians have been avoiding the city altogether, preferring the safety and cheapness of Virginia and Maryland. Much of the city has been left to the blacks and the havenots. There's a high crime rate and the streets can be dangerous at night. But this is changing too and people are starting to buy up and renovate old downtown houses while nowadays the black population is probably better off and better educated than in any other city in the country.

For all its problems, Washington is a very pleasant city to visit. There is a tremendous amount to see (mostly free), it's cleaner and greener than most US cities, and it's good to walk around. But beware the great heat and humidity of summer. The most agreeable time to visit is spring when the magnolias and dogwoods are in full bloom everywhere.

ACCOMMODATION

The Bed and Breakfast League, 2855 29th St NW, 232-8718, has a few rooms in a vintage townhouse in a quiet residential area by the grounds of the Swiss Embassy. $33 single, $42 double, including breakfast.

Columbia Guest House, 2005 Columbia Rd NW, 265-4006. Singles from $20, doubles from $15 per person. Phone first.

Connecticut Woodley Tourist Home, 2647 Woodley Rd NW, 667-0218. Singles from $18, doubles from $25. Laundry facilities. Connecticut Ave bus stops round the corner.

Days Inn, 100 S Bragg St, nr I-395 and Duke St, Alexandria, VA. Tel: (703) 354-4950. 5 miles from downtown, 1 block from bus stop. $39 single, $43 double, extra persons $4. Pool, colour TV, bath.

Ebbitt Hotel, 1000 H St NW, 628-6034. Close to Greyhound and Trailways; within walking distance of White House, Smithsonian, etc. Bath, air conditioning, TV. $33 single, $42 double.

Harrington Hotel, 11th and E Sts NW, 628-8140. Downtown, between Capitol and White House. Air conditioning, bath, radio and TV (some colour). Singles $38, doubles $50. 'Very central and clean.' 'Expensive for what it is.'

International Guest House, 1441 Kennedy St NW, 726-5808. 4 miles from downtown. $13.50 per person in double room, includes breakfast and evening snack. 'Friendly and clean.' 'Very kind people; you can meet travellers from all over the world here.'

Presidential Hotel, 900 19th St NW, 331-9020. Downtown and nr the Intl Visitors Center; accommodates many foreign travellers. Singles $28, doubles $36. 'Large, plain rooms; air-conditioned.'

Rock Creek Hotel, 1925 Belmont Rd NW at 20th St, 1 block east of Connecticut Ave, 462-6007. Air conditioning, TV. Singles $32, doubles $36. Nr Dupont Circle and Phillips Collection.

Washington International Youth Hostel (YHA), 1332 I St NW, 347-3125. 1 block from Trailways and Greyhound. $10 per person dorm, $12 non-members. $27 double, private room; $31 double, private room for non-members. Key deposit $5, linen deposit $5. 'More like a hotel than a hostel.' 'Well worth it, near White House.' 'Spartan, clean; cooking and laundry facilities.' 'The only place to stay in DC; wonderful people.' 'In the centre of the red light district; if you're female you get an amazing number of offers to carry your rucksack.'

Camping: Greenbelt Park, Greenbelt, MD, (301) 344-3943. 6 miles east of Washington along I-495, off at exit 28. $2.

Foreign Student Service Council, 1623 Belmont St, NW, 232-4979. Given two weeks' notice, some personal info and a small registration fee, they will arrange free hospitality for 2 to 3 days with a family. No point in going without prior notice.

FOOD

Old Ebbitt Grill, corner of 15th and F Sts, nr White House. Eating place of several presidents. Big steak for $8, open till 1am. 'Great atmosphere and very friendly staff.'

Shezan, 913 19th St NW. Expensive, but 'an outstanding sensual experience'. Indian cuisine; pre-theatre special $13, numerous courses from soup through dessert. Superb range of curries, atmospheric surroundings, eg framed Indian costumes on the walls.

Axum Ethiopian Restaurant, 2307 18th St NW. Spicey beef, lamb, chicken and vegetable stews eaten with unleavened bread and fingers. $6–$10 dinners.

Nanking, 901 New York Ave NW. Best and most reasonable Chinese in DC. Buffet brunches $2 per dish; dinners $6.50–$8. Closes 9pm.

Le Souperb, 1221 Conn Ave NW, between M and N. All you can eat salad bar. $3.75. Closes 8pm. 'Unbelievable.'

National Portrait Gallery Restaurant. 'Wholefood place; food cooked in open kitchen, garden open in summer. Delightful lunch $4.

Museum of American History, Constitution Ave. 'Fantastic ice cream parlour and tons of cheap good coffee; upteen refills—and lovely waiters.'

Department of Agriculture cafeteria, Independence Ave just west of the Smithsonian. 'Enter middle entrance to receive a security pass; huge selection and better than museum cafes and nowhere near as expensive.'

Sholls Colonial Cafeteria, 1990 K St NW, and Sholls New Cafeteria, 1433 K St NW. 'Live well for less money.' *The* place to eat, but closed Sun. 'Good food and the cheapest anywhere.'

US Senate Restaurant. 'Costly, not good service.' 'Excellent and reasonably priced. Try Senate Bean Soup—you'll know where they get their wind.'

OF INTEREST

The White House, 1600 Pennsylvania Ave. Although he chose the site, Washington is the only president never to have lived here. James Hoban's original design was never fully executed and the White House has been rebuilt or redesigned inside and out many times. On a tour you will glimpse but a few of the well-proportioned rooms and furnishing supplied by successive Mrs Presidents. Free tours Tue–Sat 10am–12.30pm June–Aug, Tue–Sat 10am–noon, rest of year. Queues can be long, but it's all fairly fast-moving. 'Not worth the long wait.' Avoid queueing by getting a ticket for a specific time on day you want to go at 8am at booth on the Ellipse.

The Capitol, on Capitol Hill and the point from which all streets are numbered. The city's most familiar landmark, the great domed building is fixed in frozen commemorative style, except for the chambers of the Senate and House of Representatives, which are small and pleasant auditoriums. Open to visitors 9am–10pm daily Easter to Labor Day, 9am–4.30pm the rest of the year, closed 1 Jan, Thanksgiving and 25 December. You're free to wander, but a guidebook or tour would be helpful. Free guided tours of the Congress Building are available from 9am–3.45pm. Passes for the Senate Gallery can be obtained from the Senate Sergeant at Arms. Passports or other ID are required. For the House apply to the Doorkeeper's Office on the House side of the Capitol. Senate resumes on 1 Sept.

The *Washington Post* gives details of hearings, if they are open to the public and where they are being held. The underground train linking the Capitol and the Senate Office Building can be used by all.

Washington Monument, Mall at 15th, a 555-foot high obelisk. A trip to the top affords a splendid view. 8am–midnight, Spring-Labor Day, then 9am–5pm. Elevator to the top, free, but long queues except 9am or night.

The Smithsonian Institute on the Mall is a vast complex of museums and art galleries. There are at last 51,000,000 catalogued items—ranging from Lindberg's plane to Glenn's capsule, from fossils to the Hope Diamond, from moon rock samples to the First Ladies' gowns. Admission free. Open 10am–5pm daily, to 9pm in summer. For recorded info on new displays and the day's events at the museums phone 357-2020; for general info 357-2700.

The Freer Gallery, 12th and Jefferson Dr, **Museum of History and Technology**,

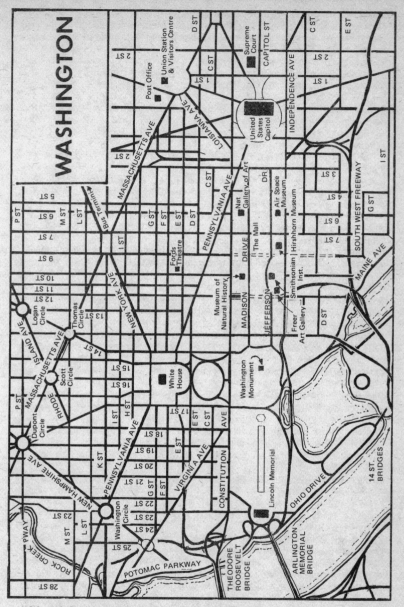

12th and Constitution Ave, **Arts and Industries Building**, 9th and Jefferson, and **Museum of Natural History**, 10th and Constitution are all part of the extraordinary galaxy of museums.

In 1974 the new circular **Hirshhorn Museum and Scultpure Garden** on Independence Ave was opened. Includes a fine art collection for the period 1930–70.

Newest of all, opened on Independence Day 1976, is the **National Air and Space Museum**, also on Independence Ave. The largest Smithsonian museum of them all, it contains an impressive array of hardware depicting the history of flight. See the 'mind-blowing' films *To Fly* and *The Living Planet* on 5-storey-high screen (75¢ each, but student reduction)—highly recommended by many readers.

National Gallery of American Art and the **National Portrait Gallery**, both part of the Smithsonian, are in the Old Patent Office Building between 7th, 9th, G and F Sts NW. It served as a Civil War hospital and was the scene of Lincoln's second inaugural ball. Greek Revival architecture with beautiful vaulted galleries. Open daily 10am–5.30pm, free. 200 years of American art, while the Portrait Gallery specialises in famous Americans with many works by John Singleton Copley, Charles Wilson Peale and Gilbert Stuart.

National Gallery, Constitution Ave between 3rd and 7th Sts NW, also part of the Smithsonian and free. Open Mon–Sat 10am-9pm, Sun 12–9pm, 1 April-Labor Day; rest of year Mon–Sat 10am–5pm, Sun 12–9pm. One of the world's superb collections of Western European painting and sculpture from 13th C to present, and American art from colonial times to now. Da Vinci, Rembrandt; French Impressionists; Flemish, Spanish, German and British paintings. Good-sized prints can be purchased cheaply in the print shop.

Library of Congress, 1st St and Independence Ave, opp Capitol, 287-5000. Open Mon–Fri 8.30am–9.30pm; Sat, Sun and hols to 6pm, free. Tours hourly Mon–Fri 9am–4pm. 76m items, including perfect copy of Gutenberg Bible (1450), first book to be printed from moveable metal type, Jefferson's rough draft of the Declaration of Independence, Lincoln's drafts of the Gettysburg Address. Also listen to vast folk music collection. Library pressings, publications, reproductions on sale in Jefferson Building. (Part of the Library and behind it is the **Folger Library**, American's finest Shakespeare collection.)

National Archives, Constitution Ave between 7th and 9th NW, 523-3000. Open daily 10am–9pm 1 April-Labor Day, closes 5.30 rest of year. Free. Preserves and makes available government records of enduring value, eg Declaration of Independence, Bill of Rights, Constitution and Watergate Tapes; listen to latter from 9.15am Mon–Fri. 'Foul-mouthed creep.'

Bureau of Engraving and Printing, 14th and C Sts SW, 447-9709. Self-guiding tours 8am–2pm Mon–Fri, free. Where dollar bills, also govt bonds and postage stamps, are made.

Supreme Court Building, between Maryland Ave and E Capitol St NE, facing Capitol. Where country's highest judicial body holds its sessions; free peek in chamber Mon–Fri 9.30am–3.30pm when court not in session; entry to building 9am–4.30pm Mon–Fri.

J Edgar Hoover FBI Building, Pennsylvania Ave between 9th and 10ths Sts NW, 324-3447. Open Mon–Fri 9am–4.15pm, free, plus 1-hr tours from E St entrance every 15 minutes. Named for the man they couldn't get rid of because he had the goods on them all. See FBI lab, fire-arms demo; won't see tapping of citizen's telephones. Queues.

Lincoln Memorial, directly in line with the Capitol and the Washington Monument. Open 8am–midnight, free. The large brooding figure, sculptured with mastery and affection, flanked by two Lincoln addresses, is in impressive sight which no visitor to the city should miss. Most awesome at night. The summertime evening concerts given here have been suspended owing to planes from nearby National Airport falling into the Potomac.

Jefferson Memorial, on Tidal Basin south of Mall, open 8am–midnight, free. Circular dome supported by Ionic columns, pretty but lacking the impact of Lincoln's. Best seen at night when floodlit. Army torchlight tattoo held here Wed summer nights; also Watergate Concerts on the steps, Sun, Tue, Thur and Fri summer evenings.

The **Pentagon** and **Arlington Cemetery**, both on the other side of the Potomac. JFK and brother Robert are buried at Arlington. The Changing of the Guard ceremony at the Tomb of the Unknown Warrior takes place every ½hr on the hr and ½hr. The **Lee Custis Mansion**, which overlooks the cemetery, was confiscated from Robert E Lee during the Civil War. It's preserved in its original state. To get there from downtown Washington catch a bus on Pennsylvania Ave outside the Post Office, or else it's a 30-minute walk across the river.

Washington Cathedral (Cathedral Church of St Peter and St Paul), Massachusetts and Wisconsin Aves NW, 537-6200. Under construction since Teddy Roosevelt laid the cornerstone in 1907, the nave was only dedicated in 1976 and work still remains to be done. Its Gloria in Excelsis Central Tower is the highest point in Washington. Woodrow Wilson, Admiral Dewey and Helen Keller are interred here. Carillon concerts and organ recitals weekly; tours Mon–Sat 10am–noon and 12.45am–3.15pm, Sun at 12.15pm and 2.30pm. Tour donation $1.

Phillips Collection, 1612 21st St NW at Q St, 387-2151. An excellent exhibition of the origins of modern art, includes Renoir's *Luncheon of the Boating Party* and works by Paul Klee, Mark Rothko, et al. Open Tue–Sat 10am–5pm, Sun 2pm–7pm, free.

Corcoran Gallery of Art, 17th St between E St and New York Ave NW, 638-3211. Extensive collection of 18th–20th C American art; European paintings, sculpture, tapestries and pottery; changing exhibits of modern art, photography and local artists. Open Tue–Sun 10am–4.30pm, Thur till 9pm, free.

Ford's Theater, 511 10th St NW, 347-4833. Where Lincoln was shot by John Wilkes Booth, 14 April 1865. Beautifully restored, and still putting on plays; phone to avoid rehearsals and performances if just looking. Open 9am–5pm, free. Opposite is the **house where Lincoln died** the next day, open 9am–5pm, free.

John F Kennedy Center for the Performing Arts, at the bottom of New Hampshire Ave beside the Potomac, 254-3600. The finest music, drama, dance and film from the US and abroad. Seniors and students get half-price tickets. Tours daily 10am–1pm, free.

National Zoological Park in Rock Creek Pk, entrances along the 3000 block of Connecticut Ave NW, 673-4800. Giant pandas (fed 9am and 3pm) and white tigers. Open daily 9am–6.30pm April–1 Sept. closes 4.30pm rest of year. Free. Bus L2 or L4.

Voice of America, 330 Independence Ave, 655-4000. Free tours 8.45, 9.45, 10.45, 1.45 and 2.45. Watch and listen to live broadcasts. 'Fascinating; not just another radio station.'

Mount Vernon, 8 miles south of Alexandria via the George Washington Memorial Pkwy, (703) 781-2000. Home of George Washington and a fine example of a colonial plantation house, built 1740. Original furnishings, plus key to the Bastille, George's false teeth, etc. George and Martha are buried here too. Open daily 9am–5pm 1 March–31 Oct. 9am–4pm rest of year, $3 adults, $2.50 seniors, $1.50 kids 6–11. Take bus 11A.

Enroute you should pause at **Alexandria**, an old tobacco port founded in 1749 with surviving 18th C houses.

Georgetown, west of Rock Creek Park and north of K St NW. A town of shady streets and old town houses, older than DC itself. Very fashionable these days, with antique shops, expensive restaurants and boutiques—though also now surplus stores and English pubs, for Georgetown attracts poor young trendies as well as rich old trendies.

The **Chesapeake and Ohio Canal** passes through Georgetown, and the towpath makes for good cycling, walking or jogging. Barge trips from Georgetown June–Sept, 299-3613.

TOURS

Tourmobile, 554-7950, offers Washington and Arlington tour for $6, $3.25 kids 3–11, and with Mount Vernon $15.25, kids $8, admission included. Passes are good for a day of unlimited reboarding and you can begin at any sight. Look for 'Tourmobile Sightseeing Shuttle Bus Stop' sign.

Gray Line, 4th and E Sts SW, 479-5900; DC Transit, New York Av nr 15th St SW, 637-2437; and Washington Boat Lines, 554-8011, all offer sightseeing tours/cruises.

A tour is not really necessary for the Washington sights which are all easily reached on foot, nor hardly for Arlington if you're feeling remotely fit. And for Mount Vernon it's cheaper to take DC Transit bus 11A, $1.20.

ENTERTAINMENT

The monthly *Unicorn Times*, free from record stores, is an 'excellent' guide to what's on. See also Fri's *Washington Post*.

Georgetown is the social hub; the minimum drinking age is 18 and alcohol tax is low.

The Washington area is the nation's bluegrass capital; The Red Fox Inn, Bethesda, MD, The Birchmere in Arlington and Partners II in Centerville are three of the best. Also visit Shakey's Pizza Parlors for bluegrass.

For threatre, etc., try the National Theater, 1321 E St NW, 628-3398, which does Broadway shows; the Arena Stage, 6th St and Maine Ave SW, 448-3300, with one of the best rep companies in the US; the Washington Project for the Arts, 1227 G St NW, 347-8304, for ballet, modern dance and experimental theatre; the Folger Theater, 201 E Capitol St, 546-4000, for Elizabethan drama; the John F Kennedy Center for the Performing Arts, 2700 F St NW, 254-3600, for drama, music, dance and film (half price for students and seniors, also standing room tickets on sale 30 minutes before performances); and Wolf Trap Park, 1551 Wolftrap Rd, Vienna, VA, 938-2900, for outdoor ballet, symphonies, as you sit on the lawn—bring sweater, blanket and picnic; take Greyhound from Chevy Chase Circle and Kennedy Center.

INFORMATION

Note: for all its abstract regularity, the street plan can be confusing. The streets are arranged on a grid pattern, the avenues overlaying this to form yet another pattern of diamonds. The focal point of the system is the Capitol, from where Washington is divided into quadrants: NE, NW, SE, SW. For reasons understandable to Euclid and a few others the effect of the overall system is that a house number and street name may occur up to four times within the city, the particular address you want only being identified by the compass quadrant. So be sure NE, SW, etc., is specified after every address.

The Convention and Visitors' Bureau is at 1129 20th, NW, 659-6423.

DC Transit Office is on New York Ave., near the corner of 15th, 637-2437.

Travelers Aid, 1015 12th St NW, 347-0101, nr bus stations; another at Union Station.

International Visitors Service (IVIS), 1825 H St NW, 872-8748, plus volunteers at Dulles and Baltimore-Washington airports and Union Station. 24-hr language assistance, info on accommodation, restaurants, currency exchange and bilingual doctors.

Main Post Office, N Capitol St and Massachusetts Ave NE, opp Union Station; also a Post Office at 12th and Pennsylvania Ave.

People's Drugstore, 14th St and Thomas Circle NW, open all-night.

Visitors Center, Union Station, falling down and so closed, but might reappear.

Loos: 'Distinct lack of public conveniences', make sure you go before you go out'.

TRANSPORT

The new subway system has been decribed by readers as 'something out of *2001*', 'not as good as BART', 'excellent, but where do they hide the stations?' It can take you to most of the visitor spots and costs 65¢ from 9.30am–3pm and after 6.30pm, but otherwise depends on the length of the journey, ie you get screwed at rush hours. Transfers for bus service.

Buses also cost 65¢ but are *cheaper* during rush hours.

For metro and bus info, ring 637-2437 from 6am to 11.30pm. The metro packs up at midnight, opens again 6am.

Trailways, 1201 New York Ave NW, 737-5800.

Greyhound, 1110 New York Ave NW (at 12th St), 505-2662.

Union Station serves AMTRAK and other trains, 1st St and Massachusetts Ave NE. AMTRAK: 484-7540; Metroliner service (3 hrs to NY): 484-5580.

Look in the *Washington Post* for shared expense rides, especially early Sept when students returning to college.

AAACON Auto Transport, 1025 Vermont Ave NW, 737-7030.

MARYLAND

The first inhabitants of the Old Line State came to the New World in search of religious toleration. They landed in southern Maryland on territory granted to the Catholic Lord Baltimore by Charles I from whose wife, Henrietta Maria, the state takes its name. The western mountainous area, settled heavily by British and Germans is influenced by the North, while the eastern shoreline can often smack of the Deep South. The latter is a land of old ante-bellum mansions, famous for hunting and delicious Chesapeake Bay crab and oysters.

If you have time, visit the tobacco auctions in Hughesville, La Plata, Upper Marlboro, Waldorf or Waysons Corner. The auctioneer's patter is spectacular. Maryland credits itself with the second largest steelworks in the world, the Bethlehem Steel Corporation at Sparrow's Point. Believe it or not, the official state sport is jousting.

BALTIMORE. One of the nation's major seaports, and the eastern terminus of the first railroad in America, the Baltimore and Ohio. Baltimore, of all the major Eastern seaboard cities, is the one people probably least want to visit. Undoubtedly Baltimore suffers from being only 40 miles from the nation's capital which offers more to visitor and resident alike. Baltimoreans, however, take great pride in their historic past, as well as in the magnificent newness of downtown Baltimore. And there's always the excellent seafood fresh out of Chesapeake Bay.

Both writer H L Mencken and baseball star Babe Ruth were Baltimore natives, and the latter has a museum in his honour on Emory Street.

Equidistant from both Washington and Baltimore are Annapolis, the Civil War battlefield of Antietam, and much of the old Chesapeake and Ohio Canal.

ACCOMMODATION
Abbey Hotel, 723 St Paul St at Madison, 332-0405. Singles without bath $21, with bath $25, doubles with bath $29. 'Clean, adequate rooms; fairly central.'
Congress Hotel, 306 W Franklin St at Howart St, 539-0227. Singles without bath $17, with bath $22, doubles with bath $25.
Howard House Hotel, 8 N Howard St at Baltimore St, 539-1680. Singles with bath $30–$35, doubles with bath $52. 'Best moderately priced hotel downtown.'
YWCA Corner House Hotel, 128 W Franklin St at Cathedral St, 6th floor, 685-1460. Singles without bath $21, doubles without bath $28, doubles with bath $33, suites with 4 beds and bath $48. Women and children only.

FOOD
Crab is the city's speciality, often served by the dozen, on a newspaper and complete with mallet to break them open.
Bo-Brooks, 4807 Belair Rd. Good crab house. About $6–$12 per dozen depending on season.
Bertha's, South Broadway and Lancaster in Fells Point. Meals from about $5. *The* place.
Burke's, E. Lombard, nr the dock area. 'Clean, safe, workingman's bar. Beer 95¢, crab cakes $3.'
Harbor Place, Pratt and Lombard. Fast food about $4, restaurant-style $5 up. Crab cakes, Polish sausage, etc. 'Best in town.' Beautiful view of harbour.

OF INTEREST
Edgar Allan Poe's House, 203 N. Amity St. Poe's tomb, 'sadly forlorn', is to be seen in the churchyard of Westminster Church.
Fort McHenry, end of Fort Ave. Take a No. 1 bus to get there. The fort was bombarded for 25 hours by the British during the War of 1812. Held prisoner on board a British warship, Francis Scott Key, seeing at the end of the bombardment that the Star Spangled Banner was still flying over the fort, felt moved to write what was to become the national anthem. After trying to sing it, you wish the British had either not captured Key or had been better shots. Today the fort's ancient cannon still cover the harbour. On Thursday nights at 6pm there is a military ceremony performed in War of Independence uniform. Open 9am–5pm. 'Catch the boat across to the fort, leaves every ½hr from Inner Harbor; very worthwhile.'
Flag House, Pratt and Albermarle Sts, is the house where Mary Young Pickersgill sewed the flag which so inspired Francis Scott Key. Tue–Sat 10am–4pm. $1.
The Maryland Historical Society, 201 W Monument St has the original of the *Star-Spangled Banner*. Also on display: period rooms, a Confederate room, and a Chesapeake Bay maritime museum. Tue–Sat 11am–4pm, Sun 1–5pm. Free.
The Baltimore Museum of Art, Charles and 31st Sts, the Peale Museum, 225 N Holiday St, and the Walters Art Gallery, Charles and Center Sts, are worth visits.
USS Constellation, Pier 2, foot of Pratt St. A 1797 frigate—the nation's oldest warship. $1.50 entrance. While down here, visit the National Aquarium, Pier 3, entrance $4. 'Modern and interesting design; the shark tank is amazing.'
Washington Monument, Mt Vernon Pl. 75 feet high, the monument was built between 1815 and 1829. Fri–Tue 10.30am–4pm. 25¢.
Mount Clare Station, Pratt and Poppleton Sts. The first railroad station in the US. Erected 1830. From here Samuel F B Morse sent the first telegraph message 'What hath God wrought'. Railway museum costs $1.50. Open 10am–4pm, Wed–Sat.
Lexington Market, Lexington and Eutaw Sts. Modernised, but was one of the oldest markets in the US.

INFORMATION
Travelers Aid, 601 N Howard St, 685-3569, and at Baltimore-Washington Intl Airport. Also 24-hr emergency service, 685-5874.

International Visitors Center, 837-7150 weekdays, or through Travelers Aid nights, weekends, holidays. Interpreters, translators and other help to foreign travellers.

TRAVEL
Trailways, 210 W Fayette St, 752-2115.
Greyhound, Howard and Center Sts, 744-9311.
AMTRAK, Penn Station, 1515 N Charles St, 539-2112.

ANNAPOLIS. Situated on Chesapeake Bay, the city of Queen Anne is the capital of Maryland and was briefly capital of the young Republic. At the State House George Washington resigned his command of the Revolutionary Army after his victory over British forces. The waterfront is 18th century and clustered behind it is one of the most beautiful of America's colonial towns.

Annapolis is synonymous with the United States Naval Academy where a tour of the grounds costs $1 with free admission to its interesting museum.

The bars on the wharf are good for a beer and overhearing the fish stories of Chesapeake Bay. Help yourself to a basket of hot crab, delicious and cheap, and catch the Clam Festival in late August.

ASSATEAGUE ISLAND. Situated off Maryland's Atlantic coast, and now a national seashore, the island is the home of the threatened peregrine falcon and the snow goose. Roaming the island are the Chincoteague wild ponies, descendants of shipwrecked horses. Assateague is a 37-mile long narrow barrier island with Maryland's Assateague State Park at the northern end and the Chincoteague National Wildlife Refuge at the southern end, in Virginia. Limited camping is available in both parks. 'Delightful area.'

Nearby is **Ocean City**, Maryland's only oceanside resort, and summer vacation spot for Washingtonians and Baltimoreans. The town has a lively boardwalk and a wide beach, but lacks some of the gaudiness of Atlantic City. Plenty of boarding house accommodation and good for summer jobs.

ACCOMMODATION
Hi-Hope Hotel, Talbot St. Singles $35 per week, doubles $46 per week. 'Cheapest in town, also the most basic.'

ANTIETAM BATTLEFIELD. Their overwhelming defeat at the second battle of Bull Run in 1862 marked the nadir of the Union's military fortunes. Robert E Lee crossed the Potomac and advanced north into Maryland. British Prime Minister Lord Palmerston, expecting further Southern victories, was preparing to intervene on the side of the Confederacy. General George B McClellan, Commander in Chief of the Northern army, met Lee in battle at Antietam Creek, 45 miles west of Baltimore. After a bloody struggle, McClellan halted the Southern advance, and with Lee back in Virginia licking his wounds, all foreign thought of intervention was postponed. Five days later, on 22 September, a more confident Lincoln issued his Emancipation Proclamation, freeing all slaves throughout the United States.

The scene of the battle is now a cemetery, with a museum at its entrance open daily. It can be reached by Route 65 out of Hagerstown.

CHESAPEAKE AND OHIO CANAL. Until the advent of the railways, America made use of a considerable system of canals throughout the Northeast and Midwest, one of these being the Chesapeake and Ohio, running along the Maryland border from Washington DC to Cumberland. The canal was opened by President John Quincy Adams in 1828 and is now a National Historic Park extending for 185 miles, the longest of all national preserves. Disused but leafy and beautiful, it's well worth a hike along its banks.

NEW JERSEY

The Garden State, when first glimpsed after crossing the Hudson River from Manhattan, is an incredible wasteland, a lunar cesspool, not to be missed. **Newark** is an industrial slum whose chief products are pollution, racial violence and corrupt city officials. It is certainly not America the beautiful.

But away from the sludge and slums in the Newark-New York area there are many parts of New Jersey that can bear the description Garden State with something less than irony. Inland there are the rolling Appalachians to walk and camp in, with the Delaware River for canoeing, while along the sea there are excellent beaches and boardwalks extending well south of Atlantic City. **New Brunswick**, home of Rutgers University, is a small friendly town just a few miles down the New Jersey Turnpike (toll) from Newark, and Princeton is just a bit further.

And even opposite Manhattan there are the **Palisades** where the George Washington Bridge (a favourite leap for suicides) meets the Jersey shore. The Palisades are a 15-mile-long line of white chalk cliffs rising as high as 500 feet above the Hudson. The most impressive view is as you cross the bridge, but on the New Jersey side you can enjoy the **Palisades Interstate Park** with its picnic grounds and beautiful woods.

PRINCETON. Princeton is a beautiful New England town that ran away and is alive and well in New Jersey. The leafy residential streets, the gothic architecture of the Ivy League university, contribute to a pleasant atmosphere of urban seclusion.

Both Albert Einstein and Thomas Mann lived here, while Scott Fitzgerald was one of the more luminous graduates of Princeton University and Woodrow Wilson was president of the university between 1902 and 1910. Tours of the campus start at Maclean House, 452-3603. Highlights include the art gallery and Nassau Hall, built in 1756, where the Continental Congress met in 1783, and used as barracks during the Revolution by both American and British troops.

ACCOMMODATION
Expensive, but this is the home of the Bed and Breakfast League, 20 Nassau St, (609) 921-0440. They may be able to help.

ATLANTIC CITY. The home of salt water taffy and the Miss America contest took on a new lease of life in 1977 when casino gambling was legalised here. Until then this was a city in rapid decay, its once smart residential areas had become slums and its grand hotels were crumbling about the famous boardwalk. Once the best loved seaside resort in America (the US version of Monopoly uses Atlantic City street names), the glamour wilted when the better-off bathers made for hotter climes south and west.

Now all is hustle and bustle again as every block is torn apart and rebuilt to cater to the bus and carloads of gamblers pouring into town from all over the East. Already a dozen or so casino hotel resorts have sprung up and more are coming shortly.

Atlantic City is still on the seedy side however, although the beach is as fine (and crowded) as ever. Gambling is restricted to the licenced resort hotels.

To escape the crowds and gaudy *joie de vivre* of Atlantic City, try the 2694 acres of **Island Beach State Park** where you can do whatever it is you're doing entirely on your own.

ACCOMMODATION
Atlantic City is more expensive than the rest of the Jersey shore, but cheap lodgings can be had in boarding houses within the rectangle described by the Boardwalk and Atlantic, Pennsylvania and Albany Aves. The area beyond Atlantic Ave is prone to crime and not recommended.
Capri Hotel, 21 Georgia Ave. $18 per person, single or double. Refrigerator and sink in room.
Oscar's, on Georgia Ave opp the Capri. An old but brighter place with singles at $32, doubles at $40.

OF INTEREST
The Convention Hall on the Boardwalk is the largest in the world, seating 70,000 in the main auditorium. It also has the world's largest pipe organ to match.
Central Pier, Tennessee Ave, was once the longest but has been destroyed 3 times by fire. But ride the elevator which spirals up and down the 380-ft observation tower at the pier's end for panoramic views, 60¢. The several piers jutting out into the sea used to be the focus of Atlantic city's beachside amusements. The Steel Pier, once famous for its diving horses, now houses the bicycle concession; only Steeplechase Pier offers games and rides for children.

Lucy the Margate Elephant, 9200 Atlantic Ave. A building in the shape of an elephant, originally built of wood and tin in 1881 to house a bazaar. Now being restored. Tours $1.50.

INFORMATION
Visitors Bureau, Convention Hall, Pacific and Mississippi, 345-7536.

TRAVEL
Transport of New Jersey (TNJ) runs buses to New York and Philadelphia and with Trailways and Greyhound shares the terminal at Arctic and Arkansas Aves, 344-8181.
Conrail links with Philadelphia; station on Bacharach Blvd, 784-1177.

WILDWOOD. A smaller version of Atlantic City, practically at the tip of the southern peninsula of the state. The beach is 1000 feet broad in some places, there are 2 miles of boardwalk, six amusement parks and plenty of wild nightlife. 'If you're over 25, you're too old for Wildwood.'

For contrast, a side visit to **Cape May** is recommended. It's a well-preserved sedate Victorian resort town favoured by vacationing presidents in the 1870s and 1880s and without the usual cluster of T-shirt shops and amusement arcades.

ACCOMMODATION
Guesthouses are the cheapest solution here.
Glenwood Hilton, Pacific and Glenwood, 'full of incredibly friendly young people'.
Blue Danube, 314 Poplar Ave, 522-3743, mostly doubles and triples.
The Morrells, 135 E Pine Ave, 'Clean and friendly'.
The Waldorf, Baker Ave. $40 per week. 'Strictly run, full of English and Irish. Kitchen facilities.'

NEW YORK

Everything about New York is big. It has the biggest industrial, commercial and population centre in the United States all rolled into one great metropolis, which together with the vast upstate area contributes mightily to the nation's manufacturing and agricultural output.

In colonial times New York was one of the most sizeable chunks of land in North America, hence its nickname, the Empire State. The battle for control of the Hudson River Valley was fought out between the British and the Dutch, while it was from the French that the British eventually wrested the northern regions of New York. Yet it says something about the vast extent of the state, much of it still wilderness even today, that as late as 1700 the most formidable empire in New York was that of the Iroquois Confederacy of the Five Nations based on Syracuse and controlling the water routes to the coast and therefore trade. Their power was broken only in the middle of that century when the British defeated the Indians and their French allies at Ticonderoga, Niagara and Montréal.

The Empire State is in fact two worlds, New York City and that great area of land stretching over miles of cities, towns, countryside, mountains and wilderness to Canada and the Great Lakes. Don't allow the common tag to confuse the two in your mind: there's a lot of beauty beyond the Bronx.

NEW YORK CITY. The nation's largest city, New York is also the business entertainment and publishing capital of the United States, the busiest port in the world, and host to the United Nations. More than 26 million people, as diverse as the United Nations itself, live and work in the New York metropolitan area stretching out into New Jersey and Connecticut. It isn't possible within this book to give more than the merest introduction to New York, and if you plan to spend some time here, we recommend you buy the excellent *Michelin Guide*.

Though the city is composed of five boroughs, Queens, Brooklyn, the Bronx, Richmond (Staten Island) and Manhattan, it's the last of these you're really talking about when you say New York: that long stretch of granite lying between the Hudson and East Rivers where skyscrapers tower over an intense mangle of social extremes.

New York's explosive variety and its appeal to so many different types of people make it an exciting place to visit. Chances are that whatever you expect to find before you get here, you will find in actuality, but so much more besides. New York offers the finest in theatre, cinema, music, museums, shopping, restaurants and general tourist attractions, as well as an object lesson in social deprivation. It can be extremely hot and humid in summer, very cold and windy in winter; it can be very dirty, or very dangerous; but it is a city which is totally outrageous, vitally alive, enthusiastic, and, above all, resilient.

Partly as a result of the spectre of bankruptcy which still haunts the city, recent times have seen a dramatic revival in New York's flagging civic pride. Many neighbourhood campaigns are under way to make streets and subways safer and cleaner; 'I love New York' badges, T-shirts, Big Apple banners and similar paraphernalia are widely bought and worn everywhere.

MANHATTAN NEIGHBOURHOODS

The Financial District: This is the oldest part of the city, a maze of narrow winding canyons now, but where Peter Stuyvesant erected his wall to keep the Indians out. That's where Wall Street gets its name. The New York Stock Exchange is here on Broad St, and the American Stock Exchange is on Trinity Place. George Washington was inaugurated first President of the United States at Federal Hall, Wall and Nassau Sts, in 1789. From Battery Park you can take the ferry to Staten Island or the Statue of Liberty. Towering over all is the second tallest building in the world—the 1,350-foot twin towers of the World Trade Center on a 16-acre site at West St. The district is a monumental necropolis on Sundays, great for cycling or a picnic on the steps of City Hall.

Chinatown: The public telephones are housed in miniature pagodas, and the local grocery shops are great for snow peas or bok choy. Restaurants are good, plentiful and relatively cheap. Chinese New Year is celebrated with the explosion of firecrackers the first full moon after 21 January. Mott and Mulberry are the major streets.

Little Italy: Just northwest of Chinatown in the area of Mulberry and Grand St. Good restaurants, bakeries and grocery shops, and a live place in June with the Feast of St Anthony, again in September with the Feast of San Genaro. Then you can ride ferris wheels in the middle of the street, eat lasagne and zeppoles, and buy large buttons that beckln, 'Kiss me, I'm Italian.'

The Lower East Side: Orchard and Delancey Streets have attracted waves of immigrants, Eastern European Jews in the 19th century, Puerto Ricians and Cubans now. Some older Jews still remain, and Sunday is their big market day, a good time to swoop in for bargains. Note that many stores are closed on Saturdays.

The East Village: St Marks Place and Second Avenue took the overflow from increasingly pricey Greenwich Village and is the hang-out for students, artists and writers. But also for some of the more wasted drop-outs, who in need of a fix might rob you at night, so tread carefully. Former inhabitants of the East Village include W H Auden and James Fennimore Cooper.

Greenwich Village: New York's original bohemian quarter and one-time home of such figures as Max Beerbohm, e e cummings, Eugéne O'Neill and Alan Ginsburg, but not what it used to be. Lots of expensive plastic cafes now to cater to the tourists, but 10th, 11th and 12th Streets remain calm, lined with brownstones for the chic-chic rich. New York University faces onto Washington Square, with its Arc de Triomphelike arch, where there's lots of live music, everything from casual guitar strumming to classical violin; a great variety of people to watch, and chess tables out for those who want to take it slow. During the summer, street fairs are common up and down the Village streets. The latest 'in' place is the area south of Houston Street: SoHo. Writers and artists who can no longer afford the village proper have been moving here and a number of restaurants, bars and fringe theatres have opened. 'Loft jazz' has taken over the old warehouses and SoHo is now the place to go for a night out. Canal Street, on the fringe of SoHo is good for cheap shopping, especially in clothes (jeans) and electronics.

The West Side: One-third of all the clothes worn in the US are made here in the garment district, between 14th and 42nd streets. The lower section around 20th Street is called Chelsea and becoming fashionable. The flower district is dug in around 27th Street. To forget the grime of the city walk along here among the ferns, tropical plants and examples of every imaginable flower in season. Further uptown, around Herald Square and 34th Street there are the large department stores like Macy's, Gimbel's, Ohrbachs (good for bargain fashion buys) and Altmans. Just a block away are the Empire State Building and Madison Square Garden. The Garden is where sports events, exhibitions and pop concerts are held; beneath it is Penn Station where you can catch trains out to Long Island, or to Boston, Washington or Chicago.

Midtown: This is the core of the apple, the part everyone gets to sooner or later. East and West, between 42nd and 59th Streets, is the heart of the theatre district, cinema district, shopping district and porno district, to name a few. The United Nations Building is on 44th Street, right over on the East River.

Times Square, or 'Hell's Bedroom' as New Yorkers call it, is the heart of the city's squalid sex scene. Despite police 'pussy posses' and earnest attempts on the part of City Hall to clean up the area the streets remain dirty and dangerous, and the peep shows, porn cinemas, pimps, hookers and junkies still flourish. The 'legitimate' theatre area is between W 42nd and W 50th Streets to the east and west of Broadway. The lights are still bright and at night the streets are thronged with people.

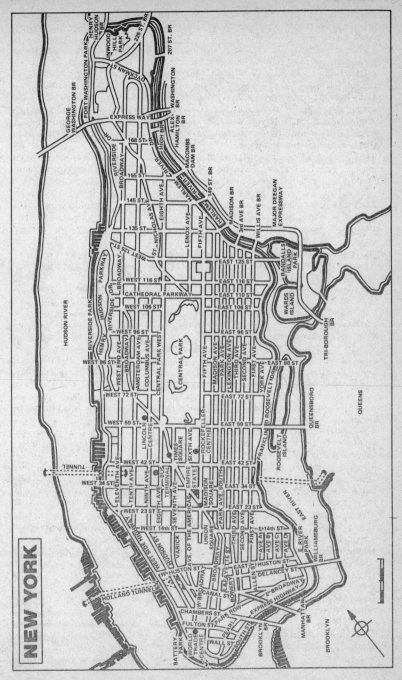

NEW YORK

Fifth Avenue is the dividing line between East and West, an elegant stomping ground perfect for window shopping, being seen, or looking at those who come to be looked at. Here you'll find Rockefeller Center and St Patrick's Cathedral, and when Britain decides to sell the Crown Jewels they will be up for sale in Tiffany's on the corner of 57th street.

Central Park: An enormous and enjoyable expanse of grass and granite outcrops bearing striations from the last retreating glacier, the park extends from 59th to 110th Street with ponds, gardens, tennis courts and zoo. On Sundays the park is crowded with New Yorkers walking, sailing model boats, jogging, riding, cycling, roller skating, skate boarding, playing baseball, reading the *Sunday Times* or, annoyingly, playing radios unbelievable loudly in an unending competition to see who has the loudest player in NYC. Look for free concerts and dramatic performances in the park during summer.

The Upper East Side: The 70s and 80s in this area are among the most coveted addresses in New York. The Metropolitan Museum of Art and the spiraling Guggenheim are here. East 86th Street is the heart of Yorkville, the German part of town with beer halls and oom-pah-pah bands. Beginning at 96th Street and running north to 145th is East Harlem, the largely Puerto Rican section, with a sprinkling of stranded Irish and Italian families desperately trying to learn Spanish.

The Upper West Side: Columbus Circle, at 59th Street and Broadway, marks the cultural hub of Manhattan where you will find the Lincoln Center, which includes the Metropolitan Opera House and the New York State Theater. At night it's pretty crowded; by summer's day it's a pleasant place to sit and eat ice cream. Around 72nd Street is a young, semi-posh and lively neighbourhood; on the corner with Central Park West is the impressive Victorian Dakota building where John Lennon was shot. Higher up Central Park West is the Natural History Museum, and still further is Columbia University at Broadway and 116th Street. Here and around Morningside Heights, is the haunt of Columbia staff and students.

Harlem: This is the all-black scene, stretching from 125th Street up to 155th, and taking in everything from miserable tenements to fashionable residential rows. 125th Street is where it all happens, some amazing gaits and still a few pink Cadillacs to be seen by the intrepid honky. But money for drugs is in short supply and the night visitor particularly may find himself broke in the gutter. If you're understandably worried about your safety, drop in at the black-operated Penny Sightseeing Company, 303 West 42nd Street (247-2860) which does 'Harlem As It Is' tours.

ACCOMMODATION

For very cheap accommodation read the *Village Voice*, best bought at 8am Wed, Sheridan Square, and the notice boards at the Loeb Student Center, Washington Square. Shops near Columbia U are sometimes good for sub-lets. Also try the fraternity houses around NYU and Columbia. Single accommodation is expensive in NYC but rates for doubles and triples go down markedly, so think groupwise if possible.

Allerton Hotel, 130 E 57th St, 753-8841. For women only. Excellent location, tight security, whistle-clean rooms for $26 single, bath down the hall. Single with bath $38, doubles with bath $60.

Carter Hotel, 250 W 43rd St, between Broadway and 8th, 944-6000. Singles with bath from $34, doubles with bath from $45. Nr Madison Sq Gdn and Port Authority Bus Terminal. Simple, clean rooms; above the 18th floor many have French doors opening onto tiny balconies with vast breathtaking views (but dangerous for children). Free parking in the building an important plus. Tatty porno district a modest minus.

Clinton Hotel, 19 W 31st St, 279-4017. Without bath, singles and doubles from

$16; with bath, singles and doubles from $22. 'You pays your money and you takes your chances.'

Fashion Institute of Technology, 230 W 27th St, 760-7885. $12 single, $80 per week mid-June to end-July. Ask for Housing Director. Priority to FIT students.

International Center, 511 W 20th St, 243-4922. Student hostel, $14 dorm-style, breakfast included. Free use of kitchen, unlimited hot showers. Highly recommended. 'Safe, friendly, personal atmosphere, well-located in Chelsea area.' German and French spoken. Midnight curfew, and closed 10am-5pm.

International Student Center, 210 W 55th St at Broadway, 757-8030. $10 in dorms of 4–6 persons with attached bathroom. Limited number of stoves available. Advisable to take own sleeping bag. 'Friendly place in the heart of the city.'

International Student Hospice, 154 E 33rd St, between Lexington and 3rd Aves, 228-4689. Men only. Students $16; non-students in private room $28. Between Empire State Building and East Side Airline Terminal, 'clean and quiet in safe area'.

Mansfield Hotel, 12 W 44th St, off Fifth Ave, 944-6050. Without bath, singles $30, doubles $40; with bath, singles from $44, doubles from $48. Vincent Price lived here for 3 years. 'A definite feeling of warmth here, like a small European hotel.'

Martha Washington Hotel, 30 E 30th St, 689-1900. Women only. Without bath singles from $23, doubles from $35; with bath, singles from $33, doubles from $45.

New York University, Housing Office, 54 Washington Sq S, 598-2083. $12 single, $9 per person in double, bedding not provided. From mid-June to end-Aug. Priority to NYU students.

Pickwick Arms Hotel, 230 E 51st St, between 2nd and 3rd Aves, 355-0300. Singles without bath $22; from $34 single and $45 double with bath. 'Clean, simply furnished, no air conditioning,' 'Safe area, within walking distance of UN, Grand Central Station.' 'Excellent central location; small basic rooms, slightly shabby.'

Rio Hotel, 132 W 47th St, 757-3870. $18 single, $22 double without bath; from $28 single or double with bath. 'Central but a bit smelly.' TV and air conditioning in better rooms.

Rosoff's, 147 W 43rd St, 582-3200. Doubles around $40. 'Small but dignified rooms.' Rosoff's has been a landmark restaurant since 1899 when Sarah Bernhardt, Lillie Langtry and the Barrymores were regulars. It's right in the theatre district and remains a charming (and pricey) place famous for its fresh fish. The upstairs rooms are a not so famous bargain.

Travel Inn Motor Hotel, 515 W 42nd St, Between 10th and 11th Aves, 695-7171. Singles from $44, doubles from $52. All rooms with bath, air conditioning, colour TV. Use of pool, sauna and free indoor parking. 'Can be quite inexpensive if several share a double room—the floors are comfortably carpeted.'

McBurney YMCA, 215 W 23rd St, 741-9226. Men only. Singles $19, some with TV. 'Reasonable rooms but mainly frequented by older people; handy for Washington Sq and Greenwich Village.'

Vanderbilt YMCA, 224 E 47th St, 755-2410. Men and women. Singles $19, cheaper per person in multi-bed rooms. TV in rooms. 'I was very impressed with the Vanderbilt after experiencing Sloane House YMCA.'

West Side YMCA, 5 W 63rd St, 787-4400. Men and women. Same rates as Vanderbilt.

William Sloane House YMCA, 356 W 34th St, 760-5860. Men and women. Singles $19, doubles $24, a bit more without student card. Extra for TV. $5 key deposit. Also known as Slow House, it takes ages checking in and out—but otherwise good for groups. 'Rooms small and bare.' 'Ah yes, but conveniently situated.' 'Good place for meeting fellow travellers.' 1 block from Madison Sq Gdn and nr Empire State Building. NY Student Center and BUNAC are here.

FOOD

New Yorkers eat out often and the city is littered with inexpensive restaurants tucked away in unlikely corners and patronised by the local neighbourhood. In short, for the best value, try and eat where the locals eat in whichever area you happen to be at feeding time. Avoid mid-town coffee shops. Chinatown is one of the cheapest areas. The list below is in no way comprehensive; some cheap places are given, others are not so cheap but possibly more interesting.

Amy's, 61st and Broadway, also 210 E 23rd St, and one open 24 hrs on Broadway around 72nd. Fast foods with a Middle Eastern flavour. 'Their yoghourt sundae is terrific.' Around $3 up.

Horn & Hardart, 42nd St and 3rd Ave. The last of the automats, where the food comes out through the wall. 'Erotic.'

Burger Joint and Pizza Place, Broadway and 76th; also Burger Joint Too (sic), 24th and 2nd Ave. Good and inexpensive.

Ray's Pizza, 11th St and 6th Ave, Greenwich Village. 'This is the best.'

Something Different, 1488 First Ave, 570-6666. 'Serves only desserts, and they are excellent. Entertainment too: waitresses serve and then sing on a small stage. Lights and piano, Uproarious fun.'

Madras Woodlands, 310 E 44th St. Veggie Indian, $5 up. There are now also several Indian restaurants on Lexington around 27th and 28th Sts, $3.50 up.

Szechaun Restaurant, 2656 Broadway, Upper West Side. A favourite with Columbia students, this is NY's oldest Szechuan; spicy; full bar. From $5. Otherwise, Chinatown is the place:

Quon Luck Restaurant, Mott St. 'Try the lunchtime specials, 3-course meals only $3.'

Chee Kee Restaurant, 59 Bayard St. 'An excellent, cheap and nice place to eat—the cheapest place possibly in Chinatown, average $3.75 for all-in meal.'

Kim Hop Hing Coffee Shop, 205 Grand St. 'Bustling with Chinese. The shop doubles as bakery and butchers. Wonderfully exotic food, most dishes $2, very substantial—in Little Italy a coffee would cost almost that much.'

La Bonne Soupe, 48 W 55th St. Cheap French Midtown restaurant, especially if you stick to the thick soups served with bread and wine, $5.

Idra, 166 W 4th St, Greenwich Village. Good Greek food and atmosphere, belly dancing upstairs on Fri and Sat nights. Main course from $5.

Molfetas, 207 W 47th St. Cheap Greek in the otherwise pricey Theatre District.

Ukranian Restaurant, 140 2nd Ave at 9th St. Several Ukranian places along 2nd Ave, but this is the best. Borscht from $1.50 a bowl, entrees $5.

Katz's, 205 Houston St, Lower East Side. You can sample the meat before deciding which sandwich. A New York Jewish institution.

The Belmore Cafeteria, 407 Park Ave S, Midtown. Probably NY's best cafeteria, where all the cabbies go, open 5.30am–2pm, hot meat sandwiches from $3.

OF INTEREST

Empire State Building, 5th Ave and 34th St. The office at the bottom will give a report of the atmospheric conditions at the top. Make sure it's a clear day. $2.75 to go up, discounts for students with ID. Not the tallest building any more (although they're planning to remedy that by adding a new piece to the top) but the view, night and day, is still fantastic. 'Go up at night, unforgettable views and less crowded, open till midnight.' On the Concourse level downstairs you'll find the **Guinness World Book of Records** exhibit. Daily 8.30am–6pm. $3 entry, 'not worth it, buying the book is a better investment'.

World Trade Center, Church, Vesey, West and Liberty Sts. The view from the 107th floor observation deck—more than a quarter mile high—is spectacular. $2.75.

Chrysler Building, 405 Lexington and 42nd St. Lovely example of 'art deco' architecture. Was the world's tallest building for one whole year.

Rockefeller Center, 5th Ave to Ave of the Americas and 48th to 52nd Sts. Tours of the whole building including the observation roof and backstage at Radio City cost $3 and run from 10am to 4.45pm starting from 30 Rockefeller Plaza. The observation room is open 9am–9pm. If visibility is poor, tickets are available for readmission.

United Nations Building, 1st Ave and 44th St. Hour-long tours are run every 10 minutes, 9.05am–4.45pm. $3, students $1.75. The General Assembly usually meets at about 10.30am and 3.30pm and tickets for the meetings are issued at the admission desks in the main lobby no earlier than 30 min before the meeting, and are free on a first-come-first served basis. Be sure to arrive early.

Seagram Building, 375 Park Ave, at 53rd St. Designed by Mies Van de Rohe. Brief free tour, Tue.

Flatiron Building, Madison Sq at 22nd St. The first iron-framed building and predecessor of NY's skyscrapers. The thin end of the wedge, and still a curiosity worth seeing.

New York Stock Exchange, 20 Broad St at Wall St. The exhibition gallery and Vistors' Room are open daily 9.30am to 3.30pm. Visit too the nearby **American Stock Exchange**.

Statue of Liberty. Boats leave Battery Park frequently year-round, during summer every ½hr 9am–5pm, $1.75. 'Allow 3hrs for roundtrip if you want to go up into the head, longer for the hand.' An elevator takes you halfway up Ms Liberty (25¢), or you can take the steps. 'Beware oven-like temperatures on hot days.' There's a free museum. A gift from the French government, the statute will be 100 years old in 1986. Alas, she's falling apart, and though there's no danger to visitors, extensive renovations costing $25m will begin in 1984 and she'll be off-limits for about a year. It's possible her raised arm will have to be temporarily removed.

Ellis Island. Once the last stop for over 12 million European immigrants entering the US between 1892 and 1924, and consequently a place of enormous significance and poignancy for many Americans. Ferry operates daily from Battery Park. Tours run by National Parks Service once there. $2.75.

The Staten Island Ferry. Nobody should miss what is almost certainly the best travel bargain to be found in North America. It costs just 25¢ rt. Frequent departures from Battery Park, at the tip of Manhattan. Passes close to the Statute of Liberty. Superb view of the Manhattan skyline, many people's (among them poet Walt Whitman) favourite view of New York.

Steuben Glass Center, 5th Ave and 58th St. Too expensive to buy but always superb to look at.

Coney Island, a gaudy fun place for generations, with crowded beach and famous amusement park. While here visit the **NY Aquarium**, 'fantastic'. Both the BMT and IND subways will get you there. (See Beaches).

Cathedral of St John and Divine, 112th St and Amsterdam Ave. Otherwise known as St John the Unfinished. Work began in 1892, was suspended in 1941 when America entered the war. Enthusiasm then waned and funds dried up, and meanwhile Americans forgot how to build Gothic cathedrals. But now Londoner James Bambridge, who built Liverpool Cathedral and oversaw the reconstruction of Wells, has been brought in to train Harlem youths as master stonemasons—their apprenticeships will make them employable for the rest of their lives; Bambridge does not expect to live to see its completion, 'but I'll get it set up right so that the work will go on properly for however long it takes'. When completed, it will be the largest Gothic cathedral in the world. Tours are available. 678-6888.

Lincoln Center for the Performing Arts, 62nd–66th Sts and Columbus Ave, 877-1800. Largest arts centre in the world, containing opera house, concert hall, theatre and museum. Hour-long tour $4.50. The Metropolitan Opera House, in the Center, has its own tours at 3.45pm—except when there's a matinee—conducted by volunteers from the Met Guild. Look for free concerts and other happenings during the summer.

Woodlawn Cemetery. In the Bronx, and the last stop on the subway. The society cemetery; 400 landscaped acres of opulent mausolea and monuments to men who started from nothing and worked their way to the right to a place at Woodlawn. Cast includes Westinghouse, Bat Masterson, associate of Wyatt Earp, Fiorello La Guardia, F W Woolworth, J C Penney, and B Bulova, the watch tycoon.

South Street Seaport, 766-9020, by Fulton St fish market. A five-block restoration of New York 200 years ago, undertaken for the Bicentennial. The ship museum costs $3 adults, $1.50 children. There are different entertainments nightly.

Brooklyn Heights. A neighbourhood of brick, brownstone and wooden houses, high up overlooking New York harbour. New York as it was 100 years ago. You can walk here across the **Brooklyn Bridge** from South Street Seaport.

MUSEUMS AND ART GALLERIES

Metropolitan Museum of Art, Central Park, 5th Ave and 82nd St, 535-7710. One of the world's greatest collections and the largest of its kind in the Western Hemisphere. There are approximately 700 masterpieces tracing the evolution of art from the 13th to the mid-20th century, plus the largest Egyptian collection outside Egypt. Wed–Sat 10am–5pm, Sun and hols 11am–5pm. Closed Mon, open Tue till 8.45pm. Suggested donation $3.50 adults, $1.75 seniors and students.

Museum of Modern Art, 11 W 53rd St, 956-6100. Outstanding collection of contemporary American and European art. Entrance $3 adults, $2 students, $1 under 16 or over 64. Costs as much as little as you want to pay on Tue. Open Mon–Sat 11am–6pm, Thur till 9pm, Sun noon–6pm, closed Wed. Films at 2pm and 5pm.

Guggenheim Museum, 5th Ave at 89th, 860-1300. Contemporary art housed in a spiral structure designed by Frank Lloyd Wright. Open Wed–Sun and hols 11am–5pm, Tue 11am–8pm, closed Mon. $2 adults, $1.25 students and over-62s, free for all Tue 5pm–8pm.

Museum of the City of New York, 5th Ave at 103rd St, 534-1672. Fascinating story of city's growth from a small Dutch community. Free. Open Tue–Sat 10am–5pm, Sun and hols 1pm–5pm, closed Mon unless hol, then closed following Tue. Also walking tours to various parts of the city Sun 2pm, late April–early Oct, $4.

Witney Museum of American Art, 975 Madison Ave, corner of 75th St, 570-3600. Devoted exclusively to 20th-century American art. Open Wed–Sat 11am–6pm, Tue 11am–8pm, Sun noon–6pm, closed Mon. Adults $2 but free Tue 6pm–8pm; seniors, students and under-12 free at all times.

The Cloisters, Fort Tryon Park, 191 St and Fort Washington Ave, 923-3700. A branch of the Metropolitan devoted to medieval European art. On top of a hill overlooking the Hudson, the museum gives the impression of a 12th-century monastery. One of the lesser known but more enjoyable galleries. Open 1 May–30 Sept Tue–Sat 10am–4.45 pm, Sun and hols noon–4.45pm, closed Mon; rest of year same hrs except Sun 1–4.45 pm. Adults $3.50, seniors and students $1.75. Best reached by express subway.

Frick Collection, 5th Ave at E 70th St, 288-0700. Once a town house, the museum boasts a fine collection of European paintings and furniture. Open 1 June–31 Aug Wed–Sat 10am–6pm, Sun and hols 1–6pm; rest of year open additionally Tue 10am–6pm. Adults $1, students and seniors 50¢; everyone $2 Sun. Under 16 must be accompanied by adult, under 10 not admitted. 'Unsuspected highlight of NY.'

Natural History Museum, Central Pk W at 79th St, 873-1300. Huge, scattered over 19 buildings. An imaginatively presented presentation of the origins of man and natural history collection from all continents and seas, though especially strong on Africa and North America. Open daily, including hols, 10am–4.45pm, Wed to 8pm. Entry by donation. In the same complex, the **Hayden Planetarium**, 873-9928. 1hr star shows. Open Mon–Fri at 1.30pm and 3.30pm, Sat and Sun at 1, 2, 3, 4 and 5 pm. Closed hols. Adults $3.50, seniors and students $2.50, kids 5–12 $1.75, under-5s not admitted.

Museum of the American Indian, Broadway at 155th St, 283-2420. One of the finest collections of Amerindian art and artefacts in the US. Open Tue–Sat 10am–5pm, Sun 1–5pm, closed hols. $1.50 adults, 75¢ students and seniors. 'A treasure house.' This is part of the **Washington Heights Museum Group** which includes the **Hispanic Society of America** with Spanish and Portuguese sculpture, paintings and decorative arts (690-0743), the **American Numismatic Society** with over 600,000 coins and medals (234-3130), and the **American Academy and Institute of Arts and Letters** (368-5900), each with various hours but all free.

Intrepid **Sea, Air and Space Museum**, W 46th and St and 12th Ave, Pier 80, 245-0072. Just opened: restored aircraft carrier with planes, also space exhibit. $5.

TOURS

Since the city is best explored on foot, and bus tours are very expensive, the authors consider that the only tours really worth taking are the boat trips around Manhattan and the bus and foot treks around Harlem. Circle Line, Pier 83, W 43rd St, 563-3200. Costs $9. First boat leaves 9.45am. The trip lasts three hours. Worthwhile only on a clear day. 'Make sure you sit on the left side of the boat.' 'Can get chilly.'

Hudson River Day Line, 279-5151, leaves Pier 81 at the foot of W 41st St. Costs $8. Frequent departures.

This company also runs a daily trip up the Hudson calling at Bear Mountain, West Point, and Poughkeepsie. Departing Pier 81, 10am, returning 7pm. Till Labor Day return tickets cost $11. Prices increase at weekends.

For 'Harlem As It Is' tours go to the black-operated Penny Sightseeing Company, 303 W 42nd St, 247-2860. $11. 'Very disappointing; probably better to take a Grayline tour of Harlem—cheaper ($9), and includes St John the Divine Cathedral.' The Grayline Bus Tours of the city are probably only worth taking if you do not intend to stay long, though do consider them for Harlem.

Island Helicopters haul you aloft from their pads at 34th St on the East River or 30th St on the Hudson River 683-4575. Tours start at $17 per person, minimum 2 persons, for 7 minutes of swooping over the East River and UN Building. 'A real experience if you've never been up in a light plane or copter before.' 'Try to sit next to the pilot.'

Not strictly tours, but certainly worth knowing about are the Culture Bus Loops. No 1 covers Manhattan, No 2 Lower Manhattan and Brooklyn. Sat, Sun, and hols $2.75. Buses run every 20 mins, and you get off and on when and as you will. Tickets can be bought on the bus and stops are marked. 330-1234.

ENTERTAINMENT

No other American city can offer more or such a variety of amusements. Entertainment, however, can be expensive for the stranger who does not know his way around. Broadway theatres, most night clubs and some cinemas will put a strain on modest budgets. At the same time, nowhere will he find so much free entertainment.

Read the *New Yorker, Village Voice, SoHo Weekly News* or *Cue* for complete details of shows, jazz and cinemas. For up-to-date theatre information call the Cultural Information Center, 582-555.

There are free orchestral, pop, operatic concerts, dance groups, and theatrical performances in Central Pk throughout the summer. Also look out for local festivals.

Greenwich Village and SoHo are two of the most interesting entertainment areas. Good jazz and folk music, as well as eating places, can still be found among the many tourist traps in the Village, although SoHo is definitely where New Yorkers go now. Go to the better places, even if there is an admission charge; you will find the best music. Beware of places that do not advertise an admission or cover charge but extract large sums for a drink and offer inferior entertainment.

Washington Square is infested with pseudo folksingers on Sunday afternoons. The Loeb Student Center on the south side of the Square presents a series of excellent free concerts on Weds in July.

JAZZ

For a real jazz fan there is so much going on that the best bet is to go to the Information Center at Times Square and pick up the free fortnightly publication *Jazz Interactions* news sheet, which lists all the gigs.

Village Vanguard, 178 7th Ave S, 255-4037. Sleazy, unkempt, chaotic and cramped; the perfect jazz club, always worth going to, whoever's playing.

Sweet Basil, 88 7th Ave S, 242-1785. Smallish room with nice atmosphere and pleasant food; attracts the best bands.

Village Gate, Bleecker and Thompson Sts, Greenwich Village, 475-5120. Good trad jazz and frequent dollops of salsa.

Jazzmania, 40 W 27th St, 532-7666. More of a loft than a club. A place where you can dance. Informal, friendly and reasonably priced.

Eddie Condon's, 144 W 54th St, 265-8277. Grand old club, small and smoke-filled. No cover, dinner till 2am, jazz lunches Wed and Fri.

Fat Tuesday's, 190 3rd Ave, 533-7902. A lively newish place.

Ginger Man, 51 W 64th St, 399-2358. Tiny friendly club in the Upper West Side specialising in traditional jazz. Serves food.

Greenwich Village Jazz Festival, started 1982 and looks like becoming an end-Aug fixture. In Washington Sq, free. 'Attracted large crowds; great atmosphere and big names, including Dizzy Gillespie.'

The Newport Jazz Festival is held in New York end June/early July. Moved here from Rhode Island in 1972. Probably the greatest jazz festival in the world. 787-2020.

COUNTRY MUSIC/ROCK

Lone Star Cafe, 13th St and 5th Ave. A bit of Texas in New York with Lone Star beer, hot chilli, and the 'best in modern country music from the Southern states'.

CBGB'S, 315 Bowery at Bleecker. Once only country music, now mainly rock.

Max's Kansas City, 213 Park Ave S at 17th St. Beef meal downstairs, rock music up.

Hurrah, 36 W. 6wnd St Good rock/disco.

O'Lunney's, 915 2nd Ave at 48th St. Country. For Info: Rock Hotline, 757-6900.

THEATRE

Broadway prices are high but tickets go on sale at half price on the day of perform-ance at the TKTS booth, 47th St at Times Square, 'Be prepared for very long queues'. Matinee sales noon–2pm, evening sales 3pm–8pm. Get there at least 45 minutes before sale time for best pickings. There is also always something inter-esting happening 'Off-Broadway' and prices are lower. Read the *Village Voice* for 'Off-off-Broadway' plays. Keep a look-out in hotels, drugstores, coffee shops, news-stands and visitors bureaux, for 'Two Fers' (two tickets for the price of one). The New York Philharmonic, the Metropolitan Opera, and the Shakespeare Festi-val all perform in the parks during the summer. Free. Information: 472-1003.

CINEMA

On Broadway prices start around $5. There are many other smaller and cheaper neighbourhood cinemas, however. Look up under 'Other Movies' in *Village Voice* for movies under $2. Cinemas at this price include the Elgin, Theatre 80, Bleecker St Cinema, Carnegie Hall Cinema and Quad Cinema.

'The New York Experience', 6th Ave, nr Radio City. 'Film mugs you from all directions—definitely captures the spirit of New York.'

Radio City Music Hall, the largest cinema in the world, Guided tour $6.95. The famous, spectacular Rockettes perform twice daily, $12. For ticket info call 757-3100. As recently as 1977 Radio City was threatened with closure and was only saved at the eleventh hour after an enormous public outcry.

TV SHOWS

Free tickets from Tourist Information, 90 E 42nd St. Also phone up TV stations.

OUT OF DOORS

The Bronx Zoo, properly the New York Zoological Park, Fordham Rd and Southern Blvd, 220-5100. Take the subway to E Tremont. Mon-Sat 10am–5pm, Sun and hols 10am–5.30pm, 1 Feb–31 Oct; daily 10am–4.30pm rest of year. Adults $2, kids 75¢ 1 April–30 Nov; cheaper rest of year. NY's biggest zoo; children's zoo, animal rides and safari monorail charge extra.

Beaches: Coney Island and Brighton Beach, Brooklyn, reached by D Subway. Jones Beach, Queens; you need a car.

Swimming: Free pool, 57th St at 1st Ave.

Spectator sport: baseball in summer, the Mets and the Yankees at Shea and Yankee Stadia; basketball at Madison Square Garden and ice hockey at the Coliseum, Uniondale, Nassau County, in winter; pro-football at Shea in autumn; in soccer there's the Cosmos out at Randalls Island; and newest of all, for tennis devotees there's the National Tennis Center at Flushing Meadows.

'Best free entertainment in NY is watching the roller disco dancers with their *huge* transistors in the middle of Central Park—some stopping on their way home from work. There's a place in the park where you can hire skates by the half-day; there's also an exhibition night, I think Wed, when the best talent gathers.'

INFORMATION

The International Center, Abbey Victoria Hotel, 23rd floor, 151 W 51st St 245-4131. A private organisation which in certain circumstances can be of help to students and academics.

New York Student Center, William Sloane House, 356 W 34th St, 760-5860. Travel advisory centre.

New York Convention and Visitors Bureau, 2 Columbus Circle, 397-8200. Free maps, tickets to television shows, list of tourist attractions.

Travelers Aid, 204 E 39th, 679-0200. For changing foreign currency try the Perera Company, 636 5th Ave (Rockefeller Center) or Deak & Co, 29 Broadway.

There are post offices at 340 W 42nd, Lexington Ave and E 45th, in Macy's, beneath the Rockefeller Center (enter at 620 or 610 5th Ave) 8th Ave at 33rd St, 61st St east of Broadway, and on 42nd St W between 8th and 9th Aves.

TRANSPORT

You should not be deterred by the infuriating topology of New York's subway. Although dirty, very noisy, and sometimes unpleasant, the subway is one of the cheapest and best means of transport around the city.

The fare is 75¢ and you purchase a token from the booking office, depositing it at the turnstile. There are express and local trains; it is very important to know which you have to take to reach your destination. Since the whole system is very badly marked, alertness and a venturesome spirit are prerequisites. 'To be avoided by lone women late at night.' Free maps are obtainable from the booking offices. For information on subway trains and buses, call Transit Authority on 330-3000.

BUSES AND TRAINS

Exact fare (currently 75¢) needed. Transfers are available between buses marked NYC Transit Authority but not on those marked Bronx and Manhattan Surface Transit Authority. After 6pm a $1 ticket is available which gives unlimited travel until 2am.

All inter-city bus lines including Greyhound and Trailways use the Port Authority Terminal, 8th Ave and 41st St, 564-8484.

Green Tortoise, 431-3348.

At peak times expect to queue for up to an hour for tickets on the major bus companies. Advisable not to hang about the Port Authority Terminal during the early hours. 'If arriving late, you can get a cheap night's sleep at a 24 hour cinema in Times Square. Costs about $2. Watch a porno film while you doze off. Put your luggage in a PAT locker first though.'

AMTRAK operates from Penn Station, 8th Ave. and W 31st St, and from Grand Central Station, E 42nd St and Park Ave. Tickets also at AMTRAK Rockefeller Plaza Office, 12 W 51st St. 'Don't take AMTRAK if travelling between NY and Philadelphia. Take Conrail instead. A bit slower with many stops (including Princeton), but half the price.'

CARS, AND BICYCLE HIRE

Try renting a bicycle for an 'original and dangerous way to see New York'. Bike Rentals has several shops, always shifting it seems, so look them up in the phone book. Rental places usually require a credit card or a $50 deposit.

Moped Experience, 200 E 25th St, between 2nd and 3rd Aves, 689-5186. $10 a day, $50 deposit for bikes or mopeds.

Renting a car can be difficult for anyone under 25; try arguing and bargaining. See Yellow Pages for numbers.

'Most companies want driver to have licence and credit card with a sufficiently large credit limit; they won't allow splitting the cost between several people. Cash is generally useless except at international airports in conjunction with a passport.'

Automobile transporting companies, eg AAACON, will be found in the phone book, but the best in New York is Dependable Drive-Away, 130 W 42nd St, 840-6262. 'Better than AAACON, gives more time and more additional mileage. Nationwide company, so no problems. Recommended.' 'Very dependable.'

If blowing town, pick up free maps of the Great Beyond at Exxon Touring, 1251 6th Ave, between 49th and 50th Sts.

For rides, check the bulletin boards at NYU, Loeb Centre, Washington Sq, or at the Columbia University Bookshop.

KENNEDY AIRPORT

The Carey Transport Bus runs between the East Side Terminal, 38th St and 1st Ave, 632-0500 and JFK, $5 one way; takes about an hour. Buses leave every 15 mins. Carey runs a free shuttle service between the Port Authority and the Eastside Terminal. Operates approx. every half hour 11am–6pm weekdays only.

Taxis from midtown Manhattan cost $22 plus tip. There are also limousines from various hotels, $6.

An express subway service runs from 57th St and other points along the Avenue of the Americas. Costs $5, takes an hour. Otherwise, the cheapest but longest way is by taking the up-town IND. Leave the IND E or F train at Kew Gardens Union Turnpike. The Q10 bus to JFK stops outside the subway station. Total cost for one journey $1.50. Time: about 90 mins.

LA GUARDIA AIRPORT

Carey Transport bus costs $5.

Take IRT Main Street, Flushing, local subway to 74th Street, Roosevelt-Jackson Heights. From the bus station underneath the subway station take the Q33 to La Guardia.

NEWARK AIRPORT

Bus between Port Authority Terminal and Newark Airport departs every 10 minutes, takes ½hr, costs $4.

SHOPPING

The Complete Traveller, Madison and 35th. Books and travel guides to everywhere.'

Barnes and Noble Book Store, 600 5th Ave, and 17th St. and 5th Ave. Reductions on best sellers and others.

Strand Bookshop, Broadway and 12th St. Huge second-hand book store.

Hudson's. Army surplus, camping gear, etc. 3rd Ave and 13th St between Union Sq and Astor Pl. Army surplus etc. 'Cheapest in US.'

J & R Music World, 23 Park Row, 732-8600. Enormous stocks of records and tapes. Good prices plus lots of oldies.

Canal Jean Co, 304 Canal St and 504 Broadway at Spring St. Jeans, etc.

Macy's, 34th and Broadway, the largest department store in the world; Bloomingdales, 58th and Lexington, arguably the trendiest.

Science Fiction Bookshop, 58 8th Ave at 14th St. Stocks virtually every SF book in print.

Korvettes, 5th Ave and 47th St. Bargains on clothes, records, electrical and electronic goods. (Founded by Korean War veterans: Kor-vets, get it?)

Downstairs Records, 20 W 43rd St. A great place to look for that lost Deanna Durbin single.

'Low-priced clothes at Orchard St market, Lower East Side, off Canal St, Sun mornings. Traditional Jewish street market, lots of bustle and colour.'

LONG ISLAND. 'The Island', as New Yorkers call it, is a 150-mile-long glacial moraine, the terminal line of the last encroachment of the Ice Age. Extending eastwards from Manhattan, it includes two of the New York City boroughs, Brooklyn and Queens, and the built-up suburban county of Nassau, though more than half its length is occuped by the still rural county of Suffolk.

Long Island Sound quietly laps against its North Shore where hills, headlands, fields and woods have attracted some of the great houses of the wealthy. Scott Fitzgerald's Gatsby partied here, and **Sagamore Hill**, outside of Glen Cove, Nassau, was the home of President Theodore Roosevelt. In **Huntington**, further east, poet Walt Whitman spent his childhood (you can visit the house) and, nearby, the Vanderbilts had an estate which they connected to New York City with their own private motorway.

The South Shore receives the waves of the open Atlantic and is generally flat and sandy. Except right out at the **Hamptons** (Southampton and East Hampton) this shoreline has always been less exclusive than the north, but it has certainly attracted those in search of magnificent beaches which stretch in a virtually unbroken line 100 miles out from the city.

All areas of Long Island are easily accessible from Manhattan via the Long Island Railroad from Penn Central, or via the Northern State and Southern State Parkways, and the Long Island Expressway, which at the city end is so often jammed with traffic that it's known as 'the longest parking lot in the world', but which eventually sweeps beyond the pandemonium towards the remoteness of Montauk Point's majestic lighthouse.

Long Island is fraught with social experiments, and **Jones Beach** is one of the nicest of them. With millions unemployed during the Depression, President Franklin Roosevelt found work for many and fun for more by developing this four-mile stretch of the South Shore into an excellent sandy beach. On a hot summer's weekend, or the Fourth of July, up to half a million people and their cars join the seagulls for a good splash in the sun and water. Go there during the week if you want more of the beach to yourself.

Fire Island, on a long sandbar further east than Jones Beach, is nicer yet, being not so much developed as preserved as a National Seashore for its natural beauty and birdlife. An excellent place for swimming, surfing, sunbathing, fishing, cooking over an open grill and getting up to no good in the sand dunes.

Facing the calm waters of Gardiners Bay, **Sag Harbor**, once a whaling port, is now a pleasant town where John Steinbeck chose to end his days, and those wealthy enough to own sailing boats moor them. The Suffolk County Whaling Museum is on Main Street.

There are in fact several such salty and tranquil spots at this end of the island, as well as an Indian Reservation, and a few days wandering is well worth it.

Many of the place names on Long Island derive from the Indians who once lived here fishing, planting or hunting deer: the Wantaghs, Patchogues and Montauks were a few of the tribes. **Montauk Point** marks the eastern extremity of Long Island where a towering lighthouse, built in 1796 by order of George Washington, looks over three sides of water with magnificent views of the rising sun.

Curiously enough, the oldest cattle ranch in the United States is also located out here.

THE HUDSON RIVER VALLEY. Though not the key to the Northwest Passage that many early explorers hoped it would be, the Hudson has gouged a considerable valley from the mountains of upstate New York past the chalk cliffs of the Palisades to the granite slab of Manhattan, and onwards even from there, forming a great underwater trench several hundred miles long out to the edge of the continental shelf.

Much of the scenery along the valley is very beautiful and marked by many historical towns and places such as Tarrytown, West Point, Hyde Park and electrifying Sing Sing Prison.

Apart from coming here by road, consider a sail up the Hudson. (See New York City, Tours section.)

About 16 miles north of the George Washington Bridge on the eastern side of the Hudson, **Tarrytown** was the home of Washington Irving and the model for his story, *The Legend of Sleepy Hollow*. His books, manuscripts and furniture are still here, the house, on West Sunnyside Lane, open to visitors. Both he and Andrew Carnegie are buried in the Sleepy Hollow Cemetery. Also worth a visit are two restored (with Rockefeller money) Dutch colonial manors, the Philipsburg and Van Cortlandt Manors. The Philipsburg Manor has a working gristmill and, operating it, a miller from Staffordshire, England. Entrance to Sunnyside and each of the manors is

$4 or a $10 combination ticket for all three. For information call (914) 631-8200.

Not an Indian reservation but a military reservation, **West Point** is the site of the US Military Academy, founded in 1802 to train potential officers, and alma mater of such architects of victory as Robert E Lee, General Custer and William Westmoreland.

If you like brass bands and cadets walking in straight lines, this is the place for you. Museum and grounds open daily. Parade schedules can be obtained by writing to the Information Officer. Close by is the 5000 acre plus Bear Mountain State Park, good for camping and hiking.

Hyde Park, a small village 90 miles north of New York City, lies on scenic Route 9 overlooking the Hudson River. It was the home of President Franklin D Roosevelt and both he and Eleanor lie buried in the Rose Garden.

Nearby is the Frederick W Vanderbilt estate, a renaissance-style house with elaborate furnishings. See how the big-time millionaires lived. Tickets to either the FDR or Vanderbilt homes are good for admission to the other.

Just a little further up the Hudson is the quaintish city of **Kingston**, founded as a Dutch trading post in 1614. In 1777 it became the first state capital and you can visit the restored Senate House on Fair Street where the senators met before fleeing for their lives in the face of a British attack. There are several Colonial buildings in the area, including the Old Dutch Church on Main Street.

Woodstock, a magic name from the '60s, is nearby off Route 28. Many an aging hippy can be seen making a nostalgic pilgrimage to the village which came to symbolise the youth/rock cult after the rock concert to end all concerts here in 1969. Woodstock is an arty-crafty place. During the summer there are several theatrical and craft festivals in the village.

The **Catskill Mountains**, just to the west of Kingston, are reputedly the spot where Rip Van Winkle dozed off for 20 years. It's an area of hills, streams, hiking paths and ski trails. The Catskills used to be the place where wealthy New Yorkers took their holidays and where the hoi polloi still do. There is just a touch of decay and nostalgia at the resorts, an air of having seen better days. But still a marvellous retreat for walking and getting away from it all.

ALBANY. Capital of the State of New York and named after the Duke of York and Albany who later became James II of England. Not the greatest place for the casual visitor but downtown does have some interesting new architecture in the shape of the Rockefeller Empire State Plaza, a massive shopping, office and cultural complex which cost a billion dollars to build.

Situated near the juncture of the Hudson and Mohawk Rivers, and on a line with the boundary between western Massachusetts and southern Vermont, the city is a convenient halting place before visiting these states, or before exploring the local New York attractions of Saratoga, Lake George and Ticonderoga, Massena, the Adirondacks and Ausable Chasm.

ACCOMMODATION

The most inexpensive accommodation during summer is at the residence halls of the State University of New York at Albany (SUNYA), the College of St Rose and Siena College. For whom to contact, phone the Convention and Visitors Bureau, 434-1217 or 474-2418.

Wellington Hotel, State St, downtown, 436-9741. Doubles start at $28. 'Try asking for a cheaper room.' 'Used by State University to house students.'

Days Inn, 16 Wolf Rd, take I-87 to exit 2E (Rt 5), 3 miles from downtown, 459-3600. Singles $34, doubles $39. Air conditioning, radio, colour TV, pool.

Northway Inn, 1517 Central Ave, Rt 5, at junction with I-87 Northway exit 2W, 10 minute drive from downtown, 869-0277. Air conditioning, cable TV, heated pool, steambaths.

OF INTEREST

Gov Nelson A Rockefeller Empire State Plaza, between Madison and State Sts, Centre of town, 474-2418. Free, 10-building complex housing 30 state agencies and cultural facilities. The most striking feature of this ultra-brute-modern affair is the 44-storey state office tower with **observation deck** up top, panoramas 9am–5pm.

State Capital, nearby, free 1-hr tours 9am–4pm daily. Begun in 1867, the building includes the Million Dollar Staircase. The stonecarvers of the staircase reproduced in stone not only the famous but also their family and friends.

State Museum, Empire State Plaza. Geology, history, Indians and natural history. In the New York Metropolis Hall is a vast display of the NYC urbanisation process, including 1940 subway car, 1929 Yellow Cab, 1930 Chinatown import-export shop and mock-up of *Sesame Street* stage set. Daily 10am–5pm, free, 474-5842. 'Superb.'

Institute of History and Art, 125 Washington Ave. Oldest Museum in the state. Dutch period and and Hudson River School landscape paintings, 18th and 19th C furniture, etc. Open Tue-Sat 10am–4.45pm, Sun 2–5pm, free, 463-4478.

Schuyler Mansion State Historic Site, 27 Clinton St at Catherine St, 474-3953. Built 1762, home of Gen Philip Schuyler, revolutionary luminary. Gentleman Johnny Burgoyne was prisoner and Schuyler's daughter Betsy married Alexander Hamilton here. Free tours Wed-Sun 9am–5pm, April-December, otherwise by appointment only.

INFORMATION

Travelers Aid, 202 Lark St, 463-2124.
Convention and Visitors Bureau, 90 State St, 434-1217 or 474-2418.
Chamber of Commerce, 90 State St, 434-1214.

TRAVEL

AMTRAK, Albany-Rensselaer station, East St, Rensselaer. The scenic *Adirondack* passes through between NYC and Montréal.

SARATOGA SPRINGS. About 25 miles north of Albany, this favourite resort with its mineral springs bears a Mohawk name meaning 'place of swift water'. The waters are on tap at the Saratoga Spa Reservation, and, also in town, on Union Avenue and Ludlow Street, is the National Museum of Thoroughbred Racing. The nation's oldest thoroughbred racing track is at Saratoga, and from April through September the trotters race here. Saratoga Springs is also the summer home of the New York City Ballet which performs at the Saratoga Performing Arts Center, an outdoor theatre sometimes featuring rock groups too; lawn seats $6–$10.

The nearby Saratoga National Historical Park is the battlefield where American forces led by Benedict Arnold (under the nominal command of General Horatio Gates) defeated the British Army commanded by Gentleman Johnny Burgoyne in 1777, marking a turning point in the Revolution.

LAKE GEORGE. Another 25 miles north of Saratoga Springs is the town of Lake George and the lake itself which runs to Fort Ticonderoga where it constricts before opening out again as Lake Champlain.

Lake George is billed as the resort area with 'a million dollar beach', but whatever that means it's in fact horribly polluted by tourists and tourist traps. Best to keep going through the area and on to the Adironduck Park.

Fort Ticonderoga at the other end of the lake is accessible by road or by boat from Lake George town, and of interest to those who would know the methods by which the British Empire grew great. Constructed by the French in 1755, the British waited just long enough for it be made comfortable before taking it over in 1756. Perhaps requiring some repairs to be made, the British then let rebel Ethan Allen grab it in 1775, and when suitable again for officers and gentlemen, Burgoyne took it back in 1777. Guided tour, $4. There is a car ferry service from Ticonderoga across to Vermont.

THE ADIRONDACKS. An enormous park of mountains, forests and lakes, stretching thousands of square miles west of Lakes George and Champlain encompasses the year-round resort area of the Adirondacks Mountains.

Lake Placid is the sporting centre of the area and the site of the 1980 Winter Olympics. The town was also the venue for the first winter games in 1932. The forests, mountains and numerous lakes all around with cross-country trails and a climb (or chairlift) up to the top of 4867-foot Whiteface Mountain are equally suitable for summer excursions.

Ausable Chasm lies on the western shores of Lake Champlain where the Ausable River has cut a vast canyon through the rock. Boats, bridges and footpaths allow the visitor to explore it.

ACCOMMODATION
Lake Placid is generally expensive; these are the best deals:

Northway Motel, 5 Wilmington Rd, half-mile east of town, 523-3500. Doubles from $33–$41, with heated pool, radio, cable TV.

AYH, 54 Main St, 523-2008. $8. 'Housed in church, some religious overtones, but very friendly and helpful.' 1 block from Greyhound stop. Advance booking required.

OF INTEREST

Lake Placid: **John Brown Farm State Historic Site**, 2 miles out of town on Rt 73. This is where he lies amouldering in the grave (see Harpers Ferry, West Virginia). Open Wed–Sun 9am–5pm, free.

Ausable Chasm: The **tour** by foot, boat and return bus costs $6 adults, $3.75 kids under 13, available daily mid-May to mid-Oct, 834-7454.

Blue Mountain Lake, about 40 miles southwest of Lake Placid enroute to Utica and Syracuse. Lake and mountain scenery, and the **Adirondack Museum**, 1 mile north, 352-7311. Shows life in the Adirondacks since colonial times, with 1890 private railroad car, log hotel, 1932 Winter Olympics relics. Open daily mid-June to mid-Oct 10am–5pm, adults $4.50, kids under 16 $2.75. 'Allow 2–3 hrs to see it all.'

THE FINGER LAKES. These slender lakes, splayed like the fingers of an open hand across midwestern New York, were formed by the receding glaciers of the last Ice Age. Their names—Canandaiqua, Seneca, Cayuga, Owasco and Skaneateles—still speak of the Indian legend that the lakes are the impress of the Great Spirit who here laid his hand upon the earth. The lakes extend through a lush area of farmlands and vineyards.

Syracuse, to the east of the Finger Lakes, was the site chief Hiawatha chose about 1570 as the capital for the Iroquois Confederacy. Around the council fires of the longhouse met the Five Nations which for two centuries dominated northeastern North America. Salt first brought the Indians and later the French and Americans to the shores of Lake Onondaga. Syracuse was founded in 1805 and for many years most of the salt used in America came from here. The New York State Fair is held annually in Syracuse from late August through Labor Day. Well-regarded Syracuse University was founded here in 1870.

ACCOMMODATION

Dome Hotel, 200 W Jefferson St, 422-2141. From $26 single, from $32 double, with air conditioning and colour TV.

Ithaca, at the southern extremity of Lake Cayuga, encompasses within its city limits hills to rival San Francisco's as well as waterfalls, gorges and natural recreation areas. A 30-mile walking trail looping round Ithaca is the most enjoyable way to appreciate its delights. This is the home of Cornell University.

ACCOMMODATION

Wonderland Lodge, 654 Elmira Rd, 272-5252. 2 miles south of downtown, between Buttermilk and Treman State Pks. Singles from $26, doubles from $30. Air conditioning, cable TV, heated pool, coin laundry.

Elmshade Boarding House, N Albany St, 273-1701. $15 per person.

Hillside Inn, Stewart Ave, Collegetown, 272-9509. Inexpensive.

OF INTEREST
Cornell University, on the northeast side of town, is beautifully situated on a hill overlooking the lake and occupies 13,000 acres including farms and experimental lands. Free tours, 256-7419.
Taughannock Falls State Park, 10 miles north on Rt 89. If you want more nature than the city limits confine, come to this mile-long glen with 400 ft walls and 215 ft falls.

Still within the Finger Lakes region is **Corning**, 50 miles southwest of Ithaca. Corningware and Steuben Glass originated here, and it's well worth spending several hours at the amazing **Corning Glass Center**, watching it being cut, moulded, blown into any shape for every conceivable use. For information phone (607) 974-8271.

Northeast of the Finger Lakes, on the shores of Lake Ontario, **Rochester** is a grimy, crowded city encircled by insipid flowery suburbs. But one mile east of downtown is George Eastman House, (716) 271-3361, the home of the founder of Kodak and now the International Museum of Photography, which should fascinate amateur and professional alike. On the other side of town is the Eastman Kodak plant, 724-4000, which gives free one and a half hour tours.

NIAGARA FALLS. A traditional destination for honeymoon couples in search of the awesome ('Was that you or the Falls, darling?'), mere tourists also flock to Niagara to see one of the most outstanding spectacles on the continent.

On the US side are the American Falls and the Bridal Veil Falls with a drop of 184 feet and a combined breadth of 1075 feet in a fairly straight line; the Horseshoe Falls on the Canadian side describe a deep curve 2200 feet long though with a slightly lower drop of 176 feet. About 1,500,000 gallons of water would normally plummet over the three falls each second, but in summer particularly the use of the river's waters to generate electricity reduces that flow by half.

The Canadian side offers the better view (see Niagara Falls, Ontario), but (or therefore) it's more commercialised. To be honest, both the Canadian and the American sides are dumps and you should just keep your eyes on the spill.

ACCOMMODATION
Coachman Motel, 523 3rd St, 285-2295. $33 double—$2 off with coupon from Visitors Center. 'Very good location near falls; clean rooms with colour TV, fridge, bath and shower.'
Big Tree Tourist Home, 40 Niagara St, 285-9258. Singles and doubles from $24. Near Rainbow Bridge.
YMCA, 1317 Portage Rd, 285-8491. $3 for women on dorm mattress (bring your own bag), $12 for men in rooms. 'Wonderful showers, incredible security.'
Frontier Youth Hostel (AYH), 1101 Ferry Ave, corner of Memorial Parkway, 282-3700 or 285-9203. Advance booking suggested in summer. $6.50 members, $10 non-members. 'One of the friendliest and most helpful hostels in America; clean small dormitories; 10 minutes from falls.'

OF INTEREST

Old Fort Niagara. About 6 miles north in Fort Niagara State Park. The fort saw service under three flags—British, French and American, and contains some pre-revolution buildings. Displays of drill musket firing, etc.

Seeing the Falls. Walk from the US to Canada via the Rainbow Bridge. Cost 10¢ each way, and don't forget your passport. On either side you can don oilskins for a trip on the *Maid of Mists* boat which will carry you within drenching distance of the Falls. Cost $5; July 1st–Aug 31st, 9.30am–8pm; other times, 9.30am–5pm.

Prospect Point Observation Tower, 25¢.

Cave of the Winds. Don oilskins for a trip to the base of Bridal Veil Falls, $3.

Helicopter flights, from Parking Lot 3, Niagara Reservation, cost $9.

Aquarium, 701 Whirlpool St. World's first inland oceanarium, using synthetic seawater. Dolphins, sharks, etc. $5 adults, $3.50 seniors, $2.50 children 5–14.

Hydrofoil trips across Lake Ontario. Between nearby Youngstown to Toronto. $18 one way, (415) 366-2333.

INFORMATION

Travelers Aid, 826 Chilton Ave, 282-2381.
Convention and Visitors Bureau, 300 4th St, 278-8010.

TRAVEL

Buses from Buffalo 11 times a day to Niagara Falls.
Greyhound, Main St and Pine Ave.
AMTRAK, daily trains, 800-523-5720.

PENNSYLVANIA

The Keystone State as she was during the earlier part of America's history, breaching the gap between North and South, but then during the Civil War becoming a major battlefield. The Appalachians dominate the geography of the state and divide it between Pittsburgh and heavy industry and Philadelphia and what survives there of the old colonial tradition.

PHILADELPHIA. At the time of the American Revolution the City of Brotherly Love was the second largest in the English-speaking world. Both the Declaration of Independence and the federal Constitution were signed here, and for visitors interested in pursuing the Liberty Trail, Philadelphia rivals Boston in historical reminders.

Philadelphia today is the nation's fourth largest city with a population of two million, an important manufacturing and cultural centre enjoying the appeal of a recent urban face lift, its many new buildings, like Penn Center, giving a taughtness to reminders of the past around Society Hill and Germantown. Even W C Fields had something good to say about the city: 'I'd rather be in Philadelphia' is inscribed on his tombstone.

There are numerous universities and colleges in the area, hence plenty of students, hence plenty of restaurants, bars and discotheques; and the black ghettoes, Little Athens, the Italian Market and

Chinatown have their colour, as it were. Valley Forge and the Pennsylvania Dutch Country lie just to the west, and New York City is only an hour and a half away.

ACCOMMODATION
There are few less expensive hotels amidst the profusion of expensive joints (that's what a face lift does to prices). The better news is that there are many youth and student places to stay.

Apollo Hotel, 1918 Arch St, between 19th and 20th Sts, 567-8925. Singles $30 without bath, doubles $32 without bath. A bath jacks the price up by at least $12. 'Adequate rooms, though not so clean.'

Drake Hotel, 1512 Spruce St, 545-0100. Downtown, near the historical sights. Singles and doubles $31.

Hotel Milner, 111 St and 10th St, 923-0140. Downtown, with singles from $32, doubles from $38.

YMCA, 1421 Arch St, 241-1200. Singles $23, doubles $38, plus $2 key deposit. Open to men and women. 'For half the price it's expensive. Rooms are small and bare, clientele dubious, neighbourhood bad. Steer clear, try the YH, or at this price a hotel.'

Chamounix Mansion International Youth Hostel, W Fairmont Pk, 878-3676. $6 members, $8 non-members. Take 38 bus from JFK Blvd and 16th St to Ford and Cranston Rds (or take Fairmount Pk trolley), carry on walking down Ford, under bridge, turn left, walk to end of road. 'Excellent, but out of the way.' 'Very pleasant and helpful staff, and back door open all night.'

Old First Reformed Church, 4th and Race Sts, smack in the middle of downtown, 922-9663. $4, bring sleeping bag. Open 2nd week July to 3rd week August. 'Clean, very friendly, peaceful and quiet; breakfast provided.'

The following may have rooms available from May or June to the middle or end of August; some will only accept itinerant teachers and students; phone first.

Drexel University, 203 N 34th St, phone Director of Residential Living, 895-2020. Singles $14, doubles per person $10.

Temple University, Broad and Montgomery Sts, phone Office of Residential Business, 787-7223. Singles $14, doubles per person $11.

University of Pennsylvania, 3940 Locust Wales, 594-6843. Singles $23, doubles per person $16.

International House of Philadelphia, 3701 Chestnut St, 387-5125. $25 single, but discount for students.

LaSalle College, 20th and Olney Aves, phone Office of Residential Life, 951-1550. $24 single, $14 per person double, cheaper if 4 or more nights.

FOOD
The local speciality is soft pretzels and mustard, sold on the streets.

Oscars, 1525 Sansom St. 'Cheap beer and pizza. Nice atmosphere.'

Public Library Cafeteria, 20th St. 'Food half normal price but closes 3.30pm.'

Jewels, 679 N Broad St. 'Jazz bar; excellent breakfast for around $1; good atmosphere.'

The Upstairs Cafe, 123 S 18th St. Informal classy joint for salads, sandwiches, Italian-style coffee.

The Commissary, 1710 Sansom St. A wide-ranging cafeteria offering the best combination of price and variety in Philly. Salad bar, omelette bar, pasta bar, you drift from one to the other.

Jim's Steaks, 4th and South Sts. Best steak sandwiches in town, $2.50 up.

Reading Terminal Market, 12th and Filbert Sts, for shoo-fly pie, a heavy, molasses-packed Pennsylvania Dutch concoction.

OF INTEREST

First go to the Convention and Visitors Bureau, 15th St and JFK Blvd, and ask for the free *Philadelphia Shopping Guide* (good map in centre) and the Visitors' Guide Map of Philadelphia. Well-armed, you should now survey the scene: **Penn Mutual Tower**, 6th and Walnut Sts, offers views from the 22nd floor, $1.50 adults, less for seniors and kids. Or go for the free view from **City Hall's William Penn Tower**, Market and Broad Sts. 'Best way to start your visit to Philadelphia.'

In the heart of the heritage city is the **Independence National Historical Pk**, the four-block area near the Delaware River. Includes: **Carpenters Hall**, home of the first Continental Congress and **Independence Hall**, Chestnut between 5th and 6th Sts, is where the Declaration of Independence was signed. Here also is the **Liberty Bell Pavilion**. Admission to this and to other colonial buildings in the area is free. Open 9am–8pm, 5pm after Labor Day. Free tours. Throughout the summer there is a free *son et lumière* at the Hall, 9pm. **The Congress Building**, Chestnut St. Next door to Independence Hall where the legislature met when Philadelphia was the nation's capital.

The Philosophical Hall, the home of the American Philosophical Society founded by Benjamin Franklin in 1743. Franklin, and 6 other signatories to the Declaration of Independence, are buried at nearby **Christ Church**.

Betsy Ross House, 239 Arch St. Betsy Ross is said to have put together the first American flag from strips of petticoats. Admission free, daily 9.30am–6pm. Near this house, off 2nd Ave is **Elfreth's Alley**, a pleasant cobbled street lined with Georgian houses.

Society Hill. Area of restored colonial town houses. The city's original residential area, in the region of Spruce and 4th Sts. The name comes from the Free Society of Stock Traders, a company formed here by William Penn.

Germantown. In northwest Philadelphia and originally settled by Dutch and German folk. Many old houses and fine mansions, some of distinctive Dutch or German design. The best are **Cliveden**, dating back to 1763, and **Stenton Mansion**, built by Penn's secretary, James Logan.

Todd House, 4th and Walnut Sts. A house that figured prominently in Philadelphia society of the 1790s and the home of Dolley Payne, who later married James Madison. 9am–6pm.

Atwater-Kent Museum, 7th between Market and Chestnut. Open 9am–5pm, Mon to Sat. History of Philadelphia.

Fairmount Park, west along Benjamin Franklin Pkwy towards the Schuykill River. A beautiful riverside park of 8600 acres, the site of the Centennial Exposition of 1876. Walks, bike and bridle paths, outdoor concerts, and a 90-minute ride on a recreated turn-of-the-century trolley to see it all. Within the park are several **colonial mansions**, also the **Japanese House and Gardens**, the **Philadelphia Museum of Art** which ranks as one of the world's greatest, the **Rodin Museum** for soft-porn sculpture and the **Zoological Gardens** for hard-porn animals.

Benjamin Franklin Science Museum and Planetarium, 20th and Benjamin Franklin Parkway. Worth a visit. Daily, 10am–5pm, shows 2pm daily. Adults $3.75, students and kids 4–11 $2.75, seniors $1.75. Phone 564-3375.

Academy of The Fine Arts, Broad and Cherry Sts. Nation's oldest art museum and school. Good collection of American art dating from 1750. Tue–Sat 10am–5pm, Sun 1–5pm. $2 adults, $1 seniors, 50¢ students.

United States Mint, 5th and Arch Sts, 597-7350. Open Mon–Fri 8.30am–3.30pm. Small museum, self-guiding tour along viewing balcony, free unless you want to mint your own penny which costs $1.

University Museum, University of Pennsylvania Campus, 33rd and Spruce Sts, 222-7777. Outstanding archaeological exhibition, open Tue–Sat 10am–4.30pm, Sun 1–5pm, closed Sun during summer. $2 donation requested.

Valley Forge, 20 miles west of Philadelphia; take train from Reading Terminal or enquire at Visitors Bureau about buses, tours. Washington hibernated here along with his half-starved troops through the bitter winter of 1777–78. Now a National Historic Park, the place is full of Americana, including the cabins in which the troops were billeted, and a few museums. The dogwoods bloom in spring and the place has a pastoral air.

TOURS
The Liberty Walk, Philly's answer to Boston's Freedom Trail. Tourist and information centres provide a map.

Use the SEPTA Cultural Bus Loops for quick, on-off, as you please travel between the sights. Daily in summer, weekends only in winter. $1.50, or $2.75 family fare. Starts at Independence Hall and ends at the zoo.

Gray Line offers tours round Historic Philadelphia, to Fairmount Park, Valley Forge, the Pennsylvania Dutch country and to Bucks County—a land of rolling green hills, white fences, old stone houses, where dwell the rich and elegant who ride to hounds and get stared at from passing tour buses; Penn's mansion, Pennsbury Manor, is out here too. 569-3666 for information.

Tour boats operate from Penn's Landing, Delaware Ave and Lombard St, 925-7640.

ENTERTAINMENT
Check the 'Weekend' section of the Friday *Philadelphia Inquirer* or phone the Tourist Center, 864-1970, or the Cultural Affairs Council, 972-8500, for information about what's on.

The Convention and Visitors Bureau dishes out free tickets to outdoor concerts in the parks, 568-1976.

The Khyber Pass, 56 S 2nd St. Pub featuring local jazz and folk artists; imported beers cheap during happy hour.

Stars, 2nd and Bainbridge Sts, for live new wave bands, admission from $6.

The area around Walnut and 38th Sts is good for pubs, or try the Society Hill Tavern, Old Market Place.

SHOPPING
Newmarket Shopping Complex, north of Market St. 'Superb.' Live entertainment.

Third Street Jazz, 10 N 3rd St. Bargains.

Wanamaker's. Famous old department store. 'Practically a museum.'

INFORMATION
Philadelphia Convention and Visitors Bureau, 16th and JFK Blvd, 864-1970.

National Parks Service Visitors Center, 3rd and Chestnut, 597-8974.

Philadelphia Council for International Visitors, Civic Center Museum, 34th and Civic Center Blvd, 879-5248.

Travelers Aid, 3rd and Chestnut, and 1218 Chestnut St, 922-0950. Also at Penn Central Station and bus stations. Taped Daily Events messages, 864-1990.

Post Office, 2037 Chestnut St between 20th and 21st Sts.

TRAVEL
Greyhound, 17th and Market Sts, 568-4800.

Trailways, 13th and Arch Sts, 569-3100.

AMTRAK, for intercity trains, 30th St and N Philadelphia stations, 824-1600.

New Local 'speedline' train to Berlin, NJ, runs from 15th and 16th Sts.

SEPTA Information: 329-4800. Airport Express bus, every half hour, stopping along Market St, JFK Blvd, and 30th St Station. $2.50.

PENNSYLVANIA DUTCH COUNTRY. While most of the original settlers have been absorbed into the rest of the community, the Amish and Mennonites have retained their traditional identities in this

stretch of country west of Philadelphia, near the town of **Lancaster**. Rejecting the use of modern machinery and still speaking a form of Low German ('Dutch' is in fact nothing to do with Holland, it's rather a derivation from 'deutsch'), the women in their long dresses and small caps and the bearded menfolk in sombre black suits and broad-brimmed hats continue to live simply and contentedly in the past. Tuesday, Friday and Saturday, market days in Lancaster, are worth the visit. Sundays are not good for visting the area.

The area lies on Route 30, but to avoid an excess of tourists take to the sideroads. One good excursion is the 3 mile jaunt from **Paradise** to **Strasburg**, equally enjoyable either on foot or via the old railroad (daily 10.30am to 7pm; after Labor Day, 1pm to 4pm).

Keep an eye out for the Pennsylvania Dutch Folk Festival, with its soap making, sauerkraut shredding, pewtering, square dancing and folklore sessions. 'The festival is a real hoe-down, straw-in-the-hair fun affair.'

A dozen miles north of Lancaster on Route 222 is **Ephrata**, settled and later forsaken by a German community of Seventh-Day Baptists. Living as sisters and brothers, they stooped through low doorways to learn humility and walked down narrow hallways to assure themselves of the straight and narrow path. Many of their original structures, including their large Cloister of unpainted wood, now gloomy grey with time, still stand.

ACCOMMODATION
The area is overrun with tourists and accommodation therefore tends to be expensive.
Sunset Valley Motel, 5 miles east of Lancaster on Rt 23, 3 miles east of US 30, 2288 New Holland Pike, (717) 656-2091. Air conditioning, colour TV, radio. Best to reserve in summer.
Mrs Nissly, 624 W Chestnut St, Lancaster, 392-2311. 'Cheapest in town; will collect from bus station.'

OF INTEREST
The Amish Village Inc, on Pa Rt 896, two miles north of Strasburg and one mile south of Rts 30 and 896 intersection. See the Amish way of life, and the tourists. Open daily 9am–8pm.
Railroad Museum of Pennsylvania, Strasburg, Historic locos and rolling stock. Open May–October.
Pennsylvania Farm Museum, Landis Valley. A museum village with the buildings, homes, trades and tools of three centuries. On US 222 near Lancaster.

INFORMATION
Visitors Bureau, 1799 Hempstead Rd, Lancaster. Free brochures and maps.
Mennonite Information Centre, 2209 Millstream Rd, Lancaster, (717) 299-0954. Assistance in finding accommodation, tours and background on Mennonites and Amish.

TRAVEL
AMTRAK will get you to Lancaster from Philadelphia.
Connestoga Buses runs $10 tours of the area from Lancaster. 'Very worthwhile.'

HARRISBURG. The undistinguished capital of Pennsylvania, though it is just here, if you're heading west, that the landscape becomes beautiful, even dramatic, with the broad Susquehanna River cutting a gap through the hills, its course lined with sudden granite bluffs and green forest, and you sense how this was once a long time ago the edge of the frontier. Rockville Bridge, 4 miles west of Harrisburg, spans the Susquehanna as the longest and widest stone-arch bridge in the world.

The area sprang to the public's attention in 1979 after the nuclear accident at nearby **Three Mile Island** which brought into focus the whole question of the safety of nuclear reactors.

From here you're on you way to Hershey, Gettysburg or Kingdom Come.

TRAVEL
AMTRAK's crack *Broadway Limited* runs from NYC and Philly to Lancaster, Harrisburg, Pittsburgh and on to Chicago. 'Marvellous service on board.'

HERSHEY. Hershey is a company town built by a candy bar magnate. The air is thick with the odour of chocolate and almonds, and the street-lamps are shaped like Hershey's famous 'kisses'. The two main streets are Chocolate and Cocoa. Tours of Milton Hershey's factory are continuous from 9am to 4.45pm Monday through Saturday, from noon Sunday; free. Also there's a 36-ride English, German and Pennsylvania-Dutch theme park in town.

GETTYSBURG. On 3 July 1863, General Lee was defeated here and the tide of the Civil War turned irrevocably against the South. Lincoln later came to give his famous Address at the dedication of the National Cemetery.

The Battlefield is now preserved as a National Military Park where visitors may follow the struggle across Cemetery Ridge, Seminary Ridge and on to Little Round Top against which Pickett's charge of 10,000 Confederate soldiers came to nought. A panoramic impression of the three days' struggle can be gained from atop a 75-foot tower near the Eisenhower Farm where the former president lived and died. The Gettysburg National Museum contains the largest Civil War collection in the nation.

ACCOMMODATION
Criterion Motor Lodge, 337 Carlisle St, 334-6268. Located in town; air conditioning and cable TV. Singles and doubles from $27 to $31.
The Homestead, 785 Baltimore St, 334-2037. This is a bed and breakfast place standing right on the battlefield. Rooms with fans or air conditioning. Singles from $12, doubles from $16, families from $20.
Swinn's Lodging Guest House, 31 E Lincoln Ave, 334-5255. Air conditioning and TV. Singles $14, doubles $16, suite with bath $25. 'Mr Swinn is a licensed battlefield

guide and will give you free information on points of interest.' 'Will collect from bus depot.'

OF INTEREST
National Museum of Gettysburg, on Rt 134 opposite the National Cemetery. Visit here before going to the battlefield for a better understanding of your trip. Open until 8pm. The wax museum is best avoided.

INFORMATION
Gettysburg Travel Council, Carlisle St, 334-6274.

PITTSBURGH.
PITTSBURGH. Famous for steel and home of many of the country's most thriving industries, Pittsburgh has adopted the tag of 'Renaissance City'. Its skyline of blast furnaces, open hearths, steel mills and dramatic bridges is imposing, to be sure, but conjures too an image of grime and pollution which is anything but Italianate. But after an earnest campaign the city's air is now cleaner than that of any other American city, almost and it has some exciting architecture down at the Golden Triangle where the Allegheny and Monongahela Rivers join to form the Ohio. At the Civic Arena, which has a vast, retractable, dome-shaped roof, you can see everything from Broadway musicals to basketball games. Pittsburgh's terrain is an appealing mix of plateaux and hillsides, narrow valleys and rivers spanned by many bridges. With elevations ranging from 715 to 1240 feet, expect to do some climbing.

ACCOMMODATION
Hotel and motel accommodation is expensive in the Pittsburgh area and car drivers would do better to stay on the outskirts.
Best Western Viking Motel, 1150 Banksville Rd, off I-279 exit 5, 531-8900. 1½ miles from downtown, this is a bargain for Pittsburgh. Singles from $34, doubles from $38. Air conditioning, TV, bath, indoor pool.
Wherever you stay in Pittsburgh, but particularly if at any of the following, reservations are advisable.
St Regis Residence for Women, 50 Congress St, 281-9888. Women only, $10 single.
Carlow College, 3333 5th Ave, 683-5827; ask for Housing Director. Rooms are available from 1 June to 31 July, $14 single, $10 per person double.
Golden Triangle YMCA, 304 Wood St, 227-6420. $21 single, men only.
Point Park College YH, 201 Wood St, 391-4100. About 8 blocks from AMTRAK and bus terminals. $8.50. 'Friendly atmosphere, many foreign students, a pleasant refuge in Pittsburgh.'

FOOD
Common Plea, 308 Ross St. Popular restaurant with high reputation, and not cheap—but worth it if you want to splurge. Seafood and veal entrees from $11, includes 3 appetisers.
Khalil's Mideastern Cafeteria, 414 Semple St, Oakland. Greek and Turkish food at McDonald's prices.
Benkovitz Seafood, 238 Smallman St, a one-time truckers joint in the wholesale district, now moved up several pegs but keeping down its prices.
Big Z Hamburgers, Liberty Ave, 1½ blocks from Greyhound (turn right out of terminal). 'Not cheap, but plenty, and colourful surroundings. Relief to get away from bus terminal fare if just passing through.'

OF INTEREST
Carnegie Institute. This world-renowned museum tells the story of the earth and man in hundreds of displays of arts, crafts and natural history. An impressive herd of prehistoric monsters towers over strange skeleton birds at the **Museum of Natural History**.
Frick Museum, 7227 Reynolds Ave. French, Italian and Flemish Renaissance paintings.
Fort Pitt Museum, Point State Park. Recreated bastion to tell the story of the struggle between Britain and France for Ohio country. Also history of Fort Duquesne and early Pittsburgh.
Triple Treat Tour. Well recommended by previous readers. For $6 you get steamer trip, ride on Mononghela incline, and trip on trolley round the town. Tkts from Gateway Clipper Dock, Fort Pitt Blvd and Wood St.

ENTERTAINMENT
For students, Oakland is the place, although the Shadyside area still has its fair share of swing.
Read *Pitt News*—free from Pittsburgh U campus—to find out what goes on.
Rock and pop concerts at the Civic Arena, Center and Bedford Aves, Washington Plaza, downtown, 471-1312.
American Wind Symphony Orchestra, free summer performances aboard showboat docked at Point State Park.
Heinz Hall, 600 Penn Ave, downtown, 281-5000. The Pittsburgh Symphony Orchestra, Ballet and Civic Opera all perform here.
Heaven, 105 6th St, downtown, is the current hot nightspot, with dancing, 3 bars, an upper level for watching the action below. Women free on Wed when male strippers bump and grind. Otherwise, heavy $8 cover, but that includes 2 drinks.

INFORMATION
Convention and Visitors Bureau, 200 Roosevelt Bldg, Penn and 6th, 281-7711.
Travelers Aid at airport, 264-7110.
Helpline for Information and Volunteer Services, 255-1155.

TRAVEL
Greyhound, 11th St and Liberty Ave, 391-2300.
Trailways, 210 10th St, nr Greyhound, 261-5400.
AMTRAK, Liberty and Grant Aves, nr bus terminals, 621-4850.
AAACON Auto Transport Inc, 951 Pennsylvania Ave, 471-5144.

TITUSVILLE. The oil well business got off to a picturesque start out here in northwestern Pennsylvania. The story is the local Indians discovered the stuff polluting their streams, and being too dumb to invent the Model T Ford, smeared it on their faces as war paint. A savvy white man peeping from the bushes realised he'd found his pot of gold and in 1859 Col. Edwin Drake, right here in Titusville, sunk the first oil well in the world. The site is now a Memorial Park with a working reconstruction of the original rig and a museum with documents, photos and artefacts of the early boom days. Open daily, even to Iranians.

WEST VIRGINIA

It's difficult placing West Virginia into any particular region, for it belongs perhaps equally to the Northeast, Midwest and South. But in

1863 it seceded from Virginia to fight with the North during the Civil War and on that basis it finds its place here. Since then it has remained an industrial backwater with a considerable amount of poverty. Here and in East Tennessee are the authentic hillbillies—still speaking a form of Elizabethan English—who, with the coal miners of the region, have contributed much to the folklore of America. This is the Mountain State, with much beauty, many scenic drives through the Appalachians and a great place for camping, hiking and white water canoeing.

CHARLESTON. Not to be confused with Charleston, South Carolina. This is the state capital and an industrial town; not much to look at, but there's a lot of nice hills around, and you've got to start somewhere.

Travel east from Charleston to the vast Monogahela National Forest and the Green Bank Observatory.

ACCOMMODATION
Red Roof Inn, 6305 MacCorkle Ave, at junction with I-77 exit 98, 925-6953. Singles from $25, doubles from $32. Air conditioning and cable TV.
Also try YMCA, Capital and Lee Sts, 344-3487, and YWCA, 1114 Quarrier St, 346-0597—though there may not be much space for passers-through.

INFORMATION
Convention and Visitors Bureau, 342-6544.

GREEN BANK OBSERVATORY. On Route 28 in the Monongahela National Forest is the Green Bank National Radio Astronomy Observatory where American scientists are for the moment holding a one-way conversation with the rest of the universe. There are tours round the giant radio telescope.

There are scenic drives and numerous recreation areas in the preserve, as well as attractions such as Seneca Rocks, Seneca Caverns and the Blackwater Falls.

HARPERS FERRY. The National Park here preserves this small historic town where in 1859 John Brown raided the government arsenal, freed a few blacks and hoped to spark a general slave insurrection. He was captured the following evening by Col Robert E Lee and two months later publicly hanged.

At the confluence of the Shenandoah and Potomac Rivers in eastern West Virginia and readily accessible by car from Harrisburg, PA, Baltimore, MD, and Washington DC, Harpers Ferry is highly recommended for Civil War buffs and the view from nearby Jefferson Rock. There is no bus service, but the Baltimore and Ohio line runs trains out from Washington.

You might also pass through here if you're on your way to the Skyline Drive through Virginia's Shenandoah River National Park.

THE MIDWEST

The Midwest (defined here as the 12 states from Ohio west to the Dakotas) is the rich, flat underbelly of the US, its glacier-scoured fertile lands yielding massive quantities of corn, soybeans, hay, wheat and livestock. It's also the manufacturing, transportation and industrial heart of America; the Chicago-Gary area alone pours more steel than all of France. The region's mighty rivers and Great Lakes serve as liquid highways for its products, just as they did in paddlewheeler days. Although newer, most Midwestern cities have quickly caught up with Northeastern cities in terms of pollution, ghettoes and general ugliness.

But the essential quality of Midwestern life is its smalltown character, and that's where you should seek it out. Take time to meet its friendly and generous people, to get to know the prairie villages and the slow drawl of fields between them.

Mother Nature provides much of the drama here, from tornados in spring-summer to the fantastic electrical storm displays that light up summer evenings. The area is also seismically active: in 1811–1812, the biggest quakes in recorded history rolled through one million square miles, causing the Mississippi and Ohio Rivers to flow backwards.

Itself once 'the West', the Midwest in turn became the staging area for pioneer trails like the Santa Fe, Oregon and Mormon. With the advent of the railroad, the region became the distribution link between cattle ranch and consumer, a role it continues to play today.

ILLINOIS

Illinois takes its nickname from the prairie, the original ground cover

117

for the vast region lying east of the Mississippi River. On it, the grasses grew nine feet or more, which is why Illinois' corn can get as high as an elephant's eye today. (West of the Mississippi, the land gradually turns from prairie to plains: just as flat but less rain, more sun, thinner soil—prime wheat-growing land).

The Prairie State has a tradition of plain-spoken eloquence, from Lincoln, Sandberg and Hemingway to the Grange Movement farmers of the 1870s, who took as their slogan: 'Raise less corn and more hell!' Its premiere city, Chicago, is also the birthplace of the only truly American architecture. In the countryside, you'll taste Midwestern hospitality at its best, as sweet and honest as an ear of young corn. All these factors may explain why Illinois is currently sought after as the most popular film location in the world.

CHICAGO. In the aftermath of the Great Fire of 1871, a Chicago realtor put up a sign that read: 'All gone but wife, children and energy!' That unquenchable jauntiness is still Chicago's trademark. The place hurls superlatives at you: tallest buildings, largest grain market, greatest distribution point, busiest airport and train terminal, biggest Polish populace outside Warsaw, highest concentration of practicing psychics—the list is endless.

Built on a swamp the Indians called 'place of the stinking wild onions', Chicago has in 152 years become the second largest city in the US. This despite a fiendish climate (although not the windiest—Great Falls, Montana, is). Both the true skyscraper, where stress falls on the metal skeleton rather than the walls, and balloon framing, a cheap breakthrough in housing construction, were born here. At various times the home of Louis Sullivan, Frank Lloyd Wright and Mies van der Rohe, Chicago possesses the finest architectural tradition in the country. It also had the good sense to preserve its lakeshore as recreational land, giving it an extraordinary skyline along 27 miles of parklands and clean beaches.

Always pugnacious, Chicago in its gangland heyday (1920s–1940s) had wide-open criminal activity and hundreds of unsolved mob murders. One public official tried to divert attention from his Capone connections with an anti-British Empire campaign. Periodically he offered to punch King George V 'in the snoot' if the monarch ever ventured near Chicago. Mob action may be gone but the city still has a murder rate double that of Northern Ireland. As a natural corollary, Chicago also has more practicing lawyers than all of England.

With this in mind, visitors should remember that the Loop and lakeshore areas are the safest. After dark, stay clear of parks and poorly-lit streets. These cautions hold particularly true for women. The South Side is very risky at night.

ACCOMMODATION

Avenue Motel, 1154 S Michigan Ave, 427-8200. Singles from $26, doubles $30–$42. Good area; shower, colour TV, pool nearby.

Belair Hotel, 424 W Diversey Pkwy, 248-4000. Singles $17. 'Safe place, nice people. Close to North Side blues clubs.'

Hotel Cass, 640 N Wabash Ave, 787-4030. $19 up single, $23 up double. 'Fairly quiet, good value.' 'Safe.' 'Friendly service.'

Leland Hotel, 50 E Harrison, 939-2733. $8 single, $10 double without bath. 'Convenient.' 'Passable if hard up.' Not recommended for women.

Plaza Hotel, 123 S Marion Ave, Oak Park, 848–2800. $20 up single, $24 up double; low weekly rates. Easy-to-reach suburb, helpful manager. 'Oak Park far safer than Chicago.'

Tokyo Hotel, 19 E Ohio St, 787-4900. Good locale. Singles/doubles $20 with tax. 8 minutes from Greyhound. 'Shabby, clean, trying hard.' 'Fantastic views from back rooms.'

Carleton Hotel, Marion and Pleasant, 848-5000. Single $12 up, double $22.

St Regis Hotel, 516 N Clark at Grand, 644-1322. $16.50 single. 'Safe; roaches weren't that big.'

B&B Chicago, 1316 Judson Ave, Evanston 60201. 328-1321. Single $25–$35, doubles $30–$55. Luxury homes. Also B&B International; see Accommodation Background for details.

Lawson YMCA, 30 W Chicago Ave, 944-6211. Coed, $17–$20 single, pool. 'Helpful.' 'Old, squalid.'

International House, 1414 E 59th, 753-2280 or 2270. Take Illinois Central RR to 59th, walk ½ block west. Open 7 June–9 Sept. $15.25 with AYH. Science Museum nearby. 'Rooms plain, clean.' 'Be sure to get off at right station—dangerous neighbourhood.' Also try De Paul University, Jackson and Wabash in Loop area, $8.50. 'Very comfortable, spacious.' And fraternities on Northwestern (lakeside—good area), Loyola, Chicago campuses.

FOOD

Local specialties: Chicago-style deep-dish pizza and kosher all beef hotdogs.

Berghoff's, west of State at 17 W Adams, 427-3170. German menu, a Chicago tradition, big helpings. Closed Sundays.

Francis' Deli, on Clark north of Fullerton. Good Jewish food.

National Cafeteria, Van Buren at Clark. Classic 1930s/40s decor, friendly clientele of workingclass, students, seniors. Low prices.

Ronny's Steak Place, 16 W Randolph near Dearborn. 'Huge servings.' 'Good, cheap.' 'Like a converted nightclub.' Near bus terminals.

For icecream lovers: try the luscious 'frango mint' at Marshall Fields' 3rd-floor ice cream parlour, State and Randolph; and monster hot fudge sundaes at Petersen's off Forest in Oak Park.

OF INTEREST

The Loop, a 5- by 7-block city core, is defined by the steel tracks of the **elevated subway** ('El'), a transit system with a voice like a giant trash compacter yet queerly lovable withall. Besides being fast and cheap (90¢ basic fare), this dotted line of noise gives free rein to voyeurism, letting you virtuously peep at a thousand fleeting tableaux as you flash past. Within the Loop are theatres, smart hotels and shopping districts, including the once-preeminent **Marshall Fields** department store (still has the best Christmas windows anywhere).

State Street, running north-south, and Madison, east-west, bisect within the Loop at what's called the world's busiest intersection. (At 1 S State, take a peep at the delicate **ironwork, by Louis Sullivan**, FLWright's mentor.) All street numbers in Chicago begin here, each block representing increments of 100, making the city easier than most to get about in.

One block east of the Loop is Michigan Ave, its most elegant stretch the **Miracle Mile**, with a glittering, often windy view of Lake Michigan.

Bus, bike and walking **tours of outstanding Chicago architecture** available at Archi-Center, 330 S Dearborn, 782-1776. Open 9.30am–5.30pm Mon–Fri, 9am–3pm Sat. A 2-hour walk around the Loop Costs $3, seniors/students $2. Daily in summer, Tue, Thur, Sat, Sun in winter. 'Good value, informative.' A 3½-hour bus tour of **Chicago highlights** costs $12, Sat and Wed only. Many tour intineraries available.

The CTA runs North, South and West **Culture Bus routes** on summer Sundays/holidays, all starting at the Art Institute, Michigan at Adams. $1.50 buys you a Supertransfer pass to get on and off as often as you like. 'Excellent value.' 'Sit in front to hear guide properly.'

For a panoramic view of the city you can ascend **Sears Tower**, $2, the tallest and one of the ugliest buildings in the world, at Wacker Drive and Adams. Visibility is posted downstairs; on a clear day, you can see across the lake to Michigan—60 miles. Open 9am–midnight. Or take a **boat trip**—Chicago is at its best from the lake. 'Best thing I did in Chicago.' Mercury, 332-1353, and Wendella, 337–1446, boats leave from opposite sides of the Chicago River at Michigan and Wacker Dr: 1-hour trip, $4, 2-hour trip, $6. The longer the better as you sail further and proportionately less of your time is taken up with passing through the locks into Lake Michigan (which is 8 ft higher than the river). Best of all is the nighttime trip (7.30pm departure, 2 hours) for the dazzling lights. 'Boat stops in front of Buckingham Fountain—spectacular lights and colour show.'

Marina City, 300 N State St, a prototype self-contained 'vertical city' of residences, offices; resembles two upended corncobs.

John Hancock Center, 875 N Michigan. Tallest residential building in the world. Cocktail bar skywalk. Views of the city at night. $2.25 fee, seniors/students $1.50 to observation hall. Open 9am–midnight.

Adler Planetarium and Museum, 1300 S Lakeshore Dr, 322-0329. Planetarium free, Sky Show film $2, free to seniors. 'Good show, interesting photos.'

Art Institute, Michigan at Adams St, 443-3500. Offers a magnificent collection of impressionist and post-impressionist works, modern American art and the Thorne Rooms: an array of English and American homes through the ages, in miniature. Open daily 10.30am–4.30pm, Thur to 8pm, Sat 10am–5pm, Sun/holidays noon–5pm. Thur free, otherwise $3, seniors/students $1.50. Good basement cafeteria.

Frank Lloyd Wright houses. There are 25 in the suburbs; the Art Institute bookshop has good guidebooks. You need a car to see many of them, but FLW's own house and studio ($3, seniors $1.50) at Chicago and Forest Ave in Oak Park is reachable by El—to Harlem. From here, some of the houses are within walking distance. Oak Park Visitors Center, 158 N Forest Ave, 848-1978, has 10-minute slide show, leaflets, $5 guided tours on Sat–Sun.

Museum of Science and Industry, E 57th St and South Shore Dr, 684-1414. Take express bus 6. 'Magnificent place.' Free; fees for coal mine, U-boat sub. Open 9.30am–5.30pm daily in summer, to 4pm rest of year. 'Best I've ever been to—easily spend a whole day here.'

Central Police Station Museum, 1130 S Wabash, 431-0005. Mon–Fri 9am–4pm. Free. 'Death masks, including Dillinger's.'

Field Museum of Natural History, Roosevelt Rd and Lake Shore Dr, 922-9410. Anthropology, botany, zoology, geology. Open daily 9am–6pm, Fri till 9pm May–Sept; shorter hours rest of year. Free Fri, otherwise $2, seniors 50¢, families $4.

Shedd Aquarium, next to Field Museum, 939-2426. Open 9am–5pm daily May–Sept, Fri till 9pm, shorter hours rest of year. Free Friday, otherwise $2, students $1, seniors 50¢, families $4.

Chicago Historical Society, Clark St and North Ave, 642-4600. Outstanding Lincolniana—notebooks, letters—plus fashions, photos, manuscripts, furnishings. Open

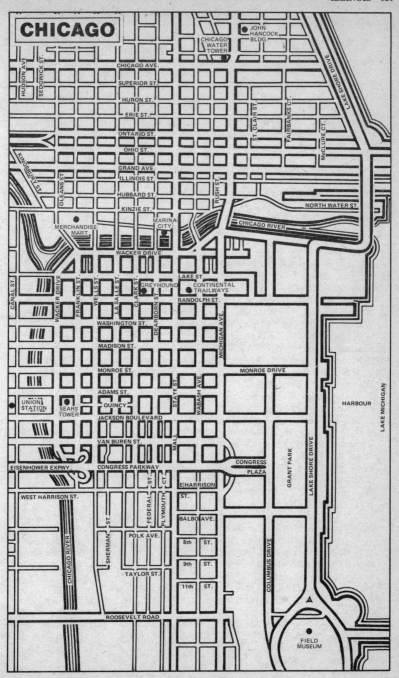

Mon–Sat 9.30am–4.30pm, Sun/holidays noon–5pm. Library, Tue–Sat only. Free Monday, otherwise $1.

Museum of Contemporary Art, 237 E Ontario St, Open Tue–Sat 10am–5pm, Sun noon–5pm. Free Tue, otherwise $2, seniors $1. Good cafe.

University of Chicago, 5 miles south. Buses 4, 28, 55 or 59; Illinois Central RR to 57th or 59th St. Fermi and colleagues first split the atom on 2 Dec, 1942, under seats of an abandoned football stadium at 59th and Greenwood. The H-bomb for Hiroshima was also built in Chicago. Henry Moore's sculpture 'Nuclear Energy' marks the site.

Water Tower, 800 N Michigan Ave. Fanciful Gothic Revival snippet which once concealed a very utilitarian pump. Sole public building to survive the 1871 fire, consequently revered by Chicagoans. Visitor Info Center inside, daily 9am–5pm, 225-5000.

Maxwell Street Market, 8 blocks SW of Loop, 1300 South at Halsted. Incredible variety and colour but *caveat emptor* and watch your wallet. Vendors like to pretend the merchandise is hot but what's hot is the live music and blues licks on Sundays.

State Street, now converted to an attractive pedestrian and public transit mall.

Michigan Avenue. 20s and 30s facades, mortared with money, opulent restraint, shops for ogling only.

Street art. Several impressively hideous works: Alexander Calder's bright red 'Flamingo' at Federal Center Plaza, Adams and Dearborn; Chagall's 'Four Seasons' 70-ft mosaic at First National Bank Plaza, Monroe and Dearborn; 'Sounding Sculpture' by Bertoia outside the Standard Oil building, 200 E Randolph St; 'Batcolumn' by Claes Oldenburg, a 5-story filigree baseball bat in full erection at 600 W Madison; the Picasso Baboon in Richard Daley Plaza, Washington and Dearborn; and Joan Miro's 'Chicago' lady in Brunswick Plaza, 69 W Washington.

Beaches. 18 sandy miles of 'em—free! Try Oak St Beach just NE of John Hancock Center, or Lincoln Park Beaches, open daily, 9am–9.30pm, mid-June–Labor Day. 'Makes Chicago seem like the seaside.' 'Quite pleasant walking along waterfront—a park all the way to Museum of Science.'

Tomb-hopping. Al Capone has two graves, one at Mt Olivet ('qui reposa'), another at Mt Carmel ('My Jesus mercy'). Graceland Cemetery has its own brochure so you can find the famous and notorious with ease.

Wrigley Field, 1060 W Addison, 281-5050. The most beautiful park in baseball. Cheap and ideal way to see the most American of games. Day games only, $2–$7.

Great Ape House, Lincoln Park Zoo, 2200 N Cannon Dr, 294-4660. Free. Daily 9am–5pm. Ingenious glass cylinder arrangement lets you see monkeyshines at close hand. NB: keep out of park after sunset.

ENTERTAINMENT

Chicago is renowned as the centre of the blues world, has the strongest folk scene in America and boasts an impressive amount of jazz activity. Pick up a free copy of *The Reader*, published Fri, and available at record shops, for entertainment choices. NB: Stick to Old Town, the Rush Street area, and the North Side at night, even if you are in an armoured car.

For inexpensive folk music:

Somebody Else's Troubles, 2470 N Lincoln, 929-0660. Cover.

Earl of Old Town, 1615 N Wells, 642-5206. Top names, no cover Mon–Tue.

For blues and jazz:

Wise Fool's Pub, 2770 N Lincoln, 929-1510. Blues and jazz greats, no cover, 2-drink minimum.

Gaspars, 3159 N Southport, 871-6680. Top talent.

Jazz hotline, 661-1881.

The Midget's Club, 4016 W 63rd, Mon–Sat. See how the smaller half lives—everything is scaled down but the drinks. A mixed crowd.

Visitor eventline, 225-2323.

Hot Tix Booth, State St Mall. 'Half-price tickets for same day performances—theatre, dance, the arts.'

Shiloh Baptist Church, 4840 S Dorchester. Sat mornings, the Rev Jesse Jackson (inspirational minister for PUSH) wails for 3 hours—the best show in town.

In Chicago as elsewhere, roller skating is popular. Hire a pair at Wholly Rollers, west side of Clark St, or at Street Skates, east side of Clark.

INFORMATION
Visitors Center: Chicago and Michigan, 225-5000 daily; 208 N Michigan, 793-2094 Mon–Fri. Good map of the Loop.

Travelers Aid at Union Station, Canal and Adams, 435-4570; at Greyhound, Clark and Randolph, 435-4537; and airport, 686-7562. Maps, brochures. 'Extremely helpful.'

Post offices: 433 W Van Buren; in Prudential Building, ground floor; at Merchandise Mart.

TRAVEL
Greyhound, Clark and Randolph, 781-2900. 'Public library nearby, with free art exhibits—good place to go if between buses.'

Trailways, 20 E Randolph, 726-9500.

Local bus CTA/RTA. 24-hr route and schedule info, 836-7000. Basic fare for buses, El and subways: 90¢ (Sun less), transfers 10¢. Supertransfer for Culture bus, all day Sun for $1.50, seniors 50¢.

AMTRAK, Union Station, Canal and Adams Sts, 786-1333. Chicago is the hub of the intercity AMTRAK system.

O'Hare Airport. To reach it, take Northwest subway from downtown, A or B train. Request transfer. Get off at Jefferson Park and put transfer ticket in stamping machine on platform. Catch 40 Express bus to O'Hare, presenting transfer and rest of fare in exact change. Takes about one hour, considerably cheaper than airport bus.

Auto Driveaway, 310 S Michigan, 939-3600. 'Friendly.' 'Very helpful.'

Metro Ride Board, 929-5139.

SPRINGFIELD. In central Illinois, Springfield is the pleasant state captial where Lincoln once lived. Worth seeing: the Old State Capitol, the beautifully restored Lincoln's home at 8th and Jackson, his tomb at Oak Ridge and the nearby reconstruction of Abe's boyhood village at New Salem. (They take you round in an ox-cart). Many free attractions, also good tours. Lodgings at the Downtown Motel, 400 N 9th, 789-1530, from $17 single, $21 doubles.

GALENA. Once an opulent riverboat and lead-mining town in northwest Illinois, Galena is now a beautiful backwater of stately homes and smalltown friendliness. Galena produced a clutch of Civil War generals, including Ulysses S Grant; each year, the townspeople reenact a battle or two. Eat at Raleighs, bed down in a 19th-century guest home. The Colonial on Park is about the cheapest, $24 up. Greyhound from Chicago or (closer) Dubuque, Iowa. If you have a car, by all means take the Great River Road south from Galena, which follows the Mississippi all the way to New Orleans. A lovely drive.

METROPOLIS. It's a bird, it's a plane, it's Clark Kent's home town in south Illinois on the Ohio River. Giant mural of Superman in the park, free kryptonite from the Chamber of Commerce, and for entertainment and the comics—the *Daily Planet*.

INDIANA

The Hoosier state has a wholesome, almost cornball ingenuousness about it, so it's not surprising to learn it's the home of Notre Dame, Tippicanoe (but not Tyler), Johnny Appleseed, Studebaker, Cole Porter, Amish villages of *Friendly Persuasion* fame, and Colonel Sanders of finger-lickin' notoriety. The rural portions have most to offer: rustic landscapes of country roads, covered bridges (notably in Parke County west of Indianapolis) and foliage that burns with colour in autumn.

Indiana cranks out lots of steel and more band instruments than any place on earth. Several rebels, with and without causes, are buried here: Eugene Debs in Terre Haute, and James Dean in Fairmont (whose gravestone behind Friends Church is walking away in ghoulish bits and pieces). It wouldn't seem the climate for it, but Indiana harbours the world's largest nudist colony, called Naked City. Nonnudists can eyeball some of its delights at the local Adam and Eve restaurant, where Miss Nude America waits table.

INDIANAPOLIS. State capital, national headquarters for the American Legion, home of the Indy 500 and crossroads of America, so called because dozens of major routes meet here. About as exciting as mashed potatoes except during the month of May, when the Romantic Music and '500' Festivals, the Indy time trials and other pre-race madness stir things up a bit. It's almost impossible to get seats for the race itself on Memorial Sunday, but a minute amount of standing room can be yours for $10, or you can elect to spend the night along Georgetown Avenue with thousands of other celebrants. Time trials begin 2–3 weeks before the main event and provide nearly the same level of thrills, decibels and mayhem as the big race; best seats run about $5, so bring beer, lunch and make a day of it.

ACCOMMODATION
Basic Inn, 5117 E 38th St, 547-1100. $20 single, $26 double.
Metro Motor Motel, 1415 N Pennsylvania St, 635-6470. $20 single or double.
YMCA, 860 W 10th St, 624-2478. Coed. $16 single. Raunchy area. Higher rates Indy week.
B&B League: has a guest home 10 miles from city centre, a breeding farm for exotic

animals. Have breakfast overlooking the tiger pen! Accommodation Background for rates, details.

FOOD

Ayres' Tea Room, 8th floor, One W Washington. 'Inexpensive, genteel.' 'Very good.'

Best Steak House, 38 E Washington. 'Cheap and good also.'

OF INTEREST

Speedway and Museum, 4790 W 16th St. 9am–5pm daily, $1. Has 50+ racing, classic and antique cars. $1 bus tours of the 2½-mile track.

Athenaeum, 411 E Michigan St. 635-6336. Mon–Fri 11am–10pm, Sat–Sun 6pm–midnight. Free. Home of Indiana Repertory Theatre, interestingly designed in 1893 by novelist Kurt Vonnegut's father.

The Children's Museum, 3010 N Meridian, 925-9263. Free. Tue–Sat 10am–5pm, Sun 1–5pm. World's largest kiddie museum: puppets, films, mummy, Tyrannosaurus; huge toy and antique train layout, etc.

Union Station, 200 S Illinois St. Built 1888, one of the finest examples of Romanesque Revival architecture in the US. Galleries, restaurants, boutiques and passenger trains.

William Henry Harrison, US President for 31 days in 1841 (he delivered a 20-hr inaugural address in freezing rain and died of pneumonia without making a single major presidential decision), lived at 1230 N Delaware; open to the public.

John Dillinger gravesite, Section 44, Crown Hill Cemetery.

Indiana State Fair, 2 weeks of hoosier hoopla in Aug. 'Huge, mad, big name groups.'

Elsewhere in Indiana:

Conner Prairie, 6 miles north of Indianapolis. Unusual 25-building village 'museum' where inhabitants live and work at 19th C pursuits and visitors are part of the action. Meals of the period, wares made by villagers for sale. Open Tue–Sun 10am–5pm, $4.50. Senior discount.

Peru, on US 31, 1 hour north of Indianapolis. Once winter home for 12 circuses, still full of performers who lovingly put on free shows in July. Two free circus museums replete with carvings from circus wagons.

Amish country: NE counties of LaGrange, Elkhart, Adams. Worth a side trip to see sober yet droll Amish life in villages like Shipshewana (on Wed or Fri auction days to put away German sausage, outrageous wet-bottom shoofly pie at the Auction Restaurant, and roast pork at Troyers); Amishville (near Berne, has camping, horse and buggy rides); and Amish Acres (near Nappanee, has 45-minute tour of Amish farm). Area is served by Greyhound and Trailways. If you want to stay longer in Amish country, try the Sycamore Springs Farm, box 224, Churubusco, 693-3603: three home-cooked meals plus room with private bath on a working cattle farm, lakes nearby and trips to the Amish auctions: $40/day.

New Harmony, SW corner near Illinois. Former utopian colony, now State Memorial. Worth a visit for Philip Johnson's moving 'roofless church' (like a rosebud half-opened to God), a trot through the 1814 labyrinth, and a fittingly utopian meal at the Red Geranium Restaurant.

IOWA

Between its watery borders of the Mississippi to the east and the Missouri to the west, Iowa raises unthinkable quantities of corn, soybeans, hay and hogs (six porkers for every Iowan) on rich rolling landscape immortalised by Iowan artist Grant 'American Gothic' Wood.

Famous for changeable weather (such as the freak blizzard which resulted in the serendipitous development of the Delicious apple), the Hawkeye State is also noted for its strong Quaker community, most famous of whom was Herbert Hoover. Iowa Quakers were a vital link in the Underground Railway and it was to Iowa that black scientist and inventor George Washington Carver fled to escape persecution.

DES MOINES. Trisected by rivers, Des Moines (population 350,000 excluding hogs) is a green and friendly place to catch your breath and take advantage of food and lodging discounts offered by the Visitors Bureau. Worth seeing is the Living Farms complex, whose visitors have included Nikita Krushchev and Pope John Paul II (the latter delivered Mass—shades of *Animal Farm*).

ACCOMMODATION
Kirkwood Hotel, 4th and Walnut Sts, 244-9191. $17–24 single, $21–34 double. Discounts to seniors, students, bus pass, Insta-Fun card. 8 blocks to Trailways. Deli and Bakery, AC, colour TV.
YMCA, 101 Locust, 288-0131. Men only, cheap, near Greyhound.
YWCA, 717 Grand, large, women only, good cafeteria.
Hickman Motor Lodge, 6500 Hickman Rd, 276-8591. Near Living History Farms. Single $10 up, doubles $13 up.
Motel 6, 4817 Fleur Drive, 285-4720. $16 single, $20 double. Close to airport; 6 bus takes you within ½ mile.
B&B: low-cost home through International Spareroom, details in Accommodation Background.

FOOD
Yellow Umbrella cafeteria, 717 Grand, 20% discount with Insta-Fun card.
Greenjeans, 406 Walnut. Under $6.

INFORMATION/TRAVEL
Visitors Bureau, 8th and High, 286-4960. Ask for Insta-Fun discount card, good May through Aug. 282-2220 is 24-hr info line.
Local bus, 239-8100. Serves downtown, the Fairgrounds.

OF INTEREST
Iowa State Fair, 10 days mid-Aug. Top-notch. Camping at E 30th and Grand, 262-7617 or 3111. Huge, good amenities, wooded area. $5/unit.
Adventureland, East of city. Hubbell exit off I-80. Thrill rides include the Tornado rollercoaster, 'largest and fastest in the Upper Midwest'. Daily Memorial-Labor Day, weekends winter. 266-2121. $10 all-inclusive. Discount with Insta-Fun card.
Living History Farms, I-35 and I-80 at Hickman exit. 278-5286. 4 operating farms, 1700s Indian, 1840s, 1900s and farm of future. $5, discount with Insta-Fun. Lots of special events, exhibits.

EFFIGY MOUNDS NATIONAL MONUMENT. In northeast Iowa, 1400 acres along Mississippi River bluffs, dotted with prehistoric burial mounds shaped like birds, serpents, humans. 'Woman mound' with 70-foot armspread is one of the largest. At most impressive when outlined by snow; area has lovely autumn colours also. Museum with artefacts, interpretive history nearby. Greyhound goes no closer than Dubuque, Iowa, or LaCrosse, Wisconsin, so car rental or hitching a must. In Dubuque, the Trappist monastery of Abbey of Our Lady of New Melleray allows free stays (offering encouraged) Sunday evening until Friday, a nice counter-point to mound exploration.

AMANA. Settled by German mystics in 1854, the Amana Colonies (7 villages located one hour apart by oxen) became the longest-lived commune in the US. Reorganized along corporate lines in 1932, Amana residents no longer practice communal living but instead produce microwave ovens and other appliances along with woollens, wine and other hand-crafted goods. You can visit the houses, factories and workshops (built along traditional German lines) but the main attraction is the solid food (heavy on pork and carbohydrates) at the Old Homestead and other Amana-run restaurants.

ACCOMMODATION
Lodging in Williamsburg cheapest at Travelodge and Cluny Haus. A more budget choice is (June 1–Aug 31) the $8 single/double at Coe College in Cedar Rapids, 399-8504, and open to anyone.
With a car, bed down at the Hotel Brooklyn, 154 Front St in Brooklyn, 522-9229: a gorgeous 1875 hotel on National Historic Register with singles $10–$18, doubles $18–$25. Eight miles from Greyhound.

GRANT WOOD COUNTRY. The largest collection of Grant Wood's works is in **Cedar Rapids**. Hometown **Anamosa** holds a GW festival in June, with the emphasis on American Gothic dress and behaviour (whatever that might be). The *American Gothic* painting itself is at the Chicago Art Institute, but you can see the famous house at **Eldon** (Wood didn't learn until later that it was a brothel). Despite appearances, the rough-hewn couple were Wood's sister Nan and her dentist boyfriend.

KANSAS

The Sunflower State has seen a heap of history. Its statehood bid was the fuse for the outbreak of the Civil War, and ferocious anti- and proslavery factions gained it the epithet 'Bleeding Kansas'. In the riproaring cattle and railroad era of mid/late 1800s, cowhands drove one million cattle a year to Abilene, there to blow their $1-a-day wages on cards, rotgut and fancy wimmen. The cow capitals gradually moved west from Abilene to Wichita and Dodge City (the last a buffalo hide centre, where in one year four million hides were shipped east).

Always noted for strong women, Kansas boasts the first woman mayor (1887), the most famous aviator (Amelia Earhart) and the most fanatical and annoying prohibitionist in Carry Nation. Carry began by singing hymns to saloon idlers, but soon found it more effective to turn saloons into kindling with a hatchet. Besides being anti-booze, Carry's vendetta encompassed tobacco, corsets, barroom paintings and foreign foods. Her last 'hatchetation' ended in ignominy: she unwisely took on a female saloonkeeper, who thrashed her soundly. Carry's zeal did keep Prohibition alive in Kansas until 1948.

Known as 'the breadbasket to the world', Kansas sells much of its surplus wheat to an eager Russia. Ironically, the original seeds for 'Turkey Red', a hard winter variety, were brought here from Russia in 1874 by Mennonites who settled here.

Despite its dust bowl overtones and tabletop flatness, Kansas exerts a peculiar attraction. Maybe that's why Dorothy in *The Wizard of Oz* was so anxious to return. 'A remarkable state, well worth making an effort to discover. At night, a magnificent and fulfilling stillness falls over the plains . . .'

ABILENE. Considering its associations with the Chisolm Trail, Wild Bill Hickok and all, Abilene's lack of westernness disappoints. Abilene is really Ike's Kansas—grain elevators, porch swings and funky little cafes like The City on NW 3rd St. The Eisenhower buildings are pompous but do stop for a look at Ike's simple boyhood home.

ACCOMMODATION
B&B On Our Farm, Wakefield, 461-5596. 20 miles from Abilene; the Thurlows will meet Trailways if desired. Folksy, friendly, just like Kansas. Reservations required. Farm house, hearty breakfast, single $18, doubles $25. Call for road directions.
Trails End Motel, PO Box 458, 1 mile from downtown, 263-2050. Single $13 up, double $16 up.

WICHITA. Meaning 'painted faces' in Indian, Wichita has Kansas' most worthwhile cowboy mockup in its Cow Town ('authentic, much better than Dodge City'), with five original and 32 replica buildings. However: 'Give it a miss after Labor Day. When crowds leave, it virtually closes up'. Noted as a manufacturing centre for aircraft and Coleman camping equipment, Wichita also harbours the brain of none other than Albert Einstein.

ACCOMMODATION
A dearth of low-cost downtown hotels. Cheap motels along Kellogg include Diamond Motor Inn, Executive Inn and Motel 6 (near airport). Also:
Western Trails Lodge, 4701 W Kellogg, 4 miles from downtown, 943-4231. $17 single, $19 double.

INFORMATION
Visitors Bureau, 111 W Douglas, Suite 804, 265-2800.

THE SANTA FE AND OTHER TRAILS. Because of its geographic position, Kansas was crosshatched with trails: the Santa Fe, Chisholm, Oregon, Smoky Hill and others. Whether travelling across Kansas or settling it, pioneers needed grit and resiliency. At Colby (US 24, 60 miles from Colorado) you can examine a sod house community, an authentic remnant of the hardships of that life. Fort Larned (6 miles from Larned off Highway 154) and graffiti-covered Pawnee Rock (northeast of Larned on 156) still stand as trail markers. Along US 50, 9 miles west of Dodge City, wagon ruts of the Santa Fe trail can be seen.

OF INTEREST
A wonderful taste of the pioneer experience can be had through Wagons Ho, a Quinter outfit that offers 4-day **wagon train itineraries** over a 55-mile segment of the Smoky Hill Trail. About $100/day includes meals, riding, pioneer dress, activities like river fordings and mail call via Pony Express. Campfire entertainment, sleeping in the covered wagons. Book: Wagons Ho, 600 Main, Quinter KS 67752, 754-3347.

MICHIGAN

Which state has 3000 miles of shoreline and the world's largest sand dune yet touches no ocean? Which state has more than 10,000 lakes and isn't Minnesota? Michigan, that's who. Rich soil and surprisingly friendly climate (considering it's Canada's neighbour) make the Wolverine State tops in cherry, blueberry and other fruit growing and third in wine production. The wine country is centred around Paw Paw in southwest Michigan.

A campers' and hikers' dream, Michigan has 29 youth hostels, thousands of campsites (including the isolated northern pleasures of Isle Royale National Park) and a rich network of farm trails and roadside produce markets on its two peninsulas. These rural charms are enthusiastically promoted by the Michigan Tourist Council (PO Box 30226, Lansing MI 48909), who publish a nice line of detailed brochures. Pictured Rocks National Lakeshore is especially beautiful; so are the sugar sands of Sleeping Bear Dunes further south.

Michigan's big cities produce quantities of steel, machinery, cereals and chemicals, making them dull choices for the visitor.
National Park: Isle Royale

DETROIT. Forget car manufacturing, Motown and race riots—as elsewhere, you can still get mugged in Detroit but auto assembly lines and good soul music are both disappearing. Unlike Chicago, Detroit has kept its ethnic neighbourhoods intact—its biggest plus. A bustling inland port, the city is working to revitalise a decaying downtown (with emphasis on flashy complexes like the Renaissance Center to snare those lucrative convention gigs).

The Motor City came by its name and fame quite by accident, largely because Henry Ford, Ransom Olds and other auto innovators happened to live and work in the area. The auto industry brought thousands of blacks to Detroit; one of them was Berry Gordy, founder in 1959 of the Motown sound (Smokey Robinson, the Supremes, the Temptations, etc), who used to make up songs on the Ford assembly line to relieve the monotony.

ACCOMMODATION
Milner Hotel, 1538 Centre, 963-3950. $18 single, $24 double. 'Large, gloomy, shabby rooms but clean.'
American Ft Wayne Hotel, 400 Temple, 831-7150. $10 with AYH card, cheaper for 2 or more. Historic 200-bed hotel, cold showers. Grotty area, ½ mile to AMTRAK.
Shorecrest Motel, 1316 E Jefferson Ave, 568-3000. Doubles $25–$35. 2 blocks from RenCen.
YMCA, 2020 Witherell, 962-6126. $15 single, $2.50 with AYH. Part for men only. Pool. Book ahead.
YWCA, 2230 Witherell, 961-9220. Women only. $16 single, $5.50 with AYH (dorm). Book ahead. 20 minutes from Greyhound.
Also try YMCA in Windsor, Canada: 'Store luggage in Detroit Greyhound locker—less hassle upon return to US'.

FOOD
Strong ethnic communities here, so head for Greektown, Chinatown and Polish community (called Hamtramck—actually an independent city within Detroit). Hart Plaza between the RenCen and Civic Center holds weekend ethnic festivals all summer long, cheap and tasty.
Sanders on Woodward. Home of the ice cream soda and best hot fudge sundaes in the Midwest, Motowners say.
New Hellas, 583 Monroe. Greek food, open daily, often to 3am.
Mykonos, 454 E Lafayette, 'Cheap lunch, Happy Hour 3–6.30'.
Parthenon on Monroe: 'very good Greek food'.
Old Shilleleigh, 349 Monroe. Low-cost Irish stew daily, pub surrounds.
Gratiot Central Market, Gratiot and Russell Sts. Produce bargains.
Wayne State U, 2nd Ave and Palmer. Outside downtown, cheap dinners.

OF INTEREST
The big **automobile assembly plants** are no longer here but in the suburbs of Dearborn, Warren, etc. At press time, there were no visitor tours available, but you might call Cadillac (554-5071), Ford (322-0034) and General Motors (575-0334) to see what's up when you arrive.
Renaissance Center, on the river 2 blocks from Greyhound. Now costs $1 to ascend this crystal quincunx, a term that elegantly describes this mirrored fortress of 4 39-story towers protecting a 73-story hotel, but the glass-fronted ride is certainly worth it, if the costly drinks at the top are not. 'Fantastic views of Detroit, Windsor, the river'. 100+ shops, restaurants, free **Money Museum** (Mon–Fri 9–4.30) in Tower 2. Across the street is **Mariner's Church**, 1848 shrine for lake sailors, whose bells still toll each time a life is lost on the lake.
Civic Center, Woodward and Jefferson Aves. Cheap thrills department: look across to Windsor from the only point on the border where Canada is *south* of the US. Street market on Sun, 75-acre park. Near here begins the 19th C trolley circuit of Washington Blvd to Grand Circus Park, 70¢ round trip.
Detroit Historical Museum, 5201 Woodward Ave, 833-1805. Free. Wed–Sun 9am–5pm. Early Detroit and the car industry.

Institute of Art, Woodward and Farnsworth, 833–7900. Free. From fine primitives to Andy Warhol, plus Diego Rivera's famous and scathing mural on factory life. Cafe in Renaissance decor, open 11am–5pm.

Greenfield Village and adjacent **Henry Ford Museum** ($8 summer, $7 winter for each; senior discounts) in Dearborn, West of Detroit. Take SEMTA bus from downtown. Greenfield is 240 acres containing 100+ genuine historic buildings amassed by Henry Ford and set up in sometimes curious juxtapositioning: Abe Lincoln's courthouse, Wright Brothers' cycle shop, Edison's lab (complete with vial said to contain Edison's dying breath). Almost everything runs or ticks or does something—a microcosm of technological Americana. Fee rides for horse carriages, steam trains, Model-T Fords, steamboats, horse-drawn sleighs. the 12-acre Ford Museum has huge transportation collection, antique aircraft.

Boat rides: various cruises to Bob-Lo Island amusement park, 962-9622. Also sightseeing boats from Cobo Hall Dock: good views of the city and Canada.

Zoos: one on Belle Isle, an island (free bridge at E Jefferson) park in the Detroit River. Free aquarium, safarilike zoo, $2. Huge zoo at Royal Park in north suburb costs $3.50, seniors free anytime.

Stroh's Brewery, 909 E Elizabeth, 259-8064. Mon–Fri, 11am–3pm. Free tours. 'Stacks of free samples.'

Windsor, Canada: a dullish city, reached via underwater tunnel on Greyhound. On return to US, backpackers beware: 'I was given a difficult time because I was backpacking and had only $100 plus ticket home. Plenty of trucks outside immigration to ask for a ride though.'

ENTERTAINMENT
Greektown, Monroe Ave and environs. 'Friendly, lively at all hours of day and night. Some good restaurants open till 3am.'

INFORMATION
Visitors Bureau, 100 RenCen, Suite 1950, 259–4333.
Visitor Hotlines, 298-6262 or 224-3755.
Travelers Aid, 1509 Broadway, 962-8251 or 6740. Free maps, very helpful.

TRAVEL
Greyhound, 130 E Congress, 963-9840.
Trailways, 1205 Washington Blvd, 963-1322.
DOT city buses, 933-1300, 24-hr service. Also trolleys from Cobo Hall to Grand Circus.
SEMTA buses, 256-8600. Service to suburbs, including Dearborn.
AAACON Driveaway, 10 Witherell St.
Gray Line tours, Cobo Hall, 224-1555.

ANN ARBOR. An hour's bus ride west of Detroit, Ann Arbor is thoroughly dominated by the University of Michigan and loves it. As a consequence, lots of good hangouts, live music, cheap eats, support services, and events like the July Art Fair.

ACCOMMODATION
Students and foreign visitors: try first at U of M's International Center, 603 E Madison, 761-9310, and U Housing Office, 763-3164 (summer dorm rooms).
Ann Arbor Motel, 3245 Washtenaw, 971-3000. Single $20 up, doubles $27 up. Air conditioning, pool, free continental breakfast, discounts at local restaurants.
Lamp Post Motel, 2424 E Stadium Blvd, 971-8000. Single $22 up, double $27 up. Same friendly management, amenities as Ann Arbor Motel.

FOOD
Count of Antipasto, 1140 S University. Food, drink, live jazz, patio.
Drake's Sandwich Shop, 709 N University. An institution, especially the desserts.
Eat upstairs in the boomerang-decorated Martian Room.

INFORMATION
Campus: 764-8207. 'Good ride board on campus.'
Visitors Bureau, 995-7281. Get a free copy of *About Ann Arbor* for the poop on food, nightlife.

MACKINAC ISLAND. An island in time as well as space, Mackinac (pronounced Mackinaw) permits no motor vehicles—your choices are horseback, bicycle, surrey or shank's mare. Restful, Victorian, especially nice during the June Lilac Festival. Chocoholics note: island speciality is homemade fudge. Boat runs every hour in summer.

ACCOMMODATION
Yoder's Bayview Tourist Home, Box 448, 847-3295. Single $22 with shared bath, doubles $25–$30. 2 rooms for 5 people, $45. Reserve 2 months ahead, or try your luck.

TRAVEL
Greyhound or car to Mackinaw City on the mainland; parking near ferry. Bike, horse rentals on island.

ISLE ROYALE NATIONAL PARK. This is the roadless, wild and beautiful 'eye' in Lake Superior's wolfish head. Free camping by permit only, including use of screened shelters around the island. 'Boil surface water at least 5 minutes.' Carry salt along—inland lakes on the island have leeches. $40 roundtrip boat fare from Houghton, 482-3310. Reservations necessary. Season is June through September only.

MINNESOTA

Something about Minnesota must attract giants, both literal and figurative. It's the birthplace of Paul Bunyan, J Paul Getty, Bob Dylan, Sinclair Lewis, Charles Lindbergh, F Scott Fitzgerald, the Mississippi River and the Jolly Green Giant of canned pea fame.

A green and wooded land of lakes (15,000+), Minnesota has a Nordic appearance and a population mix to match. Its entry into the 'who discovered America' sweepstakes is, appropriately enough, a Viking runestone which may date to AD 1000.

The state is especially lovely during Indian summer; highway markers often point out the most vivid colour displays. The Minnesota Tourism Bureau, 480 Cedar, St Paul 55101, even does a free map of fall colour routes. Or call toll-free 800/652-9747 within the state for guidance. Any time of year, North Shore Drive (US 61) along Lake Superior north to Canada is a top contender for most beautiful

camping and goggling route in America. While here be sure to go canoeing, a peculiarly Minnesotan tradition from Chippewa Indian and French-Canadian trappers days to the present.
National park: Voyageurs

MINNEAPOLIS/ST PAUL. Laced together by the curves of the Mississippi River, Minneapolis and St Paul are 'twin cities' only in geographic terms.

Minneapolis is young, Scandinavian, modern, relaxed, a working-class city freckled with lakes and built on discreetly tucked-away industry. Minneapolis was and is Mary Tyler Moore territory, as bouncy and clean as the Pillsbury doughboy, another local product.

St Paul began as an outpost with the uncouth name of Pig's Eye, described in 1843 as 'populated by mosquitoes, snakes, Indians and about 12 white people'. Perhaps to compensate for these rough beginnings, St Paul has become a conservative capital city of Irish and German Catholics, doting on history and Eastern refinement. F Scott Fitzgerald is St Paul's native son. (So is Charles 'Peanuts' Schultz, but he was evidently too brash for St Paul; in high school, his cartoons were rejected for the school yearbook.)

Minneapolis offers most for the visitor: friendly, outgoing locals, a handsome downtown with malls, skyways, parks, a meandering waterfront and swimmable lakes. Stick to downtown, however: 'I am astonished—could other US downtowns be like this, given a chance? The rest of Minneapolis that I've seen is as ordinary and soulless as anywhere else in America'.

MINNEAPOLIS

ACCOMMODATION
Continental Hotel, 68 S 12th St, 333-5441. $16.65 single with bath, $22.50 doubles.
Voyageur Inn Motel, 2823 Wayzata Blvd, 377-7100. 2 miles from downtown, $26 single, $30 up double.
YMCA, 30 S 9th St, 332-2431 or 371-8750. Coed. Single rooms only, $16. Pool. 'Shabby but central.'
B&B: Uptown-Lake District B&B League, 374-9656 or 377-7032. Period homes, reachable by bus, $15–$18 single, $25–$28 double.
Also B&B Upper Midwest, 535-7135. Guest homes in Minneapolis, other parts of Minnesota, $20–$40 singles/doubles.
Students' Co-op, 1721 University Ave SE, 331-1708 or 1078. $5/night, $25/week per individual. Kitchen, laundry, colour TV. Central. 'Smashing place to live—full of friendly lunatics. Great social life.'
Also try frat houses along SE University. And Chi Phi Fraternity, 315 19th Ave, on UM campus, 331-9297. $5.25, AYH only (can get card on campus) 15 June–15 Sept. 16A bus from downtown.
Harrison Home Hostel, 292-4129. 2 beds, $5.25 AYH year-round, near downtown with good bus connections.

FOOD
Be sure to try Minnesota specialities: wild rice, walleyed pike and Fairbault blue

cheese. St Paul's soul dish is *boya*, a Hungarian stew served on the slightest pre-
text. Happy Hour munchies are good here: try Orion Room, IDS Center, Mon and
Wed; U of Minnesota campus area bars; and Horatio Hornblower's in St Paul.
Best Steak House, Hennepin Ave and N 7th St. Continues to offer good value
steak dinners.
Dayton's Sky Room, Nicollet Ave and 7th St, top floor, and **Crepes de Nicollet**,
2nd floor: convenient, reasonably priced salads, crepes, light food.
Powers Basement, Nicollet and 5th. All-you-can-eat salad bar, cheap lunch bags.
'Very nourishing, filling and excellent value.'
Seward Cafe, on Riverside SE of Mall. 'Co-op cafe, fun place to eat.'
One Potato Two, 4th St in Dinkytown near campus. 'Filling meal to eat there or
take out, as little as $2.'
Emily's Lebanese Deli, 641 University Ave NE. Low-cost dishes, warm neigh-
bourhood place.

OF INTEREST
Besides being the longest pedestrian walkway in the US, the **downtown Mall** along
Nicollet has to be one of the most agreeable and attractive. It's full of flowers,
fountains, friendly conversations, strollers, sandwich-eaters, bus stop shelters
wafting classical music, boutiques and smart shops. Overhead an enclosed **Skyway
system** (designed for Minnesota winters) lets pedestrians cross in comfort from
building to building in a 14-square-block area. By 1985, this complex of Skyways
will connect 64 city blocks.
   Focal point of the Mall and Skyway complex is the 57-story **IDS Center** at Nicollet and 8th. Observation deck (open daily, 9am–10pm and later) on the 51st floor
lets you see for 35 miles or more over the twin cities. $2.85, seniors $1.85. **The
Crystal Court**, a 3-level arcade within the IDS complex, has a 'ceiling' of crystal
pyramids and shapes which nicely diffuse the sunlight, creating a dappled effect as
though one were strolling beneath trees. Both the effect and the vivacious cafe/
meeting-place are best absorbed mornings through lunch. Cafe has reasonable
lunch specials. Info Center in Crystal Court also.
Walks. Leaflets from Info Center at IDS Complex. Recommended: cross the Hennepin Ave bridge to the far side of the Mississippi and then return to downtown
via the Third Ave/Central Ave bridge. The area immediately across the river is
called St Anthony Main, a restored building surrounded by pathways and walkways of old railroad ties. A growing number of once defunct freight buildings are
being converted into restaurants with views back towards Minneapolis. The Third
Ave bridge takes you across to St Anthony Falls; the Minneapolis side is lined
with fine old warehouses and flour mills (walk along S 1st St to Portland Ave), eg
the Roller Mill built in 1879. Between these mills and S Washington Ave is the
Milwaukee Road Station and railways warehouses, a handsome complex which the
city has decided to preserve. If developed with the same intelligence as the
downtown area, the city and its visitors must benefit immeasurably.
Institute of Arts, 2400 3rd Ave S, 870-3046. Open Tue–Sat 10am–5pm, Thur till
9pm, Sun noon–5pm. $2, seniors free. One of the 5 great regional museums in the
US, covering a wide spectrum of fine arts from Egyptian to modern. Fine works by
Seurat, Matisse, Van Gogh, Chinese bronzes and jades. Bus 17 or 18 from Nicollet
Mall.
The Guthrie Theater, 725 Vineland Pl, 377-2224, was founded in the 1960s by Sir
Tyrone Guthrie and is one of the finest reps in the US. Excellent discounts for
seniors, students, general public rush lines and low-cost previews. Enquire.
Adjoining the Guthrie is the **Walker Art Center**, a modern collection, open
Tue–Sat 10am–8pm, Sun 11am–5pm. Free. Both reached by the southbound 1, 4 or
6 bus from Hennepin Ave between 6th and 7th Sts.
Nearby is nearest city lake in **Loring Park**: ducks, swans, croquet, free plays in

summer. You can take a miniature paddlewheeler on Lake Calhoun, $2, or a 1-hour trip along 3 lakes, starting at Calhoun, $4. Frequent sailings June–Aug, 1–8pm. Get there on the 17 bus from Nicollet Mall.

American Swedish Institute, 2600 Park Ave, open Tue–Sat 1–4pm, Sun 1–5pm. $1, students 50¢. Films at 2, 3.30pm on Sun. 33-room mansion filled with exhibits on Minnesota's Scandinavian heritage.

Minnehaha Falls and Park, south of city. 144-acre woodland with 53-foot cataract popularised (though never seen) by Longfellow in his *Son of Hiawatha*. Take 7 bus from Washington Ave.

ENTERTAINMENT

Orchestra Hall, 1111 Nicollet Mall, 371-5656. Popular, jazz, classical offerings.

U of Minnesota. The Dinkytown area near campus on the east side of the river is liveliest at night. On campus: 'the Film Society often has free or cheap screenings of recent flicks. See notice board in Student Union'.

Mini-festivals, 338-3807, Mon–Fri at noon during July, on Nicollet Mall. Many ethnic festivals May–Sept at Minnehaha Park: Norwegian, Danish, Ukrainian, etc. Check with Visitors Bureau.

INFORMATION

Visitors Bureau, 15 S 5th St. 370-9132.

Visitors Info Center in the Crystal Court of the IDS complex, Nicollet Mall. Get the free 'Do It Yourself' brochure, map of downtown and Skyways from either source. Travelers Aid, 404 S 8th St, 340-7431. At airport, 726-9435.

TRAVEL

Greyhound, 29 N 9th St, 371-3311.

Airport limo to and from downtown hotels, $4.50 per person, 726-6400.

AMTRAK at Midway Station, 730 Transfer Rd in St Paul, 339-2382.

The 16 bus runs along University Ave through both cities.

City buses costs 25¢ around downtown, 60¢ elsewhere.

ST PAUL

ACCOMMODATION

Hall Home Hostel, 1361 Lafond, 647-0611. $5.25 year-round with AYH. Reservations required.

YWCA, 65 E Kellogg Blvd, 222-3741. Women only. Singles, $15 up.

OF INTEREST

Indian Mounds Park, Dayton's Bluff, east of downtown. A pleasant picinic spot overlooking the Mississippi, believed to be a Sioux burial site.

Summit Avenue district. The Victorian mansions get grander as you work your way up Laurel, Holly, Portland and Summit Aves—just the way the family of F Scott Fitzgerald did it. Born at 294 Laurel, FSF and family lived in 4 successively posher homes before ending up at 599 Summit, where he wrote his first novel in 1919.

Science Museum 30 E 10th St, 221-9488. Omnitheater has space and science films on huge domed screen, $4.50, Seniors $3.50. Museum has multisensory displays in natural sciences, technology, $3, seniors half price. Combo ticket for $5.50, seniors $4. Open daily.

Zoo, in Apple Valley south of St Paul, 432-9000. Buses from Twin Cities' downtown. 5 zones (from tropics to oceanic) with Siberian tigers, beluga whales. Many creatures can be handled or seen at close quarters. Free 3rd Tue of each month, otherwise $3, seniors half price. Daily 9.30am–5pm winter, till 6pm summer.

INFORMATION
Travelers Aid, 355 Washington St, 222-0311.
Minnesota Info Center, 480 Cedar, 296-5029.
Chamber of Commerce, 701 N Central Tower, 445 Minnesota St, 222-5561.

TRAVEL
Greyhound, 9th and St Peter Sts.
St Paul and Minneapolis run an integrated bus system: 45 minutes, downtown to downtown. See under Minneapolis.

DULUTH. Beautifully situated on a steep hillside overlooking a finger of Lake Superior, the port city of Duluth has the world's longest aerial lift bridge, a maritime museum and that's about it.

ACCOMMODATION
Downtown Motel, 131 W 2nd St, 727-6851. Single from $27, doubles from $31, cheaper in winter.
U of Minnesota at Duluth, 726-8178. Open to general public, June 10–Aug 15. Singles $7 up, doubles $13 up, with private bath. Reserve ahead. Pool, films, tennis.

OF INTEREST
All-day **bus and boat tours** (with lunch) from Duluth Transit, 722-4426. $15. Daily June 15–Sept 15, Sat–Sun in May/June and Sept/Oct. Tour takes in harbour, bridge, lakes, ship traffic, museums, etc. Or you can take 2-hr, $5.50 cruise on the *Vista King* or *Queen*, foot of 5th Ave West, 772-6218. Frequent sailings 1 June to mid-Oct, hourly 1 July-Labor Day.

INFORMATION
Visitors Bureau, 325 Harbor Dr, 722-5501.

HIBBING. Famous for three things: Mesabi Range iron ore, Greyhound buses and Bob Dylan. Dylan got out as soon as he could and so should you. From Chisholm (Highway 73) to Hibbing, you can drive through an artificial multicoloured 'Grand Canyon', the mined-out maw of the Pillsbury open pit. Several vista points for viewing other gaping holes, some as much as four miles long and two miles wide.

VOYAGEURS NATIONAL PARK. This 219,000-acre expanse of forested lake country on the Minnesota-Canada border is just beginning to be developed for public use. The park takes its name from the French Canadians who plied this network of lakes and streams in canoes, transporting explorers, missionaries and soldiers to the West, and returning by Montréal with vast quantities of furs. You can reach the park by car, but inside there are only waterways and you'll need to rent a boat. Free primitive camping in designated areas. Other lodging at nearby private resorts. No park entrance fee.

MISSOURI

Mix equal parts of the Old South, the Wild West and the modern Midwest and you've got the flavour of the Show Me State: shrewd, salt of the earth, slightly cantankerous—nobody here believes anything unless they see it with their own eyes. The flat landscape is dominated and divided by the Big Muddy, the Missouri River, a willful, sediment-laden powerhouse. Missouri produces more tents, lead, Missouri mules, corncob pipes and space vehicles than anyone else.

It's also produced Harry S Truman, Mark Twain, Jesse James and Generals Pershing and Bradley.

In the southwest begins the Ozark Plateau, wooded, full of springs, unspoilt rivers and caverns like Fantastic near Springfield, which has seen service as a speakeasy and a KKK meeting place. Other interesting caves include Meramac (55 miles southwest of St Louis), a five-story cave variously used as a Civil War gunpowder mill, an underground railway station, and a hideout for Jesse James' gang. A portion of the Cherokee Trail of Tears runs through northeast Missouri and has been made into a scenic camping and recreational area.

ST LOUIS. Founded in 1764 by French traders, its associations are as American as apple pie. Home of both the ice cream cone and the hot dog, the latter first devoured in 1893 by hungry St Louis Browns baseball fans. St Louis is where W C Handy wrote and sang the blues, where slave Dred Scott sued for freedom, where one-time resident Tennessee Williams set his *Glass Menagerie* and where Charles Lindbergh got the bucks for his trans-Atlantic venture.

Huge, humid, full of unsavoury slums and heavy industry from meat-packing to beer-brewing, the city nevertheless has a vital cultural life, lots of free attractions and the elegant Gateway to the West arch, the seventh most popular manmade tourist draw in the US.

ACCOMMODATION
St Louis Gateway Hotel, 822 Washington, 231-1400. Single $19 up, doubles $25 up. Bath, TV. A former Hilton, huge hotel, huge rooms. 'Clean, adequate.'
Best Western St Louisian, Washington and Tucker Sts, 421-4727. Has 24 rooms for AYH members, $10.25 each. Pool, laundry, near Gateway Arch. Cheap meals also.
Washington University, 6515 Wydown, 889-5073, extension 4051. 1 June–15 Aug, open to public, $16 single with shared bath. Good facilities.
The Tripper Youth Hostel, Portage, Des Sioux, 725-1616 days, 872-7570 nights. AYH, 10-bed houseboat on Mississippi River, 2-day trips cost $70 including meals. Summer only. Advance booking required, 172 Forest Brook Lane, St Louis 63141.
Visitors Center is very helpful, will phone around for lodgings.
St Louis also has two other youth hostels and a Motel 6 near airport.

FOOD
Shamrock Bar, Laclede's Landing. 'Cheap bar food, cold Guinness, nightly entertainment.'
Jimmie's, 415 9th and St Charles. Any kind of meal, 24 hrs a day. A favourite with truck drivers.
Bogart's, 2nd and Delmar Ave. 'Good food, nice decor, very friendly.'
Bingham's, 900 North St. 'Cheapest place for beer, food at Laclede's Landing.'

Old Spaghetti Factory, Laclede's Landing. 'Massive helpings, good atmosphere, spaghetti dinners with dessert, coffee from \$3.50–\$7.'

McDonald's, on riverboat along the Mississippi. 'If you succumb to American fast foods—this joint is built along lines of a riverboat, complete with Mark Twain at the helm!'

OF INTEREST

Gateway Arch. A unique 40-person tram ('don't go if you get seasick') mounts the core of each leg of this 630-ft stainless steel arch built by Eero Saarinen, \$1.50. Once there, you overlook the city and the Mississippi. Get there before 11am to avoid long lines. Beneath the arch there's a superb theatre and **Museum of American Expansion** complex. Free. 'The museum is very atmospheric, giving vivid impressions of frontier life'. Open till 6pm winter, 10pm summer; arch tram stops ½ hr earlier.

The Old Court House, west of Arch at 11 N 4th St (free, open daily 8am–4.30pm), scene of slavery auctions and the unsuccessful attempt by slave Dred Scott to win his freedom in court; the ramifications of his case helped ignite the Civil War. Trial room no longer exists, but you may see **Dred Scott's grave** in Section 1, Calvary Cemetery.

Forest Park, midtown, 5 miles west of Gateway Arch. 52 bus from downtown will take you to Hampton Ave, from where it's a 10-minute walk. A large and well laid-out park with numerous attractions, in 1904 the site of the centennial Louisiana Purchase Exposition and World's Fair.

An electric signal from the White House simultaneously unfurled 10,000 flags, while fountains flowed, bands played, 62 foreign nations exhibited, and 19 million people visited, there to sample iced tea and ice cream cones for the first time. Of the 1576 buildings erected for the fair, only one was permanent; it's now the **Art Museum**, one of the most impressive in the US. Like most other park attractions, it's free: open Tue–Sun. The **natural habitat zoo** (also free—unusual) is open daily 9am–5pm. The outdoor **Municipal Opera** (1500 free seats at the back of the 12,000-seat amphitheatre) holds operettas, ballets, musical comedies and concerts nightly in summer. The **Jewel Box** is a floral conservatory, open daily.

Anheuser-Busch Brewery, 610 Pestalozzi at Broadway, 577-2626. World's largest brewery gives free tour with beer, pretzels and a look at Clydesdale horses. Mon–Sat 9am–3.30pm in summer, Mon–Fri 9.30am–3.30pm rest of year.

Missouri Botanical Gardens, Tower Grove and Shaw Ave. 479 acres. See the Climatron, first geodesic-domed greenhouse with computer-controlled climates maintained within. \$2.50. Daily 9am–5pm.

Museum of Quackery, 3839 Lindell Blvd, free Mon–Sat, 11am–4pm. Great assortment of fiendish devices, nasty potions, superstitions and pseudo-scientific claptrap of all sorts, side by side with medically approved fiendish devices, nasty potions, etc.

Grant's Farm, Gravois Rd at Grant Rd (outskirts), 843-1700. Free look at the largest group of lovably huge Clydesdale horses anywhere, with a few deer, buffalo, birds, etc, thrown in. Reservations a must.

ENTERTAINMENT

Municipal Opera, free seats nightly in summer, starts 8.15pm. See Of Interest.

Laclede's Landing, a 9-block area of redeveloped mills and warehouses along the river just north of Gateway Arch, is focus of nightlife. A place called 4th and Pine (at that address) has been recommended for live music 6 nights a week, good atmosphere. Along the river levee by the Arch are a number of riverboats: the *Belle Angeline* and the *Robert E Lee* are restaurants; the *Goldenrod* (good Dixieland, films, comedy theatre) is the last of the authentic showboats; the *SS Admiral*, the *Huck Finn* and the *Samuel Clemens* do night cruises with dinner dances as well as sightseeing day cruises; the *Delta Queen* and the *Mississippi Queen* make day trips from St Louis to either Cincinnati or Minneapolis/St Paul.

Sports. St Louis is the most soccer-conscious city in the US; local team is the Steamers—call 781-4030 for playing schedule.

The Fun Phone, 421-2100, gives a roundup of events, entertainment.

INFORMATION
Try the Visitors Center at Gateway Arch; helpful with accommodation too. Visitors Bureau, 1300 Convention Plaza, 421-1023 and 241-1764.
Travelers Aid, 809 N Broadway, 241-5820.

TRAVEL
Greyhound, 801 N Broadway at Delmar, 231-7800.
Trailways, 706 N Broadway, 231-7181.
AAACON Auto Driveaway, 51 Locust St, 231-7035.
AMTRAK, 550 S 16th St, 241-8806.
City buses: Bi-State Transit, 231-2345. Basic fare 75¢, 10¢ for each zone change, 10¢ for transfers.

HANNIBAL. Although born down the road a piece, Mark Twain spent his boyhood in Hannibal, and this is the place that flogs Twainiana for all it's worth. It's good-natured hucksterism for the most part. The old rogue would no doubt approve, being no stranger to exaggeration himself: 'Recently someone sent me a picture of the house I was born in. Heretofore I have always stated that it was a palace but I shall be more guarded now.'

Eschew Tom Sawyer's cave (2 miles out of town and decidedly unspooky) and take a one-hour boat trip on the Mississippi instead ($4.50, twice daily Memorial-Labor Day, less often after that, 221-3222). Mark Twain's home and museum, 206 Hill Street, is worth a look-in, especially if you like Norman Rockwell. Open 8am–6pm in summer, shorter hours thereafter. Free but donations emphasised. About 100 miles upstream from St Louis, Hannibal is easily reached via Trailways. If you want to stay overnight, cheapest lodgings are at the Mark Twain Inn, 612 Mark Twain Avenue, 211-1490, single $25 up, doubles $30 up.

Twilight Zone time: MT's birth coincided with the appearance of Halley's Comet. Throughout his life, Twain predicted he would go out as he had come in. In 1910, right on cue, the comet reappeared and Twain crapped out.

KANSAS CITY. Envelope-maker for the world, home base for TWA, Kansas City is also an important cattle market, which leads us unerringly to Arthur Bryant's, the Holy Grail of barbequedom and a prime reason for visiting the city. KC's sister city is Sevilla, Spain, which explains the preponderance of Moorish arches, Spanish tiles and ornamental fountains around town. The effect may not look like Spain to a Spaniard, but it sure as hell does to a Missourian.

ACCOMMODATION
Ambassador Apartments, 3560 Broadway, 753-7300. $25 single/double.

Hotel Schuyler, 1017 Locust off 11th St, 842-6550. $19 single, $25 double with TV, air conditioning, bath. 'Still good.'

Motor Inn Hotel, 2018 Main, 471-7872. $12.50–$15 single, $15–$18 doubles. AC, cafe, laundry, TV. Bus stop 1 block. Closest to Crown Center. Watch your step outside after dark.

YMCA, 404 E 10th St, 848-8920. Men only. Singles $15 up but 'weekly rates $35!'. Sun roof.

U of Missouri, 276-1412, and Rockhurst College, 863-4010 both have cheap digs June–July, open to the general public.

FOOD
Arthur Bryant's, 1727 Brooklyn at 18th, 231-1123. Mon–Sat 10am–11pm. It's the sauce, which you'll see ageing in the window. Get lots of sauce. World class BBQ ribs and brisket sandwiches. Go on, stuff yourself.

Dixon's Chili, 5 locales in KC. Harry Truman loved KC chili—cheap and savoury.

OF INTEREST
Nelson Art Gallery, 45th Terrace and Oak Sts, 561-4000. Huge, eclectic, strong in Orientalia. Outdoor sculpture garden is grand. Free Sundays 2pm–6pm and with student ID, otherwise $1.50 Tue–Sat, 10am–5pm.

Museum of History and Science, 3218 Gladstone Blvd at Indiana Ave, 483-8300. Free except planetarium, $1.50. Housed in the 72-room mansion of lumber king R A Long are exhibits on natural, regional history and anthropology. Crawl-through igloo, other good Native American Stuff.

The Livestock Exchange and Stockyards are at 12th and Genessee. If the smell doesn't remove your appetite, the Golden Ox nextdoor has good if somewhat pricey steaks.

Country Club Plaza, between Main St and SW Expressway. Oldest shopping mall in the US. Huge Spanish-style plaza with fountains, genuine Iberian art, beautiful night lighting, interesting food and shops (150 of 'em). At 47th and Nicholas, a copy of the Giralda Tower in Sevilla. 47th and Central: Spanish murals, exquisite sevillano tilework depicting the bullfight.

Crown Center, Main and Pershing Rd. 'City within a city', built by the greeting card people. Hotel, shops, waterfall, indoor gardens, restaurants, etc. 'Go Sat mornings when woodcarvers, artists, etc, are at work.' Often the scene of live music, events.

Independence, a few miles east of KC and one-time home of that well-known haberdasher Harry Truman. The Library and Museum contain Presidential papers; his grave is in the courtyard. Free 30-minute slide and sound show, *The Man From Missouri*, hourly at the Jackson County Courthouse.

ENTERTAINMENT
KC Fun Phone, 474-9600 for 24-hr poop on daily entertainment.

Westport, original city heart between 39th and 45th Sts, is famous for good taverns and nightlife. Nose around the Happy Buzzard, Kelly's Westport Inn, Stanford and Sons.

INFORMATION
Travelers Aid, E 12th and Holmes, 221-1559 or 421-44984.

Visitors Bureau, 1100 Main, 221-7555.

Chamber, 920 Main, 221-2424.

TRAVEL
Greyhound, E 12th and Holmes, 421-7427.

Trailways, 1023 McGee St, 221-1776.

AAACON Auto Driveaway, 4229 Locust, 756-2223.

AMTRAK, Union Station (built in Roman basilica style), Main and Pershing Rd.

ST JOSEPH. 'Wanted: young skinny wiry fellows, not over 18. Must be expert riders willing to risk death daily. Orphans preferred. Wages $25/week. Apply Central Overland Express'. Over 100 young masochists applied and thus on 3 April 1860, began the Pony Express, a 2000-mile Missouri to California mail delivery system. Only in operation 18 months, it left a lasting impression on the world. The Museum at 914 Penn Street preserves the original stables and other interesting memorabilia, well worth a visit. Same day, different year in St Joe, Bob Ford shot Jesse James for a $10,000 reward.

NEBRASKA

A huge, tilting plate of a state, Nebraska rises from 825 feet at its Missouri River eastern border to over 5000 feet as it approaches the Rockies. Through it runs the feeble Platte River, along which countless buffalo once roamed until done in by kill-crazy Buffalo Bills. As shallow as 6 inches in places, the Platte nonetheless made an excellent 'highway' and water supply for the 2.5 million folks who crossed Nebraska in Conestoga wagons, 1840–66. Even today, the most worthwhile things to see in the state are those connected with the pioneer trails west.

Like other plains states, Nebraska has perfectly miserable weather summer and winter. Its speciality is hailstones, which occasionally reach the size of golfballs. A leading producer of beef cattle, TV dinners and popcorn, Nebraska also specialises in silos, both grain and ICBM missile.

OMAHA. Once a jumping-off place for pioneers, Omaha is the Union Pacific train headquarters and has taken over the noisome title of 'meat packer for the world' from Chicago. Friendly yes, but about as lively at night as a hog carcass. Only place the sidewalks don't roll up is near the University of Nebraska campus along Farnam Street.

This was the hometown of William Jennings Bryan, a populist who three times was the Democratic Party's presidential candidate around the turn of the century, and who finally made a monkey of himself at the notorious Scope's Monkey Trial in Tennessee. His house stands at 4900 Summer Street. Omaha is nowadays the home of Boys Town and also the underground Strategic Air Command headquarters.

ACCOMMODATION
Lodging is cheap here, as well it should be. Satellite Motel, Motel 6, Imperial 400, and Hill Town Inn are all under $30 double.
Conant Hotel, 1913 Farnam, 341-1313. Opposite Greyhound. Single $19 up, doubles $22 up. TV, AC. 'Excellent rooms.'
YMCA, 430 S 20th 341-1600. $14 up single, dorms $7. Coed, pool, restaurant, 5 minutes from Greyhound. 'New, clean, pleasant.'

FOOD
Bohemian Cafe, 1406 S 13th St, 342-9838. 'Czech food and atmosphere—the duck is
superb.' Under $6. Daily 11am–10pm.
The Old Market Spaghetti Works, 502 S 11th St. Lots of carbohydrates, easy on the
pocketbook.

OF INTEREST
Joslyn Art Museum, 2218 Dodge St. Housed in art deco building, Indian and other
art; pictures painted during the Maximilian Expedition up the Missouri River in
1833–4 are worth seeing. Closed Mon. $1.
Union Pacific Historical Museum, 1416 Dodge, 271-3530. Free, open Mon–Fri
9am–5pm, Sat 9am–1pm. Lots of Lincolniana, including replica of his funeral car
with original furnishings, plus oddments like used hanging rope, Indian warbonnet
with human hair, etc.
Union Stockyards. Livestock auctions Mon, Tue, Wed. Tours possible if booked in
advance.
The Old Market, 10th and Howard. Cobbled streets, warehouses recycled into
smart shops, galleries, restaurants. 'Most interesting place in Omaha.'
Falstaff Brewery, 25th and Deer Park Blvd, Mon–Fri at 2pm; and **Storz Brewery**,
1807 N 16th, Mon–Fri at 10am and 11am. Free tours, samples of suds.

INFORMATION
Visitors Bureau, 1819 Farnam, Suite 1200, 444-4660.
Events hotline, 444-6800.
Student center, U of Nebraska, 60th and Dodge Sts, 554-2800. Accommodation,
rides, general info.

TRAVEL
Greyhound, 1802 Farnam, 341-1900.
Trailways, 16th and Jackson, 342-7303.
AMTRAK, 1003 S 9th St.
City bus, 75¢.

ALONG THE PIONEER AND PONY EXPRESS TRAILS. The
Oregon, Mormon and other pioneer trails plus the Pony Express
routes followed the Platte River, which today is paralleled in large
part by Interstate 80 and by Highways 30 (east) and 26 (west).

Moving east to west: at **Gothenburg** in midstate, you can see two
original Pony Express stations (one at 96 Ranch) and an old
stagecoach stop with bullet holes still in the walls. At Lafayette City
Park, free camping. **North Platte**, long-time home of scout and show
biz personality Buffalo Bill Cody, holds a Wild West Show and Congress of Rough Riders of the World near Scout's Rest Ranch State
Park. B Bill got his nickname for killing 4280 buffalo in 17 months
while employed by the railroad to supply meat for its crews. The ranch
house itself (free) is a pretty but prissy-looking Victorian affair. At
Bayard further west, the Oregon Trail Wagon Train company offers
two- and three-day treks which circle Chimney Rock. Meals
(including pioneer items like vinegar pie and hoecakes), wagon
driving or riding, and other activities from an Indian 'attack' to prairie
square-dancing for about $60 a day. They also do three-hour covered
wagon tours to Chimney Rock and back, up to 16 persons for $40, and

cookouts. Book through Oregon Trail Wagon Train, Rt 2, Box 200-B, Bayard 69334; call 586-1850.

Scotts Bluff and **Chimney Rock**, off US 26 in western Nebraska, are two rock formations that served as landmarks for the frontier families. Scotts Bluff is climbable, has a half-mile trail poignantly lined with pioneer graves every 200 feet or so, and clearly defined wagon ruts. The Park rangers give daily lectures in summer and the pioneer campsite can be visited. Spectacular views from the bluff.

NORTH DAKOTA

Virtually border to border farmland, North Dakota grows lots of wheat, flaxseed and cattle, which in turn produce more butter than any other state. Its superlatives aren't exactly the kind to make you rush up here: it has the world's largest concrete buffalo *and* concrete cow and the longest road without a curve—110 miles of tedium on Route 46. But do explore the Badlands and the simple pleasures of what Teddy Roosevelt called 'the roughrider country', in the west, accessible via Greyhound to Medora.

National Park: Theodore Roosevelt.

FARGO. University town and active arts community, Fargo is also the place where a dramatic encounter between a UFO and an Air Force plane took place in 1948. Ask a local to tell you the story.

Very cheap lodgings at Power Motor Hotel, 400 Broadway, 232-2517, two blocks from bus depot: $8 up single, $10 up double.

BISMARCK. Capital and craftily named by the Northern Pacific railway after Otto von B in the hope of getting German marks to capitalise railroad construction (it worked), Bismarck has the world's largest kodiak bear in what appears to be the world's smallest bear cage.

ACCOMMODATION
Patterson Place, 422 E Main, 258-4801. TV, air conditioning, near Greyhound. Single $16 up.
Kuilman Motel, 2009 E Main, 223-2636. AC, colour TV, phones. $19 single, $24 double.
Motel 6, State St near Highway 83 North, 255-1851: $16 single, $20 doubles.

FOOD
Little Cottage Cafe, 2513 E Main. Try the delicious stuffed porkchops and the ethnic soups.

OF INTEREST
State Capitol Building. Famous sons and daughters in the Roughrider gallery: Eric Sevareid, Peggy Lee, Lawrence Welk, Roger Maris.
The Historic Society Museum (on grounds) has an Indian collection called one of the

finest in the world. Many personal effects of Sitting Bull. Not to be missed: the Indian craftsmens' coop—outstanding and authentic artefacts for sale.

Hayrides and sleighrides, 255-0768 and 258-3004. Moneywise only in groups but call anyway to see if you can join one. An offbeat rural pleasure.

Events. In June and July, a week-long **covered wagon train** wends its way from Jamestown west to Ft Lincoln near Bismarck, an uncommercial local affair, visitors freely welcomed. **United Tribes powwow**, 3 days mid-Sept. Colourful, musical.

INFORMATION/TRAVEL
Visitors Bureau, 402 Bowen Ave, 222-4308.
State Travel Division, toll-free in state, 800/472-2100.
Greyhound routes cover Fargo, Jamestown, Bismarck, Badlands, Roosevelt National Park.

LEWIS AND CLARK TRAIL. By auto or on foot, you can retrace the explorers' route of 1804 south along the Missouri River. Points of interest include: **Ft Lincoln** (from which Custer and the 7th Cavalry rode out to defeat), **Ft Mandan** (where Sacajawea joined Lewis and Clark), buffalo wallows, **Knife River Indian village**, **Ft Yates** (Sioux national headquarters) and Sitting Bull Historic Site, where the leader was originally buried. Great hunters, 600 Sioux braves once killed over 6000 buffalo in three days in 1882. An excellent Indian campground one mile west of Ft Yates at Long Soldier Coulee Park, open year-round.

BADLANDS AND ROOSEVELT NATIONAL PARK. There are three units, spread over 75 miles of rough terrain. Described as 'grand, dismal and majestic', the Badlands formations are best seen early morning and late afternoon. (Not to be confused with South Dakota's Badlands, which are bigger and badder.) The south unit near Medora has a 38-mile loop with scenic overlooks, buffalo and prairie dogs, and a campground at Cottonwood. Horseback rides (all day under $20) to Badlands from Medora Stables—worth it. Teddy's Elkhorn Ranch is very remote; the ranch ultimately showed a net loss of $21,000 but he loved the area, saying: 'I owe more than I can ever express to the men and women of the cow country.' Sully Creek Campground, two miles from Medora: 'Primitive, can get cold but very convenient to Roosevelt if one has a car.'

OHIO

Ohio makes everything and more of it than anybody else: comic books, coffins, Liederkranz cheese, bank vaults, vacuums, false teeth, playing cards, rubber, jet turbine engines, soap, glassware— you name it. Small wonder that Ohio also produced America's first billionaire: John D Rockefeller. They're always tinkering in Ohio, birthplace of the cash register, the fly swatter, the menthol cigarette and the beer can, not to mention the Wright brothers, Thomas Edison, John Glenn and Neil Armstrong.

Get out of its highly industrialised cities and you'll discover a surprising amount of green and gentle countryside, full of lakes, wineries (50 of them), farms with roadside produce and local colour from Amish villages to oddities like Hinckley, buzzard capital of the world (where you can satisfy that craving for a buzzard cookie).

CINCINNATI. Probably unique in being a place which grew to cityhood on steamboat traffic, as many as 8000 boats a year docked at Cincinnati to take on passengers, lightning rods and lacy 'French' ironwork destined for New Orleans bordellos. Besides their practical value, steamboats were raced incessantly, causing huge sums of money to change hands and equally astonishing losses of life—in one five-year period, 2268 people died in steamboat explosions. Settled by Germans, Cincinnati became a leading producer of machine tools, Ivory soap, beer, gin and a variety of ham favoured by Queen Victoria, all without losing its livable, likeable essence.

ACCOMMODATION
Hotel Cincinnatian, 16 W 16th St at Vine, 241-0180. Without shower, rates begin at $8.50. Doubles $11–$21. 'Good value.'
Dennison Hotel, 716 Main, 241-7035. $9 single, $14 double without bath. 'Rundown, dirty, bearable.' Close to Greyhound.
YMCA, 1105 Elm, 241-5348. Men only, pool, restaurant.
Home hostel, 541–1972. $2.25 night with AYH; only 2 beds so plan ahead.
El Rancho Rankin, 5218 Beechmont Ave, 231-4000. 1 mile from downtown. $11–$16 single, $13–$21 doubles.
Milner Hotel, 108 Garfield Pl, 241–3570. Single $20 up, doubles $25 up. Near library, a bit seedy.

FOOD
Cincinnati's Germanic tradition means it has a number of beer gardens. It's also noted for local chili, served '3, 4 or 5-way', eg with spaghetti, beans, meat, onions, Cheddar cheese. Burpy, but good. Chili parlours everywhere: Skyline at 7th and Vine is one of the champs. Also try Charlie's Downstairs in Shillito's Department Store; Empress and Queen City Chili.

OF INTEREST
Carew Tower, 5th and Vine Sts. From the 49th floor, take a gander at Cincinnati, the Ohio River and Kentucky opposite. 50¢.
Riverboats. At public landing, foot of Broadway. Revitalised riverfront area, including seating at the Serpentine Wall for pleasant boat-watching. Cincinnati is home base for the *Delta Queen* (genuine relic on the National Register of Historic Landmarks) and the *Mississippi Queen*, its younger sister. Cruises heavily booked and rather pricey; about $80/day the cheapest. You can take in arrivals, departures and attendant hoopla and steam calliope-playing for free.
These are real paddlewheelers as opposed to the ignoble beasties that ply the waters in hundreds of US towns and cities. Also the *Majestic*, last of the original showboats: $5 and up for live theatre nightly, 241-6550. On the Covington, Kentucky, side is the *Mike Fink*, a riverboat restaurant with delectable New Orleans-style

seafood bar. Not cheap but you may feel like splurging on catfish, crab legs and French-fried peaches.

Cincinnati Zoo, 3400 Vine St, 281-4701. Called 'the sexiest zoo in the US' for its successful breeding programme: lots of gorillas, rare white Bengal tigers (blue eyes), an Insectarium. $3.75, seniors $1.50. Daily 9am–6pm summer, 9am–5pm rest of year.

Harriet Beecher Stowe Memorial, 2950 Gilbert Ave. Open Wed and Sun, June–Sept, 10am–12am, 1pm–5pm. Long-time resident Stowe conceived *Uncle Tom's Cabin* here, doing her research by visiting a Kentucky plantation and talking with anti-slavery advocates. Cincinnati was a key stop on the Underground Railway (the name given to that network of helping hands which assisted Southern slaves northwards to freedom). Economic ties to the South and strong abolitionist sentiment made the city a ferment of divided loyalties.

Hudepohl Brewery, 5th and Gest, 721-7273. Try a local specialty. Tours and free suds, Mon–Fri 10am–2pm.

ENTERTAINMENT
Mt Adams is Cincinnati's hilly Greenwich village; lots of action, day or night. Downtown, try Sleep-out Louie's, 230 W 2nd for live music and Joe's Bar in Terrace Hilton, 15 W 6th St, for good Happy Hours, live Dixieland.

INFORMATION/TRAVEL
Travelers Aid, 700 Walnut St, Room 307, 721-7660.
Visitors Bureau, 200 W 5th St. 621-2142.
Greyhound, 1065 Gilbert, 352-6000. A long walk from city centre.
Trailways, 721 Reading Rd, 241-2620. Equally distant, in industrial area.
AMTRAK, 1901 River Rd, 579-8506.
City buses, 621-4455.
Cheap and Cheerful Car Rental, 222 W Central Parkway at Plum, 621-RENT. Good used cars.

COLUMBUS. Writer O Henry once did three years for embezzlement in a Columbus cell, confinement producing some of his best stories. Local humourist James Thurber attended Ohio State and set his play, *The Male Animal*, there. This capital city sits in a region intriguingly called Leatherlips, the name of a Wyandot Indian chief who was executed by his people for siding with palefaces. But it's famous OSU coach Woody 'win at all costs' Hayes, not Leatherlips, who symbolises this football-obsessed city.

ACCOMMODATION
Hotel Norwich, 4th and State Sts, 221-3373. Single $18 up, doubles $22 up. Bus stop at door, laundry. Near Greyhound. 'Adequate, clean.'
YMCA, 50 W Long, 224-1131. Coed. $16 single, pool, restaurant.
Buckeye B&B, PO Box 130, Powell OH 43065. 548-4555. Has attractive home in downtown Italian district for $20 single, $35 double.
Home Hostel, 235-7669. $2.25 AYH only, 8 beds. Meals provided. Booking not required.
Also try the International Students Residence Hall, Ohio State campus, about $5/night.

FOOD
Good eating places in the German village, bus from High St.
Also at North Market, 29 Spruce, a century-old centre for produce, walkaway foods. Open Tue, Thur, Fri, Sat 7am–5.30pm.

OF INTEREST
Ohio State University library: largest collection of Thurber's works, drawings.
Ohio Theatre, 29 E State St. A 1930s cinema with wonderful Titian red, gold-spangled baroque interior. 'Amazing decor; organist rises up through the floor.' Call 469-1045 for film schedule.
Zoo, 9990 Riverside Dr. 889-9471. Outskirts, in Powell. Daily, $3. Impressive collection of great apes, including the first gorilla ever born in captivity.

INFORMATION/TRAVEL
Visitors Bureau, 50 W Broad, 221-6623.
Greyhound, 111 E Town St, 221-5311.
Trailways, 800 N High, 224-9159.
City bus, 228-1776. Free around downtown area.

CLEVELAND. Superman was born in Cleveland in 1933, brainchild of two teenagers who in 1938 sold all rights for $130 and commenced upon a lifetime of generally fruitless litigation. This earthly urban version of Krypton, like the doomed planet, is an entirely suitable birthplace for the 'Man of Steel'—at once an industrial powerhouse, but looking like Dresden after the war. Iron and steel are the big money-earners; also shipbuilding, for Cleveland is on Lake Erie—the Great Lakes a great fissure through the core of America—with ocean-going ships tied up along its waterfront. John D Rockefeller spun his oil business here into one of the largest personal fortunes the world has ever known. Downtown is thick with corporate headquarters, Lake Erie thick with pollution, the Cuyahoga River so rich in petrochemicals that it sometimes catches fire, while the symphony orchestra and municipal art museum (both in the first rank) and other cultural endeavours soak up the gravy.

ACCOMMODATION
Dorn Hotel, 1416 Prospect Ave, 241-8607. Very clean. Singles begin at $16 with shared bath.
YMCA, 2200 Prospect Ave, 696-2200. Coed. $16 single. Huge, pool, restaurant.
YMCA, 3201 Euclid Ave, 881-6878. Takes women and couples. $20 single, pool, restaurant.
B&B: International Spareroom has an informal couch and sleeping bag room, $8.45 in Cleveland Heights, friendly family. See Accommodation Background for address, details.
Lots of nice motels under $20 single, way out in suburban Cleveland: Red Roof Inns and Knights Inn are 2 of the best.

FOOD
Hungarian restaurants are Cleveland's pride: various along 12,000 block of Buckeye Rd; best is Balaton. Also in Shaker Heights.
The gastronomic cross-section at the West Side Market, W 25th and Lorain Ave, has old world vibes, inexpensive and mouth-watering selection. Daily except Sunday.

OF INTEREST
Museum of Art, 11150 East Blvd at University Circle, 421-7340. Free and first-rate, second only to the NY Metropolitan in value. Closed Mon.
Salvador Dali Museum, 24050 Commerce Park Rd off Chagrin Blvd, Beachwood,

646-0372. Free, by appointment only, Tue-Sat, 10am–12am, 1pm–4pm. Largest collection of the master surrealist's works anywhere.

Shaker Historical Museum, 16740 S Park Blvd, Shaker Heights, 921-1201. Free, open Mon-Fri 2pm–4pm, Sun 2pm–5pm. Once the site of a rural commune begun by the Shakers, a religious sect who turned their backs on industrialisation for 10 minutes—and along came Cleveland! Today's Shaker Heights is a ritzy suburb with good (and not always expensive) restaurants.

Dunham Tavern Museum, 6709 Euclid Ave, 421-1060. $1, Tue–Sun 12.30pm–4.30pm. Restored 1824 tavern and former stagecoach stop, now filled with Americana.

INFORMATION/TRAVEL
Travelers Aid, 1001 Huron Rd, 241-5861.
Greyhound, 1465 Chester Ave, 781-0520. 'High crime area—take extreme care, even in restrooms.'
Trailways, 1470 Chester Ave, 861-3161.
AMTRAK, Lakefront Station, 200 E Memorial Shoreway, 861-0105.

ZOAR. In Northeast Ohio are many Amish and Mennonite villages including Zoar, settled in 1817 by German religious separatists committed to communal life and celibacy. After flourishing for 75 years, the community eventually disbanded when their hotel operation brought in outsiders, fancy clothes, candy and discontentment to the Zoarites. You can take bed and breakfast at the historic Cider Mill, 874-3133, for $25 single, $30 double, and amble about the formal garden (inspired by the *Book of Revelations*) and the two town museums.

SERPENT MOUND STATE MEMORIAL and MOUND CITY NATIONAL MONUMENT. South of Chillicothe near Locust Grove and three miles north of Chillicothe are these two Indian sites in south central Ohio. The first is the largest serpent effigy mound in the US, built by the Adena culture c1000 BC. Unforgettable, majestic and truly amazing that it's still around at all. In summer, green grass covers the enormous coils, making them even more sinuous. The Mound City group dates somewhere between 1000 and 300 BC: 23 burial mounds, described as 'the city of the dead'. Both areas are free and open daily. Haunting, worth a side trip. Greyhound gets you as far as Chillicothe.

SOUTH DAKOTA

The Coyote State is living proof that bad weather (from 40 below zero to a blazing 116 degrees) can't be all bad—its citizens live longer than in any other state except Hawaii. To look at its tourist brochures, you'd think the place was full of nothing but jolly Anglo hunters, ranchers and fishermen. It has, however, a large (mostly Sioux) Indian population on nine reservations, regarded as 'uppity Injuns' (and worse) for their quixotic determination to win back more of their traditional lands. It was the discovery of gold in the Black Hills (verified by that catalytic figure, General Custer) that spelled doom for the fierce Sioux nations: today gold continues to be South Dakota's leading mineral.

Concentrate on the scenic western section: Mt Rushmore, the Black Hills, the Badlands. Because of distances and lack of public transit, it's difficult to sightsee without a car. Wyoming's Devil's Tower is only 35 miles from the South Dakota border, but you'll need a car to reach it as well.

National Parks: Wind Cave
Badlands

RAPID CITY. A strategic spot for exploring the Black Hills and Badlands, itself a hodgepodge of tourish claptrapery. Don't miss the Sioux Museum, however.

ACCOMMODATION
College Inn Motel, 123 Kansas City St, 800/742-8942 (toll-free in South Dakota). Air-conditioned dorm rooms, shared shower/bath, $16 up. Also private rooms, $25 up. Near bus depot. 'Clean, well furnished'. Pool, laundry, cafeteria.

Marion's Guest House, 830 Quincy, 342-1790. $14–$16 single, $16–$19 double, shared bath. Laundry, TV, lounge. 6½ blocks from bus. 'Charming guest house—made very welcome.'

YMCA, 815 Kansas City St, 342-8538 (phone first). $3.25 with AYH. 1 June–30 Aug only. 12 cots (no bedding) in coed room. 7 blocks to bus. Postcard in advance will reserve.

If you have wheels, the little burg of Custer is more attractive: Shady Rest Motel, 673-4478, has nice little $15-$30 cabins with kitchenettes.

FOOD
Sprouts, 5th and Kansas City St. 'Clean, vegetarian. Good salad bar under $3.'

INFORMATION
Visitors Bureau, Rushmore Plaza Center, 343-1744. Useful maps. Ask for the South Dakota Vacation Guide, with a dandy section on panning for gold and rockhounding.

OF INTEREST
Sioux Museum and Crafts Center, St Joe and West Blvd. Free, open Tue-Sun 9am–4.30pm. Wonderful collection of historical objects, excellent crafts, all the contemporary Sioux artists from Oscar Howe to Herman Red Elk. Sioux are noted for beadwork, stone pipes, quillwork.

Caves: many in Rapid City region, all charging $3.50 admission.
Diamond Crystal Cave is closest: 'Quite long but very pleasant walk.' '**Bethelem Cave Drive** is superb though bumpy. Best cave in Black Hills.'

TRAVEL
Gray Line tours, $20 up: 5 different itineraries of Black Hills, Rushmore, Badlands, Custer Game Refuge: June until mid–Oct. No Badlands tours after Labor Day. Daily 9am, return 5pm, pickup from various hotels including Alex Johnson.

Jack Rabbit Tours, 348-3300, $18 up. Same season as Gray Line. Fully narrated 9-hour Black Hills tours. Bookable from Greyhound Depot. Will pick, deliver from lodgings, including Marion's Guest House. 'Quite extensive—well worth the money'.

Black Hills Car rental, 333 6th St, 342-6696. 2 blocks from Trailways. 'Cheapest in town', about $17/day plus mileage.

DEADWOOD. Twenty-eight miles northwest of Rapid City via I-90, Deadwood calls itself 'where the West is fun!' but 'where the West is wax' might be more like it. Once the stomping ground for Calamity Jane, Wild Bill Hickok, Deadwood Dick and the rest, but amazingly ordinary today.

ACCOMMODATION
Fairmont Hotel, 628 Main, 578-2396. $10 single, $12.50 doubles with bath. 'Basic, adequate'.

Super 8 Motel. 'Pool, sauna, friendly, very clean'. Good rates especially with 4-5 people and after Labor Day.

OF INTEREST
Number 10 saloon. See the chair where Wild Bill Hickok (who blew away 7 men himself) was gunned down while holding a poker hand of 2 aces and a pair of eights—still called 'a dead man's hand'. Hickok was never punished for any of his killings, several of which were clearly murders; *his* killer was hanged, however.

Adams Memorial Museum. Free. 'Interesting'. Gold train, Wild Bill's marriage certificate and a sea of other crap.

The Trial of Jack McCall. Nightly except Sun. Starts with dramatic capture of Hickok's killer, continues with trial in town hall. 'A laugh.'

Mt Moriah 'Boot Hill' cemetery. Good place to do gravestone rubbings: Calamity, Wild Bill are here.

Nearby:

Lead (pronounced Leed), a steep little mining town with the largest gold mine in the western hemisphere, the Homestake. Surface tours May to Oct, $2. Half million ounces of gold are mined each year; about 14 million tons remain. 'Free ore sample'.

Spearfish, for 45 years the home of the Black Hills Passion Play. June through Aug, 8.15pm on Tue, Thur, Sun. $4 to $8. Huge cast in outdoor setting.

THE BLACK HILLS. They are poorly named: picture instead high and ancient mountains cloaked with spectacular pine forests, a green citadel above the vastness of tawny plains and considered sacred ground by the Sioux.

OF INTEREST
Wind Cave National Park, 11 miles north of Hot Springs, 745-4600. 28,000 acres. Discovered in 1881, the cave, some 10 miles deep, is named for the winds that whistle in and out of it, caused by changes in barometric pressure. Open daily, tours 1¼ to 3-hour, $1–$2. Dress warmly. Above ground and free, superb animal watching and photographing: deer, buffalo, antelope, prairie dog towns. Dawn, dusk are best times.

Custer State Park, 255-4514. Free if you drive through on Highway 16A, otherwise $3. Plus $5 to camp. About 2000 buffalo, through which you can take a thrilling 1-hour jeep ride for $4; daily in summer, by appointment otherwise. Also wild burros that panhandle. 'Any tour through the Black Hills should include **Needles Highway**, spectacular valcanic pinnacles. Someone once wanted to carve these into Wild West heroes, the genesis of the Rushmore idea'.

Jewel Cave National Monument. Dog-tooth crystals of calcite sparkle from its walls:

$1 scenic tour, but take the historic tour, $2, more strenuous and fun, with candle lanterns.

Mt Rushmore. Free including a 12-minutes film, evening amphitheatre programmes. It took 14 years to complete the 60-ft-high granite faces of Washington, Jefferson, Teddy Roosevelt and Lincoln, carved by Gutzon Borglum and paid for with South Dakota schoolkids' pennies. Most beautiful in morning light and when floodlit, summer eves 9.30am–10.30pm.

Crazy Horse Monument, north of Custer on Route 385. A great Oglala Sioux leader, Crazy Horse resisted white encroachment on Indian lands and at 33 was shamefully killed during a conference with US Army Officers. If ever finished, this monument to him will dwarf Rushmore, ultimately standing 385 ft high and 641 ft long. Sculptor Korczak Ziolkoski logged 36 years and blasted away some 7 million tons of rock before dying in 1982. His family vows to carry on; check locally before setting out.

BADLANDS NATIONAL PARK. Like hell with the fires put out: 207 square miles of weird and beautiful buttes, canyons and brilliantly coloured rock formations of clay and sand washed from the Black Hills. At sunset the sandstone slopes turn all shades of pink and purple. Bones of sabre-toothed tigers, three-toed horses and Tyrannosaurus rex have been found in this arid land once covered by swamps. 'Absolutely amazing—the surprise package of our tour. Come into it at dawn with the sun at your back— it'll blow you mind, it's that good.' 'Well worth the 10-mile hike along rough track to watch the sunset and spend the night at Sage Creek primitive campground. No water on site.'

OF INTEREST
Kadota, an authentic Western backwater town east of the Badlands on I-90, is the best place to stay overnight to make the favoured dawn drive through the Badlands, emerging at Wall. Excellent visitor centre at the Cedar Pass Badlands entrance: includes film show. To stay, West Motel, Highway 16 and I-90 Business Loop, 837-2427; $18, 'clean rooms, friendly staff'.
Wall. World-notorious for Wall Drug, a genial drugstore-cum-tourist trap and practical jokers' haven, whose 3000 billboards can be found as far away as Paris and the South Pole. Sip free ice water, buy a rattlesnake ashtray, puzzle over a jackalope. Wall also has livestock auctions on Thur, free chance to hear auctioneers' great patter. In Wall, the Sands Motel, 604 Glenn, 279-2624, has $18.50-$29 singles/doubles, senior and offseason discounts also.

MITCHELL. If passing through, take time to see the Corn Palace, a vaguely Russian fantasy of onion domes, dazzling pointillistic murals formed of coloured korn kernels. Extraordinary. In Mitchell also, the Oscar Howe Art Center, housing work by the most noted Sioux artist of our times; free. Area lodging: Skoglund Farm near Canova. (They will pick you up from Greyhound at Salem.) 247-3445. $20/night includes two full meals plus coffee at a friendly family operation. Horses to ride, animals to pet on a working cattle ranch.

WOUNDED KNEE. 'I did not know then how much was ended.

When I look back from this high hill of my old age, I can still see the butchered women and children lying heaped and scattered all along the crooked gulch as plain as when I saw them with eyes still young. And I can see that something else died there in the bloody mud, and was buried in the blizzard. A people's dream died there. It was a beautiful dream. The nation's hoop is broken and scattered. There is no centre any longer, and the sacred tree is dead.'—Black Elk

The symbolic end of Indian freedom came at Christmastime, 1890, at the so-called Battle of Wounded Knee when the US Cavalry opened fire with rifles and field guns on 120 Indian men and 230 Indian women and children. Most were murdered instantly; some wounded crawled away through a terrible blizzard. Torn and bleeding, many did not crawl far: a returning army burial party found numerous bodies frozen into grotesque shapes against the snow.

A shabby monument marks the spot 100 miles southeast of Rapid City, a few miles off Route 18 near Pine Ridge.

But their unquiet mass grave nearby continues to serve as a rallying point for this century's Indians. In 1973, at the second battle of Wounded Knee, two Indians died in the 71-day siege of the American Indian Movement, and the chapter is far from over.

NB: although the reservation has a motel, museum and other tourist facilities, don't expect uniformly friendly attitudes toward white faces.

MOBRIDGE. On a high hill across the Missouri from Mobridge in north-central South Dakota is Sitting Bull's grave. One of the events preceding the massacre at Wounded Knee was the murder of Sitting Bull, the great Sioux leader, organiser and victor at Little Bighorn. It was carried out by Indian policemen under the eye of the US Cavalry. The authorities always felt uncomfortable with Sitting Bull alive, regarding him as a subversive figure. Mobridge has a sculpture of Sitting Bull by Korczak Ziolkowski and ten fine murals by Sioux artist Oscar Howe in the municipal auditorium.

WISCONSIN

A liquid sort of place, Wisconsin: famed for beer, milk (one cow for every human) and water of all sorts—Wisconsinites gave names to 14,949 of their inland lakes before giving up in despair. Other places had gold rushes: Wisconsin had a 'lead rush'.

Politically, the Badger State has swung from the rapaciousness of early lumber barons to the progressive decades of the 'fighting LaFollettes', from Commie witch-hunter Joseph McCarthy to present-day liberal Gaylord Nelson.

Unlike other Midwest states, the cities here are clean, amiable and altogether charming. Of course, so is the countryside, but watch out for mosquitoes the size of aircraft carriers: the price you pay for all those lakes.

MILWAUKEE. There's a comfortable, old-shoe feeling about Milwaukee, enhanced by its reputation for good beer, 'brats' and baseball. Remarkably short on grime and slums, long on restaurants and festivals, the city is a good natured mix of ethnic groups, especially Germans, Poles and Serbs. In quantity of beer produced, Milwaukee has now been aced out by, gasp, Los Angeles, but for quality this is still Der Platz.

ACCOMMODATION
Wisconsin Hotel, 720 N 3rd at Wisconsin, 271-4900. Single $18–$25, doubles $28–$40. Old hotel, renovated recently. Near AMTRAK, museum.
Hotel Plankington House, 609 N Plankington, 271-0260. Large downtown hotel, single $24 up, doubles $28 up.
YMCA, 915 W Wisconsin Ave, 276-5077. $19 single, $30 twin. Coed. Pool, restaurant. 'Very new, clean.'
Youth Hostel, 6750 W Loomis Rd, 10 miles SW of downtown, 529-3299. $4.25 AYH, open 1 May–31 Oct. On good 64-mile bike route.

FOOD
Besides Wisconsin's famous cheeses, Milwaukee is noted for 'beer and brats', the latter a particularly succulent variety of German bratwurst, served boiled in beer and tangy with sauce. If you don't go to a Brewers baseball game and gorge in the sun on beernbrats, you've blown it. Also try local frozen custard at places like Kopps and Gilles. German and Serb restaurants are best bets ethnically but also check to see if Milwaukee is celebrating one of its ethnic feasts at the lakefront.
Ponderosa Steak House, 425 W Wisconsin Ave. Under $6, huge portions. 'Like Tad's but better.'

OF INTEREST
Breweries: 24 in town. The big 3: Schlitz, 234 W Galena, 332-4194 (tours daily at 1pm and 3pm, 'most beer'); Miller, 4251 W State, 931-2153 (Mon–Sat, 9am–3.30pm, April–Oct, 'best beer, least given'); and Pabst, 901 W Juneau Ave, 347-7326 (hourly Mon–Fri 9am–3.30pm, Sat 9am–11pm, Sept–May, 'most flavourful, unlimited suds', 'worst tour, worst beer').
Public Museum, 800 W Wells St, 278-2700. Daily 9am–5pm. Walk-through European village of Milwaukee's 33 ethnic groups—charming. The Polish and Serbian houses are beautiful. $2. Also other exhibits, silent films.
Art Museum, 750 N Lincoln Memorial Dr, 271-9508. $1, seniors and students 50¢. Closed Mon. Strong in Haitian primitives, 19th C German, contemporary American works.
Mitchell Park Conservatory, 524 S Layton Blvd, $2. Three 7-story glass domes house luxuriant botanical gardens, open daily.

ENTERTAINMENT
Fun-Line, 799-1177.
Sample the 6000+ taverns—most are rollicking, unpretentious good fun. Caesar's Inn on the south side is the Brewers baseball team hangout. 'TGI Fri: excellent potato skin dishes, great decor.'
Summerfest, 2-week festival June/July, by lakefront. 'Groups, beer, funfair, massive.' Festa Italiana in July, one of the biggest pastafazools anywhere: 'delicious'. Aug–Sept: German, Irish, Polish Feasts.

INFORMATION/TRAVEL
Visitors Bureau, 756 N Milwaukee, 273-3950 or 7222.
Greyhound, 606 N 7th, 272-8900.
AMTRAK, 433 W St Paul Ave, 933-3081.
Local bus, 344-6711.

MADISON. Located 77 miles due west of Milwaukee, state capital Madison is a college town wrapped picturesquely around Lakes Mendota and Monona. The 1000-acre lakeside campus of the University of Wisconsin is about as pretty as you can get. A great range of cheap eats in Madison, beginning with two open-air Farmers Markets. Bring your bike or rent one.

ACCOMMODATION
The Towers, 502 N Frances, 257-0701. $14 single, $12 each for doubles. 15 May–15 Aug only. Kitchen, sundeck, lots of amenities. 'Clean, central.'
Wisconsin Center Guest House, 610 Langdon, 256-2621. $24 single, $28 double. On fraternity row. Great frat parties in the vicinity, Thur–Sat.
Exel Inn, 4202 E Towne Blvd, 241-3861. Single $22, Doubles $30.
YMCA, 306 N Brooks on campus, 257-2534. $5.25 with AYH, 15 May–15 Aug only; other times, give it a try anyway. Coed, 12 beds, pool, tennis. Reserve ahead.

FOOD
Recommended: Brat and Brau, Regent St, for all-you-can-eats; Paisan's on University Square and Rocky Rococo, The Mall, for good pizzas; Ovens of Brittany, State and Johnson, terrific breakfasts.

OF INTEREST
It all circulates around the **campus**—a must for its facilities, social action and people. The **library** is noted for is Duveen collection of Alchemy.
'Take a **lakeside walk** around to opposite shore and the nature reserve. 3 hours there and back. Great views.'
Vilas Park Zoo, free. Summer Sun, 10.30am–noon, show up for your free camel ride.
Nearby:
Wisconsin Dells, 53 miles north of Madison. 'Magnificent rock and river scenery but terribly commercialised. Only visible by boat.' Boat trips, $6 to $9. Inexpensive all-you-can-eat at the Paul Bunyan Lumberjack restaurant, north woods decor.
Baraboo, about 40 miles north of Madison. In May 1884, the five Ringling Brothers began their world-renowned circus in a modest way, behind the Baraboo jail. Their former winter quarters is now the site of the excellent **Circus World Museum**, 426 Water St: daily 1-ring performance, 152 rococo circus wagons, 19th C sideshow, calliope, etc. $7, seniors $5.60. 4 July, Baraboo has an oldtime circus parade with lions, tigers, 500 horses pulling the antique wagons. Glorious. In Baraboo, eat at the Main Cafe, 4th and Broadway, for superb homecooked food, Wisconsin veggies, dynamite French apple pie.

THE MOUNTAIN STATES

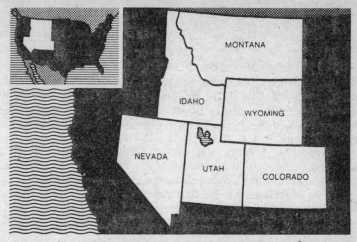

After the endless horizontality of the Midwest, the carefully mani-
cured patterns of fences and townships and agriculture, the landscape
of the Mountain States bursts upon you, young and rangy and wild as a
colt. These are exuberant mountains, still in their teens: the Rockies,
the San Juans, the Grand Tetons. Even now, crossing them is a pilgrimage, an event; just imagine how the sharp white beauty of their
teeth must have made pioneer hearts sink into their boots.

The topography doesn't limit itself to mountains, either. In this
six-state cluster, you are treated to geysers, glaciers, buttes, vast river
chasms, vivid canyons in paintbrush colours. The greater portion of
this beauty is protected in National Parks and Monuments, among
them: Rocky Mountain, Yellowstone, Craters of the Moon, Glacier,
Devil's Tower, Zion and Bryce Canyon. Counterpoint to all this
natural grandeur is provided by Las Vegas, Reno and Hoover Dam/
Lake Mead, without a doubt the most wondrously artificial trio of
spots on earth.

Las Vegas excepted, weather throughout the region is dry and hot
in summer, cold and snowy in winter. Even summer evenings can be
cold, so plan accordingly.

COLORADO

'They had a careless way of firing revolvers, sometimes at each other,
at other times quite miscellaneously—so I left'.—Horace Greeley,
1860

Like other mountain states, Colorado had a lusty, shoot-em-up past
filled with goldseekers, gold diggers, cattlemen and con men. Many

155

former mining towns remain, some recycled into ski resorts, others tarted up for tourism but still with settings of unparalleled grandeur.

Although its main revenues come from the manufacture of such mundanities as cement and luggage, Colorado is a prime tourist destination and with good reason. Known as the nation's backbone, the state has 54 peaks over 14,000 feet and terrain that averages 8600 feet above sea level.

The eastern section up to the Rockies has little to offer, being a monotony of rangeland, strewn with dun-coloured tumbleweeds and fenced 'hog tight, horse high and bull strong', as the cowpokes put it. Concentrate instead on the western half, where you find two National Parks, awesome scenery and an extraordinary display of summer wildflowers (some 5000 species). Colorado's chain of 24 hostels are among the best in the US and include ranches, historic hotels and ski lodges. Another plus are the five railroads that operate in the state, four of them narrow-gauge, all of them spectacularly scenic. For those willing to plan ahead, Colorado offers over 40 guest ranches with weekly rates from $250 up.

National Parks: Rocky Mountains
                   Mesa Verde

DENVER. Impressively situated against a backdrop of snowy peaks, Denver has metastasised into a huge manufacturing, transportation and distribution centre, complete with smog and urban sprawl. At the turn of the century, this was the Haight-Ashbury of America, a mecca for spiritualists, healers and New Thought advocates of all sorts. Today the mile-high city, in its role as a major Federal and military centre, churns out Strangelovian memoranda and bureaucratic gobbledygook instead. There is an indifferently modern, half-finished look about Denver: 'You get the impression the entire city centre is still under construction. Denver is to building sites what Dallas is to parking lots'.

ACCOMMODATION

Harris Hotel, 1544 Cleveland Pl, 825-6341. $14 single, $17 double, shared bath. Cafe, laundry, TV. Bus stop ½ block. 'Very conveniently situated.'

Kenmark Hotel, 532 17th at Welton, 623-6113. Singles $15 up, doubles $17 up. 'Dirty, hot.' May be sold for redevelopment so call first.

Regal 8 Inn, 3050 W 49th Ave, 455-8888. $20 single, $30 for 4 people. Air conditioning, pool, cafe, TV, phones. Bus stop 1 block. Discounts: senior, student, bus pass. 'Handy for hitching west.'

Park Hill Motor Hotel, 3975 Colorado Blvd, 333-4246. $16 single, $20 double with bath. 'Older style motel.'

11th Ave Hotel, 1112 Broadway, 839-5776. $14–$17 single, $17–$20 double. Bus stop in front, 4 blocks to Capitol. TV, phones. Very clean.

New Broadway Motel, 1620 S Broadway, 744-3361. $21 single, $22 double with bath.

Youth Hostel, 1452 Detroit St, 333-7672. Open June–Sept, $5 AYH. Bike rentals, kitchen, day storage, free pool nearby. An 1895 mansion, 'very friendly'. Take 15 bus from 17th St, 2 blocks from Greyhound. NB: so-called 'hostel' on Franklin is a Moonie lair—steer clear.*

B&B Colorado, PO Box 20596, Denver 80220, 333-3340. Single or double, $20 to $40, homes in Denver and vicinity, also Colorado Springs, Steamboat Springs, Boulder, Aspen, Durango and elsewhere.

FOOD
Try Rocky Mountain trout, the local specialty. This is also the home of 'Rocky Mt oysters', an indelicate dish made of French-fried bull testicles.

Casa Bonita, 6715 W Colfax. Cheap all-you-can-eat Mexican/American food in a 1100-seat 'village' rocking with gunfights, mariachis, puppets, cliff-divers, etc. 'A mini-mini Disneyland. We talked about it for days after.'

The Old Spaghetti Factory, 18th at Lawrence St, dinners with drink and dessert, $3–$6, in colourful surroundings.

Duffy's, 1635 Court Place near YMCA. 'Good service, excellent value.'

Cafe Nepenthes, 1416 Market St, veggie coffeehouse, live music most evenings.

OF INTEREST
Note: Denver's once-free museum situation is now disappointingly expensive.

Art Museum, 100 W 14th Ave, $2, students with ID $1. Striking, fortresslike tiled building, 6 floors of well-displayed art from totem poles to Picasso. 2nd floor, American Indian collection. 'Very good special exhibits.' Tue–Sat 9am–5pm, Wed till 9pm, Sun 1pm–5pm.

State Capitol, 14th St and Broadway. This dome has been gold-leafed 3 times since 1907, and you can ascend to the top free, closed weekends. Brass marker identifies surrounding peaks by name. The 13th step of the Capital is exactly 5280 feet (1 mile) above sea level.

US Mint, 320 W Colfax Ave, 837-3582. Free tours Mon–Fri 8am–3pm except at end of fiscal year, late June/July. Long lines, get there early. Stamps out 20 million coins a day: 'no free samples'.

Natural History Museum, City Park. Now $3, $1.50 seniors. 9am–4.30pm Mon–Sat, noon–4.30pm Sun. Recommended by readers for its detailed dioramas, meteorite and mineral collections, dinosaur displays. Fee for planetarium, adjacent. 'We thoroughly recommend the Laserium show.'

Larimer Square, 13th to 17th Sts. Denver's restored Victorian and highly commercial 'heart'. Bring brass or take a pass.

Nearby:
Coors Brewery, 13th and Ford, Golden, 277-2337. 15 bus from downtown. Free tours and suds, Mon–Sat 9am–4pm. Ask for short tour if you want to get right down to the Coors. 'Very nice people.'

Buffalo Bill Grave and Museum, follow I-70 west to turnoff near Lookout Mt. Open daily 9am–5pm, April–Oct, Tue–Sun 9am–4pm, otherwise. Lots of Wild West show and Pony Express artefacts of this flamboyant figure who symbolised the make-believe West. Among other things, you learn here that scalping was unknown to most Plains Indians until introduced by white scalp hunters. $1. Beautiful views from the summit.

ENTERTAINMENT
Free music: band concerts, City Park, nightly June–July. Also Wed performances in Aug by Denver Symphony Orchestra but 'arrive early to hear the orchestra, not the PA system'. Lunchtime concerts in fair weather at 17th and California also.

Red Rocks Amphitheater, SW edge of Greater Denver in Morrison. Summer classical, pop concerts in outdoor setting. 'Any concert here is a must—the most beautiful setting in the world with spectacular views over the prairies and Denver.'

The Folklore Center, 608 E 17th Ave. Denver has a strong folkie tradition; fans should visit this workshop/craft store/concern hall.

Hannigan's Greenhouse, 2120 S Ogden at Evans, 777-2189. 'Interesting, effective combination of horticulture, art and drama. First time I've seen a play performed in a greenhouse! Well worth a visit.' Near U of Denver campus.

INFORMATION
Visitors Bureau, 225 W Colfax Ave, 892-1112. Also at airport. Open daily summer, Mon–Sat winter. Walking tours, maps, useful info on city, state. 'Will book accommodation for you.'
Foreign Visitors Aid and Info, International Hospitality Center, 980 Grant St, 832-4234.

TRAVEL
Greyhound, 623-6111, and Trailways, 534-2291, 1055 19th St at Curtis. 'Helpful info desk in the bus station.' Trailways service across the Rockies from Denver to Salt Lake City is one of the most scenic routes in North America. 'Two routes to choose from. We went via Glenwood Springs and the scenery was certainly magnificent. The best part is the first 3 hours out of Denver.'
City bus, 778-6000. Downtown DART bus is 50¢, free during offpeak. Other buses 70¢ to $1, cheaper off-peak. $2 to Boulder, hourly from Greyhound depot.
Car rental: Cheap Heaps Rentacar, Colorado St; also Rentawreck, 3737 Klamath, 477-1635. Compacts Only, 3970 Monaco, 388-0948 has new cars, lower rates than Hertz, etc, but no longer offers unlimited mileage.
AAACON Driveaways, 1615 California St, 825-9191. Schaell Driveaway, 8962 W Colfax. 'Fantastic, friendly service, superb car.'
National Ride Center, 837-9738. Fee. 'I got a ride to San Francisco the same day for $12.'
AMTRAK, Union Station, 17th and Wynkoop Sts, 893-3911.
Denver and Rio Grande Western RR, also at Union Station, the only private railway through the Rockies, operates tri-weekly service to Salt Lake City via Glenwood Springs, connections to Ogden. Trip takes 15 hours, costs about $70, big discount with a foreign passport—show it. Enthusiasts break their flight across America to catch it; Mon, Thur, Sat, 7.30am departures. 'Fantastic views.' 'The best bit is to Glenwood Springs. May be worth going this far by train and then travelling by bus if you have a pass.'

ROCKY MOUNTAINS NATIONAL PARK. To the Indians and early trappers, these were the Shining Mountains, gleaming with silvery lakes, golden sunrises, blue-white glaciers and snowpacks. Later settlers prosaically dubbed them 'Rocky', but there is nothing prosaic about this wildlife-rich range of mountains and valleys crowned by a cross-section of the Continental Divide. Over 60 peaks are 12,000 feet or more and even the untrained eye can see the clear traces of glacial action and the five active glaciers that remain. **Longs Peak** at 14,256 feet is highest.

Be sure to take the **Trail Ridge Road**, which follows an old Ute and Arapaho trail along the very crest of a ridge. Along its 50 miles, you actually overlook 10,000-foot peaks, alpine lakes, spruce forests and wildflower-spangled meadows. Particularly delightful when the flowers are at their peak, June-July; indeed, snow keeps this and other park roads impassable until the end of May and from late October on.

Other routes lead hikers to a variety of long and short trails. One excellent trail is the 7½-mile hike from **Glacier Gorge** junction or **Bear**

Lake to Loch Vale, across to Haiyaha Lake and back via Dream and Nymph Lakes to the starting point. Horseback riding is also popular; animals can be rented at Estes Park and Grand Lake.

Roads enter the park from east and southwest. From the east (eg from Boulder and Denver), they converge on the town of **Estes Park**, about two miles from the main entrance. $2 part fee, $1 when Trail Ridge Road is closed.

ACCOMMODATION

Campgrounds in the park (the nearest to east entrance is about 2½ miles) cost $5 per night: Moraine Peak, Glacier Basin require booking; Aspen Glen, Longs Peak and Timber Peak are first-come, first-served. Free backcountry camping permits available through the park, Estes Park CO 80517. 'Glacier Basin has a bus to the main hiking area. Campsites have no shops or showers so it is difficult without a car.'
In and around Estes Park:
Commercial campgrounds outside park have showers and are nearer things. They may be more suitable if you are without wheels. This area is also rich in guest ranches: Wind River, Sylvan Vale, and Sky Corral Ranch are among the most reasonable.
Rocky Mt Motel, 945 Moraine Ave, 586-3485. Doubles from $22. 'Clean, carpeted, excellent views.'
Hotel Hupp, 109 E Elkhorn Ave, 586-5800. Singles with shared bath from $13. 'Cheapest in town. Shabby, clean, comfortable.'
H-Bar-G Ranch Hostel (YH), 6 miles from Estes Park at the head of Devil's Gulch, 586-3688. $4.50 with pass, memberships for sale at hostel for $14. A former dude ranch with splendid views, 75 dorms in log cabins. Bring your own food. Tennis, volleyball, BBQ facilities. Unlimited stay. Lou the warden is very good about picking up/delivering hostelers to park, etc. Closed Labor Day through May. 'Exceptionally good place, you'll want to stay longer than you intended.' 'The best.' 'To book ahead, go to Denver Visitors Center; they may save you the $1.50 phone charge.'
Shadowcliff AYH, Grand Lake (SW entrance to park), 627-9966. $4.75 members, $2 get 3-day pass for non-members. Open 1 June–10 Oct. 32 beds. Kitchen. 'Brilliant Scandinavian-style hostel cliff overlooking lake. Nice village too, a western town with a real saloon bar—the Lariat.'
Elkhorn Lodge, 600 W Elkhorn, 586-4415. ½ mile from Estes Park. $13 single $16 double.

FOOD

The Gaslight Pub, opposite Estes Park bus depot. Disco, darts, large and inexpensive portions. 'Excellent.'

TRAVEL

The best way of getting to and from park and seeing it fully is by car; see car rentals under Denver.
Gray Line runs buses from Denver and Boulder to Estes Park; around $13 one way, $25 return. Also a 10½-hour tour from Denver, about £35.
Hitching to and in the park is good.

BOULDER. Although it's become too popular for its own good, Boulder still makes a scenic and lively alternative to Denver for explorations in northern Colorado. A student mecca, at its grooviest along the Pearl Avenue Mall: 'Fun on Sundays, clowns, magic shows, good eats, lots of young people.' 'Quite a magical place and altogether more interesting than Denver.'

ACCOMMODATION
Chautauqua Association, 900 Baseline Rd, 442-3282. 'About $30/night for 2 adjoining rooms plus bath in lodge. Weekly rates, cottages also. Worth the money for superb views of Boulder, the mountains. Very friendly, peaceful.'

Wagon Wheel Motel, Salina Star Rt, 2½ miles west of town, 444-0382. Singles $24 up, doubles $26 up.

Youth Hostel, 1107 12th St, at College Ave, 442-0522. $6.26 summer, $7.75 winter AYH. $2 rental, $5 deposit for linen, blanket, etc. Kitchen. 20 minutes to mountains. 'Friendly, relaxed.' 'Ill-equipped kitchen.' 'Rather cramped.'

FOOD
Boulder is the only city in the US to own its own glacier, which serves as a delicious water supply. Drink up! Other local specialties: Hagen-Daaz ice cream and the infamous Packerburgers, served at U of Colorado's Alfred Packer Memorial Grill, named after the only man ever convicted of cannibalism in the US. Alf's orgy took place in 1886, when he and 5 others were trapped by blizzards at Slumgullion Pass for 60 days. Alf got 17 years from the judge, who said: 'There were only 6 Democrats in Hinsdale County and you son-of-a-bitch, you ate 5 of them!' Postscript: Packer became a vegetarian after release from prison. Packer Grill has other cheap eats, too.

Colacci's, 816 Main. Excellent Italian food, huge portions—shared.

Bananas, 3116 Walnut. 'Fun place to eat—natural ingredients, bright atmosphere, menus the shape and colour of bananas.'

OF INTEREST
Arapaho Glacier, 28 miles west. 1 mile long and 100–500 ft thick, the Arapaho moves at a sedate 11 to 27 inches per year. Public hike each Aug to the glacier, community breakfast and dinner also.

National Center for Atmospheric Research, 1850 Table Mesa Dr. Free slide show and look at operating weather station and computer room, daily.

U of Colorado. Ersatz Spanish architecture, big party school. Fiske Planetarium, on campus: 'Worth a visit, especially the laser show.' Various cheap eating places on campus too.

Ghost and mining towns all around, including Ward, now a commune, and Central City, restored for tourism.

ENTERTAINMENT
Blue Note Cafe, 1116 Pearl. Nightly 7.30pm, cover varies for jazz, occasional big names.

The Mall, Pearl St. 'Superb spectacles any summer evening—all free.'

TRAVEL
Great Western Rentacar, 3445 Walnut, 449-3902. 'Cheapest in town.'

COLORADO SPRINGS.
Founded by bonanza kings and intended as a resort and retirement centre, the Springs grew to become second largest city and a military headquarters for the US Air Force Academy, NORAD and Ft Carson. Trash features like motel sprawl cannot dim the glory of its setting at the base of Pike's Peak. Constant winds at the Peak blow the snow like a banner, an exhilarating sight. The city makes a good base to explore Garden of the Gods, Cripple Creek and Royal Gorge.

ACCOMMODATION

Buffalo Lodge, 2 El Paso Blvd, 634-2851. Singles $16–$20, doubles $18–$24, kitchen $3 extra. AC, pool, TV, bus stop 1 block.

Youth Hostel, 17 N Farragut Ave, 471-2938 or 634-9657. $5.25 members, need sleeping bag. Some private, semi-private twin bed rooms. Kitchen, laundry. 1 mile from Greyhound. 'Take local bus—it's all uphill.' 'Most luxurious hostel in world!' No curfew at night.

Motel 6, 3228 N Chestnut St, 471-2340. $16 single, $20 double. View of Pike's Peak from rooms. AC, pool.

Indian Hostel Annex, 471-2938 or 632-5056. 24 beds, $5.25 year-round. Outings to Inter-tribal village, 10 miles away, for dancing, music, tribal customs. 1½ miles from Greyhound.

Outlook Lodge, Box 5, Green Mt Falls 80819. 684-2302. 15 miles from Colorado Springs, no bus service. Cosy 1889 Victorian lodge at the foot of Pike's Peak, single $23 up, 3–4 to one room, $32. Includes continental breakfast. Open Memorial-Labor Day.

OF INTEREST

Pike's Peak; Lon Chaney of horror movie fame was once a guide to this 14,110-ft peak. To walk or ride horseback, take the Barr National Recreation Trail. The 18-mile auto highway ($3 toll) climbs 7039 ft; recommended for experienced mountain drivers only—but what a view. Lunchroom at top. Pike's Peak cog railway, 685-1045, open May–Oct is $12.50, but the Manitou Incline Railway ($3.50) is more than enough for most. Both at 515 Ruxton Ave.

Garden of the Gods, NW of Colorado Springs off Highway 24. 940 acres of stunning red sandstone formations, especially striking at sunrise or sunset. Inspirational vibes; *America the Beautiful* was written here. Free. 'Outstanding scenic beauty—next best thing to Grand Canyon.' 'Well worth a visit.'

Nearby:

Canon City and Royal Gorge: The town from which Tom Mix launched his cowboy career and also known through the films *Cat Ballou* and *True Grit*. Little of interest except the art shop at the Colorado State Penitentiary and Royal Gorge, site of the highest suspension bridge in the world, an acrophobe's nightmare. Lousy with tourist claptrap of all sorts (including the sickening aerial tram), but the viewpoint is stupendous and free.

Cripple Creek, on the opposite side of Pike's Peak. Reached either by the picturesque but difficult Gold Camp Road, 36 miles of gravel and curves (Teddy Roosevelt called it 'the trip that bankrupts the English language') or 18 miles via Highways 24 and 67. In its heyday, Cripple Creek yielded more than $25 million in gold in one year and had the honour of being called 'a foul cesspool' by Carry Nation for its merry brothels and 5 opera houses. Despite tourism the place has considerable charm. Don't miss the salty cemetery (wry epitaphs, heart-shaped madam's tombstone, etc) and the superlative melodrama, twice daily Tue–Sun, June–Aug. Stay overnight at the Imperial Hotel, 689-2922, a Victorian relic with shared bath singles from $17, there to partake of the melodrama downstairs and the excellent buffet dinners. The Mollie Kathleen gold mine ($4.50) is 'very worthwhile—free gold ore' and the 4-mile roundtrip on the narrow-gauge Cripple Creek and Victor RR are fun (from museum on Bennett Ave, June–Oct).

ASPEN. 210 miles west of Denver on Highway 82, Aspen is a tasteful, beautiful ski resort and classical music festival site, set amid National Forests. Most things cost the earth in Aspen but reasonable accommodation can be found here, unlike the case with its patrician sister resort, Vail.

ACCOMMODATION
NB: rates are highest in winter, lowest spring and autumn.
Mountain Chalet, 333 E Durant, 925-7797. Dorm rooms (4 bunks) $18–$21, other rooms much higher. Hearty breakfast included. Pool, sauna, fireplace lounge in attractive alpine lodge. Senior discounts.
St Moritz Lodge, 334 W Hyman, 925-3220. Dorms $15 to $20, shared bath, full lodge privileges. Partial kitchen. Library, sauna, pool.
Copper Horse, 328 W Main, 925-7525. 'Very clean, modern, good facilities.' $15 dorm, includes full breakfast. Single with shared bath $23 (summer), double $27.
Endeavor Lodge, 905 E Hopkins, 925-2847. Dorms $15 winter, $12 summer, $10 otherwise. Jacuzzi, kitchen, lounge. Bus stop 2 blocks. Relaxed.
Highlands Inn, 1650 Maroon Creek Rd, 1½ miles from town, 925-5050. With AYH, dorms are $9 (summer), $13 (winter); without AYH, $12 to $18. Jacuzzi, sauna, light breakfast, pool, free bus to Aspen, many amenities. Also 'hiker' rooms for 2, $25–$30 summer.
Camping: free at E Maroon, 1 mile NW of Aspen on Highway 82. 13 sites. Also in the White River National Forest, which covers nearly all of Pitkin County.

FOOD
Recommended: Pour la France on Mill: 'Sit on street and watch the world go by'; Hickory House on W Main: 'Good breakfast, lunch, reasonably priced' and Burger Bros on Hopkins: 'Best value in Aspen.'

OF INTEREST
Chairlift, 1 hour to 15,000 ft. $8, closed after Labor Day till start of ski season. 'Stupendous views.'
Aspen Music Festival, 9 weeks late June–Aug. Rivals Tanglewood's Berkshire Festival in prestige and importance. 'The combination of setting, fresh air and music blew my mind.' Many open rehearsals and other free events.

INFORMATION/TRAVEL
Chamber of Commerce, 925-1940.
Trailways between Denver and Salt Lake City stops at both Aspen and Vail. Re the latter: 'Extremely expensive lodgings and no campgrounds.'

ACROSS WESTERN COLORADO. The northern most route will take you throuth **Steamboat Springs**, an expensive ski resort ('fun and friendly—great skiing'), and ultimately to **Dinosaur National Monument**, which overlaps into Utah. The monument presents striking and lonely canyon vistas (used by Butch Cassidy and Co as a hideout) and the fossil remains of stegosaurus, brontosaurus and other big guys, exposed in bas relief on the quarry face, with more being excavated before your eyes. 'Not at all gimmicky; fascinating to anyone even vaguely interested in paleontology or geology.' NB: quarry, visitor centre is in Utah; see that section.

The major route west is the Interstate 70, which passes through the Eisenhower tunnel (longest in world), Eagle and **Glenwood Springs**, an invigorating place to pause for a dip in the world's largest open-air thermal pool. Wyatt Earp's sidekick at the OK Corral, Doc Holliday, lies buried here, his headstone reading: 'He died in bed.' The Interstate continues its scenic paralleling of the Colorado River all the way to Grand Junction, the last town of any size in Colorado and gateway to the towering spires and canyon wilderness of **Colorado National Monument** ($1 per car, 50¢ on foot, camping available).

Further south is the **Black Canyon of the Gunnison National Monument** ('a very special place—deer wander regularly through campsites') near Montrose, and the high adventure of the journey through Ouray and Telluride to Silverton and well south to Durango. This stretch is served by Trailways and is highly recommended. **Ouray**, the 'Switzerland of America', is noted for the Camp Bird Mine, which produced $24 million for the Walsh family and remains productive today. With some of the loot, papa Walsh bought his daughter the Hope Diamond.

'Try getting a ride in the back of a pickup truck between Ouray and **Telluride**. The views are spectacular, the road, hair-raising'. Dizzy Gillespie once said, 'If Telluride ain't paradise, then heaven can wait', as wait it did for Butch Cassidy, who pulled his first bank job here. Its interesting buildings from the mining era have earned it National Historic Landmark designation. Telluride is also well-known as a ski resort (inexpensive, too) and festival centre, including the remarkable Labor Day Film Festival (now ranked second only to Cannes) and summer music events from bluegrass to reggae.

ACCOMMODATION
Camping at Dinosaur National Monument, $3; motels at nearby Dinosaur, CO and Vernal, Utah. See also Utah.

At Glenwood Springs: Rex Hotel, 420 7th St, 945-6248. $14–$16 singles, $18–$20 doubles, cheap weekly rates, some kitchens. Senior discounts near bus stop, rail depot.

Glenwood Hot Springs Lodge, 401 N River Rd, 945-6571. Older main lodge has cheap rooms with central showers, $17 and up. 'Have to share a double bed, but rooms are clean and service friendly.' Site of largest mineral pool, plus cafe.

At Grand Junction: Melrose Hotel, 337 Colorado Ave, 242-9636. $12–$16 single, $16–$20 double, 1½ blocks from Trailways. 'Clean and very friendly.'

At Montrose: Mesa Hotel, 10 N Townsend, 249-3773. $10–$15 singles, $12–$16 doubles, TV. 1 block to bus. Discounts for multiple night stays. Run by friendly multilingual Basque couple. 'Best value I've seen in North America.'

At Ouray: Baker's Manor Guest House, 317 2nd St, 325-4574. $16 single, $18 doubles, all with shared bath. Call for street directions. Discounts for family, multinight stays. 'Clean, very friendly.'

At Telluride: New Sheridan Hotel, 231 W Colorado Ave, 728-4351. Doubles from $30 in this restored opera house with a bar that appeared in *Butch Cassidy*. Discounts for offseason, seniors.

Oak St Inn, 134 N Oak St, 728-3383. Variously a Methodist Church and a dance hall, now a comfortable lodge with communal saunas, fireplace lobby, restaurant/bar. From $16 shared bath (cheaper with AYH card); higher in winter, when rates are by room only. 'Simple but clean rooms. Absolutely worth staying in Telluride.'

Dahl Haus, 122 S Oak, 728-4158. Singles $20 up, doubles $28 up, priciest in winter. Light breakfast included, winter. Also homecooked dinners for small charge. Close to shuttle bus, ski lift. Homey.

Sundance's San Juan Boardello, 206 E Colorado, 728-4819. Per-room rates, $25 to $30; continental breakfast. Antique building where Butch Cassidy actually slept. Coffee, juices served at bar. Nice atmosphere with library, use of stereo and records, lobby with fireplace open all night.

At Silverton: Teller House Pension, 1250 Greene St, 387-5423. $19 single, doubles $25 up. Hostel dorms $10 (need bag); with AYH, $7. Rates include full breakfast with meat at French Bakery, part of Teller House, Bus stop 2 blocks. Rates same year-round. 'Excellent YH—big breakfast. Town worth visiting.'

OF INTEREST
Glenwood Springs Hot Pool, Glenwood Lodge. Therapy pool heated to 120 degrees, swimming pool to 100. $4, after 9pm, $2.50. Water chute costs $3. 'Exhilarating.' 'Especially superb at night.'
Watch the **Santa Fe train** pass through about 9pm. 'Incredibly long and very atmospheric in the darkness.'
Million-dollar highway, between Ouray and Silverton. A 6-mile stretch, numbered among the most spectacular in the US.
Silverton-Durango Narrow-Gauge RR, 247-2733. See Durango, Of Interest.

TRAVEL
Dinosaur National Monument. No direct transit, but Trailways and Frontier Airlines serve Vernal, Utah, where you can rent a car or hitch.
Glenwood Springs: served by Denver and Rio Grande Western RR and by Trailways. 'Day trip from Denver; take Trailways 10am service to Glenwood Springs. Glorious Rocky Mt scenery along the way. If the bus is not late, you arrive at 3pm. Swim, eat strawberry waffles at the Pancake House behind Trailways and catch 7.35pm bus back to Denver, arriving at 11.55pm. A long day, but worth it.'
Gunnison Canyon: locals say hitching isn't good. Ben's Taxis from Montrose is pricey (about $50), but go as a group and negotiate.
Ouray and south: Trailways route from Grand Junction to Durango passes through Montrose, Ouray and Silverton. 'Unparalleled scenery; exceeds the Denver-Salt Lake City run. Canyons through 11,000-ft red rock mountains. Best from mid-Sept when aspens have changed to gold.' 'Wrecked cars 500 ft below, left as warning to other motorists.'
Telluride: jeep trail to Ouray over 13,000-ft Imogen Pass: 'Astounding'.

DURANGO. Located in the southwest corner of the state, Durango is as authentically western as a Stetson hat (which incidentally was invented in Colorado in 1863). Billy the Kid and other outlaw types used to make Durango their headquarters; before that, the Spaniards came looking for gold, found it and lost it again when local Ute Indians got fed up with them. Western hospitality is common currency here, markedly so at the local youth hostel. Durango's location 40 miles east of Mesa Verde makes it a natural base for sightseeing.

ACCOMMODATION
8th Ave Motel, 343 8th Ave, 259-3598. $14.50–$24 single, $16–$32 doubles. Kitchenettes, TV. Bus stop 1 block. Discounts for midweek, offseason. 'Clean, comfortable, friendly.'
Silver Spur Motor Hotel, 3416 N Main, 247-5552. Single $14 up, double $16 up.
Mt Shadows Motel, 3255 Main, 247-5285. $15–$25 single, $15–$35 doubles.
Youth Hostel, 543 E 2nd Ave, 247-5477 or 9905. $6.25 summer, $7.25 winter for AYH. 3rd night free if you produce a copy of this Guide. 1 block to train, 9 blocks to bus. After-midnight bus arrivals should contact Art Olson through the station manager and he'll pick up. 'Olsons very friendly, willing to help.' 'Without a doubt the best hostel Ive seen—clean, well-equipped, nice garden and BBQ.' Hostel rents bikes, arranges trips, knows of any temp jobs going and in general serves as the social/cultural nerve centre of Durango. 'Terrific atmosphere—don't miss it.'

Camping: free at Jay-Cee Campground, near downtown across river. 'Nobody asked for a fee—others had same experience.'

OF INTEREST
The main local attraction is the *circa* 1882 **narrow-gauge railway to Silverton**. The train runs 45 miles and climbs 3000 ft through the sawtoothed San Juan Mts. Round trip takes all day, costs $20 (more if you reserve seat in the elegant parlour car). Runs twice daily, early May through mid-Oct, weather permitting. Some advise buying ticket day prior or booking well in advance, 247-2733. Others say arriving at station at 7.15am suffices. Alternatively, take the am Trailways bus to Silverton and then catch the train back to Durango, paying on board. 'Plenty of seats on south-bound journey.' 'Beautiful scenery, worth every dollar.'
Great Western Museum, 4 miles north of Durango on Highway 550. Adults $1. Open 8am–5pm daily. 'Private museum of a lifelong packrat. Fun.'

FOOD
Panhandler Pies, 948 Main. 'Reasonable, friendly.'
Durango Diner, 957 Main 'Cheaper than Panhandler, good chili.'
If you're feeling flush, try fresh trout at the Palace Restaurant.

ENTERTAINMENT
Clancy's Pub, the Golden Slipper and Farquarts are all recommended for boozing and live music.
Diamond Circle Theater in the Strater Hotel has well thought-of period theatre, Mon–Sat, June–Sept, about $7.50.

TRAVEL
Durango is served by Frontier and Pioneer Airlines from Denver.
Durango Dodge does the cheapest car rentals.
Trailways schedules to Durango are infrequent, so plan ahead.
The hostel tells us: 'We try to organise groups for shared-cost trips to Mesa Verde, hiring a car probably being the best way to see the park, although hitching works about 80% of the time'.
San Juan Tours is expensive ($20) and restrictive, but fine for the unadventurous. San Juan Tours leave Durango RR station 8.30am, return 3.30pm. Reserve ahead, 247-2733. 'Worth it.'
The Trailways run to Cedar City, Utah, is enthusiastically recommended. Departs 12.40am, but daylight after Green River: 'Magnificent canyons, buttes, mountains and desert, and when you arrive you've got Zion and Bryce Canyon to explore'.

MESA VERDE NATIONAL PARK. 'Far above me, set in a great cavern in the face of the cliff, I saw a little city of stone, asleep.'—Willa Cather.

No matter how limited your tourist plans for the West might be, a visit to Mesa Verde, the finest of the prehistoric Indian culture pre-serves, is a must. The eight-square-mile area rises 2000 feet above the surrounding plain and is gashed by many deep canyons. On the surface of the tableland now covered in junipers and piñon trees, the Indians once tilled their squash, beans and corn, while from the depths of the canyon they drew their drinking water from springs. Originally they built their pueblos on the surface, but later for security dug their homes into the sheer canyon walls.

The largest of the cliff dwellings is **Cliff Palace**, which looks like a walled medieval town and contains more than 200 living rooms, 23 kivas and eight floor levels, all within a single cave. Scattered throughout the 20 large canyons and numerous side canyons are many hundred ruins. The dwellings were occupied from the beginning of the first millenium and were vacated in 1276 after the failure of the crops and the drying up of the springs.

To really enjoy the park, it is essential that you first obtain and read the park service pamphlet giving a brief and interesting account of the centuries of human habitation here. A visit to the museum, with its extensive exhibits of tools, clothing, pottery and dioramas depicting the Anasazi way of life, is also a must for understanding the culture.

Although **Cortez** is closest to Mesa Verde, Durango (see above) is preferable—transport is more frequent, accommodation more varied, and Durango itself a better place to be. Nevertheless, a few details on Cortez and environs follow.

ACCOMMODATION
In Cortez and vicinity:
Hotel Cortez, 243 E Main, next to Trailways, 565-3431. $12–$19 singles, $17–$20 doubles. Cafe, storage. Weekly rates. 'Fine rooms, very clean.'
El Capri Motel, 2110 W Broadway, 565-3764. Singles $25 up, doubles $33 up. AC, pool, cable TV. Offseason discounts. 2 miles to bus depot.
Wilson's Pinto Bean Farm, Box 252, Yellow Jacket CO 81335. Call 562-3052. The Wilsons will meet Trailways at Cortez. A working farm with animals, orchards and huge Indian ruins—you're allowed to look for arrowheads and potsherds. Room, 3 meals daily, friendly and knowledgeable hosts, all for $175/week, less for teens, kids. 40 miles from Four Corners.
At Mesa Verde:
Far View Motor Lodge, from $32 single/double. Rooms have private balconies with a panorama of 4 states. Cafeteria. Open mid-May to mid-Oct. Best to reserve. 529-4221.
Park campsites, $2. Showers, store, laundry. 'Gets very cold at night; need warm sleeping bag as well as tent.'

OF INTEREST
Four Corners. The meeting of Colorado, Utah, Arizona and New Mexico is commemorated with a rather ugly slab of inscribed concrete upon which countless folk sprawl to have their pictures taken. But in summer, Indians from Navajo and other tribes come in their pickups and sell their handcrafted wares, often at much better prices than you'll find in the tourist centres or trading posts.

TRAVEL
Cortez is reached by Trailways at the most unearthly wee morning hours. You can also fly in on Frontier Airlines.
Bus to the park (passes not valid) departs 7am, returns around 5pm, costs $8. Within park, free shuttle buses to Wetherill Mesa, June through Aug. Check all timetables for the park in advance.
'Hitch or rent bikes to see park attractions'; rentals at Spruce Tree Terrace, mid-May to mid-Oct, $2/hour.

IDAHO

Rugged with mountains (50 peaks over 10,000 feet), slashed with wild
rivers and deep chasms (including the Snake River and Hell's Canyon,
deepest in the US), dappled with fishing lakes and hot springs, Idaho
is like Colorado without the people or the public transit. The state
was settled by French trappers, later by a mix of Basques, Mormons
and WASPS who came to run livestock, mine silver, log timber and
grow lots of delicious Idaho spuds. Idahoans are a taciturn lot; interesting, then, that the most famous figures associated with the state
were noted for eloquence. One was Chief Joseph of the Nez Perce
Indians, who surrendered by saying: 'From where the sun now stands,
I will fight no more forever.' The other, writer Ernest Hemingway,
was an adoptive Idahoan who chose to live, write (parts of *For Whom
the Bell Tolls*), commit suicide and be buried in Idaho.

The most scenic section is the panhandle, located along the northern route taken by Greyhound and crowned by the shattering beauty
of Lake Coeur d'Alene—well worth a stop. The southerly route takes
you within 80 miles of the Craters of the Moon and along parts of the
Snake River but is minimally interesting otherwise.

National Park: Yellowstone (though this is mostly in Wyoming)
Important note: for main entrances to park, see Montana.

IDAHO FALLS. A dull spot noted for its potatoes, chinchilla ranches
and little else, the city is 100 miles from Yellowstone and 86 from
Craters of the Moon. You would be wiser to break your journey at
Pocatello (better connections to Craters, also close to Ft Hall,
headquarters for the Shoshone, Nez Perce and other Indian tribes) or
at **Twin Falls**, which sits on a far prettier stretch of the Snake River;
nearby are the Shoshone Ice Caves and Craters of the Moon is 80
miles.

ACCOMMODATION
In Idaho Falls: Thrifty Lodge, 255 E St, 523-2960. Doubles under $30.
Motel 6, 1448 W Broadway, 523-9265. $16 single, $20 double, pool.
Quality Inn Westbank, 475 River Parkway, 523-8000. Singles $16 up, doubles $20
up. Overlooks Snake River.
Near Pocatello: Motel 6, 291 W Burnside Ave, Chubbuck, 237-6667. Same prices as
above.
At Twin Falls: Motel 6, 1472 Blue Lake Blvd N, 733-6663. On Snake River, 3 miles
from downtown. Same prices as above.

OF INTEREST
Pocatello. At Ft Hall, the Shoshone, Nez Perce and Bannock Indians hold various
Sun Dances and other festivals July and Aug. Buffalo barbeques, too.

TRAVEL
Greyhound links Yellowstone, Idaho Falls, Pocatello, Twin Falls and Boise west to
Oregon. Bus service also from Idaho Falls to Grand Teton National Park in

Wyoming. No public transit to Craters of the Moon, but Salmon River Stages runs 3 times weekly from Pocatello to Arco, 18 miles outside park.

CRATERS OF THE MOON NATIONAL MONUMENT. A grotesque grey landscape of extinct cones, gaping fissures and cave-like lava tubes, the most extravagant of which can be seen from one 7-mile loop road in the 83-square-mile preserve. US moon astronauts practiced their rockhounding skills here. Camping $2/night on very hard ground, mid-April to mid-October. No transit to park; see Travel, above, for ways and means. NB: this chilling region, which looks like the day after an atomic attack, is appropriately the home for much nuclear testing and tinkering. Keep within park limits!

COEUR D'ALENE. Set on an utterly lovely lake whose depth and fire remind one of sapphires, this little city with the poetic name is 32 miles east of Spokane, Washington. Lake excursions from the city dock; fishing is wonderful.

ACCOMMODATION
Garden Motel, 1808 Northwest Blvd, 664-2743. Singles $15 up, doubles under $30. Cheaper in winter. Colour TV, indoor pool. 'Most welcome, helpful, clean. Very scenic area.'
B&B: a nice home with $16 single, $22 double through Northwest B&B: see Accommodation Background for address, details.
Camping: free on east shore of lake at Bell Bay.

MONTANA

Touted as the 'Big Sky' country, Montana is an immense, Western-feeling state, rich in coal, copper, sapphires and chrome, a grower of wheat and cattle, and a regular record-breaker when it comes to the hottest, coldest, windiest and snowiest weather in the US. And wouldn't you know it—Gary Cooper was born here. Yup.

Its only sizeable minority are the Indians—about 30,000 Crows, Northern Cheyennes, Blackfeet, Flatheads, Grox Ventres, Chippewas and Crees. And Montana's the place where the Indians put paid to the whites, not only at the Little Bighorn but at the Battles of Big Hole and Rosebud as well. Indians on the seven reservations offer numerous events and facilities to non-Indians and are generally very friendly, possibly because racism isn't as rampant here as elsewhere in the US.

While in Montana, try to catch a rodeo, and don't overlook the work of artist Charles M Russell, whose cowboy days are brilliantly depicted in oils and bronze at Great Falls, Helena and other towns.

One of America's great train journeys is the *Empire Builder* route across northern Montana, especially the portion that loops around

Glacier National Park—both east- and westbound trips are in daylight.

National Parks: Glacier, Yellowstone (mostly in Wyoming)
Important note: while most of Yellowstone lies in Wyoming, three of the main entrances and the gateway towns of West Yellowstone and Gardiner are in Montana and are best reached via Greyhound from Montana cities or from Idaho Falls, Idaho. Read *both* Montana and Wyoming sections when trip planning for the park.

BUTTE. A company town, dominated by the giant Anaconda Copper Company. Its locale in southwestern Montana makes it a good base to explore the ghost towns and Indian battlefields roundabout.

ACCOMMODATION
Grand Hotel, 124 W Broadway, 723-5486. Near bus depot. Singles $11–$17, doubles $16–$22. Large rooms, comfortable and clean. 'Terrific hotel, friendly owners.'
Finlen Motor Inn, Broadway at Wyoming, downtown, 723-5461. $20 single/ doubles.

OF INTEREST
1½ hour **pit tours of the Kelley mine**, at 1pm Mon–Fri, June–Aug. Free but registration by 12.30pm, call 949-5595, is needed.
Berkeley Mine observation platform has free viewing of the pit and surrounding countryside till 8.30pm, on Park St East.
Mining museums at both the College of Mineral Science and nearby on Park St; both free, open daily Memorial-Labor Day.
Luigi's Bar, 1826 Harrison Ave, Mon–Sat till 2am. A world of weirdness, presided over a local showman/madman Luigi. Great entertainment for price of a drink.
Nearby:
Anaconda Mining Co in Anaconda. Free tours of world's largest smelter and 585-ft Big Stack, begin at main gate twice daily, Mon–Fri, June–Aug.
Ghost towns. About 60 miles SE of Butte is **Nevada City**, a restored village of 50 buildings, reached by car or the Alder Gulch Short Line train, and open daily 8am–8pm in summer only. A combo ticket for train and museum is $3, $2.50 one way. 'Don't miss the deafening collection of organs, pianolas, etc, and the old RR carriages.' 'Costs $1, lots of patience to pan for gold outside RR station, to end up with a few tiny specks of the yellow stuff.' Sister city to Nevada is **Virginia City**, a highly commercialised enterprise, 2 miles away.
    Between Virginia City and **Bannack** (Montana's first boom town and territorial capital) was the 'Vigilante Trail'. In 6 months, 190 murders were committed here and gang activity got so notorious that miners secretly formed a vigilante committee; when they caught up with the gang leader, it turned out to be their Sheriff, who was duly hanged on his very own gallows. 'Bannack: the best old Western town I've seen. Still has gallows, jail. View from top of Boot Hill unbelievable.' **Castle** (Calamity Jane's home town) and **Elkhorn** (300 old buildings still standing) are other interesting destinations.
Big Hole National Battlefield. Site of the Nez Perce victory over US troops in 1877. Chief Joseph and his band were in flight to Canada, having refused to accept reservation life. Pursued by troops, they fought courageously and intelligently under Joseph's masterful military leadership. Despite their win, they were pursued and ultimately beaten at Bear Paw, less than 40 miles from the Canadian border. Big Hole A/V programme is free, open daily.

BILLINGS.

BILLINGS. Largest and most sophisticated city, Billings is on the Yellowstone River and makes a good stopover point for travellers from North or South Dakota enroute to Yellowstone.

ACCOMMODATION
Hotel Lincoln, 2520 1st Ave N, near Greyhound, 245-8000. Singles $13–$16, doubles $19–$22. 'Excellent.'
Eastern Montana College, 657-2333. 15 June–1 Sept, shared bath rms for $10 single, open to general public. Cheap weekly rates.
B&B: through B&B League, an unusual host home ($25 single, $35 double) owned by a western author/historian. See Accommodation Background for details.

OF INTEREST
Chief Black Otter Trail. North of the city: spectacular views, Indian scout grave, and a monument to settlers.
Western Heritage Center, 2822 Montana Ave. Closed Mon. Worthwhile collection of exhibits on Calamity Jane, Gen Custer, Indians. Donations encouraged.
Pompey's Pillar, 30 miles east of Billings. A National Landmark along the Lewis and Clark trail. Huge sandstone formation 'signed' by Capt William Clark in 1806 and named by him in honour of Sacajawea's son Pompey. $1, seniors 75¢, open daily 8am–6pm, June–Aug.

INFORMATION/TRAVEL
Visitors Bureau, 306 N Broadway, 252-8855.
'I thoroughly recommend the Greyhound run from Billings to Bismarck, ND— superb views of Roosevelt National Park; our driver described points of interest enroute.'

CUSTER BATTLEFIELD NATIONAL MONUMENT.

CUSTER BATTLEFIELD NATIONAL MONUMENT. Here on the Little Big Horn River, just under 60 miles east of Billings, General George Custer imprudently attacked the main camp of the Sioux, Hunkpapas and others. The date was 25 June 1876. 'I did not think it possible that any white man would attack us, so strong as we were,' said one Oglala chief. A Cheyenne recalled that after he had taken a swim in the river he 'looked up the Little Bighorn toward Sitting Bull's camp. I saw a great dust rising. It looked like a whirlwind. Soon a Sioux horseman came rushing into camp shouting: "Soldiers come! Plenty white soldiers!"'

Before they could be moved to safety downstream, several women and children were killed, including the family of warrior Gall. 'It made my heart bad. After that I killed all my enemies with the hatchet.' Brilliantly led by Sitting Bull and Crazy Horse, the Indians routed the soldiers and surrounded Custer's column, killing them all. Who killed Custer is not known. Sitting Bull described his last moments: His hair 'was the colour of the grass when the frost comes. Where the last stand was made, the Long Hair stood like a sheaf of corn with all the ears fallen around him.'

ACCOMMODATION
Nearest camping is 3 miles west on Crow land at Little Bighorn Camp. Also rooms at the Sun Lodge Motel, 638-2651, also Crow-run.

TRAVEL
Bus service from Billings, 65 miles away, to Hardin (15 miles west of battlefield) and the Crow Agency, 3 miles away.
In Hardin, you can rent cars at Hardin Auto, 665-1211.

GREAT FALLS. Home base for Charles M Russell and an outstanding collection of his work; also home base for a fearsome array of Minuteman missiles at Malstrom AFB. A likeable hick town, home of the August State Fair and a useful stopover if heading north towards Canada or Glacier National Park. (Kalispell, the western gateway to Glacier, is actually a better way to Glacier.)

ACCOMMODATION
Elmore Motel, 6 6th St S, 452-8595. $18 single with bath, $20 double. 2 blocks from bus depot. 'Clean, safe, friendly people.'
Rainbow Hotel, 20 3rd St, 727-8200. Downtown. Singles $18 up.
YWCA, 220 2nd St N, 452-1315. Women only. Kitchen. $8; weekly rates.

OF INTEREST
Russell Studio and House, 1201 4th Ave N, 452-7369. Cowboy painter Russell lived and worked here. Outstanding collection of his paintings, bronzes and wax models. Daily 15 May–30 Sept; Tue–Sun rest of year. $1.50 for museum, donation for his studio.

TRAVEL
Buses twice daily to East Glacier Park.

BROWNING. About 30 miles east of Glacier/Waterton National Park, Browning is the headquarters for the Blackfeet Indian tribe, a handsome and hospitable people. Their 40-unit teepee village, museum, campground and other facilities are well worth spending time in.

OF INTEREST
Museum of the Plains Indian, ½ mile west of town at Highways 2 and 89. Free, daily June–Sept. Covers Indian history from pre-Columbian days to modern times. 'Intelligently set out and meticulously explained. Highly recommended.'
The Blackfeet Indians celebrate Indian Days the 2nd weekend in July; ceremonies, dances.

TRAVEL
Browning is served by AMTRAK's *Empire Builder* when East Glacier station is closed in winter.

GLACIER/WATERTON NATIONAL PARK. Glacier in Montana and Waterton in Alberta together form the Glacier/Waterton International Peace Park, the first in the world to cross an international boundary. The park is the rival of Yosemite, Yellowstone and Grand Teton for scenic beauty and the affection of enthusiasts.
Going-to-the-Sun Road, 50 miles of remarkable loveliness, crosses the park from east to west and is open mid-June to mid–October. Otherwise the hiker must emulate the indigeous Rocky Mountain

goats and bighorn sheep often seen here and follow the trails (more than 1000 miles of them), winding among the rugged peaks and cirque glaciers. Diverse and lavish wildflowers, 200 trout-filled lakes and wildlife from birds to moose are among the attractions. Park naturalists lead parties to **Grinnell** and **Sperry Glaciers** but hikers and riders are free to explore the backcountry and camp. One trail goes over the **Triple Divide**, the unique point from which waters flow northeast into Hudson Bay, southeast to empty into the Gulf of Mexico, and west to end up in the Pacific.

Generally warm in summer with occasional storms and invariably cold nights; by October, the park is liable to be snowed in. Excellent trout fishing; if you don't fancy catching your own, Eddy's is famous locally for good and inexpensive trout dinners.

ACCOMMODATION
Bear Creek Ranch, PO Box 151, East Glacier Park, 226-5962. Open 1 June–15 Sept, with AYH $5.25. Also private, semi-private rooms, suites, family rooms. Historic log ranch, meals on tap. Remote. Also North Fork hostel at Polebridge on west side of the park.
Tamarack Lodge and Motel, Hwy 2, Martin City (8 miles outside west entrance), 387-5568. Singles $15 winter, $20 summer; doubles $20 and $28. Cafe, laundry, TV. Senior discounts.
Frontier Hotel, 24 First Ave W, Kalispell (west side of park), 755-6929. $10 single, $13 double.
Many lodges at East and West Glacier, just outside park. Best prices for doubles, triples or quads, so it pays to bunch up. A few operate dorms at $12 or so per person. Also within the park are a number of large, expensive lodges which do have overflow rooms; when available, they run about $10–$15 night.
Park campsites, $3–$4. Backcountry sites free with permit. Some sites closed to tent campers because of bears. Park fee is by the week, $2 per car, free for seniors.

TRAVEL
In summer, AMTRAK stops at East and West Glacier, the latter also served by bus from Great Falls. Brown Bus lines from Kalispell goes to East and West Glacier daily in summer, Mon, Wed, Fri in offseason.
Horse rental at East and West Glacier. Also llama pack trips from Great Northern Llama, Box 303, Whitefish MT 59937. Call 862-5258. About $40/day, everything included, trips for 2–5 people, late June through Oct.
River raft trips begin at $18 half-day; most include lunch. Blue and white water. At West Glacier, try: 387-5340 or 888-5571. At Whitefish, call: 862-5208.

GATEWAY CITIES TO YELLOWSTONE NATIONAL PARK: BOZEMAN, GARDINER, WEST YELLOWSTONE. Of *Zen and the Art of Motorcycle Maintenance* fame, **Bozeman** is a college town, agricultural centre and headquarters for the Montana wilderness association, which in summer conducts numerous walking and horseback trips for visitors into remote areas. It lies on the Butte to Billings Greyhound route; south from Bozeman, Highway 191 dips in and out of Yellowstone Park, coming at length (90 miles) to West Yellowstone.

Gardiner, a small village on Yellowstone's central north border, has the only approach open year-round.

West Yellowstone, a few blocks from the western entrance to Yellowstone, has numerous lodgings, shuttlebus service to Old Faithful, bike rentals, car rentals and other amenities for exploring the park. Hitching is also good and relatively safe.

ACCOMMODATION
In Bozeman: Mt View Motel, 1010 E Main, 586-5414. Singles $14 up, doubles $18 up.
Thrifty Scot Motel, 1321 N 7th, 587-5251. Singles $19–$24, doubles $24–$40, complimentary breakfast, AC, TV, storage. 6 blocks to Greyhound.
Sunset Motel, 810 N 7th, 587–5536. $16 singles, $20 doubles.
In Gardiner: cheapest is Town Motel, 848-7322, about $22–$30/night.
In West Yellowstone: Madison Hotel, 139 Yellowstone Ave, 646-7745. Singles $13–$25, doubles $15–$28. 2 doors from bus depot. 'Romantic old loghouse, bearskins on walls.' Hotel part *circa* 1912, reflects early, pre-auto days of Yellowstone. 'Very good value.' 'Helpful.'
Alpine Motel, 120 Madison, 646-4544, $6–$21 single, $24–$30 doubles. Cafe next door, kitchen, TV. Near bus depot. Discounts to bus pass holders. 'Clean, completely modern.'
KO–Z Motel, 15 Electric St, 646-7593. $15–$22.
Westward Ho Motel, 646-7331. Singles $17 up, doubles $25 up.
Carpenter's Workshop, 5 minute walk from Greyhound. Cabins with bunks, no bedding, $7.50/person. 'Basic but very friendly.'

FOOD
In Gardiner: The Pit Stop Cafe, near entrance to Yellowstone, on 3rd St. Excellent, inexpensive beef BBQ, open Mon–Sat till 9pm.
In West Yellowstone: Rustlers Roost, on Electric St, 3 minutes from Madison/Alpine lodgings. 'Best we found in area.' Soup/salad bar (all you can eat) plus main course, $6 up.

OF INTEREST
See Yellowstone Park entry, under **Wyoming**.

TRAVEL
Bozeman: bus leaves Bozeman for West Yellowstone at 5.30pm, makes return trip 8am. Bus pass not valid. TWA bus also from Bozeman daily, about $15 one way.
Car rental: 'If travelling from Bozeman and returning, try hiring a car for a round-trip in 24 hrs. Four of us did and it worked out cheaper than busing.' American International Rentacar, 540 E Main St, 586-4884. 'VW van, total cost with 4 people about $25 including gas.'
West Yellowstone: Payless Car Rental at Travelers Lodge, 225 Yellowstone Ave, 646-7773. '$25 per day, 25¢ per mile, 100 free miles per day.' 'Helpful about drop of car in Bozeman.' 'Rent from Westwood Hotel, 5 minutes from Greyhound. Small cars around $30/day, 150 miles free.' If you want someone to share car rental with, stand outside bus station in West Yellowstone.
Greyhound: from Salt Lake City to West Yellowstone, 8am and 11.30pm. 'Entertaining driver, varied scenery.' Also see Yellowstone Park entry for additional travel details, and tours to and from park.

NEVADA

'Stark' describes the Silver State. It's a flat and monochrome universe of sagebrush, raked with north-south mountain ranges that rise like angry cat scratches from the dry desert floor.

Neveda's the place for misanthropes. About 800,000 people rattle around in a state that measures 110,000 square miles, and 50 percent of them live in and around Las Vegas. Despite its small population, Nevada became a state in 1864 on the strength of the gold and silver from the Comstock Lode, which helped finance the Union side of the Civil War. After several boom-and-bust cycles, Nevada got on a permanent roll when three things happened: the building of Hoover Dam in 1931, which drew thousands of workers into the state; the legalisation of gambling the same year, which grew to become the largest single source of revenue; and government nuclear testing in the 1950s, which provided good jobs (and generous amounts of irradiation).

Nevada's trademarks may be glitter, fallout and quickie divorces, but it's also a land of ranches, Basque and Mormon communities and natural wonders like the Valley of Fire, weirdly beautiful Pyramid Lake, and the oldest tree in the world—a bristlecone pine in Wheeler Park.

LAS VEGAS. There is a point at which overwhelming vulgarity achieves a certain grandeur, and Las Vegas is living proof. Just remember to see it at night. In the blue velvet hours, it's an opulent oasis of neon jewels, endless breakfasts and raucous jackpots, a snug clockless world that throbs with totally unwarranted promise and specious glamour. As daylight approaches, the mirage wavers and melts away and the oasis becomes a banal forest of overweight signs, tacky and oppressive.

Best approaches for nighttime views are via Highway 93 from Hoover Dam (Greyhound's Flagstaff run comes this way) or on the 7.20pm *Desert Wind* train from Los Angeles.

The splashiest casino-hotels are along The Strip, where it all began on 1940; three miles away is downtown (called 'Glitter Gulch'), a high-wattage cluster of 15 casino-hotels. Glitter Gulch tries harder with looser slots, cheaper eats and a more tolerant and friendly attitude towards newcomers and low-rollers. However: lots of cheap lodging and food deals on The Strip also, so it's a tossup.

ACCOMMODATION

Lodgings are cheaper in winter than summer, cheaper midweek than weekends. Avoid holidays if you can. Sometimes astonishing bargains, even at big flashy hotels on The Strip. If you find it difficult to get a room on a summer weekend, try one of the big places—more likely to have vacancies and it can still work out cheaply for 2 or more people.

Also compare freebies (eg coupons for gambling, shows, meals) between hotels— they can make a big difference to your overall expenses. Local radio, giveaway papers advertise the latest bargains, as do the *LA Times* classifieds.

Downtown (close to bus, train stations):

Budget Inn, 301 S Main St, 385-5560. Near Greyhound. 'Spotless.' $20 single/
double, $25 on weekends. TV, air conditioning.

Victory Hotel, 307 S Main St, single/double with shower from $17, more with TV.
'Cheap, helpful.'

El Cortez Hotel-Casino, 600 E Fremont St, 385-5200. Rates same year-round,
$19–$25, all AC.

Crest Motel, 207 N 6th near Fremont, 382-5642. '$20 double with free breakfast,
lunch and $200 funpack. We spent 5 hours using up the freebies.'

On The Strip:

Circus Circus, 2880 Las Vegas Blvd S, 734-0410. 800 AC rooms, TV, pool, amazing
themed amenities including 3-ring circus. From $25 single/double: occasional deals
even lower. Check papers.

Stardust Hotel, 300 Las Vegas Blvd S, 732-6111. Possibly the cheapest (and most
garish) on The Strip: 1380 AC rooms, 3 pools, tennis courts, Greyhound stop. From
$25 single/double.

King Albert, 184 Albert Ave, 732-1555. Near MGM Grand. Weekday singles/doub-
les, $20–$32, weekends $38–$42; with kitchenettes.

B&B: various through B&B International, International Spareroom. See Accommodation Background for details, addresses.

FOOD

As a ploy to keep you gambling, many casinos dish up cheap and/or free meals to
keep your strength up. You don't have to gamble to take advantage, either. Do read
the fine print, however; some of the largesse has strings attached. Free or cheap
breakfasts are commonplace. Many of the cheapie 'lunches' and 'dinners' actually
serve breakfast food, so be prepared to like eggs and toast. The local paper prints a
list of the all-you-can-eat buffets and other cheap deals at all hotels and casinos; you
shouldn't spend more than $2 at breakfast, $3–$6 at lunch/dinner. Don't expect
quality (some of it is barely edible), just quantity. Most frequently mentioned:
Union Plaza Hotel, downtown, massive $1.50 breakfasts, 'excellent'; Mint Hotel,
downtown, all-you-can-eat lunches/dinners, $2.50–$5, 'good'; Circus Circus, The
Strip, with breakfast, lunch and dinner deals for $1.50, $3, and $4; and Holiday
Casino, The Strip, 'huge buffet under $4.'

OF INTEREST

Mint Hotel, 100 Fremont, has glass elevator to Top of the Mint, worth a ride for the
views of Glitter Gulch, The Strip, the desert and mountains beyond.

Caesar's Palace, The Strip. Outrageous fixtures—Cleopatra's Barge, a Temple of
Diana with moving sidewalk, etc. Superb Omnimax theatre nextdoor, $4.

Circus Circus, The Strip. Designed so a continuous 3-ring circus (11am–midnight)
performs right over the gaming tables and the oblivious gamblers. Ringside seats in
the Carson City room.

Historical note: until 1962, the casinos were segregated; Sammy Davis Jr and others
performed on The Strip but had to lodge and gamble in the black folks' district.

INFORMATION

Tourist Center, 302 Fremont, downtown, 384-5896. Also near The Strip at 3150 S
Paradise Rd, 733-2323. Collect free Funbooks, coupons, etc, here.

Important: carry proof of age to Las Vegas. You must be 21 to enter casinos
(although you can eat if not).

ENTERTAINMENT

Las Vegas is moving from emphasis on big-name superstar shows to flashy special
events (from boxing to gymnastics), soft sex shows and lounge revues (many as
cheap as $7 with 1 drink thrown in). Very few free shows but do check with Visitors
Center and in local papers. The Castaways Casino comes recommended for its
lavish free and cheap drinks policy.

TRAVEL

Greyhound, 200 S Main St, downtown, 382-2640. Also at Stardust Hotel on The Strip. To use 'Fun Bus' offers, you must arrive/leave from Stardust. Greyhound has tours to Scotty's Castle in Death Valley, and to Hoover Dam (discount with bus pass).

Trailways, 217 N 4th St, 385-1141, downtown. Also bus lines to Reno, Death Valley and Phoenix from here and Greyhound terminal. We've had many complaints about the friction between Greyhound and Trailways in Las Vegas, Flagstaff and Phoenix; be sure to ask *before* checking in bags if Trailways will honour Greyhound bus pass and vice versa.

Local bus, 384-3540. Bus 6 does 24-hour circuit, downtown to The Strip, $1 one way.

AMTRAK, Union Plaza, 1 Main St. Daily service. LA-Salt Lake City/Ogden, Utah, via the *Desert Wind*. Highly social train; recommended.

Drive-a-Junk, 643-1100; Oldies but Goodies, 736-7059; and Greyhound Rentacar, 736-2416. The latter uses new cars, can be booked in Britain; from $100/week.

Auto Driveaway, 3305 Spring Mt Rd, 873-9110. 'Often have cars for the LA area.'

McCarran International Airport, 5 miles south of downtown. Lavish, carpeted. 'Large couches, ideal for dossing.' Don't play slots here.

'Scenic Airlines (739-1900) does 3 different trips from Las Vegas to the Grand Canyon. Best value probably the 7-hr air-ground tour over Hoover Dam and all along the canyon in a small plane. Expensive at $190, but well worth it for a unique experience. Book in advance.'

HOOVER DAM and LAKE MEAD. Proof that engineering can be elegant as well as massive, Hoover's 728-foot Art Deco wall holds back miragelike Lake Mead, irrigates over one million acres, and keeps the lights on in LA and elsewhere. Well worth a cool trip to the powerplant ($2.50), but you can also see Hoover *en passant* via Greyhound on the Flagstaff run. Various Greyhound tours from Las Vegas, some with boat trip also.

RENO. Although it tries hard to peddle greed, instant gratification (eg quickie marriages/divorces) and Las Vegas-style artificiality, Reno doesn't quite make it. Little glimpses of culture, humanity and scenic beauty keep cropping up: its treelined parkway along the Truckee River, for instance; its friendly university; its jazz festivals; its good Basque restaurants. Close to the beauties of Lake Tahoe and a day's drive from San Francisco, 'the Biggest Little City' makes a pleasant base to explore Virginia and Carson Cities.

ACCOMMODATION

Senator Hotel, 136 W 2nd St, 322-2125. Singles $15 up, doubles $20 up; $2 discount for *Moneywise Guide* carriers 'because they send us so many nice people'. Clean, quiet, friendly; near casinos. Free drink and other coupons.

Windsor Hotel, 214 West St, 323-6171. A clean little hotel, 2 blocks from casinos. Singles $19 up, doubles $22 up; weekly rates.

B&B: through Pacific B&B, 701 NW 60th St, Seattle WA 98107. 206/784-7920. Home is under $30 for double.

FOOD

As with Las Vegas, cheap food in most of the casinos. But also Basque meals at the

Basque Restaurant, 235 Lake St; Louis' Basque Corner, 301 E 4th St at Evans; and the Reno Business Club, 432 E 4th St.

OF INTEREST

Harrah's Auto Collection, 788-3242. Free shuttle from Harrah's Casino. $5, seniors $3.75. Daily 9am–6pm. Mind-boggling collection of 1200 classic autos: Bugattis, 1886 Riker electric, an 1838 Phantom Corsair Coupe, entertainers' custom vehicles, plus rail cars, boats. Restoration underway and can be seen also.

Harold's Club gun collection. Free look at Jesse James' .44 Colt, Wild Bill Hickok's .32 Smith and Wesson, solar cannons, crossbows and other lethal things. Open 24 hrs.

Nevada Historical Museum, 1650 N Virginia St, near campus. Free, daily 9am–5pm. Outstanding Indian artefacts, including Washoe Indian Basketry, plus 3 slide programmes.

Nearby:

Virginia City. A $25/week reporter for the local *Territorial Enterprise*, Mark Twain wrote of this semi-ghost town in its boisterous prime: 'It was no place for a Presbyterian, and I did not remain one for very long'. Full of tourist trappings but still fun, especially the 10 rococo saloons left from the 1870s. The Sundance has the oldest original bar; the Union Brewery Saloon is the most untouristy. Explore the cemeteries, the museums on C Street and take a 25-minute run on the charming Virginia and Truckee RR to Gold Hill, $2.25, all-day pass $5. (Bring a picnic lunch.) If you're taken with the area, shared bath rooms at the Gold Hill Hotel and Tavern are pretty reasonable.

Carson City. Loaded with Victorian gingerbread and refreshingly situated in the green Sierra foothills, this is the smallest capital city in the lower 48. Mark Twain lived at 502 N Division St with his brother, who was first territorial secretary of state. Free sights include a rare collection of natural gold formations at the Carson Nugget; the former mint (now a museum); and the Virginia and Truckee RR museum on S Carson St.

Further afield: ghost towns aplenty, from Yerington (where Wovoka, the Piaute 'messiah', created the Ghost Dance cult) to Marietta and Hawthorne (tip one at Joe's Tavern, an institution).

Union City, just off the Greyhound/Trailways route from Reno to Salt Lake City via I-80. A genuine ghost town where Mark Twain dabbled at prospecting, Unionville is now in private hands. Its owners offer an evocative stay for $20 per bedroom, $40 for an entire house, breakfast included. Owners will do additional meals and pick you up at Greyhound freeway stop at Imlay also. Hot springs, trout fishing, hiking. Book at Old Pioneer Garden, Unionville 79, Nevada 89418. Call 538-7585.

For **Lake Tahoe, Nevada Side**, see Tahoe, California.

INFORMATION

Visitors Center, 133 N Sierra St, 329-3558 or 768-3030. Mon–Sat.

TRAVEL

Greyhound, 155 Stevenson St, 322-4511. If you have a bus pass, take a day's excursion to Lake Tahoe and Truckee, or to Carson City and Virginia City. Gray Line also does a tour (pass valid) to Virginia City. 'Bus from Reno to Tahoe is excellent, scenic.' Trailways, Ralston and W 2nd St, 323-6123.

AMTRAK depot, E Commercial Row and Lake, 329-8638. The run from Sacramento via Truckee is dazzling. Also check for special 'Fun Train' cheap fares.

Rent-a-Ride, 786-0448; Drive a Dent, 825-9515; Ruff 'n' Ready, 359-9036 (in Sparks).

UTAH

Although the US government owns 70 percent of Utah's land, the

Beehive state is, for all intents and purposes, under Mormon control, a unique situation indeed considering the American insistence on separation of church and state.

The Church of Jesus Christ of the Latter-Day Saints began in 1827 when New Yorker Joseph Smith was led by an angel named Moroni to some gold tablets. Translated (with Moroni's help and two seer stones called Urim and Tummim) into English, the writings became the scriptures of the *Book of Mormon*. The fledgling sect was pushed from New York westward but didn't encounter any significant antagonism until Smith introduced polygamy at Nauvoo, Illinois. A hostile mob promptly killed Smith and his brother. The mantle fell to Brigham Young, who ably led his band west to the bleak wilds of northern Utah, which no one, not even the local Ute Indians, seemed terribly interested in.

The industrious Mormons established their new state of Deseret and applied repeatedly to the US government for admission to the Union but were turned down over the issue of polygamy, which was still going strong. (Brigham himself ultimately had 27 wives and 56 children.) After years of wrangling, in 1890 the Mormons gave in and banned polygamy among themselves. A number of dissenters left and their descendents can be found living quietly and polygamously in Mexico, Arizona and elsewhere.

The importance of Mormonism makes Utah—especially Salt Lake City and environs—sharply different and in many ways better than other states. Hardworking Mormons have built clean, prosperous, humanistic cities and settlements. On the negative side, it's hard to find a decent meal or a drinkable cup of coffee anywhere. Mormons discourage the use of coffee and stimulants and apparently feel the same way about seasonings. Liquor laws, once extremely stringent, have eased somewhat but getting a drink in a restaurant is still a baroque procedure.

Bear in mind when visiting any of Utah's five National Parks, all in the south, that you are in an area studded with magnificent monuments of the greatest historical, geological and scenic importance. Take a tour or rent a car, allowing yourself ample time for exploration. Utah makes a good point from which to explore attractions on the Utah-Arizona border and further south, such as Monument Valley, the Navajo reservation and the north rim of the Grand Canyon (via Kanab). A boat trip through the flooded canyons of the Glen Canyon National Recreation Area is also an unforgettable (albeit pricey) experience.

National Parks: Zion
Bryce Canyon
Canyonlands
Capitol Reef
Arches

SALT LAKE CITY. Not just a state capital but the Mecca/Vatican/ Jerusalem for three million Mormons worldwide, Salt Lake City has a joyful, almost noble air about it. Founder Brigham Young had a sharp eye; the city is cradled by the snowy Wasatch Mountains, a setting of remarkable grace. Add to that streets broad enough for a four-oxen cart to turn in, a tree for every citizen, clean air and ecclesiastical architecture that succeeds in being impressive without being dull, and you have quite a place. Lots of interesting things for 'gentiles' (non-Mormons) to see and do: 'Unlike any other American city I saw.'

Great Salt Lake lies 18 miles west of the city, a mere remnant of a prehistoric sea that covered 20,000 square miles, outlines still visible from the air.

ACCOMMODATION
Budget Bob's Motel, 534 N 300 West, 532-9071. Singles $10–$13, doubles $2 more. TV extra. 'Friendly.'

Carlton Hotel, 140 E South Temple St, 355-3418. Singles $16–$25, doubles $19–$30. Student, bus pass discounts. Near bus depots. 'Friendly', 'clean', 'good value', 'awful'.

Hotel Little, 167 S Mina St, 363-3803. 2 blocks south of Temple. Singles $10 up, doubles $14 up. 'No AC but good value.' 'Smelly rooms.'

Temple Square Hotel, 75 W South Temple, 355-2961. Above Trailways, prime locale, luxurious and pricey: singles $30 up, doubles $38 up. But: discounts to seniors, bus pass, foreign travellers. 'Backpackers not welcome even with Ameripass.'

Avenues Residential Club, 107 F St, 363-8137. Homey Hostel, $9 up to $15–$22, cheaper for AYH. 'Clean, friendly.' Kitchen. 10 blocks to Temple Square.

YWCA, 322 E 3rd South, 355-2804. $10 members. Shared rooms. Laundry, cafeteria. 'No late buses.'

Desert Inn, 50 W 5th South, 532-2900. Singles $25 up, doubles $28 up. Comfortable, well-furnished, AC, TV, coffeeshop.

FOOD
Old Spaghetti Factory, 189 Trolley St. Spaghetti, drink, dessert under $4, 'filling, tasty'.

Marianne's Deli, 2nd South opposite Salt Palace. Closed Mon eves. 'Genuine ethnic serving SLC's German population. Good salami, sausages, sauerkraut, meals from $3.'

Lotsa Hotsa Pizza, opposite Temple Square. 'Succulent—pizza slices under $1, other specials $2.50.'

Also recommended: Coffee shop below Carlton Hotel ('cheapest in town') and Wags in the ZCMI Center.

OF INTEREST
Visitors Center in Temple Square: 'Guided tour conducted by Mormons who must have been trained to sell insurance. Intimidating.' Pick up the excellent walking tour booklet.

LDS Church office building, 50 E North Temple. Open Mon–Fri 9am–6pm, Sat 9am–5pm. Free guided tours include library and genealogical records plus 'fantastic view from 26th floor'.

Mormon Temple. This monumental structure in Mormon Gothic took exactly 40 years and $4 million to build. Notice the golden statue of angel Moroni on one of the towers. 'Even if you're only passing through, go see the Temple. Fantastic the way it's lit up.' Not open to the public but the nearby **tabernacle** is. Free organ recitals (noon, Mon–Fri, 4pm Sat–Sun) show off the remarkable acoustics and the 10,814-pipe organ.

Free guided tours of the tabernacle hourly ('nauseating'). This of course is the home of the famous 375-voice Tabernacle Choir whose broadcasts you can attend gratis on Sun at 9.25am (phone 531-2534 to confirm time). Also free choir rehearsals on Thur at 8pm and evening concerts by the Youth Group in the open-air auditorium behind the Temple. Free tickets from Visitors Center.

Additional Mormonabilia: **'This is the Place' monument** at Pioneer Trail State Park, Emigration Canyon, at east edge of city. Also restored pioneer settlement, etc. 'Mormons are obsessed with the pioneers but they don't try to convert you—in fact, I found Mormonism quite fascinating.'

Brigham Young's grave in the cemetery on 1st Ave between State and A Sts.

The Beehive House and adjoining **Lion House**, 67 E South Temple. Free tours of the Beehive, BY's first residence. Lion house is not open to the public but it's where the 27 wives lived, in tiny cells off both sides of an upper hall. After supper, the great man would climb the stairs and chalk an X on the door of his lady for the night. Sometimes a rival would erase the X and chalk another on her door before the absent-minded stud came back upstairs. In this fashion, BY brought 56 new Mormons into the world.

Symphony Hall, at Salt Palace Center. Glorious glass wedge of a place; free tours, 533-5626; can also see rehearsals by special arrangement.

Shopping: Brigham Young established the first department store in the US, the Zion Cooperative Mercantile Institution (ZCMI). Now a huge affair, at one time it was the biggest covered mall in the country. Also good browsing at Trolley Square. Buses 27, 32, 33 from Temple Square.

Great Salt Lake, 18 miles west. 1500 square miles and 25% saline, the Mormons used to put joints of beef in the water overnight, retrieving them 'tolerably well pickled'. Float on the waters but shower afterwards. 2 state beaches with camping on South Shore and at the tip of Antelope Island. Several bison live on the island. 'Well worth a visit.' Bring repellant—lots of mosquitoes.

Bingham Canyon Copper Mine, 22 miles SW. Dramatic, 2-mile-wide hole (world's largest), site of immense open-pit copper mine. Free and 'well worth it'. Be there 2pm–4pm for blasting.

Hogle Zoo near Emigration Canyon. Free looks at Carnivore Mall, 1000 animals including a 'liger''—a lion/tiger cross.

ENTERTAINMENT
Promised Valley Playhouse, 132 S State St. Free musical, *The Promised Valley*, summers Tue–Sat at 8pm, tells the story of the Mormon trek west. 'Amusing, enjoyable; not an attempt at conversion.' Tickets at Visitors Center. .

Days of '47 Festival, 3rd week in July. Rodeo, parades, free concerts. 'Fun.'

Park City, ski resort 35 miles east, features fibreglass bobsled run. You control speed. 'Beats any rollercoaster.' $5 per run.

INFORMATION
Visitors Info centres at Temple Square, in suite 200 at Salt Palace, at old council hall on Capitol Hill. 521-2822.

TRAVEL
Greyhound, 160 W South Temple, 355-4684. 'The road to the station is pretty seedy.'

Trailways, 77 W South Temple, 328-8121. Their run to Denver is highly recommended and written about elsewhere.

Airport buses 18 and 18A to downtown, 50¢. 531-8600 for info.

AMTRAK, 400 W South Temple, 364-8562. 'Timetable is confusing—there *are* through carriages for SLC—no need to change at Ogden as we did.'

Denver and Rio Grande *Zephyr*, SLC–Denver. 'Foreigners showing passports get $20 reduction on fare.'

Ugly Duckling Rentacar, 2375 W North Temple, 355-5655: 'for local use only. Compacts Only (same address and phone) has best weekly rates.'

Gray Line tours: Bingham Canyon and Great Salt Lake, $16, leave 2pm, return 6.30pm. Tickets at Temple Square Hotel. 'Bus to San Francisco drives along the lake anyway.'

PROMONTORY. About 75 miles north of Salt Lake City is the **Golden Spike National Historic Site**, marking the spot where North America's first transcontinental railroad was completed in 1869. The governor of California celebrated the event by driving a golden spike into the last tie; each 10 May at 12.45pm, the ceremony is reenacted.

DINOSAUR NATIONAL MONUMENT. This park overlaps two states (see also Colorado) but the major attractions lie mostly in Utah. Vernal has a superb Field House of Natural History; nearby is Dinosaur Gardens (14 lifesize dinos) and the Visitors Center with dinosaur quarry, where you are eye level with half-exposed brontosaurus and other remains. The road from Vernal to Daggett is called 'the Drive through the Ages' for the billion years of earth's history that lie exposed on either side. Numerous campgrounds in and around Dinosaur National Monument, emphasis on RVs though.

ZION NATIONAL PARK. Though not as famous as Yosemite or the Grant Canyon, Zion ranks with them for outstanding landscapes: a huge, painted gorge of magnificent and constantly changing colours, its floor an oasis of green. At one point the North Fork of the Virgin River pours over the 2000-foot drop of the **Narrows** abyss, whose walls are just 20 feet apart. Cottonwoods grow on the lush canyon floor and here it is possible to camp. So delightful was the sight that the first Mormons called it Zion, later corrected by Brigham Young, who proclaimed 'It is not Zion', and 'Not Zion' it remained for some years.

There is an 8-mile road along the canyon floor for starters, but for a better look you are advised to walk. There are numerous short trails, sometimes dotted with guide boxes containing leaflets on local flora and geological features. You can do any of these on your own, though a ranger leads hikers along **Narrows Trail** in summer. Before setting off on any trail, long or short, check with rangers for advice on availability of drinking water in certain areas, sudden summer cloudbursts with attendant flash flooding, and rockfalls.

'We liked the **Shining Pools footpath**, a gentle stroll for a hot day— beautiful waterfall, a cool and welcome swim.' 'Try walking up to **Angels' Landing**, 5-mile round trip rising 1488 feet. Incredible views.' 'Angels' Landing walk—strenuous but very rewarding.' (NB: sheer drops along path—*not* for acrophobes.) The best view of the **Great**

White Throne, a colossal multicoloured butte, is from the Temple of Sinawava. $2 park entry fee, good for one week.

ACCOMMODATION
Lodging, camping and gas station in park. Camping: 373 sites, unreserved; arrive by noon to snag one, $4 each.
Motels and groceries at Springdale, 2 miles from south entrance.
Cedar City, 20 miles north of Zion, 6 miles from Cedar Breaks National Monument (called 'Little Bryce' for its spires, perhaps more intensely coloured than anywhere else—good camping) makes a good base. In summer Cedar City has weekend Shakespeare at Southern Utah State College; cheap standing room seats and free 'green show' nightly at 7.15pm.
Lunt's Hotel, 141 N Main, 586-9465. In Greyhound building. Singles $7.50–$11, doubles $11–$14. Weekly rates. 'Modest but clean and friendly,' say the owners.

TRAVEL
Greyhound from Salt Lake City and Las Vegas to Cedar City. Also Trailways goes from Las Vegas to St George and from Page to Mt Carmel Junction.
Color Country Tours, Cedar City 586-3777. They do 1-day tours to Zion (Tue, Thur, Sat) and Bryce Canyon (Mon, Wed, Fri). About $33 Zion, $35 Bryce. Mid-May to Mid-Oct. Also one-way fares to Zion, Bryce, etc, and overnight trips to Grand Canyon north rim twice a week. No meals. 'Very friendly tour guides.' 'Very good—if in a small group, almost like having a private taxi—driver will take you exactly where you want to go.' On overnight trips; 'markedly reduced if accommodation isn't included. Able to stay in campsites'.
Within Zion: 2-hr tram rides, $2.50, daily 9am–5pm.
Hitching between Cedar City and Zion is slow.

BRYCE CANYON NATIONAL PARK. Bryce's landscape belongs to God's Gothic period—delicately chisselled spires, colonnades and crenellated ridges in vivid to pastel pinks, madders, oranges, violets. Most stunning when seen against the sun: west rim in morning, east rim in afternoon. Named for Ebeneezer Bryce, an unpoetic soul who described the canyon as 'a hell of a place to lose a cow'. From the pine-covered clifftops (site of the Visitors Center and other facilities), the horseshoe-shaped amphitheatres reveal surreal formations that have been likened to houses, sunburned people and petrified sunsets. For hiking, descend the canyon to the **Peekaboo Trail** or for a short trip along the **Navajo** and **Queen's Garden trails** which link at the bottom. About 1½ hours for a quick trot. There is a 16-mile auto road but the views are less spectacular. On full-moon nights, take the free 'moon walks' down Navajo Trail. 'Wall Street is more spectacular than Queen's Garden.'

ACCOMMODATION
Bryce Canyon Pines Motel, outside Panguitch on Rt 12, 6 miles from Bryce entrance, 834-5336. Singles $29 up. Discounts for bus pass. AC, pool, cafe, homey dining room with good home cooking. Horseback riding. State liquor store. Open all year, highest rates 1 May–15 Oct.
Blue Pines Motel, 130 N Main, Panguitch, 676-9482. At Trailways depot. $14 single. Pool table, TV, 'Clean, friendly.' If full, ask about sleeping bag space.

Pink Cliff Motel, Junction Highways 12 and 22, Bryce Canyon, 834-5303. $29 up single, $32 up double.
Camping in Bryce: 2 developed sites, $2, fill early. Also nearby in Dixie National Forest.

TRAVEL
Panguitch is served by Trailways between Salt Lake City and Flagstaff. Tours of the park from Cedar City.

MOAB. A former uranium mining town on US 163 in east-central Utah, Moab makes a convenient centre from which to visit Canyonlands, Arches and Capitol Reef National Parks. It's also fairly good for Natural Bridges, the Glen Canyon area and Monument Valley.

Arches contains waterhewn natural bridges and over 90 arches of smoky red sandstone carved by the tireless wind. 'Our most memorable National Park.' **Natural Bridges** is noted for three rock bridges, the foremost a 268-foot span; less well-known features are the hundreds of Anasazi cliff ruins and the world's largest photovoltaic solar generating plant (free viewing), which runs the park's electrical system.

The outstanding characteristic of **Canyonlands** is its variety of colour and forms: towering spires, bold mesas, needles, arches, intricate canyons, roaring rapids, bottomlands and sandbars. The park is rich in petroglyphs, pictographs and ruins: the Maze district with its Harvest Scene and the Needles district south of Squaw Springs campground are particularly good. 'Superb view from Dead Horse Pt, just outside park.'

Capitol Reef, rising 1000 feet above the Fremont River and extending for 20 miles, is the most spectacular monocline (tilted cliff) in the US. The bands of rock exposed along its length are luminous, rich and varied in their colour, and often cut with petroglyphs of unusual size and style. Its formations were named 'sleeping rainbows' by the Navajos.

The soaring pink sandstone arch of **Rainbow Bridge** and the beauties of boating in **Glen Canyon** can be undertaken from Moab, but closer bases would be Page, Arizona, and Kanab, Utah.

On Navajo land, **Monument Valley's** landscape of richly-coloured outcroppings was the scene of many a John Ford western. Two campsites: 'the best is in the Tribal Park among the mesas—quiet, hot showers, $3/car'.

ACCOMMODATION
In Moab:
Prospector Lodge, 186 N 1st West, 259-5145 or 9922. 3 blocks from bus; if arriving late, phone ahead for pickup. $17–$24 single, $20–$26 double. AC, movies, senior and offseason discounts. 'Helpful.'
Virginian Motel, 70 E 2nd South, 259-5951. $25 single/double.
Camping: two free Lions Club campgrounds in Moab. Arches National Park sites are free (but no water), 1 Nov–1 March, $3 otherwise.

In Kanab:
Twin Pines Motel, 249 S 100 East, 644-2982. $17–$21 single, $23–$29 doubles. AC, cale TV, liquor and grocery store adjacent. 2 blocks from bus. Offseason and extended stay discounts. (Clean, and very helpful owners.'
At Capitol Reef:
Rim Rock Motel, 3 miles east on Highway 24, 425-3843. Singles $20 up, doubles $26 up. Large rooms, superb views; also surprisingly good restaurant. Many hiking/riding/jeep tours from lodge.

FOOD
Monument Valley Cafeteria, 7th Day Adventist Hospital, off Hwy 163. Behind Rock Door Canyon. Open daily. Vegetarian fare, excellent Navajo tacos, good desserts.

TRAVEL
Jeep tours, horseback trips, long and short raft trips, even covered wagon expeditions are available from a variety of operators, in Moab, at the parks and in other gateway towns. Lin Ottinger's Tours are recommended: 137 N Main, Moab, 259-7312. $25/day, including lunch for Arches or Canyonlands; small groups. Horsehead pack trips does 2-hr rides into Arches for $25.
Bryce Canyon Trail rides has various rides from $6/hour to $30 all day.
Trailways from Flagstaff to Salt Lake City via Lake Powell stops at Kanab.

WYOMING

Cowboy machismo and women's rights might seem an odd mixture, but Wyoming is nicknamed the Equality State for good reason: it had the first women's suffrage act, the first female voter, governor, justice of the peace and director of the US mint.

A horsy, folksy, gun-totin' state, Wyoming still has far more cattle and sheep than people. Its ranches are so huge they're measured in sections instead of acres.

Everyone know about the twin treasures of Yellowstone and Grand Teton National Parks. But Wyoming also contains Devil's Tower, now imprinted on the world's retina as an extra-terrestrial landing pad; and Salt Creek, world's largest light oil field and site of the infamous Teapot Dome scandal in 1927.

National Parks: Grand Teton
Yellowstone (largely in Wyoming but also in Montana and Idaho; see those states for additional information).

CHEYENNE. Once fondly called 'hell on wheels' for its volatile mix of cowpokes, cattle rustlers and con men, capital city Cheyenne now contents itself with having the purest air and the most frequent hailstorms in the US. A little of the old buckaroo flavour returns each July during the week-long Frontier Days rodeo, largest in the US.

ACCOMMODATION
Albany Hotel, 1506 Capitol Ave, 638-3507. By the bus, train depots. $16 night for single with shower.

Super 8 Motel, 1900 W Lincolnway, Highway 30 West. 10 minutes to state capitol. 635-8741. Singles $18–$24, doubles $23–$30. Also Motel 6 at 1765 W Lincolnway, 635-1675. Need a car for both.

FOOD

Albany Cafe, next to hotel. Good lunch counter with cheap breakfasts. Bar is 'good for meeting people. Not a pickup bar, not gay, not expensive, good music. Can this be true?'

Mayflower Cafe, 112 17th St. 'Juicy 3-course steak dinner for $5; good quality and value. Live cowboy band nextdoor.'

OF INTEREST

Frontier Days, 'the Daddy of 'em All' rodeo, late July. 3 parades, chuckwagon races, and perhaps the best rodeo in the US. Tickets are pricey: $6–$12. During rodeo, the whole town goes wild on Sat night but forget it at other times: 'Cheyenne is dead as a doorpost on Sat night.'

State Museum, Central Ave at 23rd St. Free. Worthwhile cowboy, Indian and pioneer museum, open daily in summer. Mon–Sat rest of year. Also the Frontier Days Museum, Frontier Park, has splendid collection of horse-drawn vehicles, Oglala Sioux beadwork; $1. Daily in summer.

TRAVEL

Greyhound, 1503 Capitol Ave (634-7774) and Trailways, same building, 634-2128. AMTRAK, 121 W 15th St at Capitol, 635-2088.

DEVIL'S TOWER NATIONAL MONUMENT. Only recently accorded intergalactic notoriety in *Close Encounters of the Third Kind*, Devil's Tower was declared the nation's first national monument in 1906 in recognition of the special part it played in Indian legend. A landmark also for early terrestrial explorers and travellers, the monolith is a fluted pillar of sombre igneous rock rising 865 feet above its wooded base and 1280 feet above the Belle Fourche River. Open year-round. You can climb the tower (about eight hours) or walk around it (about one hour): 'creepily impressive, much more so than the movie'. In the park are prairie-dog villages, an outdoor amphitheatre and ranger programmes in summer.

ACCOMMODATION

Campsites at the monument open May–Sept. Also free camping in Moorcroft at City Park, 1 mile west of town, and at the rest area west of Moorcroft on I-90.

Cowboy Motel, 101 S Yellowstone Ave, Moorcroft, 756-3444. Bus stops right outside. Rooms begin at $15. Also service to Devil's Tower (pricey).

Arrowhead Motel, 214 Cleveland St, Sundance, 283-3307. $24–$30 all with bath. 'Most clean and attractive. Friendly, helpful and bright.' AC, colour TV, cafe opposite. NE of Moorcroft, equidistant to Devil's Tower.

TRAVEL

Trailways serves Moorcroft and Sundance, both about 33 miles from Devil's Tower. Though the monument is in NE Wyoming, it's most easy to reach from the Black Hills of South Dakota, especially if you rent a car in Rapid City.

Hitching not recommended in Wyoming or Montana. 'Difficult, with long waits.'

YELLOWSTONE NATIONAL PARK. Established in 1872, the oldest and perhaps the most well-loved of the national parks,

Yellowstone comprises 3472 square miles, covering the northwest corner of Wyoming and dribbling over into Idaho and Montana. Three of the five entrances are in Montana; they and the gateway cities of Gardiner, Bozeman and West Yellowstone are discussed in the Montana section. Wyoming park entrances are from the east via Cody, from the south via Jackson/Grand Teton National Park, and from the southeast via St Anthony Falls, Idaho. Bear in mind, however, that Greyhound serves the park only via the Montana entrances at Gardiner and West Yellowstone.

Yellowstone is one of the world's most impressive thermal regions. Besides **Old Faithful** (which blows a three-minute, 200-foot plume every 65 minutes or so), there are some 10,000 geysers, hot springs, colourful paint pots and gooey mud pools—an uncanny array of colours, temperatures, smells, disquieting sounds and eruptions. Don't miss **Minerva Basin** or the **Grand Prismatic Spring**: its pool is a surreal window of gold-flecked turquoise, like a painting by Magritte.

One of your priorities should be the **Grand Canyon of the Yellowstone River**, whose 1200-foot gorge is 'one wild welter of colour', as Rudyard Kipling put it. 'Breath-taking—even better than the Arizona one.' Also do not miss **Yellowstone Lake**, famous for its trout, more so for its 2100 miles of shoreline and sublime scenery.

A wildlife sanctuary, the park is filled with deer, moose, bison, bear and other creatures. Because so many people fed the bears (often being hurt in the process, besides perverting the animals' way of life), the park has removed many of them to remote areas. Over 100 who had become real menaces had to be shot—all due to human meddling. If you do sight bears, do not feed them, get close to them, or come between an adult and cubs. They are wild, and meant to stay that way.

Cars were not admitted to the park until 1915; today, nearly 750,000 of them enter, with attendant traffic jams, accidents, pollution and parking problems. But as in other parks, the two million visitors per year tend to congregate in the same places, leaving much of the park refreshingly empty.

Challenging hikes include the 3½-mile walk to the sumit of **Mt Washburn** (but stay on trails, don't take shortcuts). If you have more time, rent a canoe at West Yellowstone and canoe/camp the **Lewis River** to the **Shoshone Lakes**—a pristine, wildlife-filled journey. Many campsites along route and at the lake. 'Don't forget Canyon and Upper Falls—on a par with Grand Canyon!'

The park is open year-round ($2 per car, 50¢ on foot), but the official season runs June to September, after which bus service and other facilities cease and there is a real chance of snow. Offseason months, the only roads and entrance open are via Gardiner. However, you can take a snow coach from West Yellowstone. Yellowstone in winter is enchanting: the wildlife move in close to the warmth of the geysers and thermal springs—awesome to see them in the swirling mists. You can actually ski or snowshoe close to bison and elk.

ACCOMMODATION
Lodging outside the park is discussed under West Yellowstone and Gardiner, Montana. See also Cody.
Within the park:
Camping. 2453 designated sites, $6/night. Usually filled before noon in summer, first-come, first-served. Note: some are closed to tent campers because of problems with bears. 'If you're prepared to sleep in the car, you can use the high bear risk campsites.' 'Arrive before 8pm if you want a shower—or use hotel as we did.' Camping can be very cold, even in July, so bring a warm sleeping bag; bag and blankets also useful for cabin rentals. Do not sleep with food near you! Backcountry camping free with permit. You need to buy a map. Mid-Sept to mid-May, free camping at Mammoth Campground—it's the only one open in offseason. Lots of amenities.
Cabins. Cheapest are the budget shelters (hot/cold running water) at Old Faithful Lodge and Cabins, $10.50: budget cabins are $16 for 1–2 persons. Open 5 June–25 Sept.
Also: Old Faithful Snowlodge, budget shelters $10.50, budget cabins $16–$30, rooms without bath $21–$30. Open 2–15 May and 25 June–31 Aug.
Also: Roosevelt Lodge, rustic shelter $9.50, Roughrider cabins $10.50 and family cabins (½ bath) for $21–$30. Open 10 June–Sept. 'No frills, clean beds, woodburning stove and fuel. Nice—western.' You're strongly advised to book well ahead, especially for Aug. All lodging, call (307) 344-7311.

FOOD
Six concessions in the park, none particularly cheap. If you can manage, bring in groceries from West Yellowstone.

TRAVEL
Tour of Lower Loop from West Yellowstone departs 8am, returns 5.30pm, costs $15 with bus pass, about $25 without. Also tours of Upper Loop. 'Clerks at West Yellowstone very helpful with advice.' You can also make your own combinations.
Shuttle service from West Yellowstone to Old Faithful: 'Interesting commentary.' Free.
Hitching within the park is rated 'very easy'.
Bike rental, 132 Madison Ave, West Yellowstone, costs $7/day. Cheaper per week. 'In fine weather, seems the best way to get somewhere and enjoy the scenery at the same time. 30 miles to Old Faithful, Norris' Geyser Basin.'
Car rental is a good idea, especially after Labor Day. See also West Yellowstone for details.
Horses for rent at Mammoth Hot Springs, Canyon and Roosevelt, $10/hour and up. Cheaper at Diamond Pt Ranch, 6 miles from West Yellowstone.

CODY. It may look like endless motels, but be not dismayed. Cody possesses a superlative, four-in-one museum complex and an Old Trail Town that are well worth your attention. About 60 miles east of Yellowstone, Cody is of course the namesake of William F, also known as Buffalo Bill, bison hunter/Army scout turned showman. His Wild West show was one of several that earned a living by touring the US, Canada and Europe with a mawkish show of brave cowboys and savage redskins—very popular at the time. Royalty loved it;

Queen Victoria gave Cody a diamond brooch, saying his show was so exciting she found it 'almost impossible to sit'. Annie Oakley and Sitting Bull were among Buffalo Bill's prize 'exhibits'; the mythology created by these shows was later recycled by Hollywood.

East of Cody, the vividly coloured strata of **Shell Canyon** along the winding stretch of Highway 14 between Shell and Sheridan is highly scenic; to reach Custer's Last Stand in Montana, turn north at Sheridan.

ACCOMMODATION
Pawnee Lodge, 1032 12th, 587-2239. Singles $12.50–$18; 2 to 4 people, $18–$32. Air conditioning, cafe nearby, TV. Bus stop 2 blocks. Close to museum.

Irma Hotel, 1192 Sheridan Ave, 587-4221. Luxurious and expensive ($30 up single, $34 up double), but a grandly historic place built by Buffalo Bill and named after his daughter. If you don't stay, at least stop by for a drink at the incredible French cherrywood bar, a gift from Queen Victoria after BB's command performance in England. Merchants' lunches and even dinners are very good value at the Irma Grill, open Mon–Sat.

Camping: free at Legion Park on I-25, north edge. Summer only, 1 night limit.

OF INTEREST
Buffalo Bill Historical Center, et al, 720 Sheridan, 587-4771. Daily 7am–10pm June through Aug, shorter hours thereafter. $3 for 4 museums. Besides Cody memorabilia, see BB's boyhood home, barn, bunkhouse. The **Plains Indian museum** is huge, imaginative and head and shoulders above most Indian collections. The **Whitney Gallery of Western Art** has bluechip western painters: Remington, Catlin, Russell and Bierstadt's work on Yellowstone. Over 5000 firearms in the **Winchester Gun Museum**.

Rodeos. Early June through Aug, nightly rodeos at 8.30pm, 2 miles west of town. $5–$7. Also the Cody Stampede, each 2–4 July.

Old Trail Town, 3 miles west in Shoshone Canyon. A well-conceived collection of historic buildings and relics from all over Wyoming—Cassidy and Sundance's hide-out to Jeremiah Johnson's grave. 'Non-gimmicky.' Open year-round. Donations.

GRAND TETON NATIONAL PARK. Twenty miles due south of Yellowstone lies the totally different world of the Grand Teton Mountains. As awe-inspiring as Yellowstone, this park reminds one of Alpine Europe rather than the American West. The Tetons rise without preliminaries from a level valley to sharp pinnacles 7000 feet high, separated by deep glaciated clefts. On their crags and flanks, you see remnants of the last great glaciation that once covered North America, 10,000 years ago. Besides peaks, valleys like Jackson Hole, the lakes and the winding Snake River add up to a stirring environment. Jackson Hole, Jenny Spring and Solitude Lakes make good if icy swimming.

Warm clothes and tough shoes are essential here. This is mountaineering country; several schools have their headquarters in the area. Permits for climbing must be obtained from a park ranger, and it's not for novices.

One of the best ways to absorb the Tetons is to float down the Snake

River on a large rubber raft steered by boatmen. In the forests at river's edge you may see some of the elk which form the largest herd in America.

ACCOMMODATION
Both accommodation in the park and in nearby Jackson tends to be more costly than at Yellowstone and vicinity.

The Hostel X, Box 546, Teton Village, 12 miles north of Jackson, 733-3415. Rooms have double bunks with private bath, carpeted but simple. $28 for 1–2, $36 for 3–4. With AYH, 10% discount. Game room, pool, lounge with fireplace (can cook), movies in evenings. Arranges tours.

Snow Job, Box 371, Wilson 83014. 1 Oct through 31 May. B&B for $16 single, $21 double in home 7 miles from Jackson. Shared bath, TV. No kitchen privileges. A very economical and pleasant place for ski/snow season.

OF INTEREST
Jackson: 'not to be missed—a real tourist trap, but worth the visit. Good craft, art galleries, cowboy bars (The Silver Dollar, Million Dollar). Daily shootout in town square at 7pm. Ask at Chamber for accommodation (some reasonable prices)'. While here visit the **Jackson Cold Storage**, 125 S King, open Mon–Sat 8am–6pm, for a free tour (and samples) of their buffalo jerky-making operation. Delicious and makes superb backpacking food. In Nov–April, about 10,000 elk graze near the edge of town. Local Boy Scouts collect and sell their antlers, some of which end up as aphrodisiacs in the Far East.

Sleigh rides in winter, $2.50. Also elk feeding. Jackson is the river trip centre for the Snake. Two covered wagon outfitters offer trips from 2–4 days in the scenic Tetons. Wagons West is cheapest at $65/day and up, all inclusive. Book: LD Frome, Outfitters, RFD, Afton WY 83110; call 886-5240.

TRAVEL
Frontier Airlines flies into Jackson.

Rock Springs Stages, daily at 8.30am, links Rock Springs (well south on the Greyhound route) with Jackson. Not good connections, however and Rock Springs is 'a dump—spend as little time as possible here'.

Shuttle bus service around the park and to Yellowstone.

Car rentals in Jackson.

Hitching described as 'very easy'.

THE PACIFIC STATES

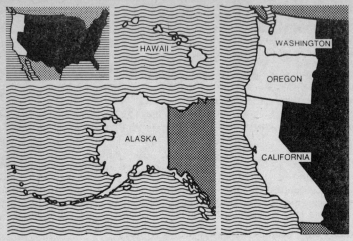

The Pacific states have everything and more. From ancient redwoods to modern cities, from lumbermen to film stars, from Polynesian huts to Arctic igloos, and in every state much of the most exciting scenery in America. The Russians, British, French, Spanish and Mexicans have all had claims here, and though Americans swept west under the conquering banner of Manifest Destiny, some of the old influences survive.

But the Pacific is also where the rainbow ends, where expectations must finally prove themselves. Enthusiasm reigns, and that is probably the region's most enjoyable quality—though the final results are still awaited.

ALASKA

Aleut for 'great land', Alaska is a great-hearted state with a penchant for superlatives: biggest, coldest, costliest, highest peak, fewest people, longest coastline, richest animal life, longest *and* shortest days.

Jeered at as 'Seward's Folly' when President Lincoln's Secretary of State bought it from the Russians for 2¢ an acre in 1867, Alaska is breathtakingly beautiful and well worth visiting, particularly in summer when daytime temperatures are moderate and there's lots of daylight. Campers and hikers be forewarned: mosquitoes are another of Alaska's superlatives.

Bus passes aren't valid in Alaska but Trek America (see under Travel in Background USA) offers tours. Bus passes *are* good through Canada: 'Ameripass valid up to Beaver Creek in the Yukon, near the Alaska–Canada border—about $35 on to Fairbanks'. Overseas visitors should consider the British Airways standby flights from London to Anchorage.

The land route of the Al-Can Highway from British Columbia to Fairbanks and Anchorage is adventurous, but the finest approach is by boat from Seattle or Prince Rupert. State-run, inexpensive ferries ply the Inside Passage year-round, giving you closeup looks at glaciers, islands, fjords, whales and stopover privileges at the various ports of call.

Prices in Alaska range from 'tolerable' in the southeastern panhandle to double those in Seattle/San Francisco and elsewhere. 'Some things are not much more than the lower 48, but be prepared for some nasty shocks.' Gasoline is on a par with California. Conventional lodging is very costly, but spartan youth hostels do exist and there are campgrounds everywhere. (Come prepared for plummeting temperatures at night.) Stick to locally-grown produce and seafood to keep food costs down.

National Park: Denali (formerly Mt McKinley)

THE INSIDE PASSAGE and THE PANHANDLE. Warmed by the Japanese Current and protected from the open sea by a necklace of islands, this southeastern waterway enjoys the state's mildest weather (a relative term meaning it rarely gets below zero in winter). Besides access by cruise ships, the state operates a nine-ferry system called the Alaska Marine Highway, an appropriate name since five of the seven ports in the Panhandle have no highway access to the outside world. 'Just the sight of a humpback whale breaching is enough to make the journey a memorable one.' 'Good vessels, interesting places to stop over, many opportunities to meet people.' 'In summer, Tongass Forest interpreters give free talks, film shows, on board. An imaginative and interesting service.'

First port of call is **Ketchikan**, still a salmon centre, now more dependent on cruiseship traffic. Weatherbeaten houses on stilts and the harbour give it a New England flavour, but it never rained like this in Massachusetts. The record is 202 inches a year here.

Sitka, once capital of Russian America and beautifully sited at the foot of Fuji-like Mt Edgecùmbe, has a reconstructed Russian cathedral, full of icons, plus interesting gravestones from this period. There is also a large and well-preserved assemblage of totems, and nearby waters are picturesque with icebergs and the great blue-green glaciers of the Chatham Strait.

Capital city **Juneau** climbs steep wooded hillsides with wooden stairways and a kaleidoscope of architectural styles. Mendenhall Glacier, 14 miles away, has camping and can be driven to. From

Haines, the old Dalton Trail leads off to the Klondike, several ghost towns and the amazing overhang of Rainbow Glacier.

In its sourdough heyday, **Skagway** was big-city size. Now down to 800, it's reaping a new gold rush of tourists to photograph its well-preserved wooden sidewalks, falsefront buildings and memorials to Soapy Smith, the local bad guy. Best during the oldtime fervour of Sourdough Days, celebrated in September. Skip the superexpensive and overtouristy vintage railway to the Yukon: 'Overrated—only the 20 minutes in/out of Skagway are really spectacular'.

ACCOMMODATION

Gilmore Hotel, 326 Front St, Ketchikan, 225-2174. Singles/doubles $30 up.

Hostel at 1st Methodist Church, Grand and Main, Ketchikan, 225-3331. $2.25, open Memorial-Labor Day. Showers. Open 7pm til 8.30am only. Mattresses on floors. 'Friendly.' Note: Alaska now has 7 limited service hostels, 4 in the Panhandle, the other 3 at Nome, Anchorage and Delta Junction.

United Presbyterian Hostel, Sawmill Creek Blvd and Baranoff St, Sitka, 747-6332. $2.25, open 1 June–1 Sept. No kitchen.

Alaskan Hotel, 167 S Franklin, Juneau, 586-1000. Singles $34, doubles $39 with shared bath, cheaper by week in winter. Sauna, jacuzzi, some kitchenettes. Oldest hotel in state, Victorian decor.

Hostel at Northern Light United Church, 11th and B Sts, Juneau, 586-9559. Open 1 June–1 Sept, $2.25. No kitchen or showers.

Hotel Halsingland, Ft Seward Dr, Pt Chilkoot (near Haines), 766-2000. Ask specifically for their economy rooms at $28–$35. Offseason discounts. Bus stop in front. Cafe, laundry. 'Classy—cheapest in town.'

Eagles Nest Motel, 1183 Haines Hwy, Haines, 766-2352. $38 singles, $46 doubles, colour TV.

Bear Creek Camp and Hostel, between Haines and Chilkoot, 766-2259. $5.25 summer. Meals available, hot showers, kitchen.

The Bunk House, 5th Ave, Skagway, $10 night, showers extra. 'Good place, welcomes all ages.'

Skagway Inn, 983-2289. $32–$40 singles and doubles.

Camping: free at all state parks but one-time $10 permit required. Also: $1 at Mendenhall Lake near Juneau, views of glacier. Free camping on steep Chilkoot Trail from Skagway; historic route taken by the miners.

OF INTEREST

Ketchikan: marvellous **Tlingit totems** at Saxman Park, Totem Bight Historical site and Totem Heritage Center, 601 Deermount St.

Sitka: National Monument traces the history of **Russian involvement** in Alaska. See in conjunction with the Eskimo and Russian exhibits in the **Sheldon Jackson Museum**, $1.

Juneau: Alaska Historical Society and Museum, 4th and Seward Sts. Noted for its Eskimo exhibits. Also see the **State Museum** on Whittier St for good artefacts; free. In summer, nightly **salmon bakes**, **walking tours** of historic Juneau, through the Chamber of Commerce at 3rd and Seward, 586-2201.

Glacier Bay National Monument, 50 miles NW of Juneau. Beautiful and untouched wilderness of seals, whales, bears and 20 glaciers. Access by boat or plane only; expensive.

Haines: Old Ft Seward, now a centre for the Chilkat dancers. Don't miss Indian artists at work on totems, masks, and soapstone, Mon–Fri 9am–5pm, Memorial to Labor Day. Near Haines is the world's largest concentration of **bald eagles**; best months Oct–Nov.

INFORMATION

Visitors Bureau, 131 Front St, 225-6166, Ketchikan.

Chamber of Commerce, 3rd and Seward, 586-2201, Juneau; and Visitors Center at State Office Building, 465-2010.

Elsewhere, look up Chambers of Commerce in the phonebook.

TRAVEL

Alaska Marine Highway system, Pouch R, Juneau, 907/465-3941.

Contact for reservations, schedules and other info. From Seattle to Skagway about $155; Juneau–Haines, $15; Juneau–Sitka, $22. '25% discount Oct–Apr.' No charge for stopovers. Meals, staterooms cost extra, can run about $70/day (with fare). 'Tolerates camping out and sleeping bags on top-deck solarium for those who have the gear and can't sleep on reclining seats.' 'Boat deck is heated, has camping beds, showers, lockers provided free.' 'Cafeteria good value, but taking your own food definitely advisable.' 'Only 2 ferries make the complete Seattle–Skagway run, twice weekly in summer. Two ferries work Prince Rupert–Skagway. Winter services much reduced due to maintenance.' (Also see Seattle.)

Train from Skagway to Whitehorse, 110 miles, $55, 6½ hours.

Buses from Haines to Anchorage, 3 times weekly. Skagway–Whitehorse runs also.

THE ALASKA HIGHWAY. Gravel or dirt-surfaced for about 1000 of its 1523 miles, the Al-Can is actually rougher in summer than in winter. Beginning at Dawson Creek, British Columbia, it covers 915 bumpy miles to Whitehorse in the Yukon; at Tok, it splits in two, one branch towards Fairbanks, the other, Anchorage.

ACCOMMODATION

Plenty of expensive motels along the way. Also numerous campgrounds; bring a tent.

TRAVEL

'Soon after Dawson Creek, the Highway peters out into a dusty, pot-holed track until you get to Alaska. Make sure your car is in good running order and carry a few of the more essential spare parts. Garages charge what they like for spares.' Fill up whenever you hit a gas station—they are few and far between.

Hitching: long waits. Don't get let off at Tok Junction (which gets below-zero temps in Sept): 'horror stories abound of people getting stuck'. Alaskan law requires motorists to pick up hitchhikers when it is very cold out, but we don't recommend you put it to the test.

Greyhound bus service. Year-round, fewer schedules in winter. Informative drivers; informality reigns.

INFORMATION

Milepost ($8), published by Alaskan magazine, is an essential mile-by-mile guide to the Highway, both Alaska and Canada portions.

Free is *Worlds of Alaska*, from Division of Tourism, Pouch E, Juneau, 99811; useful info on all aspects of the state.

ANCHORAGE. Largest city (200,000) and unremarkably modern since its rebuilding after the 1964 quake, Anchorage makes a good excursion base for Mt McKinley and the islands of southwestern Alaska. Besides its transportation links, Anchorage has a fairly rambunctious nightlife.

ACCOMMODATION

Fireweed Hotel, 604 W 26th Ave, 277-2911. 'A long way from downtown.' Singles $18 up, doubles $26 up. Coin laundry.

Inlet Inn, 539 H St, downtown; and elsewhere. No-frills budget chain, singles $25–$40, doubles $30–$45. Well kept.

Hostel, Minnesota Dr and 32nd Ave, 276-3635 or 276-9522 (7am–11pm). $6.25. On 6 bus route from airport. Laundry, limited cooking, near stores. 'Good place, easy to meet people.' 'Clean, very crowded July–Aug.' 8am weekday, 9am weekend checkout, strictly enforced.

YMCA, 609 F St, 277-8522. Dorms, men only, $12. Free Rescue Mission nextdoor. 'Very disreputable characters, drunks, etc' in both places.

B&B: through Stay With a Friend, 3605 Arctic Blvd, Number 173, Anchorage 99503.

OF INTEREST

National Forest office, 540 W 5th Ave; free films, including one of the 1964 earthquake taken from a boat in Valdez harbour near the epicentre. 'Very frightening and eye-opening—film also shown in Valdez.' NB: 'Still regular tremors—one at 5.5 while we were here!'

Alaska Arctic Indian and Eskimo Museum, 819 W 4th Ave, 279-5857. Open summer Mon–Sat 10am–10pm, Sun 12–5pm.

Historical and Fine Arts Museum, 121 W 7th Ave, 264-4326. Daily summer, Tue–Sun rest of year. Til 9pm on Tue, Thur. Free. From prehistoric to contemporary arts and crafts. Fascinating displays of Anchorage post-earthquake.

Portage Glacier, 40 miles away. Bus service. Also tours available from Anchorage, calling at Alyeska Ski Resort on the way.

Homer, southwest of Anchorage, is recommended as a friendly youth hangout and a place to find seasonal cannery work. 'Fantastic scenery.' 'Salty Dog Tavern on the spit is the "in" place.'

INFORMATION

Visitors Bureau, 4th Ave and F Sts, 274-3531. 276-3200 for recording. Also call 276-2787 for events hotline.

TRAVEL

Alaska Airlines and Wien Air Alaska (from Portland, Seattle or San Francisco) serve Anchorage, Fairbanks, Ketchikan, Sitka, Juneau and other towns. Cheap stopovers between point of origin and your furthest destination, about $15 each. Also check promotional fares.

The Alaska RR runs between Anchorage and Fairbanks via Denali National Park, 265-2494. 'Has express and a slow train—slow one much nicer, more room and stops at the most outlandish places.' 'Train slows down for photographers at the best spots.' 'One train per week, Oct–May.' Also a daily train from Anchorage south to Portage and Whittier; 'can see Portage Glacier from it'.

Local bus, 264-6543. 'Nascent bus system, friendly service, 50¢.' Circular route around town uses London double-deckers. No service Sunday, very little at night. 'Not a good town to be without a car.'

DENALI NATIONAL PARK. Mount McKinley has twin peaks, South being higher at 20,320 feet. Named for one of the assassinated presidents in US history, the mountain is unfortunately shrouded in cloud 60 percent of the time. This giant, tallest in North America, surveys a vast kingdom of tundra, mountain wilderness and unusual wildlife (caribou, Dahl sheep, grizzlies, etc). One hundred miles of gravel road allow you to see much of the park by bus (by car, only 12 miles unless you have a campsite reserved), but hiking or horseback riding one of the numerous trails radiating from McKinley Park Hotel is the best way to enter into the spirit of the place. Best views of the mountaintop at Wonder Lake—'have to go at least 8 miles into the park to see the mountain'. Free shuttle buses to Wonder Lake, Eielson Visitors Center and other points. No food or gas in park except at park entrance. Don't overlook a trip to Yentna, the 'Galloping Glacier'—most beautifully coloured on earth.

ACCOMMODATION

McKinley Park Station Hotel, 683-2215. 2 miles from main entrance, has costly rooms but for the adventurous, dorm-style cabins, old railroad cars with berths, from $10 without bath. Rumours of 'bunk beds for $2 as temporary Youth Hostel—no light or water but you can use hotel toilet facilities'. The rail motif extends to dining room, lobby. Perennially packed but a very Alaskan place. Wildlife coach tours from the hotel, $25 with lunch and recommended. Open June–Sept.

TRAVEL

Free and frequent shuttle bus service to all 7 campgrounds in park till Labor Day, reduced after that.
Rail, bus and air service from Anchorage, Fairbanks.

FAIRBANKS.

FAIRBANKS. Warmest place in Alaska in summer, Fairbanks was once a frontier town with 93 saloons in one three-block stretch. Today it booms with oil from the Pipeline and is the second largest city, located at mile 1523 of the Alaska Highway and 130 miles south of the Arctic Circle. Try to time your visit for one of its many festivals: the Eskimo/Indian Olympics (dancing, blanket toss, etc) each August and the Solstice Festival, 19–21 June, are among the wildest. Play or watch midnight baseball at the latter. 'Definitely the rough frontier town—drunken Indians everywhere.' 'Surprisingly nice—lots of trees.'

ACCOMMODATION

The oil boom makes lodging/food especially high here. However: Fairbanks Hotel, 517 Third Ave, 456-6440. $25 single, $31 double, shared bath, $31 and $35 with private bath. Bus stop nearby. Small, clean, no frills.
B&B through International Spareroom, comfortable home near Alaskaland, University, on bus lines: $26 single, $33 double, shared shower, will do evening meals also.
Fairbanks Rescue Mission, on Cushman above 12th. Free. 'Safe and homely, more like a youth hostel.' 'Also a Salvation Army shelter on 1st Ave.'
Youth Hostel camping: $2 night, with use of more expensive campground facilities adjacent; near Alaskaland.
Cripple Creek Resort Hotel, Ester City, 5 miles from U of Alaska. Open May–Sept. Group transit available. About $30–$35 single/double. Former mining camp with traditional, family-style meals, gold panning, saloon, riding. Unusual and popular.
U of Alaska Student Union building: info board for digs, rides, etc.

OF INTEREST

Eskimo Arts and Crafts at U of Alaska Museum. 479-7505. 4½ miles NW of city.

Over 125,000 items, free open year-round 9am–5pm 15 May–31 Aug, 1pm–5pm rest of year.

Alaskaland, 2 miles outside city near airport. The 40-acre site was developed to commemorate the Alaska Centennial in 1967 and portrays state history with goldrush cabins, a sternwheeler, Indian and Eskimo villages and a mining valley. Closes end of Aug. Pricey but gets praise: 'Alaska Salmon bake—about $13, some nights, all-you-can-eat. Lovely!'

Eagle Summit, 108 miles along the Steese Highway, from where you can watch the sun fail to set on 21 and 22 June.

TRAVEL

Air (see Anchorage)

Train to McKinley and Anchorage, 465-7736.

Local bus, 456-EASY. 'Very limited, most journeys $1. Fairbanks very difficult without a car.'

CALIFORNIA

There's more of everything in California: more people (24 million), more money (it's the world's sixth richest 'country', producing 12 percent of the nation's GNP), more cars (two per person), more scientific activity (a lion's share of the Nobel laureates and 80 percent of the pure sciences research). A key partner in the emerging Pacific Rim economic powerhouse, California leads in both agricultural and industrial output, from avocados to aerospace, computer hardware to entertainment and the arts.

All that economic wealth is apt to overshadow the state's true riches, which were here long before Indians, gold miners, movie stars and hot tubbers: its natural beauties, staggering because they are so many and varied. A partial list: rich groves of redwoods containing the tallest trees on earth, 1264 miles of shoreline and beaches, the mountain wonders of Shasta and Whitney, the stark superlatives of Death Valley, the glorious glacier-cut landscape of Yosemite. Most of it is easy of access and can be enjoyed in a benign Mediterranean climate.

The California climate is also one of possibility, of change, a yeasty blend of new ideas, new consciousness and new cultures (25 percent of America's foreign-born citizens and aliens live here). It's been said that what America is becoming, California is already.

All these factors make a powerful drawing card. It's no wonder California is the leading tourist destination for Americans and foreigners alike.

National Parks: Kings Canyon
Lassen Volcanic
Redwood
Sequoia
Yosemite

ACCOMMODATION OVERVIEW

Perhaps in response to its popularity, California offers a great variety of lodging options, many of them dead cheap. This is but a brief summary to keep city listings from getting too long. If you plan to be here for any length of time, you should pick up *The Moneywise Guide to California*.

1. Youth hostels. Operating hostels number about 25, with 7 in San Diego County, 4 in Los Angeles County, 7 around the Bay Area and a sprinkling elsewhere near Yosemite, Mt Shasta and the redwoods. New hostels open all the time; others are in a state of flux because of precarious funding. Always enquire locally—even the AYH handbook cannot keep pace with developments.

2. Bed and Breakfast agencies. Especially recommended are B&B International and International Spareroom, both with statewide homes and listed in the Accommodation background. Other suggestions: California B&B, Box 1551, Sacramento, (916)442-7298 (statewide, $15 to $65); California B&B Inn Service, Box 1256, Chico, (916)343-9733 (statewide, $20 to $45); Digs West, 8191 Crowley Circle, Buena Park, (714)739-1669 (Greater LA, $25–$45); Home Suite Homes, 1470 Firebird Way, Sunnyvale, (408)733-7215 (Northern Cal, $16–$55); Megan's Friends, 1230-A Fourth St, Los Osos, (805)528-6645 (Central coast, $20–$45); Rent A Room International, 1032 Sea Lane, Corona del Mar, (714)640-2330 (Greater LA–San Diego, $25–$30).

3. Motel 6. The chain began here and has over 90 units in California. One unit will book ahead to another but you pay for the call. Their 6pm 'show up or lose your money/reservation' policy is extremely firm, so be sure you can arrive on time. Advance booking a must for popular spots like Lake Tahoe and Palm Springs. No Motel 6s in San Francisco or the downtown or western sections of Los Angeles.

4. University lodgings. The following campuses have summer lodgings open to students and (in many cases) to the general public: UC Berkeley, Pacific College (Fresno), Cal State Fresno, UCLA, US International University (San Diego), San Diego State, San Francisco State, San Jose State, and Stanford (Palo Alto).

5. Camping. National Park and Monument fees range from $2 to $6; State Parks, the same. Many State Parks (especially along the coast) have hiker-biker sites for 50¢, first-come, first-served. Countless free, primitive camping opportunities in National Forest and other wilderness areas. Most require permits. 'State campsites are a good deal if you have a carload of people. Very good facilities.' 'Police will allow sleeping on Southern Cal beaches (ie, for foreign tourists anyway) but be careful—many are hangouts for gays with attendant queer-bashers.'

SAN DIEGO.

SAN DIEGO. A breezy, casual seaport and resort city, famous for top-notch Mexican food, lavish Happy Hour spreads and good beaches (all of them a busride from downtown, however). Strategically located 100 miles south of Los Angeles and as close to Tijuana as any sane person should want to get, San Diego has other pluses: a plethora of hostels and cheap B&Bs; grandly varied scenery nearby; and first-rate museums, most with free days. Despite its size and overpowering military presence, San Diego has a small-town flavour and friendliness that is very pleasant.

ACCOMMODATION

Clarke's Lodge, 1765 Union St, 234-6787. Single/double $25, student discounts. 8 blocks from Greyhound. 'Very clean', 'very friendly', 'excellent value'. In-room coffee, pool, colour TV, free phone.

Wilsonia Hotel, 1545 Second Ave at Beech, 237-9686. Singles $12–$17, bus stop outside, 6 blocks from Greyhound.

YMCA, 1115 Eighth Ave, 232-7451. Coed, singles $14, twins $21, communal showers. Mixed reviews: 'clean, friendly', 'lots of weirdos, unsafe area at night'. The Armed Forces Y on Broadway has a cheap dorm for AYH ($4.25, need sleeping bag) but it's a pit.

YWCA, 1012 C St, 239-0355. Women 18 and over, dorms $6, singles from $11. Close to transit, out of worst area. 'Good, clean, laundry and cooking facilities.'

Blue Bird Motel, 4444 Pacific Hwy, 296-9155. Near Old Town. Bus stop 1 block. Singles $20 and up.

Pt Loma Hostel, 3790 Udall St, 223-4778. 6½ miles from downtown; take 35 bus. $5.50 members, $7.50 non-members. Comfy. 'Well equipped, near cheap markets, rents bikes, surfboards.' 20 minutes from beach.

FOOD

Chuey's, 1910 Main St, 234-6937. Take 32 bus to door. Mon–Fri 11am–9pm, Sat 11am–5pm. String beef tacos, other outstanding Mexican dishes $2 to $6. The Best. Honestly. Nearby murals at Chicano Park on the Coronado Bay Bridge make a fitting post-*comida* stroll.

Runner-up for best Mexican food is El Indio Tortilla Shop, 3695 India St, an artists' district. Heavenly chicken burritos, 50 takeout items, park across the way.

Franco's Deli, 819 C St. 'Excellent pizza, cheap specials, all day breakfasts. Small, very friendly, clean.'

Farmers bazaar, 215 Seventh Ave, 233-0281. Central produce market, low prices, top-quality.

Tug's Tavern, 4650 Mission Blvd. Mexican food. 'Cheap dinners—under $2, less on Thur nights.' 'Very friendly.'

Happy Hour suggestions: Cafe del Moro in Balboa Park (incredible margaritas); Saccio's Fish Factory and Anthony's Harborside on the waterfront; and Cullpepper's at 5th and Spruce, Imperial House at 505 Kalmia (live jazz piano, best munchies Thur–Fri), and Ten Downing, 1250 Sixth Ave, all downtown.

OF INTEREST

Broadway pier, 235-3534, west end of Broadway. Free 45-minute tours Sat–Sun, 1pm–4pm, of Navy ships, moored here in rotation. 'I saw US frigate, control room, bridge, guns.' Harbour excursions, 233-6872, from the pier, frequent 1-hr trips $4.

Old Town, a snippet of the city's original heart, along San Diego Ave. Free walking tours from the Plaza, recommended to make the few historical remnants come to life. Up the hill is Presidio Park; its Serra Museum ($1.50) houses documents, maps, archaeological finds from the nearby dig.

Balboa Park. Take the bus or bike to this superlative 1400-acre park, whose pink-icing Mexican Churrigueresque buildings were designed for the 1915–16 Panama–California Exposition by Bertram Goodhue. 12 museums and galleries, a zoo, carousel complete with brass ring, pipe organ and other concerts, free sidewalk entertainment, free facilities for everything from volleyball to frisbee golf. Tue is free for **Museums of Art, Natural History, Aerospace**; Wed for **Museum of Man** (good Indian displays); others are always free. **Space Theater/Science Center** does cost $4, seniors/students $2.50. Science portion is smallish, no great shakes but the 360-degree films are exhilarating. 'Worth it if addicted to OMNI-Max films.' 'Very interesting—Columbia flight and other NASA space trials.'

The famous **Zoo** has 4000 creatures, $5 fee, $8 if you take the bus tour and children's zoo options. Don't miss the walk-through hummingbird aviary, the koalas and the primates. 'Good zoo but not quite as good as expected.' 'Need 5 hours to see it all.' Open 9am–9pm mid-June through Labor Day, 9am–4pm Nov–Feb, 9am–5pm rest of year. Take 7-B bus from YMCA.

Also at Balboa: summer light opera at the **Starlight Bowl** ('$6—very well worth it'), free Sun afternoon music at the organ pavilion, and the Pacific Relations cottages.

Sea World, 1720 S Shores Rd, 222-6363, on Mission Bay north of downtown. Expensive at $12 so you'd better like performing whales, dolphins, seals. 'Fantastic, moving, especially Shamu the killer whale.' 'Don't miss seal and otter shows.' 'An all-day affair.' Daily 9am–dusk.

Cabrillo National Monument, Pt Loma, K bus from Broadway. Splendiferous view from the site where Juan Cabrillo first landed in California in 1542. Excellent tidepools, nature walks, films on whales, exhibit hall. Open 7am–7.45pm summers, til 5.15pm winters.

Wild Animal Park, 30 miles north off I-5 near Escondido, 234-6541. 1800 acres of freely roaming animals which you view from a 50-minute ride in a monorail. 'Lots to see—don't miss bird shows. Best monorail run is 4.30pm—most animal activity.' 'Amazing scale—has concerts outside.' $8 includes entrance, monorail, all live shows.

Beaches: closest to downtown is **Pacific/Mission Beach**, funky in patches but great surfing, swimming, socialising, body watching, beachfront bars and restaurants. Surfboard, skate, bike rentals. Eat chili dogs at Sluggo's, brunch at World Famous, get happy at Jose Murphy's or Halligan's. Bus 34 from Broadway.

Posh **La Jolla**, 15 miles north, has the corner on natural beauty, from sculptured rocks at Windansea to the St Tropezlike La Jolla Shores and limpid La Jolla Cove. Takeout from Clay's Texas Pit BBQ, 623 Pearl, would make fine accompaniment. UCSD is here but don't bother unless you want to stay at the International Center ('very good, friendly, $9 a night').

ENTERTAINMENT

San Diego's music scene is hotting up; liveliest clubs include Zebra, in Gaslamp Quarter; Spirit, the New Wave headquarters at 1130 Buenos Ave, 276-3993; and Bacchanal, 8022 Clairemont Mesa Blvd. All have cover; check *The Reader* (free weekly) for details.

High-calibre Shakespeare festival at Balboa Park (June–Sept) has nightly performances except Mon. Cheap tickets on sale 8pm; free revel with Queen Bess, jugglers, etc, on the lawn before each performance.

INFORMATION

Plaza Center, 324 Broadway, 234-5191 (only info centre open on Sat); Visitors Bureau at 1200 Third Ave, Suite 824, 232-3101; at House of Hospitality in Balboa Park; in Old Town; and along highway.

Travelers Aid, 122 Fourth Ave, Suite 201, 232-7991 or 297-4314.

Mexico: consulate at 225 W Broadway, 234-8443 for tourist cards, info.

Mexican Tourist Office, 600 B St, Suite 1220, 236-9314.

TRAVEL

Greyhound, 120 W Broadway, 239-9171. (Pickwick Hotel upstairs has $25 and up doubles but getting rather mangy and dubious: 'Ask for bug spray—you'll need it').

Trailways, 310 W C St, 232-2001. Caveat emptor: 'Trailways pass valid to Tijuana but not back to US'.

Tijuana Trolley, 231-1466. Every 15 minutes, leaves across from AMTRAK. $2 return, 50¢ around downtown. 'Buy a return—you won't want to stay long.' 'Quick, comfortable.' Much cheaper than Mexicoach, Greyhound, etc.

AMTRAK, 1050 Kettner Blvd, 239-9021. Romantic 1915 depot with twin Moorish towers. About 8 runs daily to LA, 2 hrs, 45 min.

Local bus, 233-3004 or 239-8161. 80¢ to $1.25. Covers city, north to La Jolla, south to Tijuana. Cheap airport bus, $1. 'Very efficient, easy to understand.'

Rental cars: Greyhound Rentacar, 232-7268 or 800327-2501. Under $100/week, unlimited free mileage; can be booked from Britain also. Numerous used car rentals, including: Cheap Heaps, 811 25th St, 235-8733 from $9/day.

Gray Line, 231-9922, runs to Sea World, Animal Park.

AAACON Transport, 3338 Lincoln Ave, 280-4411.
Auto Driveaway, 1122 Fourth Ave, 233-6249.
Ride board at Travelers Aid, 232-7991.

ANZA-BORREGO DESERT and EASTERN SAN DIEGO COUNTY.

The biggest state park in the nation is in San Diego's backyard and reached by a scenic 90-mile climb through forests, mountains, and the charming gold-mining village of Julian, ultimately spiralling down 3000 feet to the Sonoran desert floor.

It can be done by bicycle (tough) or rental car but there's also cheap bus service via the Northeastern Rural Bus, 765-0145 (several times weekly from El Cajon, east of San Diego, to Julian, Borrego Springs and other points).

At once desolate and grand, the Anza-Borrego desert encompasses sandstone canyons, rare elephant trees, pine-covered mountains, oases and wadis. Springtime brings a profusion of wildflowers, which you can see year-round at the excellent sound and light presentation at the Visitors Center, 767-5292. Camping is allowed anywhere; there are also a dozen state and county sites (free to $6, depending on amenities). Best months are November–May; it's terribly hot thereafter. If you don't want to camp, stay in Julian at one of the two hostels rather than in expensive Borrego Springs. Either way, don't miss out on the spectacular apple pie and chicken pie at the Julian Cafe.

PALM SPRINGS.

A class act, from its artfully weathered New Mexican adobes to its privileged setting on the lee side of 10,831-foot Mt Jacinto. Even the Indians are millionaires here, but don't let that put you off. During the hot, dry summer, prices melt like ice cubes and almost everything has air conditioning and a pool.

ACCOMMODATION
Each hotel seems to set its own dates for low season, very approximately June through Sept. Rates always lowest Sun–Thur. To find the best deal, check newspaper specials, ask the Visitors Bureau, call around and don't be afraid to dicker. Except for Motel 6, winter rates are generally shocking.
Motel 6, 595 E Palm Canyon Dr, 327-2044. Lush setting, pool, book ages ahead, rates year-round are $16 single, $20 double.
Desert Hotel, 285 N Indian Ave, 325-3013. Extremely basic, no pool, near Greyhound. $17 up single. 'A bloody dump.'
Carlton Hotel, 1333 N Indian Ave, 325-5416. After 6 July, rates from $18 double.
Sunbeam Inn, 291 Camino Monte Vista, 325-3812. 8 July–30 Sept, singles/doubles are $25 up. Cheerful, small, has pool.

FOOD
In summer, they practically give the food away; check local paper, giveaway tabloids for Early Bird, brunch and other specials.
Nate's Deli, 283 N Palm Canyon Dr, 325-3506. Good noshing, especially the Nate's Special if you're extra hungry. A local institution.

OF INTEREST

Aerial Tramway, off Highway 111, 325-1391. 18 minutes, 8516 ft, and 5 climatic zones later, you're on Mt Jacinto. In summer, it's 30–40 degrees cooler, so bring a jacket. At the top: free film, unfree food/drinks, mule rides, backpacking and free camping (shelter cabin near Mt Jack's peak), plus events. 'Can see part of San Andreas Fault from top.' Closed for maintenance approximately 8 Sept–15 Oct; call first. Otherwise 8am–9.15pm weekends, from 10am on weekdays. $7.

Desert Museum (impressive modern art, Indian basketry), Living Desert Reserve (1200 acres of native plants, 'after sundown' room with nocturnal beasties) and Indian Canyons (waterfalls, palms) are closed the entire summer.

Nearby:

Cabot's Indian Pueblo Museum, 67–616 E Desert View Ave, in Desert Hot Springs, 329-7610. Eccentric 5-storey pueblo, built of found objects by Cabot Yerxa. Inside are the prospector/packrat's mementos of the Battle of Little Bighorn, Eskimo, Indian relics. $2. Open year-round, Wed–Mon.

INFORMATION/TRAVEL

Chamber of Commerce, 190 W Amado Rd, 325-1577; and at airport, 327-8411. Pick up the *Desert Weekly* and *Palm Springs Monthly*, both free and packed with info, special offers.

Greyhound, 311 N Indian Ave, 325-2053. On the Phoenix–LA route.

Local bus, 323-8157. Cheap shuttle around town also.

Desert Stage Lines, 367-3581. Buses to Joshua Tree and Twentynine Palms.

Rentacar, 320-5781.

AAACON, 454 N Indian Ave, 325-1166.

JOSHUA TREE NATIONAL MONUMENT. In the high desert 54 miles east of Palm Springs is this 870-square-mile sanctuary, full of startling rock formations, animals from mountain lions to kangaroo rats, colourful cacti and giant 50-foot yucca lilies with manlike arms and twisted bodies. They were named in the 1850s by Mormon pioneers, who recalled a line from *The Book of Joshua:* 'Thou shalt follow the way pointed for Thee by the trees'.

The park and all campsites except two are free but you need to bring food, water and firewood. Good exhibits, museum and ranger-guided tours from Park Headquarters at Twentynine Palms and the Visitor Center at Cottonwood Springs. From 5185-foot Salton View, you get a splendid panorama of the Coachella Valley, the Salton Sea and Palm Springs.

LOS ANGELES. Galaxylike, Los Angeles is invisible by day, a banal *ad nauseam* of freeway exits, housing tracts, Main Streets that aren't, the whole of it crowded under an exhausted sky that reeks of car exhaust and chlorine. But when the stars come out, so does LA, the biggest star of them all. Just like regular cities, Los Angeles has a mandatory 'view' spot, and that should be your first night's destination. From the perspective of Mulholland Drive, cantering along the spine of the Santa Monica Mountains, you see a megawatt Milky Way: 7.5 million people, 90 cities, 40,000 streets, 4000 square miles of organised chaos, pulsing with power and purpose.

LA is a water junkie, the one commodity that has enabled it to become the decentralised, auto-oriented place you see today. Mulholland Drive is in fact named for the engineer who brought LA its first big fix of H_2O at the turn of the century.

The city began in 1781 as a racially mixed agricultural community and got its first real influx of people on the strength of its oranges. Today the Big Orange makes its money from aerospace, the entertainment industries, oil, chemicals and shipping. Its ethnic mix includes cities within cities of Hispanics, Japanese, Jews, American Indians, Haitians, Armenians, blacks, Koreans and more, adding a great deal to the cultural and gastronomic life of the region. (It's also a headache for the LA school system: over 80 languages are used in it.)

If you haven't yet acquired a car, this is surely now or never. You will no doubt get lost, spend uncounted travellers cheques on gasoline and fruitless hours looking for parking, but there's a sly exhilaration to driving LA freeways. It's like urban surfing. Once you've experienced the silken seamless pull of traffic, conquered a complex exchange as cars confidently curl on and off into new trajectories, and got a taste of life in the fast lane, you'll probably agree.

SURVIVAL

Parts of LA are mighty rough, no getting around it. Unfortunately, the Greyhound/RTD terminal is located in one of the worst Skid Row areas. Try to avoid arriving at night, especially if you're female. Head west on 6th or 7th Sts away from the terminal and the war zone, which lies between Los Angeles and San Pedros Sts and between 3rd and 10th or so. Main, Spring and Broadway are 'buffer' streets: some blocks OK; others, watch your step and your wallet.

If you travel by Trailways or AMTRAK, you'll arrive at Union Station, a pleasanter spot in a better neighbourhood. However, you are then some distance from any lodging. Walking at night from Union Station is not recommended.

ACCOMMODATION

LA's interests and pleasures are so far-flung that it takes the logistical planning normally devoted to a military campaign to get to them. First decide what your must-see items will be and *then* choose one or more lodging bases. Lodging is divided into 5 areas: downtown, West LA (covering Hollywood, Beverly Hills, Westwood, UCLA), the airport district, the coast and Anaheim/Disneyland vicinity. Please note that downtown LA receives the lion's share of lodgings and food only because of its importance as the arrival/departure centre for ground travellers. Its tourist attractions are relatively few and parts of it are quite unsavoury. If planning to stay for any length of time, stay elsewhere. When arriving/departing by plane, the airport district and Beverly Hills are best. You may be surprised to learn that the latter has good bus service and several bargain hotels.

Downtown:

Motel de Ville, 1123 W 7th St, 624-8474. Doubles $27-$32, some cheaper rooms without bath. Colour TV, air conditioning, pool. On busy, well-lit street. 'Good value.'

Hotel Huntington, 723 Main, 627-3186. Cheap but very questionable. Bad area. Singles $8 up, doubles $11-$18. 'Door would not lock, bugs in rooms but clean sheets, friendly people.'

Milner Hotel, 813 S Flower, 627-6981. Singles $22 up, doubles $27-$38, includes

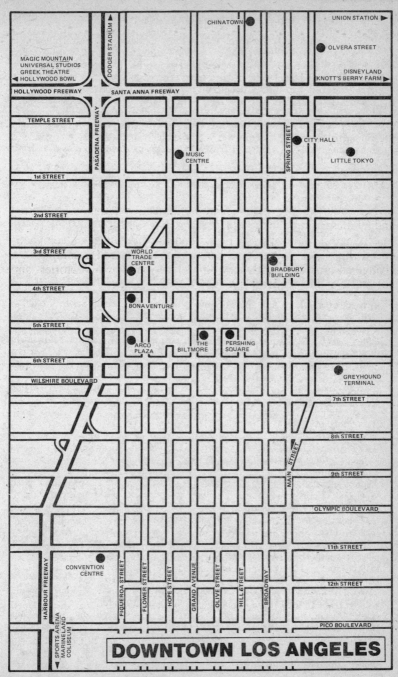

CHINATOWN

UNION STATION ▶

OLVERA STREET

MAGIC MOUNTAIN
UNIVERSAL STUDIOS
GREEK THEATRE
◀ HOLLYWOOD BOWL

DODGER STADIUM ▲

DISNEYLAND
KNOTT'S BERRY FARM ▶

HOLLYWOOD FREEWAY   SANTA ANNA FREEWAY

TEMPLE STREET

PASADENA FREEWAY

SPRING STREET

CITY HALL

MUSIC
CENTRE

LITTLE TOKYO

1st STREET

2nd STREET

3rd STREET

WORLD
TRADE
CENTRE

BRADBURY
BUILDING

4th STREET

BONAVENTURE

5th STREET

ARCO
PLAZA

THE
BILTMORE

PERSHING
SQUARE

6th STREET

WILSHIRE BOULEVARD

GREYHOUND
TERMINAL

7th STREET

8th STREET

MAIN STREET

9th STREET

OLYMPIC BOULEVARD

11th STREET

HARBOUR FREEWAY

CONVENTION
CENTRE

FIGUEROA STREET

FLOWER STREET

HOPE STREET

GRAND AVENUE

OLIVE STREET

HILL STREET

BROADWAY

12th STREET

▲ SPORTS ARENA
MARINELAND
COLISEUM

PICO BOULEVARD

DOWNTOWN LOS ANGELES

continental breakfast. Good weekly rates. 'Good clean rooms, very friendly and safe, good bar at back.'

Rainbow Hotel, 536 S Hope St, 627-9941. A congenial place near Central Library, out of the war zone. Discounts with student ID, affiliated with the Y and accepts vouchers. Much cheaper with shared bath: single $22, double $26. Inexpensive cafeteria, good Japanese food downstairs. 'Excellent rooms. To qualify for low weekly rate in double room, 2 people must be of same sex, dorm style.'

Rosslyn Hotel, 112 W 5th St, 624-3311. Close to Greyhound yet good locale. Single with shower/TV/phone, $22. Doubles $26 up. 'Friendly, helpful, clean.'

Clark Hotel, 426 S Hill St, 624-4121. Discounts for Greyhound bus pass. Singles without bath begin at $18, doubles at $22. Friendly. Near bus stop, post office.

San Carlo Hotel, 507 W 5th St, 628-2291. On Pershing Square. Singles with shared bath from $19.

West LA:

St Regis Motor Hotel, 11955 Wilshire Blvd, 477-6021. Prices from $26 single. 'Close to nicer parts of LA.'

UCLA Housing office, 825-4491. Leads to campus lodging and to frat digs with kitchen facilities. Summer only. Weekly preferred but you may be able to get nightly rates. Try frat houses also along Hilgard, Strathmore, Landfair and Gayley Sts.

American Student Hostel Association, 11024 Strathmore, 208-9055. Summer only, open 24 hrs, about $8/night. 'Friendly owner, very basic, bring sleeping bag.'

Howard's Weekly Apartments, various locations at 1225 N El Centro, 1738 N Whitley and on Pass Ave in Burbank. Call 466-6943 to book. Rentals on per-week basis but occasional lets for 3 days come up. A grand deal with clean linen, maid service, free parking, hall phones, coin-op laundry and nice apartments. Doubles $107/week. 'A suite for 4 costs $140/week. Very modern and clean. This must be the cheapest place in Hollywood!'

Hollywood YMCA-Hostel, 1553 N Hudson Ave, 467-4161. Y section $15–$18 single; hostel part is $6.25 without card, $4.50 with. In after 9pm, out by 8.30am. 'Men have beds but women only the floor!' Must be 18 years. Cafe, no kitchen. 'Pleasant, convenient, 2 blocks from Trailways.'

Beverly Vista, 120 S Reeves Dr, 276-1031. Singles $19 up with shared bath, a simple and safe place, excellently located near Beverly Wilshire Hotel. Direct bus from airport to Beverly Wilshire. A winner. Book ahead.

Hotel del Flores, 409 N Crescent Dr, 274-5115. Singles begin at $20, 2 night minimum stay. Very clean, pleasant management, superb and safe location.

El Patio Motel, 11466 Ventura Blvd, Studio City, 760-9602. Convenient to Universal Studios. $25 single/double. Quiet, AC, TV.

Airport district:

Westchester Family YMCA-Hostel, 8015 S Sepulveda Dr, 776-0922. Open 1 June–15 Sept only. 2 miles north of airport. From downtown, take 871 bus from Olive St. 'Good clean hostel with plenty of facilities.' $5.25 members, $6.25 non-members. Up at 7.30am, out by 8.30am, can stow gear. Breakfasts, $2.50.

Sands Motel, 5330 W Imperial Hwy, 641-7990. A good bargain for groups or families. 'Suite of 3 rooms, 3 double beds, $60 for 6 people. Thick carpets, shower, TV. Free shuttle to airport, very good value.'

The coast:

Action Youth America, Carson and Clark Sts, Vet Stadium, Long Beach, 420-8696. Bus 11 from downtown LA. Dorm lodgings in mobile homes, $12/night includes coffee and orange juice. Run by Brits. 'Excellent.' Year-round.

Catalina Island (boat from Long Beach, San Pedro or Newport Beach). Free camping in isolated caves and coves; permit required from Island Conservancy, 206 Metropole Ave, 510-1421. Pack in water, food. Spectacular wildlife. Also on Catalina, The Island Inn, 125 Metropole Ave, Avalon, 510-1623. Singles/doubles $25 up, cheapest place on this picturesque island.

Colonial Inn, 421 8th St, Huntington Beach, 536-9184. A new AYH affiliate, $6/night, most rooms semi-private. 4 blocks to surfing beaches, near pier with Greyhound, Orange County bus stop. Year-round. Kitchen. With the money you save, you can hang out at The Golden Bear, a 300-seat club that gets the very best music acts.

Anaheim/Disneyland vicinity:

Rates lowest Sept through May, sometimes 40% lower. Also cheaper midweek and on non-holidays. Rooms $16–$20 in offseason; same rooms $26–$35 in summer. Rates nearly identical for singles/doubles, so it pays to double up.

Numerous motels surrounding Disneyland along W Katella and S Beach Blvd. Frequently mentioned are: Princess Motel, near Disneyland Hotel, 'very clean', 'best motel I stayed in'; Aloha Waikiki, 400 W Katella, 'pool, TV, weekly rates, very clean and bright, 10 minutes walk to Disneyland'; Sir Rudimar Motel on Katella; Rustic Motel at 916 S Beach Blvd, 'clean, comfortable'; and Polynesian Motel, 641 S Brookhurst St.

FOOD

LA bursts with great ethnic restaurants and takeaway places. This is also a good opportunity to dive into guacamole dip, served throughout California and made with local avocadoes.

Downtown:

Grand Central Market, 315 Broadway. Huge, Latin-flavoured *melange* of stands with great buys: 'absolutely amazing food prices', and intermingled with standup bars and Mexican nosheries: 'good place for breakfast, lunch and dinner'. Dave and Dori's Continental Snack Bar and El Macho Taco (326 S Hill) are standouts.

Clifton's Cafeterias, 648 S Broadway, 515 W 7th St and (in Beverly Hills) at 10250 Santa Monica Blvd. Vast array of cheap dishes, soothing decor from a redwood forest with real waterfall to the Art Deco touches at 7th St.

Carl's Jr, 8th floor, Bonaventure Hotel, 5th and Figueroa. An inside look at the high-powered Bonaventure ambience, all for the price of a cheap burger. Take the outside elevator to the 35th floor for a post-burger thrill.

Phillipe's, Alameda and Ord Sts, near Union Station. Cool, 1940s place with the best French dip sandwiches, cheapest coffee, biggest breakfasts in town. Recommended.

La Luz del Día, Olvera St at one end. Skip the open-air stands and march right in for a pork tostada, under $2 for a real feast. Friendly, clean, large menu.

Finney's Cafeteria, 217 W 6th St. One of LA's interesting juxtapositions: an often-filmed Byzantine cavern of tiles, pillars and vaulted arches, serving cafeteria-style grub on bright orange trays. 'Still does full breakfast for 99¢.'

The Original Pantry Cafe, 9th and Figueroa Sts. Always open. An inexpensive favourite with Angelenos since 1924; long lines. 'Biggest steaks we had in the US.'

West LA:

Norm's Restaurant, Vermont and Sunset, Hollywood (and elsewhere). After 3pm, all-you-can-eat specials 'from $5 and it's good food'.

UCLA-Westwood: 'Student cafes on campus, all meals very cheap and good.' The Haven, 1045 Westwood Blvd, 'delicious, enormous salads, very reasonable prices'.

Ye Olde King's Head Pub, 116 Santa Monica Blvd. 11am–2am. Good fish and chips, English beer, live bands. 'Great to hear nothing but English voices.'

La Barbera's Restaurant, 11813 Wilshire Blvd. World class pizza, oozing with special cheese. From $6. 'Good lasagna, good atmosphere.'

Happy Hours around LA: In the downtown area, sample the Roaring Lion and other food places within ARCO Plaza; also the Pacific Dining Car at 1310 W 6th.

In Hollywood, hit the Nickodell, 5511 Melrose near Paramount Studios and Simply Blues Bar, top floor at Sunset and Vine: 'Weekdays 5pm–7pm, they do steak, spare ribs for 25¢ each—a ploy to drink their expensive beer.'

OF INTEREST

To make things a bit easier, Greater Los Angeles is broken down into 6 sightseeing sectors. Try to cluster your sightseeing by sector rather than attempting to get to Universal (25 minutes north of downtown) and Disneyland (80 minutes south) in one day. Notice that the airport district is innocent of attractions. If you're short of time, concentrate on West LA, the coast and your probable 'must sees' of Disneyland and Universal Studios.

Downtown is inland; west of it are Hollywood, Beverly Hills, Westwood/UCLA, lumped together as West LA here. The big boulevards of Wilshire, Santa Monica and Sunset run from downtown 16 miles to the ocean and serve as express bus corridors. Northwest of downtown is Glendale/Burbank. The coast, from north to south, includes Malibu, Santa Monica, Venice, the Palos Verdes peninsula, Long Beach (and into Orange county), Huntington, Newport and Laguna Beaches. In the southern interior you'll find San Juan Capistrano, Anaheim with Disneyland, neighbouring Buena Park with Knott's, etc. The San Gabriel Valley and Pasadena are northeast of downtown and get the most smog.

Downtown:

City Hall, 200 N Spring St, Open 10am–4pm weekdays, 11am–3pm weekends. Good views on smogless days.

Olvera St and El Pueblo de Los Angeles State Park. 44 acres representing what's left of the original pueblo—pretty underwhelming, really. A couple of adobes (Avila is oldest in city), Mexican souvenirs, food stalls, morose vendors, enlivened by occasional Latin events or live music. Free walking tours, Visitor Center, 130 Paseo de la Plaza, 628-0605.

Bonaventure Hotel, 5th and Figueroa Sts. Half castle, half spaceship, with mirrored towers that are quicksilver by day, fiery at sunset. Elevators scoot up and down the smooth cylinders like waterbugs, seemingly held in place by surface tension. The interior is busy, noisy, anticlimatic, but do take an elevator ride or have a drink on top. Summer concerts free Mon, Wed, Fri noons on 4th floor pool level; call 972-7481 for details.

Biltmore Hotel, 515 S Olive St, on the site of an ancient Indian, later Spanish, trail, the Biltmore is a beautifully renovated structure, 16th C Italian in feeling, with sumptuous ballrooms, lobby, chandeliers. JFK stayed in their $2400/day suite when he won the Presidential nomination in 1960.

Little Tokyo. A small district but charming, its 1st to 3rd St/Main to Central boundaries marked by trees and Japanese calligraphy that says 'May peace prevail on earth'. Over 50 restaurants, whose bravura displays of wok and teppan cooking are as fascinating to watch as to sample. Nice garden with koi pool on the New Otani Hotel rooftop; take elevator to garden level.

Chinatown, Hill and N Broadway Sts. The old Chinatown was pulled down, the new offering good food but little else.

Union Station, 800 N Alameda St. Built in 1938, the last great rail station in America is a hugely appealing blend of Spanish Revival and Moderne features, still glamorous and very Southern Cal. Phillipe's is close by and equally atmospheric (see Food).

West LA:

Bullock's Wilshire, 3050 Wilshire, 2 blocks east of Vermont. The construction of this elegant 1928 building with Moderne and Art Deco touches marked the beginning of Wilshire's 'Miracle Mile' and anticipated LA's trend towards drivers rather than pedestrians. Don't miss the murals on 1st and 2nd levels and in the motor court.

Silverlake district and Griffith Park. Funkily delightful district whose palm-dotted hills are a wonderful sight in horizontal LA: ABC studios, a mixed ethnic-gay neighbourhood, a lake, and to the north, Griffith Park: 4063 acres with zoo (lots of koalas), cricket grounds, hiking and horseback trails. Also the Greek Theater (June–Sept) and the Observatory and Planetarium, with its James Dean associations (*Rebel Without a Cause*). Free telescope viewing, superb spot at night. Frequent laserium ($5, call 997-3624) and planetarium ($3, call 664-1191) shows. To Griffith, take 'Observatory' bus at Vermont and Hollywood Blvds.

Hollywood. Although 2519 bronze stars in the pavement have replaced the real stars on its streets, Hollywood is still the guardian of the celluloid dream, its very tackiness and Chandleresque aura of decay eloquent in a way that Burbank could never be. While distances are great, walking is very rewarding and the best way to take in the wacky human and architectural drama. Among the highlights:

Grauman's (OK, OK, Mann's) **Chinese Theater**, 6925 Hollywood Blvd, 464-8111. Opened in 1927 with the premiere of DeMille's *King of Kings*, christened by Norma Talmadge who accidentally stepped in wet cement that night, thereby beginning a Hollywood tradition. Most of the stars whose signatures, *bons mots* and anatomical impressions you see are dead, their graffiti now a queerly moving graveyard to glamour long past. Opposite is another temple to the old Hollywood—**Frederick's**, a luscious purple passion pit of a place, busy selling the sleazy sex goddess trappings since 1947. Half a block away from Grauman's is a third temple, this one to gluttony: **C C Brown's**, archetypal American soda fountain and home of the hot fudge sundae.

Sunset Blvd. A linear 'city' in its own right, Sunset around the 7000 block becomes **The Strip**, noted for eyecatching signage, music clubs, trendy restaurants, record stores and studios. Between Fairfax and Doheny are more than 50 constantly changing billboards, 20% of them hand-painted, all of them cryptic or controversial.

Paramount Studios, 5555 Melrose Ave. Now surrounded by TV and recording studios, Paramount still maintains a medieval, walled-city look. Inside are bits and pieces of sets, cities within cities—wonderfully unreal. Ask the gatekeeper for permission to stroll about.

Farmers' Market, 3rd and Fairfax. Near Art Museum. The produce is sheer poetry and the smell from 2 dozen eating places will drive you crazy; not cheap, however.

LA County Museum of Art, 5905 Wilshire Blvd, 937-2590. Open Tue–Fri 10am–5pm, Sat–Sun 10am–6pm. Free 2nd Tue of the month, otherwise $2, seniors/ students $1. Combo ticket with La Brea also.

Excellent moderns, ancient, medieval, Renaissance and Oriental collections. Free sculpture garden—don't miss the *Attack of the Killer Lipsticks*. The tar pits are somewhat dull but the adjacent discovery museum rates higher: 'Well laid out, fascinating.'

Museum of Rock Art, 6427 W Sunset at Cahuenga, 2nd floor, 463-8979. Remarkable collection of 1960s poster art, rare videotape footage (Elvis, the Beatles, etc) and much more. $4, well spent.

Laurel Canyon, in the hills leading to Mulholland, a swish, lovely area with the ruins of Harry Houdini's mansion along the way.

Hollywood on Location, 8644 Wilshire Blvd, 659-9165. This is worth renting a car for if there are several of you. For $19, you get a detailed itinerary, maps and precise info on 5 to 10 location shoots around LA for a given day, from movies to TV series like *Magnum PI*. Also info on movie-making vocabulary, descriptions of the people involved and what they do. An outstanding behind-the-scenes look at actual shooting, not just sets. Reserve one day in advance; Mon–Fri only.

Beverly Hills. Home of the celebrated and the filthy rich, more and more of whom seem to be Arab. Salubrious, emerald green, full of huge estates but short on sidewalks: 'Walking around here is subversive—everyone drives'. To see **stars' homes**, take the 50¢ local bus or the $10 organised tour (coach leaves from Grauman's Chinese, 'beats walking'). **Rodeo Drive** between 300 and 800 has residents like Carl Reiner (714) and Gene Kelly (725), luxurious shops in the 300–400 blocks. Window-shopping and strolling are popular evenings, especially Sat 8pm–11pm, when even the Rolls-dependent locals take a turn on foot.

Westwood Village and UCLA. Tucked in with the campus, Westwood Village is a huge and handsome mall, one of LA's few walking districts, and chockful of cinemas, shops, street buskers and socialising places. 'Fri and Sat nights are like a circus—sword-swallowers, dancers, musicians—even fortune-telling cats!' Celebs also frequent Westwood: 'I saw Melissa Gilbert and Moon Unit Zappa, to name just two'. The campus area is a live party spot: 'Frat parties along Gayley from 21 Sept on—free beer, spirits, food, entertainment and the best-looking women in the world'. On a quieter note, **Westwood Village Cemetery**, 1218 Glendon, has the most visited grave in LA, that of Marilyn Monroe. Natalie Wood is also buried here.

Glendale/Burbank:

Universal Studios Tour, 100 Universal City Plaza, 877-1311 or 877-2121. $11 for 2½ hour tour, taken by tram through the 420-acre lot. Free shows, stuntman demos, videotaped shenanigans after the tour so stick around to get your money's worth. 'Most motels in Anaheim can arrange a tour bus ($24, tour included) to collect and bring you home—well worth it.' 'Get right-hand seat on tram—most scenes, Jaws, etc, to the right.' 'Not on a par with Disneyland.' 'Better than Disneyland.' Open daily 8am–6pm summer, 10am–3.30pm winter. Take Greyhound (pass valid) to North Hollywood, then 15-minute walk. Also express bus 35, every ½ hour from Pershing Square downtown to Lankershim, then take road to the right.

NBC Studios, 3000 W Alameda Ave, Burbank, 840-3537 or 3572. $3 tour every ½ hour, daily, through working TV studio; also free tickets to TV tapings. 'As a bonus we sat in on Bob Hope and Brook Shields rehearsing.'

TV shows. Free at all 3 studios, usually requires queuing twice, first to get tickets, then to get in. Best to try Visitors Center first ('We got tickets to Johnny Carson'); you'll also find TV reps giving tickets away outside Grauman's in summer. ABC ticket office, 557-4396; CBS, 852-4002.

Forest Lawn Memorial Park, 1712 S Glendale Ave, Glendale, 254-3131. Also friendly branches in the Hollywood Hills, near Artesia and in West Covina, each with its own artwork, patriotic themes and style. This is the American way of death as depicted in Evelyn Waugh's *The Loved One*: odourless, spotless, artistically uplifting, almost fun—at least for the survivors. It's hard to keep from giggling at the crass wonder of it all, from repros of the Greatest Hits of Michelango and Leonardo da Vinci to the comic-book approach on the 'Life of Jesus' mosaics. Take a copy of Ken Schessler's *This is Hollywood* along if you want to find where the notables are planted—no one will tell you. Free, open daily 10am–5pm.

Magic Mountain, Magic Mt Parkway, Valencia, 992-0884. 45 minutes north by freeway. $12 for unlimited rides. Newest madness at this hard-core ride park is the Free Fall, a sickening 10-storey drop. Its colossal rollercoaster is still second largest in the world. Open daily 9am–midnight in summer, 10am–6pm on Sat/Sun/hols rest of year.

The coast:

Malibu clings to a narrow stretch of coastline north of Santa Monica, cluttered with pricey real estate, fast food joints and 4 lanes of traffic. Good surfing, scenic camping at Leo Carrillo State Beach to the north.

J Paul Getty Museum, 17985 Pacific Coast Hwy, Malibu, 454-6541. A grandly fake reproduction of a grandly vulgar villa at Herculaneum, filled with 3rd-rate late Roman copies of earlier 2nd-rate Roman, Hellenistic and late Hellenic statuary. Upstairs are Renaissance and later paintings, tapestries, furniture. Far more interesting than the artwork is the awed, almost reverent reception given to even the murkiest statue by the American viewing public. (Perhaps the reverence is for Getty, once the world's richest man). If you come on RTD bus 175, get a pass from the driver and you may walk into the museum. Otherwise, you must drive in, by prearrangement only; call the day before. 'If pressed for time, hire a taxi and pay $10 to be taken 500 yards—worth it in the end. Lovely paintings.' Museum is free, open Mon–Fri 10am–5pm, June–Sept; Tue–Sat, 10am–5pm, Oct–May. Near the Getty is the road **Topanga Canyon**, where the young and hip with pots of money dwell in laid-back splendour.

Santa Monica, crowded with Brits and somewhat like an English seaside resort, with a good albeit crowded beach ('excellent swimming'), a ramshackle pier and interesting mural art. Free goggling at **Gold's Gym** and the **Ice Capades Chalet**, the former for bodybuilders, the latter for Olympics calibre skaters.

Venice, south of Santa Monica, has a wide white beach ('lots of gays') with good swimming and non-stop action along its roller-skating, mural-lined, people-watching Ocean Front Walk. Built in 1904 and modelled on the original, Venice's canals are now filled in but traces of its Italian blueprints remain along Windward Ave with its lovely *gelato*-coloured Corinthian columns. NB: Venice's aura of artistic decay becomes just plain seedy, even dangerous, after dark.

Marineland, 6610 Palos Verdes Dr S, on Palos Verdes peninsula. 541-5663 or 377-1571. Performing killer whales, dolphins, etc. Outstanding is the swim-through coral reef, in which you can rub shoulders and dorsal fins with 3000 fish, bat rays, sharks (all presumably vegetarians). Reef costs $4 extra but they furnish wetsuit, snorkel, hairdryers, etc. Park costs $10, daily 10am–7pm summer, Wed–Sun 10am–5pm rest of year. Long bus trip from downtown; better to stay in Long Beach or at the Youth Hostel on Palos Verdes peninsula, 831-8109.

R M S Queen Mary, Pier J, Long Beach, 435-4747. Boarding costs $3, boarding plus tour $8, which includes Jacques Cousteau's Living Sea museum. After 5pm, boarding is reportedly free. **The Spruce Goose**, Howard Hughes' wooden flying boat that laid an egg, may or may not be on view near the QM for your visit.

Catalina Island, 26 miles off Long Beach. A romantic green hideaway, 85% in its natural state. Well worth a trip to see the perfect harbour of Avalon and its delightful vernacular architecture, plus the natural beauties of the place. Snorkelling is best at Lovers Cove but look out for sharks. 'Beautiful.' Ships cost $20 round trip, depart from Long Beach, San Pedro and Newport Beach. Phone (213)775-6111 (LA), (714)257-7111 (Long Beach), (714)673-5245 (Newport).

Huntington Beach. Surfer capital, a famed party beach, home of good music at The Golden Bear and now possessing a good youth hostel. 'The local surfers love to take a complete novice in hand so don't hesitate to ask how it's done.'

Newport Beach. Terribly yachty and formal except on Balboa Island, a mecca for boy/girl-watching. 'Try the Balboa bars and the frozen bananas at the icecream kiosks.' T-K Burgers at 2119 W Balboa Blvd is the most popular hangout for the non-deckshoe set.

Laguna Beach, 30 miles south of LA, buffered against urban sprawl by the San Joaquin Hills, has a decided Mediterranean look, from its indented coves to its trees and greenery right down to the waterline. The long white sand beach has superb snorkelling, surfing (for experts) and safe swimming at Aliso Beach Park. In winter, whale watching and tidepooling are likewise excellent. Long a haven for artists, Laguna is famous for its 7-week Pageant of the Masters each July–Aug, but the accompanying Sawdust Festival (crafts, live music, jugglers, food) is more accessible and more fun. While here, plan to eat at The Cottage, 308 N Coast Hwy, or The Stand on Thalia St, recommended by a Lagunian for its 'great Mexican food, smoothies and tofu cheeseless cake'. 'Laguna has excellent atmosphere, very picturesque.'

Orange County/Anaheim:

San Juan Capistrano, 12 miles inland from Laguna and 22 miles south of Santa Ana. This mission town is well served by Greyhound, Orange County buses and AMTRAK, so you have little excuse for passing up its mission, easily the best in California. The chapel, oldest building still standing in the state, is almost Minoan in proportions, feeling and colour. Also on the grounds are the romantic ruins of the great church tumbled by an 1812 earthquake and now a favoured nesting place for the famous swallows. Indian graveyard, jail, various interesting buildings. Well worth your dollar. Take a lunch.

Knott's Berry Farm, 8039 Beach Blvd, Buena Park, 827-1776. The gift shops outnumber the rides and attractions about 10 to 1 but its Montezooma's Revenge and

Corkscrew rollercoaster (both with 360-degree upside-down loops) are nauseatingly effective, allowing you to meet yourself (and possibly your lunch) coming back. 'Hurts, but must be tried.' Lots of special celebrations (eg Indian pow-wow in Sept), rock concerts, discount promotions; check the papers. Open daily til midnight in summer, $11.

Movieland Wax Museum, 7711 Beach Blvd, Buena Park, 522-1154 and 583-8025. 200-plus movie and TV stars captured (not always successfully) in wax but the new thrill is the Black Box, 3 full-size walk-through movie sets from *Alien*, *Altered States* and *Hallowe'en*, containing $1 million worth of horrid special effects 'with the sole purpose of soiling your underwear'. Daily 9am–9pm, until 10 weekends. $8.

Disneyland, 1313 S Harbor Blvd, Anaheim, 999-4565. Best of the theme park genre, over 57 attractions in 7 themed parks. Except for Space Mountain and the runaway train, rides are quite tame. 'Tomorrowland is best—see it first.' 'Don't miss America the Beautiful 360-degree film.' Bands perform in daytime; at night, you can watch the dazzling electric parade, fireworks and name performers (eg Pointer Sisters, Sergio Mendes). Most pleasant on a balmy summer evening—less heat, fewer queues, but some rides do operate daytime only. Admission: now a standard 'Passport', $13 with unlimited rides. Open daily until midnight, mid-June to Labor Day, shorter hours thereafter. 'Get there as early as possible—lines for good rides become enormous by noon.' 'Avoid Saturdays!' 'Take a full day.' Transport: Greyhound (pass valid) to Anaheim, take Orange County bus thereafter. But plan ahead: 'Don't leave luggage at Greyhound—station closes at 9pm, Disneyland at midnight.' RTD express buses from downtown LA, $3 one way, 1½ hours. Frequent departures. Also bus from LAX airport to the park and major hotels, $8 one way.

San Gabriel Valley/Pasadena:
Huntington Library, Art Gallery and Botanical Gardens, 1151 Oxford Rd, San Marino, 792-6141 or 681-6601. Free, Tue–Sun 1pm–4.30pm. A rich 200-acre bower, landscaped with 9000 plants and trees. In the Georgian mansion, works like Lawrence's *Pinkie*, Gainsborough's *Blue Boy*, and an abundance of other treasures, large and small. Library has largest William Blake painting/poetry collection in the world, a Gutenberg, other priceless books and mss.

Norton Simon Museum, 411 W Colorado Blvd, 449-3730. 5000-piece collection of Rembrandts, Bouts, Goyas, Picasso lithos, Degas, etc. $2.50, seniors/students $1, more on Sunday. Open noon–6pm Thur–Sun.

ENTERTAINMENT
BAM, free monthly paper, lists gigs up and down the West Coast. Also pick up *The Reader* and *LA Weekly*, free, full of entertainment listings. All available at record/bookstores, newsstands.

The Twofer LA Co, 1133 Westwood Blvd, Westwood, 824-4773, offers ½ price tickets to major/minor theatres in LA. Small surcharge.

Jazz line, 306-2364, 24-hr recording.

Clubs: The Palomino, 6907 Lankershim Blvd, North Hollywood, 764-4010. The place for country acts, expensive cover but great atmosphere.

The Troubadour, 9081 Santa Monica Blvd, 276-6168, aging but legendary launching pad for top rock acts; small and smoky. Cover plus 2-drink minimum, cheaper on Mon hoot nights.

Roxy, 9009 Sunset Blvd, 878-2222. Act Deco, top rock and MOR, stiff cover and 2-drink minimum.

Whiskey a Go Go, 8901 Sunset Blvd, 652-4202. Cream of the rock triumvirate. Cover, naturally.

Bla Bla Cafe, 12446 Ventura Blvd, Studio City, 769-7874. Rock, comedy, coffeehouse vibes, lowest cover in town.

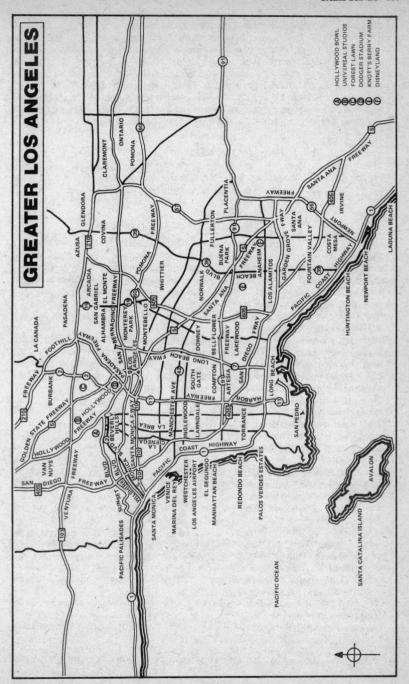

GREATER LOS ANGELES

Madame Wong's, 949 Sun Mun Way, Chinatown, 624-5346. New Wave music, lots of dance action and raunchiness. Cover, 2 drink minimum.

Tower Records, 8801 Sunset Blvd, is enormous and never seems to close. Vast selection. However: 'from a list of 13 American jazz records, they could not produce one—an abortive, time-consuming visit'. Moral: call first.

Hollywood Bowl, summer concerts, on Highland Ave just SW of Hollywood Freeway. Special RTD buses from a dozen points in the LA area. 'Classical concerts under the stars, high in the Hollywood Hills, with a background of crickets chirping, is one of the most impressive experiences to be had in LA. Buy a cheap seat in back and move down to a vacant seat at the front as performance begins.'

INFORMATION

Greater LA Visitors Bureau, 505 S Flower St, B-level, ARCO Plaza, 628-3101. Open 9am–5pm Mon–Fri, 10am–4pm Sat. 488-9100 is events recording. Very helpful, multilingual staff; pick up free TV taping tickets, addresses of stars' homes but forget their map. Close by is an RTD office; stop here for a Visitor Pass, complete schedules and the RTD Self-Guided Tours booklet, the minimum you need to ride the buses. Other visitors bureaux in Hollywood, Anaheim, at the airport.

Travelers Aid, 646 S Los Angeles St, 625-2501. 6 airport kiosks too.

Mexican Tourist Bureau, 9701 Wilshire Blvd, Suite 1201, Beverly Hills, 274-6315.

TRAVEL

Greyhound, 208 E 6th St at Los Angeles St, 620-1200. Inside, a huge, clean but cheerless terminal with no cafe; outside, the meanest streets anywhere—a zoo. Don't plan any overnights here. 'Friends twice approached by vicious druggies and tramps outside station—be careful.'

Trailways, Union Station, 800 N Alameda, 742-1200. 'Luggage may be left in depot 72 hrs, thereafter 50¢ a day.'

RTD buses, occupying lower level of Greyhound terminal, 626-4455 (always busy-keep trying). Basic fare $1, minibus system around downtown, 50¢. Get an RTD pass, $2/day, minimum 3 days, maximum 15 days. Available only at RTD centres: 425 S Main; in ARCO Plaza (see Info); in Hollywood at 6249 Hollywood Blvd. 'Excellent value.' 'You must show your passport—ISIC not acceptable.'

Orange County bus (OCTD) system interlocks with RTD, 636-7433.

Santa Monica (451-5445) also has buses to beach from downtown.

AMTRAK, 800 N Alameda, 624-0171. Also stations in Fullerton, Santa Ana, San Juan Capistrano and San Clemente, all south of downtown. The *Coast Starlight* between LA–Seattle is highly recommended for scenery and socialising—if you can get a ticket.

Los Angeles International Airport (LAX), Century and Sepulveda Blvds, 646-5252 or 536-6218. 15 miles from downtown. Bus service via RTD (express 607—check first). Also airport shuttle (much more costly).

Car rentals: Greyhound Rentacar, 800/327-2501. Can also book from Britain. Under $100/week with unlimited mileage. Used cars through Rentawreck in West LA, 478-0676 or 800-854-3380. Reader recommended: Thrifty Rentacar and Rent-a-Convertible, 933-9508. 'Rush hour driving—forget it!' 'Interesting just driving around Beverly Hills, Sunset Blvd, Hollywood, passing prostitutes, hustlers and drag queens. Also can drive to beach where parties go on all night.'

AAACON Transport, 707 S Broadway, 523-4200.

Auto Driveaway, 4800 Melrose Ave, 666-6100.

Ride board: floor B, Ackerman Union, UCLA.

Ride center, 461-3829; also Ride Center USA, 451-5526.

Gray Line, 481-2121.

DEATH VALLEY. Covering two million acres, most of them about a

million miles from nowhere, Death Valley has cornered the market on hottest, driest and lowest (282 feet below sea level) place in the US. One July day in 1972, Furnace Creek had a ground reading of 201 degrees while the air was a balmy 128 degrees. Always dramatic, the desert can bring forth storms of wildflowers as suddenly as it does storms of sand.

Death Valley lies 300 miles northeast of Los Angeles and 135 miles northwest of Las Vegas; the only bus is from Las Vegas. Park lodging boils down to camping (free in summer but can be very uncomfortable), the costly Furnace Creek Ranch (over $40 a night) and the Stove Pipe Wells Motel, 25 miles from Furnace Creek and not much better at $35 up double, higher in winter. 'During summer, arrive by 6pm. Otherwise no key.' A better bet is the gas station/motel at Panamint Springs, 10 miles west of the park. Doubles with shower $29 and up. 'A welcome relief in the middle of nowhere.'

Late October to early May are the most pleasant times to gaze at the tortured panoramas from **Zabriskie Point** and **Dante's View**, climb the **Ubehebe Crater**, explore **Scotty's Castle**, and slide on the sensuous sand dunes at **Stove Pipe Wells**. Scotty's Castle is no prospector's shack but a $2 million, 18-room Spanish fortress with an 1100-pipe organ, a large waterfall in the living room and other astonishing features. It was built by colourful con man Walter Scott and bankrolled by his 'gold mine', insurance agent Arthur Johnson.

Park headquarters at **Furnace Creek**, 786-2331, has a museum, descriptive literature, food and a cool oasis of date palms. Free rangers' hikes and programmes daily, less often in summer.

SEQUOIA-KINGS CANYON NATIONAL PARKS. These two parks, established around 1890 and jointly administered since the Second World War, straddle a magnificent cross-section of the high Sierras, including 14,495-foot **Mt Whitney**, highest peak in the lower 48. But that's not all: here you'll find the beautiful and impetuous **Kings River**, lots of wildlife, remnants of Indian camps and the most impressive groves of Sierra sequoias anywhere on earth. Like their coastal redwood cousins, these giant patriarchs were in danger of being destroyed by short-sighted logging in the mid-1800s. But the wood proved too brittle for commercial use, fortunately, allowing you to see 3000-year-old **General Sherman**, the world's most massive living thing, in all his 275-foot-high, 2145-ton glory. If you're pressed for time, at least walk the 2-mile **Congress Trail** into the heart of the **Great Forest**. The trail begins at the Sherman tree.

Road access to the parks is from the west and southwest but they can be entered on foot from the east: Kings Canyon from Independence and Sequoia from Lone Pine. (You can drive from Lone Pine to Whitney Portal, elevation 8367 feet, and climb from there but you'd better be fit.) There is also bus service to trailheads on both sides of the Sierras from Visalia. The eastern side of the Sierras along Highway 395 is truly stirring but remember it's a summer-only proposition. 'Road to Owens Valley gives very pretty views and climbs to about 8000 feet above sea level.'

ACCOMMODATION
Outside parks:
Dow Villa Hotel, 310 S Main, Lone Pine, 876-5521. Hospitable place, good rms with and without bath, $15–$25. Use of jacuzzi, pool. Hotel on first-come, first-served basis. Attached motel $32 up.
Willow Motel, 138 Willow St, Lone Pine, 876-4115. Singles $18 up, doubles $20 up. Colour TV, shower, kitchens $5 extra.
Camping: '9 miles west of Lone Pine towards Mt Whitney—breathtaking scenery'.
M Bar J Ranch, PO Box 121, Badger, 337-2513. Open Apr–Oct. Near both parks, friendly ranch with daily (about $50) and weekly ($300 up) rates, all meals, riding (into parks, etc), entertainment included. Will meet bus/plane in Visalia, 40 miles away.
Hotel Reedley, 1726 11th St, Reedley, 638-6315. About 25 miles from park entrance. Wildly furnished hotel, no 2 rms alike. $25 up single or double; good value.
Fresno and Visalia can serve as western bases; Fresno has 2 Motel 6s, a good YWCA on M St and campus rooms in summer. It is 55 miles east of parks.
Within the parks:
Camping at 10 sites, $3. Free backcountry camping with permit. Also free camping on Sequoia National Forest lands near park. 'Buckeye Flat campground—pleasant, rustic. We saw a bear in camp.' Rustic cabins without baths from $16 single or double at Giant Forest, in Sequoia, (209)565-4373, and Grant Grove, in Kings (209)335-2314. Book ahead. Also costlier cabins, cottages. Giant Forest open all year, Grant May–Oct.

INFORMATION/TRAVEL
Parks open year-round. $3 fee covers both. Access in winter via highways 198 and 180. Visitors Centers at Ash Mountain, 565-3341, Lodgepole, 565-3338, and Grant Grove. The latter 2 have libraries, so you can read among the big trees.
Sequoia-Kings Hospitality Service, 565-3373 or 3381. Mid-May to Oct, once daily bus to park meets Greyhound, AMTRAK and airport in Fresno.
High Sierra Stage, The Rucksack Mt Shop, 1043 S Mooney Blvd, Visalia, 732-4404. Only bus service to numerous trailheads on west and east sides of both parks. Very cheap; on-call service in summer, charters in winter.
Within parks: bus tours. Also interpark bus from Giant Forest to Cedar Grove. Bike and horse rentals.

YOSEMITE. An Oxford don once said, 'Think in centuries'. At Yosemite, it's inescapable. Here you can trace the tracks of creation: valleys a million years old, carved from granite by the icy knife of a glacier. Nearly 1200 square miles of incredibly varied beauty— luminous lakes and dashing streams, groves of redwood elder statesmen and aged incense cedar, jagged sierra terrain, resilient meadows filled with wildlife and spangled with poppies and lupines.

People bemoan the popularity of Yosemite, but not even 2.5 million visitors per year can ruin it. Almost half of them choose to jam the park during July and August, and 80 percent content themselves with a stay in **Yosemite Valley**, leaving vast areas untrampled. Despite its congestion, you shouldn't miss Yosemite Valley's supreme vistas of **Bridalveil Falls** and the steel-blue shoulders of **Half Dome** and **El Capitan** from **Tunnel View**. A mountaineers' mecca, Half Dome is the sheerest cliff in America; El Capitan, the biggest block of exposed granite in the world.

Other high priorities: fantastic views from **Tioga Pass**, **Glacier Point** (summer only—go at sunset or on full moon evenings), tranquil redwood groves near the south entrance at **Mariposa**.

Open year-round, Yosemite is at its most sparkling in spring and early autumn; in summer, waterfalls fade to a trickle, a factor perhaps compensated for by the warm weather and the abundance of ranger programmes.

ACCOMMODATION

More than any other spot in California, you must book cabin, lodge or camping accommodations in advance to avoid disappointment. Most are through Yosemite Park and Curry Co, Yosemite 95389; (209)373-4171; send one night's lodging.

Within the park:

Tent cabins at Curry Village, $15 for 1–2 persons. 'Was too cold to get undressed when I was there in Sept.' Showers nearby, often overtaxed. Also at Housekeeping Camp, 1 mile south of Yosemite Village, $17 and up, summer only. Other cabins at Curry Village, Yosemite Lodge, White Wolf Lodge. Housekeeping units have a stove (sometimes outside), cost a little more. No bedding or utensils.

Cheapest hotel rooms at Wawona Hotel, an old charmer 4 miles inside the south entrance and 27 miles from Yosemite Valley on Highway 41, 372-1300. Without bath, singles/doubles from $25. Also at Wawona, cabins from $27, call 375-6256. Note: after 1 Nov, rates at more expensive lodges, cabins, drop as much as 47% Sun through Thur: a good deal.

Campsites: 2000 of them, $2–$6 at improved sites, 50¢–$1 at basic walk-in campgrounds. Without advance booking, walk-ins are it: 'If you haven't booked, it's the only option—park is full even after Labor Day.' Walk-ins at Muir Tree ('less crowded'), Sunnyside. Further out at Tenaya Lake and Tuolumne, open June–Sept/Oct only. Backcountry camping free with permit but so popular there's a quota 15 June–15 Sept. Again, write ahead. Bears can be a problem: use 'bear cables' or hang food high in a tree when camping. Don't leave food in cabins, either.

Outside park:

Lodging at Fresno (see Kings-Sequoia) and Merced. Also Youth Hostel supposed to open 'soon' at Midpines, 20 miles from park entrance. Call (408)298-0670 for info.

International Spareroom (see Accommodation Background for address) has $13 loft (need sleeping bag) room with breakfast on mountain stream inside south gate of Yosemite. Northwest B&B has $20 single with pool in Sanger, 1 hour's drive from Yosemite, 45 minutes from Kings Canyon. Accommodation Background for address.

FOOD

Food is costly and often poor in the park. Readers recommend Yosemite Valley's burger shop and pizza house. Grocery stores, restaurants, cafeterias at Yosemite Valley, Curry Village, Wawona, Tioga Lake, White Wolf, Fish Camp, El Portal and Tuolumne Meadows.

INFORMATION
Park open year-round except at Tioga Pass, the eastern entrance. $4 cars, $1 per hiker or bus passenger. 'Keep your ticket—checked on exit for it.'
Visitors Center, 372-4461, at village mall in Yosemite Valley. Free maps, brochures, Yosemite Guide newsletter with free daily events.

TRAVEL
Yosemite Transportation System, 373-4171, has bus service (pass not valid) daily from Merced, Fresno AMTRAK stations and Greyhound. Arrives park 5.45pm. Sept–May, service from Merced *only*. Round trip $28 from Merced. Also once daily in summer from Lee Vining, east of the Sierras. 'Book in advance to be sure of a place.' 'Inconvenient service—better to hire a car from Merced.'
Greyhound/Trailways serve all cities and towns along Hwy 99. Greyhound also serves towns along Hwy 395 east of the parks: Lone Pine, Independence, Bishop, Lee Vining, north to Nevada.
Rental cars: Merced Motors, 722-7451 (1 block from Greyhound); Aide Rental, 722-3918. Also consider renting a car in San Francisco (Greyhound Rentacar is best—see SF Travel) to drop off in Los Angeles, stopping at Yosemite and other scenic spots enroute.
Suggested route for most scenic approach to Yosemite: take I-580 to I-5, do not turn off until Hwy 152 East (Los Banos), then take Hwys 99, 145 and finally 41. (About 5 hrs.) The payoff is the utterly spine-tingling exit from Wawona Tunnel into Yosemite Valley.
Hitching: 'a bit slow between Merced and Yosemite'. Yosemite is 67 miles east of Merced.
Within the park: bike rentals at Yosemite Lodge, Curry Village. Free shuttle bus service to most points of interest, 8am–10pm in summer, shorter hours in winter. Also bus tours with commentary.
Recommended walks: 'Hike Yosemite Valley, Glacier Pt, Illilouette Falls, Panorama Trail, Nevada Falls, Vernal Falls, Happy Isles for best photos. 14 miles, 3200-ft ascents and descents.' 'Walk up to Nevada Falls via John Muir Trail and then down by Misty Trail. Take a swimsuit—icy mountain pools. Good for those with less time. Met a bear—terrifying.'

SAN FRANCISCO. The name evokes a litany of images: hills, Haight-Ashbury, bridges, cable cars, fog, ferryboats, earthquakes, gays, painted Victorians. But the city is greater than the sum of its cliches. Ethnic and geographic factors have conspired to make San Francisco a city of neighbourhoods in the European manner. East meets West here, but ethnic differences are encouraged instead of assimilated, giving the place a cosmopolitan flavour that comes as a welcome relief after the monotony of much of urban America.

San Francisco claims a peerless setting on the tip of a green and hilly thumb of land, which shelters a huge and intricate bay from the roaring Pacific ocean. A narrow strait connects the two bodies of water, made more dramatic by the shimmering bridge that spans the gap. Like everything else, distance lends enchantment. San Francisco from afar is a shining citadel that wears its fog like a coquette, heartbreakingly lovely. Closer examination reveals the city's imperfections, from slums to cold corporate canyons to unattractive porno districts. Never mind: even with its ills, San Francisco is still way ahead of whoever's in second place.

It's hard to have a bad time here: the wealth of things to see, the diverse food experiences and most of all, the San Franciscans themselves, making visiting a delight. People don't migrate here to be successful but to be (or learn to be) happy and human. Their efforts make San Francisco a city of good manners, full of little kindnesses and occasional gallant acts of altruism and love, whether it's saving whales or cable cars.

Temperatures are mild year-round; spring and autumn offer the brightest weather but come prepared for brisk winds and romantic but chilly fog anytime.

San Francisco's situation in the heart of the Bay Area is perfect for exploration of the Wine Country, Santa Cruz, Berkeley and other points of interest, most of which can be reached within two hours and by public transit.

SURVIVAL

Like Los Angeles, San Francisco's Greyhound depot is located in a scruffy-to-rotten district, predictably worse at night. Accommodation within the large triangle formed by Market St, Divisadero and Geary is in a high crime area which spills over onto the other side of Market where Greyhound (and additional accommodation) can be found. The worst sector is the Western Addition, whose boundaries are Geary, Hayes, Steiner and Gough: stay out, day or night (no reason to visit anyway).

Other dicey streets at night are the first 4 blocks of Turk, Eddy and Ellis. That doesn't mean you shouldn't stay here—just be aware and exercise caution, particularly after dark.

ACCOMMODATION

NB: many small hotels lock their doors at 7.30pm and will not receive guests after 10pm, so check in early to get your key. If arriving late in the city, phone ahead. 'Accommodation info available at Greyhound also.'

Ansonia Residence Club, 711 Post St, 673-2670. Coed, ages 18–35. Singles from $20, with bath $25. Rates include 2 meals a day, room phones, lots of amenities and international clientele. 'Very clean.'

Hotel Arlington, 480 Ellis, 673-9600. Singles without bath $16 up, doubles $22. 'Clean, friendly, helpful.' 'Recommended.' Bus stop at door, 2 blocks from airport bus terminal.

Hotel El Dorado, 150 9th St, 552-3100. All shared bath, doubles $25 up. Continental breakfast, 'tasty'. 'Young relaxed atmosphere, cleanest we stayed in.' TV room, washing facilities.

Obrero Hotel, 1208 Stockton at Pacific, 986-9850. Brass beds, shared baths, shiny clean. $20 single, $27 double, $40 triple, all with huge meaty breakfast. Basque dinners available; in North Beach.

Golden Gate Hotel, 775 Bush St, 392-3702. Cheapest on Nob Hill, singles without bath from $22, doubles from $25. Offseason weekly discounts. Comfortable, well located.

Olympic Hotel, 140 Mason, 982-5010. Same management as Windsor, better locale. Singles without bath $16 up, single/double with tub, $30. ½ block from bus stop, near Hilton. 'Very nice, friendly.' 'Very clean rooms, excellent value.'

Riviera Hotel, 420 Jones St, 441-9339. 4 blocks from Greyhound. Singles without bath from $17, doubles from $22.

Stratford Hotel, 242 Powell, 421-7525. On Union Square, low standards of cleanliness and security, recommended *only* if you get the cheap rate ($7–$10) for

AYH/YMCA/ISIC—flash your cards. 'Depressing, dirty, no soap or towels.' 'Friendly.' Don't accept rooms in annex: 'Dirty, full of undesirables.'

Western Hotel, 335 Leavenworth, singles $13 up, doubles $15–$22, includes 'good simple breakfast'. Chinese owners called 'very friendly', 'rude and offhand'; rooms called 'scruffy', 'not that scruffy'.

Will Rogers Hotel, 589 Post, 441-9378. Singles without bath $25, with bath $30. Bus stop front door.

Windsor Hotel, 238 Eddy, 885-0101. About same price as Olympic, single with bath $20 up. 'Clean and central but rough neighbourhood.' ½ block to bus stop.

Hotel St George, 395 Eddy, 928-9684 or 771-1774. Singles $10, doubles $15; by week, $60 and $70. Free afternoon snack. Newly decorated.

Crossroads Guesthouse, 28 Rausch, 864-1777. $6/night, brand new, highly recommended, combining the cost and camaraderie of a hostel with hotel philosophy: no curfew, chores or early reveille. 13 bright bunkrooms (need bag), sleep 6, each floor with kitchen. Private garden, reading room with library, foreign papers. 'Best place I ever stayed', 'Great place to get info and tips', 'Warm welcome, helpful owners', 'Very clean'.

European Guest House, 761-763 Minna, 861-6634. $5–$7 night for sunny 6-bunk rooms if you can get one. Also floor space, same price. Run by former Greyhound driver and near Greyhound. Clean, friendly and safe but becoming a victim of its own popularity. 'Incredibly overcrowded—up to 20 sleeping on floor.' 'Get there by 5pm for a bunk.' 'At least floor's carpeted.' Maximum stay 1 week, out by 10am. Kitchens.

YWCA, 620 Sutter, 775-6500. Women only. 'Expensive at $16 up but clean, smart, in "posh" area.' NB: there are 3 YMCAs but prices are now $18 up, locales not that good, reports generally unenthusiastic, alternatives plentiful. The Embarcadero Y may honour hostel rates; call 392-2191 to enquire.

SF Youth Hostel, Building 240, Ft Mason, 1 block north of Bay St at waterfront, 771-7277. Take bus 47 from Van Ness. $6 members, $8 non-members. Kitchen, dorm overlooking the Bay, laundry. 'Chore expected in am', 'great facilities', 'Arrive early—fills quickly', 'friendly staff'. 3 day maximum. Ft Mason itself has many attractions and is well located.

FOOD

Food is one of the things San Francisco does best—don't leave without trying Dungeness crab and sourdough bread (just don't sample them at Fisherman's Wharf). Other specialties: Anchor Steam beer, Irish coffee, and Green Goddess salad (invented and served at the Palace Hotel). Outstanding and cheap are the wide variety of ethnic restaurants, beginning with standard Cantonese and running through Basque, Greek, Salvadorean, Russian, Vietnamese and more.

Breakfast: Sear's, 439 Powell (try French toast made from sourdough bread); Eagle Cafe, Pier 39, for old-fashioned prices, big helpings ('good breakfast').

Italian: Little Joe's, 523 Broadway (spectacular chefs, huge portions—ask to split spaghetti con pesto or roast chicken); Tommasso on Kearny for pizza; Basta Pasta, 1268 Grant ('yummy'); La Pantera and Capp's Corner, 2 of the family-style trattorias in North Beach.

Oriental: best tempura at Sanppo, 1702 Post; critically acclaimed Hakka Chinese at Ton Kiang, 683 Broadway ('enormous portions, ungimmicky', 'good food'); wonderful Vietnamese specialties at Tu Lan, 8 6th St. Pick Chinese restaurants by the number of Chinese you see eating there. At lunch, ask for 'wo choy' (daily special), usually 3 courses plus soup for 3 people, under $10.

Steaks: Sirloin and Brew, 1040 Columbus, 3 blocks from Fisherman's Wharf. Fish/chicken/steak plus all-you-can-eat salad, all-you-can-swill bear/wine/sangria. Cheapest 4pm–5.30pm, about $5. 'Great deal', 'Alcoholic's paradise.' Also Tad's Steak House, 120 Powell, steak/ribs plus salad, veggies, bread for $7. 'Excellent food.'

DOWNTOWN SAN FRANCISCO

¼ MILE

FISHERMAN'S WHARF

JEFFERSON ST

BEACH ST

NORTH POINT ST

BAY ST

FRANCISCO ST

CHESTNUT ST

LOMBARD ST

GREENWICH ST

FILBERT ST

UNION ST

GREEN ST

VALLEJO ST

BROADWAY

PACIFIC AVE

JACKSON ST

WASHINGTON ST

CLAY ST

SACRAMENTO ST

CALIFORNIA ST

PINE ST

BUSH ST

SUTTER ST

POST ST

GEARY ST

O'FARRELL ST

ELLIS ST

EDDY ST

TURK ST

GOLDEN GATE

MCALLISTER ST

GROVE ST

HAYES ST

FELL ST

COLUMBUS AVE

TELEGRAPH HILL

THE EMBARCADERO FREEWAY

STEAMSHIP DOCKS

RUSSIAN HILL

NORTH BEACH

LEAVENWORTH ST

JONES ST

TAYLOR ST

MASON ST

POWELL ST

STOCKTON ST

GRANT AVE

KEARNY ST

MONTGOMERY ST

SANSOME ST

BATTERY ST

FRONT ST

DAVIS ST

CHINATOWN

NOB HILL

BEALE ST

FIRST ST

SECOND ST

THIRD ST

UNION SQUARE

FOURTH ST

FIFTH ST

SIXTH ST

MARKET ST

MISSION ST

HOWARD ST

FOLSOM ST

HARRISON ST

SAN FRANCISCO SKYWAY

BRYANT ST

BRANNAN ST

45 43 41 39 37 35 33 31 29 25

Seafood: Swan Oyster Depot, 1517 Polk, locals' choice for chowder, cracked crab, steamed clams.

Atmosphere: Tommy's Joynt, Van Ness and Geary, 'great decor, huge buffalo stew'; Hamburger Mary's, 12th and Folsom near European Guest House, 'best hamburgers, good music, friendly atmosphere, run by gays'; Sam Wo, 813 Washington, eat upstairs, order wontons and watched crazed waiter Edsel Ford Fong work out; Athens Coffee Shop, 39 Mason, bouzouki music, delicious things in big pots, interesting crowd.

Sweet tooth: Just Desserts, 3 locations ('best cheesecake, chocolate cake in the city'); unusual ice creams at Polly Ann's, 3142 Noriega near Golden Gate Park (try American Beauty rose); Italian ices at Gelato Classico on Filbert St; French sorbets (raspberry and pear are heaven) at Oakville Grocery, 1555 Pacific Ave; and paletas at Latin Freeze, 3338 24th St in Mission District (Latin ice-lollies from strawberry to hibiscus flower).

OF INTEREST

Standard 'sights' are not as important in San Francisco as elsewhere, largely because so much of the city is interesting enough to qualify as a sight. The best way to take it in is to alternate walking with bus-riding. Spend at least half your time away from the tourist ghetto of Fisherman's Wharf, Pier 39, Ghiradelli, etc, all of which are aimed at the tourist-as-consumer. Although the gallant cable cars are undergoing an overhaul which will keep them out of service until mid-1984 or possibly beyond, remember that the other public transit options are not only good but rate as attractions themselves. If you don't whiz under the Bay via BART, sail across it on a ferry, or inch up and down the hills with a chatty MUNI driver, you've missed a critical part of the San Francisco experience.

Unlike LA, San Francisco is fairly compact, easy to understand and well equipped with transit to give your legs a much-needed break on its 43-plus hills. Attractions are outlined here by neighbourhood.

Union Sq:
City heart, named on the eve of the Civil War and in 1906 an impromptu campground for earthquake refugees. Nearby is **Maiden Lane**, once a red-hot red-light district, now a charming cul-de-sac with the only **Frank Lloyd Wright building** in the city at 140. Striking tunnel entrance and interior ramp; interior photos 9.30am–10am only. North at 130 Sutter is the progenitor of the modern glass skyscraper, the 1918 **Hallidie building**. Superb **stores** from Gump's to Woolworth's (yes!) in this district, along with theatres (Geary) and **cinemas** (Market). At Market and New Montgomery is the **Sheraton-Palace Hotel**, whose lacy skylighted garden court was the sole remnant in this luxurious structure to survive the quake. Singer Enrico Caruso was staying in the Palace when the quake hit; he rushed out, said 'Give me Vesuvius!' and left SF in haste.

Nob Hill:
North of Union Sq is the grande dame of SF hills; prior to the quake it was crowded with mansions, of which only the **Pacific Union Club** was left standing. If you're dressed for it, take the elevators to the view bars atop the **Fairmount** and **Mark Hopkins**.

Chinatown:
More than 65,000 Chinese live on Grant and Stockton between Bush and Broadway, the largest settlement outside the Orient. Grant is largely given over to tourism; explore Stockton, Washington and little side streets to see more authenticity. At 837 and 857 Washington are **herbal shops**. You can see fortune cookies being made at **Mee Mee**, 1328 Stockton. **Portsmouth Sq** between Clay and Washington was where the city began, where R L Stevenson lounged about, and where today's Chinese and Caucasians practice tai ch'i in the morning.

Financial district:
Montgomery St is 'the Wall Street of the West'.
Wells Fargo History Room, 420 Montgomery. Vivid collection of stagecoaches, gold rush and pioneer stuff, including mementos of Black Bart, SF's own Bad Boy who robbed Wells Fargo 28 times in 7 years. Free, Mon–Fri 1pm–3pm.
Bank of America building, 2nd tallest west of Chicago. Good free viewing gallery, 52nd floor, closes 5pm. Restricted viewing from 27th floor of the **Transamerica Pyramid**, 600 Montgomery. Both closed weekends.
Embarcadero:
Vaillancourt Walk-through fountain, a 710-ton assemblage of 101 concrete boxes, unveiled in 1971 to cries of 'loathsome monstrosity', 'idiotic rubble', etc.
Hyatt Regency Hotel, Embarcadero Plaza. Glittering 7-sided pyramid, its lobby filled with trees, birds, flowers, fountains and Sat–Sun with free music. Ride the twinkly elevators to the 20th floor for costly drinks, superb view. 'Romantic, delightful—$4.50 cocktails.' 'Required to buy drink.'
North Beach:
Originally the centre of the riproaring Barbary Coast, today still peddling flesh in its endless topless/bottomless clubs along Broadway. More than 'mammary lane', North Beach is crowded with Italians, Basques, Chinese and is also the birthplace of the beat movement. **Jack Kerouac** wrote *On the Road* at 29 Russell St. **City Lights Bookstore**, where poets Ginsberg, Ferlinghetti, etc, began to howl, is still going strong at 261 Columbus. Lots of good clubs, coffeehouses, bars—a nighttime focus.
Telegraph Hill/Russian Hill:
Romantic Telegraph Hill is topped by **Coit Tower**, a monument to early SF's volunteer smoke-eaters from Lillie Hitchcock Coit, one of SF's finest eccentrics and engine-chasers. Elevator $1.25, usually open 10am–6pm.
Russian Hill was the gathering place for Bohemian writers, artists and poets, from Ambrose Bierce to George ('cool grey city of love') Sterling. It boasts not 1 but 3 streets that make it the most vertical district in SF: famous **Lombard**, with its 8 switchbacks and 90-degree angles (almost impossible to photograph); **Filbert** between Hyde and Leavenworth; and **Union** between Polk and Hyde.
Fisherman's Wharf/Pier 39:
Minuscule amount of wharf, surrounded by a frightening quantity of souvenir crap, overpriced seafood, dreary wax museums and bad restaurants. (The working wharf is a series of 3 finger piers, just past Johnson and Joseph Chandlery.) Pier 39 is a fair walk to the right of the Wharf, a carefully hokey construct of carnival and commerce. But people love the free high diving act and other high and low jinks: 'convincing UFO exhibit'.
Aquatic Park, 3 blocks left of Fisherman's Wharf. Both the 5 vessels moored here and the nearby **National Maritime Museum** (daily 10am–5pm, crimshaw, pix, sailing ships' figureheads) are free and charming, 'especially the restored ferry'. You can board 3 of the ships. Elsewhere are docked the 1886 *Balclutha*, the liberty ship *Jeremiah O'Brien* and WWI sub *Pompanito*, all with boarding fees. Also at Aquatic: free swimming beach (cold but fairly clean, swimmers report), with free showers. Nearby is open-air seating where wonderful conga and jam sessions take place on fine Sat–Sun afternoons.
Between Aquatic and Fisherman's are **Ghiradelli Sq** and **The Cannery**, both mazes of specialty shops, restaurants and contrived street colour with a thin veneer of historicity over all.
Mexican Museum, Building D, Ft Mason, 441-0404. Free. Don't pass up this rich panorama of folk, colonial and Mexican-American works, from masks to pottery to Siquieros lithos. Outstanding special exhibits.
The marina/Pacific Heights:
The flat marina district gives way to hills, climbing to Union St, now a trendy shopping and social district. From here on up is Pacific Heights, with its surpassing

collection of **Victorian mansions**, many of them colourfully painted. Webster, Pine and the 1900 to 3300 blocks of Sacramento contain many piquant examples.

Palace of Fine Arts, Marina Blvd and foot of Lyon St, 563-7337. Built for the 1916 Panama-Pacific Exposition, in the classical papier mache mode, the palace was restored in 1967 and now houses the **Exploratorium**, with its hearing, seeing, touching and exploring exhibits in the field of human perception. Try to see the super-popular Tactile Labyrinth (extra fee). Free on Wed, otherwise $3. Open Sat–Sun, noon–5pm, Wed–Fri 1pm–5pm, Wed 5pm–7pm. 'Don't miss it!' 'Both amazing and ordinary.'

Golden Gate Bridge, perhaps the most famous suspension bridge in the world, the 1½ mile vermillion span linking SF with the green Marin headlands and Hwy 101. You can walk or bike for free (dress warmly); pedestrian walk closes at sunset. At midpoint, you'll be 220 ft above the water, a drop that has drawn at least 717 suicides. By car, bridge is free northbound, $1 ($2 weekends) southbound. 'Take bus to bridge, then walk down through wooded area with lovely plants, stroll along beach all the way back to Fisherman's Wharf. Lovely way to spend a day.'

Golden Gate Park and West SF:
An exceptional and informal park of 1017 acres, filled with a vast array of plantings, foot and bridle paths. Lots of free things: Sun concerts on music concourse; lovely Conservatory of flowers; Stow Lake and Strawberry Island; feeding buffalo in the west end; Sun juggling workshops near Conservatory; Strybing Arboretum. The Japanese tea garden is delightful if you go early or late to miss tour buses. Free Mon, and from 8am–9am, 5pm–7pm. Otherwise $1.

The **Aquarium**, $2.50, has huge open tanks; feeding times are 1.30pm for fish, every 2 hrs for dolphins. Fee includes admission to **Science Museum**, **Hall of Man**. Also in the park: the **De Young**, 558-2887, and **Asian Art Museums**, 558-2993, the former with a vast, eclectic and well-endowed collection, getting all the blockbuster shows. The latter is an overwhelming array of Orientalia, especially the jade. Both free 1st Wed of the month, $2.50 otherwise, seniors $1.25. Fee is for both plus **Palace of the Legion of Honor** (if seen same day).

Haight-Ashbury. South of the Golden Gate Park panhandle. Famous in flower-power days, now being spiffed up in what is sometimes called the 'creeping gentrification' of the city. Take a stroll down hashbury lane: **Janis Joplin's pad** at 112 Lyon, **Jefferson Airplane's hangar** at 2400 Fulton and glory be—the **Psalms Cafe**, still in business at 1898 Haight. South and east of Haight is **Noe Valley**, a sunny version of Greenwich Village, whose main drag **Castro St** is synonymous with gaydom. Note: SF's gay communities are not ghettoised; rather, you'll find gays and lesbians working and living throughout the city.

Twin Peak provides (on clear days) the finest view of San Francisco. It helps to have a car but without wheels take the K, L or M bus to Castro Station, transfer to 37 Corbett bus, get off at Parkride and Crestline, walk from trail opposite 88 Crestline.

Seal Rocks area:
In SF's northwest corner, seals, pelicans and cormorants, plus a panorama from a walk-in *camera obscura*. On the lower level of Cliff House, visit the **Musée Mecanique**, 386-1170, a droll collection of vintage arcade machines, from Fatty Arbuckle to zee French flasher! Free but bring dimes and quarters. Daily 11am–5.30pm.

Palace of the Legion of Honor, just north of Seal Rocks, is a replica of its Paris namesake and houses French 18th–20th C paintings, Rodin sculptures and fine art posters by David Lançe Goines, the Bay Area's Toulouse Lautrec. Fee $2.50 (see de Young).

Fleishhacker Zoo, Sloat and 49th Ave, 661-4844. $3. 10am–5pm daily. Largest gorilla habitat anywhere; feeding times for carnivores, 2pm; elephants 4pm.

Civic Center:
Between Franklin, Larkin, McAllister and Hayes. Its centre is City Hall, unhappy scene of the 1978 dual murder of the mayor and a gay supervisor by a former

supervisor; both crime and minimal punishment provoked rioting, outrage and jolted SF's 'tolerant mecca for gays' image.

The War Memorial Opera saw the signing of the UN charter on 25 April, 1945.

Museum of Modern Art, Van Ness and McAllister, 863-8800. All the bluechips: Miro, Klee, Jasper, Pollock, etc. Free Thur eve, otherwise $3, seniors $1.50.

St Mary's Cathedral, Geary and Gough. Almost extra-terrestrial in feeling, with a free-hanging meteor shower over the altar. 'Well worth seeing.' Free.

The Mission district:
Weekend evenings, Chicano youth strut their mechanical stuff with their highly customised vehicles in the phenomenon known as **low riding**. On Mission between 16th and 24th or so; enquire locally. The area is rich in **murals**. See for yourself at the minipark between York and Bryant on 24th; in Balmy Alley between 24th and 26th; and on Folsom at 26th. **Mission Dolores** at 16th and Dolores is a simple, restored structure with an ornate basilica peering over its shoulder. Open May– –Sept daily 9am–3.30pm. $1. Interesting cemetery, drop in anytime, free.

The Bay:
Cruises around the Bay: cheapest are the Blue and Gold boats, 546-2810, from Pier 39, 'exactly same route as Red and White fleet, less flashy boat'. Student discounts. 1¼ hours. Frequent departures. Dress warmly and wait for clear weather. Better still, ride the ferries to Sausalito, Tiburon and Larkspur; departures from Fisherman's Wharf, the Ferry building, about $7 return.

Helicopter flights over the Bay, Alcatraz, bridge, from Pier 43, 981-4832 or China Basin, 495-3333. $15 for 5 minutes. 'Go in morning for best photos.' 'Phenomenal. Worth it on a clear day.'

Alcatraz, Piers 41, 43. $4, more if you book through TICKETRON. 2-hr trip to 'the Rock', which housed Al Capone, Machinegun Kelley and other incorrigibles from Civil War days to 1963. Dress warmly and visit the toilet before your trip. Tours year-round, 9am–3pm, every 45 minutes. 'Buy tickets the day before.' 'Long queues—get there early.'

ENTERTAINMENT
Whatever your sexual proclivities, it takes quite a bit of cash (and often a smart appearance) to explore the singles bars, meat-rack taverns and gay watering holes of SF. Your best strategy is to go at Happy Hour when drinks are cheaper (of course pickings are fewer but you can't have everything). Union St is noted for hetero, Castro-Polk for gay action. You may get more action than you counted on: SF has the highest VD rate in the state, not even counting herpes.

Best sources of info for events, clubs, music are the free *BAM* monthly, the free *Bay Guardian* (comes out Wed) and the pink Datebook section of the Sunday *Chronicle-Examiner*.

Clubs, coffeehouses and watering holes:

Vesuvio Club, 225 Columbus, once headquarters for Kerouac, Dylan Thomas; colourful, atmospheric, fairly cheap drinks.

Henry Africa's, 2260 Van Ness, the original fern bar/meat-rack tavern, complete with Harley Davidson, toy trains. 'Try the fresh fruit daiquiris.'

Pier 23 Cafe, The Embarcadero, 362-5125. Bay view, funky atmosphere, good Dixieland, no cover. 2 drink minimum.

I-Beam, 1748 Haight, 668-6006. New Wave, punk bands from 9.30pm, big dance floor, cover cheapest Tue.

Mabuhay Gardens, 443 Broadway, 956-3315. The Fab Mab punk palace with dancing late, odd theatrics early. Cover and 1-drink minimum.

Bajone's, 1062 Valencia, Mission District, 282-2522. Low cover, 1 drink minimum per set for salsa, jazz, R&B. Memorable jam sessions at times. Call for hours.

Serious music, dance, theatre offerings are abundant; see the Datebook. The symphony has inexpensive open rehearsal seats; enquire at 431-5400. Also: 'You can usually get a standing ticket for $5 at the Opera House; after 1st act, grab a free seat. Productions of a high standard.'

SHOPPING
Tower Records, Columbus and Bay, 885-0500. Vast selection, open until midnight daily. For deeply discounted records and rare stuff, go to Rather Ripped Records and Rasputin's in Berkely.
Vintage clothing and factory overruns: many marvellous shops. Try along Clement, at the Thrift Town on Mission, and at Second Hand Rose at 3326 23rd. 'Ragsamatazz, 2036-A Union St, good quality factory outlet for designer clothing.' 'In Hispanic shops, be prepared to bargain. Got $180 camera down to $139. Never pay until you get the goods.'

INFORMATION/SURVIVAL
Visitors Bureau, 1390 Market at Powell, 626-5500. Open daily, long hours in summer. Multilingual, helpful. 391-2000 events message.
Redwood Empire Association, 360 Post, 421-6554. Ask for free guide—good info on counties north of San Francisco.
Travelers Aid, 38 Mason St, 781-6738 and at Greyhound, 50 7th St, 868-1503.
Mexican Tourist Info, 50 California St, Suite 2465. Issues tourist cards while you wait.
Haight-Ashbury Switchboard, 1338 Haight, 621-6211. Info, crash pads, ride board. Also free SF Survival manual.
VD Hotline, 495-OGOD. Dept of Health, 250 4th St, 558-3804, has walk-in VD clinic, 9.30am–6pm.
General: SF is a Moonies mecca; they may 'invite' you to their camp, 120 miles north, or to dinner, etc. Nip their overtures in the bud with a forthright 'piss off'. 'Very convincing, hard to get away from.' 'Also watch out for hit artists around North Beach.'

TRAVEL
If you plan to be around the Bay Area for a week or more, buy a $3 copy of the Regional Transit Guide, which shows the cheapest and best way(s) to get anywhere in a 9-county area. Or pick up the free MUNI, BART, Golden Gate, etc, maps and booklets.
MUNI city transit, 673-MUNI. 700-mile network of buses, light rail. All 3 lines of the famed cable cars are *hors de combat* until mid-1984, possibly beyond. (You can still see and photograph cable cars at the Hyatt on Union Sq and near the Hyde St Pier). MUNI buses have frequent service, friendly drivers and good transfer system; $1, free transfers, seniors 25¢. Sunday/holidays flat fee for unlimited riding. Also cheaper shopper shuttles weekdays 10am–3pm, downtown. Sightseer's special: the 22 Fillmore bus from Union St over Pacific Heights: 'a dazzler'.
BART, phone 788-BART in SF, 465-BART in East Bay. Sleek, carpeted, comfortable Bullet-Beneath-the-Bay, connecting SF with Oakland, Berkeley, etc. Fares $1 up, cheap excursion fares also. Long waits at rush hours, on Sun. Transfers valid between BART, MUNI. 'Worth it just for the experience.'
Golden Gate Transit, 332-6600. Operates bridge, ferries to Sausalito and Larkspur and buses to Marin, Sonoma counties. Headquarters in Transbay Terminal, 425 Mission St. Ferries leave from Ferry Building, about $4 one way.
A/C Transit services East Bay from Transbay Terminal, 653-3535. Often faster than BART in rush hours.
San Mateo Transit (Samtrans), Transbay Terminal, 761-7000. To Palo Alto, San Mateo. Has cheapest ($1) buses to airport. (Some runs do not accept luggage.)
Express airporter bus, Taylor and Ellis, 673-2434. Daily 24-hr service, every 15 minutes in daytime. $4 up.
Gray Line, 771-4000. City tours, Muir Woods, Sausalito. Bus pass discount.

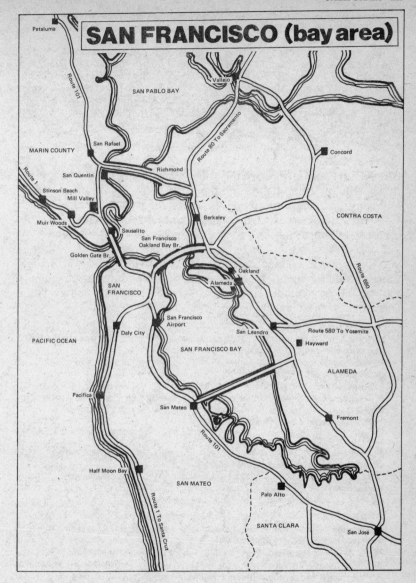

SAN FRANCISCO (bay area)

Green Tortoise Bus, 386-1798. Counterculture service to East Coast, Baja, Seattle in diesels with sleeping platforms; funky, relaxed, personalised.

AMTRAK, 556-8287, free shuttle from Transbay to Oakland depot where you get daily service on *Coast Starlight* and *San Joaquin* (to Merced, Fresno, near National Parks). Also commuter train, 700 4th St at Townsend, 495-4546. Frequent trains, SF–San Jose only.

San Francisco International Airport, 15 miles south. 761-0800 or 876-2811.

Plagued with Moonies but good art exhibits in North terminal. 'When looking for cheap flights, go directly to airlines instead of travel agencies. Be pushy.' Airport bus service; see above.
Rental cars: Greyhound Rentacar at Greyhound depot or call 800-327-2501. Unlimited mileage, about $100/week, can book from Britain also. Rent-a-Heap-Cheap, 777 Van Ness, 776-5450: 'Can take cars only within a 50-mile radius of SF.'
Ride boards, sharing: Underground ride service, 864-5663; Women's Ride Center (women only), 431-1414; KALX, 642-5259; KSAN, 478-9700. In Berkeley: 524-5404 or 5405. Also Grey Rabbit North, 428-2905. Both have on-demand buses to points north, east, south.
AAACON Transport, 1095 Market St, 864-8800.
American International Driveaway, 1600 Baker, 346-8615.

BERKELEY and OAKLAND. Easily reached by BART or bus, these two neighbour cities make good day trips; Berkeley for its university and accompanying cultural and social dividends, Oakland for its Jack London Square and excellent lakeside museum. Both cities are short on cheap lodgings, long on streets that are unsafe to walk at night.
Concentrate on the area in and around the university, the closest you'll come to the fabled Berzerkley of free speech, anti-war, radical fame: 'Rather bohemian atmosphere, good for buying secondhand rare books, homemade trinkets or discussing Marxist ideology with a stranger in a coffeehouse'.

ACCOMMODATION
'Try Berkeley fraternities—easy access to city and cheap if not free. Filthy but at that price who cares?' Located on and around Piedmont Ave.
International House, on campus, 642-9470. Summer only, 1 week minimum. Room and board about $180/week.
Shattuck Hotel, 2086 Allston Way, Berkeley, 845-7300. Old, comfy, lots of seniors. 'Friendly, safe.' Singles without bath $20 up, doubles all with bath, costlier. Bus stop at door.
YMCAs in Berkeley and Oakland, $15 up.

FOOD
Brennan's, 720 University Ave, Berkeley, 841-0960. Downtown bar with Guinness, cheap and simple foods—a local hangout.
Berkeley reader recommendations: Oscar's on Shattuck, 'really good burgers, meals under $4'; Blondie's Pizza on Telegraph, 'slice for $1'; and university cafeterias on campus ('except the main one—expensive').

OF INTEREST
On campus: both the Campanile (25¢) and the Lawrence Hall of Science (free bus) have excellent **views** of Berkeley and the Bay.
Main library has world's largest collection of Mark Twain materials. 'Try the browsing room—British papers, headphones to listen to records.' **Lowie Museum of Anthropology**, $1, excellent Indian costumes, crafts. Mon–Fri 10am–4pm, Sat–Sun noon–4pm. **Art museum**, 642-0808: video, performance art, modern works, 50¢. 'Not worth it.' **Pacific Film Archives** has massive library of flicks, 642-1412. **Lawrence Hall of Science**, Grizzly Park Blvd, 642-5132. $1–$2.50. 'Top of the mountain, excellent view, amazing museum, spent whole afternoon playing computer games.' Open late Thur and free after 4pm then. The **football stadium** sits directly on the Hayward fault, a branch of the San Andreas; a large vertical crack may be seen through the upper tier.

Off campus: Tilden Park, free, above city in the Berkeley Hills. Open until 10pm, lake swimming, riding, boating.
Oakland: Jack London Sq, 10 minutes from BART City Center station. Visit the cabin from London's Klondike days, have a drink at the First and Last Chance Saloon, where London and R L Stevenson used to tipple. 'Village is excellent reconstruction of the wharf area.' **Lake Merritt**, downtown Oakland, is the largest saltwater lake within a US city; overlooking it is the **Museum** at 1000 Oak, 273-3401. Art, history and natural science of California—free and good. Closed Mon, open late Fri.

ENTERTAINMENT
Pacific Film Archives, nightly showings, more at term time. Free on Sun, otherwise $3 to $4. Runs the gamut from Japanese samurai to vintage 1930s classics.
Larry Blake's, 2367 Telegraph, 848-0886. 'Lively restaurant/bar with good local bands.' Lively part is downstairs.
Freight and Salvage, 1827 San Pablo Ave, 548-1761. Country, blue-grass, ethnic groups and Tue night hoots for aspirants. Cheaper weeknights.
Folk dancing at Ashkenaz and Dionysos, both on San Pablo Ave.

SURVIVAL/INFORMATION/TRAVEL
Berkeley Support Services, 2235 Milvia Ave, 848-3378, has info, plus rough and ready crash pad, emphasis on rough. In warehouse area, not recommended for women.
Free clinic, 2339 Durant, 548-2570 (24-hr).
Humphrey Go-BART, free shuttle buses from Berkeley BART stations to campus, Botanical Gardens, Hall of Science, etc.

MARIN COUNTY. Linked to San Francisco by the slender red bracelet of the Golden Gate bridge is Marin County, owing its green lushness as much to wealth as to rainfall. The western edge facing the Pacific is wild, wind-buffeted, solitary and beautiful. Among its treasures are the 65,300-acre **Pt Reyes National Seashore**, which has an earthquake trail to trace the scars of the San Andreas, grand bird and whale-watching, and **Drake's Beach**, where Sir Francis may have landed when he claimed all of Nova Albion for Elizabeth I.

Next to Pt Reyes are other public wilderness sanctuaries, among them popular **Stinson Beach** (closest swimming beach to San Francisco) and **Muir Woods**, 6 miles of trails through a hushed and fragrant cathedral of *sequoia sempervivens*, some as tall as 240 feet. **Mt Tamalpais**, heavily used by hikers, commands fantastic views; its trails link up with those at Stinson, Muir Woods and elsewhere.

Inner Marin is full of affluent communities including plush **Tiburon**. Offshore from Tiburon lies **Angel Island**, successively a duelling ground, military staging area for three wars, quarantine station for Asians, and a missile site, now a State Park with four tent campsites, friendly deer, bicycling and ghostly ruins to explore. Former whalers' harbour **Sausalito**, perched near the Golden Gate bridge, has the finest view of San Francisco, lots of costly, cutsie bars and shops and a houseboat colony, its last vestige of colourful bohemianism. 'A fantastic way to get a feel for the area is to take a ferry to Sausalito and walk back across the Golden Gate bridge. Once across, you can catch a bus back to downtown.'

ACCOMMODATION
The hostel situation in Marin: Golden Gate Hostel, 941 Ft Barry, 331-2777 or 561-7277. Open year-round, 3 miles from bus stop near tunnel, now without shuttle service; call them. $4.50, $6 non-members. Handsome former officers' quarters, rec room, kitchen, laundry. Bring food. The hostel at Pt Reyes, 669-9985, now accepting groups only; its road was completely swept away in the 1982 flood and groups must be escorted in. Muir Woods hostel, 771-4646, should be open summer 1983 with trailer accommodation. Located near hot springs.
Angel Island camping, $7.75, must book by mail to Distribution Center, Dept of Parks and Recreation, PO Box 2390, Sacramento CA 95811. Daily in summer, weekends winter. Fireplaces, water, chemical toilets.

TRAVEL
Golden Gate buses about $1 1 way to Sausalito; ferry $3–$4 1 way from Ferry Building, Piers 1 and 2. 'Ferry passes by Alcatraz.' To see the infamous San Quentin prison, take the Larkspur ferry, which cruises by it. Its inmates have included Black Bart, Caryl Chessman and Sirhan Sirhan. Greyhound also serves Marin County cities, about the same prices; check at depot for schedules. Gray Line does more costly tours to Marin (see SF Travel). Ferries to Angel Island from SF Piers 41, 43½. Call 435-1915 and 546-2815. Also ferries from Tiburon to Angel Island, call 435-2131.

WINE COUNTRY. Both **Napa Valley** and its less famous neighbour **Sonoma Valley** are noted for superlative wines, producing everything from world class cabernets to sassy jug wines. Just two hours by car from San Francisco, these scenic valleys are well worth visiting. Besides wine tasting, you can visit spas in **Calistoga**, watch gliders and hot air balloons over the vineyards, visit Jack London's Beauty Ranch near Glen Ellen and maybe even pause a moment at the Tucolay Cemetery near Napa, where Mammy Pleasant is buried. A 19th-century black civil rights advocate who owned a string of San Francisco brothels, Mammy Pleasant gave more than $40,000 to finance John Brown's raid on Harper's Ferry and herself travelled about the South to stir black sentiment for him. Her headstone reads: 'Mother of civil rights in California, friend of John Brown'.

Bus service to Napa and Sonoma is good, but renting a car is a capital way to see the valleys. That way, you can alternate wine-tasting with stops at the altogether marvellous farms, roadside stands, cheese factories, delis and other tasty locales both valleys are famous for.

ACCOMMODATION
Valley Hotel, 1308 Main St, St Helena, 963-9982. Clean friendly hotel with basic rooms, bath down the hall for $15 single, $25 up double.
Triple-S Ranch, 4600 Mountain Home Ranch Rd, Calistoga, 942-6730. About $20 for 2, $5 less by the week. Pool, hiking trails, restaurant (well known for good food, served 1 April–31 Dec, dinner only).

FOOD
Pick up the farm trails brochures for both Napa and Sonoma at the Chambers of

Commerce, 1900 Jefferson St in Napa and 543 1st St E, Sonoma. To round out a picnic, you could stop at the Sonoma and Vella Cheese Factories in Sonoma, the French bakery (also Sonoma), the Napa Valley Olive Oil Co at 835 McCorkle Ave near St Helena for sausage and olives, and the Twin Hill Ranch near Sebastopol for applesauce bread. There are numerous delis and stores with picnic makings (Guigni's in St Helena is a standout and rated 'terrific') but restaurant fare tends to be dauntingly expensive in most instances.

OF INTEREST
Wineries: Over 50 in Napa Valley alone. The tiny ones tucked away on side roads are informal and fun, but you need a car. The big 7 wineries, south–north, are: **Christian Brothers** (run by a Catholic order, a castle with catacombic aging cellars); **Mondavi** (Cliff May building, 'technical tour', picnics on lawn); **Inglenook** (mix of old and new buildings, 1 owned by Francis Ford Coppola); **Beaulieu** (good tours); **Martini**; **Beringer** (its Gothic Rhine House is a landmark) and **Krug** (varietals to jug wines). All have free tasting and tours approximately 10am–4pm daily.

For champagne, hit **Kornell Brothers** in Calistoga. Around Sonoma are 4 more standouts, from **Sebastiani** to **Buena Vista**, the latter the original winery of Agoston Haraszthy, the Hungarian 'count' who brought European vinestock to the US. (Buy their Green Hungarian; Mozart Festivals here in summer). 'Christian Brothers' last tour of day is more like party night than wine-tasting—you get half glasses to taste!' 'Christian—one of the best—lets you try as may wines as you like.'

Silverado Museum, 1490 Library Lane, St Helena, 963-3757. Free daily noon–4pm except Mon. 8000 mementos of Robert Louis Stevenson, who with his bride Fanny spent 2 idyllic summer months in an abandoned mining town on the slopes of Mt St Helena. If you're an RLS buff, you should also go to **RLS Park**, 7 miles northeast of Calistoga along Hwy 29. Free, day use only, wonderful picnicking and hiking. Bring your own water/wine.

Sonoma is still centred around its lush plaza, where in 1846 Yankee rebels raised a grizzly-bear flag and established the short-lived Republic of California, giving way 40 days later to US control. Lots of interest in the village, from a Basque bakery to the mission to **Lachryma Montis**, home of General Vallejo, who once governed much of Northern California.

TRAVEL
Greyhound serves Napa to Calistoga 5 times daily; if you get down at St Helena, it's an easy walk to 3 wineries immediately north of town. Service also to Sonoma.

Gray Line from SF does all day tours.

'It's not difficult to plan your own day trip to Napa Valley if you have a bus pass, and it works out very cheaply. Leave SF at 8.30am, reach St Helena at 10.55am. Cross the Main St to Guigni's grocery and have them make you up an enormous sandwich of turkey, salami or roast beef with salad for $2.50 or so, then walk out of town as far as Beringer Brothers for guided tour of winery (no charge, frequent departures) and wine tasting. Buy a bottle of chabli and carry it back into town. Opposite the post office is a little park, well equipped with picnic tables, toilet, fountain and lots of grass. Enjoy your lunch and return to bus stop. It's possible to catch the next bus to Calistoga (end of line), spend 3/4 hr glimpsing the mud baths for which this little spa is noted, and get the 3.30pm bus back to SF, arriving 6.10pm. A memorable day out for the price of your picnic and a bottle of wine!'

EL CAMINO REAL. In the 18th century, El Camino Real (the Royal or King's Highway) was the road which linked the 21 missions between San Diego and Sonoma. The missions still stand, the road does not, but Highway 101 follows it for much of the way. Well served

by bus, El Camino Real/101 has long dull stretches and much traffic. Far more interesting (although slower) is to trace Highway 1, which edges the coast with great drama and beauty. Parts of it are served by bus. Several of the towns along El Camino Real and Highway 1 are described below.

SANTA CRUZ. Located 75 miles south of San Francisco via Highways 101 and 17 or 90 miles via scenic coastal Highway 1, Santa Cruz is an offbeat city of 35,000, full of frilly Victorians as well as sun-tanned bodies, most of whom attend the redwooded UC campus. Jumping nightlife, lots of movies and bookstores and the best pier, beach and boardwalk combination make Santa Cruz worth seeking out. You might want to bicycle or drive from San Francisco down Highway 1, stopping at the well-spaced youth hostels at Montara and Pigeon Point Lighthouses and finally Santa Cruz.

ACCOMMODATION
St George Hotel, 1520 Pacific, 423-8181. Near Greyhound. $15 single, $25 double if you can get in. 'Full by 3pm.'
Hostel, PO Box 1241, 423-8304 or 425-9915. Currently open summer only, supposed to be year-round eventually when it gets a permanent home. San Francisco Hostel can help you with details.

OF INTEREST/FOOD/ENTERTAINMENT/TRAVEL
A great eating-out town, very sophisticated and surprisingly cheap. Excellent Szechuan at Chef Tong's, 111 Soquel and the Swan-Heavenly Goose, 1538 Pacific Mall. Don't miss the Happy Hours at The Catalyst, 1011 Pacific, 423-1336. Legendary, especially Fri: 'The whole town is there!'
Good Happy Hours also on campus at the Whole Earth Restaurant, Fri 4pm–6.30pm.
The best sights are free: the **pier**, **boardwalk**, **beach**, pretty **Pacific St Mall**, **street murals** (Chamber has maps) and **Victorians**.
Local bus, 462-6080. Lots of routes, runs late nights, weekends. Free shuttle buses in summer to beach and around town.

THE MONTEREY PENINSULA. Some 121 miles south of San Francisco is the heavily touristed Monterey peninsula, whose residents have commercialised and plasticised the hell out of their environment but have failed to ruin it entirely. The good things that are left are genuinely superlative: the Big Sur coast, Pt Lobos, the Mission at Carmel, the Monarch butterfly get-togethers at Pacific Grove. Make the overpriced ($5) 17-Mile Drive, the saccharine delights of downtown Carmel and Cannery Row your lowest priorities.

ACCOMMODATION
Monterey Hotel, 406 Alvarado St, Monterey, 375-3184. Single with shared bath $20 up, doubles $22–$30. Plus key deposit. The ceilings may be cracked but rms, linens are spanking clean, help friendly. A grand old place (last in Monterey), living on borrowed time. Downtown, good locale.
Hostel, 404 El Estero (office), open summer only, call 373-4166 for this season's location.

Asilomar Conference Center, 800 Asilomar, Pacific Grove, 372-8016. Beautiful site on Steinbeck's 'Great Tidepool', group oriented but rms also for individuals. Ask for older section, $23 single or double, some with shared bath. Cheap, hearty meals also.

Camping at Big Sur: $6/night at 9 campgrounds but 'excellent sites only 50¢ for hikers and bikers'.

OF INTEREST

Monterey makes much of its Spanish/Mexican past and it does have 45+ **18th and 19th C buildings**, a few outstanding; get self-guiding walk brochure from Visitors Center, 380 Alvarado, 649-3200.

To get a sense of what it must have been like in Steinbeck's time, take an early morning walk from **Fisherman's wharf** along the water line to **Cannery Row**, especially evocative when the fog swirls around. Several blocks up from the Row, you may still see the weathered and wistful cabins of the cannery workers, now captured by flowering vines, and somehow overlooked as a source of tourist revenue. (Give 'em time.)

Pt Lobos, 4 miles south of Carmel. Bus service. $3 per car, walkers free. 1250 acres of natural beauty: coves, islands, fearless animals and birds. Best of all are China Cove and the beach beyond (take a lunch). R L Stevenson used to wander here, using its headlands as a model for Spyglass Hill in *Treasure Island*.

Carmel and the Mission. You could call Carmel 'quaint', but quaint was never this calculated. Some of the Hansel and Gretel cottages are winsome, however. 1 mile and several light-years away from downtown Carmel is the free Mission (donations 'nice'), heavily restored but lovely and very right, its great star-shaped window framed by vines, fountains and flowers. Good artefacts, museum.

Big Sur is the 90-mile stretch of deeply scissored coastline between Carmel and San Simeon, almost pristine and wholly soul satisfying. Do stop for the obligatory drink and sea-gazing at Nepenthe; the lower deck (the bar is called Phoenix) actually has a more wonderful view. Big Sur was home to the beats and Henry Miller and today continues to be inhabited (sparsely) by rugged individualists from Ansel Adams to Linus Pauling.

TRAVEL

Monterey transit, 899-2555 or 424-7695. 75¢, free transfers. All downtown routes stop at Munras/Tyler/Pearl St triangle. Serves Monterey, Pacific Grove, Carmel and limited service to Big and Little Sur as far as Nepenthe (very cheap at about $3). Also interlocks with Salinas Transit, 758-7331, which in turn gets you to Santa Cruz County.

Coastline bus, 649-4700. Monterey–Big Sur–Morro Bay–San Luis Obispo via Hwy 1. Twice daily. Stops on request, maximum fare $20, Monterey to Big Sur, about $5. 'Can stop at several points for 1 to 4 hrs.'

Auto Driveaway, 2260 Fremont, Monterey, 372-0720.

SAN LUIS OBISPO and SANTA BARBARA COUNTIES. Called the central coast, this region stretches from Big Sur south to Santa Barbara. Among its highlights are **San Simeon**, site of Hearst Castle, built by William Randolph Hearst, newspaper magnate and 'Citizen Kane' of Orson Welles' film. Of Spanish character, the castle houses his $75 million art collection, which includes now-priceless tapestries, rugs, jade, statuary, even entire antique ceilings and fireplaces from all over Europe. 'A two-hour trip into paradise.' Further down the coast, **Morro Rock** makes a monolithic landmark at water's edge, the

first in a series of volcanic peaks that march picturesquely through San Luis Obispo County. You can follow them along Highway 1 (the bus route also). The abundance of beaches and camping opportunities in this county, plus the amiable character of the inland mission town of **San Luis Obispo**, makes this area appealing.

One hundred miles further south, **Santa Barbara** beckons. Far and away the loveliest of coastal cities, from its setting against the Santa Ynez Mountains to its beautiful Spanish adobe architecture. Despite its wealth, Santa Barbara is a non-stuffy, youthful city, with a big UC campus, sophisticated music and nightlife and the best sidewalk cafe idling anywhere in the US. 'Beautiful unspoilt beaches.' 'Elegant little town with a lot happening.'

ACCOMMODATION
For Hearst Castle, camping at San Simeon and further south at Atascadero Beach. Also: the Point Motel, 3450 Toro Lane, 772-2053, 20 miles south of Hearst Castle on Morro Beach. Superbly sited, 5 rms, single/doubles $20 to $40 (3 have kitchens). Rates same year-round, weekends. Store, BBQ, cable TV, good access to beach.
In Santa Barbara: Victoria Hotel, 24 E Victoria, 966-7361. $16 up single, shared bath. 5 blocks to Greyhound.
Hotel de Riviera, 125 W Carrillo, 965-9140. ½ block from Greyhound. 'Friendly, quaint and old-fashioned hotel, doubles without bath under $30. In keeping with relaxed character of the town.'

OF INTEREST
Hearst Castle, book through TICKETRON or day of tour; get there early. $8 each, 4 different tours, each 1¾ hours. 'Take tour 2 or 3—smaller groups, more personal and informative.'
Mission Santa Barbara, upper end of Laguna St. Noble facade with columns and towers, many unusual architectural touches from Moorish fountain to Mexican skulls in this 1786 'Queen of the Missions'. More beautiful still is the **County Courthouse**, 1120 Anacapa St, a 1929 Hispano-Moorish treasure, inside and out.
Nearby is the Presidio Cafe, one of SB's great patio lolling places. Also try Joe's Cafe, 512 State: 'bustling atmosphere, lashings of food at low prices—a favourite students' meeting place'.

SACRAMENTO.
Now the capital, Sacramento was nothing but a one-man barony until 1848, when gold was found nearby and the place mushroomed into prominence with the Gold Rush. Halfway between San Francisco and Lake Tahoe at the confluence of the Sacramento and American Rivers, the city is a pleasant, Midwestern-feeling place to pause. Its sights are all downtown, making it a satisfying city for the on-foot traveller.

ACCOMMODATION
Berry Hotel, 729 L St, 442-2971. Near Greyhound, singles $18, doubles $20, all with private bath. 'Threadbare but friendly.'
Motel 6, 1415 30th St, 452-5581. Close to Sutter's Fort, reachable by bus. $16 single, $20 doubles. Pool, AC, noisy (freeway nearby).
Residence Club, 2130 22nd St, 453-0205. Prices begin at $17 single, shared bath, and include 2 meals a day. Doubles $25 up. AC, phones, bus stop ½ block. Quiet residential neighbourhood.

Capitol Park Hotel, 9th and L Sts, 441-5361. 1½ blocks from Greyhound. From $20 single, $28 double with private bath. 'Very central, clean.'

OF INTEREST

Old Sacramento, 29-acre historic district on Sacramento River. Over 100 renovated buildings, 41 of them 19th C originals. Especially evocative at night. Standouts are: the canvas and wood **Eagle Theater**, the original of which washed away in the great flood of 1850; the **Pony Express monument** at 2nd and J, marking the beginning of the 2000-mile service from Sacramento to St Joe, Missouri; the **Hastings Museum**, the western terminus for the Pony Express and the first meeting place of the California Supreme Court; and the **Sacramento Union** newspaper at 121 J, whose ink-stained wretches included both Bret Harte and Mark Twain. Fanny Ann's Saloon ('cheap and pleasant change from burgers') makes a visually interesting break from sightseeing.

State Railroad Museum, 2nd and I Sts, 445-7373. Daily 10am–10pm, $2. The crown jewel of Old Sac, an enchanting collection of rolling stock (with special effects walk-throughs, 19th C sounds, sights and even smells), displays and a show-stopper film. Don't miss it.

Sutter's Fort, 2701 L St, 445-4209, and **State Indian Museum** on Ft grounds, 324-0971. Both daily 10am–5pm. Reconstruction of the 1839 fort (first white outpost in California interior) has rather ordinary vignettes, $1. Far more gripping is the free look at the cultures, artefacts of 50 tribes in the Indian museum. It holds interesting special events (eg Acorn Day) also.

State Capitol, 10th St at Capitol Mall. Excellently restored, well worth a look—first floor museum rooms especially. Picnicking on the 40-acre tree and flower-covered lawn is recommended—all Sac does it.

Old Governor's Mansion, 16th and H Sts, 445-4209. Charming wedding-cake Gothic, open 10am–5pm. $1, seniors 50¢. 'Best sight in city', 'good tour and stories'.

Nearby:

Mother Lode country, with its vivid gold and ghost towns and Sierra scenery is well worth exploring. **Coloma** is the spot where James Marshall found the nugget that set off the Rush, but **Nevada City**, **Folsom**, **Sutter Creek**, **Amador City** and numerous others have more to offer historically and aesthetically. Rent a car if you will, or take Greyhound/Trailways to several of the villages. Others are served (in a patchwork fashion) by a mix of local buses; Amador Stages is headquartered in Sac.

INFORMATION

Visitors Bureau, 1100 14th St at K, 449-5291. Maps, 'gold' nugget lapel pins, etc. Also visitor info at 1031 2nd St in Old Sac, 446-4314.

Travelers Aid, 331 J St, suite 160, 443-1719 (24-hr).

TRAVEL

Greyhound, 715 L St, 444-6800. 'Gambler's buses to Tahoe, Reno—if you can afford to lay out the fare, on arrival Harrah's Casino gives you $14 worth of chips and $3 food voucher. Details in local papers—a great day out.'

Trailways, 1129 I St, 443-2044.

Local bus, 444-7591. Downtown, suburbs and to Davis. Also K St tram, 25¢, runs from Old Sac along the mall to 14th St.

AMTRAK, 4th and I Sts, 444-9131.

Car rentals: Renta-Heap-Cheap, 444-2710; Rentawreck, 441-3863.

AAACON Transport, 1400 S St, 442-2914.

Boat trips: Delta Travel, 372-3690, has lazy, scenic weekend trips (7 hrs) April–Nov from San Francisco to Sacramento via Sacramento River through Delta country. Under $40 roundtrip, including return by bus.

LAKE TAHOE. Located two hours east of Sacramento, Lake Tahoe is

the largest (and no doubt the bluest) alpine lake on the North American continent, situated in a valley of the Sierra Nevada which straddles the California/Nevada border. Snow-capped peaks circle the lake, whose infrequent communities range from ski-bunny resorts like Incline Village to the urban sprawl of South Lake Tahoe and Nevada neighbour Stateline. The Nevada side touts gambling, the California side, gamboling in the crisp clean outdoors. Delightful but disproportionately crowded in midsummer and ski season. 'The best walk in the area is 15 miles up Mount Tallac, from 6000 to 9700 feet—beautiful.'

ACCOMMODATION
Norden Ski Inn and Youth Hostel, Old Hwy 40 in Norden, 426-3079. 35 miles NW of Lake Tahoe. Cheapest and least crowded in summer: 3-tiered bunks (need bag) awfully cramped when full. $6.25 AYH. Also private rooms, $18 single, $22 double year-round. Sundeck, restaurant, 3 miles from Greyhound. Cheap horseback riding, sailing through hostel. Close to Donner Park.
In South Lake Tahoe: rates by far the cheapest Nov–Apr, Sun–Thur; high season is 1 July–Labor Day, and that means high.
Shenandoah Motel, 4074 Pine Blvd, 544-2985. Under $30 single/double in summer, on weekends; as low as $19 double, mid-Sept to mid-May, Sun–Thur. Colour TV, 4 blocks from Nevada casinos.
Camping in wilderness areas and around the lake, numerous, from free to $7/night.

OF INTEREST/TRAVEL
Greyhound, 1099 Park Ave, 544-2241. LTR busline also in terminal. 'For magnificent views of the lake, take the LTR bus (pass valid) to Truckee and Reno. Stops for 30 minutes in **Virginia City** enroute, allowing time for sightseeing.' '**Truckee** itself worth a stop: wooden buildings and boardwalks, a frontier atmosphere.' 2 miles west of Truckee is **Donner Summit and State Park**, where in 1846–7, the 89-member Donner party was trapped by 22-ft snows. Only 47 survived the ordeal, many of them by resorting to cannibalism.

MOUNT SHASTA and LASSEN VOLCANIC NATIONAL PARK. 160 miles northwest of Sacramento stands 14,162-foot **Mount Shasta**, the white-haired patriarch of Northern California: radiant, almost overwhelming, the mountain dominates the villages in its shadow. Mount Shasta City is closest, Dunsmuir perhaps the prettiest. Cheap lodging in Mount Shasta City, including a hostel.

Younger, shorter, hotter-headed sister to Mount Shasta is **Lassen Peak**, which last erupted in 1917—a wink of an eye in geologic terms. Brilliantly bizarre moonscape, nasty mud pots, pools of turquoise and gold, sulphurous steam vents reveal volcanic activity, especially in the Bumpass Hell area. You are free to climb the 2½ miles to the three craters of Lassen: main road takes you near, trail is easy, fine views of Shasta and the devastation to the northeast. Excellent summer programmes; Ishi, the last Stone Age man in America, was found near Lassen and the Manzanita Lake info centre has photo displays of him. Open year-round but snows keep most sectors inaccessible from late

October to early June. $1 per car, 50¢ otherwise. 'Yosemite is tame by comparison.'

ACCOMMODATION

Shasta Hostel, 200 Shelton, Mt Shasta City, 926-4896. Rustic cabins, $5 summer, $6 winter, kitchen. Greyhound 1 mile, food ½ mile.

Swiss Holiday Lodge, 50 Mt Shasta Blvd, 926-4587. Pretty chalet, tremendous view of Mt Shasta, singles $17–$20, doubles $19 up. Highly rated.

Cheaper still are nearby Pine Needles Motel (has sauna, pool, colour TV for $15 up) and Mission Motel.

Camping at Lassen: Juniper is free, 8 others are $3, most open May through Sept. Sulphur Works is closest to bus service, has nearest hot springs.

TRAVEL

Greyhound/Trailways both service Interstate 5 to Dunsmuir, Redding, Mt Shasta City, etc.

Mt Lassen Motor Transit, 529-2722 or 527-5456 in Red Bluff, serves Lassen Park and east to Susanville.

AMTRAK serves Redding and Dunsmuir.

Car rental: Affordable car rental, 243-1310; A Rent-a-Car, 221-RENT. Both used car rentals in Redding.

REDWOOD NATIONAL PARK. This 106,000-acre park begins 43 miles north of Eureka, incorporating a long stretch of shoreline and three State Parks in a patchwork administration. Often foggy and rainy, its groves of *sequioa sempervivens* include the tallest trees in the world—one measures 368 feet yet its diameter is only 14 feet. Other tremendous stands of redwoods lie between Leggett and Fortuna; while more visited, they also offer warmer, drier camping. The **Avenue of the Giants** (see it via the half- and full-day tours on the Squirrel Bus) is especially moving. Both park areas are free.

ACCOMMODATION

Orick Motel, Hwy 101, nr park. 488-3501. 4 minutes' walk from Ranger station and bus drop. $25 rms for 3 people.

Prairie Creek Motel, 488-3841, 2 miles north of Orick on 101. Singles or doubles, $25–$30. 'Friendly English couple.' 'Can't recommend highly enough.'

Camping: developed and primitive sites, all in the State Park sections of Redwood National Park, most at $6/night. Also free and 50¢ sites to bikers/hikers at various locations. At Prairie Creek: 'Free site is right next to a protected herd of elk (wild and dangerous—if they want your tent, don't argue), plenty of raccoons as well as the odd bear. Lots of trails.' Best camping in the southern redwoods is at Standish-Hickey (50¢ hiker/biker spots) and at Humboldt Redwoods State Parks. Some hot showers. The latter park has the best colour displays in autumn.

TRAVEL

Greyhound passes through the park, stopping at Orick (park entrance), Ranger Station, other places on demand enroute.

Tall trees shuttle from Orick Ranger station, 488-3461, to tall trees grove. Memorial to Labor Day, $2. 'Superb walks through redwood forest.'

HAWAII

As though to balance the tropics against the arctic, Hawaii was admitted to the Union in 1959, hard on Alaska's heels. A far-flung archipelago, Hawaii's five main islands contain every Polynesian cliche: glorious flowers, an infinity of palm-fronded beaches with your choice of wave height and sand colour, volcanoes, pineapples, and handsome people with features that reflect a pan-Pacific racial mix.

But paradise is also pasteurised and paved over, a process that began in the 1820s when New England missionaries imposed their morality, clothing standards and a truncated 12-letter version of their alphabet on the friendly islanders.

There's a lot of liquid real estate between Hawaii and the mainland: 2400 miles, to be exact. But air fares are fiercely competitive these days, and another plus is the availability of good, cheap lodgings and bed and breakfasts, many with kitchen facilities. Inter-island air and hydrofoil fares are reasonable, making it feasible to island-hop from **Oahu** (with its cosmopolitan capital, Honolulu) to the rural and volcanic delights of **Hawaii**, the Big Island. Beach and tranquillity buffs should head directly for **Maui**, **Kauai**, and **Molokai**. Landscape varies strikingly from island to island. Another pleasant variable is the fact that each island has a wet (east) side and a dry side, allowing you to change climate (and topography) at will. NB: bring something warm and/or a nylon windbreaker for mountains and for evenings.

Camping choices at county, state and national sites are many and range from free to $2 a night; most require a permit in advance. Rustic cabins are available on Hawaii, Kauai, Oahu and Maui; inexpensive but book way ahead. Bed and breakfast is popular, cheap and recommended: $14–$25 single, $19-$42 doubles with B&B Hawaii, Box 449, Kapaa, 96746 (822-1582); and $12.50 up with Pacific-Hawaii B&B, 19 Kai Nani Place, Kailua 96734 (call 262-6026). Both services have homes on all five main islands.

National Parks: Haleakala
Hawaii Volcanoes

OAHU. Most urbanised and brutalised of the islands, but don't write Oahu off entirely. It absorbs the brunt of four million visitors a year; in doing so, it's won a few battles (billboards are banned, flowers are planted everywhere) and lost a few (highrise forests in Waikiki, plastic leis for tour groups).

Good bus transit around the island, allowing you easy access to areas outside Honolulu. Two mountain ranges define Oahu. Honolulu lies on the southwestern flanks of the larger, the Koolau Range. Northeast of the city, the **Nuuanu Pali pass** cuts through the Koolau Mountains, offering splendid views of the spot where King Hamehameha the Great defeated the Oahuans in 1795 in his campaign to unite the islands. Thousands of defeated warriors were forced over the precipice to their deaths. Near Hauula on the north-east coast, a tough one-mile climb along a rough mountain ravine brings you to the **Sacred Falls**, one of the loveliest sights on the island. The falls drop 87 feet into a pool in the gorge, while above you loom the 2500-foot walls of the mountain. On the west or leeward side is **Makaha Beach**, site of international surfing competitions November through December. To the south, Sea Life Park and Hanauma Bay are both worth seeing.

Don't come to **Honolulu** looking for miles of beaches, Hawaiian village charm or quiet. You'll find Waikiki is postage-stamp in size and covered with bodies in unbecoming shades of red. Honolulu's pace, while not at the gallop of hypertensive Los Angeles, is brisk, its traffic thick, its pavements crowded. Honolulu is a place to act the tourist, to shop at the International Marketplace, to sip maitais and eat puupuus (Hawaii's hors d'oeuvres) and raise hell when the sun goes down. Flossy hotels aside, lodging can be very cheap here. To keep costs even lower, raid the city's huge and colourful produce and seafood markets and try Japanese box lunch takeouts and noodle stands.

Although they are somewhat buried in the barrage of tourist ballyhoo, Honolulu's cultural attractions (from museums to its Chinatown) are numerous and its historic sites—Pearl Harbor and Punchbowl Crater in particular—are tasteful and moving.

ACCOMMODATION
Waikiki is crowded with low-cost digs, many with kitchens, most a couple of blocks from the beach. Reservations advised in summer.
Edmunds Hotel Apartments, 2411 Ala Wai Blvd, 923-8381. $14 up single, $16 up double, 2-bedroom apartments $20 up. TV, maid service. Homey, recommended.
Hale Waikiki Apartment Hotel, 2410 Koa Ave, 923-9012. Studios with kitchens, $15 to $20. 100 yards from beach. Maid service, weekly rates.
Big Surf Hotel, 1690 Ala Moana Blvd, 946-6525. $13 up single, $16–$25 double, near boat harbour. Air conditioning, refrigerators.
YMCAs; several. Only coed is at 250 S Hotel St. The YWCA Fernhurst Residence, 1566 Wilder Ave, 941-2231, is recommended for women. Bed plus 2 meals daily, $16, cheaper by week. Shared bath, many amenities. Bus to downtown, Waikiki.
Hostel, 2323A Sea View Ave, 946-0591. Near U of Hawaii, take bus 8, transfer to bus 4 at Metcalf. $4.75; must reserve ahead. Cafeteria nearby. City bus won't take backpackers.
Outside city: Alohaland Guest House, 98-1003 Oliwa St, Aiea, 487-0482. $20 shared, $25 private bath; $30 double with private bath. Full breakfast, $2.50. Minimum stay 3 days, senior discount. 1 block from bus lines to Honolulu, other parts of Oahu.

FOOD
Lots of all-you-can-eat smorgy places, notably Perry's, for no-nonsense breakfast and lunch buffet. Good ethnic eating at the Japanese delis, Chinese takeaway counters, noodle shops. Also tap into Honolulu's lavish Happy Hour spreads; the one at the Colonial House Cafeteria in the International Marketplace is great. 2.30pm–6.30pm daily.

Hawaiian munchies are called puupuus and reflect ethnic diversity—from egg rolls to falafel. This is the home of the maitai, a nobly proportioned ration of rum, passionfruit juice, chunks of fruit and a baby orchid. Luaus: eschew the big hotels, read the *Waikiki Beach Press* and other local papers for the local church luaus— cheaper (about $10), friendlier and much better food and entertainment. For Hawaiian specialties, try Helena's, 1364 N King St. Inexpensive way to sample generous portions of butterfish, laulau, poi, etc. Lastly, be sure to sample shave ice, Hawaii's better answer to the snowcone.

OF INTEREST

In Honolulu:

Bishop Museum and Planetarium, 1355 Kalihi, 847-1443. Daily 9am–5pm. $3. Incredible feather cloaks (treasured as booty by the ancient kings), Hawaiian and Polynesian artefacts.

Foster Botanical Garden, 180 N Vineland Blvd, 538-7528. Daily 9am–4pm. Free, cool oasis of orchids, rare trees, flowers.

Honolulu Zoo, 151 Kapahulu Ave, 923-7723. Free, 9am–5pm daily, world's finest group of tropical birds. On Wed nights, June through Aug, stays open until 7.30pm, free entertainment at 6pm. Bring a picnic like the locals do.

Iolani Palace, King and Richards Sts. Only royal palace on American soil, used just 11 years by the Hawaiian monarchs. Queen Liliuokalani wrote *Aloha Oe*, easily the most famous Hawaiian song, while imprisoned here. $3; very popular. Free noon concerts Fri.

Kodak Hula Show, Kapiolani Park, Tue–Fri, 10am. Free; array of Hawaiian, Tahitian dancing, costumes to blow colour film on; get there early for seats. Also free shows at: **Ala Moana Shopping Center** (2pm Tue and Thur), **Reef Hotel** (Sun eves); **King's Alley** (Wed, Fri, Sun) and elsewhere; check with Visitors Center.

Academy of Arts, Ward and Beretania, take 2 bus from Waikiki. Open Tue–Sun, varying hours. Free: 25 galleries from Polynesian to *avant-garde*. James Michener collection of *ukiyo-e* woodblock prints is one of world's best. Many changing exhibits, plus films, classes, lectures, etc.

Outside Honolulu:

Pearl Harbor. Departures from Halawa Gate. 20-minute film on Pearl Harbor at the Visitors Center, followed by free Navy boat tours of the harbour and the *USS Arizona* **Memorial**. You can look down through the limpid water to see the ghostly outline of the *Arizona*, wherein lie 1177 sailors who died on 7 Dec, 1941, in the Japanese air attack. Shivery. Daily except Mon. Take 8 bus from Waikiki, transfer at Ala Moana to 50 or 51. 1-hr bus ride.

Sea Life Park, Makapuu Pt, 923-1531. 16 miles from Waikiki. Now $7—about half the price of mainland aquatic parks and better, too. The huge reef tank gives you skindiver's view of brilliant fish, coral, sharks. Various shows, pettable porpoise, etc. Daily 9.30am–5.30pm. Bus service.

Polynesian Cultural Center, 38 miles from Waikiki at Laie. $14 admission—ouch! Daily except Sun, 923-1861. Run by Mormons, but the shows, dances, villages are quite authentic: Tahiti, Fiji, Samoa, Tonga, the Marquesas and the Maoris are all represented. Spend all day to catch shows at 12.30pm, 3.30pm. Evening pageant costs still more, ditto meals, so bring picnic lunch. Tickets in Waikiki at 2222 Kalakaua, Suite 915.

Dole Pineapple Cannery, Iwilei Rd, 538-3663. $2 tour, May–Sept only. 'All the pineapple juice you can drink.'

INFORMATION

Visitors Bureau, 2270 Kalakaua Ave, 923-1811.

TRAVEL

Good bus service around the island, 50¢ any distance, free transfers. Also good in Honolulu.

MAUI. Twenty-five flying minutes southeast of Honolulu is Maui, trendiest of the islands and famous for such diverse things as sweet onions, potato chips, humpback whales and Maui wowie, a potent variety of local marijuana. Two volcanic masses form the island, joined by a wasp-waisted isthmus. Maui is marked by an extra-ordinary variety of terrain and climate, from the cold dryness of 10,013-foot **Haleakala volcanic crater** to the lush wetness of **Hana**, which requires a new vocabulary of greens to describe it. The former whaling port of **Lahaina** is touristy and social; the upcountry euca-lyptus land around **Makawao** is rural and mellow, Hawaiian cowboy country. Once past the endless condos of Kihei and Wailea, there are superb beaches and camping opportunities at **Makena** and further south.

At **Haleakala National Park** the 'House of the Sun' has the largest dormant (at least it hasn't erupted in 200 years) crater in the world, 21 miles in circumference and big enough to swallow all of Manhattan Island. The terrain is marvellous: graceful cones and curves of deep red and purple, amid which sit ethereal silversword plants. At times, huge cumulous clouds pour over the crater lip and pile up like whip-ped cream. On days when the summit is clear of clouds, pilots of Honolulu-to-Hilo flights obligingly dip down inside. At dawn and dusk, the Spectre of Brocken effect can sometimes be seen, where one's own shadow is projected in gigantic form onto the cloud form-ations within the crater. Sunrise at the crater is like a slow-motion fireworks display, best seen near the Puu Ulaula observation centre. Holo Holo Tours, 661-4858, does a sunrise tour that includes a light breakfast, around $35.

ACCOMMODATION AND FOOD

Food is costly so stick to local products: seafood, pineapple, lettuce, tomatoes, onions. Try Maui's new wines, made near Haleakala, and of course the outrageous potato chips.

Pioneer Inn, 658 Wharf St, Lahaina, 661-3636. Cheaper rooms (fan only), $19 up single, $22 up double. A balconied old charmer that captures the ramshackle, social feeling of Lahaina; excellent food, bar, cookout facilities, good place to meet people.

Maui YMCA/Camp Keanae, 18 miles from Hana, 244-3253. Isolated, beautiful setting, 100 beds (need bedding), $4.50. Meals during camp session; otherwise, pack it in.

At Haleakala: small amount of free tent camping plus 3 hiker cabins, so popular they're booked on a lottery system. Now $2; access on foot or by horseback only. Worth enquiring about cancels when you get here. Enroute to the crater: good food at Bullock's, home of the 'Moonburger'.

Other camping cabins at Poli Poli Spring and Waianapanapa State Park, near waterfalls, Seven Pools. Tent camping free at State Parks, $1 at county sites.

OF INTEREST

Lahaina: viewing place for **humpback, sperm whales**, who mate and calve in the channel. The Cetacean Society runs tours, late Dec–March. Also see the **whaling museum** on the brig *Carthaginian*; its A/V show has whale songs.

Hana area: 54 miles of bad but beautiful road keep Hana private; Charles Lindbergh loved it and is buried here. Lodging is exclusive, so day trips or camping near Seven Pools is about it. 'Don't miss the **Oheo stream** and **Seven Pools**; crystal clear, just like paradise.' Stoke up before (and after) tackling the Hana Highway at Paia's E–Z Cafe and Mama's Fish House, both excellent.

HAWAII. Big Island for its size, Orchid Island for the 22,000 varieties that grow wild and in nurseries, Hawaii is the youngest and fieriest of the archipelago. Long used to volcanic eruptions, Hawaii these days is erupting with development also, largely at Kona, Kailea and Hilo. But like the Hawaiian lava, which flows slowly enough to permit escape, the commercialisation of the Big Island doesn't seem to be as headlong as elsewhere. If there is such a thing as the 'old Hawaii', you may discover it in this richly rural setting, full of cattle and coffee ranches, macadamia nut plantations, a place where the aloha spirit hasn't frayed too much and people still get together to 'talk story' and watch the sunset.

It was at Kealakekua Bay that Captain Cook ended up as part of a Hawaiian Happy Hour menu. Originally greeted as a god when he landed in 1779, Cook tarnished his deity image with various outrages against the natives. When he took a chief hostage, he and four crewmen were promptly clubbed to death.

Bus service around the island—good thing because it's huge.

Only in America—drive-in volcanoes, at **Hawaii Volcanoes National Park**. Compared with the Mount St Helens variety, these shield volcanoes erupt in a relatively controlled manner, allowing the curious to literally stand at volcano's edge to watch redhot lava flows and fissures that spray curtains of fire into the air. This comes about because lava from 13,680-foot Mauna Loa, Kilauea and others is extremely fluid, hot (2000 degrees) and low in gas. The volcanoes obligingly erupt in a lavish way every couple of years, with attendant quakes, fissures yawning open, steam explosions and lava flows (1979 was a very good year, eruption-wise). Between times, you will see, hear and smell milder but still impressive activity.

ACCOMMODATION AND FOOD

Start the day with Kona coffee and macadamia-nut muffins (or pancakes, etc)—delicious and local. Luaus on all the islands have become terribly commercialised mass feeding operations, but perhaps you'll find them slightly cheaper and less obnoxious here. Scan the local paper for church or other groups with luaus open to the public. The roast pig really is ambrosial, and poi—well, you eat it to say you've eaten poi. Avoid high prices at Volcano National Park and eat instead at Volcano Cafe, 1 mile from park headquarters on Hwy 11. Reasonable, very tasty food.

Dolphin Bay Hotel, 333 Iliahi, Hilo, 935-1466. Well-furnished, $19 singles, $25 doubles. Studios/apartments $30 up. All with kitchens, fans. 4 blocks to bus stop, town bay. Wonderful garden with pick-your-own breakfast.

Polynesian Pacific Hotel, 175 Banyon Dr, 961-0426. On 'hotel row', pool, cafe, BBQ, spa, on Hilo Bay, $18 single/double.

Manago Hotel, village of Capt Cook in Kona area, 323-2642. Shared bath $13–$15,

private $21–$24. Cafe with great home cooking, Japanese and American. 1400 ft up in coffee country, simple place overlooking the spot of Cook's demise.
In Volcano National Park:
Volcano House, 967-7321. Steep at $31–$42 single, $34–$45 double; possibly worth it if you get a volcano view room. Restaurant overlooks glowing crater; avoid it at lunch, but at least stop for a Pele's Delight in the bar. Excellent and free eruption flicks in the lobby nightly at 8.30pm, 9.30pm.
Free camping in the park.

OF INTEREST
Beaches are few and varicoloured: black at Kaimu and Punaluu, white at Hapuna, Magic Sands (west side).
Manta ray watching, Kona Surf Hotel. Nightly, the hotel spotlights the ocean where huge rays come to feed; free and thrilling.
Ka Lae, most southerly point in the US and site of the oldest known settlement, *circa* AD 750. Has green sand and a haunting heiau or ancient temple.

KAUAI. Once sleepy and undiscovered, the island of Kauai now has its share of supermarkets, condos, huge resorts and loads of canned tours. Ignore all that to visit **Lumahai and Haena beaches** (settings for *South Pacific* and just like the postcards) and the Oriental landscape of **Hanalei Valley**, all on the wet side. The dry side's attractions include huge **Polihale State Park**, a great beach for camping, shelling and fishing; and the photogenic village of **Hanapepe**, where the eating is superb at Mike's Cafe and the Green Garden. Wonderful mahi-mahi (dolphin fish) and lilikoi (passionfruit) chiffon pie. Between Highway 543 and Pt Allen is a poignant touch of local life, the jewel-like Japanese cemetery. Island nightlife is best at the jumping Club Jetty on Lihue's waterfront, a real South Seas throwback. For a taste of mountain terrain, stay at the Kokee Lodge cabins, $25/night in Kokee State Park. In Lihue, Ocean View Motel (singles/doubles $15 up), 245-6345, offers rooms with refrigerators.

OREGON

In 1804–1806, Lewis and Clark explored this region, following the mighty Columbia River to its mouth. Their favourable reports brought a flood of pioneers along the 2000-mile Oregon Trail by the 1840s. A remarkably homogeneous bunch they were, too: conservative WASP farmers, mostly from the Midwest and South, all running from the economic depression of 1837–1840, all looking for good soil, rainfall and a climate without snow or malaria.

Oregon became a US territory the year of the California gold rush and promptly lost two-thirds of its males to the gold fever. A few struck it rich; more returned home and started selling wheat and lumber to the miners. At one point, Oregon wheat was actually made legal tender at $1 a bushel.

The heavily forested Beaver State has suffered in recent years from the decline in lumber demand but still produces half the plywood in the US (the process was invented here). Tourism is now the third-largest industry. Biggest visitor magnet is the 400-mile coastline, protected as a series of almost continuous state beaches. At times cold, foggy and windy, they offer a kaleidoscope of magnificent sights: offshore rocks, driftwood-piled sands, cliffs, caves, twisted pines and acres of rhododendrons. Coastal villages seem to specialise in weatherbeaten charm and have kept crass tourist traps to a minimum.

Picturesque barns, covered bridges and historic villages make the area from the coast east to the Willamette Valley fun to explore. Unless you're bent on speed, avoid the dull ribbon of Interstate that unseams the valley north to south.

Both the youth hostel and the bed and breakfast networks are alive and well in Oregon. Biking is extremely popular here. Just remember that it and other outdoor activities can be rained out or rained on at any moment. Most of the time, it's a slow mournful drizzle, the kind that drove Lewis and Clark nearly crazy during their winter sojourn at Fort Clatsop.

National Park: Crater Lake

PORTLAND. In 1843, a couple of canoeists enroute to Oregon City liked what they saw here and staked a 'tomahawk claim' by slashing trees in a 320-acre rectangle. The naming of the town was similarly impromptu: settlers flipped a coin (the losing name was Boston).

Voted as having 'the highest quality of life' of any US city of 500,000 or thereabouts, Portland modestly revels in its sparkling mountain and riverside setting, its luxuriant rose gardens (ten-day Festival of Roses in June) and its low-key neighbourliness. Lots of good eating and social action in this city of booklovers, art lovers and ardent joggers. The downtown core is pedestrian-oriented, full of sculpture, waterfalls and patches of park.

Portland makes an ideal base to explore the Columbia River Gorge to the east, and to follow the river and Highway 30 west to Astoria—one of Oregon's prettiest and most varied drives. The city is 40 miles south of Mount St Helens and tours can be taken from here as well as from Seattle to the north.

ACCOMMODATION
Imperial Hotel, 400 SW Broadway, 228-7221. Singles $21–$37, doubles $33–$40. 6 blocks to bus. Colour TV, comfort. The lunch special at the hotel's bar is legendary.
Jack London Hotel, 415 SW Alder, 228-4303. Cheap ($11–$15 single, $13–$17 double) but a tough part of town. Bus stop across street. TV, cafe. 'Seedy', 'Dirty'. Recommended for adventurous males only.
Park Avenue Hotel, 623 SW Park, 238-6088. Singles $9 shared bath; $14 with bath, TV, phone. 'Friendly, modern.'
Portland State U, 1802 SW 10th and Montgomery, 224-2727 after 8pm. About $20 double.

YWCA, 1111 SW 10th Ave, 223-6281. 'Very excellent YWCA—clean, helpful, quiet.' Single, shared bath $11. Near Greyhound.

Paramount Heathman Hotel, 712 SW Salmon, 228-5262. $19–$27 single, $24–$34 double. Bus stop in front. Senior, bus pass and weekly discounts. 'High standard of cleanliness and comfort.' 10 stories: 'Ask for upper floor to see Mt St Helens'.

Campbell Hill Hotel, W Burnside and SW Vista. Modest, in decent neighbourhood. Singles $10 and up. Cafe.

B&B: numerous choices through Northwest B&B, PT International, B&B League, International Spareroom; see Accommodation Background for addresses. Northwest has homes around Portland, on coast in Cannon Beach, Seaside, Arch Cape, Lincoln City, Newport, Bandon; in The Dalles, Salem, Eugene, Ashland, etc. $14–$20 single, $25 up doubles.

FOOD

The tastiest thing in Oregon is free—the drinking water. Grocery prices are high, even for local produce. You'll do better at the myriad produce stands along many roadsides. Don't miss local specialties: blackberry and boysenberry pie, razor clams (hideously expensive but you could get a licence and dig your own), scallops, smelt and Dungeness crab.

Old Spaghetti Factory, 126 SW 2nd. Daily. Your reliable spaghetti plus bread, salad, drink, dessert, under $6.

Dan and Louis' Oyster Bar, 208 SW Ankeny. Daily. Outstanding oysters, stew, marine atmosphere. A local favourite.

Saturday market, 222-6072. Under west end of Burnside Bridge, SW 1st and Ankeny. Stalls with homemade everything, Sat–Sun. 'Wonderful!'

Hot Potata, 422 SW 13th. Inexpensive place with zany decor and humour. Great soups and hot (stuffed) potatoes.

Old Portland Post Office Cafe, 439 NW Broadway. Open Mon–Sat. Across from Trailways and a real find: order the creole gumbo and the hush puppies. Also good breakfasts, Southern style.

OF INTEREST

Washington Park, west of town, has **Japanese Gardens**, 223-1321, with 5 traditional styles, especially lovely with the white cone of Mt Hood framed by maple leaves and pagodas. $2, teahouse also. One block away is the **Rose Test Garden**—free, over 8000 rosebushes. Take bus 63 from downtown. From here you can take 'the world's smallest railroad' ($1.25) through the forest to the **Zoo-OMSI** complex. The zoo, open daily 9.30am–dusk ($2, seniors $1) has huge chimp collection, large elephant herd. The Oregon Museum of Science and Industry (OMSI) is open daily 9am–5pm, 248-5900. $3, seniors $1.50. Includes planetarium shows. Walk-in heart, ship's bridge and 'transparent woman who narrates story of the human body'.

Art Museum, 1219 SW Park, 226-2811. $1, seniors free. Tue–Sun, noon–5pm, Fri 5pm–10pm. European, 19th and 20th C American, pre-Columbian, West African and Pacific Northwest Indian works.

Port. Free bus tour (2 hrs) of port, showing bulk cargo operations, 2 marine terminals. Tue, Wed at 1pm (mid-June to mid-Sept), 231-5000 extension 207; reservations required. Very popular.

Outside Portland:

Columbia River, east along the gorge. Unusual rock formations, Bonneville Dam, 11 waterfalls including Multnomah, and dramatic cliffs that loom 200 ft high along this extremely scenic stretch to The Dalles, via Greyhound. 'Spectacular.'

Hwy 30, west. A beautiful 100-mile drive to Astoria, that romps up hill, down dale, beside the Columbia and its wooded islands, and past roadside stands, houseboats, picturesque backwaters, juicy blackberries—there's even a pulloff to see **Mt St Helens**. Westport, with its Huck Finn ferry across the river, makes a good lunch stop.

ENTERTAINMENT

Washington Park is the local gathering place; free shows, concerts, opera, musical theatre in summer most evenings, some afternoons. Bring a picnic; call 248-3580 to check what's playing and when.

Saturday Market, 108 W Burnside under the bridge. Sat 10am–5pm, Sun 1pm–5pm, April to Christmas. High-calibre crafts, delightful free entertainment, savoury munchies. A treat. Nearby is Old Portland, your standard restored historic district.

Cafe Euphoria, 315 SE 3rd St. 'Big tavern, once a warehouse, features name folk acts, local rock bands.'

Pap Haydn's, 5829 SE Milwaukie, 232-9440. A Viennese coffeehouse, dynamite pastries, also food. Tue–Thur until 11pm, Fri–Sat until midnight.

Wilde Oscar's, 318 SW 3rd, 223-8620. Pub with Wilde motif, congenial mix of straights and gays, meat pies, long beer list.

INFORMATION

Information Center, 824 SW 5th Ave, 228–9411. Also at Front and Salmon Sts, 222-2223.

TRAVEL

Greyhound, 509 SW Taylor, 243-2323.

Trailways, 500 NW Broadway, 228-8571.

Tri-Met buses in 'Fareless Square' downtown are free; 65¢ elsewhere, 233-3511.

DART (223-2139) does airport to downtown for $4 one way.

AMTRAK, 800 NW 6th Ave, 248-1146 or 241-4290.

Rent-a-Junker, 3583 SE 82nd, 771-2273. Very cheap; need to stay within 100-mile radius with older models. 3-day minimum.

Contact center, 3214 SE Holgate, 231-4841. Rides, survival info.

Gray Line, 400 SE Broadway, 226-6755. Lots of tours: Mt St Helen, Mt Hood, the Columbia River, coast, around town.

THE OREGON COAST. US 101 runs along the Pacific coastline from southernmost California to northernmost Washington, but the Oregon piece of it—especially the pristine 225-mile stretch between the Cal border and Newport—is surely the loveliest. The southern portion is also warmest and driest (about half the rainfall north of Newport), making it a good camping choice. 'Best way to see this is by camping—buy a tube tent—light, compact, about $12.' The special experiences of the Oregon coast include driftwood hunting, whale watching, razor clamdigging, rockhounding (from agates to jasper) and looking for glass floats. The Japanese Current and westerly winds combine to wash these beauties onto shore with regularity; look for non-rocky beaches with moderate slope and go very early to beat other float-hunters. December through March are the best months, but the green, amber and turquoise glass balls wash in year-round. Swimming is dangerous in many areas and invariably cold everywhere; enquire locally.

Gold Beach is on the banks of the Rogue, an officially designated wild river and prime rafting/fishing area. Good smoked salmon here. Further along, the panorama of **Humbug Mountain** and the rock-strewn ocean are worthy of a stop; hiking to the top is three miles.

Excellent campground with low-cost biker/hiker section. At cranberry-growing **Bandon**, you have a cheese factory, the makings of an art colony and lots of scenic beauty, with a good co-op and a youth hostel as added pluses. US 101 turns inland here to Coos Bay, although you can follow secondary roads nearer the coast to spectacular scenery at **Sunset Bay** (camping) and **Shore Acres State Parks**. Biggest town in SW Oregon, **Coos Bay** is a fishing and lumber port with a grimy bay, good for a night's stopover, a meal at the Hurry Back, and possibly a look at local myrtlewood factories.

The Oregon Dunes (some as high as 500 feet) stretch for 40 miles to Florence; camping duneside is possible but crowded at Honeyman State Park, but the Umpqua Lighthouse State Park (hiker/biker section), six miles south of Reedsport, is better. Between rhododendron-happy Florence and Yachats are the **Sea Lion Caves**, reached via elevator and reeking of sea lion fish halitosis. Open daily, $3.50; you can also see the huge creatures more distantly from an outside point just north of the caves.

Yachats (that's *Yah*-hots) is well worth a pause, especially if you arrive in smelt season, May–September, or better yet, at the annual Smelt Fry in early July. It's child's play to eat a dozen of the small silvery fish, and fun to watch the catch, too. Good non-fish offerings at the Yachats Pie and Kite Shop, the Adobe Hotel and others. Enroute to Newport is a likeable tourist trap called **Sea Gulch**, a village of antic lifesize figures. The carving is done freehand—with a chainsaw!—and you can watch. Fishing and beach town **Newport** is lively, on a sheltered and beautiful bay, a good place to eat Dungeness crab and browse with other holidayers. 'A friendly young community on NW cliff, where there are quaint wooden summer cottages facing the ocean.' Neighbouring **Depoe Bay** is noted as an excellent whale-watching spot, November–March; along its seawall, geyserlike sprays of ocean water often arch over the highway. Beverly Beach to the south is the nearest campground and has hiker/biker spots.

Near Tillamook, take the **Three Capes Road**, a 39-mile loop through a succession of scenic vistas, villages and lighthouses to **Three Arch Rocks National Wildlife Refuge** with its herd of Stellar sea lions. **Tillamook** itself provides cheese and wine-tasting daily at the Blue Heron and Tillamook Cheese Factories. Further north, **Cannon Beach** merits a pause: monolithic Haystack Rock, a charming art-mad village, great camping at Ecola State Park and a cosy youth hostel are some of its pluses. Its annual Sand Sculpture Derby in spring is one of the most inventive anywhere—can be cold as the devil, though.

Seaside, with its boardwalk, arcades and popular swimming beach, is a cotton-candy sort of town, noted for great scallops at Rose's Cafe, and cheap seafood at Norma's. At **Ft Stevens**, a historic park with a picturesque shipwreck, you run out of coastline and turn eastward to

Astoria, a miniature San Francisco at the mouth of the Columbia River and worth seeing for the goings-on at Ft Clatsop (the restored fort where Lewis and Clark spent the winter of 1805), the rococo Flavel House and Shallon Winery. Try scallops at Pier 11 and Finnish limpa bread at the local bakeries.

ACCOMMODATION

Sea Star Traveler's Hostel, 375 2nd St, Bandon, 347-9533. Open 1 Apr–31 Oct. $4 AYH.

The Tioga, 275 N Broadway, Coos Bay, 269-1270. $12 single, $14 for 2. Bus stop beneath hotel. Laundry. Old but well-maintained, 'clean, quiet and pleasant'.

Seagull Youth Hostel, 438 Elrod, Coos Bay, 267-6114. Open 30 May–6 Sept. $5.75 fee includes substantial homecooked breakfast and dinner, and you don't need to be AYH member. 6 blocks to Greyhound. 'Just great—owners will do anything to make your stay something to be remembered.'

Adobe Motel, Yachats. Doubles start at $20, to $42 with ocean view, fireplace. Excellent meals, agate hunting and smelt fishing on their beach. Call 547-3141.

Hostel, 3rd and Hemlock Sts, Cannon Beach, 436-2603. Near beach, centre of town. Open June–Sept, $6. 'Includes 2 meals, bunk, shower. Very cosy, like being in a family.'

Camping: State Parks $2–$5 plus $2 for out-of-staters. Many sites have hiker/biker sections for 50¢ to $1. Tugman State Park near Lakeside comes highly praised: 'Best campsites in the US'. Greyhound will drop you where you like. Warm sleeping bag and tent advised, also food as parks usually distant from shops. Free camping near Florence in the dunes and in Suislaw National Forest.

TRAVEL

Greyhound covers US 101 from California border to Lincoln City, then dipping inland to Portland. At Tillamook, it resumes US 101 along coast to Astoria. Local bus services in Coos Bay, Astoria.

CRATER LAKE NATIONAL PARK. In a densely forested part of the Cascade Range in southern Oregon, **Crater Lake** is a sapphire gem set in the crater of extinct **Mount Mazama** volcano. Once 12,000 feet high, the volcano blew some 6500 years ago; its colourful cliffs, 500 to 2000 feet high, are all that is left. The waters of the lake, fed solely by rain and snow, cannot be bettered for intensity and brilliance. At 1932 feet, it is one of the world's deepest also. In the lake are **Wizard Island**, itself an extinct volcanic cone, and **Phantom Ship Island**. Boat-excursions visit Wizard, where you can hike to its 760-foot summit and down into its 90-foot-deep crater. The 33-mile **Rim Drive** is open mid-June to October, but also recommended is the one-mile hike down to the lake from Cleetwood Cove and the 1½-mile Discovery Point Trail. From high points in the park, you can see Mount Shasta, 100 miles to the south. Wonderful bird-watching, wildflowers and nature programmes. Crater Lake is even more beautiful offseason, when the snow and the conifers are reflected in the deep blue iris of the lake.

ACCOMMODATION AND FOOD

Mazama campground $5, at the junction of West and South Entrance roads, open mid-June to Oct, depending on snow conditions. Free campsites in the backcountry and at Lost Creek campground, 3 miles SE of Main Rim Drive, open 1 July–1 Sept. The Nature Trail begins here. Grocery store at Rim Village; also excellent fishing, no licence required.

Crater Lake Lodge, Rim Village, 594-2511. Cheapest are the sleeping cottages; without bath, $20 single, $27 double.

Outside the park:

Ft Klamath Lodge in Ft Klamath, Hwy 62, about 22 miles south of Crater Lake, YH for $4.25 summer, $5.25 winter. Restaurant nearby. Has family rooms.

Lodging also at Klamath Falls and Medford; try Motel 6 or Motel Orleans, a very good and low-cost chain.

TRAVEL

Daily bus service from Klamath Falls to Crater Lake, 15 June–15 Sept. On its Hwy 95 run, Greyhound travels from Klamath Falls to within 15 miles of the park.

SOUTHERN OREGON. South and west of Crater Lake are a cluster of worthwhile destinations, made more appealing by three well-placed hostels and other good lodging in the area. **Ashland** is for Shakespeare buffs, with three theatres and an eight-month play schedule, and for ski buffs as well. Good B&B, hostel. Not far away is **Jacksonville**, an intelligently restored gold mining town. Stagecoach rides to see the 80-odd homes, cemetery, etc, but a minimum of touristy touches. A fine place to stay would be the Wolf Creek Tavern, 866-2474, off Interstate 5 near Gold Hill. $19 single, $23 double for atmospheric rooms in a 19th-century stage stop; great bar, music room, dining room, presided over by mob-capped attendants.

This region is dominated by the **Rogue River**, and a prime way to enjoy its white water and other country pleasures is at the Rogue River Horse and Buggy Farm, an AYH affiliate. Further south is Cave Junction (with a hostel), a base for **Oregon Caves National Monument**, 20 miles away. The caves ($3.75) are deep in the marble heart of Mount Elijah and full of stalagtites, flowstone formations and strenuous hikes.

ACCOMMODATION

Ashland Hostel, 150 N Main St, Ashland, 482-9217. Open year-round, $4 AYH, $6 non-AYH. Close to buses, Shakespeare Festival. Kitchen, laundry; in historic home.

Rogue River Horse and Buggy Farm, 4533 Rogue River Hwy, 582-4226. Open year-round, $4.25 summer, $5.25 winter. One family room. Kitchen. All manner of outdoor things to do, presided over by knowledgeable history buff/farmer who raises gentle, gigantic Belgian draught horses. 10 miles to Greyhound in Grants Pass.

Fordson Home Hostel, 250 Robinson Rd, Cave Junction, 592-3203. $3.25 summer, $4.25 winter; must reserve ahead for the 3 beds. Also camping $1, pit toilets and solar showers. 10 miles to Oregon Caves, close to winery, bikes for use, many extras on this 20-acre homestead.

WASHINGTON

Like its neighbour Oregon, the Evergreen State is rainy and green from the Cascade Mountains west, flat, dry and tawny from the mountains east. Likewise, it has but one preeminent city, Seattle, which enjoys a tenacious rivalry with Portland.

Once a stronghold of the radical labour movement (the Wobblies were headquartered here), Washington these days builds more Boeings, raises more apples, processes more seafood and stores more nuclear waste than almost anyone else.

Washington used to be filled with a large and varied Indian population, which accounts for some of the enchanting names scattered about the state: La Push, Muckleshoot, Enumclaw, Snohomish, Humptulips, Queets, Sedro Woolley and Walla Walla.

Most of the natural grandeur of the state is nicely within reach of Seattle: Puget Sound and its hundreds of islands, the Olympic rain forest, Mount Rainier National Park, and hot-tempered Mount St Helens, 75 miles south. A few important sights are further flung. Grand Coulee Dam is in eastern Washington. North Cascades National Park, an expanse of alpine scenery with canyons, glaciers, peaks and grizzlies, lies along the British Columbia border. You will also enjoy southwest Washington and the Long Beach peninsula, more conveniently reached from Astoria, Oregon.

Rain is endemic to the Northwest, but Seattle gets most of its 34 inches per year between October and April; the Olympic rain forest gets up to 150 inches annually.

National Parks: Olympic
                Mount Ranier
                North Cascades

SEATTLE. The 'Emerald City' has achieved one of the most becoming arrangements of hills, houses, water and mountains that you'll find in America. To the southwest, the skyline is dominated by snowy Mount Rainier. To the west, the city's great deepwater harbour opens onto island-studded Puget Sound and the Olympic Mountains. Urbanisation is further subdivided by lakes and parks, from tiny to massive, girdling the downtown district into a compact and pleasing shape. The look is an idiosyncratic mix of sleek and traditional, of contemporary ranch houses and bohemian houseboats. But it's not just looks. Seattle has a certain flair. What other city would make a Wagnerian opera cycle (sung in German and English) its major cultural event? Or outfit its waterfront with vintage 1927 Australian streetcars and its airport with a meditation room?

Considering it's a major gateway to and trade partner with the Orient, Seattle shows few Asian influences other than restaurants. It does have a rough and rollicking quality, perhaps a legacy from its close ties with Alaska since the days of the Klondike gold rush.

ACCOMMODATION

Central Hotel, 1516½ 5th Ave, 223-9174. $13–$18 single, $15–$20 double, TV, storage. ½ block to bus. 'Bit like old peoples' home but clean and friendly.'

St Regis Hotel, 2nd end Stewart, 622-6366. $16 single, $22 double, extra person $3. Colour TV. 'Basic but comfortable.'

Vance Hotel, 620 Stewart, 623-2700. Single $32 up, doubles $38 up. Senior discount. Cafe, TV. 'Rather expensive but very comfortable, worth the money.' 1 block from Greyhound.

Downtown YMCA, 909 4th Ave, 382-5000. $18 single, $13 each for twin rooms, higher with colour TV. 'Excellent, very clean.' '4th floor more comfortable, better facilities than 3rd floor at same price.'

Gatewood Hotel, 102 Pine St, 382-4180. Old Victorian, AYH-affiliated. $7.25 member, $9 non-member. $3 key deposit. 1 block to Pike Market, open year-round. 'Noisy but clean and cheap.'

College Inn Guest House, 4000 University Way NE, 633-4441. $24–$30 single, $36–$45 double, all shared bath. Continental breakfast plus all-day coffee, tea. Tudor style, antique furnishings, on charming street near University. Buses to downtown.

Airport Motel, 139th and Pacific Hwy, 244-0810. $17 single, $27 triple. AC, colour TV, kitchenettes, transport to/from airport.

B&B: lots of options including B&B International, Northwest B&B, International Spareroom, addresses in Accommodation Background. Also: Pacific B&B, 701 NW 60th, 784-0539; Traveller's B&B, Box 492, Mercer Island, 232-2345. Rates $16 up single, $25 up double; Traveller's has more luxurious homes, $30 up double. Besides Seattle, guest homes in Puget Sound, Tacoma, Olympia, Ocean Park, Chinook, Spokane, Victoria and Vancouver Island, BC.

FOOD

Washington is famous for superb fruit (especially apples and berries), Dungeness crab, Olympia oysters, razor and littleneck clams, and Seattle is a prime place to sample all of them. Excellent Chinese, Thai, Japanese and Vietnamese restaurants also. Pike Place Market is *the* place to buy both fresh produce and walkaway items: it's a warren of ethnic treats from Filipino lumpia to Spanish tapas. Also try the Seattle Center Food Fair: 'Where else can you sample Mongolian cooking next to a Vietnamese coffeeshop?' Washington now has 26 wineries, 8 around Seattle, which are winning modest acclaim.

Iron Horse, 311 3rd Ave, opposite King St station, 223-9506. 'Burgers delivered by model trains! Great railroading atmosphere.'

The Old Spaghetti Factory, Elliot at Broad St, near Pier 70. Complete meal under $6. 'Amazing violin-playing machine.'

Cafe Loc, 407 Broad St, near Seattle Center monorail terminal. 'Good Vietnamese food.' Tiny, pleasant, cheap. Try the spring rolls. Mon–Fri 11am–8pm, Sat 4pm–8pm.

Emmett Watson's Oyster Bar, 1916 Pike Place, behind the Soames-Dunn building. Best oysters anywhere, also good ceviche (marinated fish). Inexpensive.

Java, 8929 Roosevelt Way NE, 522-5282. Low-cost Indonesian food in a beautiful setting, worth the trek.

Breakfast recommendations: Sourdough Bakery at Pier 58, 'Excellent value, large wholesome meals'; The Dutch Oven, 1404 3rd Ave, 'Excellent, under $3.50'; Tess' Kitchen, near 6th and Stewart, 'Good food, fast'.

OF INTEREST

Mount St Helens. The Indians called it 'Louwala-Clough' or 'Smoking mountain' and they knew what they were talking about. On 18 May, 1980, the mountain erupted, blowing away a cubic mile of earth, killing 70 people and 2 million mammals, birds and fish, sending smoke and ash to 60,000 feet to circle the globe. Since then, Mt St Helens has erupted sporadically but on a smaller scale; quakes and ominous rumblings are commonplace. Plan on spending all day for your trip, whether from Seattle or Portland.

Options include: Omnidome, Pier 59, 622-1868, in Seattle. On a 100-foot screen, see an awesome film of the eruption and aftermath, $2.50. 'It's as if you're flying round the mountain during its eruption', 'Do not on any account miss this extraordinary 30-minute film'. Trailways does a 9-hr tour from Vance Hotel on Tue, Thur, Sat for $20. Book ahead. Gray Line does a similar one, slightly cheaper. Air flyovers from Toledo near the mountain, about 1 hr for $40, circle crater and give best views of flattened trees, mud-choked rivers and the grey-blue devastated landscape. Two Forest Service Centers on I-5, north and south of the volcano. Check in with them first or call 696-7500 to enter the volcano zone. Three main routes usually open to cars; hikers can make a difficult but worthwhile hike from Meta Lake to Independence Pass, which overlooks ruined Spirit Lake. Chilling views of desolation and crumpled human artefacts.

Seattle Center, 625-4234, 1 mile from downtown; take monorail from 4th and Pine terminal, a 95-second ride for 50¢. A legacy of the 1962 World's Fair, the Center has been recycled into the city's cultural life. Among its attractions: the 605-ft **Space Needle** ($2 for glass elevator), best at night when all below is lit up. 'Kitschiest souvenir shop in Seattle on top.' **Sky Ride** floats across the Center; 6-min rides from 11am–11pm in summer, noon–11pm weekends in winter. **Pacific Science Center**, next to Space Needle, 382-2887. $4, seniors $3 (free on Wed). Fee includes IMAX film of Columbia space shuttle. Daily. 6 buildings: laserium, planetarium, computer rooms, seismograph, Indian longhouse, lots of science toys. Eve show lasts 1 hr: 'Laserium *Rock It* is exciting presentation'. The Center also has many shops, eateries and entertainment from opera to rock and folk festivals.

International District, between Main and Lane, 4th and 8th Sts. Seattle's Chinese/ Japanese district, bright with Buddhist temples, restaurants, herbal shops and the Bon Odori Festival in Aug.

Pike Place Market, Pike and 1st. Begun in 1907, this colourful maze of stairways and levels boasts over 200 businesses, including dozens of restaurants, standup bars and takeway places, plus local produce and seafood. Also bookstores, coffeehouses, bars, second-hand shops, craftspeople and 'excellent free entertainment by buskers and street musicians'. Daily 9am–6pm except Sun, many places open later.

The waterfront is accessible and interesting, although the 'working piers' for the Alaska halibut and salmon fleet and the large freighters tend to be more remote. Piers 60 through 68 do have fishing and cargo traffic, however. Piers 48 to 70 contain ferry lines to Alaska, the islands, etc; a waterfront park; Ye Olde Curiosity Shop, a delightfully macabre melange of shrunken heads, mummies, fleas wearing dresses, etc, ('must be seen'); an aquarium on Pier 59 ($2.50, 'marvellous'); harbour tour lines; a firefighting museum; and other amusements. 'Vintage Melbourne trams run along waterfront, 60¢ with free return within 1½ hrs.'

Pioneer Square, around 1st and Yesler, heart of old downtown. The original 'skid road' (whence 'Skid Row'), nicely restored but still a gathering place for bums and blots-on-the-town; good walking tour map available. Do see the **Klondike Gold Rush National Historic Park** at 11 S Main, 442-7220: exhibits, free films. 'Watch Chaplin's *The Gold Rush* free on weekends.' 'Free gold panning demos.'

Underground tours, 610 1st at Doc Maynard's, 682-4646. Booking required, 1½ hrs, $3. When Seattle burned down in 1889, the city simply built the new on top of the old. What's left below is an odd warren of storefronts, brothels, speakeasys, tunnels where sailors are popularly supposed to have been shanghaied, etc. 'Highly amusing account of Seattle's early sewage system. Never thought crap could be so funny.' 'Interesting ripoff.'

Art Museum, Volunteer Park, 14th Ave E, 447-4710, $1, students/seniors 50¢. Free on Thur. Open Tue–Sat 10am–5pm, Sun noon–5pm, Thur until 9pm. Orientalia,

Northwest Mystics school, superb jade. Free concerts in park, summers. 'Next to the park is beautiful **Lake View cemetery** divided by nationality—Chinese, Japanese, Polish, etc. Also **Bruce Lee's grave**, covered with letters to him, martial arts trophies, mementos, flowers, etc, left by devotees.'

U of Washington, 15th Ave NE. Info centre on NE 40th. 'Beautiful, like Berkeley.' On campus, an Arboretum and Japanese teagarden, gift of Seattle's sister city, Kobe.

Government Locks, connecting Puget Sound and Lake Union, built in 1916 are second only to the Panama Locks in size. Buses 17, 43 go there. Free tours, 1pm. 'Best free sight in Seattle. Boats and leaping salmon passing through all day.' 'Some salmon nearly jump onto the footpath!' 'Interesting historical/ecological display in building.'

Harbour boat rides. Tours available or ride the agreeable commuter ferries to a variety of destinations. A good way to get a look at the working aspect of the port.

Nearby:

Boeing Aircraft Factory, 3303 Casino Rd S, Everett, 35 miles north of Seattle. 237-2384 or 342-4801. See jumbo jets in the making in the largest (volume) building in the world. Very heavily booked in summer; free tours Mon–Fri, 9am and 1pm, June–Sept; at 1pm, rest of year. Also can book through tour companies; 4-hr trip plus lunch about $17, 624-5813.

USS Missouri, at Bremerton; ferry trip $3 round trip. Free shuttle to ship, guided tour of shipyards, subs, aircraft carriers. Daily 8am–8pm. On this WWII battleship, the Japanese surrendered: 'Actual surrender spot covered with plaque under plastic. Press nearby button to hear Gen MacArthur wind up WWII.'

ENTERTAINMENT

The 5th Avenue, *circa* 1916 vaudeville house patterned after Imperial China's architecture in the Forbidden City and elsewhere, recently renovated for $2.6 million, now hosts Broadway shows, etc. Free tours of its interior Wed, 12.30pm and 1pm, 628-5101. Absolutely smashing place.

Seattle Opera, Symphony Orchestra, 447-4711, at the Seattle Center; student tickets as low as $5. Also call 447-4736. Rock and pop acts appear at the Paramount on Pike and 8th; not cheap but good acoustics.

Pioneer Square, Volunteer Park and the campuses of U of Washington and Seattle University (downtown at E Cherry and Broadway) are all nuclei for daylight and after-dark entertainment. Read the *Post-Intelligencer*, the *Seattle Times*' Tempo mag for listings. Tempo has a 'Hot Tix' column with discount and free stuff.

INFORMATION

Visitors Bureau, 1815 7th Ave, 447-7276.

Travelers Aid, 909 4th, 447-3888.

Washington State info, call 800/562-4570. Free and useful maps from Dept of Transportation, Transportation Building, Olympia 98504. Canadian Government Office of Tourism, 447-3811.

TRAVEL

Greyhound, 8th and Stewart, 624-3456.

Trailways, 1936 Westlake, 624-5955. Has airport bus to/from downtown hotels, $4. 'Most helpful staff.'

Local bus, 447-4800, free within 'Magic Carpet' downtown area; 60–90¢ outside. Inexpensive 1 and 3-day pass combos for unlimited riding.

Get Metro Map and Fun Book at 821 2nd St.

Gray Line, 343-2000, from the Westin Hotel, Space Needle, other points.

Seattle Harbor Tours, Pier 56, 623-1445, May through Oct, $3.50.

Ferry service:

To Victoria, British Columbia, Pier 69, on the *SS Princess Marguerite* 623-5560, leaves 8am, returns 9.45pm, one way $18, return $29. 'Worthwhile—good views of Seattle.' 'Beautiful run—touch of real class. Sit in bar lounge at sunset and feel like a king.'

To Alaska and the Inside Passage: Alaska Marine Highway System, Pier 48. Book as far in advance as possible.

To islands, Olympic peninsula: Washington State Ferries, Pier 52, 464-6400 or 800-542-7052, to Olympic peninsula, Bremerton ($3 round trip), Vashon Island and other points. 'Excellent way to see the Sound and the islands around Seattle.' Ferries for the San Juan islands departs from Anacortes (north of Seattle), 293-2188. See San Juan section.

AMTRAK, King St Station, 3rd Ave S, 464-1930. The *Pioneer* goes to Ogden/Salt Lake City, the *Coast Starlight* to Oakland/SF and LA, and the *Empire Builder* to Minneapolis and Chicago. Also trains to Vancouver, BC.

Airport buses: city bus 174, 75¢. Also Gray Line 'hustlebus', 343-2000, about $4.

AAACON Transport, 1904 3rd Ave, 682-2277. 'Great place to start a ride down the coast.'

OLYMPIC NATIONAL PARK. Occupying 1400 square miles in the centre and along the coastline of the Olympic peninsula, this fifth largest national park is about 80 miles west of Seattle. US 101 circles the park but only a few roads penetrate inward; its wilderness is further cushioned by vast tracts of national forest around it. A hikers' park indeed.

Massive glacier-cut peaks are the park's signature note; the highest at 7954 feet was named **Mount Olympus** by an English sea captain in 1788. Use the Port Angeles entrance to get here. 'Don't miss the 18-mile drive from sea level to one mile high at Hurricane Ridge— what views of Mount Olympus and its glaciers!' 'Make every effort to see this park—fantastic.'

One thinks of rain forests as a tropical phenomenon, but west of Olympus in the Bogachiel, Hoh, Quinault and Queets river valleys is the great **Olympic rain forest**, a cool-weather Amazon that gets 142 inches of rain in an average year. Jewelled with moisture, tree limbs cloaked in clubmoss, this incredible forest is suffused in a pale green luminosity, primordial and eerie. Best access is via the 20-mile drive up the Hoh River. Don't overlook the intelligent displays at the Visitor Center and the views along Quilcene Creek.

The pristine, rocky **coastal strip** contains dense forest almost to ocean's edge. Most easily seen at its southern end where US 101 passes close to shore, but the best part is up by **Lake Ozette**, only reached by trails. Here the undergrowth is extravagant and the ground so soggy that much of the trail leads over boards. Bears sometimes lumber down to the water in search of a meal. About 4 miles from the lake is **Capa Alava**, an utterly beautiful spot, especially when silhouetted at sunset.

Admission to the park is free, as is camping and the use of huts along the trails. No food stores within the park; best to purchase at Port Angeles.

ACCOMMODATION
Lake Crescent Lodge, 20 miles west of Port Angeles on US 101, 928-3211. Inside park, on lake. Informal resort with dining room, amenities, boat rental. Lodge rooms $27 double shared bath, cottages $30 up double. Open Memorial–Labor Day.

INFORMATION/TRAVEL
Park headquarters, 600 E Park Ave, Port Angeles, 452-4501.
Greyhound does several trips daily from Seattle to Pt Angeles (about $30) and has limited daily service to small towns bordering the park.
Gray Line does summer tours, 457-4140.
From Seattle, take ferries across Puget Sound and Hood Canal.

PORT TOWNSEND and THE SAN JUAN ISLANDS. Port Townsend is proof that western Washington isn't uniformly soggy; it lies in the 'rain shadow' of the great Olympic mountains, and gets a mere 18 inches a year. Sunny weather, a vital cultural life, ebullient Victorian charm and architecture and the presence of two hostels nearby make **Port Townsend** an excellent place to base yourself for exploration. Good food and friendly faces at the Blue Parrot and the Lighthouse Cafe; jazz Wednesday evenings at the Town Tavern.

In 1859, the US gained the 192-island chain of the **San Juans** in the great 'Pig War', precipitated when a British pig recklessly invaded an American garden and was shot. The resulting squeal of outrage had US and British troops snout to snout on island soil. But diplomacy won out. With Kaiser Wilhelm the unlikely mediator, the US got the San Juans and the British got bangers, one supposes.

Connected by bridges to the mainland and each other are the islands of **Whidbey, Fidalgo** and **Camano**. The city of Anacortes on Fidalgo is a major ferry terminus. Despite their easy access, these islands are quite rural. Further north and well served by ferry are **Orcas, Lopez, Shaw** and **San Juan**. All have excellent camping, super-lative shorelines and scenery with good clamming and some fine beaches. Shaw lacks fresh water; Lopez is best for bicycling and has one of the few good swimming beaches at Spencer Spit.

ACCOMMODATION
In Port Townsend and environs:
Palace Hotel, 1004 Water St, 385-0773. Rooms with shared bath, $21 up single, $26 up double. TV, brass beds, antique decor. Bus stops at door.
Ft Worden (385-0655) and Nordland (385-1288) Youth Hostels, the former 2 miles ('lovely surroundings') from Pt Townsend, the latter 20 miles away on Marrowstone Island. Both $3.75 with kitchens. Open most of the year.
On the San Juans:
Palmer's Chart House, PO Box 51, Deer Harbor, Orcas Island, 376-4231. $30 per person, all homecooked meals included. Plus trips on the Palmer's 33-ft yacht, weather permitting. Open year-round, warm place with lots of amenities and pampering. 1-hr ferry ride to Orcas from Anacortes, Palmers will pick up. Reservations needed. Highly recommended for an unusual American experience.
Elite Hotel, 35 First St, Friday Harbor, San Juan Island, 378-5555. AYH affiliated. $6.25 members. Booking needed. Hot tubs, saunas by the hour. Ferry from Anacortes.

TRAVEL
Greyhound/Trailways to Anacortes, 83 miles north of Seattle. Ferries from Anacortes daily to Shaw, Lopez, Orcas, San Juan and also Victoria, BC. Ferry and land combinations are extremely numerous; you'll do best to study the free ferry schedules, maps and get *Carfree Tour Guide*: call 464-6400 or 800-542-7052.

MOUNT RAINIER NATIONAL PARK. It was the enterprising 18th century British Admiral Rainier who got this 14,410-foot mountain named after himself. Today it's surrounded by a national park that should interest the most jaded peak peeker. Rainier is located 80 miles south of Seattle and clearly visible from there.

Mount Rainier gets 575 inches of snow in an average winter; except for its most rugged spires, little of the mountain shows beneath the glittering whiteness. Ice nestles in the crater itself, and more than 40 glaciers cap the peak. Best of all are the lush conifer forests that cover its lower slopes, these interrupted by meadows brilliant with wildflowers in July and August.

The **Wonderland Trail** wanders for 90 miles around the mountain, passing through snowfields, meadows and forests, with shelter cabins at convenient intervals. The full walk can take over a week, but there are lesser trails for those with lesser ambitions. Near the park's southeast corner is the **Trail of the Patriarchs**, leading through groves of massive red cedars and Douglas firs.

The best place for seeing wildflowers is to march up from **Paradise Valley**. A 2½-mile hike leads to ice caves at the foot of Paradise Glacier. You can, of course, continue up from here, a distance of 16 miles to the summit. Once there, you'll notice from the steam venting from the crater that the volcano is not quite dead. (It was only 5000 years ago that Rainier blew a sea of redhot mud over 125 square miles of Puget Sound.)

July through September are often warm and clear, making sunsets and sunrises over the mountain unforgetable. Even in summer it does rain and other months clouds, rain and fog are quite common. Always dress warmly and bring raingear. Camping $3, entrance $2 per car, 50¢ per hiker.

A reader suggests the **Cascade foothills** north of Rainier as a closer alternative: 'Drive 30 miles east to North bend, then follow south fork of the Snoqualmie River for 15 miles. Take dirt track marked Lake Talapus to car park. From there, a 2-mile hike to the lake. Gorge yourself on blueberries, swim and dive off rocks, kill bugs—on a sunny day, this beats any city tour. This is the real America.'

ACCOMMODATION
Campgrounds open summer only except for Sunshine Point near Nisqually Entrance. Come warmly equipped; at higher altitudes, there will be snow on the ground and more may fall, even in July.

Paradise Inn, 475-6260, at 5400 ft. Open mid-June to early Sept. Single/double $19 to $35, cheaper with shared bath.

National Park Inn, 569-2565, at 2700 ft. Open year-round. Single/double $18 without bath, up to $33 with bath. To reserve rooms at National or Paradise, write Reservation Manager, Mt Rainier Hospitality Service, 4820 S Washington, Tacoma 98409.

Outside park:

Lodge Youth Hostel, Hwy 706, ¼ mile from Nisqually entrance, 569-2312. $5.25 summer, $6.25 winter with AYH. Kitchen; nearest food supply 5 miles away in Ashford.

TRAVEL

Gray Line 343-2000, runs daily bus service (late May–Oct) from Seattle into the park, with stayovers and return service at your option. $27 return.

LONG BEACH PENINSULA. On its long sandy finger of land in extreme southwest Washington, the Long Beach peninsula harbours an immense clam and driftwood-filled beach, covered with huge dunes (great for escaping the wind) and backed by pines amid which hide hundreds of old-fashioned beach cottages. Besides the windswept beauty of the area, visit the free Lewis and Clark Interpretive Center near Cape Disappointment lighthouse, a superb audio-visual evocation of the hardships and wonders of that epic journey. The display ramps lead you to the same magnificent ocean overlook that climaxed Lewis and Clark's trip in 1805.

The peninsula boasts two extraordinary eating experiences (based on local ingredients, too) at the Ark in Oysterville and the Shelburne Inn at Seaview. Also try My Mother's Pies in Long Beach for extravagant deep-dish berry, rhubarb and other pies.

ACCOMMODATION

Shelburne Inn, Box 250, on Pacific Highway and J Sts, Seaview, 642-2442. $24–$34 summer, $20–$26 offseason. In a National Historic Register structure of forest green, superb restaurant, antique furnishings.

Ft Columbia Hostel, Box 224, Chinook, 777-8755. Open June–Oct. $3.25 AYH. Kitchen, also breakfasts for 75¢, dinners $1. Lovely, isolated site overlooking Columbia River in park with museum, old fort. 6 miles from Astoria, Oregon, across a toll bridge ($1.50 each way for cars, hitchhikers free). Near Chinook is Bead Heaven Beach, site of an old Chinook Indian village. Good bathing, arrowhead hunting.

THE SOUTHWEST

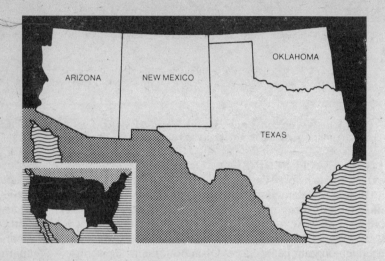

Much of this area, particularly Arizona, New Mexico and west Texas is just as one would expect from seeing Westerns—whether shot in Spain or otherwise. Purple mountains, searing deserts, cactus, cowboys and Indians. In contrast are the lush farmlands of east Texas and eastern Oklahoma, and the northern plateaux and mountains of New Mexico.

Hardly passing through an intervening industrial stage, since the Second World War the Southwest has leapt from a simple economy into the nuclear-aerospace-electronics age and is now a boom region of the nation. But at the same time, Indian reservations cover large parts of Arizona and New Mexico and the Spanish influence is apparent right up to the Red River.

For several decades after it was blazed in 1822, the Santa Fe Trail served emigrants and trade between Missouri and the Southwest. Before Greyhounds and the railroads, the first scheduled trans continental service was the Butterfield Stage Route between Missouri and San Francisco. It made stops at San Angelo and El Paso, Texas, and Tucson, Arizona. Now the major thoroughfare is Route 66, passing through Tulsa, Oklahoma City, Amarillo, Albuquerque and Flagstaff. To enjoy the Southwest, stay off it as much as possible.

ARIZONA

A land of vast silences and arid beauty, the Grand Canyon State also contains sharp and sometimes troubling contrasts. One-quarter of

Arizona is Indian land, containing the incredibly ancient and artistically evolved cultures of the Hopis, Navajos and others, yet Indians in this state were not allowed to vote until 1948. Arizona's works of nature are among the grandest, beginning with the Grand Canyon and continuing through 17 other highly variegated national parks, monuments and recreation areas. At the same time, the works of man range from banal to short-sightedly destructive: insipid, water-greedy cities, borrowed London bridges, dam-drowned canyons.

Distances being huge, natural wonders scattered and bus service thin, we advise you to allow yourself ample time, preferably with wheels. Camping and bed and breakfast are easy to find, youth hostels less so. The southern section from Tucson east is the richest historically, being the stomping grounds for Wyatt Earp, Billy the Kid, Apache chiefs Geronimo and Cochise, and assorted prospectors, padres and gunslingers. Northern Arizona, with its stark mesas and richly coloured canyons, offers the greatest drama scenically. Glen Canyon and Monument Valley, both spilling over into Utah, should be high on your list after the Grand Canyon and Canyon de Chelly.

National Parks: Grand Canyon
Petrified Forest

PHOENIX. Huge, hot and horizontal, Phoenix is quite possibly the world's worst city for pedestrians. This electronics/retirement/aerospace community doesn't make a convenient gateway to anywhere (although at the rate it is sprawling, it may one day ooze right up to the lip of the Grand Canyon).

About 55 miles southeast lies **Casa Grande Ruins National Monument**, a four-storey dwelling built *circa* AD 1300 by the Pueblo Indians. Far more spectacular are the ruins at **Tonto National Monument**, 60 miles east on scenic Highway 88. 'The **Apache Trail** follows Route 88 to Tortilla Flats and Roosevelt Lake through superb desert scenery with views of the Superstition Mountains and Weavers Needle. Make a day trip of it'.

ACCOMMODATION
NB: In general, expect much higher rates Oct–May in Phoenix and Tucson.
Apache Hotel, 515 N Central, 254-1127. $11–$13 single, $13–$17 double; low weekly rates, Laundry, TV. 5 blocks to Greyhound. 'Friendly owners. Avoid rooms opposite heat-conserving wall—unbearably hot.' 'Great value.'
Downtown 6 Motel (formerly Chalet Lodge), 938 E Van Buren, 252-3447. Pool. $19 single with bath, doubles $24–$35.
Portland House Hostel, 506 E Portland St, 252-6344. $5.25 summer AYH, no smoking. Men only. 'Half mile from bus station, modern.'
Valley of the Sun Hostel, 1026 N 9th St. $5.25 members, $7.25 non-members. Kitchen. Close to museums.
YMCA, 350 N 1st Ave, 253-6181. Coed, 1 floor for women. Dorm style, $13 single. Pool, cafeteria. Fairly new, clean.

Motel 6, 2323 E Van Buren, 267-1397. AC, pool, $16 single, $20 doubles. 2 miles to downtown.

B & B: B & B in Arizona, 8433 N Black Canyon, Suite 160, 995-2831. Modest singles $15–$20, doubles $25–$30. All worth private bath, full breakfast. Host homes in Phoenix plus Tombstone, Bisbee, Nogales, Tucson, Flagstaff, Sedona, Page, Lake Havasu, Williams, Grand Canyon Village, etc. Also: Mi Casa-Su Casa, PO Box 950, Tempe; 990-0682. Homes are $18–$23 single, $25–$30, many with private bath. Homes in Phoenix, Tucson, Flagstaff, Sedona, Nogales, and other areas. Other B & Bs through International Spareroom; see Accommodation Background for address.

FOOD
Essentially an expensive gringo golf/tennis/dude ranch resort area, Phoenix offers little in the way of good Mexican food except at La Casita Cafe, 1021 S Central Ave, 273-7477. The University area around Tempe has low-cost bars and nosheries with student flavour. For a splurge, try mesquite-cooked steaks; the Indian art of cooking over mesquite wood originated here. Pinnacle Peaks (30 miles away) is where locals go for cheap and excellent mesquite barbeque.

OF INTEREST
Always phone first or check with Visitors Bureau; sights are very far apart and it is over 100 degrees outside in summer.

Pueblo Grande Museum, 4610 E Washington, 275-3452. 50¢. Open Mon–Sat 9am–4.45pm, Sun 1pm–4.45pm. The ancestors of current-day Pimas and Papagos, the Hohokam people built this complex, irrigated city about 200 BC and disappeared about AD 1450. This is both museum and dig.

Heard Museum, 22 E Monte Vista Rd, 252-8848. Outstanding silverwork, weavings, basketry plus Barry Goldwater's collection of 450 Hopi kachina dolls. $1.50 students 50¢. Open Mon–Sat 10am–5pm, Sun 1pm–5pm. Has Indian Fair in April.

Architectural buffs: **Frank Lloyd Wright's winter home and school, Taliesein West**, is in Scottsdale (phone 948-6670 for fee, directions, hours). Also in Scottsdale, **Paolo Soleri's gallery/studio** (948-6145). 60 miles north is his futuristic vertical city in the making, **Arcosanti.**

Art Museum, 1625 N Central, 257-1221. Open Tue–Sun, donations. Besides art from medieval to Western, the place has live music Fri from noon, other activities.

Camelback Pt Park, take Echo Canyon Park Rd. Phoenix' most visible landmark offers scenic views, picnicking, good trails. Open daily 7am–sundown.

ENTERTAINMENT
Big Surf, 1500 N Hayden Rd, Tempe, 947-2477. Open mid-March through Oct; call for hours. $4, seniors $2, surfboard fee extra. 2½-acre body of water with perfect man-made waves, 4–5 ft high with special periods for surfers, swimmers. 300 ft water slide, palms, waterfalls. 'Most indulgent moment of my holiday; drinking Pepsi, watching girls surfing on machine-made waves in the middle of the desert.'

INFORMATION
Visitors Bureau, 2701 E Camelback Rd, 957-0070. Mon–Fri. Also at airport, open daily.

TRAVEL
Greyhound, 525 E Washington, 248-4040. Exercise caution in this district.

Trailways, 24th Ave and Camelback, 246-4341. New terminal, on opposite side of city from Greyhound. NB: we've had negative reports about friction between Greyhound/Trailways here; don't check bags in until you're sure your bus pass is accepted.

City bus, 257-8426. 60¢–$1.50. Scanty service, none at night or Sundays.

Gray Line, 248-6030 and Arizona Tours, 257-1490, do local tours.

AMTRAK, Union Station, 401 W Harrison St, 800/421-8320. The *Sunset Limited*, LA-New Orleans, stops here.

Rental cars: Greyhound rentals (can book from England), ask at Greyhound depot. Also Rent-a-Relic, 257-1328 and Rentawreck, 352-4897. 'Canyon Mazda has $30/day plus gas, 263-9791.'

AAACON Transport, 222 W Osborn Rd, 264-0201.

Phoenix Airport, via city bus 17, 4 miles out of downtown. Limo service about $4. 'Airport is fairly comfortable to sleep in.'

Horseback trail rides into the Superstition Mt Wilderness: Gold Canyon Stables, 982-7822, and Peralta Stables, 982-5488, both in Apache Junction.

TUCSON. Once capital of the Arizona territory and now a university city, Tucson retains a Western informality as it grows past the half-million mark. Folksiness notwithstanding, Tucson is, like Phoenix, a big tough town with its share of crime, poverty and drugs. Watch your step, particularly at night, in downtown, and if you are female.

Most worthwhile sights in the area are well away from downtown: the Desert Museum, Mission San Xavier del Bac, Saguaro National Monument, Old Tucson and the interesting Yaqui Indian tribe. A highly spiritual and musical people, the Yaqui rites combine native and Catholic traditions. Their public performances (centred round Pascua village south of Tucson) are especially magnificent during Holy Week and at Christmas.

Both Tucson and Phoenix are in the Sonoran Desert, surrounded by giant saguaro forests, cacti and mountains—all within driving (not walking) distance. Tucson is 65 miles north of Nogales, an agreeable town on the Arizona-Mexico border.

ACCOMMODATION

Congress Hotel, 311 E Congress St, 62-8848. $10–$12 single, $15 doubles. TV. 'Very nice, nr Greyhound.' 'Best value in USA.'

Sahara Motor Hotel, 919 N Stone, 622-3541. $20 up single, $25 up double with private bath; pool, bar. 'A treat.'

Motel 6, 960 S Freeway, 624-6345. Nr downtown, reachable by bus. $16 single, $20 double, air conditioning, pool.

YMCA, 516 N 5th Ave, 624-7471. Men only, $13 night.

YWCA, 302 E University Blvd, 884-7810. Women only, reasonably clean and safe, near campus. $10 and up. Book ahead.

Salvation Army Hospitality House, 1021 N 11th Ave, 622-5411. Clean dorm style, showers. Arrive before 9am. Free up to 2 nights.

FOOD

Best pickings around the U of Arizona; try Cafe Finjaen at 931 E University.

Also recommended: Food Conspiracy Co-op, 412 N 4th; Caruso's, 434 N 4th, 'Great lasagna, $4 and up'; El Minuto Cafe, 354 S Main, 'Excellent and cheap Mexican food, basic decor."

OF INTEREST

Mission San Xavier del Bac, 9 miles SW on Papago reservation. Built in 1797 and called 'the white dove of the desert' for its cool beauty, the mission has weathered 3 political jurisdictions, 2 explosions and 1 large earthquake, still serving as church/school for the 11,000 Papagos. The mural-lined interior is especially rich. Free; guided tours.

Old Tucson, 12 miles west. A 1939 Western movie set, where hayburners from *Rio Bravo* to *High Chaparral* have been filmed. Corny family fun: $6 gets you gunfights, bank raids, museums and unlimited rides on stagecoaches, antique trains/cars/carousel. Without a car, Gray Line is it. 'Low budget tourist trap.'

Arizona-Sonora Desert Museum, 14 miles west of city. $5, daily till sundown. Detailed look at Sonoran desert plants and animals in native habitats, from tunnels that let you peer into snake and prairie-dog households to outdoor settings with Gila monsters, mountain lions, etc. 'Don't miss this place.' Visit early am or late afternoon to see maximum animal activity. Gray Line tours.

Worthwhile museums on **U of Arizona campus**: **State museum**, free daily with archaeology, Navajo, Apache, Pueblo artefacts; the **Historical Society**, Park and 2nd, 'Free, excellent displays of Southwest history'; and **Flandrau Planetarium**, free exhibits on space, astronomy. 'Part of tracking system for Voyager mission and space shuttle. Also laser shows ($2.50) with Pink Floyd, others.' 626-4556 for programme info.

Saguaro National Monument, 2 sections, east/west of Tucson 17 miles. Found only in southern Arizona and Sonora, Mexico, these giant cacti get to be 35 ft tall, up to 200 years old. From late May, waxy white flowers tip the cactus arms—a charming and improbable sight. East Park (Rincon) costs $1, has oldest stands, allows free wilderness camping. West park is free, day-use only.

ENTERTAINMENT

Near U of Arizona campus: The Shanty, 4th Ave and E 9th, 'Good friendly pub and student watering hole'; Gentle Ben's, 841 N Tyndall, 'Beer garden—need we say more?'

The Bum Steer, 1910 N Stone Ave. 'A must. Good luck lads and don't forget Happy Hour.'

INFORMATION/TRAVEL

Visitors Bureau, La Placita Villa (downtown shopping mall), 791-4768 and 884-9555 for events line.

Greyhound, 2 S 4th Ave, 792-0972. 'Girls near depot should stay on the move. This is the local prostitutes' pitch—clients are very persistent and extremely unpleasant.'

Trailways, 201 E Broadway, 882-0005.

AMTRAK, 400 E Toole St, 623-4442.

Rental cars: Budget, 623-5742, Compacts Only, 790-0989 and 886-6656.

Local bus, 792-9222. Within city only, limited service, less at night, on weekends.

Gray Line, 622-8811. Year-round, Mon, Wed, Fri, Sat, $8–$17. No bus pass discounts; admissions are extra. Tours to Xavier Mission, Desert Museum, Old Tucson, Saguaro National Monument.

TOMBSTONE, BISBEE and APACHE COUNTRY. This rugged
terrain, once subject to the raids of Mexican revolutionary Pancho Villa, was originally Apache territory and the stronghold for chiefs Cochise and Geronimo, who fought the US Cavalry until 1886. Cochise remained free and lies buried somewhere in the **Coronado National Forest**, about 60 miles east of Tucson (lots of free camping in this and other sections of the National Forest). Geronimo (whose name has achieved a peculiar immortality as the traditional 'jump cry' of US paratroopers) was imprisoned in Oklahoma and died there in 1900.

Tombstone, a short-lived (1877-90) silver town and desperado den, now lives off the quantity of tourists it traps. Weekends you can witness staged versions of the famous Wyatt Earp/Doc Holliday gun-fight at the OK Corral. (The actual deed ingloriously took place in an alley.) The Bird Cage Theater ($1) where Lola Montez danced, is still standing. Montez, an exotic dancer and adventuress whose delicious breasts caused Bavarian King Ludwig I to salivate and later to abdicate, trod the boards here and elsewhere. Best thing in Tombstone is the free Boot Hill Cemetery north of town. You may also enjoy the world's largest rosebush (4th and Toughnut), whose white flowers perfume half of Tombstone. 'Whole place a little false but great fun.'

Twenty-five miles south of Tombstone sits **Bisbee**, a steep mining town of great character and considerable charm. Over $2 billion in silver, gold and copper came from these hills, but today Bisbee is famous for a special variety of turquoise, which you can see at Bisbee Blue Jewelry. Don't miss the mine tour or the delightful Art Deco courthouse. Much cooler here than Tombstone and surrounds because of the 5500-foot elevation.

ACCOMMODATION
In Cochise: Cochise Hotel and Waterworks, PO Box 27, Cochise 85606. 384-3156. Booking mandatory for this authentic relic of the Old West. $14 single, $23 suite, complete with brass beds, quilts, chamberpots (plus modern plumbing). Homecooked meals by the irascible proprietress. No AC, bring your own booze.
In Tombstone: free camping at the City Park, east of Allen St, follow the signs. Year-round, 2-night limit. Also look for the old freight wagon behind the library: 'Wheatherproof, ideal for sleeping.' NB: When sleeping outdoors, remember this is rattlesnake country.
In Bisbee: Copper Queen Hotel, 11 Howell Ave, 432-2216. Beautiful, regal, once the headquarters for everyone from Teddy Roosevelt to 'Black Jack' Pershing, hot on Pancho Villa's trail. Singles $18 up, doubles $22 up, all private bath. Good sidewalk cafe, pool. 'Many rooms with antique furniture—a trip back in time when this was a bustling mining town'.

FOOD
OK Coffee Shop, 3rd and Fremont on Highway 80, Tombstone. 'Best in the West. Cheap too. Flo's chicken dumplings are great!'

INFORMATION/OF INTEREST
Tombstone Chamber of Commerce, on Highway, 457-3552; lots of traveller info about the area.
Tombstone Epitaph, the town's local newspaper. Saved from bankruptcy by the U of Arizona and now publshed by students; pick up a copy.
Copper Queen Mine, in Bisbee. Daily tours, 1½ hours $3.50. On a train; cold so dress warmly. 'Extensive, informative, good value.' Adjacent is the Lavender Pit, free viewing of its huge purple maw from Hwy 80. Also $2.50 bus tours.

FLAGSTAFF. Located 79 miles south of the Grand Canyon, Flagstaff should be considered a jumping-off point for such scenic splendours as Oak Creek Canyon and Montezuma Castle to the south; Petrified Forest and Canyon de Chelly to the east; and Sunset Crater and Wupatki to the north. Avoid layovers—the town itself offers little to do or see. 'Must qualify as the most boring place on earth in which to be stuck waiting for a bus.' Somewhat closer to Grand Canyon is Williams, which has some lodgings and good camping.

ACCOMMODATION
In Flagstaff:
Note: rates begin falling after Labor Day and are cheapest 31 Oct–May. Summer rates given below.
Du Beau Motel, 19 W Phoenix, 774-6731. 'Basic but very clean and comfortable with shower, toilet, no TV.' $15–$20 doubles.
Flamingo Motor Hotel, 560 W Highway 66, next to Greyhound. 779-2251. Singles $19 up, doubles $24 up. 'Clean, well-kept.' 'Budget car rental in lobby.' Cheaper rooms offseason, without TV. 'Very friendly.'
Weatherford Hotel and Hostel, 23 N Leroux, 774-2731. $7.28 members, $9.36 non-members. Near AMTRAK, Trailways, has free shuttle to Greyhound in daytime. Shared rooms. 'Terrific.' AYH meals $2.50 each but downstairs cafe 'expensive'. Also kitchen, Ugly Duckling car rental and camping gear rental on premises. However: 'Breakfast is a ripoff, car rental likewise. Arrange rental yourself with company or take the $10/day, 10¢ a mile offer.'
Town House Motel, 122 W Santa Fe Ave, next to Trailways, 774-5081. Single with shower, TV from $16, doubles from $19. 'Good.' 'Friendly, clean, comfy.' On main road, noisy.
Pine Hotel, 114 E Santa Fe Ave, 774-9969. $13 single, $18 doubles, flash your passport—owner favours international visitors.
Sierra Vista Hotel, 9 E Phoenix Ave, 774-6371. Near AMTRAK. Spartan but tidy. Singles $15 up, doubles $25 up.
Other cheapies along Santa Fe including Chalet Lodge, Alpine Motel. Also good but car needed are Motel 6, Regal 8, Wonderland Motel.
In Williams:
Patio Motel, 128 E Bill Williams, 635-4791. Singles $16 up, doubles, $22–$35. Cable TV, AC, coffeeshop. 'Clean, neat.'
Sun Dial Motel, 200 E Bill Williams, 635-2562. $18 up single, $24 up double.

FOOD
Often mentioned: Choi's on E Aspen, 'excellent', 'best value'; The Alternative, 12 N Beaver, 'good cheap food, great steak'; Grand Canyon Cafe, 110 E Santa Fe, 'superb value—3-course meal under $4'; and Mary's Cafe on Highway 89, 'huge homemade cinnamon rolls'. Capparelli's near Trailways and Alpine Pizza on N Leroux are also praised for good Italian food.
In Williams, eat at Rod's Steak House, 301 E Bill Williams. Not super budget but hearty, delicious and very western meals.

OF INTEREST
Walnut Canyon, 10 miles east. Lush canyon filled with cliff-hanging ruins. The day-use trail is strenuous in places. 'Wildlife and Indian relics, very worthwhile and not crowded.'

INFORMATION
Chamber of Commerce, 101 W Santa Fe, 774-4505.

TRAVEL
Greyhound, 399 S Malpais Lane, 774-4573. 'A mecca for Europeans.'
Trailways, 114 W Santa Fe Ave, 774-6661. Day excursion service from Flagstaff to Grand Canyon at 7.30am and 10.30am, returning about 5pm. $16, with bus pass $10. 'Comfortable.'
Nava-Hopi bus service, 774-5003. From 26 April to 25 October serves Grand

Canyon 3 times daily beginning at 7.30am. About 2-hr trip; but pass valid. Serves Bright Angel Lodge on South Rim. Also has once-daily trip from Williams to Bright Angel; if travelling west, it might be more convenient to take the noon bus from the Canyon to Williams. In winter, buses leave Flagstaff 9am, return 6pm.

Gray Line does half-day tours to east and west ends of South Rim. 'Tours don't leave you enough time at the canyon.'

Car rental: recommended, especially among 3 or more people. Cheapest is Ugly Duckling, 23 N Leroux, 528-2329 at $10/day, 10¢ a mile plus insurance. 'Still cheapest but watch out—we got stopped for expired licence plate and UD got a $20 citation.' Book directly with agency. Also try Thrifty and Payless near Greyhound; and Budget, 779-0306, which has cheaper weekend rates. 'Car rental—the best way to tour Grand Canyon in a hurry in a small group.'

AMTRAK, 1 E Santa Fe Ave, 774-8679. *Southwest Limited* services Flagstaff on the LA-Chicago run.

Horseback riding: Hitchin' Post Stables, 448 Lake Mary Rd, 774-1719. 6 miles from town. 'Great ride through beautiful Walnut Canyon.'

Hitching: reported as 'good', 'easy' to and from the Canyon. 'Just as quick as the $16 bus trip.' Elsewhere, best to rent a car.

OAK CREEK CANYON and SEDONA. Going down US 89A from Flagstaff, the road makes a switchback descent into this brilliantly tinted canyon carved by Oak Creek. From the **Oak Creek natural area** a footpath takes you along the floor, through a dense growth of pines, cypresses and junipers, crossing repeatedly the swift-running brook. After the 16-mile descent you come to **Sedona**, a pretty artists' colony and setting for many of Zane Grey's Western novels. Just south on Route 179, the landscape opens up into striking vistas punctuated by mesas and serrated sandstone cliffs of red, pink, ochre and buff. Spend some time at the Frank Lloyd Wright Church of the Holy Cross, a stunning concrete shadowbox set against rust-coloured cliffs. The view from inside is nearly as moving, often accompanied by Gregorian chants.

ACCOMMODATION
Northern Star Motel 295 Jordan Rd, Sedona, 282-3641. Summer $28 single, $30 double, winter $20 and $22. AC, TV, kitchen. 1 block to bus, close to restaurants, shops. 'Clean, neat.'

TRAVEL AND OF INTEREST
Trailways passes through here on the Flagstaff—Phoenix run. 'Beautiful drive. Stop for a swim at Slide Rock, a small gorge with cold pools.' 'Well worth a visit. Schnebley Hill approach is outstanding.'

MONTEZUMA CASTLE NATIONAL MONUMENT. Further along the 89A route is **Tuzigoot National Monument**, a pueblo ruin atop a mesa overlooking the Verde River. But for a better example, cut across to US 17 for **Montezuma Castle** (AD 100–1400), far more picturesque and intact. Neither castle nor connected with Montezuma, this was a cliff dwelling inhabited by Sinagua farmers. 'Ask at visitors centre for directions to Clear Creek campground, $2 a night. Friendly owners. You can swim in the nine-foot pool formed by the stream nearby.'

PETRIFIED FOREST NATIONAL PARK. This 94,000-acre park actually contains the varicoloured buttes and badlands of the **Painted Desert** as well as Indian petroglyphs at Newspaper Rock, pueblo ruins, two museums and a large 'forest' of felled and petrified logs. The trees date to the Triassic period and were probably brought here by a flood, covered with mud and volcanic ash, preserved by silica quartz and laid bare once again by erosion. Most of the fossilised remains are jasper, agate, a few of clear quartz and amethyst. Like the red, yellow, blue and umbre tones of the Painted Desert, these vivid colours are caused by mineral impurities. An excellent road bisects the park north to south. Park fee is $1 per car; camping for hikers only (with permit) at two spots. The museum-restaurant at the north end contains murals by noted Hopi artists.

ACCOMMODATION
No lodging in the park.
Arizona Rancho Motor Lodge, 57 Tovar St, Holbrook, 524-6770. 19 miles from park. AYH affiliate, hostel price is $6.25 year-round. 3 blocks from Greyhound. 'Friendly, clean', 'comfortable', 'Mrs Taylor is very helpful.' Now supposed to sponsor low-cost hostel tours to the Petrified Forest, Indian reservations and elsewhere; ask.
Brad's Motel, 301 W Hopi Drive, Holbrook, 282-3641. 3 blocks from Greyhound. Singles $17 up, doubles $22 up. 'Friendly, helpful.'

TRAVEL
Greyhound and Trailways operate along I-40 to Holbrook. Of late, Roy Baker's Tours (524-6535) of the area have been criticised by readers; enquire at the Holbrook Hostel instead.

NAVAJO and HOPI RESERVATIONS. The **Navajo** nation occupies the northeast corner of Arizona (plus parts of Utah and New Mexico), an area the size of West Virginia. On it dwell a shy, dignified, beauty-loving people, the largest and most cohesive of all Native American groups. Nearly all Navajos are fluent in their native tongue, a language of such complexity that Japanese cryptographers were unable to decipher it during the Second World War, when the US military used Navajos to send secret information. Originally a nomadic culture, the flexible Navajos adopted sheepherding and horses from the Spanish, weaving and sandpainting from the Pueblo Indians, and more recently such things as pickup trucks from the whites. The reservation, while poor, is a fascinating mix of traditional hogans and wooden frame houses, uranium mines and trading posts, all in a setting of agriculturally marginal but scenically rich terrain, anchored by the four sacred peaks of Mounts Blanca, Taylor, Humphrey and Hesperus.

Amidst the 150,000 Navajos is an arrowhead-shaped nugget of land upon which sit the three mesas of the **Hopis**, a strenuously peaceful and traditional tribe of farmers and villagers. Now numbering about 6500, the Hopis have planted corn and ignored Spaniards, Navajos and Anglos alike for nearly a thousand years, their religion and culture still poetically and distinctly non-Western.

Route 264 crosses both reservations, allowing you access to the Hopi mesa villages and the Navajo settlements and capital at **Window Rock** on the Arizona-New Mexico border. Neither group is particularly forthcoming with whites, but you can bridge their suspicion by respecting their strong feelings about photographs, alcohol, tape recorders and local customs. Always ask permission to take pictures; if you are allowed, expect to pay for it and live up to your bargain. If you are lucky enough to witness dancing or healing ceremonies, behave as the Indians do to avoid giving offence.

Oraibi on the Third Mesa vies with the Pueblo Indians' Acoma as the oldest continuously inhabited settlement in the US. To enter the village, you must ask permission of the chief and pay a fee— absolutely no cameras, however. One of the most intriguing Hopi villages is **Walpi**, high atop the narrow tip of the Second Mesa. Dating from the 17th century, this classic adobe village of kivas and sculptured houses remains startlingly alien. 'Hire a four-wheel drive to get up very steep roads, dirt tracks.'

Monument Valley, scene of countless John Ford films and full of Navajo sacred places, sprawls across Arizona-Utah state lines and can be reached via Highways 160 and 163 from the south. Perhaps easier is the access from the Utah side. Page, Arizona (also site of Lake Powell and its 90 flooded canyons) makes a good base for Monument Valley exploration. A car is almost a necessity, both here and elsewhere on the reservations. There is some bus service via Nava-Hopi from Window Rock to Tuba City, which stops at Kearns Canyon in Hopiland.

Besides looking at the masterful rugs, pottery, jewellery and other crafts, be sure to sample Indian food. Navajo specialties include fried bread, mutton stew and roast prairie dog. Interesting Hopi dishes are *nakquivi* or hominy stew and the beautiful blue cornmeal bread served with canteloupe for breakfast. The Hopi Cultural Center Restaurant on Route 264 is open daily; besides its mind-bending views and fine crafts, the menu explains the cultural and religious significance of each Hopi dish. An interesting way to absorb the mind-set of a special people.

CANYON DE CHELLY NATIONAL MONUMENT. Surrounded by Navajo land, Canyon de Chelly (about 60 miles north of Highway 264 and pronounced 'Shay') has the powerful beauty of a bygone Garden of Eden. Occupied successively by the Basket Makers, the Hopis and the Navajos, the canyon was just one of the targets in the 1863 US Army campaign to subdue or annihilate the Navajos. Kit Carson and his men eventually overwhelmed the stronghold at Canyon de Chelly, killing livestock and Indians, destroying hogans and gardens, even cutting down the treasured peach trees, a move which shattered the Navajos. Canyon de Chelly is again inhabited by Navajos, who live among 800-year-old pueblo buildings. Both are totally upstaged by the fantastic walls of the canyon itself, 1000 feet of sheer orange verticality.

A road runs along the rim with several lookouts to view **White House Ruin, Spider Rock** and **Three Turkeys Ruin**, so named from the Navajo pictographs on its walls. The only descent you're allowed to navigate solo is the White House Trail; all others require a Navajo guide.

ACCOMMODATION
Free camping, 90 sites in Cottonwood Campground with flush toilets, all year.
Justin's Thunderbird Lodge, Chinle at National Monument entrance, 674-5443 and Canyon de Chelly Motel, 674-5288, are both $40 single, $42–$44 double from 1 April–1 Oct; other times, T-bird is $30–$32, Canyon de Chelly $26–$28. Full baths, AC, TV; cafeteria at T-bird.

INFORMATION
Visitors Center, open 8am–5pm year-round. Although a National Monument, Canyon de Chelly is on Navajo land and is therefore subject to certain restrictions designed to limit intrusion on Navajo privacy.

TRAVEL
No public transport to either the monument or Chinle. Inside the monument, jeeps tour the canyon floor for a good look at ruins and pictographs, $16 half day, $30 all day with lunch; through Thunderbird Lodge. As mentioned earlier, except for White House Trail, all hikers must have park ranger or an authorised Navajo guide; about $5/hour. This goes for 4-wheel-drive rentals also.

SUNSET CRATER and WUPATKI NATIONAL MONUMENTS. US 180, the most direct route from Flagstaff to the Grand Canyon, is also the dullest. A better choice is to travel US 89 past Sunset Crater and Wupatki, turning off for the Canyon at Cameron.

Long a volcanic region, **Sunset Crater's** most recent eruption occurred about AD 1064, leaving a colourful cone on a jet black lava field. The crater makes an interesting hike; from the top, over 50 volcanic peaks, including the San Franciscos, can be seen. Camping $3; lava tubes to explore. The volcanic ash from Sunset made good fertiliser, and a number of Indian groups built pueblos nearby at **Wupakti**. There are over 800 ruins on mesa tops, a ball court, dance arena, and a museum to interpret the finds at this long since abandoned settlement. Day use only.

THE GRAND CANYON. This, the most popular natural attraction in the US, is a glorious geologic strudel, a calendar that marks the millennia in rainbow striations. Wind, frost and the Colorado River have gnawed a magnificent, 217-mile-long canyon from the landscape, filled with 270 animal species and containing four of the seven known life zones. The proportions of the one-mile-deep canyon are deceptive; most visitors find it difficult to believe that it is never less than four times wider than it is deep. The cross-sectional prospect from **Grandview Point** helps to set the matter straight.

The Grand Canyon has three parts: the South Rim (open year-round, access via Highway 64/180 from Williams and Flagstaff), the North Rim (open mid-May to mid-October, access via Highway 67 from Jacob Lake) and the Inner Canyon (open year-round, access on foot, by mule or boat only). To get from the North Rim to the South Rim is 215 miles by car or an arduous 20-mile hike up and down. This means the choice between North and South Rim should be made at an early stage.

Pros and cons: the **South Rim** is easy to reach, has the best views plus the lion's share of the lodgings, amenities and crowds. The **North Rim** is unsurpassed for abundance of animal life, uncrowded serenity (less than 10 per cent of the three million visitors per year get here), cooler temperatures and special autumn colouration.

If you're at all fit, you'll want to hike to the **canyon floor**, or at least part of the way. 'Hard work, but an awesome and breath-taking spectacle.' Do read the hiking tips under Of Interest before setting out; the heat, the stiff 4500 foot climb, the high altitude of the entire area and the need to carry large amounts of water are all factors you must prepare for.

Park fee is $3 per car, $1 per person. 'No traveller should miss the Grand Canyon: a spiritual experience.'

ACCOMMODATION
Rates within the Grand Canyon generally hold true all year around. For any of the South Rim lodgings, call 638-2631; for North Rim, call 638-2611. Book well ahead, even after Labor Day. Failing that, be on hand between 3.30pm–4.30pm for no-shows: the lodges always hold a few rooms for people on the last buses from Flagstaff and Williams. Campsites are filled quickly June through Sept so get there *very* early.
South Rim:
Bright Angel Lodge and Cabins, $27 single, $30 up doubles, $6 extra person. Modest lodge rooms, rustic cabins, all with bath. The cheapest by far so reserve ahead. Older and cheaper rooms without bath being phased out, but ask.
Grand Canyon Youth Hostel, PO Box 270, 76 Tonto, 658-9018. New 20-bed hostel with plans to expand, located along a path behind Ranger HQ across from El Tovar Hotel, $7 AYH, $9 without. Dorms. Open year-round. 'Very friendly, clean.' 1 night limit. Conflicting reports about booking: 'No reservations accepted—arrive at 4pm when it opens.' 'Can book through Phoenix or Flagstaff hostels.'
The other lodgings (all year-round) in ascending order of singles/doubles cost: Motor Lodge ($30–$40); Original Yavapai ($35–$40, 'good clean rooms, extremely helpful staff'); New Yavapai ($40–$50); Thunderbird, Mushwhip and Kachina Lodges ($50–$60) and El Tovar Hotel ($60–$65).

Camping: Mather open year-round, $5 for car, less for tent campers, backpackers. 'Always places reserved for people without own transport.' 300 sites, one available through TICKETRON, can book up to 2 months in advance. Shower, laundromat, near supermarket. In summer, 'tent not needed', but by mid-Sept, 'cold, sleeping bag plus tent essential'. Other campsites at Trailer Village and Desert View (latter is 27 miles east, summer only). Lower rates reported in Sept. Cheapest strategy is to share tent/space rental with others. Can also rent sleeping bags, tents ($10–$15) and leave luggage with Bright Angel Lodge for 50¢/day. 'Reservations taken 7am on the day before you want to camp.'
Outside park to the south:
Ten-X Campground, 11 miles from Canyon Village. Sites $1–$5, open year-round. 'We arrived well after dark, left well before dawn and avoided paying.' Also: 'Free camping allowed on National Forest land. Go 6 miles south on South Entrance Rd, turn at forest track on left opp Squire Inn. OK as long as you remain within ½ mile of public telephone.'
Down the Canyon:
Free camping at 4 hike-in sites, which require both a permit and a trailhead or campground reservation, often made months in advance. 'As soon as you arrive, go to Visitors Center and put your name on a list for an overnight permit.' 'Be at Visitors Center by 7am for a chance at unclaimed permits.' Call 638-2401 or 638-2474 to reserve. Keep in mind there's a heavy fine for those caught camping without a permit.
Phantom Ranch, on canyon floor, 638-2401. Has rustic cabins (about $45 double but includes meals) and dorm bunks for $12. Leave excess luggage on the rim for a fee. 'Now air conditioned, very comfortable.'
North Rim:
Grand Canyon Lodge, 638-2611. Late May to mid-Oct only. $31–$43. Cheapest are Pioneer Cabins, 4 people for $42. Western cabins slightly more, but have superlative views, more comfort. Can reserve also in Cedar City, Utah: 801-586-7686. Campsite reservations, trail info at the lodge, but no place to check luggage.
Camping: first-come first-served at Bright Angel Pt, summer only, $3. Often necessary to camp outside park on National Forest land the night before, arriving at North Rim early am to nab campsite.
Outside park to the north:
Camping at De Motte (5 miles) and Jacob Lake (32 miles). Lodging at Kaibab Lodge, May–Oct, 19 miles north, 638-2389. $24 single, $32 doubles. On Hwy 67.
Jacob Lake Inn, 44 miles north, 643-5532. Year-round, cheaper Dec–April. Singles/doubles $22.50–$32.

FOOD

Expensive and generally poor everywhere in the park, even at the cafeterias. 'Best' bets: Babbitt's supermarket, Bright Angel restaurant (especially their specials), Grand Canyon Lodge at North Rim (breakfasts and lunches $3–$7) and the home-cooked meals at Phantom Ranch. The ranch also prepares pack lunches and has a snack bar.

INFORMATION

Road conditions, weather and Grand Canyon park activities, 638-2245 (24-hr). Visitors Center, 638-2411, has info, maps, excellent bookstore and a museum. Closes 9pm in summer. Ranger programmes are highly recommended; they conduct guided hikes, do evening slide shows, etc. In winter, programmes are inside the Shrine of the Ages building. Also recommended: 'The sunrise and sunset photo walks by the Kodak rep.'

TRAVEL

For bus service and car rental to and from South Rim, see Flagstaff. To and from the

North Rim: Parks Bus company from Cedar City, Utah, 177 miles north, operates mid-June Sept only. Gray Line does tours from Flagstaff, Phoenix, Las Vegas and other points, some of them surprisingly reasonable.

Air tours from LA, Las Vegas (see entry), Phoenix, Flagstaff and Williams. 'Northland Aviation, Flagstaff airport, has 1-hr 40 minute flights, passing over Sunset Crater and along 87 miles of the Grand Canyon and back across northern Arizona desert by a different route. Very good value: 2 persons in plane, $70 each; 3 for $60 each.'

Hitching: 'Save your money by walking 3 miles out of Flagstaff and hitching. Will get a ride easily.' 'Hitching to North Rim is OK—we did it in less than 24 hours from Zion in Sept.'

Within the Canyon:

Bus tours from Bright Angel Lodge now $6.50–$12, called 'a waste of money'.

Two free shuttlebus services: operate May–Sept every 15 minutes, throughout Grand Canyon Village and around South Rim. Get on and off at will. Also to scenic West Rim as far as Hermit's Rest.

Mule rides into the Canyon: from South and North Rims (summer only). Outrageously popular and booked up, but many no-shows so try anyway. 1-day trips $28–$40 with lunch; overnights $130–$140. 'Unforgettable.' 'Must be the best way to see the Canyon.' 'Go to Bright Angel Lodge desk at 6.30am the day before you wish to go and you'll get a place.' The mules won't carry anybody who is over 200 pounds, pregnant, under age 12, acrophobic, non-English speaking or any combination thereof. Call 638-2401 or book: Reservation Dept, South Rim, Grand Canyon National Park AZ 86023 or Grand Canyon Scenic Rides, Kanab Utah 84741.

Bike rentals at West Rim drive, summer only.

Boat trips down the Colorado River, rewarding but very costly average $100/day, 3-day minimum. Must be booked ahead; use mule ride addresses.

Air tour of Canyon. Helicopter (638-2619) and plane (638-2616) flights into the Canyon, $55 and up from airport near the Visitor Center. 'Not to be missed.' 'Both copter and plane go below rim but plane is better value—slow enough to take good photos.' Book ahead if you can. (See also earlier entry.)

OF INTEREST

Tips: Whether you descend the Canyon or not, guard against heat exhaustion and dehydration by drinking the park-recommended juice mixture. Water alone will not satisfy your body's requirements, as the rangers will tell you. Other hiking tips: wear a hat, don't wear sandals, always check beforehand to make sure your trail is open. For hiking into the Canyon, plan to carry 4 litres of water per person per day. Also carry food, permit, pocket knife, signal mirror, flashlight, maps, matches and first-aid kit. Calculate 2 hrs up for every hr going down. (If you do get lost or injured, stay on the trail so they can find you.) The park service warns against hiking to the Colorado River and back in one day. Readers add: 'Do take notice of time estimates.' If you plan to camp at the bottom, you need a minimum of equipment—it reaches 100 degrees in summer. 'Hardly worth the effort to carry tent.' A final recommendation: 'When camping at the bottom, start the ascent at 3am, escaping the midday heat, seeing sunrise over the Canyon, and catching the 9.45pm bus back to Flagstaff.'

Along the South Rim, the most remarkable views are from Hopi, Yaki, Grand View and Desert Views points. A 9-mile trail from Yavapai Museum to Hermit's Rest follows the very edge of the Canyon. Pick up relevant leaflets from the Visitors Centers before setting out. The South Rim is also the starting point for the South Kaibab and Bright Angel Trails to descend into the Canyon.

Bright Angel Trail has water at 3 points (May–Sept only) and is 7.8 miles to the river. 'A good one-day hike—Bright Angel to Plateau Point and back, 12 miles. Great scenery.' 'Try to leave yourself 8 hrs for comfort.' 'Water is essential.' **South**

Kaibab Trail is 6.3 miles down, no campgrounds, no water and little shade: don't attempt in summer. 'Colorado River is nice to paddle in—too strong for anything else.'

From the North Rim, the North Kaibab Trail is 14 miles with water at 4 points. A good day hike would be to Roaring Springs and back, about 6–8 hours. The entire Kaibab Trail is 21 miles and connects North and South Rims. Views from the North Rim include Cape Royal (nature talks in summer), Angel's Window, overlooking the Colorado River, and the much-photographed Shiva's Temple, a ruddy promontory of great beauty.

NEW MEXICO

Travel industry hyperbole aside, New Mexico *does* enchant. It possesses a dramatic desert landscape, heightened by the scalpel-sharp clarity of the air; natural wonders like the Navajo's Shiprock and the Carlsbad Caverns; and the finest array of Indian cultures, past and present. In human terms, New Mexico is incredibly ancient, having been inhabited for over 25,000 years. More significantly, it is the only state which has succeeded in fusing its venerable Spanish, Indian and Anglo influences into a harmonious and singular pattern. You will notice the benign borrowings everywhere, from sensuous adobes tastefully outfitted with solar heating to the distinctive New Mexican cuisine.

New Mexico inspires awe for more than its beauty. On 16 July 1945, at the appropriately named Jornada del Muerto (Journey of the Dead) Desert, the world's first atomic bomb belched its radioactive mushroom into the air. Today, the state is a leader in atomic research, testing, uranium mining and related fields. Blithe as locals may be about nuclear materials (the Alamogordo Chamber of Commerce still sponsors an annual outing to Ground Zero), think twice before visiting the Alamogordo-White Sands region. Your genes may thank you some day. Instead, concentrate on the fascinating and diverse Indian populations: the 19 Pueblo villages, each with its own pottery, dance, arts and style; the Navajos, whose capital is at Window Rock; the Jicarilla and Mescalero Apaches, noted for dancing and coming of age ceremonies. Celebrations open to the public are so numerous that you could plan an itinerary around them. The State Tourism office publishes a good free booklet, *Indians of New Mexico*, which will help you do so.

National Park: Carlsbad Caverns.

ALBUQUERQUE. Named for a ducal viceroy of Mexico, Albuquerque is not as pleasing as its euphonious name would lead you to believe. It contains one-third of the state's 1.3 million residents and rather more of the state's trash features, from tacky motels to urban sprawl. (At least it's all in one place.)

Albuquerque does make a good base for day trips to the Indian pueblos and to the Sandia Mountains. The best times to visit are during the June Arts and Crafts Fair, the September State Fair, the October Hot-Air Balloon Fiesta and at Christmas, when city dwellings are outlined with thousands of *luminarias* (candles imbedded in sand, their light diffused by paper).

ACCOMMODATION
Central Ave is the north-south divider; railroad tracks divide east-west.

Plaza Hotel, 125 2nd St NW, 243-4421. Nr bus depot. $24 up single, $28 up doubles. A former Hilton, recommended for its decor. Try bargaining.

Town House Motor Hotel, 400 Center SE, 247-0703. Singles $15 with bath, colour TV; doubles $18. Free transport. 'Very good value, friendly. Tea, coffee provided in your room.'

Spanish Gate Motel, 2411 Center NW, 247-2751. Singles $13-$16, doubles $15-$18. AC, pool, kitchen, TV. Offseason, weekly rates. Close to bus. 2 blocks from Old Town.

Grand Western Motor Hotel, 918 Central SW, downtown, 243-1773. Single $16 up, doubles $19 up.

Canterbury Hostel, 1906 Central SE, Near University. $5.25 members, $7 nonmembers. Kitchen. 'Handy, homely and small, opens 5pm, closes 10am.' 'Recommend you sleep on the veranda. Very lax. Only rule: not allowed to sleep with the opposite sex unles they ask you!'

FOOD
G/M Steak House, 222 Central SW, 1 block from bus/train. Under $5 for steak dinner. 'Good, very friendly.' 'Closes at 8.30pm however.'

Lindy's Coffeeshop, Central at 5th. 'Cheap, close to bus station, friendly, free coffee *ad infinitum*. Opens 6am.'

Standard Truck Plaza, 1915 Menaul Blvd NE, at I-40 and I-25. Fairly near Old Town. Authentic Mexican food; get red or green chile.

OF INTEREST
Old Town, 1 block north of Central Ave NW. Shops, restaurants and occasional live entertainment. The only nugget of Spanishness left in the city. 'Well worth a visit.' On the plaza is the 1706 **Church of San Felipe de Neri**.

U of New Mexico, Central NE and University. Pioneer in pueblo revival architecture, has free exhibits, often on Indians, in the Maxwell Museum.

Indian Pueblo Cultural Center, 12th St near I-40, 1 mile east of Old Town, 843-7270. $1. Excellent exhibit, sales rooms by the 19 Pueblos and a good way to compare techniques and styles. High quality, prices to match. 'Only thing of interest in this town.' Also Indian dancing Sat-Sun, 1 and 3pm, June-Sept. Restaurant on premises serves traditional pueblo food—give it a try.

National Atomic Museum, Building 358, Wyoming Blvd SE at Kirkland AFB, 264-4223. Free, daily 9am-5pm. Disquieting look at selection of defused nuclear hardware, plus 'oops' items like the A-Bomb the US accidentally dropped on Palomares, Spain, in 1966. Regular screenings of *Ten Seconds That Shook the World*.

Sandia Peak Aerial Tramway, NE of town, take Tramway Rd off I-25, 298-8518. At 2.7 miles, the world's longest tramway, climbing to 10,378 ft. $6.50 round trip, $5 students. Fantastic panorama which sometimes includes hang gliders and hot air balloons in the area.

Hot Air Balloon Fiesta, 883-0932: about 500 balloons from around the world assemble for 9 days in early Oct. High points are the mass ascensions on opening and closing weekends: get there 6am–7am. Also balloon rides during fiesta, but cheaper at other times ($75 for 30 minutes).

Christmas: Chamber of Commerce does free night-time bus tours of the outstanding *luminaria* displays, a medieval Spanish custom which began as small bonfires lighting the way to the church for the Christ Child.

INFORMATION
Chamber of Commerce, 401 2nd St NW, 842-0220.

TRAVEL
Greyhound and Trailways share a building at 302 2nd St SW. Clean, safe, new depot with all-night cafe, 'a little pricey'. 243-4435 Greyhound, 842-5511 Trailways.
Local bus, 766-7830. Fun Bus on weekends, $1; get on, off as often as you like.
Gray Line, 243-5501, does tours to Sandia Peak, the Indian pueblos in area and to Santa Fe.
AMTRAK, 314 1st St SW, 842-9650.

CARLSBAD CAVERNS. Largest and very possibly the most beautiful caves in the world, the Carlsbad Caverns began their stalagtite-spinning activities about 250 million years ago. In contrast, the famous Mexican freetail bat colony has been in residence a mere 17,000 years. Once numbering three million, give or take a bat, the colony is now down to 200,000, due in part to increased use of insecticides. It was the eerie sight of bats pouring like smoke from the cave openings that led to Carlsbad's discovery in 1901.

The caves became a National Park in 1930, but the big bucks locally came from the sale of 100,000 tons of prime bat shit to California citrus growers. Naturalists estimate that half the bats in the wild have rabies; thus it might pay you to keep your throat and other parts covered at least 50 percent of the time when the little boogers are zooming overhead.

Oh yes, the caves. The cross-shaped **Big Room** is 1800 feet by 1100 feet; nearby you'll see a formation called **The Iceberg**, which takes half an hour to circle. Sheer size is not the important factor but rather the variety of colours and formations and the intricate filigree of these caverns (five percent of which are still living and growing), which awes you. Don't touch the formations, much as you might like to; a number of them have been turned black by ignorant handling.

ACCOMMODATION
Motel 6, 3824 National Parks Highway, 885-8807. 24 miles from caves. Pool, AC, TV. $16 single, $20 doubles.
Carlsbad Inn, 601 S Canal St, downtown Carlsbad, 22 miles from caves. 887-3541. $18 single, $25 doubles, pool, sauna, restaurant.
La Caverna Motel, 223 S Canal St, 885-4640. $20 single, $24 double, cafe, TV, 15 minutes from Greyhound, 8 blocks from bus stop.
Camping: free in Carlsbad National Park (wonderful spring flowers but look out for snakes in summer); $1 at Lake Carlsbad campground, Muscate Lake. Beautiful setting, nr city, has showers.

OF INTEREST
Cave tours: longer trip 3 miles, about 2½–3 hours. 'Get there early—after 2pm,

you'll have to take the shorter 1¼ mile trip. Still worth seeing.' 'Free nature walks around cavern entrance at 5pm, something to do while waiting for bats.' Carlsbad costs $3, $1 per person from bus. Temperature inside cave is 56 degrees, refreshing in summer but bring a jacket.

Bat facts: bats are in residence spring through late Oct only and are at busiest May–Sept. They leave the cave 6pm–8.30pm to fly 120 miles, consume an aggregate ton of insects, return at dawn to spend the day sleeping in cosy bat-fashion, 300 per sq ft. Call Visitor Center, 785-2233 for more bat-data. 'No one should miss the incredible sight of a million bats flying a few feet over one's head. Just like Dracula, in fact.'

TRAVEL
Greyhound from El Paso, about 3 poorly-timed schedules daily in summer, very irregular after Labor Day. 'Have to pay $2 single fare from White City to Caverns. Last pickup at Caverns is 2.50pm.' Bus between Carlsbad (town) and caves, once daily, 887-1108.

Texas, New Mexico and Oklahoma Coaches, in El Paso (915) 532-3404, has daily service to Carlsbad.

Hitching: 'There's about a 15-minute wait 7 miles from Caverns while changing bus. Try hitching. If successful, get ticket refund in El Paso.' 'If you hitchhike to Cavern, get in free with whomever gave you a lift.' 'For girls, not worth the risk.'

SANTA FE. That rarity of rarities, Santa Fe is a city for walkers, full of narrow, adobe-lined streets that meander round its Spanish heart, the old plaza where the Santa Fe trail once ended. Long a crossroads for trade routes and the oldest seat of government in the US, Santa Fe has witnessed a remarkable amount of history. But the age of the place doesn't prepare you for its beauty, the friendliness of its locals, the vitality of its artistic and cultural life. Santa Fe is one of the few places in the US whose character and venerable charm is natural and not reconstituted.

ACCOMMODATION
De Vargas Hotel, 210 Don Gaspar Ave, 983-3391. Behind bus depot. Single $20 with bath, $18 without, doubles $26 and $24. 'Old, clean, attractive.'

Santa Fe Motel, 510 Cerrillos Rd, 982-1039. 10 minutes from Greyhound. Singles $26, doubles $30 with bath. 'Was able to bargain price down.'

Motel 6, 3007 Cerrillos Rd, 471-2442. Great at $16 single, $20 double, but far from downtown on 'motel row'. Other cheapies along Cerrillos, too.

Bed and Breakfast of Santa Fe, 218 E Buena Vista, 982-3332. Varied listings from a modest $7.50 dorm for bicyclists to $25 rooms and studio efficiencies near the plaza. Also costlier digs, so reserve ahead for the bargains.

Council on International Relations, Suite 3, Mezzanine, La Fonda, 100 E San Francisco on the plaza, PO Box 1223. 982-4931, mornings only. Open 30 June–10 Sept, 9am–noon and 2pm–5pm weekdays, 9am–noon Sat. Rest of year, 9am–noon weekdays only. Closed holidays. Can arrange lodging plus breakfast with family for $10/night (foreign visitors *only*) but you must arrive morning or early afternoon. Best to book ahead for this singular programme. 'Really kind and helpful.' 'Excellent programme.' CIR also has free language bank.

Camping: all sites well out of town so car needed. Reader recommended: 'Carmel Rock, 14 miles north. $3.50 each, clean facilities, very cold at night in Sept.'

NB: no hostels, crash pads or YMCAs in Santa Fe; bus station closes at 9.30pm. Late arrivals, have room waiting. 15 June–15 Sept, call Lodging Hotline, 988-4252 between 4pm–10pm for help.

FOOD
While you're here, sample a bowl of *posole*, the hominy-based stew served with spicy pork that New Mexicans love. Also recommended: Josie's, N Marcy, 1 block north of plaza, 'Very generous helpings of well-cooked Mexican food, $3–$4. popular with locals'; Woolworth's luncheonette (an adobe also) on plaza: 'Cheapest place in town—clean. Breakfast $2 up.' The Shed, 113½ Palace, in *circa* 1692 adobe. Good New Mexican lunches, $2–$5. Crowded. Order their blue corn enchiladas and lemon souffle.

OF INTEREST
The Plaza: city heart, popular gathering place since 1610, and end of both the Santa Fe and El Camino Real trails, the Plaza has seen bullfights, military manoeuvres, fiestas and sights as diverse as Billy the Kid exhibited in chains and the annual Indian Market in Aug in which 40 Southwest tribes take part. Fronting the Plaza is the **Palace of the Governors**, oldest public building in America and seat of 6 regimes. Within its walls, territorial governor Lew Wallace hid out while Billy the Kid vowed to kill him; while cloistered, Wallace wrote *Ben-Hur*. Open daily, the Palace has historical exhibits inside, Indian crafts for sale outside under its arcade. Nearby is the free **Museum of Fine Arts**, beautifully housed.

A city of **churches** is Santa Fe. Among them: **El Cristo Rey**, noted for its size and stone reredos; the **San Miguel chapel**, probably the oldest church in the US; the French Romanesque **St Francis cathedral**, built by Archbishop Lamy (subject of Willa Cather's *Death Comes for the Archbishop*) to house La Conquistadora, a 17th C shrine to the Virgin Mary; the **Loreto Chapel**, a Gothic structure whose so-called 'miraculous' spiral staircase is of mild interest; and the charming **Sanctuario de Guadalupe**, where 18th C travellers stopped to give thanks after their hazardous journeys from Mexico City to Santa Fe.

Museums: numerous, most free, outstanding and devoted to Indian or Southwest art/ethnology. First priority should be the **Wheelwright**, Camino Lejo, 982-4636, open Mon–Sat 10am–5pm, Sun 1pm–5pm, with its marvellous sand paintings made by Navajo singers during various curing rituals. Also on Camino Lejo are the **Laboratory of Anthropology** (Indian crafts) and the **Museum of International Folk Art**, 827-2544 ('Well worth the walk'). NB: despite its compact size, you may find yourself flagging, due to Santa Fe's altitude—7000 ft. Pace yourself.

Interesting neighbourhoods: Canyon Rd for its adobe art galleries, studios and shops; Barrio de Analco, across the Santa Fe River and originally settled by Indian labourers; Sens and Prince Plazas, good shopping areas.

Events in Santa Fe: 2-day **Indian Market** in Aug, **Spanish Market** July. Both in Plaza. Besides selling wares, the Indians sell food, demonstrate weaving and other crafts, and dance. The open-air **opera house** is remarkably beautiful, open July–Aug, and standing room seats are very cheap. Locals dress warmly and drink hot chocolate. The annual **Fiesta**, held mid-Sept since 1692, is the oldest non-Indian celebration in the US; great community spirit. 'Zozobra or Old Man Gloom, a 40-ft dummy, is burned amidst dancing and fireworks. Most spectacular!' 'Fantastic.'

INFORMATION
Chamber of Commerce, 200 W Marcy St, 2 blocks from plaza, 983-7317. Very helpful with details of the Indian pueblos roundabout, their dances, ceremonials, etc. Good maps, booklets. 'Ready to help.'

Also check the Council on International Relations (see under Accommodation): 'overwhelmingly hospitable.'

TRAVEL
Greyhound, Trailways share a depot, 126 W Water St, 982-8564. Closes 9.30pm. 'Trailways route to Denver much prettier than Greyhound's.'

AMTRAK stops at Lamy, 16 miles south. 'Do not get off at Lamy—no transport. Instead get off at Albuquerque and take the bus.'

Gray Line does 1-hr Roadrunner tours of Santa Fe from Plaza. 'Well worth $5—tour goes to Wheelwrights Museum—excellent craft shop.' Also tours to nearby pueblos, Los Alamos, Bandelier National Monument.

Bike rental, nr bus station. 'Useful for museums on Old Pecos Rd.'

Car rentals: cheapest may be Payless (662-3131) or Southwest Auto (988-8981).

TAOS. Set against the rich palette of the crisp white Sangre de Cristo Mountains, the earth tones of a soaring Indian pueblo and the turquoise sky of northern New Mexico, Taos has long been a haven for artists and writers like Georgia O'Keefe, John Fowles and D H Lawrence. Given its powerful attractions, naturally Taos has become a little precious and more than a little expensive. But get to know its traditional Indian and Hispanic communities and you'll glimpse the real Taos still. About 72 miles from Santa Fe and served by Trailways.

ACCOMMODATION

Indian Hills Inn, 2 blocks from South Plaza on Santa Fe Rd, 758-4293. Singles $20 up, doubles $30 up.

El Pueblo Motor Lodge, N Pueblo Rd, 758-8641. Singles $19–$25, doubles $25–$30. Pool.

If you want to stay in the area, cheaper deals are found in Arroyo Seco, a small town 10 miles NE near ski areas.

Abominable Snowmansion, PO box 3271 in Arroyo Seco, 776-8298, is an AYH-affiliated old adobe with dorm style bunks. AYH prices are $7 summer, $9.50 winter, plus all meals for $9/day. Non-members, bed and breakfast is $12 summer, $15 winter. Cosy, friendly lodge atmosphere.

Camping: various free sites in the Carson National Forest, from 3 to 12 miles away from Taos.

OF INTEREST

NB: although Taos has just 3400 people, its attractions are scattered, making a car very useful.

Kit Carson lies buried in the cemetery 2 blocks north of the plaza; his home (1843–68) is a period museum, open daily $1.50.

Art galleries. Best of local artists at The Stables, next to Kit Carson Park. For O'Keefes, go to The Gallery of the Southwest. Navajo paintings of R C Gorman at the Navajo Gallery on Ledoux St.

Mission of St Francis of Assisi, 4 miles south. A masterpiece of the Spanish Colonial period, the mission has a sculptural quality beloved by painters from O'Keefe on down. The interior suffers from over-restoration but do see the reredos and Ault's mysterious painting, *The Shadow of the Cross*. Check locally for open hours before setting out.

Milicent Rogers Museum, 4 miles north, $2 daily, 9am–5pm, May through Oct, Tue–Sun 10am–4pm otherwise. Fascinating collection of death carts and *santos* (carved saints) of the Penitentes, New Mexico's fanatical religious brotherhood. Still active, the Penitentes once practiced flagellation and other mortifications during Holy Week.

Taos Pueblo, 2½ miles north. Best access via Hwy 68. This eye-satisfying 5-storey pueblo, punctuated with beehive ovens and bright *riatas* of during corn and chilis, preserves an 800-year-old architectural tradition. Its 1300 occupants are equally traditional, having banned electricity, piped water, TV and other contrivances. Noted almost solely for their dancing and devotion to ceremonials, the Taos Indians celebrate numerous fiestas, the biggest being the 29–30 Sept Fiesta of San Geronimo (races, dancing). 'Craft market also with good prices.' Also of interest are the ruins of the old Spanish Mission church, burned by the Indians in 1680. In 1847, the Taos Indians also showed the Anglo invaders they meant business by filling the new governor full of arrows and scalping him in the bargain.

˜ Today visitors are tolerated until 6pm; private quarters not open to viewing. $2 per car, 75¢ per walker. Photography permit is $5 and you must also ask permission to take individuals' portraits. No cameras at ceremonial dances. No bus to the pueblo but hitching is easy. Richard's Taxi (758-4710) does round trips for about $4 per head. 'A spiritual experience—well worth it.'

TRAVEL
Trailways runs to Taos town 3 times daily; Ameripass valid.
Gray Line tours to Taos from Santa Fe, covers pueblo; bus pass discount.

INDIAN GROUPS ELSEWHERE IN NEW MEXICO. There are 19 Tewa-speaking Indian groups in all, called collectively the Rio Grande pueblos. Among the most interesting: **Acoma**, the 'Sky City', 60 miles west of Albuquerque, occupies a huge and spectacular mesa, the ground so stony that the Indians had to haul soil 430 feet for their graveyard. Inhabited since AD 1075, the pueblo vies with Oraibi in Hopiland as oldest settlement in the US. Noted for high quality pottery with intricate linear designs. Photo fee and restrictions. Food but no lodging. **Santa Clara**, between Santa Fe and Taos, is famous for its black polished pottery. More outgoing and open to visitors than other pueblos, the Santa Clarans have fewer restrictions on photography. This is an excellent place to take in the dancing at the late July festival. Furthest west of the pueblos is the **Zuñi**, which figured prominently in the Spanish conquest. Spurred greedily on by the lies of an advance scout, Coronado thought he had 'the seven golden cities of Cíbola' but instead found the Zuñi pueblo. Renowned as silversmiths, stone craftsmen and dancers, the Zuñis still measure their wealth in horses. Camping available on their lands. One of few pueblos where outsiders can watch the masked dances.

The **Jicarilla Apaches** in the northwest and the **Mescalero Apaches** in the southeast have numerous tourist facilities, including camping on their lands. Their ceremonies are very striking, especially the female puberty rites which take place during Fourth of July week. Non-Indians may respectfully watch the principal activities. Just outside Jicarilla land is the town of Cuba, which has an excellent hostel called the Circle A Ranch, PO Box 382, 289-3350. On the Durango-Albuqerque Trailways route, it costs $6.25 summer, $7.25 winter for members. Open daily June through September, weekends in winter. 'Lovely adobe ranch, felt part of the family.' The hostel is 40 miles from **Chaco Canyon**, a massive 11th-century ruin, its largest pueblo containing 800 rooms and 39 kivas (sacred chambers). Contemporary with Mesa Verde, possibly more remarkable and certainly less visited.

SILVER CITY. Located in the southwest mining country on a Trailways route from Deming, Silver City also sits in the Gila Wilderness, a wild and lovely terrain of blood-red gorges, ghost towns and Indian ruins. In this region, Geronimo eluded 8000 US Cavalry troops for eight years.

ACCOMMODATION
Bear Mt Guest Ranch, PO Box 1163, Silver City, 538-2538. A wonderful room/board ranch with a year-round calendar of nature and arts events led by its owners, from wildflower tours to painting expeditions. AYH members $5.25, all 3 meals for $17 additional. Discounts also to seniors, other groups. Otherwise, $38.40 single, $60 double (includes 2 meals, private bath). Also housekeeping cottages $32 up. Owners will meet buses at Deming, Silver City.

La Casita, Rural Route 10, Box 137, Glenwood, 539-2124. 1 mile from Gila Wilderness. 40 miles from Silver City where bus goes. B & B $20 single, $30 double, 4 beds $50. Delicious cooking, dinner available by prior arrangement. On farm near hot springs. Open year-round. Close to ghost towns, wildlife.

OKLAHOMA

Originally set aside as an Indian Territory, in 1893 Oklahoma was thrown open to settlers in one of the most fantastic landgrabs ever. One hundred thousand homesteaders impatiently lined up on its borders, and at the crack of a gun at noon, 16 September, raced across the prairie in buckboard, buggies, wagons and carts, on bicycles, horseback and afoot to lay claim to the 40,000 allotments drawn up by the federal government.

Some crossed the line ahead of time, giving Oklahoma its nickname, the Sooner State. The territory was admitted to the Union in 1907.

Apart from prairies, the state has generous forests and low rolling mountains in the east. Agriculture, oil and the aviation and aerospace industries bring in most of Oklahoma's revenue. Oklahoma City installed the world's first parking meters way back in 1935.

National Park: Platt

OKLAHOMA CITY. Oklahoma City was established in a single day when 10,000 landgrabbers showed up at the only well for miles around in what had till then been scorched prairie-land. The city has become an insurance centre for farming and other enterprises in the area and like other parts of the state got rich on oil. Eighteen oil wells slurp away in the grounds of the Capitol Building.

ACCOMMODATION
Travelodge, 5th and Walker, 5 blocks from Greyhound, 235-7455. Now $26 up single, $32 up double. Some readers feel 'it's worth the money'.

Tivoli Inn, 202 W Sheridan, downtown, 232-1551. Singles $17-$19, doubles $22–$27.

Trend Hotel, 527½ NW 9th, 239-9623. $27 single, $30 double, 25% discount with Visitor Center coupon book (see Info). Comfortable, colour TV.
YMCA, 125 NW 5th St, 232-6101. $10/night, men only. Air conditioning, pool.

FOOD

Steaks and cafeterias, that's what Oklahoma City is famous for. The best and cheapest of the former can be had near the stockyards at Cattlemen's Cafe, 1309 Agnew, which never closes.
Good cafeterias in the State Capitol building, the Furr's chain, and Anna Maude's in the First Life Insurance Building, 119 N Robinson.

OF INTEREST

State Capitol, NW 23rd and Lincoln Blvd. 18 derricks make politics pay; one of them is 'whipstocked' (drilled at an angle) to get at the oil beneath the Capitol, itself an unimpressive structure. N Capitol at 2100 N Lincoln is the **Historical Society**, free displays of Oklahoma history, lots of Indian relics.
Frizzell Coach and Wheel Works, E 10th and I-35. Free tours Mon–Fri 9am–5pm of the only firm which still makes authentic 19th C stagecoaches, a nice bit of Americana.
National Cowboy Hall of Fame and Western Heritage Center, 1700 NE 63rd, 6 miles north of downtown along Route 66, 478-2250. $3, open daily. Sitting right on the Old Chisholm Trail, this complex is a joint venture by the 17 Western states and it's magnificent. The art gallery includes many works by Russell, Remington, Norman Rockwell, Bierstadt. Huge relief map of all the old Pioneer trails is especially good. Indian dancing in summer. Inquire at Travelers Aid about free ticket offer.
Indian City USA, near Anadarko, 65 miles SW of Oklahoma City on Highway 62. Authentic recreation of Plains Indian villages, done with help of U Oklahoma Anthropology Dept. Dancing, demonstrations, ceremonies, camping, swimming. Also Indian Hall of Fame, etc. $4 for village, museums free.

INFORMATION

Tourism Bureau, 4 Santa Fe Plaza, 232-2211. Be sure to get their 'Ride the Good Times' discount coupon book; excellent deals on motels, eats, attractions.
Travelers Aid, 601 NW 5th, 232-5507. Both TA and the Chamber at 1 Santa Fe Plaza, 232-6381, have been praised for the hospitality shown international visitors. 'Volunteers show strangers around town and introduce them to the non-commercial side of America.' Enquire.
Native American Center, 232-2512. Info on summer pow-wows in area.

TRAVEL

Greyhound/Trailways, 427 W Sheridan, 235-6425. Crummy area. Also used by MKO and other bus companies; compare schedules and prices.
Local bus, 235-7433.
Rental Cars: Wrecks for Rent, 670-2102, and Rent a Klunker, 842-2602. For new cars, try Sears Rental Car, 525-5477.

TULSA. Once known as the 'oil capital of the world', Tulsa has slid technologically sideways to 'aerospace capital of . . . Oklahoma'. Its setting among rolling green hills on the Arkansas River is prettier than OKC but it's just as windy. (The whole state is notorious for wild weather.)

Oklahoma generally and Tulsa in particular are in Bible Belt country, and here you'll find Oral Roberts University, founded by the evangelist as a learning centre but looking more like an airport. 'Reminiscent of 1950s science-fiction comics.'

ACCOMMODATION
YMCA, 515 S Denver, 583-6210. Men only, $12 night.

Downtowner Motor Inn, 121 W 4th, 2 blocks from civic centre, 583-6251. Cheerful rooms, $20 up single, $28 up double. Pool, TV.

Hiway House, 5311 W Skelly Drive, 446-4535, 6½ miles SW on Route 66 enroute to OKC. Singles $10 up, doubles $12–$25. Also on Skelly Drive are a Motel 6 and the inexpensive Windsor Motel.

FOOD
American Fare, Williams Center, 2 blocks from Greyhound. 'Amazing shopping centre overlooking ice rink. Cheap breakfasts, better value than Greyhound crap.'

Both Tulsa and OKC have Casa Bonitas, a crazed mixture of Mexican village and dining area with waterfall, mariachis, puppets, dancers, etc. Good value, all-you-can-eat Mexican dinners (see Denver for more comments). Another good local chain is Heritage House, with all-you-can-eat smorgies. Both probably difficult to reach without wheels.

OF INTEREST
Gilcrease Institute, 2500 W Newton, 581-5311. The treasurehouse of Western art, plus 250,000 Indian artefacts, interesting maps and documents like the original instructions for Paul Revere's ride, the first letter written from the North American continent by Chris Columbus' son, Aztec codex, etc. Free: Mon–Sat 9am–5pm, Sun 1pm–5pm.

Sun Oil Company, 17th and Union Ave, 586-7601. Free 1-hr bus tours; Mon–Sat, 10am and 2pm, Sat 10am only.

Tsa-La-Gi Village, 456-6007, 54 miles SE of Tulsa nr Tahlequah. Replica of a 17th C Cherokee village complete with Cherokee-speaking cast of medicine man, braves, kids, villagers. 45 minute tours $2.50, 5 May through Labor Day weekend. Closed Mon. Also Cherokee museum, $1, open year-round Tue–Sun. Outdoor drama *The Trail of Tears* performed June through Aug Mon–Sat 8.30pm in a lovely amphitheatre, telling the story of the tragic march 1838-1839 in which 4000 of 16,000 Cherokees died of hunger, disease and cold. Haunting music, dance. $6–$9 tickets.

INFORMATION
Visitors Center, 616 S Boston, 585–1201.
Travelers Aid, 125 W 3rd St, 592-9231.

TRAVEL
Greyhound, Cincinnati and 4th Sts 582-2111.
Trailways, Cheyenne and 6th Sts, 584-4427.
Local bus, 584-6421.
Car rental: Renta-Wreck, 836-6467.

TEXAS

Texans may have had to pass the Stetson of 'biggest state' to Alaska but they haven't lost their talent for beer-drinking, braggadocio, barbeque and making Dallas-sized mountains of money. This state has the size, colour and raw energy of a Texas longhorn steer, and it'll wear you out if you try to cover it. As the old jingle has it, 'The sun is riz, the sun is set, and we ain't out of Texas yet!' Better to focus on its two cities of any charm—San Antonio and Austin—and perhaps the tropical coast around Galveston or Corpus Christi.

Always intensely political, Texas has seen six regimes come and five go, from Spanish, French and Mexican, to a brief whirl as the Republic of Texas and finally Confederate. Through it all, Texas remains good ole boy country, a terrain of hardbitten little towns and hard-edged cities whose icons are Willie Nelson, the Dallas Cowboys and LBJ.

National Parks: Big Bend
                    Guadelupe Mountains

SAN ANTONIO. About 75 miles south of Austin sits thoroughly Hispanic San Antonio, the only Texas city to possess a proper downtown, much less one with attractions worth walking to. The action centres round the San Antonio River and its pleasant green Riverwalk, where fiestas, music and fun of one sort or another take place year-round.

This city of 800,000 began in 1691 as an Indian village with the wacky name of 'drunken old man going home at night', which the Spaniards bowdlerised to San Antonio. Despite the early Spanish (and later Mexican) presence in Texas, settlement lagged and authorities began admitting Americans. By the 1830s, six of seven inhabitants were Anglo and the resultant friction caused skirmishes and ultimately the Battle of the Alamo. During its 13-day seige, 200 Americans gallantly fought to the last man against the 5000-man Mexican army of Santa Anna. Afterwards, the rallying cry of 'Remember the Alamo' helped Sam Houston and his troops defeat the Mexicans and establish the Republic of Texas, 1836-1845.

ACCOMMODATION

Alpha Hotel, 315 N Main Ave, 223-7644. Now reported to be a dubious bargain at $18 single with shared, $24 with own bath. 'Very spartan, no facilities, disgustingly filthy.'

Manor Hotel, 26 Pecan St, ½ block from Greyhound, 223-8434. $10 single, $12 double for room with toilet, sink. Mixed reports so ask to see room first. 'Free ice, friendly clerk.' 'Appalling.'

Travelers Hotel, 220 Broadway, 226-4381. Downtown. Singles $20 up, doubles $25 up.

Bluebonnet Hotel, 426 N St Mary's St, 222-1221. Across from Greyhound. AC, tours from door. $26 up single, $30 up double.

El Tejas Motel, 2727 Roosevelt Ave, 533-7123. Close to missions, 3 miles from downtown. Bus 42 to door. Single $22–$25, doubles $28–$35, extra person $2. Air conditioning, Pool, TV.

For those with a car: 2 Motel 6s, plus Western 6 at 5522 Panam, 661-9137.

FOOD

NB: San Antonio, with its 52% Latin population, has far better Mexican food than most Mexican border towns.

Along Riverwalk: Big Bend Restaurant, 'good chili, taco and coffee, $3. Comfortable chairs and shade—essential when it's in the 90s.' Kangaroo Court, 'Great choice of beers including Lone Star dark—near as US gets to real ale.'

Mi Tierra, 218 Produce Row in El Mercado. Open 24 hrs, dynamite Tex-Mex food. Order the *chalupa compuesta* and the supercheap *caldo* (soup).

Chili Bowl, 220 Fredrickson Rd. Low-priced tamales with chili, possibly best in town.

Produce Row Oyster Bar, El Mercado. Excellent seafood.

OF INTEREST

The Alamo. Texas' most visited tourist attraction, the restored 1774 presidio-mission is free and open daily 9am–5.30pm, Sun from 10am. Interesting Hollywood touches like the mural inside: heroes Bowie, Crockett and Travis have the faces of John Wayne, Richard Widmark and Lawrence Harvey (stars of *The Alamo* film). Pass up the $2.50 slide show across the way—ear-splitting and redundant. 'In the Alamo itself you get a guided tour, film, etc, just as luridly patriotic as the film opposite.'

Also in Old San Antonio: **San Fernando Cathedral**, Main Plaza, where Alamo heroes are buried. The beautiful **Spanish Governor's Palace**, Military Plaza, is open daily, 50¢, 9am–5pm, Sun 10am–5pm.

La Villita, between S Presa and S Alamo Sts, downtown restoration of the city's early nucleus, with cool patios, banana trees, crafts demos and sales.

Paseo del Rio or **Riverwalk**. The jade green river is echoed by greenery on both sides, cobblestone walks, intimate bridges at intervals, and lined with restaurants and bars with good Happy Hours and late hours. A civic as well as tourist focal point: 'Free lunch, evening concerts in summer.' 'Free dancing along the Riverwalk.' Watch where you stroll, however: 'Stinks in places—with excrement—not dog's!' Small boats ply river from Casa Rio Restaurant, $3 for 25-minute circuit: 'Not worth it.'

Brackenridge Park, 3 miles NE of downtown. Take bus 9. 2 art museums, free Chinese sunken gardens, a skyride, riding stables, and a zoo/aquarium ($2—'worth the money but packed').

Hemisfair Plaza. The free Hall of Texas Culture has displays on 25 ethnic groups; the view from the 700-ft Tower of the Americas is worth $1 fee.

San Antonio has 5 **missions**, counting the Alamo. Unless you're mission-mad, skip the others and sees **Queen Mission San Jose** (take the hourly S Flores bus marked 'San Jose Mission'). Interesting granary, Indian building, barracks. Try to time your visit for Sun mass when the mariachis play. Costs $1 per mission, combo for 4, $2.

Lone Star Brewery, 600 Lone Star Blvd, does tours hourly, accompanied by beer and rootbeer. For $1.25, you gain admission to the museum: enormous collection of horns, animal heads and copies of *Rolling Stone* (O Henry's tabloid, not Jann Wenner's).

Circus Museum, 210 W Market in library annex, 299-7810. Free, 20,000 items, including Tom Thumb's carriage, miniature circus and other Barnum and Baileyana.

INFORMATION

Information centers at St Mary's N near Greyhound, 227-2020, and across from the Alamo, 226-2345. Both 'very helpful'.

Travelers Aid, 226-7181.

ENTERTAINMENT

Mexican Festival, 3rd week in Sept, Riverwalk. 'Entertainment was electric.'

Arneson Theater, 299-8610. Showcases everything from flamenco to jazz to country; river separates you from stage. Fiesta Noche del Rio variety show is $4, June–July evenings.

Numerous fiestas, music events and blowouts (most free) throughout the year; during St Patrick's week, San Antonians dye both their beer and their river green!

TRAVEL
Greyhound, 500 N St Mary's, 227-8351.
Trailways, 301 Broadway, 226-6136.
El Centro bus circles downtown frequently for 10¢; other buses, 60¢.
AMTRAK, 1174 E Commerce St for the *Sunset Limited*, LA-New Orleans; and W Commerce St at MP Railroad for *Inter-American*, Laredo-Chicago.
Airport bus, 227-2029. 'Express 10 runs every 40 minutes, last one 8.20pm costs 75¢.'
Rental cars: used cheapos from Rent-a-Dent, 734-9431.

AUSTIN. Capital city but decidedly unstuffy, Austin (named for 'the Father of Texas') is in the running with San Antonio for most enjoyable city in the state: 'a cultural oasis in a "biggest and best" desert—colleges, lots of young people, non-stop flow of music'. Sights here are secondary; Austin is a place to eat well, drink deep and party hard.

ACCOMMODATION
Alamo Hotel, 400 W 6th at Colorado, 476-4381. $21 up for single with shared bath, $24 up for double with private bath. Good bar downstairs.
The Castilian, 2323 San Antonio St, 478-9811. $19 single, $23 double with kitchenette, 1 June–10 Aug only. Private residence hall, coed, overlooking University. Cafe, AC, pool; very nice. Bus stop ½ block.
Congress St is cheap hotel/motel row: closest to bus depot is the Imperial 400 at 901 S Congress, 444-3651 ($23–$30). Also try San Jose Motel, 1416 S Congress, 444-7322 ($17 up doubles) and the Ace Motel, 2601 S Congress, 442-1329 (singles/doubles $22).
With a car: 2 Motel 6s and a Western 6, all on Int'l Hwy 35, which runs north-south through the city.

FOOD
Great pickings, but you'd better like Texas Barbeque, Mexican food and Texas chili. Lots of student hangouts along Guadalupe, including: Flapjack Canyon, 'Excellent full meals under $6' and Taste Alternative, 'Health foods'.
Texas Chili Parlor, 1409 Lavaca St. World class chili joint and saloon, free music.
The Filling Station, 801 Briton Springs Rd, 477-1022. 'Menu printed on oil cans, beer from gas pump. Get ethyl-burgers or a gasket basket! A must.'
Texas BBQ: Rudy Mikeska's, 300 W 2nd downtown; Reese's, 2728 S Congress; The Pit, 2403 S Congress; and Loyd's at 5423 Cameron Rd.
Austin's a prime Happy Hour town: try Beans, 311 W 6th (superb food too); the 3 Chelsea St Pubs; and El Arroyo on 1624 W 5th (picturesque Mexican patio).

OF INTEREST
Capitol building. Free tours, unrestricted entry to public areas, including galleries from which you can observe debates.
O Henry Home, 409 E 5th St. Free. Tue–Sat 11am–4.30pm, Sun 2pm–4.30pm. Personal effects of the popular short-story writer, who lived here 1884-1895.
U of Texas, Guadalupe and 24th St, north of Capitol. Huge, rich, its 27-storey tower the site of the deranged Charles Whitman 'sniper massacres' in 1974. Highly social school. Has several museums and the LBJ Library at 2300 Red River Rd, free, daily 9am–5pm. A/V displays, replica of the Oval Office and tapes of LBJ's twang.
LBJ's birthplace, home, ranch and grave are west of Austin, in and around **Johnson City**.
Daughters of the Confederacy/Republic of Texas Museums, E 11th nr Capitol. Free. 'House in mock German castle used as a setting in an O Henry story; indispensable museum to anyone interested in Texas or Civil War history.'

ENTERTAINMENT
Austin is the centre of the progressive country and western scene; check *The Daily Texan* and the free monthly, *Austin Arts and Leisure*, to see who's playing where. The Austin Opry House, owned by Willie Nelson, gets the top country acts; also check the Lock, Stock and Barrel on Anderson Lane for live groups nightly, great Happy Hours.

Soap Creek Saloon, 11306 N Lamar, is a low-down dive with great music. Cover charge.

Club Foot, 4th St and Brazos. '*The* place to go—great live music nightly. About $2 cover except when big bands play. Austin is the most fun place in the South for young people.'

Guadalupe Ave, called The Drag, is hot spot for student—and non-student—action.

Barton Springs, Zilker Park. Open-air swimming hole (not a chlorined pool) fed by underground springs. 'Reached by lovely 40-minute riverside walk, beautiful setting'. $1.25, 'but if you smile and ask for the loan of a swimsuit you might get in free'.

INFORMATION
Chamber of Commerce, 901 W Riverside Dr, 478-9383.
Tourist information centre, open daily in State Capitol Building, 475-3070.

TRAVEL
Greyhound, 401 Congress, 476-7451 or 472-5423.
Trailways, 1001 Congress, 478-4655.
Local bus, 385-6860.
AMTRAK, 250 N Lamar.

DALLAS/FORT WORTH. Big D pushes culture but its finest achievements are Neiman-Marcus, the glittering emporium of the conspicuous consumer, and Tolbert's Chili Parlor, where the serious chiliheads go to eat a bowl of red before they die. Like its premier families, the Hunts and the Ewings, what **Dallas** does best is make money. The city itself is enormous, vacuously modern and dull: 'Great if you like parking lots'.

An airport larger than Manhattan is the umbilical cord linking Dallas with **Fort Worth**, its cattle- and agriculture-based sister city, which, surprisingly enough, has a lot more going for it. Fort Worth's wealthy have underwritten a number of top-notch museums and art collections, most free and conveniently clumped in Amon Carter Square. As befits an overgrown cowtown, the honky-tonk country and western scene is alive, well and more cowboy than urban. Forty miles and a heap of freeways separate these two behemoths, so don't plan to lodge in one and visit the other.

ACCOMMODATION
Huge caveat: the downtown situation for cheap lodgings in both cities has got worse and is essentially zilch. Suggest you book the Ys in Ft Worth, rent a car to get to one of the 8 Motel 6s ringing both cities, or make your stay extremely brief.

In Dallas:
Plaza Hotel, 1933 Main St, 742-7251. Single $30 up, doubles $44 up; discounts for

seniors, students. AC, cafe, TV, reminiscent of European hotels. 'Comfortable.' Bus stop on corner. Brass Derrick restaurant on corner is quite cheap.

Salvation Army, free flop, 5 blocks from YMCA in 600 block of Ervay, which no longer has beds but has info on Salvation Army.

Sands Motel, 3722 N Buckner Blvd, 328-4121. $20 single, $24–$30 doubles.

In Ft Worth:

YMCA, 512 Lamar St, 332-3281. Men only, $12 single, key deposit, cheap weekly rates.

YWCA, 512 W 4th St, 332-6191. Women only, $10 single, key deposit, 10 blocks from bus station.

Rancher's Inn, 2530 W Freeway, 335-5515. 1 mile west of downtown. Single $16 up, doubles $22 up.

FOOD/OF INTEREST

In Dallas:

Tolbert's Chili Parlor and Museum of Chili, 802 Main St, Open Mon–Sat. Go on Sat to hear live band. Primo chili shrine, not particularly cheap but recommended if the Texas chili culture interests you.

Chiquitas, 3810 Congress St. Mexican food, popular with Dallasites. 'Delicious, excellent service, not costly.'

Kennedyana: John F Kennedy's **route** that fateful 22 Nov 1963 went along Commerce to Houston and Elm, where he was shot from the **Texas Schoolbook Depository**, 4th floor, 2nd window (2 blocks from Greyhound, easily reached during a rest stop). Overlooking the scene is an **obelisk**; a memorial **Cenotaph** is at 1 Main Place. A $2 **museum** at Elm and Record shows 25 minutes of film on the assassination, funeral, Oswald's murder by Jack Ruby: 'Not worth it.' JFK spent his last night on this planet in the **Ft Worth Hyatt Regency**.

Architecture: both the **Hyatt Regency** and **Reunion Tower** at 300 Reunion Blvd get high marks: 'Best thing in Dallas,' 'Especially beautiful at sunset.' The **Adolphus Hotel**, Commerce and Akard, was built by a brewer and has a 40-ft beer bottle on top. At White Rock Lake ('large rec areas with boats, bikes for hire') is the **Hunt family home**, a copy of Mt Vernon only 5 times larger, in which Hunt installed a pay phone for visitors (that's how the rich get richer).

Neiman-Marcus Dept Store, Main and Ervay. Of it, Lucius Beebe said: 'Dallas, for all its oil, banks, insurance wouldn't exist without Neiman-Marcus. It would be Waco or Wichita, which is to say: nothing.'

South Fork Ranch from *Dallas* TV series, well east of Dallas. Mon–Fri, 9am–5pm, $5 for close look. 'Looks better on TV.' 'Just as seen on TV.'

Six Flags Over Texas, 20 miles west in Arlington, 461-1234. $13 fee includes all rides, shows. Open daily mid-May to 1 Sept; weekends thereafter. If this 100-ride amusement park can't make you lose your cookies, you're ready for astronaut school. New and nauseating is the 'Texas Cliffhanger', a 10-second free-fall from a 128-ft tower. Also 5 hours of air-conditioned shows. Get there on Greyhound bound for Ft Worth, bus pass valid.

In Ft Worth:

Ft Worth Stockyards area, along Exchange Ave and N Main St, on North side. Pungent and still active with Mon–Thur cattle auctions (free viewing). 'Original stalls and railway exist, storefronts and boardwalks renovated. Gives a feeling of the past.' Nearby is **Billy Bob's Texas**, 626-1906, a gigantic honky-tonk with 42 bars, a real indoor rodeo ring and 14,000 sq ft of dance floor: John Travolta, eat yer heart out.

Water Gardens, downtown by Convention Center. 'Beautiful fountains you can climb, where *Logan's Run* and *The Lathe of Heaven* were filmed.'

Amon Carter Square: 3 free museums, the **Western Art Collection**, with masses of

Russells and Remingtons; the **Kimbell Art Museum**, itself an architectural *tour de force* by Louis Kahn, housing Oriental, pre-Columbian and late Renaissance works; and the **Modern Art Museum**, with everything from O'Keefes to Warhols. **Museum of Science and Industry** costs 50¢, has sophisticated talking exhibits.

INFORMATION
Visitors Bureau, 1507 Pacific Ave, Dallas, 651-1020.
Visitors Bureau, 700 Throckmorton, Ft Worth, 336-8791.

TRAVEL
Greyhound, Commerce at Lamar, Dallas, 741–1481.
Trailways, 1500 Jackson at Ervay, Dallas, 655-7000.
AMTRAK, Union Station, 400 S Houston, Dallas, 653-1101. 'Very helpful tourist info in terminal adjacent to Reunion Tower. The bars upstairs in terminal also worth a visit—cheap and wonderful architecture.'
Local bus, Dallas, 826-2222, 25¢ in downtown.
Local bus, Ft Worth, has free service round downtown.
Airport buses, 574-2142, will cost you dearly from either city: about $7 one way.
AAACON Transport, 912 Commerce, Dallas.

HOUSTON.
The newer skyscrapers that crowd Houston's skyline have sleek skins of black sun-reflecting glass, the same material used for astronaut helmet visors. Seems appropriate, since this city of 1.6 million is inextricably linked with NASA and the first moon landing.

But space money is petty cash compared to Houston's real wealth, which comes from oil refineries and its port activities. Unless you have an air-conditioned car, ample time and money, skip humid and expensive Houston: 'This vast exploding city confused me and seemed to confuse everyone else too.' 'Freeways jammed day and night; apart from downtown area, it's scrubby and dusty.'

ACCOMMODATION
Montagu Hotel, 804 Fannin St, 237-1504. Singles $19 up, doubles $24 up, including key deposit. 'Clean.'
Texas State Hotel, 720 Fannin at Rusk, 227-2271. Single $15, double $20, more for private bath. Transport to/from airport. 5 blocks from Greyhound.
Dorm Hotel, 2019 Franklin St, 228-8132. Men only, dorm for $6 night with clean linen, shower.
Houston East End Hostel, 5530½ Hillman, Apt 2, 926-3444. Texas' only hostel! $5.25 members, storage rental, bike rental. Laundry facilities. Take bus 82 from downtown bus terminal (4 miles away). Call first.

FOOD
Lots of good places, most totally inaccessible without a car.
Downtown: Glatzmaier's Seafood Market, on Travis south of Old Market Square. Incredible, messy feasts of gumbo, crab, crawfish. Order a 'New Orleans poor-boy'—massive bun stuffed with Gulf oysters and shrimp. Nearby is Huber's, same menu, also low prices, newspapers for tablecloth.
Around the Galleria Mall (a flossy 3-level affair with ice rink, miles west of downtown on Westheimer), try Helmet's for 'gorgeous strudel', Farrell's for 'great party atmosphere'.

OF INTEREST
NASA-LBJ Space Center, 483-4321. 24 miles SE via I-45. No public transit, 3-hr Gray Line tour costs $12 with bus pass discount: 'Cheaper to Rent-a-Heap-Cheap

and take your time.' Also, hitching is 'worst I've ever come across—took us 2 hrs to get a lift'. Center open daily 9am–5pm (no admittance after 4pm), free. Once there, wander about on your own to see spacecraft, Skylab trainer, moon rocks, vacuum chamber, NASA films. Or take guided tour: 'No need to book Mission Control tours—just register at info desk.' Sat–Sun, tours on first-come, first-served basis; other days, they advise booking. 'A total waste of time—Mission Control was a lot of torn-out consoles.' 'Very informative.'

Astrodome, 799-9544, south of downtown. Largest indoor stadium in the world, modestly called 'Taj Mahal', 'Eighth Wonder', etc, in its literature. Tours $2.50, 5 times daily, obligatory when no event. More worthwhile to combine a visit with a Houston Astros baseball game or other happening (from dog shows to dirt-bike races). Cheapest seats in the Pavilion but also: 'We recommend $3 Gold Level seats behind home base.' Take S Main 8600 bus from Main St.

Astroworld, opposite A-Dome. Six Flags clone with 100 rides, $12, open April––Nov, varying hours.

Port of Houston. Now a deep channel runs 50 miles south to the Gulf of Mexico, making Houston a major port. From the observation platform at Wharf 9 you can watch huge ships in the Turning Basin. 1½-hr boat trips, 225-0671, available Tue–Sun except Sept, a free look at the bayou and a stunning perspective of the skyline. Book well ahead in summer.

Museum of Fine Arts, S Main and Montrose Blvd, 526-1361. Exhibition wing designed by Mies Van der Rohe. Renaissance art plus renowned Hogg collection of 65 paintings, watercolours by Frederick Remington. Free. Open Tue–Sat, 10am–5pm. Sun noon–6pm.

Hermann Park. Free zoo, planetarium and Museums of Natural and Medical Science. **Zoo's** strong suit is a macabre vampire bat colony. You're allowed to see them quaff their daily blood at 2.30pm—fascinating, repellent. **Natural Science Museum** has moon landing equipment.

Sam Houston Park, downtown at Allen Parkway and Bagby St. Nice melange of historic Greek Revival, Victorian, log cabin and cottage against a canyon of office buildings. Daily tours $2. Not far away is **Tranquility Park** at Bagby and Walker, named in honour of lunar landings. 'Truly an oasis in the desert.'

ENTERTAINMENT

Miller Outdoor Theatre, Hermann Park, 641-4111. Free symphony, ballet, plays, drama and musicals in summer. 'Get there 30 minutes early for good position.'

Astrodome (see Of Interest) also features rock shows. Huge video screens afford a good view. 'During intermission girls often do impromptu strips (really!) when the video camera points at them.' Feb sees the Rodeo and Livestock Show, (naturally) the world's largest.

Gilley's, 4500 Spencer Highway, Pasadena, 30 miles from Houston. $5 cover minimum, a place to be shined on: 'Not much fun unless you're a beer-swilling macho cowboy or you're into beer-swilling macho cowboys. Full of tourists with kids.'

INFORMATION

Visitors Council, 1522 Main St, 658-4200.
Travelers Aid, 5501 Austin, 522-3846.

TRAVEL

Greyhound, 1410 Texas St, 222-1161.
Trailways, 2121 Main St, 759-6560.
AMTRAK, 902 Washington Ave, 224-1577. The *Inter-American* to Chicago and the *Sunset Limited* between New Orleans and LA call here.
Local buses, 651-1212. 40–60¢. 'No service after 9.30pm.'
Gray Line, 757-1252. Various tours: 'NASA tour limited—not worth the money.'

Houston has 2 airports: International is 25 miles away, costs $6 via Trailways shuttle. 'Houston is a good base to get to Mexico City.'

GALVESTON. History rich, hurricane prone Galveston was once headquarters for pirate Jean LaFitte, who liked its location on Galveston Island 50 miles south of Houston and—who knows?—its 32 miles of sandy beaches (so handy for bullion burying). Houston's Ship Channel eventually siphoned off the big shipping business, leaving Galveston at its architectural peak: a resplendent little city of scarlet oleanders, nodding palms and fine 19th century mansions. Come here to gorge on bay shrimp, dabble in the warm Gulf of Mexico and imbibe the placid, slightly decayed, Southern feeling of the place. Camping on the beach and at the State Park. Access via causeway, also by free ferry from Port Bolivar to the east.

FOOD/OF INTEREST
Tuffy's, South Jetty. 'Best seafood in a seafood area.'
Hillman's Seafood Cafe, Rt 146 just south of Rt 517. Amid a grand setting of mesquite trees, boats, windmills, eat low-cost filé gumbo and bay shrimp.
Some of the **architecture** worth seeing: **Ashton Villa**, 24th and Broadway, $3, an elegantly restored 1859 Italianate mansion. Tour includes slide show about the 1900 hurricane that claimed 5000–7000 lives. **The Bishop's Palace**, 14th and Broadway, extravagant 1886 home ranked among top 100 in US for its interest, $2. **The Strand** contains a fine concentration of 19th C ironfront buildings.
Sea-Arama, Seawall Blvd at 91st St, 744-4501. $8 gets you dolphins, exotic fish, snakes, birds, divers cavorting with 20 sharks. Open daily 10am.

INFORMATION/TRAVEL
Information Center, 2160 Seawall Blvd, 763-4311.
Greyhound, Moody and Ball Sts, 765-7731. About 6 buses daily from Houston, bus pass valid.
'Rollerskate, bike rental shops on Seawall Blvd. Useful shower/changing facility on Stewart Beach. $2 all day use, has lockers.'

CORPUS CHRISTI and THE SOUTH TEXAS COAST. A large port city with a leaping population, **Corpus Christi** makes a good gateway to **Padre Island**, a long lean strip of largely unspoilt National Seashore that points toward the Texas toe. Once inhabited by cannibals, the shifting blond sands of Padre have seen five centuries of piracy and shipwrecks and no doubt conceal untold wealth. The natural wonders of the 110-mile-long island are quite sufficient for most people, however: it's a prime area for bird watching, shelling and beachcombing for glass floats. You can camp free at a number of idyllic and primitive spots. All are at the South Padre end, reached only via Highway 358. Camp on the seaward side of the dunes; the grassy areas may have rattlers.

Besides Galveston and Padre, the South Texas coast has hundreds of miles of coastline and various other islands. Not all are scenic, but you might enjoy the undeveloped camping at **Brazos Island**.

North and east of Padre Island and Corpus Christi is the **Aransas Wildlife Refuge** where you can go by boat from Rockport and see (in season and at a distance) the world's remaining 73 whooping cranes. In **Rockport**, get down to marvellous seafood and gumbo eating at Charlotte Plummer's. Corpus Christi, South Padre and the entire area are rich in roadside stands that sell cheap, fresh boiled shrimp and tamales, the local speciality.

South Texas border towns with Mexico are numerous but not particularly appealing. Avoid **Laredo**: "A dump with ripoff hotels." **Brownsville/Matamoros** is probably the best and certainly most convenient to South Padre. 'Got free tourist card from Mexican consulate at 10th and Washington Streets in 5 minutes.'

INFORMATION/TRAVEL/OF INTEREST
Tourist Bureau, 613 S Shoreline Blvd, Corpus Christi, 882-5603.
South Padre Tourist Bureau, 943-6434.
Greyhound serves Corpus Christi and Laredo from San Antonio.
Trailways serves Houston-Corpus-Brownsville and also up to San Antonio and over to Laredo.
Confederate Air Force Museum, Harlingen, just north of Brownsville. $3, open Mon–Sat 9am–5pm, Sun noon–5pm. Impressive array of WWII combat aircraft. 'Very good—also includes 20-minute film plus displays, uniforms, etc.'

EL PASO. Biggest Mexican border city, El Paso feels neither Latin nor Texan. Backed by mountains, El Paso's main focus is the Rio Grande River, where early Spanish expeditions used to cross. The river also serves as the border and a casual, non-bureaucratic one it is. Other than sampling the sleazy delights of Ciudad Juarez, there's little reason to tarry in El Paso. It can serve a a base for Carlsbad Caverns (in New Mexico) and **Big Bend** and **Guadalupe Mountains National Parks**. The latter, 110 miles east, includes El Capitan, a 1000-foot cliff, and 8751-foot Guadalupe Peak, highest in Texas. 'Unless your journey necessitates going via El Paso, take another route.'

ACCOMMODATION
McCoy Hotel, 123 Pioneer Plaza, 533-1681. Singles $10–$15, doubles $12–$19. Air conditioning, storage, laundry, TV. 1 block to bus depot. Senior discounts, also 10% off to any foreign visitor with visa. 'A good night's sleep.' 'Very friendly.' 'Dirty.'
Gardner Hotel, 311 E Franklin Ave, 532-3661. $11–$16 singles, $15–$20 doubles. AC, storage. 5 blocks to Greyhound/Trailways. 'Old, Shabby but quiet and clean.'
YMCA, 701 Montana Ave, 533-3941. Coed, $14 single, $18 twin, pool, restaurant. 'Good—clean.'
YMCA, 315 E Franklin St, 532-4957. $12 single, $18 doublel Close to bus station, games room. 'Friendly and clean.'
Camping: free at Lake Meredith Recreational Area, 5 miles from city. Some sites with shade ramadas. Store, food, flush toilets, water.

FOOD
Tony's Mexican cafe, 706 N Piedras, always open. Cheap. Sample their cabrito (roast kid).
Tigua Reservation Cafeteria, Almeda Ave, 859-3916. Daily till 6pm summer, 5pm

winter. Besides its crafts and rather small and restored mission, the reservation has a good eating place with excellent red and green chili, other traditional dishes. Worth a stop, if only for the food. 'Reservation costs $1 to get in, $1.50 for dancing, very small and perhaps not worth it.'

OF INTEREST
General consensus is to skip the **Aerial Tramway**, $2. 'View is sweeping but totally uninspiring.' 'Very difficult and steep climb without a car, buses infrequent.'
Ciudad Juarez. Simply stroll across the bridge, 5¢ toll each way. 'Mexican immigration didn't even give us a glance.' You can also ride the bus over but why bother. If you do, hold on to your passport and don't surrender your DSP 66 to the US authorities. CJ is a junky, souvenir-oriented city, either ridden with whores or totally lacking in this important commodity, depending on whom you talk to.
Deeper into Mexico: Mexican buses leave El Paso Greyhound depot on the hour; Mexican customs and through-tickets to Chihuahua and Mexico City are dealt with there also. El Paso-Chihuahua, about $9 US.

INFORMATION
Visitors Center, 5 Civic Center Plaza, 544-3650 and 541-4911. Helpful staff with good lodgings listings.
Mexican Consulate, 601 N Mesa, Continental Bank, Suite D.

TRAVEL
Greyhound, 111 San Francisco St, 542-1355. To Carlsbad Caverns, the Greyhound surcharge is $6 for bus pass holders, otherwise $30. If you go to White City and hitch the 7 miles to the caverns, no surcharge. 'Journey to Carlsbad past El Capitan peak is marvellous desert scenery.'
Trailways, 200 San Antonio St, 533-5921.
Local Bus, 533-3333.
AMTRAK, 700 San Francisco St. Served by the LA-New Orleans *Sunset Limited*.
Rental cars: Rent-a-relic, 592-2500.

THE SOUTH

Included in this section are all the states of the Confederacy except Texas, though with Kentucky, a slave state that remained loyal to the Union, added. The Civil War crippled the South and the region is still wrestling with its history. Life is slower here, progress has been more painful, and conservatism and worse more evident.

However, the situation is changing and a 'New South' is fast emerging. Experts pinpoint the Southlands as the new boom area of the United States, the area that has everything America is going to need in the future: plenty of food, plenty of oil, coal and natural gas, a warm climate and a tremendous concentration of governmental and military installations. Although Southerners still do not earn as much as other Americans, it is interesting to note that it is now the number one area in retail sales, and more and more major companies are moving away from the Northeast and Midwest and into the Southern states where labour is cheaper.

Even at her greatest moments, Dixie was as much the victim as the beneficiary of the plantation system. Though the gentry lived at a level of elegance often wistfully recalled today, and contributed significantly to the leadership, politically and culturally, of America, they did so at the cost of the blacks they enslaved, the small farmers whose initiative they thwarted, and a narrow-based agricultural economy whose profits were invested in crinolines rather than steam engines.

The South is a complex blend of old and new. Much of the renowned Southern charm and hospitality remain, but you will also find progressive cities like Atlanta, and brand new chunks of twentieth century real estate as in Florida. The countryside is varied and frequently immensely attractive and the climate usually kind, although it can be overpoweringly hot and humid in summer.

ALABAMA

This is the old, traditional Deep South, best known to the world for ultra-conservative politician George Wallace and the civil rights struggles in places like Birmingham and Selma. But the times they are a'changing. Racial integration advances and cotton is no longer king. Steel (Birmingham) and rockets (Huntsville) are now major industries, closely followed by tourism, thanks to the Gulf coast and the Tennessee Valley lake country in the northern part of the state.

Summers are hot and humid and winters are generally mild with only the occasional really cold day.

MOBILE. The old quarter of this busy Gulf port preserves a blend of Spanish, French, and ante-bellum architecture, most beautiful in March when the azaleas bloom. Those who have been through Mardi Gras here say it's second only to the celebration in New Orleans, 150 miles west. Fort Conde was the name the French gave to Mobile in 1711. For eight years thereafter, this was the capital of the French colonial empire.

The area is not as attractive as it once was. Hurricane Frederick caused great destruction a few years ago and many charming old buildings were lost, replaced by typical strip rubbish. Also, if the wind is not in the right direction you will have to endure the smell of the paper mills which wafts over downtown.

ACCOMMODATION
Since the hurricane, there's a dearth of really cheap downtown accommodation.
Days Inn, I-65 and US 90, 3651 Government Blvd, 666-7750. Southwest of city centre. $27 single, $32 double.
Best Western Admiral Semmes Motor Hotel, 250 Government St, 432-4441. Singles from $32, doubles from $38. In downtown historic area. AC, TV, in-room movies, pool.

FOOD
Wintzell's Oyster House, 605 Dauphin St. Dinner $5 up. 'Very popular place.'
Western Sizzlin' Restaurant, Government St. 'Interesting and cheap; great variety on offer.'

OF INTEREST
Nice to wander around the old squares and streets, dating back to the 1700s when the French held sway in Mobile. **Bienville Sq, De Tonti Sq,** and **Church Street East Historic District** are the best preserved parts. Among the houses open to the public are **Fort Conde Charlotte House,** and **Oakleigh,** an ante-bellum mansion furnished by the Historic Society.
USS Alabama, a World War II battleship, moored on the Tensas River at Battleship

Parkway. The battleship is now a state shrine. Can be explored 'from bow to stern'.
Cost $2. Accessible with the Ameripass from downtown Mobile.
Mardi Gras is late Feb, early March.
Dauphin Island, directly south of Mobile is a quiet place where you can camp, swim
and wander.

INFORMATION
Convention Dept, Mobile Chamber of Commerce, 108 S Claiborne St, 433-6951.
Travelers Aid, 450 Government St, 432-6566.

BIRMINGHAM. The steel town of the South, Birmingham has the
largest furnaces south of Pittsburgh and a night sky that glows with the
flames. The great civil rights marches of 1963 that culminated with the
March on Washington were set off here. Birmingham elected its first
black mayor in 1979.

The heat and industrial pollution in summer make Birmingham
unpleasant for any length of time; it's best to be here in late April,
early May, when the roses and dogwoods are in bloom. The city
stretches for 15 miles along the Jones Valley, and the best views are
from atop Shades and Red Mountains.

ACCOMMODATION
Cabana Hotel, 1631 2nd Ave N at 17th St, 252-7141. Downtown. AC, TV, radio,
bath. Singles $24, doubles $28.
Econo Lodge, 2224 5th Ave, 324-6688, nr downtown. Colour TV, pool. Singles $28,
doubles $32.

OF INTEREST
'The birthplace of Birmingham', **Arlington**, an ante-bellum home, is at 331 Cotton
Ave SW. Civil War relics. $2. 'Something out of old Dixie.'
The world's largest iron statue, **Vulcan**, all 53 feet of him, plus a 127-ft pedestal,
dominates nearby Red Mountain. Cast from Birmingham iron, the massive head
alone weighs 6 tons. Vulcan carries a green torch in his hand and after a traffic
fatality in the area the flame changes to red. Elevator to the top, daily
8.30am–10pm, 50¢.

INFORMATION
Convention and Visitors Bureaux, 1909 Seventh Ave N, 252-9825, and in Suite 940,
First Alabama Bank on 20th St. 'Both are very friendly and try to make you think
there's a lot to do in Birmingham.'
Travelers Aid, 360 8th Ave S, 322-5426.

MONTGOMERY. Now only the capital of Alabama, Montgomery
was the capital of the entire Confederacy until the honour was transferred to Richmond. The Senate Chamber is kept just as it was the day
secession was voted, and the tree-shaded streets lined with ante-bellum homes help carry you back a hundred and more years. But the
plantations are gone, and Montgomery county has now gone over to
cattle ranching. Cows ain't so uppity, y'understand.

Forty-five miles west is **Selma**. Early in March 1965, using whips
and tear gas, George Wallace's state troopers attacked a civil righs
march here, forcing President Johnson to give Federal protection to

Martin Luther King's march later in the month from Selma to Montgomery. Even so the Ku Klux Klan managed to murder two of the marchers enroute. One marcher who survived was Andrew Young, America's ex-ambassador to the UN.

ACCOMMODATION
Tourway Inn, 205 N Goldthwaite St, 265-0541. Nr Civic Center, in historic district. AC, cable TV, pool. Singles from $30, doubles from $40.

FOOD
Morrisons', 150 Lee St, near bus terminal. 'About $3 for a filling meal. The classiest cheap meal I had in the US.'

OF INTEREST
State Capitol. A gold star marks the spot where Jefferson Davis was inaugurated as president of the Confederacy in February 1861. Note also the impressive murals depicting state history and the graceful hanging spiral staircases.
First White House of the Confederacy, across the street from the Capitol. Contains memorabilia of Jefferson Davis and family. Mon–Fri 8am–11.30am and 12.30pm–5pm, weekends 8am–5pm. Free.
St John's Episcopal Church, where Jefferson Davis worshipped on a Sunday.
W A Gayle Space Transit Planetarium. Simulated space journeys. Tue, Thur 3.45pm, Sat and Sun 2pm and 3.30pm, $1.50.
East of Montgomery is the noted **Tuskegee Institute**, a co-ed university founded in 1881 by former slave Booker T Washington. One of the Institute's alumni was George Washington Carver, who became famous for his research on peanuts.

INFORMATION
Visitor Information Center, 220 N Hull St, 265-1731.

HUNTSVILLE. Hominy grits and one-horse carriages give way to apfelstrudel and rocket research in this one-time sleepy town that was turned over to the late Wernher von Braun and the Penemunde crowd.

Visiting the hush-hush Redstone Arsenal ist verboten, aber der Space Orientation Center at Marshall does a nice PR job with displays of rockets, satellites, engines and control mechanisms. Films, too, but not *The Blue Angel* (open daily 9am–5pm, $5).

Huntsville is in northern Alabama, about halfway between Birmingham and Nashville, Tennessee.

ARKANSAS

The Land of Opportunity, as Arkansas calls itself, was admitted to the Union as a slave state in 1836. Its long hot summers and in the east in particular its rich alluvial soil well suited the cultivation of tobacco, corn and cotton, and this became plantation country.

But western Arkansas, with its hills and forests, and the colourful Ozark Mountains to the north, smacked more of the frontier, and settler opinion caused the state to hesitate before seceding from the Union. The Ozark and Ouachitas areas retain a strong folksy flavour with a distinct mountain culture which has left its mark on national folk art, legend and music.

National Park: Hot Springs

LITTLE ROCK. This one-time hunter and trapper outpost is now the State capital, and known to its residents as 'City of Roses'. It was back in 1957 that Little Rock came to the world's attention with the attempt to ban nine black children from the segregated Central High School. There's nothing much to see by visiting the school now, nor by visiting Little Rock for that matter.

Hot Springs National Park is only an hour's drive away. This is an area of spas and thermal baths, and it's a good place for water sports, hiking and camping.

ACCOMMODATION

Sam Peck Hotel, Capitol Ave at Gaines, 376-1304. Downtown. 'Phone from bus or train station and they'll pick you up.' Singles from $30, doubles from $35. Air conditioning, TV, pool.

OF INTEREST

The only city to have three capitol buildings. The hand-hewn oak log territorial capitol is in the Arkansas Territorial Capitol Restoration; the capitol used from 1836 to 1912 is an attractive Greek revival style building and then there is the building currently in use on W Capitol Ave.

The Territorial Capitol Restoration, E 3rd and Cumberland Sts. A collection of 13 restored buildings from the Little Rock of the 1820s. 9am–5pm. $1.

THE OZARKS. Although not especially high as mountains go, the Ozarks offer attractive wooded hills, rocky cliffs, gushing springs and rivers. It's a good area for white water canoeing, fishing, hiking, cycling and camping, or just getting away from it all for a few days. The **Ozark National Forest** is bounded on the east by the White River and to the west by the Buffalo National River, and includes **Blanchard Springs Cavern**, **Cove Lake** and **Mount Magazine**, the highest point in the state.

Summers are very hot and you will need mosquito repellant. Best months to visit are August and September when it's cooler, driest and bugless.

The small university town of **Fayetteville** is a good centre for visiting the area. Also worth a stop is the Victorian spa town of **Eureka Springs** in the northwest corner of Arkansas; it looks like a village in the Bavarian Alps and indeed has its own version of an Oberammergau passion play every summer. From Eureka Springs you can also visit the **Pea Ridge National Military Park**, the site of the 1862 battle which saved Missouri for the Union.

FLORIDA

Although Florida was one of the hard-core Confederate states, this followed from her plantation system along the panhandle, the southern part of the state having been that much wilderness. The Florida of today dwells little on Dixie, but gets its impetus from tourists who have been piling in since the Miami land boom of the 1920s, though more spectacularly since the Second World War—and now from across the Atlantic, as Florida competes with Spain for northern Europe's summer holiday-makers.

Now as then the Sunshine State is booming and both industry and agriculture thrive. But all is not fun in the sun, and these days there's a distinct touch of paradise lost around southern Florida, where the crime rate is soaring and the drug trade is fast becoming the leading industry. Spanish is as common as English in Dade County where about 40 percent of the population is now Hispanic, mainly refugees from Cuba and Haiti. Add to this the fact that most Floridians did not grow up in the state and have no developed sense of community and you have some real problems.

For the visitor the drawbacks are the sky-high winter prices, the threat of summer hurricanes, the year-round omnipresent bugs and some of the crassest commercialism to be found anywhere. Yet a visit is still recommended: bad as well as good, Florida is just so different from the usual North American landscape. Consider the tropical sunsets, the primeval Everglades, the palms, mangroves and other tropical vegetation, the miles of sand beaches all washed by warm seas, the citrus groves, Disneyworld, even the gaudy resorts. It all has to be seen to be believed.

Note: all hotel prices are for the summer/autumn season. Winter/spring rates are generally double. Shop around for cheap car rental deals, particularly off season, and also good air fares to and from the Northern states.

National Park: Everglades

MIAMI. You'll hear Spanish spoken all the time in Miami, on the street, and on radio and television, for this is the area which bore the brunt of the recent refugee exodus from Cuba and Haiti, adding considerably to the already sizeable Hispanic population of this sprawling, depressing city.

Given the rising murder rate and the racial tensions which exist in Miami now, not just between Hispanic and Anglo, but also in the poor black ghetto of the misnamed Liberty City, it's best to follow the tourists across the causeway to Miami Beach, or even further away south to the Keys, or head north up the Gold Coast to calmer waters . . . or anywhere.

ACCOMMODATION
Willard Garden Hotel, 124 NE 14th St, 374-9112. Downtown location, convenient

for buses; clean, helpful, ultra-secure hotel, with library and TV room. Singles from $17, doubles from $20; lower weekly rates.

Hotel Miramar, 1744 N Bayshore Dr, 379-1865. $25 single, 'Friendly, clean.' 'Not what it used to be, and the pool is a joke.'

FOOD
The area around Miami College, off 4th St NE, has plenty of small cafes and restaurants with reasonably priced food.

OF INTEREST
Seaquarium, Rickenbacher Causeway. Oldest and best: dolphin, sharks and killer whales, plus TV star Flipper. Take bus B from downtown Miami. Open 9am–6.30pm. Adults $7, kids $3.50. Phone 361-5703.

Vizcaya, south on US 1. An Italian-style palace created by millionaire James Deering, now the **Dade County Art Museum**, 10am–5pm, adults $4.50, seniors and students $3, kids $2.50. Gardens only, $2.50 for all. Phone 579-2708. Also *son et lumiere* Fri and Sat, 8pm.

Monkey Jungle, 14805 SW 216th St in Goulds, 22 miles southwest of downtown and 3 miles west of US 1; 235-1611. Monkeys run wild, you view them from cages: look smart and they might give you a cream bun. From marmosets to gorillas, with orangutans and gibbons in between. Daily 9.30am–6.30pm, adults $4.50, seniors $4, kids to 12 $2.50.

Parrot Jungle, junction Red Rd (SW 57th Ave) and Killian Dr (SW 112th St), 11 miles southwest of downtown; 666-7834. Huge cypress and oak jungle filled with exotic birds, some on roller skates. Daily 9.30am–5pm, adults $5, kids $2.50.

Museum of Science and Planetarium. 3280 S Miami Ave. Florida's natural history from prehistoric times. Also Indian exhibits. Museum is free, planetarium costs around $3, depending on show; 854-2222.

Planet Ocean, 3979 Rickenbacher Causeway, 361-9455. HQ for International Oceanographic Foundation. Walk through a cloud or experience a hurricane. 10am–6pm, $5, kids $2.50.

Coconut Grove, in the southern suburbs, for a look at a 'Florida-style-subtropical Chelsea scene'. Galleries, boutiques, boat hiring. Get there via bus 14 going south to Main Highway. The flogboards in Coconut Grove are said to be good for rides going north.

Swimming, etc. Water-ski lessons to be had by the hour; surfing at Haulover Beach Park and South Miami Beach, but beware the waves are small; and good swimming at Cape Florida State Park, Matheson Hammock, Tahiti Beach, Lummus Park, etc.

INFORMATION
Miami-Dade County Chamber of Commerce, 1200 Biscayne Blvd, 377-4711.
Miami-Metro Information Center, 499 Biscayne Blvd.
Travelers Aid, 2190 7th St NW, 643-5700.

TRAVEL
Greyhound: NE 2nd Ave and 10th St, 374-7222.
AMTRAK station: 8700 NW 37th Ave, 371-7738. *Silver Meteor* and *Silver Star* service from NYC.
Trailways: 99 NE 4th St, 373-6561.
To and from airport: buses 3 and 20 run downtown. Otherwise take a Yellow Cab (885-1111), or a limo (526-2300), which is a bit cheaper.

MIAMI BEACH. Situated on a long, narrow island, across Biscayne Bay from Miami, Miami Beach came to be regarded as the ultimate in opulence, the dream place for retirement, or a bar mitzvah. Fifty years ago this was a steamy mangrove swamp. Now it's a long strip of hotels of varying degrees of grandness, plus of course the beach.

It's still a favourite retirement spot but the really rich have moved further up the coast. In their wake have come the Cuban refugees and the North European package tours, making it harder to get the good hotel rates which used to be available here during the summer. Still worth bargaining however.

ACCOMMODATION
Clevelander Hotel, 1020 Ocean Dr, 531-3485. Singles $15, doubles $18. 'Still excellent value!' Fridge, cooker, colour TV, pool.
Haddon Hall Hotel, 1500 Collins Ave, 531-1251. Fridge, cooker, colour TV, pool, patio. 'Friendly, clean; supermarket handy.' 'Seems like a home for senile Yanks except in summer when it operates as YH.' Singles $21 with bath.
South Miami Beach YH in Clay Hotel, 406 Espanola Way, 534-2988. $8 per night, members. Kitchen facilities. 'A bit shabby; in Cuban neighbourhood; not far from beach.' 'Cheap, clean; very friendly and helpful staff.'
Waikiki Resort Motel, 18801 Collins Ave, 931-8600. $11–$20 per person in double from 1 May to 14 Dec, twice that during high season. Kids under 12 free if sharing with 2 adults. 400-ft private beach, 3 pools, colour TV in rooms.

OF INTEREST
Sun, sea, sand and gaudy hotels.

FORT LAUDERDALE. This is a double attraction, with a six mile ocean beach on one side (probably the finest on the Gold Coast), and 165 miles of lakes, rivers and canals on the other, hence Fort Lauderdale's tag, 'The Venice of America'.

Along with Daytona Beach, Fort Lauderdale is a major target for students over the Christmas and Easter holidays, though the police are never far behind. Sports cars, mini-bikinis and cases of beer are what the scene is all about, though you might find it more pleasant to boat around the quieter canals.

Fort Lauderdale is 30 miles up the coast from Miami.

ACCOMMODATION
Lamplighter Motel, 2401 N Ocean Blvd, 565-1531. $25 per room in summer. 'Spacious rooms with big kitchens; TV, AC, pool, opposite beach. Charming landlady will do her best to please; will collect guests if required; highly recommended.'
Ocean Way Motel, 1933 N Ocean Blvd, 566-8261. $35 single or double, $5 per additional person. Includes bath/shower, fridge, AC, colour TV; some rooms include complete kitchen facilities. 'Beautiful apartments just across the road from the beach; owner very helpful, offers free lifts to bus station, supermarket.'
Wedgewood Motel, 2307 N Ocean Blvd, at 23rd St, 563-6615. $25 single, $30 double. Take 10 bus from downtown, or late night pick up from bus station on request. 'Friendly, clean, 2 minutes from beach.' 'Good value but ability to speak German required for conversation with fellow guests.'

OF INTEREST
Jungle and Everglades cruise. 3 hrs and 30 miles on the *Jungle Queen*. Departs Bahia Mar Yacht Basin.

TRAVEL
AAACON Auto Transport, 1806B E Sunrise, 771-4059.
Greyhound, 515 NE 3rd St; Trailways 130 NW 1st Ave.
AMTRAK, 200 SW 21st Terrace. The *Silver Meteor* and *Silver Star* stop here between New York and Miami.

KEY WEST. You pick up the toll-free Overseas Highway at Key Largo for the 100-mile run down to Key West. Enroute the road hops from island to island and at times you can travel up to 7 miles with only the sea around you. It's worth a brief stop in **Key Largo** to visit the **John Pennekamp Coral Reef State Park** and to pay a brief tribute to Humphrey Bogart. The *African Queen* now sits outside the Holiday Inn here and you can visit the Caribbean Club Bar where the movie *Key Largo* was filmed.

Key West itself is the southernmost and second oldest town in the United States. Hemingway once lived here and it remains a favourite place for writers and artists—and gays creative or otherwise. Key West is not typical America. Easy to imagine you've somehow made it to a Caribbean island; even the food—turtle steak, conch (pronounced 'conk') chowder, Key lime pie—suggests this. Don't miss sunset over the Gulf of Mexico—the whole town turns out to watch the show, both heavenly and earthly, for sundown here is usually accompanied by some kind of people-performance, whether it be a waterski display, a magician or a folk singer. 'Key West was virtually deserted when we were there in September and October; very quiet and idyllic.'

ACCOMMODATION
Bavaria Hotel, 501 Southard St, corner of Duval St, 294-9323. Half block from bus station. $22 single or double with TV, $19 without TV, summer rates; half the price late September to mid-December.
Plantation Guest House, 914 Eaton St, 294-8446. $14 single, $19 double, add $2 for AC. 5 blocks from Greyhound, though will collect. Kitchen, swimming pool, tropical garden. 'Clean, good atmosphere, lots of friendly people.'
Tilton Hilton, next to bus station, $17 single, $21 double. 'Adequate and laid back.'
Camping at Key Long and John Pennekamp Coral Reef State Parks, $6 per site. Also Bahia Honda State Park: 'Good camp site, less touristy than Pennekamp.'

FOOD
La Creperie, 124 Duval St. 'Reasonably cheap and very good omelettes and crepes.'
Smooth Sailin' Cafe, 120 Duval St. 'Excellent sandwiches.'

OF INTEREST
Hemingway Museum, 907 Whitehead St. The author wrote several major novels in this 1851 house. The present owners bought the house as a home, but on discovering more and more Hemingway memorabilia, decided to turn it into a museum instead. 'Full of the overfed descendants of Hemingway's cats.' Open 9am–5pm. $2 (50¢ discount if you take Conch Train).
Coach Tour Train. Takes you about 14 miles in 1½ hours and costs $5. Info: 294-5161. Includes: Hemingway's house, Truman's Little White House, Audubon House where the artist stayed while sketching birdlife over the Keys, the turtle kraals, the

shrimp fleet, etc. Conch tour offers discounts on sights, eg 50¢ off on Hemingway's house. Tours of the area are also available by **glass-bottomed boat**. And try **snorkelling trips** over the coral reefs. 'Well worth splashing out $12 or so—and maybe even hire an underwater camera.'
'Explore the island by foot if you have more than one day in Key West, or rent a bike.'
There's an early morning bus from Miami (Ameripass valid) which gives you most of the day at Key West with time for a Conch Train ride before catching the evening bus back again. 'The most amazing bus journey I have made.'

EVERGLADES NATIONAL PARK. The Everglades lies farther south than any other area of the US mainland and is the last remaining sub-tropical wilderness in the country.

World-famous as a wildlife sanctuary for rare and colourful birds, this unique, aquatic park is characterised by broad expanses of sawgrass marsh, dense jungle growth, prairies interspersed with stands of cabbage palm and moss-draped cypresses, and mangroves along the coastal region. The level landscape gives the impression of unlimited space.

The western entrance to the park is near Everglades City, but the only auto road leading into the area is Route 27 from Homestead in the east running 50 miles to Flamingo. A drive along here, with its various points of interest, should be enough to satisfy your curiosity. But the more adventurous may explore the park by boat with overnight camping to be arranged with a park ranger.

Year-round temperatures generally keep within 60 to 80°F, though summer days can be hotter and very humid. You are advised to bring sunglasses and insect repellant. Accommodation, restaurants, sightseeing and charter boats and other services are to be found at Flamingo. The Royal Palm Interpretive Center provides information on the park.

ACCOMMODATION
Everglades Motel, 605 S. Krome Ave, Homestead, 247-4117. $20 single or double, summer. AC, colour TV, coin laundry, small pool.
Campgrounds in the park at Lone Pine Key and Flamingo, $3 pn. In addition there are 19 back country sites accessible to the intrepid by boat.

TOURS
Grayline Tours from Miami and Miami Beach, but for a group of people it would be better and cheaper to hire a car for a day.
Also available: air-boat rides and ordinary boat rides from various bases in the park. Trips last 1–5 hours and cost from about $6.

THE GULF COAST. This is the quieter, less visited side of the state, better for that perhaps, and certainly the beaches are as golden and the sea as warm as on the Atlantic side.

Fort Myers was originally a military post in the Seminole Indian Wars. Now its streets are lined with majestic royal palms, its gardens filled with exotic flowers, and it is worth pausing here enroute between Miami (144 miles to the southeast) and Tampa (122 miles to the northwest) to visit Thomas Edison's winter home.

OF INTEREST

Thomas Edison's Winter Home, 1 mile southwest on Rt 867 at 2350 McGregor Blvd, (813) 334-3614. The inventor lived here from 1886 to his death in 1931. 'Good value for $3 (under 18 $1) for an excellent guided 2 hour tour including display of early lightbulbs with bamboo filaments and Ford cars presented to Thomas by his good friend Henry.' Open Mon–Sat and hols 9am–4pm, Sun 12.30pm–4pm.

Jungle River Cruises. 3-hr cruises up the Caloosahatchee River, daily except Mon, $5, to wild life in the Everglades.

About 250 miles north and west of Miami are the cities of **Tampa** and **St Petersburg**. Usually referred to in the same breath, these two sit facing each other across Tampa Bay. Tampa is the nation's eighth busiest port and home port for one of the world's largest shrimp fleets. The latin quarter, Ybor City, is an important cigar producer.

The more sedate St Petersburg has become a large retirement community. Known as 'Sunshine City', St Pete offers, in addition to geriatrics, excellent beaches and an abundance of watersports.

ACCOMMODATION

Peak season here is Jan–April when prices are at least 25% higher than the summer rates below. All addresses are in Tampa.

Belmont Motel, 734 S Dale Mabry, on US 92, 1¼ miles south of I-275, exit 23. 877-5843. Singles from $24. doubles from $26, fridge, colour TV, air conditioning, kitchens, pool. Lone women not accepted.

Days Inn, 2901 E Busch Blvd, on Rt 580, 1¾ miles east of jct I-75, exit 33. 933-6471. $32 single, $35 double. AC, colour TV, coin laundry, pool. 10 minutes from Busch Gardens.

America Motel, 3314 S Dale Mabry, 837-9510. Single $16, doubles $22. $1.50 extra for kitchenette. Nr Belmont Motel.

OF INTEREST
TAMPA

The waterfront. Watch the banana boats docking and unloading at Kennedy Blvd and 13th St. The walk along Bayshore Blvd will bring you to a string of southern mansions.

Busch Gardens, just of Rt 580, 988-5171. $11 adults, under-4 free, open daily in summer 9.30am–10pm, closes 6pm rest of year. Take an African safari to view more than 1000 animals, plus tropical gardens, rides, shows, etc.

Both the **University of South Florida** and the **University of Tampa** are here. The latter, on W Kennedy Blvd, is worth a visit to look at **Plant Hall**, the admin building and once Teddy Roosevelt's HQ in the Spanish-American War.

ST PETERSBURG

Here it's mainly variations on the beach theme. Best trips are to **Municipal Beach** at Treasure Island and **Fort DeSoto Park** across the Bayway.

Sunshine Skyway. A remarkable series of bridge and causeways carrying Rts 19 and 275 15 miles across Tampa Bay.

TALLAHASSEE. Hidden away in the hills and forests of the Florida Panhandle, the state capital usually manages to avoid too many tourists. The townsfolk also managed to avoid being captured by the

Union forces during the Civil War, the only Confederate capital east of Mississippi with that distinction. This is a city of real Floridians, not transplanted northerners, and there's still much of its 19th century architecture to see, a slower way of life to appreciate.

ACCOMMODATION
Lafayette Motel, 1525 W Tennessee Ave, 224–1145. Singles $23, doubles $27.
Ponce de Leon Motel, 1801 W Tennessee Ave, on US 90, 2 miles west of downtown, 222-4950. Singles $22, doubles $26. Pool, AC.

OF INTEREST
State Capitol, S Monroe. Modern 22-storey tower building. Tours available. The original building (1845) can be seen in front of the new one.
Tallahassee Junior Museum, at Lake Bradford. Built for kids but fun for all. Includes Indian farm, grist mill, nature trails, sheep shearing, weaving, etc. Tue–Sat 9am–5pm, Sun 2pm–5pm. $2 adults, $1 children.

Moving further west along the Panhandle, you come to **Panama City** and the commercialised resort of **Panama City Beach**. Panama City runs on Central Standard Time and so is one hour behind the rest of Florida. It used to be a peaceful fishing village and it remains quieter than most places along this coast. The developers are moving in however in the wake of their triumphs down the road at Panama City Beach.

The beach really is lovely and the sea is clear and warm, but everything is over-priced and over-populated.

Further west still, and the last city in Florida, is **Pensacola**. Since the first successful settlement here in 1698, Pensacola has flown the flags of five nations and has changed hands 13 times. The British used it as a trading post in the 18th century and business seems to have been good—here Scotsman James Panton became America's first recorded millionaire. Here too, in 1821, Andrew Jackson completed the transaction whereby Spain sold Florida to the United States.

The Spanish influence is particularly evident in the Seville Square quarter where 17th and 18th century buildings have been redeveloped but, alas, also over-commercialised. Otherwise it is the giant naval air station which dominates, and the air museum (free) is worthy of a visit.

The white sand beaches near Pensacola are among the best in Florida; after a dip you're on your way west to Gulf Islands National Seashore (see Biloxi, Mississippi) and to New Orleans.

THE ATLANTIC COAST. Most of the Florida coast from St Augustine down to Miami was deserted as little as 30 years ago, but the press of the tourist trade and the development of Cape Kennedy Space Center and Disneyworld in particular have triggered off the growth of new resorts.

Not new, however, is **St Augustine**, founded by the Spanish in 1565, 42 years before the first English effort as Jamestown, making it the oldest city in the United States. The place is pointedly aware of this and does much to commercialise its heritage. Try to ignore the billboard signs on the way in ('The Old Jail: Authentic and Educational') and give the history and atmosphere of the city a chance to make its mellow impact on you, for by Florida standards this is a different town, picturesquely set on a quiet bay.

ACCOMMODATION
Monson Motor Lodge, 32 Avenida Menendez, 829-2277. Downtown by historical area and waterfront. Singles and doubles from $27. Pool, TV, AC, 1 mile from Greyhound. 'Excellent.'
Days Inn, 2800 Ponce de Leon Blvd, at junction US 1 and Rt 16, 828-6581. Downtown, sightseeing trains stop next door, $23 single, $27 double.
North Beach Campground, 3 miles north of town. $8 per site. 'Best campground in USA—jungle-type setting.'

FOOD
Malaga St Depot Restaurant, Malaga St. 'Next door to Trailways depot. Slightly expensive, but cheaper than rest of St Augustine, and owner may let you leave bags there if Trailways closed, as it is on Sun.'

OF INTEREST
Among the old Spanish buildings in the town are the **Castillo de San Marcos**, the **Cathedral of St Augustine, Mission of Nombre de Dois, Old Spanish Inn, Oldest House**, and the **Old Slave Market**.
A 208 foot stainless steel cross marks the spot where the pioneer Spaniards landed in 1565, although the present mission church dates only from earlier this century.
Entrance to the mission grounds is free; entrance to the Castillo de San Marcos is 50¢; and entrance to the Old School House, St George St is $1.
Old Town, around St George St. A traffic free area of town where most of the old buildings are located. 'Get walking tour of old town details from Chamber of Commerce. A lot of it is disappointing however since a number of the lovely old buildings are now the home of junk and trash shops.'
Cross and Sword, Florida's official state play, is presented during the summer at the St Augustine Amphitheatre.
Fiesta Days, a time of general jollifications American-Spanish style, are held during August.
Alligator Farm, Highway A1A south of town. Established 1893, claims to be 'the world's largest'. Includes man vs gator wrestling matches.

INFORMATION
Chamber of Commerce Information Center, San Marco Ave, just beyond the Old City Gates.

TRAVEL
Various tours available—by boat, rubber-tyred 'train', or by horse and carriage. Details from the Info Center.

Daytona Beach is, like Fort Lauderdale to the south, a popular rave-up resort for university students during holiday periods. The beach is hard and flat, hence the motor races of past decades here, though now the only sorts of vehicles not on the beach are racing cars.

The racing happens at the Speedway south of town, while at the beach you just park on the sands and stroll down to the water for a dip. Dune buggies and bicycles can be hired for riding along the sands.

ACCOMMODATION
Daytona rates are highest in summer and between Christmas and Easter, lowest between Labor Day and Christmas.
Lou Ray Motel, 400 S Atlantic Ave, 252-2174. $20 double after Labor Day, cooker, fridge, etc. 'Excellent motel.'
Surfview Motel and Apartments, 401 S Atlantic, 253-9961. $22 and up. 'A 10% discount will be given at all times to those who present a copy of this Guide.' 'Very helpful indeed. Right on the beach. English owner.'
Camping nearby at Tomoka State Park or at nearby Flagler Beach. 'Peace and quiet.'
Also Nova Family Campground, on Herbert St, 2 miles east of I-95, Port Orange exit, or west from 55A ot US 1. 10 minutes from Daytona Beach. 'Shady sites, good facilities.' $8.50 per site. (904) 767-0095.

FOOD
Morrisons, Granada Plaza. $3.50 eat all you can. 'Fantastic value.'
Surfside Inn, 3125 S Atlantic Ave. 'Sunday champagne brunch $6. Eat and drink as much as you like, including champagne.'

OF INTEREST
Daytona International Speedway. Races from 30 Jan, through summer.
Hell's Angels' motorcycle race week in March.
The Beach. All 23 miles of it. Careful where you sunbathe.

INFORMATION
Chamber of Commerce, City Island, 253-7282.

ORLANDO. Standing 35 miles from the coast in the heart of the Florida lakes area, Orlando—hardly heard of a few years ago—is now perhaps the most visited place in the state owing to its access to the nearby Kennedy Space Center and especially Disneyworld. It has the mayhem atmosphere of a boom town, but choose carefully before you set out to see the sights—so many of them are waste-of-time money-grabbing Disneyworld parasitical spinoffs.

ACCOMMODATION
Numerous budget motels in the area, though they tend to cost more than elsewhere, eg Days Inn with doubles from $38.
Janie's Tourist Rooms, 436 N Lexington Ave, 841-8867. Next to Greyhound, can't miss it. $10 per person in dorm-style room, $24 single. AC, kitchen, laundry. 'Meet people from all over the world.' 'Primitive but clean, very friendly staff.' 'Provides transportation service to all local attractions, cheaper than tour operators.' 'Well recommended.'
Van's Place, 438 Lexington Ave, 849-0659. Near Greyhound. $16 single, $24 double, special weekly rates. AC, TV, bath. 'Clean, friendly and helpful.'
Young Women's Community Club, 107 E Hillcrest St, 425-2502. $6.50 per night. 'Very strict, but cheap and clean.' 'Amazing value, really friendly, and excellent cheap food.'
Camping: Twin Lakes, Kissimmee, 4 miles from Disneyworld, $8 per site. 'Cheapest sites around, but dirty facilities.'

KOA of Kissimmee camping ground, Rt 192, 8 miles east of Disneyworld, $12 per site. 'Good facilities, tent required.'

FOOD
Malcolm's Hungry Bear, 924 W Colonial Dr, 10 minute walk from Janie's Tourist Rooms and opp Holiday Inn. Open daily 7am–9.30pm. All-you-can-eat meals at lowest prices in town, plus 20% discount on breakfast if you eat dinner there. 'Fantastic variety, unbelievable value.' 'Good place to fill up your tummy after days of fast food.'

OF INTEREST
Disneyworld. At Lake Buena Vista, about 20 miles south on Interstate 4. Bus pass valid. Exceeds Disneyland as a magnificent architectural, technological and entertainment achievement. $13.25 for 1-day pass (unlimited use on all attractions), $23 for 2-day pass. 'You definitely need 2 days.' 'Great! I wish I was a child again.' 'Better than it's hyped up to be.' 'We thought the whole place was very artificial and plastic. Enormous queues for everything.' 'Visit after Labor Day to avoid queuing 1 hour for everything.' Space Mountain and Electric Parade most often recommended by readers. 'Food expensive, old and pre-packed.'

Epcot Center (Experimental Prototype Community of Tomorrow), is Disney Inc's latest fantasia, $1 billion-worth, 260 acres, linked to Disneyworld by monorail, and costing $15 for a 1-day pass. 35 audio-animatronic figures, including Ben Franklin and Mark Twain, will boggle your sense of boredom by 'bringing to life stirring moments in American history' and even walking and climbing stairs. It opened in October 1982 and may not yet be fully fledged; for the moment it's predictable and pedestrian. 'Not worth the price; very modern and technical, no place to have fun like in Disneyworld.' Served by Greyhound; pass valid.

Wings and Wheels Orlando, at Orlando Intl Airport. Airplanes and autos, all vintage and ticking over, plus film *To Fly*. Daily 9.30am–6pm, $5.50 adults, $2.75 kids.

Wet n' Wild, $7.50 entrance for water slides, wave generator. Take city bus, 60¢, to 6200 International Dr, 9 miles southwest. Tel: 351-3200.

Circus World, southwest of Orlando at Davenport on US 27 at I-4. 422-0643. $9.50 adults, $8 kids under 12. Ringling Bros and Barnum & Bailey present 'every kind of circus act imaginable' and let you fly on the trapeze, walk the tightrope and make a clown of yourself.

Sea World, on I-4 between Orlando and Disneyworld, 351-0021. $9.50 adults, $8.50 kids. Features sharks, killer whales, walruses, multimedia fish and naked dolphins. 'One or the most spectacular aquatic animal displays I've ever seen', says one reader who sounds as though he's seen thousands.

ENTERTAINMENT
Rosie O'Grady's Bar, Church St. $5 for 5 bars plus live entertainment. 'Great atmosphere; last bar closes 5am.'

Playhouse, a go-go bar. 'Topless dancing till 2am nightly. Walk to end of Church St and left for 1–1½ miles. No cover charge. Drinks $1.75 or sometimes 2 for the price of 1. Ask for a $3 dance. Girls very attractive and alluring.'

Gray Line buses to Disneyworld, Kennedy Space Center, Sea World, Circus World, etc, from Howard Johnson Hotel nr Greyhound 9am daily.

Greyhound to D'world, Epcot, Seaworld and Kennedy only, departs 10am daily.

'Amazing airport, with fake monorail operated completely automatically. Bus to town, 60¢. If broke there are some lovely couches. One of the better airports to sleep at.'

TRAVEL
AMTRAK, 1400 Sligh Blvd. The NY-Miami *Silver Star* and *Silver Meteor* pass through daily.

Cape Kennedy Space Center, on Cape Canaveral, lies just north of Cocoa Beach (good for surfing) off US 1, and is the site for Space Shuttle and manned Apollo launchings. Guided tours of the Center go every 30 minutes from 8am to 6pm, last two hours, and cost $3. Half price for groups of 20 or more, or for those under 18. Make sure, however, that on the day of your tour they are not testing or preparing for a space shot as they then cut out visits to the training buildings. There is an excellent museum at the Visitor Information Center, on SR 405, six miles east of US 1. Lots of space hardware around, also free films. 'Absolutely fascinating. I was completely disinterested in space travel before I went but am now wildly enthusiastic. As a bonus it's set in a nature reserve so you see alligators and all sorts of birds and animals. A must.'

Private vehicles may tour the base from 9am to 3pm on Sundays only. For more information phone NASA, 783-7781, or Cape Kennedy, 853-1113. For current launch information call: (800) 432-2153. Many motels in the vicinity offer 'free' tour tickets.

OF INTEREST
South of Cocoa Beach is **Patrick Air Force Base** where there's an exhibit of missiles and rockets.
Canaveral National Seashore, 57,000 acres of wilderness and including the nice Playalinda Beach. Good for boating, swimming and fishing.
Merrit Island National Wildlife Refuge. Waterfowl sanctuary across the causeway from Titusville.

TRAVEL
Buses from Orlando, but steep at $15; get together with a few people and rent a car.

GEORGIA

Named after George II, the Colony of Georgia was initially established as a buffer between Spanish Florida and the prosperous Carolinas. As an act of philanthropy and expedience, it was settled by former inmates of debtor's prisons.

When cotton became king the plantation system introduced Georgia to the way of life of the Deep South. The final months of the Civil War saw a large swath of the state devastated by Northern General Sherman's notorious March to the Sea. But unlike some other states of the Deep South, the Peach State has chosen to look more to the future than to the past, and since the Second World War has been riding the crest of an industrial boom.

Textiles are still Georgia's major industry, while peaches, tobacco and peanuts are the prime crops. The most famous peanut farmer of all, former President Jimmy Carter, is a native son and now back on his farm in Plains, in the southwest corner of the state.

Georgia's landscape ranges from the Appalachians in the west to the low-lying Atlantic coast and, in the south, the great Okefenokee Swamp.

ATLANTA. As a major railway junction by the time of the Civil War, Atlanta was already the commercial, industrial and social Queen of the South. The Union's General Sherman 'drove old Dixie down' with his devastating March to the Sea during which Atlanta was bombarded and then burned to the ground.

But Atlanta has risen again, a modern city, indeed a fast-growing Southern success story where progress counts for more than prejudice. Atlantans elected their first black mayor back in 1973, and it was here that Martin Luther King was raised and first preached. It's skyscraper skyline, while proclaiming Atlanta's leadership of the 'New South', is also boring and charmless, though Peachtree Street, financial hub of the ante-bellum South, still retains some of its presence, and, away from downtown, the city's hills, wooded streets and numerous colleges—Atlanta University, Clark College, Emory University and the Georgia Institute of Technology—create a pleasant atmosphere. On the debit side, Atlanta has one of the worst murder records of urban America.

Coca-Cola, with sales of over 160,000,000 bottles a day, was invented in Atlanta by Dr John Pemberton in 1886.

ACCOMMODATION

Bed and Breakfast Atlanta, 1221 Fairview Rd, NE, (404) 378-6026, offers rooms in desirable neighbourhoods in and near Atlanta from $26 single, $30 double—but it's advisable to reserve in advance. 'Southern hospitality in the European tradition.'

Atlantan Hotel, Luckie and Cone Sts, 524-6461. Singles from $30, doubles from $38. Nr bus station. 'Recently renovated, nice and friendly place.' Bath/shower and TV in rooms.

Georgian Terrace Hotel, 659 Peachtree NE, at Ponce de Leon, 872-6671. 'An old hotel with traditional decor, crumbling though due to lack of funds. The rooms are comfortable, the staff friendly.' Used in part as YH; with card is 'best deal in Atlanta'. $7 per person in quad, $8 in triple, $10 in double, $16 in single; about double without AYH card. AC, colour TV, shower. 'Atlanta's gays hang out here.' 'Keep an eye on the elevator boy.'

Imperial Hotel, 355 Peachtree St NE, 524-1941. Recently closed for renovation; check it out, it's been recommended in the past.

Villa International, 1749 Clifton Rd NE, 633-6783. 'A Ministry of the Christian Community.' Singles with shower $17, doubles $24.

YMCA, 22 Butler St, 659-8085. Singles from $14. No AC, stuffy and tatty rooms. 'Shabbiest YMCA I've seen.' Either this is being renovated or a new Y is being built nearby, so check.

Numerous budget motels in Atlanta area, but you'll need a car and they usually cost more here than elsewhere.

The area around Myrtle, Piedmont, Peachtree and Ponce de Leon, is where to look for lodging houses.

The Lodgings Office of Georgia Institute of Technology Mathieson Dormitory, 711 Techwood Drive, and Emory U Campus may be able to help students with accommodation lists.

FOOD

Atlanta's specialties are fried chicken, black-eyed peas, okra and sweet potato pie. Try Mary-Macs on Ponce de Leon for a bowl of pot likker with corn bread.

Farmer's Market, corner of Butler St and Edgewood Rd. Very cheap fruit. Also the cafe does good value food, eg huge pork chop sandwich, $1.

Natural East, 127 Peachtree. 'Cheap and excellent health food.'

The Varsity, North Ave at I-75. World's largest drive-in, next to Georgia Tech campus. Serves 15,000 people with 8300 Cokes, 18,000 hamburgers, 25,000 hotdogs each day. Clean, fast, cheap and good.

OF INTEREST

'You should make it clear that Atlanta, especially midtown, is now second only to San Francisco for large gay community.'

The Omni Complex, Techwood Dr NW. Sports, hotel and entertainment centre. Also known as the 'waffle iron' because of its criss-cross steel and glass exterior.

Peachtree Plaza Hotel, Peachtree. The newest piece of Atlantan extravagance. An indoor lake, outside elevator to rooftop bar.

Grave of Martin Luther King, in Ebeneezer Baptist Churchyard at 413 Auburn Ave, NE. The inscription on the tomb reads: 'Free at last, free at last, thank God Almighty, I'm free at last.' Open daily 9am–5pm.

Regency Hyatt Hotel. Built like a hollow skyscraper. A spectacular piece of civil engineering with statutory revolving restaurant at the top. The walls of the building are one suite thick and there's nothing in the middle. After 6pm you'll have to be jacketed and tied if you want to go to the top.

Cyclorama of the Battle of Atlanta. In Grant Park. One of the largest dioramas in the world. $1.20. Depicts Atlanta's plight during Sherman's March to the Sea. Also, the *Texas*, of the Great Locomotive Chase of the Civil War. To get to Grant Park, take a No 6 bus to Georgia Ave.

Further **Civil War memorabilia** in the area include the breastworks erected for the defence of the town—in Grant Park, Cherokee Ave and Boulevard SE—and Fort Walker, Confederate Battery, set up as during the siege.

State Capitol, Washington St at Mitchell. Modelled on the Washington DC capitol building and topped with gold from the Georgia goldfield at Dahlonega, brought to Atlanta by special wagon caravan.

The **Atlanta Historical Society** is at 1753 Peachtree St NE. Good archives. The **Trévor Arnett Library** on the Atlanta U campus has interesting contemporary Black art; and the **Emory U Museum**, in the Druid Hills section, specialises in American Indian artefacts and objects from Middle East excavations.

Joel Chandler Harris, author of the Uncle Remus stories, lived at **Wren's Nest**, 1050 Gordon St SW. See the briar Brer Rabbit lived in. Entrance $1.25. Mon–Sat 9.30am–5pm, Sun 2pm–5pm.

Atlanta Zoo, Grant Park. Open daily 10am–5pm. Adults $1.50, children 50¢.

Stone Mountain. In massive bas-relief the equestrian figures of Generals Robert E Lee, Stonewall Jackson and Confederate President Jefferson Davis have been cut from a 600-ft-high granite dome in this state park. A cable car runs to the top, or you can climb it. Also in the 3200-acre historical and recreational park is an ante-bellum plantation, an antique auto and music museum, a game ranch, riverboat cruises, a 5-mile steam railroad and more. Entrance to the park is $1.50 adults, $1 under 12 and then you pay for attractions individually, or you buy all-in ticket $8.95 adults, $5.50 under 12.

There's a campground in the park.

To get there take MARTA eastbound from OMNI or Five Points station to Avondale. Transfer to bus 120 to Stone Mountain, 50¢. It's advisable to get the bus back by 4.30pm.

ENTERTAINMENT
Read the free, weekly *Creative Loafing* and *Atlanta Gazette* to find out what goes on.

Piedmont Park, free open-air jazz and classical concerts, Atlanta Philharmonic Orchestra, throughout the summer. 'Not to be missed. People dance, drink; on a good evening it can be like the last night of the proms. Also watch the fireflies do illuminated mating dances.'

Six Flags Over Georgia, 10 miles west on I-20. 276-acre entertainment park. Bus goes from Luckie St. $11.50 entrance.

The Fox, 660 Peachtree. Second largest movie theatre in America. Good for concerts.

Agora Ballroom, 665 Peachtree. Rock club with big names.

688 Club, 688 Spring and 3rd St. New wave music.

INFORMATION
Chamber of Commerce, Omni Building, Marietta St, 522-4711. Very helpful. Good for maps, general Atlanta literature.

Travelers Aid, in Greyhound Terminal, 523-0585.

TRAVEL
MARTA (Metropolitan Atlanta Rapid Transit Authority) is the affectionate name given to the city's brand new and superb subway system. Transfers between subway and buses. Basic far 60¢.

Greyhound, 81 Cain St, NW, 522-6300.

Trailways, 200 Spring St, NW, 524-2441.

AMTRAK, Peachtree Station, 1688 Peachtree St, NW. The NY-New Orleans *Crescent* stops here daily.

AAACON Auto Transport, Allen Rd NE at junction I-285 and Roswell Rd, 256-2994.

SAVANNAH. The first settlement in Georgia got started here when Englishman James Oglethorpe landed in 1733. Seafaring has been important to Savannah since colonial times. Once a favourite port of pirates, these days oil tankers, freighters and pleasure boats are the traffic in the US's tenth largest port. As the smell will tell you, the other major business around here is pulp and paper.

Still, Savannah is a pretty town, spaciously laid out round a series of shady squares with many old mansions to look at. It's at its best when the azaleas bloom everywhere in spring. The historic waterfront, cobblestoned underfoot, is now renovated and the old brick warehouses host specialty shops, restaurants and nightspots.

ACCOMMODATION
Bed and Breakfast Inn, 117 W Gordon at Chatham Sq, 233-9481. In the heart of the historic district, an 1853 townhouse. $26 single, $30 double and up.

Quality Inn, 300 W Bay St, 236-6321. Close to historic district. AC, free continental breakfast, colour TV. Singles from $23, doubles from $27.

Thunderbird Inn, 611 West Oglethorpe Ave, 232-2661. $30 double and up. Nr bus station.

FOOD
Morrison's Cafeteria, 15 Bull St. Good and inexpensive. Closes 8pm.

The Pirate's House, 34 E and Broad St. 'Not cheap, but good value and genuinely historic.'

Wilkes Dining Room, 107 W Jones St. On Mon–Fri from 11am to 3pm it's all-you-can-stuff-in-your-gob for $4.

OF INTEREST
Old Savannah offers cobbled streets, charming squares, formal gardens and several beautiful mansions. Among the stately houses of the town is the **Owens-Thomas House**, at 124 Abercorn St, at which Lafayette was a visitor in 1825.
Savannah Waterfront. The old cotton trade buildings, restored, reconstructed and used as restaurants, shops and night spots.
Ships of the Sea Maritime Museum, 503 E River St. Open 10am–5pm, $2 adults, $1 seniors, 75¢ under-13s.
Telfair Academy of Arts and Sciences. The oldest art museum in the southeast and the home of a fine collection of portraits and Renaissance masterpieces. Tue–Sat 10am–5pm, Sun 2pm–5pm, closed Mon. $2 adults, $1 seniors and students, 50¢ under-13s.

INFORMATION
Visitor's Center, 301 W Broad St, 233-3067. Literature, maps, a walking tour leaflet, introductory films. The Shuttle Train Tour starts here.
Travelers Aid, 428 Bull St, 233-5729.
Post Office: Bay St at Broad; in courthouse building, Wright Sq.

OKEFENOKEE SWAMP. This large swamp area lies in southeast Georgia. Eight miles south of Waycross on highways US 1 and US 23, is the Okefenokee Swamp Park with an observation tower, boat tours and walkways enabling you to take in the cypresses, flowers, aquatic birds, bears and alligators without getting your feet wet. There is also a museum telling the story of the 'Land of the Trembling Earth' (the old Indian name for the swamp). Entrance to the park is $5.

KENTUCKY

A mixture of the Midwest and the South, both Abe Lincoln and Jefferson Davis were born here, and Daniel Boone also figured in its history when in 1769 he blazed the Wilderness Trail permitting Kentucky to be the first area settled west of the Alleghenies.

The state ranks second to North Carolina in tobacco output, and nearly half the land is forested, yet the Bluegrass country around Lexington, famous for is racehorse breeding, gives Kentucky its nickname. Bourbon whiskey is Kentucky's other great contribution to civilisation.
National Park: Mammoth Caves

LOUISVILLE. The oldest horse race in the country, the Kentucky Derby, is held here the first week in May amidst a festival atmosphere of parades, concerts and a steamboat race.

Founded by George Rogers Clark as a supply base on the Ohio for his Northwest explorations, Louisville is now a commercial, industrial and educational centre and one of the world's largest tobacco manufacturing centres. Louisville and Jefferson County distilleries produce about 25 percent of all liquor made in the US. This is also the hometown of the Louisville Lip, though the boulevard named after him is called Muhammad Ali.

Enroute from here to Mammoth Caves are various folksy attractions, including Abraham Lincoln's birthplace at Hodgenville, Stephen Foster's original 'My Old Kentucky Home' and the Lincoln Homestead nearby.

ACCOMMODATION
Milner Hotel, 231 W Jefferson St, 585-4241. Downtown. Singles from $20, doubles from $28.
San Antonio Inn, 927 S 2nd St, 582-3741. Central part of town, about 2 miles south of river. All rooms with air conditioning, TV and bath. Pool. Singles/doubles $32.
YMCA, 930 W Chestnut St, 587-7405. Small, simple singles with bath $16. Men only.

OF INTEREST
Churchill Downs, home of the Kentucky Derby. Also at Churchill Downs, there is a **racing museum**, 700 Central Ave.
JB Speed Art Museum, 2035 S 3rd St. One of the better mid-South galleries. Thomas Jefferson was the architect of the John Speed Mansion, **Farmington**, 3033 Bardstown Rd.
Several **bourbon distilleries** in the area offer tours, among them Brown-Forman, 1908 Howard St 778-5531 ext 280, Seagrams, 7th St and Central Ave, 634-1551, and Old Fitzgerald Distilleries, Fitzgerald Rd, 448-2860.
Old Louisville, between 3rd and 4th Sts, is an area of attractive Victorian homes. Some are open to visitors during the St James Court Arts and Crafts Fair in early Oct.
A pleasant way of spending an afternoon is to take a **cruise on the Ohio River** on the *Belle of Louisville*, an old sternwheeler. The boat leaves from the landing at 4th St and River Rd.
Cave Hill Cemetery, east end of Broadway. Old and beautifully landscaped, contains **grave of George Rogers Clark**.

INFORMATION
Louisville Visitors Bureau, Founders Sq, 5th St and Muhammad Ali Blvd, 582-3732.
Travelers Aid, Greyhound Bus Terminal, 720 W. Walnut St, 584-8186.

TRAVEL
Local bus system (TARC) runs only limited service after sundown, packs up at 1am. 50¢ fare, rush-hour 60¢. Info: 585-1234.
Greyhound, 720 W Muhammad Ali Blvd, 585-3331.
Trailways, 213 W Liberty St, 584-3336.

MAMMOTH CAVES NATIONAL PARK. Halfway between Louisville, Kentucky, and Nashville, Tennesee, above ground this is a preserve of forest, flowers and wildlife, below ground several hundred miles of passages, pits, domes, gypsum and travertine formations, archaeological remains and a crystal lake. The caves rival in size the better-known Carlsbad Caverns and may be explored on foot, or afloat during conducted boat trips.

Keep to the caves within the park and do not stray into the trashy/ commercial/privately-owned/exploited caves nearby. There are several campgrounds within the park. Various tours leave regularly from the Visitors Center. Cave City is the service centre for the Park. Lots of motels here.

A short drive from Cave City is Hodgenville where you can visit the modest **Lincoln Birthplace and National Historic Site**. Nearby Knob Creek Farm was Abe's boyhood home.

LEXINGTON. Lexington lies in the heart of the Bluegrass horsebreeding country, and just outside the town are the famous Calumet stables. A horse show is held here in July, races at Keeneland in April and October and trotting races in June and September. The countryside is rolling and pleasant. Confederate President Jefferson Davis was from Lexington.

If you're travelling south from here via the I-75 to Knoxville, Tennessee, you'll pass through a land of lakes and forests. Daniel Boone National Forest, covering nearly 800,000 acres, is nice for hiking and camping.

ACCOMMODATION
Phone DIAL-A-CCOMMODATION for assistance Mon–Fri 9am–5pm, 233-7299.
Days Inn, 1675 N Broadway, I-75 and US 27/68, exit 113, 293-1421. $33 single, $36 double.
Best Western Lexington Motel, 925 Newtown Pike, 252-6656. AC, colour TV, pool. Singles from $26, doubles from $33.
YMCA, 535 W 2nd St, 252-7543. Men and women.

OF INTEREST
Some of the **Blue Grass horse farms** can be visited; for a list, contact the Lexington Convention and Tourist Bureau, 252-7565. Some of the most famous are **Spendthrift Farm**, Iron Works Pike, 299-5271; **Darby Dan Farm**, Old Frankfort Pike, 254-0424; and **King Ranch**, 3000 Old Frankfort Pike, 254-1858. Also visit the **Kentucky Horse Park**, Iron Works Pike, 6 miles north on I-75, 233-4303, admission $4.50. 'Well worth a visit, especially for horse lovers. See a film, excellent museum, various shows, many different breeds, horseriding at extra cost.'
Ashland, E Main St and Sycamore Rd, was the home of politician Henry Clay, leader of the 'War Hawks' who with their eyes on Canada, led America into the War of 1812 against England.
Shakertown. Thirty miles southeast of Lexington, this community was established by the Shaker sect in 1805 and by the middle of that century numbered 500 inhabitants. The Shakers have departed, but their buildings, with the help of some restoration, still stand. The place is known locally as Pleasant Hill.

TRAVEL
Greyhound, 240 N Limestone St, 252-4261.

LOUISIANA

Basic to the development of the Pelican State have been its waterways, principally the great Mississippi, its port of New Orleans, and the Gulf itself, once roamed by pirates, now plumbed by offshore wells which make Louisiana second only to Texas as an oil-producing state. Much of its delta land is below sea level, the water held back by vast levees.

The state's history has been unusually varied, the area settled by the Spanish and French whose blood survives in the Creoles of today; later by the Acadians, French inhabitants of Nova Scotia forcibly transported to Louisiana by the British in 1775, now known as Cajuns.

The blues developed amongst rural blacks; when it moved downriver to sophisticated New Orleans, jazz was born.

NEW ORLEANS. Canal Street is the dividing line between the new city and the old. Below it are the banks, businesses and flashy buildings that mark New Orleans as the financial centre of the South, an importance based on agriculture, oil and a port that ranks second in value of trade in the United States.

But visitors are drawn by the Vieux Carré above Canal Street, where gracious homes, walled gardens, narrow streets overhung by iron-lace balconies, and delicious Creole food struggle to retain a mellow atmosphere against encroaching plastic America.

And of course there's jazz, though today Bourbon Street comes out with the wrong notes. The street is an over-commercialised strip of bars, drunks, prostitutes, skin shows, rip-off joints and gawking tourists in bermuda shorts. The locals usually avoid it, and the cognoscenti will at once make for the Jazz Museum and Preservation Hall, the place nonpareil for the traditional sound.

Two weeks before Shrove Tuesday, all heaven and hell breaks loose with Mardi Gras: street dancing, masquerades, torchlight parades and formal balls.

New Orleans has a sub-tropical climate. Spring and autumn are the best times to visit when it's warm but not as humid nor as rainy as in summer.

ACCOMMODATION
Crescent Motel, 3522 Tulane, 486-5736. $28 double, bath, pool.
LaSalle Hotel, 1113 Canal St, 523-5831. $27 double, no bath; $32 double, bath. Reduction with bus pass. 'Absolutely excellent! Near Vieux Carré. Clean, large rooms. TV, air conditioning, laundry, safe-deposit boxes.'
St Charles Guest House, 1748 Prytania St, 523-6556. B&B 5 minutes from French Quarter; 'beautiful terrace with palms', AC, pool. Without bath: singles $23, doubles $26, triples $32. With bath: singles $34, doubles $40. Reports that owners are setting up annex for backpackers, about $12 per person. 'Comfortable, clean rooms; helpful proprietor.'
Marquette House Youth Hostel, 2253 Carondelet St, 523-3014. Greek revival home near Garden District, mile south of Canal St, along St Charles streetcar line (get off at Jackson Ave and walk 1 block). Advisable to phone first for info and reservations. Male and female accommodation in separate dorms, $7 AYH

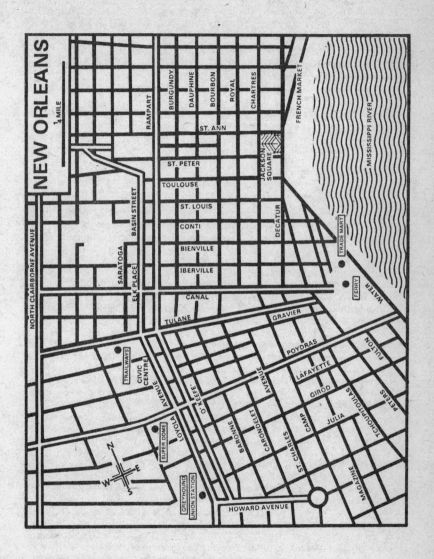

members, $9 non-members. Also 1 double room available, $22. 'Clean, friendly, comfortable and safe.'

YMCA, 936 St Charles Ave, 568-9622. Men and women, pool. Single $20, doubles $28. $5 key deposit. Small rooms.

Campus accommodation available during summer: Tulane U, 27 McAlister Dr, 865-4591; $13 single, $20 double, from 5 June to 31 July. Loyola U, 6363 St Charles Ave, 866-5471; $17 single, $25 double, from 1 June to 1 Aug.

FOOD

Bonanza Steak Bar, St Charles, nr Canal St. Steak, unlimited salad, garlic bread and coffee for $5. 'Excellent, helpful.'

Cafe du Monde, French Market. 'Coffee and hot donuts, $1.25. An experience not to be missed.'

Buster Holmes Cafe, Orleans and Burgundy Streets. Red Beans and rice, $2. 'Great Value.'

Mena's Palace, Iberville and Exhange. $2.50 seafood gumbo. 'Very friendly, show them this book.'

The Gumbo Shop, St Peter's St. 'Try delicious gumbo and jambalaya. Reasonable prices and good atmosphere.'

OF INTEREST

Vieux Carré. Some 70 blocks of the old city between the river and Rampart St. Apart from the pleasure of simply wandering around the streets, you will find in this area the majority of the city's buildings of note. Royal St is perhaps the nicest. Start wandering here, at the Tourist and Convention Commission. Historic buildings include:

Absinthe House, 238 Bourbon St. The house where the Lafitte brothers, Pierre and Jean, 'plotted against honest shipping'.

Casa Hove, 723 Toulouse St. Believed to have been built around 1720.

US Customs House, Decatur and Canal Sts.

The French Market; the Historical Pharmacy Museum, 516 Chartres; the Pontabla Buildings in Jackson Sq; Ursuline Covent, 1115 Chartres; Madame John's Legacy, 632 Dumaine St, built 1726 and achieving fame through author George Cable.

St Louis Cathedral, Jackson Sq, and the Cabildo, right next door, where the Spanish governors lived, now housing the Louisiana State Museum. The Cabildo is open daily, except Mon, from 9am to 5pm and has a $1 charge. Free on Friday.

Uptown New Orleans, around Maple, Oak and Willow Streets, down St Charles from Canal. 'Where the locals go. Good bars and clubs. Better music and cheaper.'

Cemetery freaks can tune into the weird tombs at Basin St, $1. 'Have Buddy show you the tomb of the Voodoo Queen of New Orleans.'

New Orleans International Trade Mart, at the foot of Canal St. Admission to the observation deck and the Louisiana Maritime Museum, both on the 31st floor, is $2.50, or $1.50 for under-13s, but the better view is from the revolving 'Top of the Mart Bar' where you will have to buy a drink. The platform revolves every one and a half hours. Mexican tourist cards also obtainable in the building without waiting. A free view is to be had from the spectacular Hyatt Regency Hotel, Poydras and Loyola.

Confederate Museum, Camp and Howard Sts. 'Ten out of ten.' $1 adults, 50¢ kids.

Superdome, 1500 Poydras St, 587-3663. Opened in 1975, and the world's largest covered stadium. Tour, $3.50, or $1.50 seniors and under-13s. 'The stadium is impressive but the tour is a rip-off; better to pay to see an event, if you can afford it.'

The last remaining streetcar, St Charles runs through the fashionable Garden District. Once there get out and wander among the sumptuous houses built by rich ante-bellum whites to rival the Creole dwellings in the Vieux Carré.

Cruises on the Mississippi. The SS Mark Twain is not recommended: 'filthy; bad food'. The SS President leaves Canal St and tours the harbour—the second busiest in the US. This costs $9. The *Voyageur*, which docks at Peters Rd, explores 32 miles of bayous, including Chalmet where the British lost the Battle of New Orleans, $10; and the *Natchez*, a stern wheeler steamboat, leaving from Toulouse St Wharf, 2-hour cruise, $9. Or take the free ferry to Gretna from the bottom of Canal St. Goes every 5 mins. Still on the subject of water—**Lake Pontchartrain.** Although the beach and funfair are closed after Labor Day it's a nice idea if you have transport to take the road across the Lake. 24 miles long, and for 8 of those one is totally out of sight of land! 'Well worth travelling over the world's longest bridge. It's unbelievable that a bridge could be so long.'

ENTERTAINMENT
Although the jazz revival in New Orleans has brought back many good musicians, there are also, on Bourbon St, scores of overpriced nightclubs, flashy restaurants, endless clip joints, and plenty of bad music. Choose carefully, and carry proof of your overeighteenness. *Figaro* and *The Courier* will tell you what's on.

Annual Jazz and Heritage Festival. Takes place late April. Includes jazz, dancing, crafts and entertainments. 'A good time was had by all.'

Al Hirt's, 501 Bourbon, Expensive but reliably good mainstream.

The Jamini, Chartres and Iberville. 'Very friendly locals and not the usual Bourbon St rip-off. Cheapish beer.'

Pat O'Brien's, St Peter St. 'Great atmosphere; no cover; closes 5am.' 'Home of the Hurricane Cocktail, don't miss it.'

Preservation Hall, 726 St Peter. Trad jazz. 'Arrive early.' 8.30pm–12.30am nightly, $1 entry. 'Great atmosphere, the only original jazz bands left in New Orleans, a must.'

Tipitina's, 501 Napoleon. 'The real thing.' Dixie Cups, Earl King, etc.

Pete Fountain's, 501 Bourbon. Jazz place.

The Cajun Bandstand, 1822 Airline Highway. Good Cajun music and 'lovely homemade gumbo'.

Sloppy Jim's Bar, Royal St. 'Cheap local bar, full of colourful characters. The barman is especially worthy of attention; long, drawn features and doleful eyes, he's reminiscent of Melvin the Depressed Robot out of *Hitchhiker's Guide to the Galaxy*. Probably enjoys funerals and disaster jokes. Getting drunk at his bar was great entertainment.'

La Strada, Bourbon St. Topless and bottomless men and women.

INFORMATION
Tourist and Convention Commission, 334 Royal St, 522-8772. Start here. They have a lot of useful information and excellent free coffee.

Chamber of Commerce, 334 Camp St.

Travelers Aid, 211 Camp St, Suite 400.

Post Office: at Iberville and Bienville.

TRAVEL
Train station: 1001 Loyola Ave, 525-6063. AMTRAK's *Crescent* from NY, *City of New Orleans* from Chicago and *Sunset Limited* from LA terminate here.

Greyhound Terminal, Loyola and Howard. 525-9371.

Trailways Terminal, 1314 Tulane, 525-4201.

Green Tortoise, 800-227-4766, toll-free.

There is a local bus service to the airport, $1.

City bus and streetcar flat rate 50¢. For bus tour information call: 529-1689, and for boat cruise info call: 586-8777.

Auto Driveaway, 201 Kent Ave, 885-9292.

Try Tulane and Loyola Universities for their ride boards.

BAYOU TECHE. Bayou is an Indian word meaning slow moving stream. In the 19th century, when overland transportation was difficult, planters built their homes along such navigable waterways as this. The homes are worth visiting, and the countryside and towns worth exploring for their Cajun influences, expressed most notably in dialect, folk music and food (gumbo with okra, crawfish etouffe and jambalaya). The hunters and trappers, who live off muskrat, otters and raccoons in this area account for about half of America's furs. **Lafayette** is the industrial and cultural centre of the bayoux, and the Mardi Gras celebrations here draw nearly as many people as in New Orleans. The University of Southwest Louisiana is home of the Maison Acadienne, dedicated to the perpetuation of French and Acadian traditions.

St Martinville, east of US 90, is an early Acadian town that served as the setting for part of Longfellow's *Evangeline*. The Arceneaux home is now the Acadian Museum, an excellent example of a French colonial country house, simple, but furnished to the taste of a gentleman. It stands in the lovely setting of Longfellow-Evangeline State Park just north of town. Apart from Cajuns, Royalist refugees from the French Revolution also settled here, hence the town has sometimes been called Le Petit Paris. The chapel of St Martin is the centre of town life, and amongst the tombstones round the back you can find that of the real Evangeline, Emmeline Labiche.

South of St Martinville on Route 31 is **New Iberia**, founded by the Spaniards but given its flavour by the Cajuns. Here, on East Main Street, is the old rose-bricked and columned mansion, Shadows on the Teche. Its second storey *galerie* is reached by the customary outside stairway behind a louvered screen. Built in 1830 by David Weeks, both house and family have since become the source of many stories and legends. Most of these are told on the spot by a guide; though the most fascinating inhabitant was Weeks Hall, great-grandson of the founder, who figured in Henry Miller's *Air Conditioned Nightmare*.

MISSISSIPPI

If cotton is anywhere king it's here in Mississippi. But despite some recent industrial progress and the gracious tag of Magnolia State, Mississippi remains economically and socially one of the most backward states in the Union.

'When you're in Mississippi, the rest of America doesn't seem real. And when you're in the rest of America, Mississippi doesn't seem real,' said Bob Parris, a leading civil rights worker.

But don't let that put you off visiting the state. Keep your eyes and ears open, for much of times past—ante-bellum mansions, backcountry blues—still survive here and are worth seeing and hearing.

The Natchez Trace Parkway stretches diagonally across Mississippi along the historic highway of bandits, armies and adventurers. You can drive along it, or else explore the old trails on foot. Along Mississippi's Gulf coastline there runs another old trail. This is the old Spanish Trail which ran from St Augustine, Florida, to the missions in California. US 90 from Pascagoula to Bay St Louis follows the trail through the state.

OXFORD. An unpretentious little town set in corn, cotton and cattle country in the north of the state, Oxford nevertheless stands large in the world's great literature. Novelist William Faulkner's Jefferson in his fictitious Yoknapatowpha County corresponds to Oxford and his home is here, along with several beautiful ante-bellum mansions and the University of Mississippi—Ole Miss.

ACCOMMODATION AND FOOD
Ole Miss Motel, 1517 E University Ave, 234-2424. Singles $22, doubles $27.
Smitty's Cafe, 208 S Lamar St. Sandwiches $1.50–$3, and huge helpings of Southern cooking from $3 to $9.

OF INTEREST
Visit the Tourist Information Office in the main square; you can easily cover the town on foot.
William Faulkner's Home, called Rowan Oak, on Old Taylor Rd, reached by walking down S Lamar. 234-3284. Tucked away back in the woods, unmarked from the street. U of Miss students give free tours.
Square Books, 115½ S Lamar, has an impressive collection of Southern writing and photographs of the South.

TRAVEL
Trailways, 925 Van Buren Ave.

VICKSBURG. After months of battle and siege, General Grant took Vicksburg on 4 July 1863, giving control of the Mississippi Valley to the Union forces and splitting the Confederacy in two. Amidst the since-dedicated stone monuments all about the National Military Park, it's possible to trace the course of battle, though as the park is 16 miles round, a car would help.

But perhaps the most fascinating visit would be to the Waterways Experiment Station with its working models of New York harbour, the lower Mississippi and other such places—the one of the Mississippi being several acres in size.

Enroute from here to Natchez via US 61 is **Port Gibson** (said by Grant to be 'too beautiful to burn'). Resin P Bowie, inventor of the knife made famous by brother Jim, is buried in the Catholic Cemetry here.

ACCOMMODATION
Downtowner Motel, Walnut St, $32 single, $40 double. 'Very good; pool, coffee in room and in heart of historic district.'
Camping near town at Rocky Springs Park on Natchez Trail.

FOOD
Walnut Hills, 1214 Adams St. 'Home cooking served at large round dining tables. Rowdy bar with live country music.'

OF INTEREST
Vicksburg National Military Park. Encloses three sides of the city. Old trenches, gun positions and rifle pits to be seen. Also a museum. Tour begins at the Visitors Center with exhibits and artefacts of the siege; the drive is free though you can take a guide along in your car for $10, or hire a casette for $4.50.

Courthouse Museum, Cherry and Jackson Sts. Mementoes of the 47-day siege. There are several impressive ante-bellum mansions to be seen. These include **Cedar Grove, Planters Hall** and **McRaven House**.

The *Sprague*, largest of the stern-wheelers, was a showboat until fire put an end to on-board activities. Now being restored out of town. The *Delta Queen* (1926) and *Mississippi Queen* (1973) ply the Mississippi and Ohio Rivers, calling here.

The *Cairo*, a Union gunboat sunk in the Yazoo River during the campaign, has been raised; watch the restoration on site.

Waterways Experiment Station, south of midtown via Halls Ferry Rd, the southern extension of Cherry St. Mon–Fri, 10am–2pm. Free tours.

For a tremendous view of the Mississippi River, climb up on to the **Vicksburg Bluffs**.

INFORMATION
Tourist Information Center, Clay St Exit (4B) off I-20.
Warren County Tourist Promotion Commission, PO Box 110, Vicksburg; 636-9421.

NATCHEZ.
Natchez is one of America's finest historical towns, graced by numerous ante-bellum mansions, and making little attempt at commercialising on its charm. In the 1850s one-sixth of America's millionaires lived here, great cotton planters and brokers who established imposing homes and furnished them handsomely.

The favoured architectural style was Classical Greek and Roman as promoted by Palladio, Inigo Jones and Thomas Jefferson. Natchez families have carefully preserved, rather than modernised, their treasures, and for the visitor a block's walk off Main Street is to retreat a century and more back into time.

ACCOMMODATION
Dumas Riverview Hotel, 218 John R Junkin Drive, 442-0211. $28 single, $33 double. Pool, Colour TV.
Prentiss Motel, 442-1691, on US 62 south of town. $33 single, $38 double. AC, colour TV, pool.
Days Inn, 109 US Hwy 61 S, 445-8291. $28 single, $32 double.
For those who want to blow it all: several old mansions take overnight guests, eg Dixie, 211 S wall St, 442-2525. Built 1795–1828 and showing strong Jeffersonian influence, with its original formal gardens intact. $65 per room, furnished with antiques, includes tour of home and plantation breakfast.
Camping at Clear Springs Recreation Area.

OF INTEREST
The best time to see the fine mansions is during the **Natchez Pilgrimage**, a house and garden tour of 30 of the best, in early March, or in October.

Many of the mansions are privately owned and still lived in. To get inside, appointments should be made. Three that have gone public, however, and are open daily, are:

Connolly's Tavern: Spanish-colonial style; though a frontier inn, it's elaborately furnished. Now headquarters of Natchez Garden Club, they'll help arrange appointments for private visits elsewhere. Canal and Jefferson Sts. 9am–5pm. $2.50, students $1.50.

Stanton Hall: one of the grandest of ante-bellum mansions. Headquarters of Pilgrimage Garden Club will also help with appointments. Overnight rooms available, restaurant. Pearl and High Sts. $2.50, students $1.50.

Rosalie: dates from 1820. South end of Broadway. 9am–5pm. $2.50, students $1.50. Of those houses that require appointments, the three perhaps most worth visiting are **Arlington, D'Evereux** and **Dunleigh.**

Natchez Museum, 111 S Pearl St. Outstanding collection of early Americana. Mon–Sat 10am–5pm, Sun 1pm–5pm.

Natchez-under-the-Hill. 'The remains of this infamous riverside area are to be found on Silver St. Little known by tourists and as yet untouched by preservationists.'

The **Natchez Trace** was originally a buffalo trail, later an Indian Trail, finally the main frontier road between Nashville and Natchez until the riverboats proved a superior form of travel. Andy Jackson used the Trace to lead his men against the British at New Orleans in the War of 1812. The route is now followed by the Natchez Trace National Parkway. Info Center with audiovisual program at Tupelo Headquarters Visitor Center. **Emerald Mound**, one of the largest Indian Mounds in the country is about a mile off the parkway, 11 miles northeast of Natchez.

INFORMATION

Chamber of Commerce, 300 N Commerce St. They have literature, maps, and brochures on the houses and various tours available.

TRAVEL

'I would suggest a day-tour from New Orleans, departing by bus 5am, arriving Natchez 10am, departing again 5.30pm. Leaves plenty of time to visit the 3 best houses and walk around the town. Or take a riverboat from New Orleans.'

BLUES COUNTRY. There is no one place in Mississippi, Louisiana or any other part of the Deep South that can be called Blues Country. This is just one recommended excursion into that backcountry world of weathered shanties, silent swamps, their trees draped in Spanish moss, and dusty roads where the original sound can still be heard.

'Tell me, mama, how you want your rollin' done,
sweet mama rollin' stone.
Say, you must be wantin' me, baby, to break my lowdown
back—No!
Sweet mama rollin', sweet mama rollin' stone.'

Coming down US 61 out of Natchez turn off at Woodville on to Route 24 making for **Old River Lake**, a Mississippi 'cutoff' left isolated by the changing course of the river. You have to get off the surfaced road as you near the lake, and now travelling over the bottomlands to the shanty settlements inhabited by hunters, fishermen, adventurers and self-made outcasts, you're as far removed from the rest of the world as it's possible to be in the South. Scott Dunbar used to play *Mama Rollin' Stone* on his guitar here, and his wife Celeste would cook up some good food for visitors. Maybe they still do, or somebody else does now.

Just down the river over the border into Louisiana is infamous **Angola State Penitentiary** where the blues come over the prison walls and have been heard on recordings around the world.

BILOXI. The town is along the most populated area of the Gulf coast and has commercialised on its white sand beach. Though tourism is important, this has been a shrimping community since the Civil War. In early June, the fleets are ritually blessed; at the harbour front down the end of Main Street, or in the Back Bay area, you can watch the fishermen get on with their lives oblivious to tourism.

At various times in the town's history, Biloxi has been under the flags of France, Spain, Britain, the West Florida Republic, the Confederacy and the US.

ACCOMMODATION
Sea Gull Motel, W Beach Blvd, 896-4211. $24 single, $28 double, $4 per extra person. AC, colour cable TV, heated pool. Across from the beach.
Camping at Biloxi Beach Campground, US 90 at 3314 W Beach Blvd.

FOOD
Mary Mahoney's French House Restaurant, 138 Rue Magnolia, 1 block north of US 90. In 1737 home, one of the oldest in America, not cheap but noted for its excellent regional cuisine, especially shrimp—try shrimp dolores. Entrees $8 up; also children's dishes. Reservations advisable, 432-0163.

OF INTEREST
Beauvoir. The last home of Jefferson Davis; on US 90. You can tour the house and the library cottage in which he worked. Adults $3.50, seniors $2.50, under-17s $1.50. 8.30am–5pm. Biloxi also has several other fine houses.
Fort Massachusetts, on Ship Island. Completed by the Federal government during the Civil War and still pretty intact. Ship Island is part of the new **Gulf Islands National Seashore** which includes the islands of Horn and Petit Rois, a mainland campground at Ocean Springs, and a further section 80 miles east in Florida. In both Mississippi and Florida park attractions include: old forts to tour, beautiful swimming, varied wild life, rare sea oats, and superb white sand beaches. Boats run daily to Ship Island from Biloxi. $6.

INFORMATION
Travelers Aid, Medical Arts Building, 1145 W Howard Ave, 435-4584.

NORTH CAROLINA

Verrazano, De Soto and Sir Walter Raleigh each explored the state, though it was first developed privately by wealthy Barbados planters. They sold out to the Crown in 1729 and the area became a Royal Colony.

With a jagged coastline and forested mountains, the state is a favourite with campers. It shares the Blue Ridge Parkway with Virginia. Though one of the most progressive of the Southern states, it happily retains its slow and friendly pace of life.

The Tarheel State (so named for the tar deposit left by tobacco leaves when touched) is number one in America for tobacco growing and cigarette manufacturing. Winstons, Salems, Camels and other cigarettes are manufactured in Winston-Salem in the northwestern part of the state.

National Park: Great Smoky Mountains (also in Tennessee)

THE COAST. Though jagged, the mainland coast is protected by the Outer Banks. Fresh and saltwater fishing are excellent here, but beware the treacherous currents.

The first power-driven flight was made near **Kitty Hawk** at Kill Devil Hills on 17 December 1903, by Orville Wright. Now in the Smithsonian Institution, Washington DC, the plane was aloft for 12 seconds and achieved a speed of 35 miles per hour. Orville later explained that he and his brother Wilbur had remained bachelors because they hadn't the means 'to support a wife as well as an aeroplane'. There's a free and interesting museum here. Ironically turning its back on the airborne internal combustion engine, hang-gliding is the big sport around here these days. For about $40 you can get wings and tuition and launch right off the sand dunes. The beaches here and down to **Nag's Head** are relatively uncrowded and excellent for swimming. There are numerous campgrounds.

Fort Raleigh, on Roanoke Island, is the site of the Lost Colony. Three hundred Englishmen settled here in 1587, but when some of their friends returned three years later, the entire colony had disappeared without trace. The only clue was the word 'Croatan' carved into a tree. The mystery remains unsolved. The original fort has been rebuilt.

Cape Hatteras National Seashore, 45 square miles on the Outer Banks, constitutes the most extensive stretch of undeveloped seashore along the Atlantic coastline. The inhabitants of the past would tie lanterns to their horses' necks to lure ships on to the treacherous Diamond Shoals before plundering their cargo. The tallest lighthouse (208 feet) in the US now protects shipping from what was known as the 'Graveyard of the Atlantic'.

The sand is still treacherous however and visitors should only park in designated areas. The Cape is often hit by summer hurricanes and the remains of many shipwrecks are visible. Not deterred are the bottle-nosed dolphins who often come near the beach and the greater snow geese, and other migratory birds, who stop off annually at the **Pea Island National Wildlife Refuge**. A visitor in the past was

Bluebeard who hung out on **Ocracoke Island** at the southern end of Hatteras Seashore. The famed pirate and his crew met their deaths at Teach's Hole. You can reach the island by free ferry from Hatteras.

GREAT SMOKY MOUNTAINS NATIONAL PARK. The name Great Smokies is derived from the smoke-like haze that envelopes these forest-covered mountains. The Cherokee Indians called this the Land of a Thousand Smokes. Part of the Appalachians, the area has been preserved as a wilderness and affords an excellent impression of obstacles facing the earliest pioneers on their push west. Cabins, cleared acreage and other pioneer remnants lie undisturbed in the park's valleys, while plants and animals live protected in this forest and mountain sanctuary. The highest peaks east of the Rockies (with the exception of 6684-foot Mt Mitchell in the state but not in the park) are here.

Though the park is traversed by road, the best way to appreciate its beauty is to walk its trails. The **Appalachian Trail** extends 68 miles through the length of the park, but shorter hikes, both guided and not guided, are available to dilettante naturalists.

ACCOMMODATION
Campgrounds are located throughout the park. The season is May through October, though the park is open all year and spring and autumn are less crowded, more beautiful, than summer.

OF INTEREST
Sugarlands Visitor Center, Newfound Gap Rd and Little River Rd. Information audio-visual displays. May to Oct: 8am–9pm; otherwise 8am–4.30pm.
Cades Cove, off Little River Road. Restored pioneer dwellings, history provided. Free.
Okonaluftee Museum Newfound Gap Road 2½ miles north of Cherokee. Reconstructed farmstead, exhibits of Pioneer possessions. June 15 through Labor Day, 8am–7.30pm. There is also a park info centre here.
Okonaluftee Indian Village, in Cherokee. A recreated 18th century Indian community. Also a museum and, in the summer, there's a production of *Unto These Hills*, an Indian drama. Admission to the village: $4.50 adults, under-13s $2.50. Open daily mid-May through late Oct 9am–5.30pm. Tel: 497-2111.

TRAVEL
Horses rentable at Cades Cove, Cosky campgrounds. Smokemount campgrounds, and Two Mile Branch nr Park Hdqs.
Asheville, North Carolina, the southern terminus of the Blue Ridge Parkway which runs down the Appalachians from Virginia, can serve as a base for visiting the park, though transport is better from **Knoxville**, Tennessee.

SOUTH CAROLINA

In its semi-tropical coastal climate and historical background, the Palmetto State, first to secede from the Union, marks the beginning of the Deep South. South Carolina also typifies the New South. Since the Second World War booming factories, based on the Greenville area, have replaced sleepy cotton fields and cotton itself has been replaced by tobacco as the major cash crop. Textile manufacturing and chemicals are the state's major industries, but industry has not developed at the expense of the state's traditional charm and lovely countryside.

Whereas North Carolina was originally a virtual province of easygoing Virginia, the planters of South Carolina worked both their land and their slaves to the limit, producing rice and indigo and making their fortunes in a season. Pastel mansions rose in the humming port of Charleston where, in the words of one observer, 'every Tradesman is a Merchant, every Merchant is a Gentleman, and every Gentleman one of the Noblesse. We have no such Thing as a common people among us; Between Vanity and Fashion, the Species is utterly destroyed'.

CHARLESTON. In the 20th century it started a world-wide dance craze; in the 19th it started the Civil War; and in the 18th century Charleston itself got off to a cosmopolitan start with an influx of Englishmen, Huguenots, Portuguese Jews and African blacks who created what remains one of the most charming cities in the country.

Tall townhouses in pastel colours stand along gardens, squares and cobblestoned streets. Compact and easily explored on foot, Charleston rewards the visitor with fine architecture, mellow history and excellent seafood. 'The Harrogate of America; historical, picturesque, but certainly not the liveliest place on earth.'

ACCOMMODATION
Mrs McIntosh, 184 Ashley Ave, 723-8572. $30 per room, bath, fridge, TV. 'Excellent.' 'Really lovely lady.'
268 Calhoun St at Ashley, 722-7938. $30 per room, bath AC. 'Shabby but clean.'
Heart of Charleston, 200 Meeting St, 723-3451. $38 single, $44–$50 doubles. AC, colour TV, pool. Children 18 and under free with parents.
Christian Student House, 5 Halsey Ave. 'Kind enough to put us up for the night free.'

FOOD
The Colony House, between Market and Broad Sts at 35 Prioleau St. $6 buffet luncheon weekdays, dinners from $8. Not cheap, but marvellously prepared food; try the she-crab soup. Must dress; bookings advised: 723-3424.
Market House, Little Sq, with 12 carry-out restaurants of varying fare. 'Great meeting place.'
Olde Towne Restaurant, 229 King St. Despite its name, it turns out to be Greek, with fish and meat specialties. Lunches from $3.50.

OF INTEREST
The Confederate bombardment of Federally-garrisoned **Fort Sumter** began the Civil War. Across the harbour and now a national monument. The history of the fort is depicted through exhibits and dioramas. There are 6 boat tours a day to the fort before Labor Day, and 2 thereafter. Boats leave from the foot of Calhoun St on

Lockwood Dr, and from the Municipal Marina, 722-1691. There is also a Gray Line tour which goes from the Sheraton Fort Sumter Hotel. Be careful to take a boat that actually lands on the fort! For info call: 722-1112.

Charleston is famous for its fine houses, squares and cobblestone streets. Among those worthy of attention are **Catfish Row**, made famous through Heyward's *Porgy and Bess*; the **Battery** has blocks of attractive old residences; the **Dock Street Theater**, Church and Queen: the only **Huguenot church** in the US at Church and Queen; **Nathaniel Russell House**, 51 Meeting; **Sword Gate House**, Tradd and Legare. 'The Nathaniel Russell costs $2.50 but it is probably the best house to visit. It has a famous freeflying spiral staircase.'

The Charleston Museum, at Rutledge Ave and Calhoun St, was built in 1773. It claims to be the oldest museum in the country. Open 9am–5pm. $1.50 adults, 50¢ under-19s. By contrast, the city's newest museum has a full-scale replica of the **Confederate submarine**, *H L Hunley*, 50 Broad St. You can peer into the open side of the sub and see life-like models of the crew going about their work. Free. 10am–5pm.

Gibbes Art Gallery, 135 Meeting. Early art of South Carolina. 10am–5pm.

Old Slave Mart Museum, 6 Chalmers St. Has exhibits depicting the history of the blacks. $1.50 adults, 50¢ under-13s. 10am–5pm.

Flea Market, Meeting and Market Sts. 7am–5pm, Saturdays. Fruit, veg, masses of junk. 'Lively and colourful.'

Boone Hall Plantation, 7 miles north nr US 17. Open 9am–5pm weekdays, 1pm–5pm Sun. Beautiful house, beautiful gardens. Adults $3.75, under-13s 50¢.

Charlestowne Landing, Old Town Rd. Site of the first permanent English speaking settlement in SC. See *The Adventure*, a working reproduction of a 17th century sailing vessel. The park is also the place for local events and happenings.

ENTERTAINMENT

Summers can be close, but you can cool off at Folly Beach, off Rt 171, where there's also a Pavilion and Amusement Park. 'Excellent beach, very long, deserted and clean.'

Blue Marlin, Cumberland St, nr the Market. 'Rowdy warehouse bar, busy and fun.'

RR's, St Phillips and Wentworth Sts. 'Good bluegrass, friendly folks.'

INFORMATION

Information Center, 85 Calhoun St, 722-8338.

NB Even the Chamber of Commerce is historic. Formed in 1773, it is one of the nation's oldest civic commercial organisations.

TRAVEL

There are various city tours available including, a Gray Line tour, carriage rides, double decker bus tour, and do-it-yourself cassette tape tour for auto or walking tours. Details from Info Center.

Greyhound, 89 Society St, 722-7721; Trailways 100 Calhoun St, 723-8649.

AMTRAK, Hwy 52, 8 miles west of town; bus service available. The *Palmetto* and the *Silver Meteor* call here, both from NYC, the first terminating at Savannah, the second at Miami.

TENNESSEE

Sloping westwards from the rugged Appalachians to the Mississippi bottomlands, the Volunteer State occupied a pivotal position in the Civil War. The mountain people remained loyal to the Union, while Nashville and Memphis were, and still are, solid South.

For such a folksy state, Tennessee has had its fair share of pacesetters. The Tennessee Valley Authority was one of the first large-scale Federally inspired development programmes in a nation usually suspicious of such pinko activities. The Atomic Energy Commission ticks away at Oak Ridge.

National Park: Great Smoky Mountains (also in North Carolina)

CHATTANOOGA. On the Tennessee River, Chattanooga is blessed with one of those names that rolls so mellifluously off a Southerner's tongue. Maybe with a sob too, for on the nearby mountains the Civil War Battle Above the Clouds forced the Confederates to retreat from Tennessee, opening up Georgia to the ruthless General Sherman. The landscape all around the city is beautiful.

Chattanooga was originally the spot where the great Indian trails met, and it became a Cherokee trading centre called Ross's Landing. In 1837 the Cherokee Trail of Tears began here.

ACCOMMODATION
Golden Gateway Inn, 9th and Carter Sts, 266-7331. Downtown, opp Civic Center. Colour TV, bath in rooms; pool. Singles $32, doubles $38.
Terri Motel, 450 Cherokee Blvd, 267-0281. Across river from downtown. $32 double. 'Very good.'

OF INTEREST
For both the view and the history, take the incline railway up **Lookout Mountain**. The gradient is 77.9% at its maximum. Cost, $2.50 round trip. Funicular leaves from St Elmo Ave, 4 miles from downtown. Connecting bus, 50¢. 'While at the top, follow road to park and see the cannons and memorials, and imagine the battle. The view is still better from up here.'
Chickamauga-Chattanooga National Military Park. The nation's oldest and largest battlefield park (8000 acres).
Also available: side trips to the 'heavily advertised but disappointing' Ruby Falls ($3), and to Rock City ($4). 'Beware the last bus leaves early.'
Chattanooga Choo Choo, Terminal Station. Converted home of the old train, now a railway museum, tourist centre, entertainment spot and restaurant.
Nearby: two TVA dams worth visiting are the Chicamauga on State 153 and Nickajack, seven miles west off US 41.

INFORMATION
Convention and Visitors Bureau, Memorial Auditorium, 399 McCallie Ave, 266-5716.
Travelers Aid, 323 High Street, 267-9543.

NASHVILLE. The Nashville skyline really is quite fine, but though this is the nation's Country and Western music capital, with trappings such as blaring record stores, recording studios and the Grand Ole Opry to suit, it soon becomes apparent that the emphasis is more on canning music than on-the-spot public performances.

ACCOMMODATION
Days Inn, 1–65 and W Trinity Lane, exit 87B, 226-4500. 3 miles north of Nashville. $32 single, $36 double.

Bell Hotel, 112 6th Ave N, 255-7930. Opp Trailways. Singles $15, doubles $20. 'Simple but clean in seedy area.'

Sam Davis Hotel, 7th Ave. $22 double and up, bath, AC. 'Clean, friendly.'

FOOD

Morrison's Family Buffet, 1720 West End Ave. All-you-can-eat-cheap; lunches $3.50, dinners $4.50.

Browns Bar-B-Q Pit and Soul Food, 13 Lafayette St. Black place in black area. 'Excellent cheap smoked chicken sandwiches.'

Stockyard Restaurant and Bullpen Lounge, 2nd Ave N and Whiteside. 'Excellent charcoal steak with homemade soup, salad, veg and fresh bread, $12. Plus live music and dancing downstairs.'

OF INTEREST

Fort Nashborough, 1st Ave N between Broadway and Church Sts. A reproduction of the original fort from which the city first grew. Free.

Nashvillians are hot on reproductions. Their pride and joy is a full-sized **copy of the Parthenon** in Centennial Park.

For the real thing leave the town behind and travel 13 miles east. Off US 7 is **The Hermitage**, the house where Andrew Jackson lived. He is buried in the grounds. $3.

Country Music Hall of Fame, 700 16th Ave S and Division. $3.95. 'Not worth it.' Includes tour of RCA recording studios and Elvis Presley's gold Cadillac. 'Watch out for bogus Hall of Fame on next street.'

Music Row, between 16th and 19th Avenues South, between Division St and Grand Ave. Columbia, RCA and other recording studios can be visited.

Nashville Skyline. For a beautiful night view take the elevator to the revolving bar at the top of the Hyatt Regency Hotel.

Belle Meade Mansion, Leake Ave. Once the home of the biggest horse breeding stable in the South. Tour $2.50.

Cumberland River Cruise. The *Belle Carol* leaves from the Quay near Fort Nashborough, $5.

ENTERTAINMENT

Glynnview Inn, 900 S 5th St. 'A redneck dive. Go with friends for safety to view this bizarre place—the lowest, roughest stratum of class enjoying Western music.'

Downtown nightspots are mostly on 'The Alley'. They tend to be expensive and none too good. It is suggested that you get out of downtown Nashville to Hillsborough village and Vanderbilt campus. Plenty of good eating and drinking places here.

Opryland, out of town, on Briley Pkway. 'A $28 million family entertainment complex.' $12 admission. Also here is the famous **Grand Ole Opry**, 'The home of country music.' Open Fri, Sat, $8 admission. Tickets are scarce, but you can ask to go on the waiting list for cancellations. 'If you have up to number 15 you stand a chance.' 'Nothing quite like it.'

INFORMATION

Convention and Visitors Division, Chamber of Commerce, 161 4th Ave, 259-3900. Travelers Aid, 122 7th Ave N, 256-3168.

TRAVEL

Greyhound, 8th Ave and Demonbreum St, 2 blocks south of Broadway, 255-3504. Trailways, 113 6th Av N, 242-6373.

Gray Line, one block from Greyhound, does a $2\frac{1}{2}$ hr tour.

MEMPHIS. Memphis, home of the Beale Street blues, is Tennessee's Deep South, though suburbanisation and core rot have destroyed a lot of the life of the inner city. Reconstruction of the downtown area is underway, but meantime there's precious little to look forward to here unless of course you're an Elvis fan. Memphis was home to the King of Rock n' Roll and Graceland is the town's major tourist attraction.

There are excellent views of the Mississippi as she makes a broad sweep away to the southwest just below the city.

ACCOMMODATION
Memphis Downtowner, 22 N Third St, 525-8363. Within block of Greyhound and Trailways. AC, colour TV, heated pool. Singles $33, doubles $42.
Hotel Tennessee, 88 S Third St, 525-6621. Behind Greyhound terminal. 'Cheapest place in town.' 'Marvellous value.' Singles from $15, doubles from $22. AC, TV.
Lorraine Motel, 406 Mulberry St, 525-6834. Also a cheapy, and a haunted one at that: here in 1968 Martin Luther King was assassinated. There's a shrine and small museum of Afro-American art.
Camping available in Fullerstone Park, nr Chucalissa Indian Village. 'Very good.'

OF INTEREST
Look for traces of **old Memphis** around the levees where the riverboats once docked, and at **Magevney House**, 198 Adams, thought to be the oldest house in Memphis. Free tours available, 10am–4pm Tue–Sat, 1pm–4pm Sun.
Fontaine House, 680 Adams, built in 1870, the house has been restored. Open 1pm–4pm. **Front St** is the US cotton mart. The **Memphis Cotton Exchange** is on Front and Union.
Chucalissa Indian Village, five miles west of US 61, off Mitchell Rd. An Indian village abandoned in the 1600s and now restored and excavated by Memphis State Univ. The guides are Choctaw Indians. Open 9am–5pm, Tue–Sat, 1pm–5pm Sun Closed Mon $1. 'You can get there via a 47 bus and then hitch.'
A **paddle-boat trip** on the Mississippi on the *Memphis Queen II* costs $3.50 and is reputed to be 'very dull'.
Elvis Presley's house, **Graceland**, is just south of town. $5 entry with tour. 'Extravagantly and disgustingly amusing.' 'I'm not an Elvis fan, but it was well worth it. Get there before 11am to avoid 1–2 hr queues.'
Memphis Museum, 233 Tilton at Central Ave. 'Excellent African game exhibits.' Daily 9am–5pm, closed Mon. Free.
Beale St. Ain't what it used to be, but Pee Wee's Saloon is where W C Handy blew the notes to make him 'Father of the Blues'.

ENTERTAINMENT
Blues Alley, Front and Union. Blues.
The Mall. Good rock.

INFORMATION
Chamber of Commerce, Second St, 523-2322.
Visitors Bureau, 12 S Main St, Suite 107, 526-1919.
Traveler's Aid, 1025 Derman Building, 525-5426.

TRAVEL
Greyhound: 203 Union Ave, 523-7676.
Trailways: Union Ave, and 3rd 525-5826.
Airport bus 40¢.
Grayline Elvis Tour, $8.50.

VIRGINIA

The Old Dominion State is famed for its colonial heritage, for the statesmen it has produced, its historic homes and estates, and the great battlefields on which the fate of the nation was decided in both the 18th and 19th centuries. Seven of the 15 pre-Civil War Presidents were born in the state.

Named after Elizabeth, The Virgin Queen, the colony was the first to be permanently settled by the English, and by 1619 had the first representative legislature in the New World. The American Revolution ended with the surrender of Cornwallis at Yorktown, while the Civil War closed with Lee's surrender to Grant at Appomattox. That event marked the end of Virginia's rivalry with New England for political, cultural and intellectual supremacy.

Virginia is the least southern, both geographically and in attitude, of the old Confederate states and suffers least from their usual social problems. It is a state that has a great deal to offer the visitor both from the scenic and the historic point of view. In the east, sandy beaches and the amazing 17½-mile Chesapeake Bay Bridge Tunnel linking Virginia to Maryland, in the west, the Skyline Drive and the Shenandoah National Park, while everywhere there are countless well-preserved links with the past.
National Park: Shenandoah

RICHMOND. The capital of Virginia and of the old Confederacy. Anyone who has seen the famous photographs by Matthew Brady will know it was largely destroyed by retreating Southern troops. Today it is a factory town, rank with the odour of tobacco, but nonetheless a good centre for visiting nearby landmarks.

ACCOMMODATION
Bensonhouse of Richmond, PO Box 15131, phone 321-6277. B&B agency, offering rooms in the Richmond area from $24 single, $33 double.
Days Inn, 2100 Dickens Rd, I-64 and Broad St, 282-3300. $35 single, $40 double.
Massad House Hotel, 11 N 4th St, 648-2893. $25 double. Recommended by YMCA which does not have overnights.

OF INTEREST
The State Capitol building was designed by Thomas Jefferson. Free tours.
The White House of the Confederacy and the **Confederate Museum** are at 12th and Clay Sts. Mon–Sat, 9am–5pm, Sun 2pm–5pm. $1. Nearby at 818 E Marshall St, is the **home of John Marshall**, Chief Justice.
You can also visit the **Edgar Allan Poe Museum** in the 17th-century Old Stone House and the house, on Franklin St, that **Robert E Lee** lived in during the last year of the Civil War. The latter is open 10am–4pm. Admission $1. The Poe Museum is at 1914 East Main St. Open Tues–Sat, 10am–4.30pm, Sun–Mon 1.30pm–4.30pm. Admission $2.
Hollywood Cemetery, south end of Laurel. US Presidents James Monroe and John Tyler, and Confederate President Jefferson Davis, are buried here, along with some 18,000 Confederate soldiers.
St John's Church, 24th and Broad. Built 1741 and where Patrick Henry made his famous 'Give me liberty or give me death' speech.
City Hall Skydeck, 9th and Broad, for a view of the city. Free.

Virginia Museum of Fine Arts, N Blvd. One of the country's finest art galleries. Entry by donation.

Valentine Museum of the Life and History of Richmond, 1015 E Clay St. Includes Indian stuff. 10am–4.45pm. Closed Mon. $1.

American Tobacco Co, free tours and samples. 26th and E Cary Sts. Mon–Fri 8am–4pm. 643–5341.

INFORMATION
Visitors Information Center, 1700 Robin Hood Rd, 358-5511. From here you can buy a 'passport' for $5 which includes entry to 9 museums and historic houses, and discount coupons for two plantations and parks.

TRAVEL
Greyhound: 412 E Broad St, 648-0120.
Trailways: 9th and Broad St, 643-1886.
AMTRAK, 7519 Staples Mill Rd.

FREDERICKSBURG.
North of Richmond off the I-95, four great Civil War battles were fought in the area. You can tour the Fredericksburg Battlefield where Lee's army fought off wave after wave of charging Federals from Marye's Heights. Free tours are available. The town itself has several interesting old houses standing, among them Washington's family home, Ferry Farm, and the Rising Sun Tavern, owned by George's brother, Charles, and meeting place for Jefferson, Patrick Henry and other patriots.

WILLIAMSBURG.
Early capital of Virginia, Williamsburg, planned by Christopher Wren, is perhaps the most beautifully restored colonial town in the country. The feat was achieved through financing by John D Rockefeller. The town lies just off US 64, about 40 miles southeast of Richmond.

ACCOMMODATION
All of the following offer accommodation at about $16 single, $20 double.
Mrs W Rawl, 307 Indian Springs Rd, 229-4718 'Phenomenal. Will pick up at Greyhound. Free drinks. Found alternative accommodation for me when full up.'
Mrs Fisher, 701 Monumental Ave, 229-4320.
Williamsburg Lodge, S England St, 229-1600.
Mrs A Gordon, 312 Indian Springs Rd, 229-1974. 'Will pick up.'
The Information Center can provide lists of tourist homes, and will do some phoning around for you. Students can try the U of William and Mary fraternities.

FOOD
Campus Restaurant, 433 Prince George St. 'Good value; student atmosphere.'
Williamsburg Lodge Coffee House. 'Dinner around $6 but also has a pleasant cafeteria.'

OF INTEREST
Colonial Williamsburg. Hundreds of buildings have been painstakingly restored to bring back into being the colonial capital of Virginia (or as one reader put it: to make 'a sort of Colonial Disneyland'). Perhaps the best are the Capitol, jail, Raleigh Tavern, Governor's Palace, and various colonial craft shops.
Tickets are priced according to the number of buildings and craft shops visited: 10-building ticket $10; 18-building ticket $13; kids 6–12 half-price. Phone 229-1000

for info. Finally, you can just wander for free without going into the houses at all. Go first to the Information Center. You can see a documentary film here which may make the visit more meaningful.

College of William and Mary. Founded 1693, the second oldest in the nation.

In the vicinity is **Jamestown**, first permanent English settlement in America. Not that much has been restored: the visitor must often content himself with looking at foundations. Plagues, Indians, starvation and floods hindered its development, and when finally the peninsula became an island, Williamsburg and Yorktown prospered in its stead. For a history and study of everyday life in early Jamestown visit the Information Center and Museum at Jamestown Island. The original settlement is two miles from the more recent **Jamestown Festival Park**, opened by Elizabeth II in 1957. In the park are replicas of the three ships, *Susan Constant*, *Godspeed*, and *Discovery*, a reconstruction of the first fort, and a museum.

Yorktown is the least restored of the James River historical areas. Only the battlefield remains. The French navy blockaded and bombarded the town while the Franco-American allies, outnumbering the British 2 to 1, pressed in overland.

The surrender of the British at Yorktown in reality ended the War of Independence, although it was actually a further two years before the final peace treaty was ratified. The **Yorktown Victory Center**, on a 21-acre tract overlooking the York River, built for the Bicentennial, is a permanent museum dramatising the military events of the Revolution. $2.

James River Planatations. Take Routes 5 and 10 along the river to visit several plantation homes of early American leaders.

VIRGINIA BEACH. Continuing southeast from Williamsburg and past Norfolk, you come to this fast-growing resort with a 28-mile beach running from the landing dunes of America's first permanent colonists on Cape Henry to Virginia's Outer Banks. From here you can get on to the amazing Chesapeake Bay Bridge Tunnel for the northern drive up the Atlantic coastline, stopping off to visit the Assateague National Seashore (see also Maryland).

ACCOMMODATION
All prices at Virginia Beach skyrocket from June to Labor Day. $55 for a double passes for 'economy' at a place like the Dolphin Atwater Hotel, 1705 Atlantic Ave, 428-5353. Cheaper to rent an efficiency apartment and cram everyone you know into it. For starters, go to the Visitors Center, 20th St and Pacific Ave, 425-7511. They can be very helpful in finding inexpensive accommodation.

CHARLOTTESVILLE. Located in west-central Virginia, Charlottesville, surrounded by beautiful countryside and old estates, is one of the most interesting and charming places in the state. The homes of Jefferson and Monroe are nearby, as are the birthplaces of Lewis and Clark. Much of the architecture is either directly Jefferson's or influenced by his example. The elegant University of Virginia is testimony to his humanism and architectural genius.

ACCOMMODATION
Guesthouses Reservation Service, 107 Bollingwood Rd, 979-7264. Not the cheapest accommodation, but the most gracious.
Chancellor Apartments, 1413½ University Ave, 295-5457. Over Chancellor's Drug Store. Doubles $19.

The Venerable Guesthouse, 316 14th St NW, 295-7707. $23 double, but only 4 rooms so book ahead. 'Beautiful location.'

Econo Travel Motel, 2014 Holiday Dr, 295-3185. Singles $29, doubles $34.

Town and Country Motor Lodge, Rt 250E, 293-6191. Singles $29, doubles $34. 'Very friendly and clean.'

Camping: Lake Reynovia, 1770 Avon St, 296-1910. Lake swimming, snack bar, open all year. $8 per site.

OF INTEREST

Old centre of town, around Jefferson and Main Sts. Self tour pamphlet free at Tourist Center.

Monticello. Three miles southwest of the town on Rt 53. This is the home which Thomas Jefferson designed for himself. It is an architectural masterpiece and the incorporated gadgets bear testimony to Jefferson's inventive genius. $3 adults, $1 under-12s. Open daily 8am–5pm summer, 9am–4.30pm rest of year. 'Magnificent, with fine views of surrounding countryside.'

Nearby is **Ash Lawn**, the house which Jefferson designed for his friend James Monroe. Open 9am–6pm summer, 10am–5pm rest of year. $2.50 adults, 75¢ under-12s.

Further testimony to his brilliance is the **University of Virginia**, one of the most beautiful and architecturally interesting of American universities.

Michie Tavern, near Monticello. The meeting place of such as Jefferson, Monroe, Madison and General Lafayette, now a museum of early Americana. Admission $2.50 adults, $2 seniors, 75¢ under-13s.

APPOMATTOX. South of Charlottesville on US 460 and just outside the town proper is Appomattox Court House, where Lee surrendered his sword to Grant and Grant returned it, the one act of grace concluding the brutal Civil War. The date was 9 April 1865.

SHENANDOAH NATIONAL PARK. Though only 80 miles from Washington DC, the park remains a wilderness area. The 105-mile-long Skyline Drive runs along the crest of the Blue Ridge Mountains, following the old Appalachian Trail, and with an average elevation of over 3000 feet. The southern end of the Drive meets the Blue Ridge Parkway which takes the traveller clear down to the Smokies.

The route affords a continuous series of magnificent views over steeply wooded ravines to the Piedmont Plateau on the east, and across the fertile farmlands of the valley of the Alleghenies to the west. Check the weather before doing the Skyline Drive. If it's bad, you'll just drive through clouds.

There are over 200 miles of foot trails for every grade of hiker, with shelters provided every six miles or so. But these are 'only recommended for racoon and mice lovers. Otherwise, bring a tent, or sleep away from the shelters'. Look out for pioneer dwellings and homesteads along the way.

ACCOMMODATION

Shelters are open all year and are free. Campgrounds with full facilities open May through October. Lodges and cabins also available. There's a $3 per car entrance fee to the Park/Skyline Drive. Entrances at north for Washington, south for Charlottesville, and others, east and west.

OF INTEREST
Luray Caverns, with stalactites and mites, $7 adults, $6 seniors, under-14s $2.50. 'Excessive.' 'Worth every cent.'
Blue Ridge Parkway, the southbound continuation of Skyline Drive, takes you clear down to Great Smoky Mountains National Park.

3. BACKGROUND CANADA

BEFORE YOU GO
Citizens and legal residents of the United States do not need passports or visas to enter Canada as visitors although they may be asked for identification or proof of funds at the border. All other visitors entering Canada must have valid passports. The following categories do not need a visa if entering only as visitors.

1. British and Commonwealth citizens
2. citizens of Ireland, France and South Africa
3. persons born or naturalised in any North, South or Central American country
4. citizens of Austria, Belgium, Denmark, Finland, West Germany, Greece, Iceland, Italy, Japan, Liechtenstein, Luxembourg, Monaco, Netherlands, Norway, Portugal, San Marino, Spain, Sweden, Switzerland and Turkey

Nationals of all other countries should check their visa requirements with their nearest Canadian consular office. If there is no official Canadian representative in the country, visas are issued by the British embassy or consulate.

To work in Canada, a Work Visa must be obtained from the Canadian immigration authorities before departure. To qualify you must produce written evidence of a job offer. If you plan to study in Canada you will need a special student visa, obtainable from any Canadian consulate. You must produce a letter of acceptance from the Canadian college before the visa is issued.

Smallpox vaccinations are not normally asked of visitors, unless an outbreak has recently occurred in the area from which the traveller is coming.

Visitors to the United States wishing to visit Canada briefly and return to the United States should be sure they have with them all the necessary papers to regain entry. Visitors requiring a visa to enter Canada should apply for it at the nearest Canadian embassy or consulate before leaving home. Be aware that Canadian immigration officials can be difficult—make sure that you have sufficient funds and the correct documentation, and look respectable.

Customs permit anyone over 16 to import, duty free, up to 50 cigars, 200 cigarettes and 0.9 kg (2 lbs) of manufactured tobacco.

Along with personal possessions, any number of individually wrapped and addressed gifts up to the value of $25 each may be brought into the country. Each visitor who has passed the legal age of the province or territory of entry (19 in Newfoundland, Nova Scotia, New Brunswick, Saskatchewan, British Columbia, the Yukon and

Northwest Territories; 18 elsewhere) may, in addition, bring in 1.1 litres of liquor or wine or 8.2 litres of beer or ale, duty and tax-free.

Further details on immigration, health or customs requirements may be obtained from the nearest High Commission, embassy or consulate.

GETTING THERE

From Europe. Advanced booking charter (ABC) flights are available from London and other British and European cities, to various Canadian cities including Halifax, Ottawa, Toronto and Montréal, and Winnipeg and Vancouver. Also available are several different types of package deal. Wardair and Air Canada offer packages including anything from bus passes, hotels, coach tours, rail passes, to car and camper wagon rental. The only way to discover the best fare and route for yourself is to get all available information from your travel agent when you are ready to book.

Air Canada has various economy and advanced purchase fare plans, as well as operating a North Atlantic Youth Fare for those between the ages of 12 and 24. The youth fare rate is determined by the time of year in which you are travelling, but, as a rough guide, generally costs around half of the normal scheduled return fare. Wardair, which operates out of Manchester and Prestwick as well as London Gatwick and is generally a much recommended airline, currently offers the best ABC rates.

If you are not able to take advantage of the various advance booking fares, then it would be worth your while considering flying standby on British Airways, TWA, etc, from London or elsewhere in Europe to the US and continuing your journey from there.

From Australia and New Zealand. Qantas has several classes or fares available from Sydney, NSW, to Vancouver. Additionally there is an advance purchase fare; to qualify you have to book and pay for your seat at least 45 days ahead of travelling.

It is perhaps worth investigating the possibility of flying first to New Zealand and then flying Air New Zealand to the US West Coast and then on up to Canada.

From the USA. No problem, you have the choice of bus, train, plane or car, or of course you can simply walk across on foot. It is impossible, within the confines of this Guide, to give all the possible permutations of modes, fares and routes from points within the USA to points within Canada, but, as a rough guide to fares from New York to the major eastern Canadian cities, the current fares to Toronto are: by train, $68 one-way, $102 round trip; by air, $116 one-way, $233 round-trip, excursion fare (14 days advance purchase) $156 round-trip; and by bus, $71 one-way, $99 round trip.

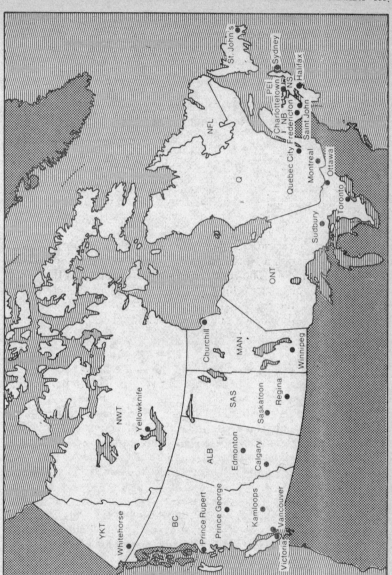

Should you cross the border by car it's a good idea to have a 'yellow non-resident, interprovincial motor vehicle liability insurance card' (phew!) which provides evidence of financial responsibility by a valid automobile liability insurance policy. This card is available in the US through an insurance agent. Such evidence is required at all times by all provinces and territories. In addition Québec's insurance act bars lawsuits for bodily injury resulting from an auto accident, so you may need some additional coverage should you be planning to drive in Québec. If you're driving a borrowed car it's wise to carry a letter from the owner giving you permission to use the car.

CLIMATE AND WHAT TO PACK

Canada's principal cities are situated between the 43rd and 49th parallels, consequently summer months in the cities, and in the southernmost part of the country in general are usually warm and sunny. August is the warmest month when temperatures are in the 70s. Ontario and the Prairie Provinces are the warmest places and although it can be humid it is never as bad as the humidity which accompanies high temperatures in the US.

Be warned, however, that nights, even in high summer, can be cool and it's advisable to bring lightweight sweaters or jackets. Naturally as you go north temperatures drop accordingly. Yellowknife in the North West Territories has an average August temperature of 45°F (7°C) for instance, and nights in the mountains can be pretty cold. Snow can be expected in many places as early as September, and in winter Canada is cold and snowy everywhere.

When you've decided which areas of Canada you'll be visiting, note the local climate and pack clothes accordingly. Plan for a variety of occasions, make a list, and then cut it by half! Take easy-to-care-for garments. Permanent press, non-iron things are best. Laundromats are cheap and readily available wherever you go. Remember too that you'll probably want to buy things while you're in North America. Canadians, as well as Americans, excel at producing casual, sporty clothes, T-shirts, etc. But if you're visiting both countries plan to buy in the US, it's decidedly cheaper. The farther north you plan to go and the more time you intend to spend out of doors, the more weatherproof the clothing will need to be. And don't forget the insect repellent.

It's important too to consider the best way of carrying your clothes. Lugging heavy suitcases is nobody's fun. A lightweight bag or a backpack is possibly best. A good idea is to take a smaller flight-type bag in which to keep all your most valuable possessions like passport, travellers cheques and air tickets, as well. When travelling by bus be sure to keep your baggage within your sights. Make sure it's properly labelled and on the same bus as yourself—at every stop!

TIME ZONES

Canada spans six times zones:

1. Newfoundland Standard Time: Newfoundland, Labrador and parts of Baffin Island.

2. Atlantic Standard Time: The Maritimes, Gaspé Peninsula, Anticosti Island, Québec Province east of Comeau Bay, most of Baffin Island and Melville Peninsula.
3. Eastern Standard Time: Québec Province west of Comeau Bay, and all of Ontario east of 90 degrees longitude.
4. Central Standard Time: Ontario west of 90, Manitoba, Keewatin district of Saskatchewan and southeastern part of the province.
5. Mountain Standard Time: rest of Saskatchewan, Alberta, part of Northwest Territories and northeastern British Columbia.
6. Pacific Standard Time: British Columbia (except northeastern portion) and Yukon Territory.

Newfoundland Standard Time is 3 hours 30 minutes after Greenwich, Atlantic Standard Time, 4 hours, and, moving westwards, each zone is one hour further behind Greenwich, so that the Pacific Zone is 8 hours behind.

From the last Sunday in April through the last Saturday in October, Daylight Saving Time is observed everywhere except Thunder Bay and Essex County, Ontario, and the Province of Saskatchewan.

THE CANADIAN SITUATION

Canada is a comparatively young country and it is well to remember this when discussing the nation and its character. In a manner of speaking, one might say that Canada, having finally acquired control of its own constitution from Britain, has only just come of age. But while Canadians may have won their own national charter, the search continues to find their true role in the world and to reach contentment within the limits of federation at home.

It is after all only a little more than a hundred years since the confederation of 1867. At this time Canada petered out into trackless forest to the north of Lake Superior, and no regular communication existed to the isolated settlements of the Red River in the west. Only the provinces of Ontario, Québec, Prince Edward Island and Nova Scotia were in at the beginning and after 1867 the other six provinces and two territories only gradually trickled into the federation. Of the last of the provinces, Saskatchewan and Alberta were formed in 1905 and Newfoundland entered the federation as recently as 1949.

In this enormous land of little commonwealths people are still few (total population 24 million) and the spaces as vast as ever. In fact, outside the well-populated southern strip of Canada, the land is even less populated today than it was 100 years ago. Today only one in three Canadians lives on the land and you can travel vast distances without seeing any sign of human habitation. The founding peoples, the French and British, make up approximately 75 percent of the population, Indians and Eskimoes account for about one percent, while the remainder is drawn from every corner of the world, the largest ethnic group being German.

Canadian internal politics are renowned for their narrowness and provincial rivalry, the deepest and most bitter rivalry being felt between Ontario and Québec.

The problem of Québec in particular has always lurked in the background and simply refused to go away. It is a problem which has existed in one form or another since the first European explorations which opened up the lands north of the 49th parallel, and in particular since that day in 1759 when General Wolfe defeated Montcalm on the Plains of Abraham, thus signalling the end of the French colony of New France and the defeat of France in North America. Since that day the French Canadian minority have regarded their history as a struggle for physical and cultural survival whilst isolated amidst an alien people.

The election of Pierre Elliott Trudeau and the Liberals in the late '60s for a time offered fresh hope and the chance of a solution to the problem. For Trudeau was elected by a majority which included not only the faithful of Ontario and western Canada, but also the young vote, previously alienated by the normally puritanical and restrictive outlook of Ottawa, and also by the many French Canadians whose loyalty to the Confederation had seemed in doubt during the turbulent early '60s.

Trudeau all along steadfastly refused to give the Québecois 'special status' but concessions were made, notably with the policy of 'two languages' (which in practice means that everyone else has to be bilingual while the French go on being as French as they please). But while Québec remains within the fold, the cause of 'Québec Libre' is very much alive. For instance on the day the Canadian House of Commons approved the constitutional reform as the first step towards acquiring a new constitution, all flags flew at half mast in Québec Province.

Worse still, Québec is not alone in speaking the language of separatism. The rapidly growing western provinces, British Columbia and Alberta in particular, also tend to feel that they could function quite happily without the east, and that anyway Ottawa spends far too much time worrying about Québec to the detriment of other national problems. The Maritimes for their part have long thought that less control from Ottawa would be no bad thing for them.

Meanwhile, his great personal ambition of bringing the constitution to Canada finally realised, the perennial 'enfant terrible' of Canadian politics, Pierre Trudeau, soldiers on, older, and possibly wiser now after a short break from office, and perhaps at last able to deal with some of Canada's other pressing problems unconnected with inter-provincial rivalries and constitutional reform.

Unemployment is at an all-time high; the value of the Canadian dollar has fallen sharply; and inflation has risen just as steeply. Poverty is rife among minority groups like the Indians, and many Canadians feel that legal reform is long overdue. Large tracts of the Northlands with all their resources have yet to be opened up and academic and technological standards are generally lower than in the US. Canadians do have a high standard of living, however, although it may be prosperity bought at the price of economic reliance upon the US. The latter has invested massive amounts in Canadian education, industry, mines and, most recently, oilfields, so much so that more cynical Canadians are left wondering if they have simply exchanged their colonial ties with Britain for economic ties with America.

The United States, on the other hand, and notwithstanding the occasional 'minor' neighbourly dispute over fishing rights, natural gas pipelines or pollution control, now takes Canada a little less for granted and consequently regards her neighbour with a little more respect. Many Americans, looking northward, see in the emerging nation a similar yet less harsh and perhaps a more liberal society. They see cosmopolitan cities like Toronto and Vancouver which are cleaner and greener than most US cities and vast open spaces and much mineral wealth beckoning them to come and explore. At the time of the Vietnam War, many young Americans did just that and many will no doubt continue to do so if Canada can continue on the road to its own peculiar brand of North American liberalism and survive intact through the current constitutional upheavals.

THE GREAT OUTDOORS

Hardly surprising with all those wide open spaces, that Canadians are very outdoors minded. Greenery is never far away and, as in the US, the best of it has been preserved in national parks. There are 28 national parks in Canada ranging in size from less than one to more than 17,000 square miles, and in type from the immense mountains and forests of the west to the steep cliffs and beaches of the Atlantic coastline. In addition there are many fine provincial parks and more than 600 national historic parks and sites.

Entrance to the national parks cost $1 for a one-day pass, $2 for four days, or $10 for the season. Many of the national parks are dealt with in this Guide. For more detailed information we suggest you write to the individual park. A list of major parks follows.

Banff, Alberta.
Cape Breton Highlands, Nova Scotia.
Elk Island, Alberta.
Forillon, Québec.
Fundy, New Brunswick.

Georgian Bay Islands, Ontario.
Glacier, British Columbia.
Jasper, Alberta.
Kejimkujik, Nova Scotia
Kootenay, British Columbia.

Mount Revelstoke, British Columbia.
Point Pelee, Ontario.
Prince Albert, Saskatchewan.
Prince Edward, Prince Edward Island.
Riding Mountain, Manitoba.
St Lawrence Islands, Ontario.

Terra Nova, Newfoundland.
Waterton Lakes, Alberta.
Wood Buffalo, Alberta/North
  Western Territories.
Yoho, British Columbia.

HEALTH

Canada does operate a subsidised health service, though on a provincial rather than federal basis. Most provinces will cover most of the hospital and medical services of their inhabitants, although three months' residency is required in Québec and British Columbia. The short-term visitor to Canada, therefore, must be adequately insured before arrival.

MONEY

Canadian currency is dollars and cents and comes in the same units as US currency, ie penny, nickel, dime, quarter, dollar bills, etc. You can tell the difference by the portrait of Queen Elizabeth on the Canadian ones! American coins are often found among Canadian change and are accepted at par. However American bills do not usually circulate and are not accepted at par. At present one Canadian dollar is worth about US $0.80. To avoid exchange rate problems it is a good idea to change all your money into Canadian currency.
All prices in this section are in Canadian dollars unless otherwise stated.

Travellers cheques are probably the safest form of currency and are accepted at most hotels, restaurants and shops. As well as American Express and Barclays Bank cheques you can also purchase cheques issued by Canadian banks before you go. **Credit cards** are widely used; Barclaycard and Bankamericard (Visa) are reciprocal with Chargex, and Access or Eurocard with MasterCharge.

Bank hours are generally 10am to 3pm, Monday to Friday, and often with a later opening on Friday. Provincial **sales tax** applies on the purchase of goods and services. In Ontario for instance the rate is seven percent, although there are exceptions such as on groceries, and restaurant meals costing less than $4. On the other hand if your meal costs more than $4 then the tax is ten percent.

ACCOMMODATION

All the provincial tourist boards publish comprehensive accommodation lists. These are obtainable from Canadian government tourist offices or directly from provincial tourist boards and have details of all approved hotels, motels and tourist homes in each town. These are really excellent publications and worth having, especially if your stay is limited to one or two provinces.

Hotels and Motels. Always plenty to choose from around sizeable towns or cities, but if you're travelling don't leave finding accommodation until too late in the day. In less populated areas distances between motels can be very great indeed. The major difference between the hotel/motel picture here and in the US is that the budget chains like Days Inn and Motel 6 have not yet made it to Canada in force. The exceptions are Friendship Inns (starting around $19 single, $25 double), Days Inns in Ontario, and Relax Inns in Alberta (starting around $18).

Another budget possibility is a scheme called Econo-Lodging Services, almost nationwide and operating out of Ontario at 101 Nymark Avenue, Willowdale, (416)493-1629. The service is free and may help you find accommodation in hotels, hostels, tourist homes or on campuses. It's aimed primarily at families, students, groups and retired persons.

Otherwise there is the scheme operated by some of the more expensive chains like Ramada, TraveLodge and Holiday Inns, whereby you purchase hotel vouchers before going to Canada. The cost is about $40 to $45 per room per night for a room which can sleep up to four people and with all the trimmings including (usually) a swimming pool. It's a good idea to make your first night's reservation before departure, but after that you can simply call ahead to make your next reservation before you leave the motel in the morning. Any unused vouchers will be refunded later. A reader writes: 'Please make our experience known to your readers. We travelled across Canada using this scheme. This way we lived well, felt safe and had a great time at a price we would have paid for a holiday in Europe'.

Tourist Homes. A bit like bed and breakfast places in Britain and Europe, only without the breakfast. In other words a room in a private home. Usually you share a bathroom and your room will be basic but perfectly adequate. Such establishments are scattered very liberally all over Canada with prices starting around $12. Certainly if hostels are not for you, and your budget doesn't quite stretch to a motel, then these are the places to look for.

Out of town there is now the firmly established farm bed and breakfast circuit. Single it's about $15, double about $25, and details are available from *Country Bed and Breakfast Places in Canada* by John Thompson, published by Deneau and Greenberg.

Hostels. The Canadian Youth Hostels Association (CYHA) has more than 50 member hostels scattered across the country. On the whole they tend to cater to outdoor types and are to be found mostly in the national parks and the Rockies. Class A hostels provide the more luxurious type of accommodation at about $3–$5; more basic establishments cost less. Nearly always you have to be a member of the CYHA ($15 per annum) or a member of the association in your own country. Some hostels are open to non-members. For detailed information and lists of hostels write to: CYHA National Office, 3425 West Broadway, Vancouver 9, BC, or else enquire via the Association in your own country.

Something else again is the programme of state youth hostels run by the government. There are more than 100 of these hostels, situated in towns and at frequent intervals along the Trans Canada Highway. The accommodation is rock bottom basic, costs about $4 a night, and includes, sometimes, breakfast and a shower. Hostels usually open, during the summer, at 6pm, close at 8am and have a three-day limit to stay. You can obtain a list of hostels from: Hostels Program, 333 River Street, Vanier City, Ottawa, K1L 8B9, or from tourist information centres.

YM/WCAs. As elsewhere, standards vary. Certainly there nearly always is a Y when you need it! But cheaper, and often better, are tourist homes and government hostels. Worth considering is the 'Y' voucher scheme. Vouchers get you accommodation at around $11 single, $16 double per night. In the better Ys, this can be good value indeed.

University Accommodation. Plenty available during the summer. Look particularly for student owned co-operatives in large towns and cities which provide a cheapish service, often with cooking facilities. In fact they are only too pleased to have summer visitors since it helps to keep the place going. University housing services and fraternities will often be able to help you also.

Camping. Like Americans, Canadians are very fond of camping and during the summer sites in popular places will always be very full. Usually, however, campgrounds are not as spacious as those in America and less trouble is taken with the positioning of individual sites. Prices are about the same. There are many provincial park campgrounds, as well as sites in the national parks and the many privately operated grounds usually to be found close to the highways. Campgrounds are marked on official highway maps.

Hiring camping equipment is relatively cheap and easy. KOA, for instance, has a Tent America/Canada plan whereby you can rent a tent for a family of four at one of their 'full-service' campgrounds for about $12 per night. You'll need to bring sleeping bags plus cooking and kitchen essentials along though. For further information write to KOA, Box 30558T, Billings, Montana 59114, USA.

See USA Background, under Getting There. Trek America tours in Canada too.

Guest Ranches and Farms. Many farms accept paying guests during the summer. Prices vary and in some cases guests are encouraged to help about the farm. For information write for *Farm, Ranch and Countryside Guide*, Farm and Ranch Vacations Inc, 36 East 57th Street, New York, NY 100022 (sending $4), or *Ontario Farm Vacations*, Ontario Federation of Agriculture, 387 Bloor Street East, Toronto, Ontario M4W 1H9.

FOOD

How much you spend per day on food will obviously depend upon your taste and your budget, but you can think in terms of roughly $1–$3 on breakfast, $2.50 upwards on lunch, and anything from $4 to $5 upwards on dinner. It is customary in Canada to eat the main meal of the day in the evening from about 5pm onwards. In small, out-of-the-way towns, any restaurants there are may close as early as 7pm or 8pm. Yes, McDonalds does operate in Canada, as do several other American fast food chains.

Canadian food is perhaps slightly more Europeanised than American and in the larger cities you will find a great variety of ethnic restaurants—anything from Chinese through Swedish and French. In Québec, of course, French-style cooking predominates and in the Atlantic provinces sea food and salmon are the specialities. For the sweet-toothed, there are the highly recommended Laura Secord Candy Stores. Good ice cream as well as chocolates!

TRAVEL

To be read in conjunction with the USA Background travel section.

Bus. Every region in Canada has different bus companies, while the trans-Canadian services are operated by Greyhound Lines. Bus travel is usually the cheapest way of getting around; Greyhound, for example, offers a maximum 'point-to-point' fare of US $99 (good for 15 days), and the Ameripass, good for unlimited travel in the US and Canada. Currently, a sevenday pass costs US $99, the 15-day pass is US $179, and the 30-day pass costs US $325. You can extend the term of your pass for US $10 per day.

One difference between US and Canadian Greyhound operations worth noting is in baggage handling. Unlike the USA, the Canadian bus companies will never check baggage through to a destination without its owner. Bags cannot be sent on ahead, for instance, if you are simply seeking a way to dump them for a day or so while you see the sights. Lockers are usually on hand at bus stations, and don't forget to collect your bags from the pavement once they have been off-loaded by the driver.

Car. The Canadian is as attached to his car as is his American cousin. In general roads are better, speed limits are higher and there are fewer toll roads than south of the border. Canadian speed limits have gone metric and are posted everywhere in kilometres per hour. Thus, 100 km/h is the most common freeway limit, 80 km/h is typical on two-lane rural highways, and 50 km/h operates most frequently in towns.

When considering buying a car for the summer it may be as well to bear in mind that car prices are higher in Canada than in the US. Anyone planning to visit both countries by car would clearly be well advised to buy in the US first. You'll need to check that the US insurance policy is good for Canada too. It's a help to have a yellow non-resident interprovincial motor vehicle liability insurance card. This is obtainable through any US insurance agent.

Note that the wearing of seat belts by all persons in a vehicle is compulsory in British Columbia, Ontario, Québec and Saskatchewan.

Car rental will cost from about $140 per week with an additional mileage charge. To hire a Volkswagen camper would cost about twice as much, but of course you wouldn't be paying for accommodation as well. Your travel agent, or airline can arrange all this for you before you go.

Third party **insurance** is compulsory in all Canadian provinces and can be expensive. 'Insurance to cover a VW camper worth $1000 with a driver 24 years of age cost $155 for three months.' British, other European and US drivers licences are officially recognised by the Canadian authorities. Membership of the AA, RAC, other European motoring organisations, or the AAA in the US, entitles you to all the services of the Canadian AA and its member clubs free of charge.

Gas is now sold by the litre and costs up to 35¢ a litre. This is about the same as the US. Gas stations can be few and far between in remoter areas and it is wise to check your gauge in the late afternoon before the pumps shut off for the night.

One hazard to be aware of when driving in Canada is the unmarked, and even the marked, railroad crossing. Many people are killed every year on railroad crossings. Trains come and go so infrequently in remote areas that it's simply never possible to know when one will arrive.

Air. There are two major airlines in Canada, Air Canada and Canadian Pacific, and both offer some discount fares to foreign visitors.

Although no longer available in the US, **youth standby fares** do continue to operate in Canada. Both Air Canada and Canadian Pacific operate such a fare and it is no longer necessary to purchase a special card in advance. Travel is on a standby basis and anyone between the ages of 12 and 22 is eligible. It is not usually available on Friday or Sunday. The discount varies with the distance travelled and can be as high as 40 percent. Complementing the youth fare both airlines also offer discounts to senior citizens of 65 and over.

In addition, there is a family plan fare where the wife, when travelling with her husband, can travel at a reduced rate; the Super Budget fare, which can save up to 43 percent on round-trip economy rates (purchase 30 days in advance, stay 7–60 days), the Freedom fare with a 20 percent saving (buy ticket seven days in advance, stay at least until the following Sunday, limited availability), and Weekend Excursion fares. The only way is to decide upon your route and then consult a travel agent or the airline to determine the best available rate.

A good buy is the no-frills skybus service operated by CP on a once- or twice-weekly basis. The Skybus operates between Toronto and Montréal and the western cities of Vancouver, Winnipeg, Edmonton and Calgary at less than half the economy fare. No food is available on board and you must pay for your seat at the time you buy your ticket. In other words, telephone reservations are not possible. Air Canada, offers Nighthawks; for the inconvenience of flying around at 2 or 3 in the morning you get a considerably reduced fare.

Rail. One of the conditions for the entry of British Columbia into the Confederation was the building of the Canadian Pacific Railway, and with the completion of the track in 1885, Canada as a transcontinental nation finally became a reality. Later came Canadian Northern and the Grand Trunk Pacific, nationalised into Canadian National in 1923 after both companies had gone bankrupt.

Until 1978, Canada possessed two great rail systems, the privately operated but viable Canadian Pacific, and the state-owned, often floundering, Canadian National. With the formation of Via Rail Canada in 1978, the routes and fare structures of both have been totally integrated.

There are several discount and excursion fares available to travellers. These include one day, three day and seven to 30-day round trip excursion rates where you can save up to two-thirds over the regular cost. Sleeping accommodation is extra and good, cheap meals are available. The fare is not valid from 15 June to 15 September. Group reductions are available to two or more adults travelling together, and there are also reduced prices for children and senior citizens. Advanced purchase fares are also available, but not between May and September. Decide on your journey and then check out the best deal with VIA Rail.

Then there is the CANRAIL Pass. This gives unlimited travel on VIA and CP trains at a fixed cost in a particular region. High season rates (June–September) are: Eastern corridor route, 8 days, $100; Edmonton, Calgary and West, 8 days, $100. For 15 days: Winnipeg and East $225; Winnipeg and West $225; Windsor Corridor $130; Edmonton, Calgary and West $130. For 22 days: Winnipeg and East $260; Winnipeg and West $260. For 30 days: nationwide only, $395.

Given plenty of time at your disposal, lots of patience, and a good book or two, the railroads still offer the best, and often the most scenic, means of crossing Canada.

Hitching. Thumbing is illegal on the major transcontinental routes, but it is common to see people hitching along access ramps. Check the 'local rules' before setting out. In some cities there are specific regulations regarding hitching but in general the cognoscenti say that hitchers are not often hassled and that Canada in general is one of the best places to get good lifts, largely because rides tend to be long ones.

The Trans Canada Highway can be rough going during the summer months so look for alternative routes, for example the Laurentian Autoroute out of Montréal, and the Yellowhead Highway out of Winnipeg. Wawa, north of Sault Ste Marie, Ontario, is another notorious spot where you can be stranded for days. The national parks can also be tricky in summer when 'there are too many tourists going nowhere'.

PUBLIC HOLIDAYS

Victoria Day	3rd Monday in May
Dominion Day	1st July
Labor Day	1st Monday in September
Thanksgiving Day	2nd Monday in October
Remembrance Day	11th November

COMMUNICATIONS
Mail. Postage stamps can be purchased at any post office or from vending machines (at par) in hotels, drug stores, stations, bus terminals and some newsstands. If you do not know where you will be staying, have your mail sent care of 'General Delivery'. You have 15 days to collect.

Telegrams. Not handled by the post office, but sent via a CP or CN telegraph office.

Telephone. Local calls from coin telephones usually cost 10¢. When making long distance calls, consult the operator by dialling 0 and be sure to have plenty of change. To place a call outside North America, dial 0 and ask for the Overseas Operator.

ELECTRICITY
110v, 60 cycles AC, except in remote areas where cycles vary.

DRINKING
Canada's liquor laws hark back to a puritan past and the harsh rules of frontier society, and often seem niggling and absurd. Liquor regulations come under provincial law, and although it's usually pretty easy to buy a drink by the glass in a lounge, tavern or beer parlour, it can be pretty tricky buying it from a retail outlet.

Beer, wine and spirits can only be bought at special liquor outlets which can be few and far between. Liquor stores keep usual store hours and are closed on Sundays. In Prince Edward Island and Newfoundland alcohol can only be obtained with a permit, but visitors can obtain permits in special shops. The drinking age is 19, except in PEI, Québec, Ontario, Manitoba and Alberta, where it is 18.

CIGARETTES
Currently cost around $1.25 for a packet of 25. Foreign brands available.

THE METRIC SYSTEM
As already noted above, Canada has begun going metric. See the conversion tables in the Appendix.

4. CANADA

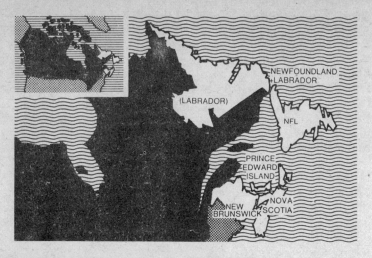

MARITIME PROVINCES

These Atlantic-lapped provinces were the early stop-off points for eager explorers from Europe and subsequently became one of the main battlegrounds for their colonial ambitions. The chief combatants were England and France and strong British and French threads run through Maritime culture.

Not surprisingly the sea is the other great influence and this is a good area to visit for picturesque seascapes, good fishing, excellent seafood and, in summer, a refreshing dip in the ocean. The economy of the Maritimes is mostly based on sea-related industries and endeavours including tourism. The climate brings warm summers but cool, snowy winters, temperatures in both seasons being moderated by the presence of the sea.

The visitor will find here a wealth of outdoor pursuits to indulge in, plus good food, comfortable accommodation and constant reminders of a stormy, but fascinating history.

NEW BRUNSWICK

Bounded on most of three sides by water, and part of the Appalachian mountain system, New Brunswick adjoins Nova Scotia, Québec and Maine. The Vikings reputedly came here some thousand years ago and when French explorer Jacques Cartier arrived somewhat more recently in time, the Micmac and Maliseet Indians lived here. Now much of the northern part of the province is inhabited by French

Acadians and French is widely spoken. (Acadia was comprised of New Brunswick, Prince Edward Island and Nova Scotia.)

From being a battleground for French and English forces, the 'Picture Province' has more recently become a stamping ground for US tourists enticed across the border by the promise of good huntin', fishin', and campin'. But if you can avoid the touristy bits along the southern coastline (and perhaps even if you can't), you will find in New Brunswick an interesting mix of French Acadian, Indian, and English cultures, beautiful scenery, and the ever-present influence of the sea.

National Parks: Fundy
                Kouchibougnac

FREDERICTON. Capital city of the province and its commercial and sporting centre. Clean and green, this is 'a good Canadian town' which got started in 1783, when a group of Loyalists from the victorious colonies to the south made their home here, naming the town after the second son of George III. They chose for their new town a spot where there had previously (until the Seven Years War) been a thriving Acadian settlement. During hostilities the settlement was reduced by the British and the inhabitants expelled.

Fredericton's great benefactor was local boy and press baron, the late Lord Beaverbrook. His legacies include an art gallery, a theatre, and the university library. The latter is named Bonar Law–Bennett Library, after two other famous sons of New Brunswick, one of whom became Prime Minister of Great Britain, and the other Prime Minister of Canada.

The town is situated inland on the broad St John River, the 'Rhine of America', once an Indian highway and a major commercial route to the sea. The whole area is one of scenic river valleys and lakes.

ACCOMMODATION
Colonial Inn, J H Horncastle, 72 Regent St, 455-3343. $16 single, $20 double.
Elms Tourist Home, Mrs J T Irvine, 269 Saunders St, 454-3410. $14 single, $20 double.
Fredericton Motor Inn, 1315 Regent St, exit 2 off Trans-Canada Hwy, 455-1430. $20 single, $30 double. Pool.
Univ of New Brunswick, Kings College Rd, 453-4891. 15 May–25 Aug, with student ID: $6 single pn, $30 pw, shared washrm. 2 miles from town centre. Also, McLeod Hse, Montgomery St, women only, $6 single and Jones House, on campus, men only, $6.
Youth Hostel, York St, 454-1233, 15 June–30 Aug. $3.25 members, $5 non-members.
Camping: Mactaquac Provincial Pk, 12 miles west on Hwy 2. $5.50 per site. Beach, fishing, golf.

FOOD
Farmers Market, George St. Saturday. 'Get there early to have breakfast at Goofy Roofy's. At $2.50, it's good value and well worth the effort.' Also good craft stalls.

The Attic Cafe, 161 Main St. 'Best value in town.' Under $5. Menu varies from quiche to mid-east cuisine.

OF INTEREST
Provincial Legislative Buildings, Queen and St John Sts. Includes, in Library, complete set of Audubon bird paintings and copy of 1783 printing of Domesday Book. Library and Gallery open Mon–Fri 8.30am–5pm, 7pm–9pm. Free.

Beaverbrook Art Gallery, opp Leg Bldg on Queen. Has works of Dali, Reynolds, Gainsborough, Churchill, etc, plus good section on history of English china. A gift to the province from the press baron and open Tue–Sat 10am–5pm, Sun–Mon noon–5pm. $1, students free.

Kings Landing Historical Settlement, at Prince William, 23 miles west of town. Showing life as it was in the Central St John River Valley between 1790 and 1870. Features homes, school, church, farm, theatre, etc. Daily 10am–6pm June–Oct $4, under 16 $1.50, family rate $9.

Opus Craft Village, 12 miles west, on Hwy 105. Artists' complex where you can see glassblowing, pottery making, leather.

University of New Brunswick. Founded 1785 and the third oldest in Canada. Buildings on campus include the Brydone Jack Observatory, Canada's first astronomical observatory.

INFORMATION
Fredericton Tourist Bureau, Woodstock Rd, 472-1907.
Provincial Dept of Tourism, Queen and Church Sts, 453-2377.

TRAVEL
Fredericton Airport is about 5 miles out at Lincoln. The limo fare is $3 into town from the airport.
Bus services connect to all major US and Canadian cities via Scotia Motor Transport.
Bike rental from: The Trail Shop, 347 Queen St. Approx $5 per day.

MONCTON.
A major communications centre and worth a brief visit for the tidal bore and Magnetic Hill. The bore is at its highest during the summer months when it sweeps up the Petitcodiac River form the Bay of Fundy reaching heights of 30 feet on the way. Bore Park is the spot to be when the waters rush in.

The other phenomenon Moncton has to offer is **Magnetic Hill,** seven miles out of town. Here you can drive to the bottom of the hill, switch off your engine and coast uphill!

There is a nice beach at **Shediac,** on the Northumberland Straight. It's a short bus ride from Moncton and there is plenty of camping space nearby.

ACCOMMODATION
Elmwood Motel, 401 Elmwood Dr, 388-5096. $20 single, $25 double. Close to Trans-Can Hwy.
Friendship Skyliner Motel, 9 miles west of Trans-Can Hwy, 384-9705. $27 up. Scenic views of Petticodiac Valley included.
Moncton Hostel, 141 King St., 388-4793. $4 dorm.
University of Moncton residences, May–Sept. $6 single pn, $30 pw.
Camping: Camper's City, Green Acres Tenting and Trailer Pk, both close to Magnetic Hill.

CARAQUET. Situated on scenic Chaleur Bay in the north of the province, Caraquet is the oldest French settlement in the area and just west of town is a monument to the first Acadian settlers who came here following their expulsion by Britain. On St Pierre Boulevard there is an interesting museum of Acadian history, and off Highway 11 to the west of town is the **Village Historique Acadien**. The buildings here are all authentic and were brought here and then restored. There are also crafts and demonstrations showing the Acadian lifestyle.

Caraquet is also an important fishing port. A good time to visit is in August for the annual Acadian festival and the Blessing of the Fleet.

ACCOMMODATION
Caraquet Youth Hostel, 30 Blvd St Pierre Ouest, 788-4793. Open 26 June–3 Sept, $2.50 members, $4 non-membs.
Camping: At Caraquet Prov Pk. $6 per site, beach, swimming.

SAINT JOHN. Known as the Loyalist City, and proudly boasting a royal charter. Saint John was founded by refugees—among them no less a personage than Benedict Arnold, reputedly disliked by his fellow Loyalists for his sharp business practices—from the rebel New England colonies. The landing place of the Loyalists is marked by a monument at the foot of King Street, and a Loyalist house stands yet at Germain and Union Streets. Before the Loyalists and the Seven Years War, the French were here. The first recorded European discovery was in 1604 when Samuel de Champlain entered the harbour on St John's Day—hence the name of the town and the river on which it stands.

Largely as a result of its strategic ice-free position on the Bay of Fundy, Saint John has become New Brunswick's largest city and its commercial and industrial centre. Shipbuilding and fishing are the most important industries and Saint John Dry Dock, at 1150 feet long, is one of the largest in the world. (Incidentally, Saint John rather than St John is the accepted form, to distinguish it more easily from St John's, Newfoundland.)

ACCOMMODATION
Bonanza Motel, 594 Rothesay Ave, 693-2310. $18 single, $24 double.
Fundy View Guests, 968 Manawagonish Rd, $10 up.
Johnson's Tourist Home, 888 Manawagonish Rd, 672-8135. $12 single up.
White House Lodge Motor Hotel, 1400 Manawagonish Rd, 672-1000. $30 double up.
YMCA, 19–25 Hazen Ave, 652-4720. $10 per night, men only.
YWCA, 27 Wellington Row, 657-6366. 'Usually free' for dorm/floor space.

FOOD
Saint John City Market, Germaine St. Good shopping place for fresh produce. Open daily except Sun.

OF INTEREST
The Loyalist Trail. A walking tour uptown encompassing some 21 historic sites

including the **Loyalist House**, the **Loyalist Burial Ground** opp King Sq, the spiral staircase in the **old Court House**, King Sq, and **Barbour's General Store**. The latter, on King St E and Carmarthen St, is a restored old country store which was originally located more than 80 miles away. It was brought downriver by barge and then, over a period of 3 years, stocked with authentic wares gathered from all over the Maritimes.

New Brunswick Museum, 277 Douglas Ave. Canada's oldest museum with relics of the Indian, French and British periods, plus the Loyalist story in full. May–Sept, open daily 10am–9pm. Sat 2pm–5pm rest of yr. $1, 6–19 25¢, over 65 free.

Fort Howe, Magazine St. Built during 1777–78, for protection against American privateers and Indian uprisings. Daily 10am–dusk. Free.

Martello Tower, Lancaster Heights. Erected during the 1812–14 war. Now houses a display of firearms and 'antiquities'. Nice too for views.

Reversing Rapids. The Town's biggest tourist attraction. At high tide waters rushing into the gorge where the St John river meets the sea cause the river to run backwards. See it all from the Tourist Bureau's lounge and sun deck on King St.

INFORMATION
Visitor and Convention Bureau, City Hall, Market Sq, 658-2815.

TRAVEL
Via Rail Terminal is on Rothsay Ave, 657-6410.
There is ferry service from Saint John to Digby, Nova Scotia. Takes cars, nice scenery enroute. A two and a half hour trip. For info: 672-4270.

CAMPOBELLO ISLAND. Going west on Highway 1 from Saint John, you can catch a ferry from Back Bay which will take you, via Deer Isle and Campobello, to Lubec, Maine. On Campobello is the 3000-acre Roosevelt Campobello International Park. Visitors can see the 34-room 'cottage' occupied by FDR from 1905 to 1921. Open daily 9am–5pm, May–October. Free. The Island is also linked to Maine by the Franklin D Roosevelt Memorial Bridge.

FUNDY NATIONAL PARK. The park fronts for eight miles on to the beautiful Bay of Fundy and extends inland for more than nine miles. The tides in the bay sometimes rise as high as 60 feet and are thought to be the highest in the world.

The sea-sculptured sandstone cliffs and the immense tides have made Fundy National Park the second most popular park in Canada. Camping sites aplenty. Access is easy from either Saint John or Moncton via Highway 114. There are beaches at Alma, Herring Cove and Point Wolfe.

NEWFOUNDLAND

Officially entitled Newfoundland and Labrador, and with a population of just over 550,000, the province is a bit off the beaten track, but it's worth taking a little time and trouble to get here. It's a province rich in historic associations and, as revealed by recent archaeological excavations, one of the oldest settled regions in North

America. The Vikings were here as early as AD 1000, settling on an isolated stretch of shoreline at L'Anse Aux Meadows at the tip of the Great Northern Peninsula.

By the time John Cabot 'discovered' Newfoundland and made it England's oldest colony (excepting Ireland) in 1497, the Vikings had long since gone and little remained of their hamlets. Newfoundland is also the youngest Canadian province, having joined the Confederation in 1949. **Labrador**, the serrated northeastern mainland of Canada, was added to Newfoundland in 1763. Until recent explorations and development of some of Labrador's national resources (iron ore, timber), the area was virtually a virgin wilderness with the small population scattered in rugged little fishing villages and centred around the now all but obsolete airport at Goose Bay.

Newfoundland Island is characterised by a wild and rugged coastline with picturesque fishing villages (some still with access only from the sea) and deep harbours and a society neither wholly North American nor yet European. Fishing is still the main industry, although mining is important and the oil industry has reached here too.

There is a daily car and passenger ferry service to Port-aux-Basques from North Sydney, Nova Scotia, and once on the island the Trans Canada Highway goes all the way to the capital, St John's, via Corner Brook and Terra Nova National Park.

National Parks: Gros Maine
                Terra Nova.

ST JOHN'S. St John's is a gentle, though weather-beaten city, built around a steep-sided natural harbour, and situated on the eastern side of the island 547 miles from Port-aux-Basques on the southwestern tip. Nearby Cape Spear is just 1640 miles from Cape Clair, Ireland, and the city's strategic position has in the past made it the starting point for transatlantic contests and conflicts of one sort or another.

Bitter struggles between the English and French for domination of the Atlantic coast culminated here in 1762 with the final capture of St John's by the British after the last brief French occupation; the first successful transatlantic cable was landed nearby in 1866; the first transatlantic wireless signal was received by Marconi at St John's in 1901; and between 1919 and 1937 the city was involved in more than 40 pioneering transatlantic airplane crossings, hosting, among others, Alcock and Brown, Amelia Earhart, Charles and Anne Lindberg, and the inaugural transatlantic flights of Pan American and British Imperial Airways.

ACCOMMODATION

Cochrane Hotel, 47 Cochrane St, 754-1260. $20 single, $25 double. Restaurant.
Skyline Motel, 337 Kenmount Rd, 722-5400. $25–30 single/double. Dining rm.

Seaflow Tourist Home, 53–55 William St, 753-2425. $15 single, $18 double, shared bath. Cooking facs, breakfast avail.

Youth Hostel, Devon House, 59 Duckworth St, 753-8603. $5 single dorm, members, $5.50 non-members. Meals available.

Memorial University of Newfoundland, Elizabeth Ave, 753-1200. May–Aug, reservations required. $12 single/double. Shared washroom, meals available.

Camping: La Manche Prov Pk, north on Hwy 10. Primitive. $3.50.

FOOD
Chess' Snacks, Freshwater St. Take-out fish'n Chips, no less. Around $2.

Memorial Univ campus, Thompson Student Centre. Not just for students.

OF INTEREST
Anglican Cathedral, Church Hill. Said to be one of the finest examples of Gothic architecture anywhere. Begun in 1816, and following two fires, restored in 1905. Features sculptured arches and carved furnishings. Tours available, 9.30am–5.30pm.

Quidi Vidi Battery, cliffside position overlooking scenic Quidi Vidi and now restored to its War of 1812 appearance. Manned by guides dressed in period Royal Artillery costume. Daily 9am–9pm, mid-June to mid-Sept. Free.

Newfoundland Museum, Duckworth St. St John's is rich in history and folklore and this particular museum has the only relics in existence of the vanished Indian tribe, the Beothucks. Open Tue–Sun 10am–6pm, Thur 6pm–9pm. Free.

Provincial Building. Fine panoramic view from 11th floor and it has an interesting small museum in the tower observation room dealing with Newfoundland's military and naval history.

Signal Hill National Historic Park. Reached from Duckworth St. Scene of the 1762 battle for domination of the Atlantic coast, and site where Marconi received the first transatlantic wireless signal. Remains of forts, and an interesting visitors centre. Open daily 9am–8pm summer, otherwise Mon–Sat 10am–5pm, Sun noon–5pm. Free.

INFORMATION
St John's Tourist Commission, City Hall, New Gower St, 368-5900.

Tourist Services Dept, Confederation Building. 737-3610.

St John's Tourist Chalet, west of town on the Trans Canada. Tartan-clad hostesses dispense helpful literature and run an accommodation service.

ENTERTAINMENT
The annual regatta on Quidi Vidi Lake at the beginning of August is the Province's event of the year.

SHOPPING
Hudson Bay Co, Water St. Eskimo soapstone carvings.

TERRA NOVA NATIONAL PARK. This area was once covered by glaciers 750 feet thick which left behind boulders, gravel, sand and grooved rock. The sea filled the valleys leaving the hills as islands. The result is the incredibly beautiful **Bonavista Bay** with its rugged coastline, fjord-like sounds, and bold headlands. But it's certainly not swimming country. The cold Labrador Current bathes the shores and it's not unusual to see an iceberg.

Inland the park is thickly forested and nature trails are provided by the park service. Lynx, brown bears, red fox, and moose are common.

(Incidentally, Newfoundland has a moose population thought to be in excess of 40,000.)

Access to the park is easy since the Trans Canada Highway passes right through it for a distance of 25 miles. Gander is but 35 miles away and there is accommodation here or else you can camp in the Park itself. St John's is many miles further south.

ST PIERRE AND MIQUELON ISLANDS. Off the southern coast of Newfoundland, these islands constitute the only remaining holdings of France in North America. Once called the Islands of 11,000 Virgins, these granite outcrops total only about 93 square miles. France was given permanent possession by the Treaty of Versailles in 1783. You can reach the islands by ferry from Fortune on Route 210.

L'ANSE AUX MEADOWS. At the northern tip of Newfoundland, and believed to be the site of the Viking settlement of AD 1000. According to legend, the Vikings defended this post against Indians until perils became too great and they withdrew to Greenland. No standing ruins of their buildings have survived, but excavations have disclosed the size and location of buildings, and many everyday objects have been found. Guides on site daily, 8.30am–8.30pm. Free.

NOVA SCOTIA

Canada's 'Ocean Playground' is famous for its attractive fishing villages, the rocky, granite shores, historic spots like Louisbourg and Grand Pré, and its Scottishness which finds expression in such events as the annual Highland Games at Antigonish and St Ann's Gaelic College. Although John Cabot arrived at Cape Breton Island as early as 1497, it was the French who first attempted colonisation of the area. That is until 1621, when James I granted the province to Sir William Alexander, and gave Nova Scotia (New Scotland) its own flag and coat of arms. The French colonists, however, prefered the name Acadia, after explorer Verrazano's word for Peaceful Land, and so the French thereafter became known as Acadians.

Several times during the 17th century Nova Scotia changed from French to British hands and back again, until, in 1713, by the Treaty of Utrecht, it finally became British. Cape Breton Island fell into British hands later, after the siege of Louisbourg in 1758.

Although about 75 percent of Nova Scotians are of British descent, French, Irish, Germans and the Chesapeake Blacks have also settled here. The Blacks came after the war of 1812, but earlier immigrants from the south were a group of 25,000 Loyalists, possibly the largest single emigration of cultured families in British history, since their numbers included over half the living graduates of Harvard. The Loyalists settled around Shelbourne.

Young people tend towards Halifax and the southern shoreline but don't miss Cape Breton Island across the Strait of Canso.

National Parks: Cape Breton Highlands
Kejimkujik.

HALIFAX. Provincial capital and the largest city and economic hub of the Maritimes. The making of Halifax has been its fine ice-free harbour so that not only does it deal with around 3500 commercial vessels a year but it is also Canada's chief naval base. Halifax was founded by Cornwallis in 1749 as a British military and naval depot and as a British response to the French fort at Louisbourg.

Although a thriving metropolis with the usual tall concrete buildings and expressways, the town does retain a certain charm with many constant reminders of its colourful past. Citadel Hill in the middle of the town is a good place to start exploring and to get your bearings in relation to both Halifax and its twin across the bay, **Dartmouth**.

Connected to Halifax by two bridges and a ferry, Dartmouth is known as the 'city of lakes' since there are some 22 lakes within the city boundaries. The town is also home to the well-respected Bedford Institute of Oceanography, which collects data on tides, currents and ice formations.

ACCOMMODATION

Bluenose Motel, 636 Bedford Hwy, 443-3171. $32 single, $34 double shared bed, $36 double 2 beds. About 5 miles north of town.

Downsview Friendship Inn, Riverside Dr, opp harness race track, 865-4343. $21 up.

Inglis Lodge, 5538 Inglis St, 423-7950. $12 single up. $18 double up.

South Park Lodge Tourist Home, 1135 S Park St, 423-8857. $15 single $20 double. Off-season rates also available.

YMCA, 1565 S Park St, 422-6437. $12.50 single (students get discount), $19 double. Sleeping bag space avail. Pool, gym, central.

University residences: St Mary's Univ, 5865 Goresbrook Ave, 422-7361. End May–late Aug, reservations required, $12 single, $18 twin, students $10, $14.

Howe Hall, Dalhousie Univ, Coburg Rd, 424-2107, May–Aug, men only. $11 single, $18 double, $50 pw.

Sheriff Hall, Dalhousie, 6385 South St, 424-2577, women only. $11 single, $18 double.

Camping: Laurie Prov Pk, about 12 miles north on Rte 2 on Grand Lake. No showers, beach, $5 per site.

FOOD

Camille's, 2564 Barrington St. Fish n' Chips (English style) from about $1.50, plus seafood of all kinds.

Peacemeal, 1581 Grafton St. Sandwiches, curry, good daily specials.

OF INTEREST

The Citadel. This hilltop fortress surrounded by a moat, was built in 1828–56 on the site of fortifications dating back to 1749. There's a magnificent view of the city and harbour and a free, 45-minute guided tour is available. The fort once served as a prisoner-of-war camp and numbered Leon Trotsky among the inmates. There is an **Army and Navy Museum** recalling the military history of the fort, and a museum featuring pioneer and MicMac Indian items. The Citadel is open July–Aug, 9am–8pm daily; Sept–June, 9am–5pm. Free.

Province House, Hollis, Prince, Granville and George Sts. Canada's oldest, and smallest, parliament house. A handsome Georgian building, built in 1818. Canada's first newspaper, the *Halifax Gazette*, was published here in 1752 by one Charles Howe. 8.30am–5pm. Free.

Maritime Museum of Canada, HMC Dockyard Annex, 1895 Upper Water St. Clipper ship and other maritime relics. Open Tue–Sun 10am–5pm. Don't forget the harbour itself.

St Paul's Church, Barrington and Duke Sts. Built 1750 and the oldest Protestant church in Canada. Has small museum. Open 10am–4pm.

Old Dutch Church, Brunswick and Garrish Sts, and only 12 by 6 metres! Erected 1756 by German settlers and Canada's first Lutheran church. The keys are with the caretaker of another unusual church, **St George's Round Church**, 38 Brunswick St.

Fort York Redoubt, Purcell's Cove Rd. Begun 1790, completed 1945, must be some kind of record. Of major importance in WWI and II in guarding the sea approaches to Halifax's harbour. Good views of coastline and McNab Island.

Nova Scotia Museum, 1747 Summer St. Social history, flora and fauna. Open weekdays 9am–8pm summer, otherwise 9am–5pm. Free.

Dalhousie University, Coburg Rd. An attractive campus, good for the usual things, and also the home of the **Nova Scotia Archives**.

Point Pleasant Park and the **Halifax Public Gardens** are both good places to be and both have a martello tower.

Historic Properties, Granville St, on the waterfront. A restored area of stores, restaurants, pubs and offices. Good for browsing or buying gifts.

Nearby:

Peggy's Cove, Liverpool, Lunenberg, Bridgewater and the rest. Picturesque fishing villages but overrun by tourists. At Lunenburg you can visit the **Fisheries Museum of the Atlantic**. On Duke St, and housed aboard 3 old ships, the museum contains mementoes of the days of wooden ships. There is also an aquarium. July–Sept, open daily 9am–8pm; otherwise 9.30am–5.30pm. $1.50, under 17 50¢, family rate $3.50.

INFORMATION

Nova Scotia Travel Info Centre at the airport, Hwy 102.

City info booths: Historic Properties, in the old Red Store on Water St, Scotia Sq, Lord Nelson Hotel and Hotel Nova Scotian. Tel: 424-4247.

CYHA, 6260 Quinpool Rd, 423-8736.

TRAVEL

Bus station: 64 Almon St, nr the Forum.

Buses depart for the airport from big downtown hotels every hour, $5.

Dartmouth Ferry Commission, 466-2215, operates passenger ferries across the harbour from George St Terminal, Halifax, and Portland St, Dartmouth.

Harbour cruises under sail available on the famous schooner *Bluenose II* from Privateers Wharf.

GRAND PRÉ NATIONAL HISTORIC PARK. The restored site of an early Acadian settlement. The nearby dykeland (great meadow— grande pré) is where the French Acadians were expelled in 1755 after failing to take an oath of allegiance to the English king.

The sad plight of the Acadians of Nova Scotia was taken by Longfellow as the theme for his narrative poem *Evangeline* (see under

Louisiana in USA section). There is a museum in the park with a section on Longfellow and a fine collection of Acadian relics, everything from farm tools to personal diaries. Also in the park is the Church of the Covenanters. Built in 1790 by New England planters, this do-it-yourself church was constructed from hand-sawn boards fastened together by square hand-made nails. The similarly homemade pulpit spirals halfway to the ceiling.

The Gardens are nice for walking and the whole park is open, June to September, 9am–6pm daily. To get there from Halifax take Route 101 going north and the park is three miles east of Wolfville. During the summer, hostel accommodation is available at the University of Acadia in Wolfville.

ANNAPOLIS ROYAL. Situated in the scenic Annapolis Valley, famous for its apples, this was the site of Canada's oldest settlement founded by de Monts and Champlain in 1604. Originally Port Royal, it became Annapolis Royal in honour of Queen Anne, after the final British capture in 1710, serving then as the Nova Scotian capital until the founding of Halifax in 1749.

The site of the French fort of 1636 is now maintained as Fort Anne National Historic Park, and seven miles away, on the north shore of Annapolis River, is the **Port Royal Habitation National Historic Park**. This is a reconstruction of the 1605 settlement based on the plan of a Normandy farm. Here, too, the oldest social club in America was formed. L'Ordre de Bon Temps was organised by Champlain in 1606 and visitors to the province for more than three days can still become members. The park is open daily until October. Thirty-five miles to the south is **Kejimkujik National Park**, an area once inhabited by the Micmac Indians. The park entrance and information centre is at Maitland Bridge. Daily admission is $1. The park is good for canoeing, fishing, hiking, and skiing in winter.

YARMOUTH. The only place of any size on the western side of Nova Scotia, Yarmouth is the centre of a largely French-speaking area. During the days of sail this was an important shipbuilding centre although today local industry is somewhat more diversified.

A good time to visit is at the end of July when the Western Nova Scotia Exhibition is held here. The festival includes the usual agricultural and equestrian events plus local craft demonstrations and exhibits.

ACCOMMODATION

McKenzie's Tourist Home, 70 William St, 742-2128. $34 double, TV. Open May–Oct.
El Rancho Motel, Lakeside Drive, 742-4363. $34 double, overlooking Milo Lake.
Ocean View Farm Tourist Home, 742-4741. Sorry no address, but recommended.
YMCA, Main and Cliff Sts, 742-7181. $3.50 members, $4.50 non-membs.

TRAVEL
Ferries go from here to Portland (10-hour trip) and Bar Harbor (5 hours), Maine.
For info on the Portland run call: 775-5616. Current fare is $35. For Bar Harbor call:
742-3513. Fare about $25.

SYDNEY. Situated on the Atlantic side of the province, Sydney is the
chief town on Cape Breton Island and a good centre for exploring the
rest of the island. It is a steel and coal town, a grim, but friendly,
soot-blackened old place. While here you can visit the largest steel
plant in North America.

Like the whole of Cape Breton Island, Sydney has a history of
struggles against worker exploitation and bad social conditions. Since
France ceded the island to Britain as part of the package deal Treaty
of Utrecht in 1715, hard times and social strife have frequently been
the norm.

A ferry goes to Newfoundland from North Sydney across the bay.

ACCOMMODATION
Bed and Breakfast, 369 Townsend, 562-3738. $18 pn.
Campbell's Mansion Tourist Home, 259, Kings Rd, $15 single, $18 double.
YMCA, Charlotte St.
Summer Hostel is on Rt 125 at Sydney Mines. 736-8255.

FOOD
Menzies Lunch, across from the Metrocenter on George St. Cheap.
Yellow Submarine, Esplanade. 'Beer and reasonably priced meals.'

OF INTEREST
Sydney Steel Plant—the largest in North America—does tours at 9.30am and
1.30pm, weekdays.
Cape Breton School of Crafts, Townsend. Offers classes in art, weaving, pottery,
etc, and holds annual crafts fair in July.
The major annual event in Sydney is the **Highland Games** in July. Kilts, pipes and
drums, sword dancing, caber tossing, etc.
Nearby:
At **Sydney Mines**, nr jct Trans-Can Hwy and Hwy 125, is the **Historic Princess Mine**.
Tour through a colliery that was mined (until 1975) for 100 yrs. Protective clothing
provided. Daily 11am–5.45pm, June–Sept. $6, under 12 $3.
Glace Bay, 13 miles east of Sydney and site of the **Miners Museum and Village**.
Includes tour of underground mine running out and under the sea and The Village
shows the life of a mining community 1850–1900. The Museum features weekly
concerts of Cape Breton folk songs. $1, children 50¢.
Baddeck. Alexander Graham Bell National Historic Park. Displays, models,
papers, etc, related to Bell's inventions. Bell had his summer home in the town.
Summer open 9am–9pm, otherwise 9am–5pm. Free.

TRAVEL
Ferries to Argentia and Porte-aux-Basques, Newfoundland, 794-7203.

FORTRESS OF LOUISBOURG NATIONAL HISTORIC PARK.
Built by the French between 1717 and 1740 and presently in the process of being restored by the Federal Government, this fortress was
once the biggest built in North America since the time of the Incas.

Louisbourg played a crucial role in the French defence of the area and was finally won by Britain in 1760, but not before it had been blasted to rubble.

The restoration project involves the rebuilding of a complete colonial town within the fortifications and it will be several years before it is completely finished. There is a museum and you will be shown around by a French colonial-costumed guide.

Accessible by bus from Sydney, 26 miles to the south, the park is open from 9am to 8pm daily during July and August. During the rest of the summer it is open from 10am to 6pm daily. Admission $2. Ages 5–17 50¢, Canadian senior citizens free, family rate $4.

CAPE BRETON HIGHLANDS NATIONAL PARK. The park lies on the northern-most tip of Cape Breton sandwiched between the Gulf of St Lawrence and the Atlantic Ocean. It covers more than 360 square miles of rugged mountain country, beaches and quiet valleys. The whole is encircled by the 184-mile-long Cabot Trail, an all-weather paved highway on its way round the park climbing four mountains and providing spectacular views of sea and mountains.

In summer however it gets very crowded and the narrow, steep roads are jammed with cars. There are camping facilities in the park and good sea and freshwater swimming.

This is an area originally settled by Scots and many of the locals still speak Gaelic. There are park information centres at Ingonish Beach and Cheticamp. Admission to the park is $1 per day. At **Cheticamp**, a rug-making centre, there is also an Acadian Museum with craft demonstrations and French-Canadian antiques and glassware. Open daily during the summer.

IONA. On the way back across the Strait of Canso, a side trip here to the Nova Scotia Highland Village may be worthwhile. The village includes a museum and other memorabilia of the early Scottish settlers. A highland festival is held here on the first Saturday in August. Summer opening 10am–5pm. Admission $1. The village is off Highway 105 and 15 miles east on Highway 223 via Little Narrows.

PRINCE EDWARD ISLAND

Prince Edward Island is Canada's smallest province measuring just 140 miles in length and with an average width of only 20 miles. The province is separated from the Canadian mainland by the Northumberland Strait. The local Micmac Indians called the island 'Abegweit', meaning 'cradled in a wave'; the French called it Isle St Jean, and when it became a separate colony and was ceded to Britain, the British named it after Prince Edward, Duke of Kent. Known now as the 'Garden of the Gulf', PEI is one of Canada's favourite family holiday spots offering the warm waters of the Gulf of St Lawrence and beautiful sandy beaches. It's also famous for potatoes, horse racing and fish.

Reach this island paradise by ferry, either from Cape Tormentine, New Brunswick, to Borden, west of Charlottetown, or from Caribou, Nova Scotia, to Wood Islands, east of the capital. Fares are low, but queues are long in summer particularly if you're taking a car.

National Park: Prince Edward Island.

CHARLOTTETOWN. The first meeting of the Fathers of the Confederation took place in Charlottetown in 1864. Out of this meeting came the future Dominion of Canada. In the Confederation Chamber, Province House, where the meeting was held, a plaque proclaims 'Providence Being Their Guide, They Builded Better Than They Knew'. The citizens of PEI were not so convinced however. They waited until 1873 before joining the Confederation. Even then, according to the then Governor General, Lord Dufferin, they came in 'under the impression that it is the Dominion that has been annexed to Prince Edward Island'.

These days things are quieter hereabouts, only livening up in summer when Canadian families descend en masse, and PEI's other tourist attraction, harness racing, gets going out at Charlottetown Driving Park. The restored waterfront section of town, Olde Charlottetown, offers the usual craft shops, eating places and boutiques. You can tour the town in a London double-decker bus, leaving from Confederation Centre.

ACCOMMODATION
Cameron's Tourist Home, 95 Edward St, 894-8174. $8 single, $12 double. 'Central.'
MacGillivray Tourist Home, 93 Edward St, 894-9354. About $15 per night. Central and close to harness racing.
Sunny King Motel, 4 miles west on Trans-Can Hwy 1, 675-2209. $35 up single/double. Pool.
Univ of PEI residences: University and Belvedere Ave, 892-4121. In summer $20 per person, $25 double.
Youth Hostel, Mt Edward at Belvedere, 894-9696. Summer only, sexes segregated, $4 members, $5 non-members. Cooking facilities.

OF INTEREST
Confederation Center. Focal point of the town's cultural life, it has an art gallery, museum, theatre and library. A summer festival is held here annually. And if you came to PEI in search of Anne of Green Gables, the Center theatre does an annual musical version.
Fort Edward. One of a series of batteries built in 1908 to guard the harbour entrance.
Province House, Queen Sq. The stones used to build the House were all brought across the Atlantic by sailing ship. The Provincial Legislature meets here. Open 9am–9pm, July, Aug.
Micmac Indian Village. At Rocky Point, across the harbour. Recreated 16th

century Indian village. Open 9am–9pm. $2. Also here is the **Fort Amherst National Historic Park.** Open 9am–8pm. Free.

Pioneer Village, nearby at Carmel. A log reproduction of an Acadian settlement with homes, blacksmith's shop, barn, school, general store, and church. Open 9am–dusk July and Aug, 9am–5pm June–Sept. $3, under 14, $1.50.

INFORMATION
Charlottetown Tourist Office, 892-2457.

TRAVEL
There is a free ferry from the docks across to Rocky Point where the beaches are.
'Everyone hitches around here.'
Acadian Bus Lines operate a route via ferry from New Brunswick, and Charlottetown is also accessible by rail from Moncton, New Brunswick and Amherst Nova Scotia.

PRINCE EDWARD ISLAND NATIONAL PARK. Situated north of Charlottetown, the Park consists of 25 miles of sandy beaches backed by sandstone cliffs. Thanks to the Gulf Stream the sea is beautifully warm. Rustico is one of the quieter beaches.

Ask about good places for clamming. Assuming you pick the right spot, you can just wriggle your toes in the sand and dig up a good meal.

At Cavendish Beach, on a golf course, is **Green Gables**, the farmhouse home of the famous Anne. Anne's creator, Lucy Maud Montgomery, was born just west of the park. The visit to Green Gables is free. The beach here however is very crowded during summer and probably best avoided. Camping sites and tourist homes abound on the island.

ONTARIO AND QUÉBEC

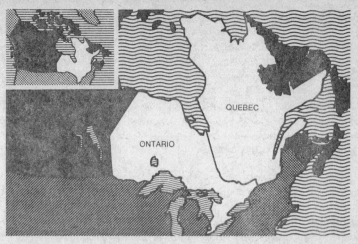

This section is devoted to those old enemies and still rivals Ontario and Québec. Both provinces evolved out of vast wilderness areas first opened up by Indians and fur traders, only later to become the focus of the bitter rivalry between the French and British in North America as Québec was colonised by the French and Ontario by the British and American Loyalists. In 1791 Québec became Lower Canada and Ontario became Upper Canada. In 1840 the Act of Union united the two and finally brought responsible and stable government to the area.

Cultural differences between the two provinces remain strong, and whatever tensions this might mean for Canada, it is stimulating for the visitor. One thing which is pretty similar is the climate. Summers can be hot and humid but winters long, very cold and snowy. Both Québec and Ontario also offer progressive, modern cities as well as vast regions of wilderness great for getting far away from whatever it is you're getting away from.

ONTARIO

The 'booming heartland' of Canada is the second largest province, claims one-third of the nation's population, half the country's industrial and agricultural resources and accounts for about 40 per cent of the nation's income. Since Confederation, Ontario has leapt ahead of its neighbours, becoming highly industrialised and at the same time reaping the benefits of the great forest and mineral wealth of the Canadian Shield which covers most of the northern regions.

Ontario was first colonised, not from Britain, but by Empire

363

Loyalists from the USA. Previously there were only sporadic French settlements and trading posts in what was otherwise a vast wilderness. The ready transportation provided in the past by the Great Lakes, all of which (except Lake Michigan) lap Ontario's shores, and now the St Lawrence Seaway, has linked the province to the industrial and consumer centres of the United States and has been a major factor behind Ontario's success story.

There is water virtually everywhere in Ontario, and in addition to the Great Lakes, Ontario has a further 250,000 small lakes, numerous rivers and streams, a northern coastline on Hudson Bay and of course Niagara Falls.

National Parks: Point pelee
                   Pukashwa
                   Georgian Bay Islands
                   St Lawrence Islands

OTTAWA. Situated at the confluence of the Ottawa and Rideau Rivers, the capital of Canada cannot claim to be one of the more lively of the world's capital cities. Although very much a government town which shuts up shop at 5pm and weekends, it does offer the visitor several excellent museums and art galleries, attractive government buildings and a fair selection of red-coated Mounties. The most colourful time of year to visit is probably during spring when more than a million tulips bloom in the city. The tulip bulbs were a gift to Ottawa from the government of the Netherlands as thanks for the refuge granted to the Dutch royal family during World War II.

Champlain was here first, but didn't stay long and it took a further 200 years and the construction of the Rideau Canal before Ottawa was founded. Built between 1827 and 1831 the Canal provided a waterway for British gunboats allowing them to evade the international section of the St Lawrence where they might be subject to American gun attacks. In winter the canal is drained to a depth of three feet and is maintained as the world's longest skating rink, four and half miles long.

Montréal is two hours away to the east, Toronto 250 miles to the southwest. On the way west you can visit the St Lawrence towns, among them Kingston and Morrisburg.

ACCOMMODATION

Bytown Hotel, 127 Metcalf St, 237-5171. $22 upwards single, $28 double. Laundry.

Carlton University Residence, Colonel By Drive, 231-3610, $16 single, $23 double, both with breakfast, laundry, cafeteria. 'Away from downtown but well recommended.' Reached by bus 1A or 7.

Hotel Eastview, about 1½ miles east of Parliament Bldgs on Hwy 17B, 746-8115. $27 single, $32 double, one bed.

Mrs Lyon, 479 Slater St, 236-3904. Bed and Breakfast. $20 single, $27 double. 'Very friendly, downtown location.'

Lord Elgin Hotel, Elgin Blvd, at Lauriel Ave. Tel: 261-6121. $38 upwards. 'Excellent hotel, conveniently situated for everything.'

YM/YWCA, 180 Argyle Ave, 237-1320, $24 single. Discount given for groups of 6 or more who stay in doubles. AC, gym, TV, pool, cafeteria. 'Clean and bright.'

University of Ottawa, 648 King Edward Ave., 231-7055. May–Aug, $8 nightly student rate, or $15 single.

Auberge Nicholas Street Gaol Hostel–YHA, 75 Nicholas St, 235-2595. $5 members, $6 non-members. Breakfast $1.25. 'Sleep in the corridors of the former jail and take a shower in a cell.'

For camping: Gatineau Park, and Camp Le Breton, at Le Breton Flats, Booth and Fleet Sts. Summer transit camp, $1 per night.

FOOD

Byward Market, north of Rideau. Health food, meat, fish, fruit, clothing.

Romona Cafe, Byward Market. 'Looks grubby, but food is good and cheap. Farmers eat here.'

Spaghetti Factory, on York and Rideau. 'Cheap.'

Yesterdays', Spark St Mall. 'Good food at reasonable prices.'

OF INTEREST

Dominion Parliament Buildings. The Gothic-style, green copper-roofed buildings stand atop Parliament Hill overlooking the river. Completed in 1921, the three buildings replaced those destroyed by fire in 1916. Conducted tours daily 9am–5pm; July and Aug, 9am–9pm, Sun 9am–6pm. When parliament is in session you can visit the House of Commons. For the best view in the city climb the 291-foot-high **Peace Tower** in the Square. The Tower has a carillon of 53 bells. During the summer the bells ring out hour-long concerts four times a week. In true Buckingham Palace tradition the **Changing of the Guard**—complete with bearskins and red coats—takes place on Parliament Hill at 10am from late June to early Sept.

National Museum of Natural Sciences, McLeod and Metcalf Sts. Eskimos, Indians, natural history, free films. Tue–Sun 10am–6pm. Free.

National Gallery of Canada, Elgin and Slater Sts. Canadian, English and European masterpieces. Mon, Wed and Fri–Sun 10am–6pm. Tue and Thur 10am–10pm. Closed Mon out of summer season. Free.

National Museum of Science and Technology, 1867 St Laurent. 'A must for those who like to participate.' Daily 9am–9pm. Closed Mon after Labor Day. Free.

Royal Canadian Mint, 320 Sussex Dr. Guided tours every half hour, 9am–11.30am, 1pm–2.30pm. Call 992-2348 to make a reservation.

Royal Canadian Mounted Police Barracks, Rockcliffe Driveway and Sandridge Rd. See why the Mountie always gets his man. Open 8.30am–3.30pm Mon to Fri. Closed hols.

Canadian War Museum, 330–350 Sussex Dr. Canada's military history from the early 1600s on. Daily 10am–5pm, May–Labor Day, Tue–Sun 10am–5pm, rest of yr. Free.

Central Experimental Farm, Maple Dr. Established 1886 and HQ for the Canada Dept of Agriculture. Flowers, tropical greenhouse, animals. Mon–Fri 9am–4pm. Horse-drawn wagon tours available.

Rideau Canal. The 124-mile waterway which runs to Kingston on Lake Ontario. The 'giant's staircase', a series of eight locks, lifts and drops boats some 80 feet between Ottawa River and Parliament Hill. Cruises on the Canal and river are available. Cost $5.50, under 12, $2.75. Contact Paul Boat Lines. Or hire a bike at Dow's Lake and ride along the towpath.

Near the locks is the **Bytown Museum.** An interesting look at old Ottawa. Weekdays Mon–Sat 10am–5pm, May–Sept. Donations. Close by, in Mayor's Hill Park, is the spot from where the **Noonday Gun** is fired. Everyone in Ottawa sets their watches by it.

National Arts Center, Confederation Sq. Completed in 1969, the complex includes theatres, concert halls, an opera house and an art gallery. Hour-long free tours, leaving the foyer at 10am, 2pm, 4pm.

National Aeronautical Collection, Rockcliffe Airport, just off St Laurent Blvd. Considered by Canadians to be the third best aeronautical collection in the world. Open 9am–9pm daily. There is a nice park at Somerset and Lyon and the **Vincent Massey Park**, off Riverside Dr has free summer concerts. If you have transport, a trip to **Gatineau Park**, five miles beyond Hull, is worth a thought. Good swimming. 'The park gives one an impression of the archetypal Canada; rugged country, timber floating down the Gatineau, etc.'

TOURS

Gray Line Tours available from National Arts Centre. For info: 741-6440.
For walking tours, contact NCC Walking Tours, 48 Rideau St, 996-4908.

INFORMATION

Capital Visitor's and Convention Bureau, 222 Queen St, in the Capital Square Building, 237-5150. Accommodation and sightseeing advice.
Read *Usually Reliable Source* and *Penny Press* for what's happening.
Post Office at Elgin and Sparks Sts.

ENTERTAINMENT

Read *What's on in Ottawa*. For late entertainment cross the river to Hull where the pubs are open longer.

Le Hibou, Sussex, nr Rideau St. Folk plays in the round. Cheapest on Mon.

Albion Hotel, off Rideau on Nicholas St. 'Hang out for U of Ottawa students.'

Bon Vivante Brasserie, St Joseph, Hull. French Canadian music.

Faces, 1071 Bank St, Andy and Flo's, 1820 Carling Ave, and Patty's Downtown/ Hiccup's Bar, 207 Rideau, are other possibilities.

At the National Arts Centre student standby tickets are available half an hour prior to performances with tickets reduced to about $5.

CBC Summer Festival, Camp Fortune, Gatineau Pk. Everything from French-Canadian folk to classical. Free.

Annual summer exhibition, Landsdown Park. Fair, animals, crafts, concerts, etc. 'Good fun.'

SHOPPING

Mile of History, Sussex Dr, between George St and St Patrick St. Small shops run by young people in old buildings.

Arthur's Place, Bank, nr Somerset. Second hand books and records.

For Indian and Eskimo stuff try Four Corners, 93 Sparks St, and Snow Goose on Elgin St.

Sparks Street Mall, 3-block traffic-free section between Elgin and Bank. Fountains, sidewalk cafes, good shopping, etc.

Byward Mkt, east of Chateau Laurier and one block north of Rideau between York and George Sts. Restored to 1830s character. As well as farm produce, speciality shops, eating places, crafts.

TRAVEL

Bus depot: Kent and Catherine Sts. Rail station is two miles from city centre. To get there catch either a 21 Ottawa Station bus or half-hourly service from Centennial Center. Leaves city half hour before train leaves, and leaves station 15 minutes after train arrival. Info: 236-7581.

The airport is six miles out. Buses run from the Chateau Laurier every 20 minutes.

One of the nicest ways of seeing Ottawa is by bike, and an extensive system of bikeways and routes is there for this purpose. Info from Central Ottawa Bikeways, 222 Queen St, 563-2788. Bicycles are available for hire at Dow Lake Boathouse and at Chateau Laurier for about $12 a day.

MORRISBURG. A small town on the St Lawrence whose main claim to fame is **Upper Canada Village**, a re-creation of a St Lawrence Valley community of the 19th C. The village is situated some 11 kms east of Morrisburg in Crysler Farm Battlefield Park.

The buildings here were all moved from their previous sites to save them from the path of the St Lawrence Seaway and include a tavern, mill, church, store, etc. Vehicles are not allowed. Open 9.30am–6.30pm June–Labor Day, mid-May to mid-June and Labor Day to mid-October, 9.30am–5pm, $3.75, ages 6–15 $1.25. Family rate $10.

KINGSTON. A small, pleasant city situated at the meeting place of the St Lawrence and Lake Ontario. Early Kingston was built around the site of Fort Frontenac, then a French outpost, later to be replaced by the British Fort Henry, the principal British stronghold west of Québec. This was, ever so briefly, the capital of Canada (1841–44) and many of the distinctive limestone 19th C houses still survive.

The town is the home of Queens University, situated on the banks of the St Lawrence. The Kingston Fall Fair, which in fact happens in late summer, is considered 'worth a stop'. Kingston is also a good centre for visiting the picturesque **One Thousand Islands** in the St Lawrence.

ACCOMMODATION

Journey's End Motel, 3 kms west on Hwy 2, 549-5550. $22 single, $30 double.
Prince George Hotel, 200 Ontario St, 549-5440. $28 single, $35 double. Central.
Queen's University, 547-5940, has rms May–Aug. Reservations required. About $8 per night single, double or triple.
International Youth Hostel, 307 University Ave. $4.50 per night members, $7 non-members. Shower and kitchen facilities.
Camping: Lake Ontario Park Campground, 4 kms west on King St. $6 for 2, 50¢ per person extra.
Rideau Acres, on Hwy 15, north of exit 104 off Hwy 401. $8 per site.

FOOD

The Farmer's Market, Market Sq, is open Tue, Thur, Sat.

OF INTEREST

Old Fort Henry, east on Hwy 2 at junction Hwy 15. The fort has been restored and during the summer 'hand-picked' college students dressed in Victorian army uniforms give displays of drilling. Open daily 9.30am–6.30pm. $2.75. You can also watch them at band practice twice a week. Wed and Sat. Admission $2.25, 7.30pm. The fort is also a military museum.

John A MacDonald, Canada's first prime minister, lived in **Bellvue House**, on Center St. The century-old house has been restored and furnished in the style of the 1840s. Known locally as the 'Pekoe Pagoda' or 'Tea Caddy Castle' because of its comparatively frivolous appearance in contrast with the more solid limestone buildings of the city. The house is open daily, 9am–6pm. Free.

Fort Frederick, Royal Military College Museum. On RMC grounds, half a mile east of Hwy 2. Canada's West Point, founded in 1876. The museum, in a martello tower, features pictures and exhibits of Old Kingston and Military College history, and the Douglas collection of historic weapons. Open June through Labor Day. $1.50.

Murney Redoubt. At the foot of Barrie St. Now the Kingston Historical Society museum. Open daily. 50¢.

Pump House Steam Museum, on Ontario St. A restored 1848 pump house now housing a vintage collection of working engines.

North of the city the **Rideau Lakes** extend for miles and miles. The Rideau Hiking Trail winds its way gently among the lakes. You can take a nice, free, ferry to **Wolfe Island** in the St Lawrence. Ferries leave from City Hall. Once on the island it is possible to catch another boat (not free) to the US.

Thousand Islands Boat Trips. From quay 5 miles east of Old Fort Henry, On Hwy 2. Trip lasts 4½ hours. Cost $9, ages 6–14 $4. There is also a shorter, 2-hr cruise at $6.50 and $4.

Departing from Crawford Dock at the foot of Brock St in downtown Kingston, there are additional tours of the harbour and Thousand Islands. About $9.50. For info: 549-5544.

INFORMATION

Chamber of Commerce, 209 Ontario St. 548-4415.
Industry and Tourism Office, 1055 Princess St, 546-1191.

SPORT

Canadian Olympic Training Regatta. An annual event, held during the last week in August, and one of the largest regattas in North America.

International Hockey Hall of Fame, Alfred and York Sts. Open daily. $1, ages 12–15 50¢. Family rate $2.

TRAVEL

Bus terminal, 16 Bath Rd, 548-7738.

ST LAWRENCE ISLANDS NATIONAL PARK. The park is made up of 17 small islands in the Thousand Islands area of the St Lawrence between Kingston and Brockville, and Mallorytown Landing on the mainland. The islands can be reached only by water-taxi from Gananoque, Mallorytown Landing and Rockport, Ontario, or from Alexandria Bay and Clayton in New York State.

It's a peaceful, green-forested area noted chiefly for its good fishing grounds. Camping facilities are provided on the islands.

TORONTO. Once this was the site of a wilderness meeting place for Indians and fur traders but it's grown a bit since then and is now Canada's second city and the thriving, provincial capital. It's a busy port and an industrial cultural and financial centre.

'Trunno', or 'Metro' as the natives call their city, is the most American of the Canadian cities, having many of the characteristics of metropolitan America without all of the problems. It's a brash, cosmopolitan city with some 25 different languages on tap around town, sprawling over 270 square miles, with many fine examples of skyscraper architecture, good shopping areas, a vibrant night life, fast highways, and yet it's a clean city, with markedly few poor areas, and the streets are safe at night. The city has several large and attractive parks. It's also an important transportation centre, controlling more than 32 miles of some of the busiest waterways in the Great Lakes system, as well as being a focal point for the Canadian rail networks. On hot summer weekends the best place to be is on or near Lake Ontario. Possibilities include the eastern beaches (accessible by Queen Street streetcar), the newly developed harbour front area between Bathhurst and York Streets and Toronto Islands out on the lake.

This is also a good centre from which to see other places in Ontario. Niagara Falls and New York State are an hour and a half away down the Queen Elizabeth Way (QEW), to the north there is Georgian Bay and the vast Algonquin Provincial Park, while to the west there is London and Stratford.

ACCOMMODATION

Mrs O E Kristensen, 183 College St, 979-2489. $20 single, $18 per person double, $15 per person triple 'when available'. 'Centrally located; very helpful lady.'

Carlton Inn, 30 Carlton St, 363-6961. $30 single, $35 double. Extra person $4. TV, movies, central.

Karabanow Tourist Home, 9 Spadina Rd, 923-4004. $25 double, special cheaper rates for YHA members. TV, no bath. 'Next to subway.' 'Clean and very helpful.'

Neill-Wycik, 96 Gerrard St E, 977-2320. 14 May–early Sept. $21 single, $27 double, also good long term rates. Try here first. Good facs, central. No AC.

St George Guest Home, 309 St George St, 922-0232. Summer rates: $17 one person, $14 per person double, $12 per person triple.

St Leonard Hotel, 418 Sherbourne St, 924-4902. $20 single, plus weekly rates available.

Women's Christian Temperance Union, Williard House, Gerard St W. 977-2123. $16 single, $15 per person double, $75 weekly. 'Women only; clean and friendly.'

YMCA, 40 College St, 921-5171. $22 single, $27 double. Pool.

YWCA, 80 Woodlawn Ave, 923-8454. $15 single, $25 double. Take northbound subway to Summerhill.

Tartu College Student Apartment Hotel, 310 Bloor St W, 925-4747. Weekly rates, reservations required.

Toronto Hostel, 223 Church St, 368-1848. $8 members, $11 non-members.

University College, 73 St George St, 978-8735. $10 single, $50 per week.

U of Toronto Housing Service, 49 St George St, 978-2542. Has list of accommodation available in student residences.

For apartment rentals try: Execupart Ltd, 175 Bloor, 924-0000, and Econo-Lodging Services, 101 Nymark Ave, 493-1629 for tourist home referrals.

FOOD

Fran Restaurants, 20 College, 21 St Clair Ave W, 332 Yonge. Spaghetti, fish and chips, burgers. Open 24 hrs. Under $5.

Loon Fong Yuen, 393 Spadina. Unpretentious Chinese. $5ish.

Queen Mother's Restaurant, 206 Queen St W. 'Arty and fun.' $7.

Organ Grinder, Esplanade east of Yonge. 'Noisy but a good laugh.' Pizza, $5 up.

Old Spaghetti Factory, near CN Tower. About $3 up. 'Very delicious. Excellent value and service.'

Underground Railroad, 225 King St E. Soul food, with Billie Holliday and Bessie Smith for background.

For fresh produce, try the St Lawrence or Kensington Markets.

OF INTEREST

Parliament Buildings, Queen's Park. Completed in 1892, the Legislative Buildings once provided living accommodation for its elected members. Guided tours Mon to Fri, 9am–3.30pm, including a ½-hr visit to the Public Gallery. Check on 965-4028 for exact schedule at the time of visit.

City Hall, Queen and Bay Sts. $30m creation of Finnish architect Viljo Revell, perhaps most impressive when lit at night. The reflecting pool in the centre becomes a skating rink in winter. There is an observation deck on the 27th floor. Tours daily every half hour from 10.15am–5.45pm. Free. Look out for free lunchtime concerts in City Sq.

CN Tower, foot of John St. At 1815 ft the tallest free-standing structure in the world. The pinnacle is crammed with radio and TV equipment, but lower down there is a revolving restaurant and an observation deck, open in summer 9am–midnight, other times 10am–11pm. Elevator to observation deck $3.50, ages 13–17 and over 65 $2.75, under 13 $1.75. To reach the Space Deck it's a further $1.50 per category. 'A life-enriching experience.' 'Good view—and drop—from 1466 ft.'

Old Fort York. On Garrison Rd, the Fort was built in 1739 and has been completely restored during the last ten years. It now houses a collection of antique weapons, tools, etc. Guided tours, 10am–5pm, admission $2.50, no student reduction.

Black Creek Pioneer Village, on the northern edge of Toronto at Jane and Steele Sts. A reconstructed pioneer village of the 18th C. Costumed workers perform daily tasks in the restored buildings. July and Aug open 10am–6pm; mid-March to June,

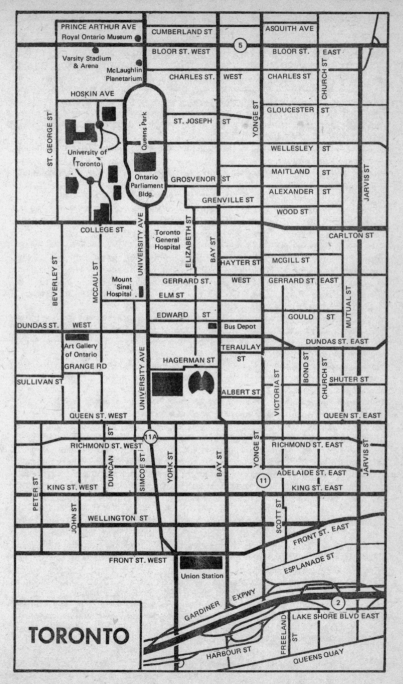

TORONTO

Sept–Oct open 9.30am (10 weekends)–6pm; 9.30am (10)–4pm, Nov–Dec $4 over 64, $2 children and students $1.75, family $8. If travelling there by subway and streetcar allow about one hour each way from the city centre.

Casa Loma, Davenport at Spadina. An eccentric chateau-style mansion built by the late Sir Henry Pellatt between 1911 and 1914 at a reported cost of $3m. It was restored in 1967 and the proceeds from the daily $2 tours go to charity. 'Fantastic.'

Toronto Stock Exchange, 234 Bay St. Visitor's Gallery has recorded explanatory guide on tap. Mon–Fri, 10am–3.30pm. Free tour daily. Free tours 11am and 2pm, 1.30pm in winter.

University of Toronto, just west of Queens Park. The largest educational institution in the British Commonwealth. Free one-hour tours of the campus available, starting from either Hart House or University College. 10.30am, 12.30pm and 4.30pm daily.

Art Gallery of Ontario, Dundas and Beverly Sts. Rembrandt, Picasso, Impressionists, large collection of Henry Moore sculptures, plus Oldenburg's 'Hamburger', and collections by Canadian artists. Tue, Fri–Sun 11am–5.30pm; Wed–Thur 11am–9pm. $2, students 75¢, 12–16 50¢.

Ontario Science Centre, 770 Don Mills Rd and Eglinton Ave E. A do-it-yourself-place. 'Breathtaking.' 'An absolute must.' Open 10am–6pm. Cost: $5, students $1. To get there take Yonge Subway to Eglinton, then 34 bus to Don Mills Rd.

Royal Ontario Museum, 100 Queen's Park Crescent W. Due to re-open 1983 after refurbishment. Mon–Sat 10am–9pm, Sun noon–8pm, July and Aug, daily 10am–6pm rest of yr. $1.50 students, children 75¢, snr citizens 50¢. Has the largest Chinese art collection outside China and fine natural history section. Next door is the **McLaughlin Planetarium**. Open Tue–Sun 10am–5pm, shows at 3pm and 7.30pm. $2.25, ages 6–14 and snr citizens $1.25.

Mackenzie House, 82 Bond St. Mid-Victorian home and print shop of William Lyon Mackenzie, first mayor of Toronto and leader of the Upper Canada rebellion in 1837. Now restored to mid-1800s condition. Open daily. $1, over 65 and under 13, 50¢. Tea served daily 2pm–4pm, $2.

Marine Museum, Exhibition Park. History of shipping and the Great Lakes from fur trading days on. Open Mon –Sat 9.30am–5pm, Sun noon–5pm. $1, under 13 and over 65 50¢.

Chinatown, along Dundas West and China Court, Spadina, south of Dundas. Usual mixture of tourist and 'real' Chinese. Good place to eat.

Ontario Place on the lakefront. Opened in 1971, Ontario Place is a complex of manmade islands and lagoons, with a marina and some attractive parkland. Free outdoor rock, folk or symphony concerts are given late afternoons and evenings at the Forum; there are free films at Cinesphere on the 'largest screen in the world'; and multimedia presentations of Ontario are shown in several unusual pavillions. There's an amazing children's fun village and fairly cheap food is available in several different eating places. Well recommended by previous visitors. $3.50, ages 13–17 $2.

Canadian National Exhibition, otherwise known as CNE or 'The Ex', held annually next to Ontario Place during the 18 days before Labor Day. Free admission to Ontario Place from the CNE during this time. A sort of glorified state fair, Canadian style, and the largest annual exhibition in the world. Cheap food in the Food Hall, and site of the Hockey Hall of Fame.

Canada's Wonderland, 30 kms north, Rutherford Rd, off Hwy 400. Ontario's answer to Disney? Includes 5 theme areas, a 150-ft man-made mountain complete with waterfalls, and all the usual rides and entertainments, May–Sept 10am–10pm. $12.95 for deluxe tkt book, jumbo tkt book $14.95. For info: 669-6400.

The best of the city's **parks** and open spaces are High Park, Edwards Gardens, Don Mills, Forest Hill and Rosedale. The ferry ride to **Center Island** in the harbour costs $1.25 return.

In Toronto's parks they invite you to walk on the grass.

Metro Toronto Zoo, 25 miles northeast of junction Hwy 401 and Meadowville Rd N. 10am–7pm. $4.

INFORMATION

Convention and Tourist Bureau, Eaton Centre, 220 Yonge St, 979-3133.
Visitors Bureau, City Square.
Community Information Center of 34 King St E, 3rd floor, 863-0505. 24 hr service.
Free Youth Clinic, 252 Dupont, 925-6223. Open 24 hrs.
Post Office at Front and Bay Sts.

ENTERTAINMENT

Check the *Globe and Mail* for daily entertainments guide.
O'Keefe Center, Front and Yonge Sts. Opera, ballet, concerts, jazz, drama. St Lawrence Center for the Arts, Front and Scott Sts. Was Toronto's project for the Confederation celebrations in 1967. Drama, dance and opera.
The Strip. On Yonge St, running between Dundas and Gerrard Sts. The usual.
Free swimming at Woodbine Swimming Pool (subway to Woodbine, bus to Lakeshore), and Sunnyside Swimming Pool (subway to Dundas W, streetcar to Queen).
The Festival of the Dragon Mall is held in Chinatown at the end of Aug.
Mariposa Folk Festival is held on Toronto Islands mid-July.
Bull and Bear, Wellesley at Bay. 'English-style pub.'
The Nag's Head, Eaton Centre. Folk music most nights.
Ye Olde Brunswick House, Brunswick and Bloor. 'Good jazz and a lively amateur night.'
Bourbon St, 180 Queen St W. Jazz, often with top-name appearances.
El Mocambo, 464 Spadina Ave. Dancing, groups. Where Margaret Trudeau and the Rolling Stones got together.
Look out for Summer Music Festival happenings in various parks. For info: 367-7251.
Harbourfront, 235 Queen's Quay. Concerts, etc, plus movie theatre showing oldies, horror movies, and other classics.
The Roxy Cinema, Greenwood Rd. Downtown movies at $2.
For free tickets to CBC TV shows, call 925-3311, ex. 4835, weekdays 9am–5pm.
Sport: in winter the Toronto Maple Leafs play ice hockey at Maple Leaf Gardens, Carlton and Church Sts, and in summer the Blue Jays play major league baseball at Exhibition Place Stadium.

TRAVEL

Standard fares operate on the integrated transport system (bus and subway) and it is cheaper to buy tokens. Current fare is 75¢, 7 tokens $4. Children under 13, 25¢. Transfers, valid between subway and bus lines, are free. Exact fare required for buses and streetcars. Sun and holidays bus pass $2. Bus drivers do not give change. Route maps available from ticket booths. The Toronto Transit Commission (TTC) offers information on 484-4544. Sun bus pass $1.50.
Bus Terminal, Bay at Dundas, 979-3511. Opens 5am.
There is an express bus services from Islington Subway to the airport. Goes every half hour and costs $2.
Airport buses leave the Royal York Hotel and the Sheraton Centre every 20 mins. $4.75.
Via Rail Canada information: 367-4300 or 366-7411.
Grayline Tours of city range from 2½ to 5½ hrs. Call: 487-5111.
Toronto Harbour and Islands Boat Tours, leaving every hr from foot of Yonge St and Ontario Pl. $5.75.
Buses to Niagara Falls go every hour from the bus station. 2-hr ride.
Toronto Driveway Service, 5385 Yonge St, Suite 34, 226-4616.

Bike rentals: George the Bicycle Man, 1606 Queen St E. About $8 daily, $20 weekly. Brown's Sport and Cycle Shop, 2447 Bloor St W, same rates.

SHOPPING
Honest Ed, Bloor and Markham. 'Just about everything at 40% reduction.'
Sam the Record Man, Yonge and Dundas. 'Huge selection of cheap records.'
Cheap clothes at Hercules, 577 Yonge St.
Do-It-Yourself Garage, 300 Greenwood (rear), 465-3901. Make your own repairs; flat rate of 50¢ for use of tools.
Yorkville Shopping Plaza, north of Queens Park on Avenue Rd. 'Lively, open till about 1am on Sat night—street theatre, music, etc.'
Eaton Centre Shopping Mall, Yonge and Dundas. An impressive multi-levelled, glass-domed complex of stores, eating places and entertainments. 'Definitely worth a visit.'
Beneath the Toronto Dominion Bank complex, Bay and King Sts, there is a wealth of shops and restaurants, bustling during the day but closed at night. Interconnects into the subway system, the Royal York Hotel and Union Station.

HAMILTON. Situated on the shores of Lake Ontario roughly midway between Toronto and Niagara Falls, Hamilton is Canada's King of Steel. The city is home to the two principal steel companies in the nation, Stelco and Dofasco, and like its US counterpart, Pittsburgh, is in the throes of an urban cleanup and renewal in the wake of the steel giants. The air and the water are cleaner here these days and many new and interesting buildings have gone up around town. Hamilton is working hard to improve its image.

The city is also blessed with one of the largest landlocked harbours on the Great Lakes, as a result handling the third largest water tonnage in the country. Although primarily a shipping and industrial centre, Hamilton does offer a variety of non-related activities to the visitor. It is also within easy reach of Niagara, Brantford, Stratford and London.

ACCOMMODATION
Clappison Corners Motel, 2000 Hwy 6 N, 689-6615. 5 kms from downtown. $25 single, $30–$36 double. Pool.
Jamesway Motor Inn, 1187 Upper James St, 385-3291. $26 double.
McMaster University, 525-9140, ex 4781. May–Aug. About $10–$12. Shared washrm, kitchen facilities, indoor pool.
YMCA, 79 James St, 529-7102. $16 single. Reservations a good idea.
YWCA, 75 MacNab St, 529-8121. $17 single, cheaper rates for longer stays, shared washrm.

FOOD
Cameo Restaurant, 60 James St N. 'Inexpensive.'
Farmers Market, central Hamilton, and the largest such market in Canada.
Duffey's Tavern, 59 Kings St E. Chinese and Canadian dishes. Much recommended.
McMaster University Common Building Refec. 'During the summer, June through Aug, it is possible to eat here. Meals about $2.'

OF INTEREST
Dundurn Castle, York St at Dundurn. Restored Victorian mansion of Sir Allen

Napier MacNab, prime minister of United Canada, 1854–1856. Son et lumière performances during summer, also Children's Cockpit Theatre, Sat and Sun 2pm. Mansion open 11am–4pm June–Labour Day, thereafter 1pm–4pm. $2, over 64 $1.50, students $1.

Art Gallery of Hamilton, Main St W at Forsythe Ave. Canadian and American art. Open 9am–5pm, or 9pm Thur, Sun 2pm–5pm. Closed Mon. Free.

MacMaster University. Has one of Canada's first nuclear reactors and a planetarium. There is also an art gallery on campus, in Togo Salmon Hall.

Canadian Football Hall of Fame, MacNab within City Hall Plaza area. Computerised information systems and push button exhibits. Open Sun–Fri 10am–4pm, Sat 1pm–4pm. $1.25, students and over 64 75¢.

Royal Botanical Gardens, York Blvd. Nature trails. Dawn to dusk daily. Free. A maple syrup and pancake festival is held here in March.

Hamilton Place, an impressive $11m showcase for the performing arts and part of the downtown renewal project. Call 525-3100 for schedules.

Hess Village, four blocks between King and Main. Restored Victorian mansions in a 19th C village. Trend shops, antiques, restaurants, etc.

Steel Company of Canada, Wilcox St. Conducted tours Tue–Fri, 9.30am and 1.30pm. Sturdy shoes required. Info: 528-2511, ex 2952.

Dofasco Inc, 1330 Burlington St E. Tours Mon–Wed and Fri. No-one under 16. Info: 544-3761, ex 2214.

INFORMATION
Convention and Visitors Bureau, 155 James St S, 525-1151.
Bus terminal: John St off King St.

BRANTFORD. Chief Joseph Brant brought the Mohawk Indians to settle here at the end of the American Revolution, the tribe having fought with the defeated Loyalist and British North American armies. Her Majesty's Chapel of the Mohawks was built in 1785 and ranks as the oldest church in Ontario and the only royal chapel outside the United Kingdom. King George III himself was pleased to donate money for the cause.

Chief Brant's tomb adjoins the chapel. The annual **Six Nation Indian Pageant**, depicting early Indian history and culture, takes place at the beginning of August. One disappointed visitor was moved to remark, 'Not a feather in sight till then.'

The town's other claim to fame is **Tutela Heights**, the house overlooking the Grand River Valley where Alexander Graham Bell lived and to which he made the first long distance telephone call, all the way from Paris, Ontario, some eight miles away. The call was made in August 1876, following Bell's first call in Boston.

OF INTEREST
Bell Homestead Museum, 94 Tutela Heights Rd. Bell's birthplace and museum, furnished in style of 1870s. Daily 10am–6pm in summer, Tue–Sun rest of yr. Free.

Brant County Museum, 57 Charlotte St. Indian and pioneer displays. Tue–Fri 9am–5pm, Sat–Sun 1pm–4pm. Closed Mon and Sun outside summer months. 75¢, students 50¢.

Brant's Ford, Lorne Park. Memorial marks the spot where Chief Brant crossed the Grand River.

Woodland Indian Cultural Centre and Museum, 184 Mohawk St.

Art Gallery of Brant, Arts Pl, at 76 Dalhousie St. Canadian artists. Tue–Fri 9am–5pm, Sat 10am–5pm. Free.
Brantford Highland Games, held early July. Pipe bands, dancing, caber tossing, etc.

INFORMATION
Chamber of Commerce, 77 Charlotte St, 753-2617. Also organises daily tours of town.

NIAGARA FALLS.
The Rainbow Bridge which spans the Niagara River connects the cities of Niagara Falls, NY, with Niagara Falls, Ontario, and whichever side of the river you stay on the Canadian side is definitely the better side from which to view the Falls. It's an awe-inspiring sight which somehow manages to remain so despite all the commercial junk and all the jostling crowds you have to fight your way past. Try going at dusk or dawn for a less impeded look, and then again in the evening when everything is floodlit. Snow and ice add a further grandeur to the scene in winter. (See Niagara Falls, NY, for further details.)

ACCOMMODATION
Tourist homes are the best bet here. Beware of taxi drivers who try and take you to motels or more expensive tourist homes. Suggest you call first, many tourist homes offer a free pick-up service from the bus depot.
R Barker, 4765 McDougall Cr, 354-5439. $22 double. 'Very friendly and helpful.' 10 mins from Falls.
Mrs F Blackburn, 4687 Eastwood Cr, 358-8429. 'May pick up. She and Mrs Barker work together.'
Mrs Dell Tourist Home, Orchard Ave. $22 double. 10 minutes from bus station. 'Very clean.'
Mall of the Mist Motel, behind bus station. $20 double. 'Good.'
Parkview Motel, Buchanan Ave. $25 double. 'Cheaper rms not as warm or well equipped, but good value and only 10 minutes from the Falls.'
Mr and Mrs H Schooley, 4487 John St, 358-3815. $12 single, $14 per person double. 'Everyone with this book will be accepted.' 20 minutes from bus station. 'Friendly.'
Scotsman Motel, 6179 Lundy's Lane 356-0041. $24 double up.
Niagara Falls Youth Hostel, 4699 Zimmerman Ave, 357-0770. $6 members, $9 non-members. Open yr-round, kitchen facilities.
Camping: Riverside Park, 14 kms south on Niagara River Pkwy, on Niagara River banks. $7 for 4, laundry, pool.
YMCA, 6135 Culp St, 345-3031. $10.

OF INTEREST
Niagara Tower. Ascend in glass elevators. Open daily.
Panasonic Tower. 665 feet tall with a restaurant at the top. $3.50.
Skylon Tower. One of the tallest concrete structures in the world. See-through outside elevator; revolving restaurant at 500 feet. $3.50, over 65 and under 18 $1.75. Open daily 9am–1am. 'Arrive first around sunset and see the Falls floodlit by night and then by day.'
'Maid of the Mists' boat trip. The boats pass directly underneath the Falls. Oilskins provided. $3.75, ages 6–12 $1.75. Elevator to the dock is 50¢.
You can also **walk under the Falls** through rock tunnels, descending by elevator from Table Rock Hse $3, ages 6–12 75¢. 'Very amusing.' 'A big con.'
Niagara Falls Museum. Exhibits of the curious objects within which people have gone over the Falls and lived, and flora and fauna of North America. Also an

excellent collection of Egyptian mummies! Open daily 9am–midnight. $3.25, students and over 60 $2, ages 6–12 $1.25.

Marineland Game Farm, 3657 Portage Rd. Dolphins and sealions. $7, ages 4–11 $4.

Fort George, at Niagara-on-the-Lake. Reconstructed 18th C military post. 10am–5pm, $1. Whole town of **Niagara-on-the-Lake** is worth a brief visit. This was the first capital of Ontario and home of the first library, newspaper and law society in Upper Canada. Has a certain 19th C charm.

Shaw Festival, Niagara-on-the-Lake. June to Sept season of Shaw productions. 20 miles from Niagara Falls. Tickets from $6. For info: 468-3201.

Whirlpool and Rapids, four miles from Falls by sightseeing tour. Aero car and Rapids Broadwalk. $2.50 round trip, ages 6–12 75¢.

TRAVEL

To reach Niagara Falls International Airport, USA, catch bus from bus station, $2.25.

A new hydrofoil service has recently been inaugurated across Lake Ontario between Youngstown, NY, and Toronto. Youngstown is about 12 miles from Niagara Falls. $15 one way.

KITCHENER-WATERLOO.

A little bit of Germany lives exiled in Kitchener-Waterloo, a community delighting in beer halls and beer fests. The highlight of the year is the Oktoberfest, a weeklong festival of German bands, beer, parades, dancing, sporting events and more beer.

Waterloo is often referred to as the 'Hartford of Canada' since the town is headquarters of a number of national insurance companies. The best days to visit K-W (a fairly easy 69-mile excursion from Toronto) are Wednesday and Saturday in time for the farmer's market where black bonneted and gowned Amish and Mennonite farming ladies and their menfolk sell their crafts and fresh-picked produce. Sixteen miles north at **Elmira**, there's the annual Maple Syrup Festival, held in the spring.

ACCOMMODATION

Mayflower Motel, 1155 Victoria St N, 745-9493. $16 up.

Waterloo Hotel, 4 King St N, 886-1110. $14 single, TV.

YMCA, 57 Queen St, Kitchener, 743-5201. 'Homely and decaying. Closed on Sun.'

YWCA, 84 Frederick St, Kitchener, 744-6507, and 186 King St, Waterloo, 744-1711.

OF INTEREST

Kitchener was the boyhood home of **William Lyon Mackenzie King**, Prime Minister from 1921 to 1930 and 1935 to 1948. His former home at 528 Wellington St, is open to the public during the summer, 9am–5pm daily.

Doon Pioneer Village, south of town on Huron Rd. Close to exist 34 off 401. Recreation of early Canadian pioneer village. Open daily 9am–5pm. $2 students $1.

GEORGIAN BAY ISLANDS NATIONAL PARK.

A good way north of Toronto on the way to Sudbury, this is one of Canada's smallest national parks. It consists of 30 islands or parts of islands in Georgian Bay. The largest of the islands, Beausoleil, is just five miles square, while all the rest combined add only two-fifths of a mile.

The special feature of the park is the remarkable geological formations. The mainly Precambrian rock is more than 600 million years
old and there are a few patches of sedimentary rock carved in strange
shapes by glaciers.

Midland is the biggest nearby town for services and accommodation
but boats to Beausoleil Island go from Honey Harbour, a popular
summer resort off Route 103. On Beausoleil, once the home of the
Chippewa Indians, there are several campsites.

ACCOMMODATION
Park Villa Motel, 751 Yonge St W, adjoining Little Lake Pk, Midland, 526-2219.
$22 up, heated pool.
Shamrock Motel, 955 Yonge St W, Midland, 526-7851. $20–$25 up.

OF INTEREST
Huronia Museum, off King St. Indian, pioneer and natural history exhibits, plus
section on shipping in the Great Lakes. 9.30am–5.30pm. $1, high school students
50¢.
Huron Indian Village, in Little Lake Pk. Replica of Indian village of the district 300
yrs ago. Mon–Sat 9am–6pm, Sun 1pm–6pm. $1.50 snr citizens, students $1.
Sainte-Marie Among the Hurons, 3 kms east on Hwy 12. Recreation of Jesuit
mission which stood here 1639–1649 plus Huron longhouses, cookhouse,
blacksmith, etc. Orientation Centre offers a colour film about the mission and the
excavation work involved in the project. Daily 10am–6pm. $1.50, students 75¢,
family rate $3.50.
30,000 Island Cruise, at Midland Dock. 3 hr trip among the islands of Georgian Bay.
Daily 2pm. $6.50, under 12 $3.
Wye Marsh Wildlife Centre, Hwy 12. Guided tours, animals, exhibits, floating
boardwalk. Daily 10am–6pm. Free.

LONDON. Not to be outdone by the other London back in Mother
Britain, this one also has a River Thames flowing through the middle,
although the pronunciation is different here. London, Ontario, also
has its own Covent Garden Market. It's a town of comfortable size,
and a commercial and industrial centre. Labatt's Brewery is perhaps
the town's most famous industry.

London also offers the visitor a thriving cultural life. It's physically
a pleasant spot, known as 'Forest City', and is situated midway
between Toronto and Detroit. The University of Western Ontario is
here and is said to have the most beautiful campus of any Canadian
university. You'll find it on the banks of the Thames.

ACCOMMODATION
Abbey Hotel, 2010 Dundas St, 451-7171. $15 single, $26 double, AC, TV.
Maple Glen Motel, 1609 Dundas, 451-2030. $18 single, $26 double. Close to airport.
YMCA, Wellington and Dundas, 432-4706. $19 single, $24 double. Also hostel
dorm during summer. M and F. 'Advisable to book. Very friendly place in a very
friendly town.'
Univ of Western Ontario, rm 118 Somerville Hse, Dept of Housing, 679-3991.
May–Aug. Reservations required. $10 single, shared washrm, laundry, pool, etc.

OF INTEREST

Centennial Museum, 325 Queen's Ave. History and culture of the region housed in a building the same shape as Canada's centennial symbol. Tue–Fri noon–8pm, Sat 10am–5pm, Sun 1pm–5pm. 50¢.

Eldon House, 481 Ridout St. London's oldest house and now a historical museum. Noon–5pm, $1.

The Museum of Indian Archaeology and Pioneer Life, Wonderland Rd N, on the university campus. Entrance: 50¢.

Labatt's Pioneer Brewery, 150 Simcoe St. Restored to 19th century appearance. Noon–5pm up to Labor Day. Free.

Fanshawe Pioneer Village, Fanshawe Pk, off Clarke Rd. Re-creation of 19th C pre-railroad village. Log cabins, etc. Daily 10am–5pm, $1, under 13, 50¢. Park admission $2.50 per car.

Children's Museum, 379 Dundas St. World cultures, communications, music and crafts. 'Excellent.' $1 adults, under 12, 50¢.

Royal Canadian Regiment Museum, Wolseley Hall, on Canadian Forces Base. History of Canadian forces from 1883. Mon–Fri 9am–11.30am and 1pm–4pm. Wed 7am–9pm. Free.

Springbank Park, Springbank Dr. Nice for walking or for taking a ride on the mini train in summer. Also the 20-minute river ride—the Tinkerbelle Cruise, 85¢.

INFORMATION

Visitors and Convention Services, 300 Dufferin Ave, City Hall, 672–1970.

ENTERTAINMENT

The Ridout, 346 Ridout St N. 'Popular tavern.' Rock bands.

Clifton Arms, 332 Richmond St. 2 bars—one with dance floor and disco, other has live blues and country music.

Western Agricultural Show. Second largest state-type fair in Canada. Held in Queens Park, mid-Sept.

TRAVEL

Greyhound, 155 York at Richmond, 434-3245.

TILLSONBURG. Some 46 miles away from London, the town springs to life at the beginning of August when the tobacco harvest begins. Tillsonburg, and nearby **Delhi**, are the main supply centres for southern Ontario's most affluent tobacco growing area. Around harvest time the towns are crowded with transients looking for work on the farms and large German, Belgian, and French tobacco farmers looking for potential pickers. At Delhi, there is the **Ontario Tobacco Museum** which documents the story of tobacco from Indian times.

ACCOMMODATION

Hillcrest Motel, 50 Simcoe St, 842-5966. $26 single, $32 double.

Riley's Motor Hotel, 145 Simcoe St, 842-5917. $24 upwards. 'Usual facilities.'

STRATFORD. In 1953 this average-sized manufacturing town on the banks of the River Avon some 50 kilometres north of London, held its first Shakespearian festival. The now world-renowned season has become an annual highlight on the Ontario calendar. The festival lasts for 22 weeks from mid-June, attracting some of the best Shakespearian actors and actresses, as well as full houses every night.

Based on the Festival Theatre, but encompassing several other theatres too, the festival includes opera, original contemporary drama and music, as well as the best of the Bard. In September the town also hosts an international film festival.

There's not much else of interest in Stratford except a walk along the riverside gardens and a look at the swans. Heading west there is Point Pelee National Park before going to Windsor and crossing to the US.

ACCOMMODATION
The Festival Theatre provides an accommodation service during the summer. You are advised to first contact them, 271-2420.
Kent Hotel, 209 Waterloo St S, 271-6756. $32 double.
Queens Motel, 161 Ontario St, 271-1400. $25 single up.
Rosecourt Motel, 599 Erie St, 271-6005. $35 double.
Youth Hostel, 23 Albert St. Summer only. $10 members, $14 non-members. Central location.

FOOD
Daniels, 107 Erie St. 'Reasonable.'
Banbury Tea Room, 21 Church St. 'Good food at good prices.'

ENTERTAINMENT
Festival Theatre. Tickets from $6.50–$22.50, Festival Theatre, and also Avon Theatre. The Festival Theatre is at 55 Queen St, and the Avon is on Downie St. Order from: Festival Box Office, PO Box 520, Stratford, Ont N5A 6V2. Call: 519-273-1600. Special student matinees in Sept but often swamped by high school parties. 'Get there early on the day of the performance for returns.'
Stratford **Farmer's Market**, Colisum Fairground, Sat mornings.

INFORMATION
Stratford Chamber of Commerce, 32 Downie St.

POINT PELEE NATIONAL PARK. About 35 miles from Windsor, Point Pelee is a V-shaped sandspit which juts out into Lake Erie. On the same latitude as California, the park is the southernmost area of the Canadian mainland.

Only six square miles in area, Point Pelee is a unique remnant of the original deciduous forests of North America. Two thousand acres of the park are a freshwater swamp and the wildlife found here is unlike anything else to be seen in Canada. On the spring and fall bird migration routes, the park is a paradise for ornithologists. There are also several strange fish to be seen and lots of turtles and small water animals ambling around.

Point Pelee is quite developed as a tourist attraction and there are numerous nature trails, including a one-mile boardwalk trail. Canoes and bicycles can be rented during the summer months and the Visitor Centre has maps, exhibits, slide shows and other displays about the park. Entrance to the park is $2 per day. There is no camping in Point Pelee, although there are two sites in the nearby town of Leamington.

SUDBURY. Sudbury is some 247 miles northwest of Toronto and the centre of one of the richest mining areas in the world. The local Chamber of Commerce will tell you that Sudbury enjoys more hours of sunshine per year than any other city in Ontario (and we have no reason to doubt them), but this is not a pretty area. Part of the empty landscape looks so like a moonscape that American astronauts came here to rehearse lunar rock collection techniques before embarking on the real thing. However away from the immediate vicinity of the town there are scores of lakes, rivers and untracked forests to refresh the soul after witnessing the ravages of civilisation.

ACCOMMODATION
Cheapest in the Ukrainian District, around Kathleen St.
Coulson Hotel, 68 Durham St, 675-6436. $20 single, $24 double.
Four Sisters Motel, 1077 Lorne St, 675-6436. $22 upwards.
Laurentian University Residence, Ramsey Lake Rd, 675-1181. About $14 single, plus weekly rates available.
Plaza Hotel, 1436 Bellevue St, 566-8080. $20 up.
Sudbury Hostel, 278 Lloyd St, 674-4373. $5 per night.
YWCA, 111 Larch St, 674-2210. $14 single.
Youth Hostel, Richards Lake, Mine Mill Camp. Accessible by downtown bus from Sudbury. Also 278 Lloyd St, 674-4373.

OF INTEREST
Free guided tours are available of the **INCO Smelter**, at Copper Cliff, 4 miles west of town, on Highway 17. The smelter is the world's largest single smelting operation and is open to visitors, May through Sept, 10am and 1.30pm, 682-2011.
The Falconbridge Nickel Mines, 12 miles east in Falconbridge, also organise tours, 9.30am and 1.30pm. No children under 12. Info: 693-2761.
Canadian Centennial Numismatic Park. A sort of giant's money box which includes a 30-foot stainless steel nickel, a 10-foot Kennedy half-dollar and a 10-foot Lincoln penny. Also a model mine. Open daily May–Oct.

INFORMATION
Chamber of Commerce, 144 Durham St S, 673-7133.

TRAVEL
Bus station situated 3 miles from town centre.

SAULT STE MARIE. First established in 1669 as a French Jesuit mission, Sault Ste Marie later became an important trading post in the heyday of the fur trade. Today 'The Soo', as locals call the town, oversees the great locks and canals that bypass St Mary's Rapids. The Soo Locks, connecting Lake Superior with St Mary's River and Lake Huron, allow enormous Atlantic ocean freighters to make the journey 1748 miles inland. Visitors can watch the ships rising and falling up to 40 feet, from special observation towers.

The town is connected to its US namesake across the river in Michigan by an auto toll bridge. If you're going north from here, 'think twice about hitching'. Lifts are hard to come by, the road is long

and empty. It's probably best to get as far beyond Wawa as possible.
Thunder Bay is 438 miles away to the northwest.

ACCOMMODATION
Beaver Hotel, 569 Queen St W, 256-8441. $17 single, $26 double.
Riverview Motor Court, 1280 Queen St E, 254-4420. $28 double up.
Royal Hotel, 2 Queen St E, 254-4321. $17 single, $26 double. 'Very good value,
close to bus station.'
Youth Hostel, 1447 Trunk Rd, 253-4241. $4.50. 16 kms out of town.
Camping: Woody's Campsites, Hwy 17N, 12 kms north. $5 for 2.

FOOD
Ernie's Coffee Shop, 9 Queen St. 'Big, cheap meals, excellent value.'

OF INTEREST
Lock Tours. 2-hr round trip cruises through both the Canadian and American
(which are the world's busiest) locks. Dep from Norgoma Dock, Foster Dr, next to
Holiday Inn. Also takes in St Mary's River. Daily in summer, $8.50, ages 13–17 and
over 64 $7, ages 6–12 $4.25. Info: 253-9850.
Agawa Canyon Wilderness Tours, from Algoma Central Railway Terminal, 129 Bay
St Rt rail excursion to wilderness, scenic areas. Daily dep 8am, ret 6pm. $24 round
trip, seniors $15.
MS Norgoma **Museum Ship**, Norgoma Dock at Foster Dr. The last of the overnight
passenger cruise ships built on the Great Lakes, the ship plied the Owen Sound to
Sault Ste Marie route from 1950 to 1963. Daily 9am–9pm during summer. $2.50,
ages 6–16 $1.25.
The Old Stone House, 831 Queen St E. Completed 1814 and a rare example of early
Canadian architecture. Restored. Daily 10am–8pm. Donations.
Lake Superior Provincial Park. A fair ride north of here—some 130 kms—but
nonetheless worth the trip to this rugged wilderness park. Includes nature trails,
moose hunting in season, Indian Rock paintings and a fine beach.

THUNDER BAY.
On the northern shore of Lake Superior and an
amalgam of the towns of Port Arthur and Fort William, Thunder Bay
is the western Canadian terminus of the Great Lakes/St Lawrence
Seaway system and Canada's third largest port. Port Arthur is known
as Thunder Bay North and Fort William is Thunder Bay South. The
towns are the main outlet for Prairies grain and have a reputation for
attracting swarms of huge, and hungry, black flies during the summer.

The city's new name was selected by plebiscite and is derived from
the name of the bay and Thunder Cape, 'The Sleeping Giant', a
shoreline landmark. Lake Superior is renowned for its frequent
thunderstorms and since in Indian legend the thunderbird was responsible for thunder, lightning and rain, that was how the bay got its
name. The city is 450 miles from Winnipeg to the west, and about the
same distance from Sault Ste Marie to the southeast.

ACCOMMODATION
Circle Inn Motel, 686 Memorial Ave, 344-5744. $28 double. 'Reasonably close to
the bus terminal.'
Lakehead Motel, 421 N Cumberland St, 344-3231. $20 single, $26 double.

Lakehead University Residence, Oliver Rd, 345-2121. May–Aug $12 single, also weekly rates.

Modern Hotel, 430 N Cumberland St, 344-4352. $20 single, $24 double.

Park Mount Hotel, 390 Adelaide St, 683-6274. $24 double up.

Longhouse Village Youth Hostel, Lakeshore Dr, and McKenzie Stn Rd, 983-2042. $8 non-members, $6 members, $4 tenting. 'Friendly, warm hostel, baths, TV.' 'The best in Canada.'

OF INTEREST

World's largest **grain elevator**. Half-hour tours available. Start from Bay South Information Center. $1. 10.15am and 2.15pm.

Thunder Bay Historical Society Museum, 217 S May St. Indian artefacts and general pioneering exhibits. Daily 2pm–5pm, June–Aug.

The Sleeping Giant. He of the Indian folk legends from whom the town derives its name. Impressively visible across the bay in Lake Superior.

Old Fort William. On the banks of the Kaministiquia River. Once a major outpost of the North West Trading Company, now a 'living' reconstruction. Craft shops, farm, dairy, naval yard, Indian encampment, breadmaking, musket firing, etc. 10am–6pm. $3, students $1.50.

Centennial Park, east of Arundel St. Animal farm, a museum and a reproduction of a typical northern Ontario logging camp of the early 1900s. Open daily. Free.

Amethyst Mine. 35 miles on Trans Canada Highway, then north on E Loon Lake Rd. One of the largest amethyst mines in North America. Gather your own rocks and then pay on the way out.

TOURS

Harbour cruises. From Port Arthur Marina, Arthur St, 344-2512. $4.50 to $7.50 depending on which cruise you take.

INFORMATION

Convention and Visitors Bureau, 193 Arthur St.

ONTARIO'S NORTHLANDS.

Going north out of Toronto on the Trans Canada Highway, you can carry on round to Sudbury, Sault Ste Marie and Thunder Bay, or else, at Orillia, you can get on to Route 11 which will take you up to North Bay, and from there to Ontario's little-explored north country. **North Bay** is 207 miles from Toronto and is a popular vacation spot as well as the accepted jumping off point for the polar regions.

There's not much in North Bay itself, but there is ready access to the **Algonquin Provincial Park**, a vast area of woods and lakes good for hiking, canoeing and camping, and also to **Lake Nipissing**. Pressing north, however, there is **Temagami**, a hunting, fishing, lumbering, mining and outfitting centre. The Temagami Provincial Forest was the province's pioneer forest, established in 1901 and providing mile upon mile of sparkling lakes and rugged forests. It's quiet country up here; even with modern communication systems, people are few. It's also mining country. **Cobalt** is the centre of a silver mining area and **Timmins** is the largest silver and zinc producing district in the world. You can visit mines and mining museums in both towns.

At **Cochrane**, 207 miles north of North Bay, the northbound highway runs out, and the rest of the way is by rail. The Polar Bear Express runs daily during the summer up to Moosonee on James Bay, covering the 186 miles in four and a half hours (cost $22 round trip). It's a marvellous ride, the train packed with an odd assortment of people, everyone from tourists to miners, missionaries, geologists and adventurers. Before boarding the train for the trip north there is the Cochrane Railway Museum to visit. Housed in an engine and four coaches, the museum traces the history of the James Bay Frontier. **Moosonee** counts as one of the last of the genuine frontier towns and is accessible only by rail or air. Since 1673 when the Hudson Bay Company established a post on nearby Moose Factory Island this has been an important rendezvous for fur traders and Indians. It's also a good place to see the full beauty of the Aurora Borealis.

This is as far north as most people get, but there's still a lot of Ontario lapped by Arctic seas. Over 250 miles north of Moosonee by air, there's **Polar Bear Provincial Park**. This is a vast area of tundra and sub-arctic wilderness. The summer is short and the climate severe. The rewards of a visit here can be great however. There are polar bears, black bears, arctic foxes, wolves, otters, seals, moose and many other varieties of wildlife to be seen in plenty.

ACCOMMODATION

All the towns mentioned above have small hotels or motels, none of them especially cheap however. If planning to come this far off the beaten track it is advisable to give yourself plenty of time to find places to stay. Remember that if everything is full in one town your next options may be several hours' driving further down the road. There are many campgrounds in this part of Ontario, but again the distances between them are often considerable.

QUÉBEC

Canada's largest province and totally different from anywhere else in North America. The larger cities, Montréal and Québec City, may be, at least superficially, bi-lingual but the remoter parts of La Belle Province are totally French and once there it is easy to imagine that you are on the other side of the Atlantic. What is more you will find the Québecois very determined to remain French and very reluctant to speak English. In Montréal you may be totally ignored if you speak to someone in English.

Québec is as large as France, Spain and Germany put together but four-fifths lies within the area of the barren Canadian Shield to the north. This remote and beautiful wilderness, coupled with the poverty of all the rural areas of the province, contrasts sharply with the sophistication of Montréal and the charm of Québec City.

National Parks: Forillon
La Mauricie
Auguittuq

MONTRÉAL. Canada's largest city is situated on an island and is built around a mountain, Mount Royal, hence its name. Situated on the archipelago at the junction of the Outaouais and Saint-Laurent Rivers, Montréal is a natural meeting point for overland and overwater routes.

Jacques Cartier arrived here in 1535 to find a large Indian settlement, Hochelaga, believed to have been where McGill University now stands. When Champlain arrived, nearly 100 years later, the Indian town had gone, and the rest was up to the French.

They succeeded so well that their city is now one of the greatest inland ports (with 14 miles of berthing space) in the world and since the opening of the St Lawrence Seaway in 1959 the city's port-based industries have greatly expanded and increased, making Montréal one of North America's most important commercial, industrial and economic centres.

More than two-fifths of the total population of Québec live in the Montréal metropolitan area. Two-thirds of these people are French-speaking, making their city the largest French-speaking city in the world after Paris and an interesting compromise blend of French and English influence in an American setting. Theatre and the arts in general flourish here and Montréal has three universities, McGill and Sir George William being English-speaking, and the Université de Montréal, French. This last institution is a hotbed of separatist militancy, as from time to time is the whole city.

ACCOMMODATION
A L'Àmeriquaine, 1042 Rue St Denis, 849-0616. $17 single, $21 double. Much recommended. 'Friendly people, large rooms, and close to Old Montréal.'
Canada World Youth, Cité du Havre, 861-8157. $5.50 members, $7 non-members. 'Difficult to reach.' Take bus 168 at Bonaventure subway stop.
Castel St Denis Tourist Rooms, 2099 Rue St Denis, 842-9719. $14 single, $18 double. 'Clean, comfortable, very French.'
Friendly Tourist Rooms. 1701 Rue St Denis, 844-2413. $12 single, $18 double.
Hotel Iroquois, 446 Place Jacques Cartier, 861-5416. $12 single, $21 double. 'Clean and friendly. Very beautiful part of city to stay.'
Kent Tourist Rooms, 1216 Rue St Hubert, 845-9835. $18 up.
Maison Impala Tourist Rooms, 302 Rue Ste-Catherine Ouest, 861-2307. $8 single, $12 double.
Maison Paradis, 6927 Rue St-Denis, 274-2673. $9 single, $13 double.
Maison de Touriste le Relais, 756 Rue Berri, 844-3611. $15 single, $20 double. 'Highly recommendable.'
Salvation Army, off Dorchester Blvd. $1.50 nightly for shower and bed.
Maison Villa de France, 57 Rue Ste-Catherine Est, 849-5043. $20 single, $25 double.
University residences: Concordia, 7141 Sherbrooke W, 482-0320, ex 528. May–Aug. $12 single, less for students.
McGill, 3935 University Ave, 392-4224. May–Aug. $16 single, also weekly rates. Shared washrm, pool, laundry.
YMCA, 1441 Drummond St, 849-5331. $20 single. Metro to Peel.
YWCA, Dorchester and Crescent, 866-9941. $19 single up. Cheaper dorm rates. 'Well situated, good facilities.'

Youth Hostel, 3541 Aylmer, 843-3317. Members $6.50, non-members $8.50. Breakfast $1.

Camping: Camping Henri, 12 kms east on Rue Notre-Dame along St Lawrence, 642-5477. $7 for 4.

FOOD
Ben's, Maisonneuve and Metcalf. Cheap food 24 hrs.

Brasserie Le Gobelet, 8405 Blvd. St Laurent. Nearest metro stop is Jarry. 'Converted barn, worth a visit for amazing decor and atmosphere, as well as for the food.'

Le Boeuf a la Mode, 277 St Paul E. Dinner about $11. 'Excellent French food.'

Concordia University Cafeteria, Bishop St 'Especially good for breakfasts.'

La Crepe Breton, Mountain St. 'Good for a night out. Large variety of crepes.'

The Mazurka, Prince Arthur at Coloniale. 'Good and tasty food. Really friendly atmosphere.'

Medasie, Rue Notre-Dame. 'Very good and reasonably priced Chinese.'

Stash's Restaurant, 461 St Sulpice. 'Good Polish food from $6.'

Atwater Market, Atwater St. Below Rue Notre-Dame. For buying your own.

OF INTEREST
Vieux Montréal. Situated on the Lower Terrace, the area includes the business and local government sectors. In recent times the buildings lining the old narrow streets have been given facelifts, funds being provided from the public as well as private purse. The squares and streets, etc, are best explored on foot. Notre-Dame, Bonsecours, and St Paul are the best streets to walk along. Not to be missed, particularly if you are not planning a visit to Québec City. Pick up the excellent walking tour leaflet from one of the city's information bureaux. To get there: metro to Champ-de-Mars, Place d'Armes or Victoria.

Notre-Dame Church, Place des Armes. Notable for its size and extravagant early Gothic Revival architecture and the gilded interior which threatens to 'out-Pugin Pugin'. 6am–9pm. Museum 50¢.

Notre-Dame de Bonsecours, St Paul E. Overlooking the harbour and known as the 'sailor's church'. Built in 1771, the oldest still standing in the city, this church was once an important landmark for helmsmen navigating the river. There is a fine view from the top of the tower. 25¢.

Place Jacques Cartier. Once Montréal's farmer's market. The restored Bonsecours Market building is on the south side of the square. This square also has the honour of containing the first monument to Nelson erected anywhere in the world. You can buy good cheap food from the stalls here, or sit out at a street cafe and listen to a jazz band.

Bank of Montréal Museum, Place des Armes. Coins, documents and general banking memorabilia tracing Montréal's history as the country's financial centre.

Chateau Ramezay, 280 Rue Notre-Dame Est. Built by Claude de Ramazey, a governor of Montréal, and now a museum depicting life in New France in the 18th C. Tue–Sun 10am–4pm. $1, students, snr citizens 50¢.

The Upper Terrace. Flanking the southern edge of the mountain, the area includes a considerable part of the city stretching east and west for several miles. At its heart was the Indian town of Hochelaga, discovered by Cartier in 1535, standing not far from the present site of McGill. This central skyscraper area through which run Sherbrooke, Maisonneuve, Ste Catherine Sts and Dorchester Blvd, is the visitor's centre, into which converge metro, bus and rail systems and where the major hotels and shops are situated. Beyond Boulevard St Laurent, Montréal is wholly French, while on the western half of the Upper Terrace is the City of Westmount, famous for its stately mansions, fine churches and public buildings.

Place des Arts, Ste Catherine St. Montréal's new integrated cultural centre.

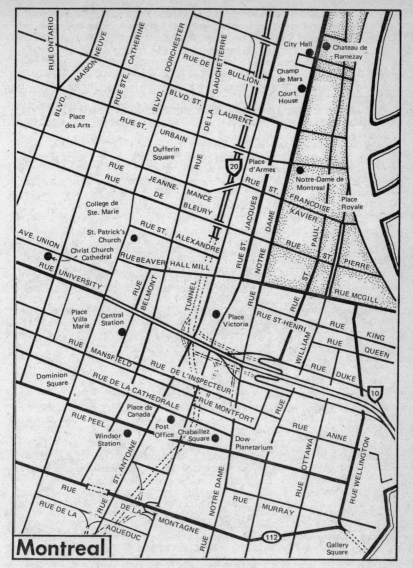

Montreal

Guided tours Tue and Thur on the hour between 1pm and 4pm. Cost 50¢, students 25¢.

Museum of Fine Arts, 1379 Sherbrooke St. Canada's oldest art institution. Founded 1860. Soapstone carvings to impressionst masters. Tue–Sun 11am–5pm. $2, ages 12–16 50¢, over 65 and under 12 free.

Museum of Contemporary Art, Cité du Havre. Tue-Sun 10am–6pm. Free.

Place Ville Marie. New civic development. Below ground there is a vast complex of underground passages linking Place Ville Marie, Place Bonaventure, and Place

Victoria, two railway stations, hotels, hundreds of shops, parking lots and the subways. Down here you can shop, eat, see a movie or catch a train to Vancouver.

Canadian Imperial Bank of Commerce, Rues Dorchester and Peel. Among the tallest buildings in the British Commonwealth. The observation deck on the 45th floor is open daily 10am–10pm. 75¢.

McCord Museum, 690 Rue Sherbrooke Ouest. The collections of McGill University including paintings, prints, costumes, furniture and native folk art. Wed–Sun 11am–5pm. Free.

St Lawrence Seaway Lookout, south end of Pont Victoria on top of Seaway Authority Building. 9am–9pm daily. Free. Watch the ships go by on one of the world's busiest waterways.

Botanical Gardens, Sherbrooke. Reached via a 118 bus. Tour on foot or by miniature train. 192 acres containing some 10,000 different species of plant and shrub. Open daily 9am–6pm.

Mount Royal Park. On a fine day the views from the 763-foot 'mountain' are tremendous, the vista taking in the St Lawrence and Ottawa Rivers, the Adirondacks in New York State and the Green Mountains of Vermont. By night the lights of the city sparkle below. During the summer look out for open-air concerts in the park. In winter there is skiing and skating.

St Joseph's Oratory. On the north slope of Westmount Mountain which is separated by a narrow cleft from Mount Royal. The Oratory dome is a marked feature of the Montréal skyline and the shrine is a popular point of pilgrimage, attracting thousands of visitors from all over North America. Also famous for its cures said to have been affected through the prayers of the 'Miracle Man of Montréal'. Either a 62 or a 65 bus gets you there.

Mary, Queen of the World Basilica, Rue de la Cathèdrale on Dominion Sq. Small-scale version of St Peters in Rome. Built 1878.

Terre des Hommes (Man and His World). Out in the Saint Lawrence on the Ile Sainte-Hélène (named after Champlain's wife). The site of Expo '67 and now a permanent cultural and entertainment centre. Many of the Expo buildings survive but the whole thing shuts up shop after Labor Day. Also includes **La Ronde**, an amusement park at the eastern end of Ile Ste-Hélène. $7.50. Daily 10am–8pm until Aug 31.

Canadian Railway Museum, St Contant, 632-2410. Twelve miles out of town. Get there on Hwy 9C or by bus from Longeuil Metro. Open Mon–Fri 9.30am–4.30pm; Sat, Sun 10.30am–5.30pm. $3, ages 13–17 $2, ages 5–12 $1.50.

Maison de Radio Canada, 1400 Blvd. Dorchester E. HQ for CBC French TV and Radio and for Radio Canada International. Bi-lingual tours. Free. Call: 285-2339.

Olympic Park, eastern Montréal. Site of the 1976 Olympic Games and now home to Montréal's football, baseball and soccer teams. Tours in French daily 11am, 2pm; in English 12.30pm, 2.45pm and 3.30pm. $3, ages 7–16 $1, snr citizens $2. Info: 252-4737, Montréal Expos (baseball). For better value go to a baseball or football game here and see the stadium plus an all-American game.

INFORMATION

Montréal Tourist Bureau, Dominion Sq, and 2 Place Ville Marie, 873-2015. Also, 155 E Notre-Dame, 872-3561, info, and advice.

Post offices: opp Notre-Dame, St Jacques E, and 1025 St Jacques.

ENTERTAINMENT

Enthusiastic Canadians have been heard to call Paris the 'Montréal of France', but the city is both a little more and a little less than the French capital incorporating elements of Soho and Manhattan as well. The best places for drinking (as elsewhere in Canada) are taverns. Beer is sold on draught but a 'men only' rule generally applies.

Le Café Théâtre du Quartier Latin, 4303 Rue St Denis, live theatre, life music plus puppet shows.
Chez Dumas, 286 Ste Catherine E, live music, no cover.
L'Imprevu, 446 Place Jacques Cartier, rock and roll bands.
Le Soleil Levant, 286 Ste Catherine W, jazz. $5 cover.
Esquire Pub, Stanley St. Reputation for good country and blues.

TRAVEL
The Metro (built for Expo) is fully integrated with the bus system and whispers along on rubber tyres between handsome, arty-crafty stations. Current fare: 75¢. For information call: 877-6260.
Bus tours, Gray Line from 1241 Peel St, Dominion Sq, 866-4641.
Bus terminal: Maisonneuve Blvd and Berri St, 842-2281.
CN Central Station is on Mansfield and Dorchester Blvd, beneath the Queen Elizabeth Hotel. Via Rail: 282-2650; Amtrak: 800-263-8130.
Mirabel Airport, 34 miles out, handles international flights, while Dorval, 10 miles west takes domestic and US flights. Limousines go from the Queen Elizabeth Hotel, Dominion Sq.
Auto Driveaways: 4036 Ste Catherine W, 937-2816, and Reliable Drive Away, 5100 Jean Talon W, 731-8507.
Bike hire: Cyclo Plein Air Inc. 352 Villeray St. About $12 per day. Peel Cycle Centre, 1832 Ste Catherine. Again about $12 per day.
Canoe Rental: Peel Cycle Centre, reservations necessary plus fat deposit. About $35 for a weekend plus deposit. Also Rosario Faucher, 4282 Brebeuf, about $20 per day plus deposit.

THE LAUENTIAN MOUNTAINS. This is a region of mountains, lakes and forests just north and west of Montréal and reached from the city via Autoroute 15 and Route 117. The proximity to Montréal and Québec City does mean that amenities are well developed but nonetheless it's nice for summer camping and hiking and best of all in winter for skiing.

Ste Agathe is the major town of the Lauentians and is built around the shores of Lac des Sables. Water sports and cruises on the lake are the most popular activities here. Other towns worthy of interest include **St Donat**, the highest point in the area, and consequently a skiing and climbing centre, **St-Sauveur-des-Monts**, an arts and crafts centre, **Mont Laurier**, a farming area, and **Mont Tremblant**, a year-round sports centre offering fishing, watersports, hiking and skiing.

In the hills to the northeast of Montréal and accessible off Highway 55 is the unspoiled **La Mauricie National Park**. The park is marked by rolling hills and narrow valleys with chains of lakes. Canoeing is especially popular here as well as cross-country skiing in winter. Moose, black bear and coyote are among the animals making their home here as do a great variety of bird species. The park is open year-round and admission is $1.

Accommodation is plentiful, although not especially cheap throughout the area. Of course it's also possible to visit the Lauentians in day trips from Montréal.

QUÉBEC CITY. The pride and focal point of French Canada is in fact two cities. Below Diamond Rock, the Lower Town, Basse Ville, spreads itself over the coastal region of Cape Diamond and up the valley of St Charles, and atop the rugged Diamond Rock, 333 feet above the St Lawrence River, is the Upper City. Built as the fortress heart of New France, Upper Québec remains today the only walled city in North America.

Here, in 1759, General Wolfe and his scarlet-coated British troops scaled the cliffs in pre-dawn darkness, surprised and overcame Montcalm and the French high on the Plains of Abraham and secured Canada for the British. The Plains are now a peaceful public park and a popular family picnic spot.

And yet Québec remains French. Only five percent of the city's inhabitants speak English and they are more friendly if you speak French. Walking through the narrow, winding streets, past the greystone walls, the sidewalk cafes and the artists on the Rue du Trésor, it is easy to imagine that you have left North America behind and somehow been catapulted across the Atlantic Ocean to the alleyways of Montmartre. It is a town best seen on foot and details of a walking tour are available from the tourist bureaux. Montréal is 168 miles west of here.

ACCOMMODATION
Maison Au Bon Accueil, 48 Rue St-Louis, 647-9350. $13 single, $16 double. 'Big decent rm. Very French.'
Au Vieux Foyer, 71 Rue St Louis, 647-9305. $15 single, $20 double. 'Central, pleasant.' No 3 bus gets you there.
Maison Château Vue, 8 Rue Laporte, 692-2692. $20 up. 'Friendly.'
Hotel Manoir Charest, 448 Rue Dorchester, 647-9320. $25 up. 'Clean and friendly.'
Auberge de la Haute Ville, 1190 Claire-Fontaine St, 523-4139. $5. 'Simple, basic. sleeping bag necessary.'
Maison Louis Herbert, 668 E Grande Allee, 525-7821. $20 single, $30 double.
Le Manoir la Salle, 18 Rue Ste Ursule, 647-9361. $15 single, $25 double.
YMCA, 835 St Cyrille St W.
YWCA, 845 Holland Ave, 682-2155.
Youth Hostel CYHA, 69 Rue d'Auteuil, 694-0755. $6.50 incl breakfast. Co-ed rooms, sleeping bag necessary. Close to Old Town.
Laval University, St Foy, 656-2921. May–Aug, $12 single, shared washrm, laundry.
Camping: Camping Motel Canadien, on Hwy 138 north of Québec and Pierre Laporte bridges, 872-7801. $9 for 2.
Camping Parc Beaumont, exit 337 Trans-Can Hwy, then north on Rte Lallemand to jct Rte 132, then 8 kms west. Tel: 837-1450. $7.50 for 4, laundry, groceries, pool.

FOOD
Open-air market, de la Couronne St. Thur, Fri evenings, all day Sat.
The area around Rue St Jean and Rue Buade is good for cheap cafes. Complete 3-course meals (répas complet) are usually the most economical.
Cafe Buade, Rue Buade. 'Excellent tasty food.'

Cafe Paysan, 2480 Ste Foy. 'Inexpensive steak and chicken.'
La Poudriere, 100 St-Louis. French cuisine in a 19th C powder shop.

OF INTEREST

The Citadel, on Cap-Diamant promontory. Constructed by the British in the 1820s on the site of 17th C French defences, the Citadel is the official residence of the Governor-General and the largest fortification in North America still garrisoned by regular troops. Changing of the Guard ceremony takes place at 10am daily and there is a museum of military objects. Museum and citadel are open 9am–7pm daily during the summer, with reduced opening times thereafter. $2 incl tour, under 18 75¢. 'Not really worth the money.' 'Very enjoyable.'

The Plains of Abraham. Battlefields Park was the scene of the bloody clash between the French and British armies. A Martello Tower, part of the historic defence system of walled Québec, still stands, and the views from up here are terrific. Also in the park is the **Musée de la Province de Québec**: original hand copy of the surrender of the city by Montcalm; also displays of Québec art and handicrafts. 'Disappointing.'

Musée du Fort, 10 Rue Ste Anne. Provincial military history and dioramas of the 6 sieges of Québec. Daily 9am–9pm July, Aug; Mon–Sat 10am–5pm, Sun 1pm–5pm rest of yr. $2.25, $1.25 students.

Chateau Frontenac, Rue St Pierre. A view of the St Lawrence is to be had from the Promenade des Gouverneurs.

Musée des Ursulines, 12 Donnacona St. The oldest girl's school in America and where, in the convent grounds, Montcalm is buried. His skull, however, is carefully preserved in the Chapel. Parts of the convent date from 1686 and there are also paintings, furniture and engravings to see. Tue–Sat 9.30am–noon, and 1.30pm–5pm, Sun 12.30pm–5.30pm. $1, under 16 25¢, family rate $2.50.

Parliament Buildings, on Grande-Allée. The main building built in 1886 is in 17th C French Renaissance style. Tours depart every half hr. Free.

The Ramparts, Rue des Ramparts, and studded with old iron cannons, probably the last vestiges of the Siege of Québec in 1759.

Notre Dame de Québec, City Hall Sq. Restored many many times, the basilica was first constructed in 1650 when it served a diocese stretching from Canada to Mexico.

Notre-Dame-Des-Victories, Place Royale, Basse Ville. Built in 1688, but 80 years before, this was the spot where Champlain established the first permanent white settlement in North America north of Florida. The church itself gets its name in honour of two French military victories. Its main altar resembles the city in that it is shaped like a fortress complete with turrets and battlements. The whole **Place Royale** area is now being restored.

Dow Brewery—Jean Talon Vaults, 15 St Nicholas St. Guided tours include a peek at pioneer brewing utensils, old posters and documents and the original brewery vaults. During the summer tours are available Mon through Fri, 10am–4pm.

Ile D'Orleans. Out in the St Lawrence and reached by bridge from Hwy 138. A little bit of 17th C France to wander around with old houses, mills, churches, etc. Also known for strawberries and handicrafts.

INFORMATION

Visitors Bureau, Place des Armes.
Québec City Tourist Bureau, 60 Rue d'Auteuil, 692-2471. They will also give you information on the city walking tour beginning at the Chateau Frontenac.

TRAVEL

For city bus information call 524-4692.
For Voyageur bus co information call CPR-522-1284.
The quickest way across the St Lawrence is via the ferry to Lévis. Passenger fare: 75¢. Nice views of Québec, especially at sunset, from the other side.

THE GASPÉ PENINSULA. This is the bit of Québec Province jutting out above New Brunswick into the Gulf of St Lawrence. The word Gaspé is derived from the Micmac Indian word meaning Lands End. Stand on the shore at Gaspé and you'll fully appreciate this for there's nothing but sea between you and Europe. Picturesque fishing villages line the Peninsula; slow, pleasant places in summer, rugged in winter. Inland it's farming country although a large area is taken up by the Gaspesian Provincial Park.

From Québec City take Route 138 with the rugged Laurentian Mountains on your left, through **Ste-Anne-de-Beaupré** and **Baie-Saint Paul** where there is an interesting museum of old-time French Canadiana, and up to St Simeon where there is a ferry crossing to Riviére du Loup. From here take Route 132 as far as **Trois Pistoles**.

Long before Canada was 'officially discovered', Basque whale hunters built ovens at Trois Pistoles to reduce whale blubber to oil. The remains of the ovens can still be seen. Carry on along the south shore of the St Lawrence through the fishing villages, catching all the while the ever changing seascapes. From **Rivière A Claude** access to the top of 4160-foot **Mount Jacques Cartier** is 'easy'. The mountain is in the Gaspesian Provincial Park and is the highest point in the province.

Or for the moment carry on round the top of the Peninsula coming first to **Gaspé** itself where Jacques Cartier came ashore in 1534 and set up a cross to stake France's claim to Canada. Nearby is **Forillon National Park**.

Forillon scenery is typified by jagged cliffs and fir-covered highlands. The park is criss-crossed by many hiking trails and on the way you may see deer, fox, bear or moose. Large colonies of seabirds such as cormorants, gannets, and gulls nest on the cliff headlands and it is possible to see whales and seals basking offshore.

Naturalists offer talks and slide presentations at the Interpretive Centre on Highway 132 near Cap-des-Rosiers. There are campsites at Cap Bon Ami, Le Havre, and Petit-Gaspé. All three have good recreational facilities including beaches.

The views around here are fantastic but none better than at **Percé**. The village takes its name from **Rocher Percé**, the Pierced Rock, which is just offshore. You can walk there on a sandbar at low tide.

From Percé boat trips go to nearby **Bonaventure Island** where there is a bird sanctuary. Before heading down to Chaleur Bay and thence back to Québec proper as it were there is still the **Gaspesian Provincial Park** to see. In the park you may catch a glimpse of the caribou herd which spends its summers here. Mornings are the time you are most likely to see them. It's a good place for fishing and hiking.

ACCOMMODATION
There are several small hotels in Gaspé, the least expensive of which are the Maison

Berube, on Montée Sandy Beach, at $15 up and Motel Anna Mabel on Blvd Gaspé, at $24 single.

There is a youth hostel in Rivière-du-Loup and student accommodation at the College de la Gaspésié in Gaspé.

Campsites are available everywhere.

THE PRAIRIE PROVINCES

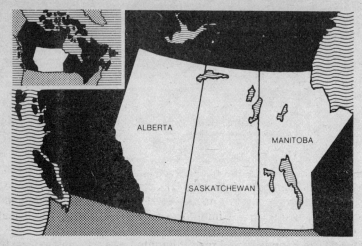

Alberta, Manitoba and Saskatchewan are for the most part wide open prairie country, although western Alberta offers, in contrast, the magnificent scenery of the Rockies. Grain once formed the basis of the economy of these provinces but today mineral wealth and tourism are also the big money spinners.

Although the major cities are fast-growing modern centres of commerce and culture, there remains a touch of the frontier about all three provinces. Vast areas of virgin wilderness are still there for the intrepid to explore and conquer and it is possible to travel for days in some places without ever seeing another human being.

ALBERTA

Once an agricultural backwater with an economy dependent solely on wheat, Alberta is now enjoying an economic boom based on the Province's multi-billion dollar oil and gas industries. The former small-town farming centres of Calgary and Edmonton are now thriving metropolises, their skylines dotted with skyscraping corporate headquarters. With 85 percent of Canada's oil and gas on tap, Albertans are enjoying the lowest taxes, the least unemployment and the highest per capita incomes in the country.

The situation is not without its political implications. The four western provinces and two territories hold less than 30 percent of the seats in the Federal Parliament and westerners feel themselves deprived of power by the more populous East. It is not only in Quebec that the language of separation is often spoken.

Of all the Canadian provinces, Alberta has the greatest variety of geographical features, ranging from the towering Rockies in the southwest to the rolling agricultural land north of the US border, and up north the near wilderness lands of lakes, rivers and forests. Although it gets hot in summer, cold weather and even snow can linger into May and come again as early as September. In the mountains of course the nights can be cool even in summer.

National Parks: Waterton Lakes
                    Jasper
                    Elk Island
                    Wood Buffalo (not developed, no access by road, no accommodation)

EDMONTON. The close proximity of the highly productive Leduc, Redwater and Pembiano oilfields to the provincial capital has made it the fastest growing city in Canada. Coal-mining, natural gas, and a couple of throw-backs to Edmonton's origins, fur-trading and wheat, are the other factors behind the boom.

During the Klondike gold rush Edmonton was a stopping place for prospectors enroute to the goldfields. The town remembers this with joy every July during Klondike Days when the place goes wild for a week. Otherwise it's a sober, hard-working spot, the most northerly major city in North America, boasting as well as skyscrapers a progressive university, the only subway system in western Canada and as a result of hosting the Commonwealth Games a few years back some of the finest sporting facilities anywhere.

Edmonton is centrally situated within Alberta and it's a good starting point for a northbound trip or for going westwards towards the Rockies. Jasper is 228 miles away, but first there's Elk Island National Park just 30 miles east.

ACCOMMODATION

Cecil Hotel, 10460 Jasper Ave, 428-7001. $19 single, $24 double. Downtown location.

Commercial Hotel, 10329 82nd Ave, 439-3981. $15 single no bath, $25 single with bath, $18 double no bath, $28 double with bath.

Grand Hotel, 10266-103 St, 429–7521. $18 single, $22 double, family rm $26.

Klondiker Hotel, 153 St and Stony Plain Rd, 489-1906. $24 single, $27 double.

Park Hotel, 8004 104 St, 433-6441. $24 single, $28 double, cheapest without bath.

Relax Inn, 10320 45th Ave, 436-9770 and 18320 Stony Plain Rd, 483-6031. $27 single, $29 double, family rates.

University of Alberta residence, Lister Hall, 87th Ave and 116th St, 432-4281. Open to non-students May–Aug.

YMCA, 10030 102A Ave, 424-8047. $15 single. New building.

YWCA, 10305 100 Ave, 423-9922. $14 single.

Youth Hostel, CYHA, 10422-91 St, 429-0140. $6.50 members, $10 non-members. 'Easy walk from downtown. Comfortable.'

Camping: Rainbow Valley CG, 3.2 kms W of Hwy 2 on 45th Ave. Tents and tent trailers only. Operated by city.

FOOD
Legislative Building. 'Cheapest restaurant in town.'
Casablanca's in Hubb Mall for cheap pizza, etc.
RATT (Room at the Top), on university campus on 7th floor of tower at west end of Student's Union building. 'Popular and inexpensive.'
Farmer's Market. Location varies according to time of year. For info call 427-2727.

OF INTEREST
Legislative Building, on the site of the original Fort Edmonton, 97th Ave and 109th St. Built at the beginning of this century, the building has an interesting free tour, daily.

Fort Edmonton Historical Park, along the N Saskatchewan River southwest of Quesnell Bridge. Reconstruction of the original and a replica of a Hudsons' Bay Co Trading Post. Open daily 10am–6pm in summer months, Sept–12 Oct, Sat, Sun and hols 1pm–5pm. $2.75, 13–17 and snr citizens, $1.50, 6–12 $1, family rate $7.50. 'Worth a visit.'

The **John Walter House**, at 10627 93rd Ave., was built of hand-hewn logs in 1874. The house was the district's first telegraph office. Nearby is a preserved shack furnished in pioneer style, and built in 1885. This was the home of one 'Little Henry', a Metis dwarf. 10am–6pm. Free.

Edmonton Art Gallery, 2 Sir Winston Churchill Sq. Emphasis is on Canadian artists. Mon, Tue, Fri, 10am–5pm, Wed and Thur 10am–10pm, Sun 1pm–5pm. Free.

Provincial Museum, 102nd Ave. Built as part of the 1967 Centennial celebrations, the museum endeavours to show the 'making of the Canadian West'. Mon–Sat 9am–9pm, Sun 1pm–9pm. Free.

Queen Elizabeth Planetarium, Coronation Pk nr 111 Ave. Summer showings daily at 3, 8, 9pm. Rest of the yr: Tue–Fri 8pm, weekends 3, 8pm. $2.75, 13–15 and over 64 $1.50, family rate $6.

Ukrainian Church of St. Josaphat, 97th St and 108th Ave. Splendid Byzantine trappings, golden ikons and old silver ornaments.

Ukrainian Canadian Archives and Museum of Alberta, 9543 110th Ave. Traces history of Ukrainian pioneers in Alberta. Includes costumes, paintings, folk art, etc. Mon–Fri 1pm–5pm, Sat, Sun 2pm–5pm.

Rutherford House, 11153 Saskatchewan Dr. Was the home of A C Rutherford, Alberta's first premier. Jacobean revival style and marks break from pioneer style and start of modern architecture. Furnished in early '20s style. Daily 10am–8pm.

AGT Tower, McAudley Plaza. Climb to the top, the 33rd storey, for a view of the town and surrounding countryside. 50¢.

Alberta Natural Resources Science Centre, off Hwy 16E at 17th St. Describes science and technology involved in processing province's natural resources. Daily 11am–9pm. Free.

Polar Park, 22 kms SE on Hwy 14. Preserve for cold-climate and hardy African animals. Cross country trails and sleigh rides in winter. Daily 8am–dusk. $3, over 64 and 7–16 $2.

INFORMATION
Visitors Bureaux, Hwy 2, Oil Derrick; Edmonton Visitors Centre, 5068 103 St, 434-5322.

ENTERTAINMENT
Klondike Days. 'Excellent entertainment' in the style of the 1890s is provided during the nine Klondike Days in mid-July. The show at MacDonald Hotel, Jasper and 98th St, during this time, is 'not to be missed'. Free entrance to the Golden Slipper Saloon. Corona Hotel, bar downstairs. 'Where most students drink; good entertainment.'

The Red Barn, RR1, about 30 miles out of town, 921–3981. 'Largest indoor barbeque in Canada. Worth a visit.' 'Very popular.'

TRAVEL
Bus station: 102nd St and 102nd Ave, 429-4751.
CN/VIA Rail Station, 104th Ave and 100th St.
Edmonton International Airport is 15 kms south off Hwy 2. Airport bus departs every 45 minutes from Hotel MacDonald and Airport Arrivals Terminal. About $5.
Edmonton Transit System Info: 432-1234. Standard fares operate.

ELK ISLAND NATIONAL PARK.

This 75-square-mile park is the largest fenced wild animal preserve in Canada. Apart from the elk, moose, mule deer and numerous smaller animals who live here, there is a herd of some 600 buffalo. Once roaming the North American continent in their millions, the buffalo was hunted almost to extinction by the end of the 19th century. The herd here at Elk Island has been built up from about 40 animals since 1907.

It is possible to observe the buffalo from close proximity, but on the other side of a strong fence. Walking on the buffalo range itself is discouraged. North America's largest buffalo herd, 12,000 strong, is contained in **Wood Buffalo National Park** in the far north of Alberta. This area, however, remains relatively undeveloped.

Elk Island is open throughout the year and the daily admission is $1. There is a Visitor Centre just north of Hwy 16 which features exhibits and displays. Walks, hikes, campfire talks and theatre programmes are also offered by the park rangers. Recreation facilities are available on the east shore of Astotin Lake including swimming, golf and hiking trails. There are camping facilities in the park.

OF INTEREST
Ukrainian Cultural Heritage Village, on Hwy 16. Russian immigrants played an important role in taming western Canada and this open-air museum portrays pre-1930s life of the Ukrainian settlers. The buildings are authentic and have been moved here and then restored. Daily 10am–6pm. Free.

JASPER NATIONAL PARK.

Jasper National Park is 4200 square miles of lofty, green-forested, snow-capped mountains, canyons, dazzling lakes, glaciers and hot mineral springs. In sharp contrast to one another, within the park are the Miette Hot Springs, one of which gushes forth at a temperature of 129°F, and the huge Columbia Icefields which send their melting waters to three oceans, the Atlantic, the Pacific and the Arctic.

Reached by Route 16 (The Yellowhead Highway) from Edmonton, Jasper lies along the eastern slopes of the Canadian Rockies running south until the park meets Banff National Park. This vast mountainous complex of national parkland is an extremely popular resort area throughout the year. Jasper National Park takes its name from one

Jasper Hawes who was clerk in the first trading-post at Brulé Lake in about 1813.

One of the park's biggest attractions is the 17-mile-long **Maligne Lake**. This is the largest of several beautiful glacial lakes in the area and the tour to the lake from the township of Jasper has been much recommended by previous visitors.

Within the park it is possible to drive through some of the West's most spectacular mountain scenery. **Mount Edith Cavell** (11,033 feet) and **Whistler's Peak** (7350 feet) are two of the more accessible points from Jasper township and the aerial tramway has put Whistler's Peak within reach of even the most nervous would-be mountaineers. In the cable car at the highest point above the ground you will be 450 feet in the air and once atop the Peak the view is tremendous. In winter this is a favourite skiing spot.

Sixty-five miles from Jasper on the Icefield Highway between Jasper and Banff (Route 93) is the **Columbia Icefield**. This is 130 square miles of impressive glacial ice. You can walk across parts of the glacier but it is perhaps best seen by snowmobile. Even on a very hot day take a sweater with you. Also to be seen along this most beautiful of highways are the several glaciers creeping down from the Icefields. **Athabasca Glacier** is but a mile from the road and snowmobile trips are available on the glacier.

The resort village of **Jasper** is the Jasper National Park Headquarters and also an important CN railroad junction. There is little of interest in the town itself, but should you arrive by train take note of the 70-foot Raven Totem Pole at the railway depot. The totem was carved by Simeon Stiltae, a master carver of the Haida Indians of the Queen Charlotte Islands, and gives its name to a famous annual golf tournament held here.

ACCOMMODATION

The Visitor's Hospitality Center has a list of hotels and tourist homes in the area; 852-4913.

Astoria Motor Inn, one block from railroad station, 852-3351. $38 up, open yr round.

Athabasca Hotel, half block from railroad and bus stations, 852-3386. $38 single, $39 double, open yr round.

Mrs F F Crowther, 703 Maligne Ave, 852-3013. $23 up double. 'Friendly and comfortable.'

Jober, 705 Geikie St, 852-3893. $23 up. 'Very good value. Will pick you up from bus station.'

A Leonardi, 315 Patricia St, 852-4385. $23 up double. 'Lovely accommodation.'

Youth Hostels: Maligne Canyon, 3 kms east and then 11 kms up the Maligne Rd. Dorm, yr round.

Mount Edith Cavell, 12 kms along Mt Edith Cavell Rd. Dorm, June–1 Sept only.

Athabasca Falls, 30 kms south on Hwy 93. Dorm, yr round.

Beauty Creek, 81 kms south on Hwy 93. Dorm, summer only.

Whistler's Hostel, 3 kms south and 3 kms west on Whistler Mtn Rd, 852-3215. Dorm.

Further hostel info for the area from: 10926 88th Ave, Edmonton, T6G 0Z1, 403-439-3089.
Camping: there are several campgrounds in the area, the nearest ones to Jasper being at Whistler's on Icefield Pkwy S, and Wapiti, also on Icefield Pkwy; also Wabasso on Hwy 93A S.

OF INTEREST
Columbia Icefield. Snowmobile trips available daily mid-May to mid-Sept, weather permitting, $7.75, ages 6–12 $3.50. Info: 762-2241.
Athabasca Snowmobile trips, $9. 'Well worth it.'
Jasper Sky Tram. 2 miles south via Hwy 93 and Whistler Mountain Rd. Daily mid-May to early Oct, 8am–9pm June through Aug, otherwise 9am–5pm. $5.75. Bus connections from RR station, 10.15am, 1.45pm, 3.15pm. Or walk there.
Jasper Raft Tours. 2-hr trips on Athabasca River. Daily 9.30am, 10.30am, 1.30pm, 2.30pm, June–Sept. $17.50, children $9. Tkts available at the Brewster Bus Depot and Jasper Park Lodge. For info: 852-3613.
Maligne Lake Boat Tours. 2-hr cruises, June–Oct. $10, family rate $25. Views of Maligne Narrows.

TRAVEL
Grayline Tours available to: Columbia Icefields, Lake Louise, Banff and Maligne Lake. Ask for Ameripass Discount.
Bus station closes between 1.15am and 3am.

BANFF NATIONAL PARK. Banff, Canada's oldest national park,
was established in 1885 after hot springs were seen gushing from the side of Sulphur Mountain. It takes in an area of 2546 square miles of the Rockies and the area's dry, equable climate, alpine-style grandeur, hot mineral springs and pools, have brought Banff fame and fortune as a summer health, and winter ski resort. **Banff** and **Lake Louise** are the main resort towns. The park gets its name from Banffshire in Scotland, the birthplace of Lord Strathcona, a past president of the Canadian Pacific Railroad.

Operating all year round are the cable cars which take the visitor high into the mountains. Both the **Sulphur Mountain Gondola Lift** and the **Mount Norquay Chair Lift** offer fantastic views. There are many trails winding up and around the mountains but it's tough going and the inexperienced should acquire a guide before venturing forth.

It is possible to walk up **Mount Rundle** or **Cascade Mountain** in a day, but you must first register with a park ranger. If you're on Mount Rundle, make sure that you're on the right trail, since it's easy to mistake the trail and get on to the less scenic one along the river valley.

The trail up Sulphur Mountain takes one and a half hours from Upper Hot Springs. You can ride the cable car down for free. At **Upper Hot Springs** there is a pool fed by sulphur springs at 100 degrees; great for swimming although it will cost you $1.25. If you need to hire a towel this will be a further 25¢. Hitching up here from Banff town is said to be 'easy'.

If you don't have much time in Banff there is a nice trail walk along the glacial green Bow River to **Bow Falls** near the Banff Springs Hotel. The hotel, the pride of Canadian Pacific, is built in the style of a Scottish baronial mansion. The scenery however really is spectacular and the area is not overrun by tourists. An alternative short walk is the trail up Tunnel Mountain which should take about an hour and a quarter from bus station to summit.

Glacial lakes are one of the most attractive features of Banff. **Peyto Lake** (named after Bill Peyto, famous explorer and guide of the 1890s) changes from being a deep blue colour in the early summer to an 'unbelievably beautiful turquoise' later in the year as the glacier melts into it. The glacier which feeds the lake is receding at 70 feet a year.

'The jewel of the Rockies', **Lake Louise** lies in a hanging valley formed during the Ice Age and is one of the loveliest spots in the world. It is a placid green lake in a terrific setting. Not for swimming in however. The water is a chilly 10 degrees centigrade. The town of Lake Louise is 36 miles from Banff on the Jasper highroad. From the town suggested trips are the 9 miles to the incredibly blue **Moraine Lake**, and the **Valley of the Ten Peaks** and back through Larth Valley and over Sentinel Park, or a walk out to the **Plain of the Six Glaciers** via Lake Agnes. You will need lots of time and a pair of stout shoes.

Be careful of the black and grizzly bears who live in the park. You may also see moose, elk, cougars, coyotes and Rocky Mountain goats. The lakes and rivers of the park are excellent for trout and Rocky Mountain Whitefish fishing.

BANFF. Situated 81 miles west of Calgary and 179 miles south of Jasper, Banff village, like Jasper village, is chiefly a park service centre. The park information centres are here as are the park's hotels and sporting facilities.

In summer the township bustles with people and activity. The energetic can do almost anything from climbing a mountain on foot or on horseback, to canoeing, fishing, cycling, golfing or boating, while less lively souls can admire the scenery and do some gentle shopping and people-watching. Banff is also a lively centre for the arts in summer. A Festival of the Arts is held in town from May until late August and includes music, theatre and visual arts. Lake Louise, the second largest resort town in the area is 48 kms north.

ACCOMMODATION
Visitors Bureau, 762-3711, will find accommodation, but charge $3.50 for the service. Not advisable to arrive in Banff on Sunday evening without reservation.
Irwin's Motor Inn, 429 Banff Ave, 762-4566. $36 upwards.
Mrs L Harnack, 338 Banff Ave, 762-3619. $16 double. 'Mrs Harnack has been in the business for 30 years and is a real professional.'
King Edward Hotel, 137 Banff Ave, 762-2251. $25–$39. 'Nr bus station. Always seems to have vacancies since it's at the town's busiest crossroads.'

Kudzin's, 337 Big Horn St, 762-3491. $12 double. 'Very reasonable, with cooking facs and no-smoking rule.'

Red Carpet Inn, 425 Banff Ave, 762-4184. $34–$45.

Tan-Y-Bryn, 118 Otter St, 762-3696. $17 single, $20 double. 'Super guest house.'

YM/YWCA Mountain Chalets, 414 Muskrat St. 762-3560. $6 bunk with own sleeping bag, $10 single, $15 double. 'Friendly and homely, log fire on cold night.' No cooking facs.

Youth Hostels: Mountview Hostel, 2.4 kms north of town, dorm tents, showers, cooking facilities.

Spray River, 4.5 kms south on Spray River Fire Rd. Yr round.

Mt Eisenhower, Hwy 1A nr Eisenhower Jnct. Yr-round.

Corral Creek, 4.5 kms east of Lake Louise on Hwy 1A. Yr-round.

Ramparts Creek, on Icefields Pkwy, 24 kms south of Jasper/Banff Nat'l Pk boundaries.

Mosquito Creek, south of Bow Summit on Icefields Pkwy. Dorm cabins.

Camping: there are 11 campgrounds in the park, the largest being on Tunnel Mtn. $4.50 per site. Reservations not accepted at any of the park campgrounds.

Youth Hostels within the park at: Ramparts Creek, Mosquito Creek, Corral Creek, Mt Eisenhower and Spray River. Details from: 455 12 St NW, Calgary, 283-5551.

FOOD

Drifters' Inn, Sundance Mall, 215 Banff Ave. 'Superb salad bar. Soup and salad $6.75, lasagne and salad $7.95.'

Guido's Spaghetti Factory, Banff Ave. 'Generous 3-course meal $5–$6. One of the best eating places in Canada.'

The Grizzly House, Banff Ave. 'Not cheap but food good in nice atmosphere. Small dance floor.'

OF INTEREST

Banff National Park Museum, 93 Banff Ave. The museum deals with the flora, fauna and geography of the park. Admission free. Open 11am–8pm, daily, during the summer.

Natural History Museum, 112 Banff Ave. Geology, archaeology and plantlife of Rockies plus films. Open 10am–10pm, July, Aug; 10am–8pm, May, June, Sept. $1.50, ages 6–16 75¢, family rate $3.75.

Peter White Foundation and Archives of Canadian Rockies, 111 Bear St. Library, art gallery, history of Rockies. Mon-Fri 1–5pm, 6–9pm, Sat 10am–5pm, Sun 1–5pm. Free.

The Indian Trading Post. A museum-like store which sells everything on display. Indian crafts and furs. Open Mon–Sat 9am–10pm.

Buffalo Paddock. On the Trans Canada Highway half a mile west of the eastern traffic circle. A 300-acre buffalo range. No entrance fee charged but you have to stay in your car.

Mount Norquay Cablecar, Mt Norquay Rd, off Trans Canada Hwy. May, June, daily 9.30am–5.30pm, June–Sept 9am–8pm. Other times weekends only. $4.50, ages 6–11 $2.25. Info: 762-4421.

Sulphur Mt Gondola Lift. 2½ miles south of Banff. Daily May–Oct. $5.50, ages 5–12 $2.75. Info: 762-2523.

Lake Louise Gondola, off Trans Canada Hwy. Daily 9am–6pm June-Labour Day. $4 roundtrip, one-way hikers' special $3, under 13 $2. Skiing Dec–May. Info: 522-3555.

Upper Hot Springs, 4 kms south via Mountain Ave. Pool has temp of 38°C. 8.30am–11pm in summer, 9am–9pm in winter. $1.25, children 75¢.

Icefields Snowmobile trips. See under Jasper.

The Banff School of Fine Arts, on Tunnel Mountain. Acts as a convention centre and holds a summer school from beginning July to mid-August. Look out for free concerts and art exhibition held there during the summer.

INFORMATION
Visitor Information Bureau, Banff Ave, 762-3711.
Park Service HQ, Banff Ave, across Bow River Bridge.
Banff Park Information Centre, 762-4256.
24-hr backcountry travel info, including weather forecast and avalanche warning, 762-3600.

TRAVEL
Gray Line Tours. Banff to Jasper, about $30; to Yoho Valley and Emerald Lake (much recommended, fantastic scenery) from Lake Louise, or from Banff.
'Unless you have a car, forget trying to see both parks.' Budget and Tilden Rent-a-car both have offices in town. Budget: 226 Bear St, 762-3345; Tilden: Lynx and Caribou Sts, 762-2688. On the other hand: 'hitching between the beauty spots is easy'.
Bike Hire: Park 'n Pedal Bike Shop, 229 Wolf St, 762-3477. Spoke n'Edge, 214 Banff Ave, 762-2854.
Canoes and rowing boats are on hire at Banff and Lake Louise, and at Lake Minniewanka and Bow River, motor boats are available. Motor boats are not allowed on Lake Louise.
Saddle horses from Martins Stables, Banff, Banff Springs Hotel and Chateau Lake Louise. Hired horses cannot be ridden in the park without a guide escort.

CALGARY. Like Edmonton, 186 miles to the north, the whole tone of this town has altered with the discovery of oil in the province. Once a cowboy town pure and simple, Calgary has now become an important oil and gas refining and distribution centre and the fastest growing town in the west. One of our readers complained however that for a 'boom town' there is markedly little to do in Calgary, unless you happen to like looking at half-finished skyscrapers. He clearly didn't visit town during the famous Calgary Exhibition and Stampede in July when the whole town reverts with joy to its cowtown image during ten days of cowpunching revels.

Despite its northerly location, Calgary gets less snow than New York City and it hardly ever rains here either. Local weather is determined by the chinook, a mass of warm air rushing in from the Pacific which can instantly send the temperature from minus 10°C to plus 15°C.

The town also is a major communications centre. It is on the Trans Canada Highway and from the town Route 2 goes south to the US border and north to Edmonton. It is also within easy reach of Banff and Waterton Lakes National Parks.

ACCOMMODATION
Red Carpet Inn, 4635 16th Ave, 286-5111. $30 single, $34 double.
Relax Inn South, 9206 Macleod Trail S, 253-7070. $29 single, $31 double, $33 triple.
Shamrock Hotel, 2101 11 St, 265-5446. $27 single, $30 double. Tavern downstairs.
St Louis Hotel, 430 8 Ave, 262-6341. $20 single, $22 double, least expensive rms no bath.
YMCA, 332 6 Ave. SW, 269-6701. $17 single. 'Good facilities including a pool; close to bus station.'
YWCA, 320 5 Ave SE, 263-1550. $16 single.

Youth Hostel, 520 7 Ave SE, 269-8235. $7.50 members, $9.50 non-members. Food available from $2. 'Excellent facilities.'
U of Calgary, Kanawaskis Hall and Rundle Hall, 284-7243. $12 single. Monthly rates also available. 'Good facilities, gym, cheap meals.'
Camping: KOA Calgary W, 288-0411, 1.6 kms west on Hwy 1 and Langdon Park, about 20 miles east.

FOOD
Calgary Tower (see under Of Interest), $4.50 for 3-course breakfast while revolving. Includes admission.
Hudson Bay Co. 7th Ave. Cheap complete meals.
Guido's Old Spaghetti Factory, 9th Ave and 66th St. 'Great atmosphere and good meal for around $7.'
The White Spot, Central St, north from Plaza. 'Good breakfasts.'

OF INTEREST
Heritage Park, 82nd Ave SW and 14th St W. Calgary was once the Northwest Mountie outpost and this and other aspects of the town's past are dealt with in the park. The reconstructed frontier village includes a Hudson Bay Company trading post, an Indian village, trapper's cabin, an 1896 church and graveyard, a ranch, school and a blacksmiths. A 1905 vintage train takes tourists round the park. $3, ages 3–15 $2. Open daily 10am–6pm. Reached by bus from downtown Calgary.
Glenbow-Alberta Institute, 9th Ave and 1st St SE. Works relating to history of west and eskimos. Daily 11am–9pm. $1, students 50¢.
Calgary Stockyards, 21st Ave and 12th St SE. Focal point for livestock in the west. Weekday auctions.
Calgary Tower, in Palliser Sq, 101 9th Ave at Centre St S. Offers fantastic views of the town and the Rockies. Open 8am–midnight daily except Sun when closes 11pm. $1.75, ages 6–12 and snr citizens $1.
Centennial Planetarium and Aero-Space Museum, Mewata Pk, 11th St and 7th Ave SW, 264-4060. Phone to check times of shows in planetarium. Museum has vintage aircraft, model rockets and a weather station, and is open Mon and Tue. $3 for planetarium.
Fort Calgary Interpretive Centre, 750 9th Ave SE. History of fort and early North West Mounted Police life, plus prairie natural history and development of Calgary. Wed–Sun 11am–9pm May–Sept, otherwise 10am–6pm. Free.
Zoo and Dinosaur Park, Memorial Dr and 12th St E on St George's Island. Has a fine aviary and a large display of cement reptiles and prehistoric monsters including one 120-ton dinosaur. Get there on the Forest Lawn bus. Daily 10am–6pm in summer, Mon–Fri 9am–4.30pm/5.30pm Sat, Sun during rest of year. $2, ages 12–17 $1.

INFORMATION
Tourist information from the city's hospitality centres at: Mewata Park, 1300 6th Ave SW, the base of Calgary Tower, and at Calgary International Airport.

ENTERTAINMENT
Calgary Stampede. Takes place annually the 10 days after the first Monday in July. Chuck-wagon racing, bronco-busting, etc. Whole town goes pretty wild. 'Definitely the best time to visit Calgary, but watch those prices shoot up.'
Summit Hotel Tavern, 4th Ave and 1st St SW.
The university runs a summer season of films. Fri 50¢. For info: 284-7101/7201.

TRAVEL
Greyhound Bus Station: 4th Ave and 1st St SW, 265-9111. Buses leave every hour for Edmonton.

'The only bus south out of Calgary to the USA leaves at 6.30am, arriving Butte, Montana, at 7pm.'

VIA Rail Station is on Centre St and 9th Ave S, 256-8033.

Hitchhiking is illegal within city limits.

For the Airport: the Airporter bus leaves every 20 minutes from major downtown hotels. Cost: $5.

DRUMHELLER. In the Drumheller Badlands, northwest of Calgary, the 30-mile **Dinosaur Trail** leads to the mile-wide valley where more than 30 skeletons of prehistoric beasts have been found. Everything from yard-long bipeds to the 40-foot-long Tyrannosaurus Rex.

As well as dinosaur fossils, petrified forests and weird geological formations such as hoodoos dolomites and buttes are to be seen in the valley. Another survivor of prehistory is the yucca plant found here, also in fossil form. The **Drumheller Dinosaur Museum**, 335 1st St SE, gives the background to the Badlands. The museum is open 9am–8pm July and August, 9am–5pm May–June, and September–October, and costs $1. The trail starts here.

WATERTON LAKES NATIONAL PARK. The other bit of the Waterton/Glacier International Peace Park (see also under Montana). Mountains rise abruptly from the prairie in the southwestern corner of the province to offer magnificent jagged alpine scenery, several rock-basin lakes, beautiful U-shaped valleys, hanging valleys and countless waterfalls.

There are more than 100 miles of trails within the park which is a great place for walking or riding. It's also a good spot for fishing and canoeing and has four campsites. Several cabins and hotels are provided within the park. Most of Waterton's lakes are too cold for swimming but a heated outdoor pool is open during the summer in Waterton township.

A drive north on Route 6 will take you close to a herd of plains buffalo. Go south on the same road and you cross the border on the way to Browning, Montana. You can also reach the US by boat. The *International* sails daily between Waterton Park townsite and Goathaunt Landing in Glacier National Park. Park admission $1 daily. **Waterton Park** townsite, on the west shore of Upper Waterton Lake, is the location of the park headquarters. The park information office is open daily during the summer and park rangers arrange guided walks and tours, and give talks and campfire programmes, etc, about the flora and fauna of the area.

MEDICINE HAT. A town whose best claim to fame is its unusual name. Legend has it that this was the site of a great battle between the Cree and Blackfeet Indians. The Cree fought bravely until their medicine man deserted them, losing his headdress in the middle of the nearby river. The Cree warriors believed this to be a bad omen, laid down their weapons and were immediately annihilated by the Blackfeet. The spot became known as 'Saamis', meaning 'medicine man's hat'.

Nowadays it's a smallish town on the Trans Canada Highway some 300 miles southeast of Calgary on the way to Saskatchewan, or else south to the United States.

ACCOMMODATION
Assiniboia Inn, 680 3rd St SE, 526-2801. $20 single, $28 double.
Trans Canada Motel, 780 8th St, 526-5981. $20 single, $24 double.
Saamis Youth Hostel, 1577 Dunmore Rd SE, 526-0974. $5 members, $7 non-members. Open yr round.

OF INTEREST
Altaglass, 613 16th St SW, where you can observe craftsmen blowing glass ornaments. 'Fascinating.' Mon-Fri 8am–4pm, Sat 9am–noon. Free.
Historical Museum and National Exhibition Centre, 1302 Bomford Cr. Indian artefacts, pioneer items and national and local art exhibits. Mon-Fri 9am–9pm, Sat 9am–5pm, Sun 1pm–5pm. $1.
Medicine Hat Air Show. Held annually in Aug. 'Fantastic.'

WRITING-ON-STONE PROVINCIAL PARK. In the south of the Province, 40 kilometres from the small town of Milk River on Highway 501, is this park which is of great biological, geological and cultural interest. The site, overlooking the Milk River, contains one of North America's largest concentrations of pictographs and petroglyphs. Inscribed on massive sandstone outcrops, these examples of plains rock art were carved by nomadic Shoshoni and Blackfoot tribes.

The site is open year round but access is only on the one and a half hour guided tours offered Monday to Thursday at 2pm, 3.30pm, 7.30pm and 9.30pm. Free.

MANITOBA

Situated in the heart of the North American continent, Manitoba extends 760 miles from the 49th to the 60th parallel; from the Canada–United States border to the Northwest Territories. Surprisingly then the province has a 400-mile-long coastline. This is on Hudson Bay where the important port of Churchill is located.

The first European settlers reached Hudson Bay as early as 1612 although the Hudson's Bay Company was not formed until 1670. You cannot travel far in Canada without becoming aware of the power of the Hudson's Bay Company and its influence in the settlement of the country. At one time its territory included almost half of Canada, its regime only ending in 1869 when its lands became part of Canada.

By 1812 both French and British traders were well established along the Red and Assiniboine Rivers and in that year a group of Scottish crofters settled in what is now Winnipeg. The present population of Manitoba includes a large percentage of German and Ukrainian immigrants although the English, Scots and French still predominate. Manitoba became a province in 1870, although only after the unsuccessful rising of the Metis (half Indian/half trapper stock) had been quashed. After the rail link to the east reached here in 1881, settlers flocked here to clear the land and grow wheat. Winnipeg became the metropolis of the Canadian west.

Though classed as a Prairie Province, three-fifths of Manitoba is rocky forest land, but even this area is pretty flat. If you're travelling across the province the landscape can get pretty tedious, prairies in the west and endless forests and lakes in the east. More than 100,000 lakes in all, the largest of which is Lake Winnipeg at 9320 square miles.

National Park: Riding Mountain

WINNIPEG. A stop here is almost a necessity if you're travelling across Canada. The country's fourth largest city, and the provincial capital, is a pleasant enough place to be, especially if your visit coincides with the annual week-long Folklorama Festival held in August, when more than two dozen ethnic groups celebrate their heritage in pavilions in different parts of town. Also in August there is the Winnipeg Folk Festival.

The city is very 'culture-conscious', offering the visitor good theatre, a symphony orchestra, the world-renowned Royal Winnipeg Ballet, a plethora of museums and art galleries. There are two local universities and Winnipeg is Canada's main wheat market as well as being one of the world's major grain markets. The city is the financial and distribution centre for the prairie provinces as evidenced by the chains of vast grain elevators, railway yards, stockyards, flour mills and meat packaging plants you will see.

The Red River divides the city running roughly north to south and Lake Winnipeg is just north of the city. Winters are very cold indeed here, but July and August daytime temperatures are comfortably in the 70s and low 80s. Cool in the evenings though.

ACCOMMODATION
Aberdeen Hotel, Carlton and Graham Sts, 942-7481, $16 single, $24 double up. 'Clean and friendly.'
Commercial Hotel, 226 Main, 943-4916. $10 single up.
Garrick Hotel, 287 Garry St, 943-7172. $16 single, $18 double.
Knappen House Youth Hostel, 210 Maryland St, 772-3022. $7 single. Also rents out bicycles.
McLaren Hotel, SE Main and Rupert, 943-8518. $15 single up. Family rates available.
Windsor Hotel, 187 Garry St, 942-7528. $15 single, $18 double. 'Very good value.'

YMCA, 301 Vaughan St, 942-8157. $13 single, co-ed, coffeeshop. 'One of the better Ys I stopped in.' Cheaper for YH members.
YWCA, 447 Webb Pl, 943-0381. $19 single, $16 per person double, coffeeshop.
University of Manitoba residence, 26 McClean Cr, 474-9942. May–Aug, co-ed, $12 single. Small fee gives access to pool and other sports facilities.
Youth Hostel, University College.

FOOD
Al's Restaurant, Albert St. 'Fantastic value at around $3.'
The Mid-Town, Portage and Smith. 'All you can eat buffet, $3.50.'
Perky's, nr Graham St 'Cheap and offers extensive choice.'
University of Winnipeg campus cafeterias open to public. 515 Portage Ave.
Tisza River Gardens, 346 Donald St, Hungarian. Reasonable.
Farmers Market, Old Market Sq. Buy your own fresh produce.

OF INTEREST
Details of a **walking tour** of historic Winnipeg are available from Manitoba Histori-cal Society, 190 Rupert St, 943-7037.
Legislative Building, Broadway and Osborne. Built of native stone, this neo-classical building houses, as well as the legislative chambers, an art gallery, a museum and a travel office. It is set in a 30-acre landscaped park. Guided tours; open daily 9am–8pm, mid-May to early-Sept.
Lower Fort Garry, on the banks of the Red River 19 miles north of Winnipeg and the only stone fort of the fur-trading days in North America still intact. The fort has been used at different times for various purposes. Originally the fortified headquar-ters of the ubiquitous Hudson's Bay Company, it has also been used as a garrison for troops, a Governor's Residence, a meeting place for traders and Indians, and the first treaty with the Indians was signed here. Tours are available. Daily 9.30am–6pm, May–Sept. $1.25, ages 5–16 50¢, family rate $3.50. There is also a museum with nice displays of pioneer and Indian goods, maps and clothes. To reach the fort take a Beaver Bus Line bus from downtown Winnipeg, leaving every hour on the hour, afternoons. $1 rt.
Upper Fort Garry Gate, the only bit remaining of the original fort, stands in a small park opposite the CN station on Main St. This stone structure was Manitoba's own 'Gateway to the Golden West'. A plaque outlines the history of several forts which stood in the vicinity.
Centennial Center, James Ave. New cultural complex consisting of a concert hall, planetarium, a theatre centre and the **Museum of Man and Nature**. The museum, 555 Main St, features Provincial history and natural history of the Manitoba grass-lands. 'Superb museum.' Includes dioramas depicting Indian and urban Manitoban history and a replica of the 17th C sailing ship *Nonsuch*. Mon–Sat 10am–9pm, Sun noon–9pm in summer; rest of yr Mon–Sat 10am–5pm, Sun noon–6pm. $1.50, students 75¢. There is also a **planetarium** featuring daily shows in summer. $2.50, $2 students, over 64 and under 13 $1.25. Info: 943-3142.
Winnipeg Art Gallery, 300 Memorial Blvd. Traditional and contemporary Canadian, American, and European works. Open 11am–5pm Tues.–Sat; noon–5pm Sun; closed Mon. Tue–Sat 11am–5pm, Sun noon–5pm. Free except for special exhibits.
Ukrainian Cultural Museum, and Education Centre, 184 Alexander Ave E. Folk art, documents, costumes, and history. Open Tue–Sat 10am–4pm, Sun 2pm–5pm. Free.
Assiniboine Park, 2799 Roblin Blvd. On the Assiniboine River with miniature railway and an English garden. Picnics and strolls in summer, sleigh ridings, skating and tobogganing in winter. Free. The annual carnival is held here on 12 Sept and includes a free fair and free supper. There is a good free zoo in the park specialising in North American wild animals. Closes half hour before sunset.

Grain Exchange, 360 Main St. Special visitor's gallery overlooks the trading on the 6th floor. Mon–Fri 9.30am–1.15pm.

Royal Canadian Mint, 520 Lagimodiere Blvd. One of the largest coin producing mints in the world. Free tours, Mon–Fri 9am–11am, 1pm–3pm.

Grant's Old Mill, about 5 miles west on the Trans Canada Hwy. Built 1829, the log mill marks the first use of water power in Manitoba. You can watch the mill working and buy samples of the finished product. Mon–Sat 10am–8pm, Sun 1pm–9pm. 50¢.

Living Prairie Museum and Nature Preservation Park, 2795 Ness Ave. A remnant of the prairie which once covered much of North America. Open daily 10am–8pm, July and Aug. Free.

St Boniface. Across the Red River, this French Canadian suburb is the site of the largest stockyards in the British Commonwealth and Symington Yards, the giant VIA Rail marshalling yards. There is also an interesting museum and the **St Boniface cathedral**.

INFORMATION

Convention and Visitors Bureau, Room 400, 365 Hargrave St.

Chamber of Commerce, 177 Lombard Ave.

Manitoba Visitors Reception Centre, Legislative Building, Broadway and Osborne, 946-7131. Maps and literature.

TRAVEL

Railway Tours. VIA Rail does tours to Churchill and back during July and August. For info: 123 Main St, 949-1830.

River Cruises on the Red and the Assiniboine Rivers. Leave from Louise Bridge. Also paddlewheel trips from Redwood Bridge and on Sundays a trip to Fort Garry. From about $5. Info: 669-2824, 589-4318.

Bus station, 487 Portage Ave, 775-8301, for Greyhound Lines and 301 Burnell St, 786-1427, for Grey Goose Bus Lines.

VIA Rail station is at Broadway and Main, 944-8785.

Public Transit Information around town: 284-7190. There is a free bus service—DASH—operating in the downtown area from 11am to 3pm.

SHOPPING

Osborne Village. Between River and Stradbrook Aves. Boutiques, craft and speciality shops and eating places.

Portage Ave is the main downtown shopping area.

Bike hire: 21-24 McPhillips, also in Assiniboine Park.

RIDING MOUNTAIN NATIONAL PARK.

In western Manitoba, the park occupies the vast plateau of Riding Mountain, which rises to 2200 feet, offering great views of the distant prairie lands.

The total area of Riding Mountain Park is about 1200 square miles and although parts of it are fairly commercialised there are still large tracts of untamed wilderness to be explored by boat or on the hiking and horse trails. Deer, elk, moose and bear are all common and at **Lake Audy** there is a buffalo herd. It's a good fishing region.

Clear Lake is the part most exploited for and by tourists and the township of **Wasagaming** (an Indian term meaning 'clear water') has campsites, lodges, motels and cabins as well as many other resort-type facilities, right down to a movie theatre built like a rustic log cabin.

The park is reached from Winnipeg via Route 4 to Minnedosa, and then on Route 10. Daily admission $1.

CHURCHILL. Churchill has been a trading port since 1689 and is still the easiest part of the 'frozen north' to see. During the short July to October shipping season, this sub-artic seaport handles vast amounts of grain and other goods for export. The distance from Edmonton, Alberta, to Liverpool, England, via Churchill, for instance, is 1100 miles shorter than the Great Lakes/St Lawrence route. The west's first settlers came to Manitoba via Churchill.

The partially-restored **Prince of Wales Fort**, the northernmost fort in North America, was built by the British in the 1770s. It took 11 years to build and has 42-foot-thick walls. Despite this insurance against all-comers, the garrison surrendered to the French without firing a single shot in 1782.

This is a good place from which to view the beautiful **Aurora Borealis**, September through April being the best months for viewing and picture-taking. The long daylight hours of summer make for less favourable viewing conditions. What you can see hereabouts in summer are the white whales who come in and out of harbour with the tides. Polar bears too are frquently to be seen raiding the town's garbage dump and have to be periodically airlifted to other regions.

ACCOMMODATION
Beluga Motel, 675-2382. $25 single, $35 double.
Polar Hotel, 16 Franklin St, 675-2727, $36 single, $44 double.

OF INTEREST
The **Eskimo Museum**, next to the Catholic Church, is worth visiting. Fur trade memorabilia, kyacks, Indian and Eskimo art and utensils. Open Mon–Fri 9am–noon, 1pm–4pm, Sun 1pm–4pm. Free.
Fort Prince of Wales. After its partial destruction by the French in 1782, never again occupied. Now partially restored. Open daily. Entrance to the fort is free but it's only accessible by boat (weather permitting) and there is a small charge for this.
From 21 June to 21 August Hudson Bay becomes a whale-hunting ground. The unfortunate victims end up at the **Churchill Whale Processing Plant.** Arrange tours with the Dept of Indian Affairs, Churchill.

INFORMATION
Chamber of Commerce, in CN RR Station. Exhibits, films, literature.

TRAVEL
Bus station, 406 Kelsey Blvd, 675-2629.
Jane's Dog Taxi, 675–2375. Travel in style by dog sled.
Nanuk Tours, from Beluga Hotel. Daily tours of Sloop's Cove (where traders with the Eskimos tied their sloops and carved their names on the rocks in the bay), Fort Prince of Wales, the harbour plus whales and bears. June–Sept. About $15.
To get here from Winnipeg see under Winnipeg.

SASKATCHEWAN

Cornflakes country. The black, broad ribbon of the Trans Canada Highway takes the traveller across the province through seemingly endless, flat expanses of wheat fields, where visibility is usually about

20 miles. But this southern part of the province is also a land of rolling ranchlands and rugged badlands, seamed by creeks and river valleys and backed by wooded hills.

Travelling north within Saskatchewan the prairies gradually give way to rolling parklands and green begins to interrupt the yellow landscape. Going still further north you come to the wilderness area of lakes, rivers and evergreen forests still much as they were before the Hudson's Bay Company began fur trading here in the late 1700s. It is only within the last hundred years that settlements and law and order have been established in the region. The province of Saskatchewan was created as recently as 1905.

Wedged between Alberta and Manitoba the province is the prairie keystone and agriculture is the major industry. However, large quantities of oil have recently been found in the south and oil exploration has lead to the discovery of helium and potash, Canada's only commercial source. Summers are hot in Saskatchewan, while winters are long and very cold with lots of snow. .

National Park: Prince Albert.

REGINA. Provincial capital, situated in the heart of the wheatlands, and the accepted stopping place between Winnipeg and Calgary. Regina became capital of the entire Northwest Territories in 1883 just one year after its founding. Situated on the railroad the town served as a government outpost and headquarters for the Northwest Territories Mounted Police until the formation of Saskatchewan as a separate province.

The town was founded and christened Regina after Queen Victoria in 1882 when the first Canadian Pacific Railway train arrived. Its earlier, more picturesque name of Pile O'Bones, referring to the Indian buffalo killing mound at the site, was considered inappropriate for a capital city.

ACCOMMODATION
La Salle Hotel, 1840 Hamilton St, 522-7655. $14 single. 'Quite good place.'
Empire Hotel, 1718 McIntyre St, 522-2544. $10–$20 per rm, open yr round.
Georgia Hotel, 1927 Hamilton St, 352-8678. $16 up.
North Star Motel, Hwy 1 E, 352-0723. $20.
YMCA, 2400 13th Ave, 527-6661. Yr-round, co-ed, $16 per night.
YWCA, 1940 McIntyre St, 525-0151. $16 single.
Youth Hostel, 1711 Hamilton St, 522-4200. $5 members, $6 non-members, cooking facilities, showers, laundry. Central.
University residence—College West Residence, University Dr and McKinley Ave, 584-4777. May–Aug. About $17 single.
Camping: Holiday Wheels Campground, just east of town on Hwy 1, 568-2810. $7 per site.

FOOD
Geno's, Albert and Gordon Sts. Also on Rae St. Inexpensive Italian.
New Venture, Cafe, Hamilton St and S Railway St 'Cheap daily specials.'

OF INTEREST

Wascana Center, mid-city parkland complex which you can tour by double-decker bus. Built around Wascana Lake, the centre includes the legislative buildings, the museum of natural history, the university campus, a water-fowl sanctuary and an arts centre.

The Saskatchewan Museum of Natural History, College and Albert. Eskimo carvings, the bird and animal life of Saskatchewan, local geology. Free. Open 9am–5pm daily. Free.

Grab a view of the prairies from the new **Power Corporation Office** building. The observation platform is on the 13th floor and is open for viewing from Mon–Fri 9am–9pm, Sat and Sun 2pm–9pm. Free.

Norman MacKenzie Art Gallery, on U of Regina campus. European and American art. Mon–Fri noon–5pm, Wed and Thur 7pm–9pm, Sat and Sun 1pm–5pm. Free.

Diefenbaker Homestead, Wascana Centre. Boyhood home of the former prime minister. Daily 10am–8pm. Free.

RCMP Barracks, western edge of town. Western HQ and training school. Museum open daily 8am–9pm. Info: 569-5777.

Buffalo Days are celebrated in Regina during the first week in August. Includes RCMP musical ride, chuckwagon races, logging contest, an agricultural exhibition and fair. $3 entrance. 'Great fun.'

INFORMATION

Tourist and Convention Bureau, 2145 Albert St, 527-6631.
Sask Travel, 3211 Albert St, 565-2300.
Community Switchboard, 523-6443. 24 hrs.

SASKATOON. Saskatoon got going in 1883 as the proposed capital of a temperance colony. An Ontario organisation acquired 100,000 acres and settlement began at nearby Moose Jaw. The society was unable to carry through its plans for the colony, but Saskatoon continued to develop as a trading centre.

The South Saskatchewan River cuts right through the middle of the town and the parklands along its bank make Saskatoon a really pretty place, especially in the summer. Just 145 miles north of Regina, and right in the heart of the parklands, the town is a quiet, easy-going place, nice for a short stay.

ACCOMMODATION

Colonial Motel, 1301 8th St E, 343-1676. $20–$30.
Patricia Hotel, 345 2nd Ave N, 242-8861. $15 single up.
Skybird Motel, 16 33rd St E, 244-4055. $20–$25.
YMCA, Auditorium Ave and 22 Ave, 652-7515.
YWCA, 3rd Ave and 24 St, 244-0944. $15 single, women and children only, pool.
Youth Hostel, 220 24th St E, 244-0944. $5.
Camping: Gordon Howe Campsite, Ave P South, 664-9328. $5.50.

OF INTEREST

The Western Development Museum, 2610 Lorne Ave. Turn of the century 'Pioneer Street'—family life, transportation, industry, agriculture, etc. The museum's collection is 'said to be the best of its kind in North America'. Daily 9am–9pm May–Sept, Mon–Fri 9am–5pm, Sat, Sun noon–5pm rest of year. $1.50, ages 6–15 50¢.

Mendel Art Gallery, 950 Spadina Cr. Soapstone carvings and a Rembrandt. Also displays of Canadiana. Daily 10am–10pm. Free.

Ukrainian Museum, 910 Spadina Crescent E. Folk art, photographs and exhibits depicting the history of Ukrainian immigrants. Tue–Sun noon-4pm. $1.50, over 65 and 6–16 $1.

Pioneer Days. Held early July on Exhibition Grounds south of Lorne Ave. The town's big event of the year.

INFORMATION

Visitors and Convention Bureau, 601 Spadina Cr, 242-1206.

TRAVEL

Bus Terminal is at 50 23rd St E, 664-3133.

Little Northcote River Cruises from bandstand behind Bessborough Hotel on Spadina Cr. Trips along the South Saskatchewan River every hour during summer. From about $5.

PRINCE ALBERT NATIONAL PARK. This 1496-square-mile park typifies the lake and woodland wilderness country lying to the north of the prairies. It's an excellent area for canoeing with many connecting rivers between the lakes.

The park is well provided with resort facilities like bowling greens and tennis courts. To get away from this take the hiking trails out into the woods or visit the pelican rookeries. Accommodation in the park includes campsites, hotels and cabins. **Waskesiu** is the main service centre. Saskatoon is 140 miles south.

THE PACIFIC PROVINCE

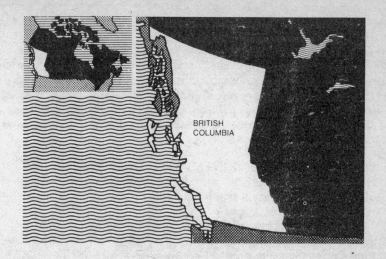

BRITISH
COLUMBIA

BRITISH COLUMBIA

Sandwiched between the Pacific Ocean and the Rocky Mountains to the west and east and bordered to the south by Washington State and to the north by the Yukon Territory, British Columbia is Canada's most westerly province and arguably the most scenic as well. This is an almost storybook land of towering snow-topped mountains, timbered foothills, fertile valleys, great lakes and mightier rivers, plus a spectacular coastline. The coast has long deep fjords dotted with many islands, and rising out of the coastline are ranges of craggy mountain peaks, in some cases exceeding 13,000 feet.

Inland there is a large plateau which provides British Columbia's ranching country. This is bounded on the east by a series of mountain ranges extending to the Rocky Mountain Trench. From this valley flow the Fraser, Columbia and Peace Rivers. The southwestern corner of British Columbia is considered one of the world's best climatic regions having mild winters and sunny, temperate summers and is consequently popular with Canadian immigrants.

This vast and beautiful province, which is about four times the size of the United Kingdom, was however a late developer. As recently as the 1880s there was no real communication and no railroad link with the east. Then as now the Rockies formed a natural barrier between British Columbia and the rest of the Confederation. Although both Sir Francis Drake, while searching for the mythical Northwest Passage, and Captain James Cook came this way, there was no real development and exploration on the Pacific coast until the mid-1800s.

Vancouver Island was not designated a colony until 1849 and the mainland not until 1866. British Columbia became a province in 1871.

The whole province still only has a population of less than two and a half million people, but in recent years they have enjoyed one of the highest standards of living in Canada thanks to the rapid development of British Columbia's abundance of natural resources. About 50 percent of provincial monies comes from timber-related products and industries but BC also has an amazing diversity of minerals on tap as well as oil and natural gas. Fishing and tourism are the other major money-makers.

National Parks: Yoho
                 Glacier
                 Kootenay
                 Mount Revelstoke
                 Pacific Rim

VANCOUVER. This rapidly-growing West Coast city rivals San Francisco for the sheer physical beauty of its setting. Behind the city sit the snow-capped blue Mountains of the Coast Range; lapping its shores are the blue waters of Georgia Strait and English Bay; across the bay is Vancouver Island; and to the south is the estuary carved out by its magnificent Fraser River.

Metropolitan Vancouver now covers most of the peninsula between the Fraser River and Burrard Inlet. Towering bridges link the various suburbs to the city and downtown area which occupies a tiny peninsula jutting into Burrard Inlet with the harbour to the east and English Bay to the west. Once downtown you are within easy reach of fine sandy beaches (or ski slopes in winter) and within the city limits there are several attractive parks. Most notable of these are the Queen Elizabeth Park, from which there is a terrific view of the whole area, and the thickly wooded 1000-acre Stanley Park.

Again like San Francisco, Vancouver is a melting-pot. English, Slavs, mid-Europeans, Italians, Americans, and the second largest Chinatown in North America. The city is Canada's third largest and the industrial and financial centre of British Columbia.

Canada's 'Gateway to the Pacific' has a harbour frontage of 98 miles but the railroads too have an important part to play in Vancouver's communcations system and one of the most spectacular rides is that into Fraser Canyon, once the final heartbreak of the men pushing their way north to the goldfields with only mules and camels to help them. If you're heading back east from here this is the route to take.

Vancouver's climate is mild, but it does rain a fair amount. January is the coldest month although temperatures then are only about

11° centigrade cooler than in July. Snow is rare and roses frequently bloom at Christmas.

ACCOMMODATION

Ambassador Hotel, 773 Seymour St, 684-2536. $16 single, $25 double. 'Central, cheap and comfortable.'

Hazelwood Hotel, 344 E Hastings St, 687-9126. $16 single, $22 double. Weekly rates available. Nr Chinatown.

Kingston Hotel, 757 Richards St, 684-9024. $15 single up, $20 double up, continental breakfast included.

Niagara Hotel, 435 W. Pender, 681-5548. $17 single, no bath, $25 single with bath, $30 double with bath. 'Comfortable and close to stores and bus station.'

Patricia Hotel, 403 E Hastings, 255-4301. $8.50–$20 single, $13–$25 double. 'Close to downtown facs.'

Robsonstrasse City Motor Inn, 1394 Robson St, 687-1674. $25 single, $25 double. 'Spectacular views.'

Sylvia Hotel, 1154 Gilford St, 681-9311. $26 single up, $33 double up. On English Bay at Stanley Park.

YMCA, 955 Burrard St, 681-0221. $14 single, 'but far from downtown'.

YWCA, 680 Burrard St, 683-2531. $22 single. 'Pool, quite nr bus station.'

Youth Hostel, Jericho Beach, 224-3208. $7 members, $9 non-members. Dinner $3.50. 'Friendly and close to beach.' Take 4th Ave bus from Community College at Greyhound.

University residences: Simon Fraser, 291-4203. June–Aug, $8 single, shared kitchen, washroom; campus restaurant nearby.

UBC Conference Centre, Gage Tower Residence, 2075 Westbrook Pl, 228-5441. Student ID necessary. About $12 single. Shared Kitchen, washroom, 15 minutes downtown and close to Wreck Beach.

Camping: Surrey Timberland Campsite, 3418 King George Hwy, 531-1033. About $6.50 per site. Store and laundry.

FOOD

Sportsman Cafe, Dunsmuir St. $5 meals. 'Delicious.'

White Spot Restaurants. Good and cheap.

The Old Spaghetti Factory, Carrall, off Maple Sq. Complete meal around $8. 'Queues, popular with locals.'

The Only Fish and Oyster Bar, 20 E. Hastings. Meals from $4.50. 'Basic but tasty meal: A Gastown institution.'

Granville Market, Granville Island underneath the Granville St Bridge. 9am–6pm except Mon. Good for farm produce, freshly baked goods and recently caught fish.

Vancouver Community and Vocational Centres, Dunsmuir and Hamilton Sts. 'Products of catering school sold to public. Good main course about $3.'

OF INTEREST

The Downtown area

Chinatown, on Pender St, between Gore and Abbott Sts. Gift and curio shops, oriental imports, night clubs and many Chinese restaurants.

Gastown, in the area of Water, Alexander, Columbia and Cordova Sts. The original heart of Vancouver. In 1867 'Gassy Jack' Deighton set up a hotel in the shanty town on the banks of the Burrard Inlet. His establishment became so popular that the whole town was dubbed 'Gastown'. In the past couple of years Gastown has undergone a revival and is now an area of trendy boutiques, good restaurants, antique shops, and pubs. There is also a 'Cost Plus' à la San Francisco.

Robson St, known locally as Robsonstrasse, between Howe St and Broughton St. European import stores and Continental restaurants.

Vancouver Art Gallery, 1145 West Georgia St. Look out for special exhibitions and lunchtime poetry readings, etc. Open Tue–Thur and Sat 10am–5pm, Fri 10am–10pm, Sun 1pm–5pm. Free.

Stanley Park. This, the largest of Vancouver's parks, occupies the peninsula at the harbour mouth and has swimming pools, golf courses, a cricket pitch, tennis courts, several beaches, a free zoo, an aquarium, an English rose garden, and many forest trails and walks. A nice way to see the park is by bicycle. You can hire a bike just outside the park entrance. Rates are around $5 ph. If you're walking, a recommended route is the **Sea Wall Walk** past Nine O'Clock Gun, Brockton Point, Lumberman's Arch and Prospect Point. Near the eastern rim of the park is a large and very fine collection of totem poles. Admission to the park itself is free but you will have to pay for the aquarium.

Vancouver Public Aquarium, Stanley Park. Open daily 9.30am–9pm until Labor Day. Entrance $4, students and seniors citizens $1.50, family rate $8. Dolphins and killer whales.

Vancouver West
Centennial Museum, 1100 Chestnut St. Traces the development of the Northwest Coast from the Ice Age through pioneer days to the present. Entrance $1.50. Mon 10am–5pm, Tue–Sun 10am–9pm.

Macmillan Planetarium, 1100 Chestnut St 'Essential to arrive early and book. Very popular.' Closed Mon. Tue–Sat, shows 1pm, 2.30pm, 4pm, 7.30pm and 9pm; Sun 1pm, 2.30pm, 4pm, 7.30pm. Cost: $2.50. Info: 736-3656.

Maritime Museum, foot of Cypress St. Exhibits include the RCMP ship *St Roch*, the first ship to navigate the Northwest Passage in both directions and to circumnavigate the continent of North America. Open daily. 10am–5.30pm. $1.75.

Old Hastings Mill Store, 1575 Alma Rd. One of the few buildings remaining after the Great Fire of 13 June 1886, this is now a museum with Indian artefacts, mementoes of pioneer days and pictures of the city's development. Open daily 10am–4pm.

University of British Columbia, at Point Grey. Has a population of some 23,000 students. There is a good swimming pool, cafeteria and bookshop. Also an **Anthropological Museum**, the **Nitobe Japanese Garden** and **Totem Park** which has carvings and buildings representing a small segment of a Haida Indian village. To get to the campus take a No 10 bus from Granville and Georgia. Coming back you want a No 14.

Queen Elizabeth Gardens, Little Mountain. When you enter the park keep left for the side with the views overlooking the North Shore mountains and harbour. There is a good view from the Lookout above the sunken gardens. Also, **Bloedel Conservatory** on top of the mountain has a fine collection of tropical plants. Entrance $1. To get to Little Mountain, from Georgia and Granville Sts take a No 15 Cambie bus and get off at 33rd and Cambie St. The return bus is No 6 Fraser bus.

Vancouver East, Burnaby
Exhibition Park, bounded by Renfrew, Hastings and Cassiar Sts, this is the home of the Pacific National Exhibition. Stadia and a Sports Hall of Fame. The PNE takes place at the end of August. $4.50 for a day's admission. 'Fantastic. Includes lumberjack competition, rodeo, demolition derby, exhibitions, fair, etc.'

Simon Fraser University, atop Burnaby Mountain. Constructed in only 18 months, the giant module design of this ultra-modern seat of learning makes it possible to move around the university totally under cover. The views from up here are superb. To reach the campus catch a Westbridge bus to SF. The last bus back to downtown Vancouver leaves about 7.30pm but hitching is said to be easy, and special hitching stations have been installed outside the university.

Vancouver North
Capilano Suspension Bridge. Going north, the bridge is on the lefthand side of Capilano Rd. The swinging 137-metre long bridge spans a spectacular

70-metre-deep gorge. Entrance to the rather commercialised park costs $2.75, $2 students. 'Not worth it unless you have time to walk one of the trails.'

Grouse Mountain. The skyride is located at the top of Capilano Rd and you can ride it to the top of the mountain for incredible views, a cup of coffee or a quick hike. Make sure the weather is clear before you go. 'Spectacular. Not to be missed. Best thing I did in North America.' The gondola costs $6 and operates Mon–Fri 3pm–11pm, weekends noon–midnight. Info: 984-0661.

Lynn Canyon Park. Less exploited than Capilano and free. The bridge swings high above Lynn Canyon Creek. Swimming in the creek is nice to and there is an 'excellent' ecology centre (75¢) by the park entrance. To get there: catch the Seabus at bottom of Granville. At Grouse Mountain take a 228 bus to Peters St and then walk. By car, take the Upper Levels Highway to Lynn Valley Rd and follow the signs. 'Peaceful and uncrowded.'

Beaches. Near UBC there is Wreck Beach, free and nude; other recommended spots are English Bay, Tower Beach (also nude), Spanish Banks (watch the tides), Locarno and Kitsilano.

INFORMATION
Tourist Bureaux: 800 Robson St, 668-2300; 650 Burrard St, 682-2222.
BC Tourist Info: 701 W Georgia, Pacific Centre, 682-2222. Free maps and info and

you can buy a book of tickets which give slightly cheaper admission to various places around the city.

ENTERTAINMENT

Read *Georgia Straight* for what goes on generally.

Hollywood Theatre, West Broadway. One of the cheaper movie houses.

For UBC's flic schedule call 228-3778. Some cinemas offer student reductions.

Vancouver loves festivals. Look out for the Rain Festival held in Gastown in April; the King Neptune Carnival in June; Vancouver Sea Festival in July; the Oktoberfest in Oct; and biggest and best, the Pacific National Exhibition held in late Aug through early Sept.

TRAVEL

Hitching is legal and usual, even for girls, in the Greater Vancouver area. Exact fare buses (currently 75¢, 40¢ for students) operate in the city. On Sundays and holidays it is possible to purchase a $1.50 pass enabling you to ride anywhere, anytime, that day.

Bus terminal: 150 Dunsmuir St, 683-2421. Closes 3am.

Train termini located at 1150 Station St, at 200 Granville St, and 1311 West 1st in North Vancouver. ViaRail info: 682-5552, 987-6216.

Gray Line Tours leave Hotel Vancouver, 872-8311 and cost from $15 for circle tour of the city in a double-decker red London bus.

Take the ultra-modern Seabus from the bottom of Granville to Grouse Mountain for stunning views enroute. 75¢ each way. Info: 324-3211.

Vancouver International Airport is reached via Hwy 99, Grant McConachie Way. Airport buses leave every 15 min from major downtown hotels. Or from opp Greyhound. One-way fare is $5. To get there by city bus take the No 60 Richmond bus, change at the second loop to a No 71.

'Downtown to Downtown' Vancouver to Victoria bus service (via ferry). Cost: about $15 rt. However, it is much cheaper to go by public transport all the way using the ferry services.

Ferries. British Columbia Ferries link the mainland with Vancouver Island: Nanaimo and Sunshine Coast ferries dep from Horseshoe Bay, 13 miles west. For schedule information call: British Columbia Ferries Infor. 669-1211, or the Visitors Bureau, 682-2222. For ferries to Swartz Bay and Gulf Island, departure is from Tsawassen, 15 miles out. Cheaper on Tue, Wed, and Thur. Buses for the ferry termini go from Georgia St. To go all the way using public transport: Take the 401 bus and request a transfer from the driver. At Ladner Exchange change to the 640 bus and this will take you to the Tsawassen Ferry Terminal. The ferry to Swartz Bay takes about 40 minutes and costs $3. Once there take the bus down Port Bay Hwy to Victoria, about $1.50. All very scenic and the cheapest way.

Harbour tours: Operated by Harbour Ferries Ltd on the stern-wheelers *Yukon Belle* and *Yukon Queen*. Fare: about $7. Info: 687-9558.

Train tour: the steam engine *Royal Hudson* makes a 6-hr round trip tour between North Vancouver and Squamish along the cliffs of Howe Sound and including stops at the Britannia Mines and Mining Museum. Fares are from $8. For departure times, etc: 987-5211.

Car Rental: Avis 757 Hornby St, 682-1621; Budget, 430 W Georgia, 685-0536; Thrifty, 1133 W Hastings, 669-5441.

Auto Driveaway: Drive Away, 2390 Kingsway, 434-9943.

VANCOUVER ISLAND. The island, and the Gulf Islands which shelter on its leeward side, are invaded annually by thousands of tourists attracted by the temperate climate and the seaside and mountain

resorts. Vancouver Island is a 'fisherman's paradise', with mining, fishing, logging and manufacturing the chief breadwinners. There are good ferry and air connections with the mainland. (See under Vancouver and Victoria.)

Victoria, the provincial capital, is situated on the southern tip of the Island. **Nootka**, on the western coast, was the spot where Captain Cook landed in 1778, claiming the area for Britain. In the ensuing years, despite strong Spanish pressure, Nootka became a base for numerous exploratory voyages into the Pacific. The Spaniards were finally dispersed as a result of the Nootka Convention of 1790 but a strong sprinkling of Spanish names on the lower coast bear witness to the past.

Long Beach, 12 miles of white sand west of **Port Alberni** on the Pacific Coast, is recommended for a bit of peace. To get there take Route 4 from Port Alberni across the mountains towards **Tofino**, the western terminus of the Trans Canada Highway. The beach is part of the new, and as yet not fully developed, national park, **Pacific Rim**. Also in the park is the Broken Island Group in Barkley Sound and the 45-mile-long Lifesaving Trail between Bamfield and Port Renfrew. There are campsites in the Long Beach area and on the Ucluelet access road.

The Pacific Ocean is too cold for swimming here, though it's great for surfing or beachcombing. But at **Hot Springs Cove** there are reputed to be the best hot springs in Canada. The least known too for you can only reach the springs by boat from Tofino and then walk a one-mile trail. The springs bubble up at more than 85° centigrade and flow down a gully into the ocean. The highest pool is so hot that you can only bathe in winter when cooler run-off waters mix with the springs. Sneakers (as protection against possible jagged rocks underfoot) are the only dress worn while bathing.

Back over on the southeastern side of the Island there is a superb drive from Victoria north to **Duncan**, and at Duncan itself the Forest Museum offers a long steam train ride and a large open forestry museum. Going further north you come to **Nanaimo**, the fastest growing town on the Island. Lumbering and fish-canning are the main occupations in town and it's worth taking a look at Petroglyph Park with its preserved Indian sandstone carvings of thousands of years ago. Nanaimo is also the starting point for the annual Vancouver Bathtub Race across the Georgia Strait in mid-July.

VICTORIA. Former Hudson's Bay Company trading post and fort and now provincial capital, Victoria is noted for its mild climate and beautiful gardens. This small, unassuming little town is located at the southern tip of Vancouver Island on the Juan de Fuca Strait. As a result of its attractive climate it's a popular retirement spot as well as being popular with British immigrants. Victoria has the largest number of British-born residents anywhere in Canada, and likes to preserve its touch of Olde Englande for the benefit of the year-round tourist industry.

Afternoon tea, fish n' chips, British souvenir shops, tweed and china and double-decker buses all have their place, but if you can get beyond all that, you will find Victoria a pleasant place to be for a time with plenty to explore around the town and out on the rest of the Island. There are ferry connections from here to Vancouver and Prince Rupert as well as to Anacortes and Port Angeles, Washington.

ACCOMMODATION
Victoria Visitor's Bureau, 812 Wharf St, 382-2127, can help find accommodation for you.
Cherry Bank Hotel, 825 Burdett Ave, 385-5380. $18 single, $25 double. 'Comfortable, central, recommended by locals.'
Craigmyle Guest Home, 1037 Craigdarrock Rd, 595-5411. $20 up.
James Bay Inn, 270 Government St, 384-7151. $20 single up, $25 double up. Nr Parliament buildings. 'Friendly.'
Bastion Inn, 1140 Government St, 388-9166. $26 single, $32 double. Coffee shop, downtown location.
Oak Bay Guest House, 1052 Newport Ave, 598-3812. $23 single incl breakfast. Communal kitchen, washroom.
Yates Hotel, 712 Yates St, 384-7187. $15 single, $20 double, restaurant, student discount. $22 double, no bath. 'Efficient and clean.''
YWCA, 880 Courtney St, 386-7511. $16 single. 'New building with coffee shop.'
Univ of Victoria Residence, Lansdown Building, 477-6981. May–Aug, students and non-students.

FOOD
Butchart Gardens, 800 Benvenuto Ave. For afternoon tea English-style, in winter served in front of open fire. Tea, scones, crumpets, etc.
The Empress Hotel, 721 Government St. Also serves afternoon tea in the lobby. Includes scones with Devonshire cream—of course. Not cheap but très elegant!
Old Victoria Fish and Chips, 1316 Broad St. $5. Also oysters.
Scots, 680 Yates St. Open 24 hr. Meals from $4.50.
Palliacci's, Broad St. Dinner about $8. 'Great food, relaxed atmosphere and live jazz nightly.'

OF INTEREST
Parliament Buildings, Government and Belleville Sts. The seat of British Columbia's government is a palatial, many-turreted Victorian building with a gilded seven-foot figure of Captain George Vancouver, the first British navigator to circle Vancouver Island, on top. Conducted tours available daily throughout summer months.
Provincial Museum of Natural History and Anthropology, next door at 601 Belleville St. British Columbia flora and fauna, Indian arts and crafts and a reconstructed 1920s BC town. July–Sept daily 10am–9pm; rest of year 10am–5.30pm. Free.
Bastion Square overlooking the harbour. There is a **Maritime Museum** in the square (open 10am–6pm. $2, students 50¢) and a number of other renovated 19th-century buildings housing curio shops and boutiques. 'Nice place for just sitting, sometimes there is free entertainment around noon.'
Thunderbird Park, Douglas and Belleville. The park contains 'the world's largest

collection of totem poles', a Kwakiutl Tribal Long House, its entrance shaped like a mask, and a flotilla of canoes fashioned from single logs of red cedar.

Butchart Gardens, 14 miles north of the city off Hwy 17. An English Rose Garden, a Japanese Garden and a formal Italian garden, are the chief features of Victoria's most spectacular park. Floodlit in the evening in summer. 9am–11pm July and Aug; 9am–9pm May, June, Sept; otherwise 9am–4pm. $6, 13–17 $3.50, 5–12 $1. For info: 652-4422. 'Definitely worthwhile.'

The Undersea Gardens, Inner Harbour. You can look through glass at a large collection of sea plants, octopi, crabs, and other sea life. Also scuba diving shows with Armstrong the giant octopus. Daily 9am–9pm May–Sept; rest of year 10am–5pm. $3.75, 12–17 and over 65 $2.50.

Sealand, 1327 Beach Dr, three miles out. Performing killer whales, and sea lions. Daily 10am–9pm June 21–Sept 9; rest of year 10am–5pm. $4.50, 12–17 and senior citizens $3. Take a No 2 bus to Oak Bay, 593-3373.

Anne Hathaway's Thatched Cottage, 429 Lampson St. 'Authentic' replicas of things English, plus 16th and 17th century armour and furniture. Tours daily 9am–9pm, 388–4353. $3.50, ages 6–16 and over 65 $2.

Craigflower Manor, 4 miles northwest on Hwy 1A. Built 1856 of native materials in simple colonial style. Tue–Sun 10am–5pm. Free.

Market Square, off Douglas St. Attractive pedestrian mall with shops, fine restaurants and bars.

Christ Church Cathedral, Quadra and Rockland Sts. One of Canada's largest cathedrals, built in Gothic style. Started 1920s but not yet complete. The bells are replicas of those at Westminster Abbey in London, England.

Art Gallery of Greater Victoria, 1040 Moss St. Includes contemporary and oriental sections. Mon–Sat 10am–5pm, Thur until 9pm, Sun 1pm–5pm. $1, free to senior citizens and kids.

Craigdarroch Castle, 1050 Joan Crescent St. Sandstone castle built in late 1880s by Scottish immigrant Robert Dunsmuir as a gift for his wife, Joan. Now a museum with stained glass windows, gothic furnishings, original mosaics and paintings. 9am–9.30pm. Donations.

INFORMATION
Greater Victoria Visitor Information Centre, 117 Wharf St, 382-2127.

TRAVEL
Harbour Cruises, from Government St opp Empress Hotel. Narrated waterfront trips. Daily. Info: 592-9667. $6, children $3.

Ferries to Vancouver leave from Swartz Bay, 20 miles out of town.

There is a centre-to-centre bus and ferry service which leaves hourly from the bus depot. Current fare is about $15 rt. For details to Vancouver see under Vancouver.

There is also a ferry service to Port Angeles, and Seattle, Washington, and from nearby Sidney to Anacortes, Washington. To Port Angeles the foot passenger rate is US$5, for a car it's US$19. The trip takes 1½ hrs and the service is yr-round with reduced sailings after Labour Day. To Seattle, the on-foot rate is $17, or $29 round trip, and $25 for a car. The crossing time is 4 hrs 15 minutes, 386-6731. To Anacortes it's US$4.95, US$21.20 for a car. Crossing time is 3½ hrs. Operates year round with reduced services in winter. Info: 656-1531.

'The ferries are very comfortable and the views fantastic. An excellent way of getting back to the USA.'

From Victoria there is also a ferry service around the Gulf Islands and a free service operates among the islands themselves. It's $1.75 from Victoria to Saltspring Island. Info: 382-6161.

KELOWNA. Going east out of Vancouver, Route 3 takes you over the Cascade Mountains and down into the Okanagan Valley, a very pretty place and an important fruit-growing and agricultural region. One-third of apples harvested in Canada come from this area. Good therefore for summer jobs, if you're looking for such work, or, if you're taking it slow, for a nice holiday, just lying by the lake in the sun. The Kelowna Regatta is held during the second weekend in August, with accompanying traditional festivities.

Beware of the local lake monster. It goes by the name of Ogopogo, and is like the Loch Ness Monster but with a head like a sheep, goat or horse.

Not to be missed are the two local wineries. Mission Wines, Westbank, and Calona Wines, in Kelowna, both offer free tours, with sampling daily: 10am–4pm. While the Kelowna Centennial Museum on Queensway Avenue has nice displays of Indian arts and crafts.

ACCOMMODATION
Slumber Lodge, 2486 Hwy 97, 860-5703. $28 single up, $32 double up. Pool.
Western Budget Motel, 2679 Hwy 97, 860-4990. $20 single, $25 double.
Willow Inn, 235 Queensway, 762-2122. $32 single, $40 double. Downtown, close to lake and park.
Hiawatha Park Campground, 3787 Lakeshore Rd, 762-3412. $10.50 for 2, additional person $2. Laundry, store.

INFORMATION
BC Tourist Information, west end of Floating Bridge, 769-4140.

KAMLOOPS. The Trans Canada Higway takes the Fraser Canyon/ Kamloops/Revelstoke route through the province. The Highway, incidentally, at 5000 miles long, is the longest paved highway in the world, and Kamloops, situated at the point where Route 5 crosses it, is a doubly important communications centre for the railroad also chooses this way through the mountains.

Kamloops is useful perhaps as a halfway stopover point between Vancouver and Banff or else a possible jumping-off point for visits to the Revelstoke, Yoho, Glacier, and Kootenay National Parks. The **Kamloops Museum** on Seymour Street deals with the region's agricultural and Indian history. Kamloops is a popular place for skiers and trout fisherman.

ACCOMMODATION
Plaza Motor Hotel, 405 Victoria St, 372-7121. $22 single up, $28 double up. Downtown location.
Thrift Inn, 2459 Trans Canada Hwy, East Kamloops, 374-2488. $27 single, $28 double, pool.
Camping: Kamloops View Campground, East Trans Canada Hwy, 573-3255. Heated pool, laundry. $8 for 2.
Orchard Ridge Trailer Park, 7155 East Trans Canada Hwy, 573-3443. $8 for 2, laundry. Overlooks Thompson River.

INFORMATION
Tourist Bureau, 166 Lorne St, 372-7722.

MOUNT REVELSTOKE NATIONAL PARK.
The park, midway between Kamloops and Banff, Alberta, is situated in the Selkirk Range. The Selkirks are more jagged and spikey than the Rockies and are especially famous for the excellent skiing facilities available on their slopes. Revelstoke is known as the pioneer ski-jumping centre in Canada.

You can get a ski-lift to the lower slopes of the mountains but the only way to the very top is on your own two legs. On the summit of Mount Revelstoke there is a nine-mile trail winding through forests and meadows with fantastic views of distant peaks, glaciers and mountain lakes.

For the car-bound, the Trans Canada runs along the southern edge of the park following the scenic **Illecillewaet River** and you can see it all without every getting out of the car.

Park services are provided in the town of Revelstoke, a quiet, pretty place set amidst the mountains.

ACCOMMODATION
In Revelstoke:
King Edward Hotel, 837-2104. $16 single, $20 double. 'Good value.' Downtown.
Mountain View Motel, 1017 First St W, 837-2057. $20 single, $24 double. Central.
Regent Motor Inn, 112 E First St, 837-2107. $18 single up, $23 double up. Downtown, recently renovated.
Camping: Canada West Campground, 2½ miles west of Revelstoke, 837-4420. $6 for 3, laundry, showers.

OF INTEREST
Canyon Hot Springs, about 15 miles east of town. 39°C mineral waters, or a swim in a pool of 30°C. Mon–Fri 8.45am–10pm, June–Aug; 9am–7pm rest of year. $3.50 per day, students and over 65 $1.75.
Three Valley Gap Ghost Town, about 10 miles west on Trans Canada Hwy 1. Nr site of original mining town of Three Valley with historical buildings moved here from various places in BC. Open daily 8am–dusk in summer. $1.50, ages 14–17 $1.

INFORMATION
Junction Hwy. 1 and Big Bend Hwy, 837-3522.

GLACIER NATIONAL PARK.
From Revelstoke carry on eastwards along the Trans Canada and you very quickly come to this park. As its name tells you, Glacier is an area of icefields and glaciers with deep, awesome canyons and caverns, alpine meadows and silent forests. There are many trails within the park and, like Revelstoke, this too is skiers' paradise. The Alpine Club of Canada holds summer and winter camps here.

The annual total snowfall in the park averages 350 inches and sometimes exceeds 500 inches. With the deep snow and the steep terrain, special protection is necessary for the railway and highway running through Glacier. Concrete snowsheds and manmade hillocks at the bottom of avalanche chutes slow the cascading snow, while artillery fire is used to bring down the snow before it accumulates to the critical depths. Travellers through the Rogers Pass in winter may feel more secure in the knowledge that they are passing through one of the longest controlled avalanche areas in the world.

Admission to the park is $1 daily and climbers and overnight walkers must register with the wardens at Rogers Pass. Park services and accommodation are in Revelstock to the west of Glacier and **Golden** to the east.

ACCOMMODATION
See also under Revelstoke:
Brookside Motel, west of Golden, 1 block off hwy, 344-2359. $16 single, $28 triple.
Glacier Park Lodge, Rogers Pass, 837-2126. Not budget but right in the park. $45 up.
Golden Lodge Hotel, central Golden, 344-5231. $12 single, $15 double.
Camping: Blaeberry Campground, 9 miles west of Golden nr Hwy 1. Showers, laundry. $6 per camp site.
Golden Municipal Park, in Golden on Kicking Horse River, 344-5412. Showers. $6 per site.
There are National Park sites at Illecillewaet River, Loop Creek and Mountain Creek.

YOHO NATIONAL PARK. Still going east, Yoho National Park is on the British Columbia side of the Rockies adjoining Banff National Park on the Alberta side. It gets its name from the Indian meaning 'how wonderful'.

Yoho is a mountaineer's park with some 250 miles of trails leading the walker across the roof of the Rockies. Worth looking at are the beautiful alpine **Emerald** and **O'Hara Lakes**, the curtain of mist at **Laughing Falls**, the strangely shaped pillars of **Hoodoo Valley**, and **Takakkaw Falls**, at 1248 feet the second highest in North America. The spectacular, rushing **Kicking Horse River** flows across the park from east to west.

ACCOMMODATION
There are four campgrounds and various cabins within Yoho. The campgrounds are at Chancellor Peak, Hoodoo Creek, Kicking Horse, Takakkaw Falls and Lake O'Hara. Sites must be reserved directly with the park. Alternatively Yoho is easily visited from either Lake Louise or Banff. Tours of the park are available from both places.

KOOTENAY NATIONAL PARK. Lying along the Vermilion-Sinclair section of the Banff-Windermere Parkway (Highway 93), going south from Golden, Kootenay is rich in canyons, glaciers and ice fields as well as wild life. Bears, moose, elk, deer and Rocky Mountain goats all live here. The striking **Marble Canyon**, just off the highway, is formed of grey limestone and quartzite laced with white and grey dolomite and is one of several canyons in Kootenay.

The western entrance to the park is near the famous **Radium Hot**

Springs. There are two pools with water temperatures at almost 60°C. Springs are open daily in summer and entrance is $1.25. Admission to the park is $1 daily; visitors must obtain a park motor vehicle license at the entrance before driving through. There are campgrounds within the park and motel accommodation is available in the town of Radium Hot Springs.

PRINCE GEORGE. If heading north either from Vancouver or from the Banff area it is likely that Prince George will be your first stopping place. Known as the 'Gateway to the North', this otherwise fairly uninteresting town has become the takeoff point for development schemes in the wilderness Northwest.

The recently opened Yellowhead Highway, Route 16, from Jasper is one of the main routes to Alaska. (The bus pass is not valid for the journey.) If travelling north from Kamloops, Route 5 picks up at the 16 at Tete Jaune Cache. From Prince George you have a choice of Route 6 winding over the Hazleton Mountains to Prince Rupert on the coast, or Route 97 to Dawson Creek and the Alaska Highway. But first a trip south to Barkerville.

> **ACCOMMODATION**
> Nechako Inn, 1915 3rd Ave, 563-7106. $24 single up, $30 double. Waterbeds available.
> Prince George Hotel, 487 George St, 566-7211. $32 single, $36 double. English pub.
> Muncipal Campground, 18th Ave. $6 site, hot showers.
>
> **INFORMATION**
> 1198 Victoria St, 562-2454.

BARKERVILLE. The boom town story that triggered off the settlement of British Columbia got started on 21 August 1862 when a broke and bearded Cornishman, one Billy Barker, a naval deserter, at that point on the verge of quitting altogether, struck the pay dirt which within a short time earned him $600,000. All from a strip of land only 600 feet long. As a result of his find Barkerville became the largest boom town north of San Francisco and west of Chicago.

The shaft that started it all is now a part of the restored gold rush town (the original settlement died before the turn of the century) at **Barkerville Historic Park** located 55 miles east of Quesnel and 130 miles south of Prince George. To get there a car is necessary.

In Barkerville you can do some panning in a nearby creek, take a stagecoach ride through the town and call in at the Gold Commissioner's office. Or visit Trapper Dan's cabin in Chinatown, the General Store piled high with miner's boots, Kelly's Bar and the barber's shop. In the evenings there are shows 'of the kind miners once enjoyed' at the Theatre Royal. A fine museum in the park tells the whole saga of Barkerville with photographs, exhibits and artefacts.

There is a camping ground near the park or alternatively there is fairly inexpensive motel accommodation in nearby **Wells**. Park admission is $4, or $2 for under 12s and over 65s. The park is open year-round with reduced opening hours and no guided tours after Labour Day.

DAWSON CREEK. A small, but rapidly growing town northeast of Prince George on Highway 97 which marks the start of the Alaska Highway (see also under Alaska). The Zero Milepost for the Highway is the centre of town.

Dawson Creek was founded as recently as 1936 when the railroad was built to ship wheat from the area. A much older settlement, **Fort St John**, about 50 miles north, was established in 1793 as a fur trading outpost and mission. Today the community thrives on the expanding gas and oil industries in the area.

ACCOMMODATION
Big Bobs Motel, Mile 1 Hart Hwy, 782-4611. $23 single, $25 double, courtesy coffee, laundry facilities.
Windsor Hotel, 1100-102nd Ave, 782-3301. $20 single up, $26 double up. Coffee shop.
Camping: Municipal Campground, 1 mile west of jnct Alaska Hwy next to golf course. $5 per site.
Tubby's Tent and Trailer Park, 20th St at Hwy 97 S, 782-2584. $5 per tent site.

OF INTEREST
South Peace Pioneer Village, 1 mile southeast on Hwy 2. Turn of the century village incl log schoolhouse, trapper's cabin, blacksmith's stop, etc. Daily 9am–5pm June–Sept. $1.
Historical Society Museum, 1634 94th Ave. Local wildlife and history.

INFORMATION
Tourist Info, 10100 13th St, 782-4868.
Tourism BC, on Alaska Hwy, west of junct Hwy 97.

FORT ST JAMES NATIONAL HISTORIC PARK. Back on Highway 16 (the Yellowhead Highway) and heading from St George to St Rupert, it's perhaps worth a small detour on to Highway 27 at Stuart Lake to visit this former Hudson's Bay Company trading post. The 19th century post features restored and reconstructed homes, warehouses and stores. The park is open daily May to October and entrance is free. It must have been an isolated, strange existence for the Hudson's Bay men here in the middle of nowhere 100 years ago.

PRINCE RUPERT. Known as the 'Halibut Capital of the World', Prince Rupert is the fishing centre of the Pacific Northwest. The season's peak is reached in early August and this is the time to visit the canneries.

This area was a stronghold of the Haida and Tsimpsian Indians and the **Museum of North British Columbia**, on First Avenue, contains a rare collection of Indian treasures. In front of the building stand three superb totem poles. The most famous of these, the Wolf Totem, portrays major historical events of local tribal life. Inside, there are more totems, masks, carvings and beadwork.

Prince Rupert is marvellously situated among the fjords of Hecate Strait and at the mouth of the beautiful Skeena River. There is also a reversing tidal stream fit to rival the falls at Saint John, New Brunswick. You get a good view of the Butz Rapids from Highway 16, enroute from Prince George. The town is also a major communications centre being the southernmost port of the Alaska Ferry System, the northern terminus of the British Columbia Ferry Authority and the western terminus of Canadian National Railways.

ACCOMMODATION

Accommodation hereabouts tends to be expensive. The Visitor's Information Bureau may be able to help find something cheaper than the hotels listed below.

Aleeda Motel, 900 3rd Ave, 627-1367. $32 single up, $40 double up, courtesy coffee.

Parkside Resort Hotel, 11th Ave, and McBride St, 624-9131. $30 single up, $35 double up. Close to centre.

OF INTEREST

Museum of Northern British Columbia, 1st Ave and McBride St. Daily 9am–9pm May–Sept, 10am–5pm Mon–Sat rest of year. Free.

Northcoast Marine Museum, 309 2nd Ave W. Fishing equipment past and present plus an aquarium. Mon–Sat 9am–5pm. Free.

Gondola Lift, Mount Hays Ski Area, on Wantage Rd. Operates in summer for sightseeing purposes. Relax and admire the views in the Eagle's Nest Lounge at almost 2000 ft. $3.

Salt Lake Ferry, from foot of McBride St. Trips across the harbour for picnicking, etc. $2.

Queen Charlotte Islands, west of Prince George. Miles of sandy beaches. A place for taking it easy and doing some boating. Accessible from Prince Rupert by plane or boat.

Hazelton. A village northwest of Prince Rupert off Highway 16, Hazelton is worth a stop for the interesting **Ksan Indian Village and Museum**. This is an authentic village and consists of a carving house and four communal houses. The houses are decorated with carvings and painted scenes in classic West Coast Indian style. Tours daily 10am–6pm, May–15 October. Admission $3, over 65, $2, students $1.50.

INFORMATION

Visitors Information Bureau, 1st Ave and McBridge, 624-5367.

TRAVEL

The nicest way to approach Prince Rupert is undoubtedly by sea. A ferry calls here from Kelsey Bay, on Vancouver Island, making the trip on odd days of the month. One-way it takes about 20 hrs. The scenery is magnficent and if you can afford it, it's a great trip, well worth taking. Ferries also leave here for Haines, Alaska. If you want a shorter trip, take the one to Ketchikan, passing through glaciers and fjords enroute, 'Very beautiful.'

THE TERRITORIES

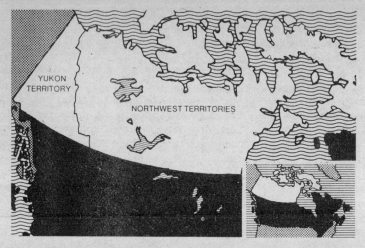

Both the Northwest Territories and the Yukon were originally fur-trading areas of the Hudson's Bay Company, only becoming part of Canada in 1870.

NORTHWEST TERRITORIES

Canada's Arctic is larger than half of the continental USA. It's a vast, mostly unexplored, lonesome area, with a population of only 34,000, scattered over 1,300,000 square miles. The territories are not however entirely lands of perpetual ice and snow. Although half the mainland and all the islands lie within the Arctic zone, the land varies from flat, forested valleys, to never-melting ice peaks; from blossom-packed meadows to steep, bleak cliffs and from warm, sandy shores to frigid, glacial banks.

European explorers looking for a water route to the Orient came here as early as the 16th century. Sir Martin Frobisher sailed here in 1576 and founded the first settlement on what we now call Frobisher Bay in 1578. Henry Hudson and Alexander Mackenzie both explored the area in search of greater trading outlets and profits.

With the more recent discoveries of rich mineral deposits and the promised exploitation of the oil and gas fields, life in the Territories is beginning to change, many believe, for the worse. Fur trapping is still the principal occupation of the native Indians while the Eskimos rely on the white fox and seal for their chief source of income. In many areas the native peoples are fighting hard against encroaching modernisation but continued development of the area's natural resources could threaten their traditional ways of survival.

It's a long long way North but once you've decided to go there are various alternatives. There are regular scheduled air services from Edmonton, Winnipeg and Montréal into the Territories. Once within the Territories flights are available to the remoter parts of the Arctic. By road, the Mackenzie Highway starts 250 miles inside the Alberta boundary travelling up to Hay river on the Great Slave Lake before striking west to Fort Simpson. from Hay River it's a further 600 miles to the capital, Yellowknife, on the north shore of the lake. There are three buses a week as far as Yellowknife from Edmonton, Alberta. When travelling in the Territories always carry ample supplies of food and fuel since it can be hundreds of miles between towns with few, if any, services enroute.

The **Mackenzie** is one of the world's greatest rivers, twisting and turning for 1200 miles from the Great Slave Lake to the Arctic Ocean, and offering access to more hundreds of navigable miles on the Slave River, the Nahami, Liard, the Peel and Arctic Red Rivers, and on Great Bear Lake. During the ice-free months (end of May to October) tugs and barges ply up and down the river. The hardiest canoeists and trailer-boaters can join them for one of the loneliest, loveliest trips in the world.

The **Great Slave Lake** is the jumping-off point for the vast developments underway to the north. **Hay River** is a vital freight transportation centre being the transshipment point between rail and river barges.

Yellowknife, the Territorial capital, and less than 300 miles from the Arctic Circle on Great Slave Lake, has two gold mines and even boasts street lighting and one high-rise building. Accommodation and food are expensive but new suburbs are springing up and business is booming. In July you can take part in a 24-hour golfing marathon made possible since the sun doesn't set here for the whole of the summer. It is also possible to visit the underground gold mines. Tourist information is available from the Chamber of Commerce, 48th Street and 50th Avenue, and from Yellowknife Tourist Information, 52nd Street and 49th Avenue. One other place to visit is the **Prince of Wales Northern Heritage Centre** which has exhibits and crafts on the history and cultural developments in the Northwest Territories.

Fort Smith, just across from the Albertan frontier, and once the Territorial capital, is a sprawling mixture of shacks, log cabins and more modern government-built establishments. The Hudson Bay Company established a trading post here in 1874, the town later becoming a stopping place for goldseekers on their way to the Yukon.

Trips to **Wood Buffalo National Park** depart from the Fort Smith Information Bureau, 56 Portage Avenue. Wood Buffalo straddles the Alberta/Northwest Territories line and was established to protect the only remaining herd of wood bison. In the park there are also plains bison, moose, caribou, black bear and a great variety of birds and fish. There are several trails within the park and rangers sponsor guided nature hikes in summer. Camping is permissable.

Two other national parks are under development in the Territories, although neither is accessible by road. **Auyuittuq National Park** is near the Inuit settlement of Pangnirtung on Baffin Island and is notable for its fjords, glacial valleys and mountains. The second new park, **Nahanni**, is northwest of Fort Simpson and is a wilderness area of hot springs, waterfalls, canyons and river rapids.

The third largest city in the Northwest Territories is **Inuvik**, way up in the northernmost corner. A boom town, ever alert for news of oil strikes, it is an interesting mixture of old timers, traders, delta Eskimos, Indians, oilmen and entrepreneurs. There are three hotels, all expensive.

The town of **Frobisher Bay**, way up north on Baffin Island, is the administrative, education and economic centre of the eastern Arctic region of Canada. Frobisher Bay has also, since 1954 and the establishment of the Distant Early Warning Line, become an important defence and strategic site and a refuelling stop for military and commercial planes.

National Parks: Auyuittuq
Nahanni
Wood Buffalo

THE YUKON TERRITORY

Fur-trading brought the Hudson's Bay Company into the Yukon in the mid-1800s but it was the Klondike Gold Rush of 1898 that really put the area on the map. Thousands of gold-seekers climbed the forbidding Chilkoot and White Passes and pressed on down the Yukon River to Dawson City. In two years **Dawson City**, at the junction of the Klondike and Yukon Rivers, grew from a tiny hamlet to a settlement of nearly 30,000.

There's not much gold around anymore, however. Instead there's silver, copper, zinc, open-pit mining and a big hunt for oil. In fact following the Gold Rush the Yukon practically settled back into its pre-gold hunting and trapping days, once again a remote spot on a map in northwestern Canada until the Japanese occupied the Aleutian Islands in the Second World War. Then another rush to the Yukon was on, this time of army engineers who constructed the **Alaska Highway** as a troop route in 1942, passing right through the Yukon and up to Alaska.

The 1523-mile Highway begins at Dawson Creek, British Columbia, and winds its way, via **Whitehorse**, the Yukon capital, and a mining and construction centre, to Fairbanks, Alaska. Services are provided at regular intervals along the route. Anyone heading up this way is advised to get a copy of *The Milepost—The All-North Travel Guide*. Published by *Alaska Magazine*, it is a mile-by-mile guide to The Yukon, Alaska, the NW Territories and northwestern BC. Above Whitehorse, many prospectors lost their lives in the dangerous Whitehorse Rapids. Later, the White Pass and Yukon narrow gauge railway took the prospectors as far as **Skagway**. The railroad is still in operation and it passes through some tremendous mountainous scenery enroute. There are daily departures from Whitehorse. The fare is US$60 and includes a meal. Reservations should be made in advance with the Seattle office: Passenger Sales and Service, PO Box 2147, Seattle, WA 98111, (206) 623-2510. In Skagway you can phone (907) 983-2252.

You can also fly into Dawson City or Whitehorse, or else travel by steamer as far as Skagway, Alaska, and from there pick up a train to Whitehorse.

Whitehorse is also the headquarters of the Territory Mounties. A visit here should include a stop at the **WD McBride Centennial Museum** on First Avenue and Wood Street to look at Gold Rush and Indian mementoes including a steam locomotive, a sleigh wagon, guns, shovels, etc. You can also ride the Yukon River through turbulent Miles Canyon on the *MV Schwatka* (named after the explorer) and visit the Whitehorse Power Dam to see the salmon leap in August.

At **Dawson City** many of the buildings hurriedly thrown up in 1898 still stand. At the height of the Gold Rush more than 30,000 people lived in Dawson, in the settlement at the meeting point of the Yukon and Klondike Rivers. The now declining population capitalises on the tourist trade with things like an old time music hall and gold panning for a dollar a go. Food and accommodation prices are high. For the real thing, visit the **Bonanza Hotel Museum**. Picks, pans, and even bags of unrefined gold are all on view. The **Shaw Mining Museum**, on Front and Queen Street, also has early mining equipment exhibits and Yukon River tours leave daily from the dock on Front Street.

In the southwestern corner of the Yukon is the mountainous **Klaune National Park**. The park has extensive icefields and Canada's highest peak, Mt Logan (19,850 feet), as well as a great variety of animals, fishes and birds. The rugged, snowy mountains of Kluane typify the storybook picture one has of the Yukon. In fact the territory is not entirely a land of perpetual ice and snow. Summers here are warm with almost total daylight during June and although winters are cold, they are generally no more so than in many Canadian provinces. The Yukon government provides and maintains more than 50 campgrounds through the territory, mostly in scenic places along the major highways. There are also several youth hostels to stay at including three in Whitehorse, as well as in Dawson, Carmack Lake (Mile 102 on the Klondike Highway) and Watson Lake. Hotel/motel accommodation is available in all the towns mentioned above but it's on the expensive side.

National Park: Kluane

5. BACKGROUND MEXICO

BEFORE YOU GO
What follows applies to nationals of the USA and Canada, of Britain and other EEC countries, also of Norway, Sweden, Switzerland and Austria, and of New Zealand and Australia. Nationals of all other countries should obtain specific information from their nearest Mexican Consulate.

A tourist card (not a visa) is necessary for entry to Mexico, is available only to persons entering Mexico on a holiday or for reasons that are strictly non-remunerative, and is easy to obtain from a Mexican Consular Office or from an authorised airline serving Mexico. All that need be produced is a valid passport, except when the traveller is under 18 years of age, in which case a parental authorisation signed by both parents and witnessed by a Commissioner for Oaths (or Notary Public) is additionally required.

Your passport, the tourist card and, if you have been in an infected area within the previous five days, a cholera certificate, must be produced at the Port of Entry.

Tourist cards must be used within 90 days of issue and are normally valid for 90 days from date of entry. However, border officials have the power to alter that from 90 to 30 days or whatever they see fit. Longer validation is often granted, up to a maximum of six months, either at the time of issue or later on in Mexico when seeking an extension, though you will be asked to present proof of sufficient means. It is advisable to obtain a tourist card in advance; you can get it at the border, but valid only for a shorter period.

Tourists wishing to visit a border town (by land) or a seaport (by sea) will be granted entry for up to three days simply upon presentation of a valid passport.

The tourist card is issued in duplicate. One is taken from you upon entry, the other as you leave. If you are a national of a country outside North America and are visiting Mexico from the US where you are on an Exchange Programme Visa, do not let US officials take your DSP 66 when you cross into Mexico.

GETTING THERE
Most travellers (and certainly the overwhelming number using this Guide) will be visiting Mexico via the US. Major American, Mexican and international airlines fly from Los Angeles, Chicago, New York, Miami, Houston, San Diego, San Antonio, New Orleans and other US (and Canadian) cities to Mexico City and elsewhere in Mexico.

Because of the 1982 peso devaluations, you should not fly from US/Canadian destinations but rather cross into Mexico and fly on domestic flights purchased with pesos, where at present your savings are substantial. For example, at press time, air fare round-trip from Tijuana to Guadalajara was US $95 (paid in pesos); to Cancun (on the southeast tip of Mexico), it was US $170. The economic situation being volatile, do check with a US travel agency before going ahead with this.

There are 12 major and a number of minor crossing points along the US–Mexico border. The most important are Tijuana (12 miles south of San Diego), Calexico-Mexicali, Nogales (south of Tucson), Douglas/Agua Prieta, El Paso/Ciudad Juarez, Eagle Pass/Piedras Negras, Laredo/Nuevo Laredo, Hidalgo/Reynosa and Brownsville/Matamoros. If you have a car, the smaller border crossings (such as Tecate, 40 miles east of San Diego) are often less bureaucratic. Car travellers should avoid Tijuana, especially on weekends—long delays, caused by extensive searches for drugs and aliens. El Paso/ Ciudad Juarez' border is often mentioned by readers as the easiest crossing: 'Mexican officials didn't pay any attention to us'. Matamoros may be the most corrupt: 'We refused to pay a bribe and were kicked out of the country'. Bribees are usually satisfied with US $5; principles notwithstanding, paying a *mordida* is usually cheaper and certainly less time-consuming than travelling to another crossing point. Matamoros is the crossing point closest to Mexico City (622 miles/996 kms); first class bus fare is about US $26. Even from Ciudad Juarez, a much greater distance, first class bus fare is only about US $35. AMTRAK goes to the border at El Paso and Laredo from where you make your own arrangements with Mexican National Railways. Trains also leave daily from Mexicali to Mexico City, but the distance makes it a dreadful trip: 'Even first class it was hell—zero sanitation, three days and four nights. A big mistake to make the journey in one go.' Extremely cheap at about US $22 first-class, $12 second-class fare.

Now refer to the Travel heading a few pages further on for information on how to continue on your way through Mexico.

GEOGRAPHY AND CLIMATE

Running from north to south, the two chains of the Sierra Madre dominate and dictate the country's geography and climate. Thrown up between these ranges and rising out of the northern deserts is the vast Central Plateau. Around the area of the capital, just south of the Tropic of Cancer, there is a further jumble of mountains, finally petering out in the narrow and comparatively flat Isthmus of Tehuantepec. From Tijuana in the northwest to Merida in the Yucatan, Mexico stretches for 2750 miles.

Between the altitudes of 5000 and 8000 feet the climate is mild. The descent to sea level corresponds to an increase in temperature, so that the lowlands are very hot in summer as well as being very warm in

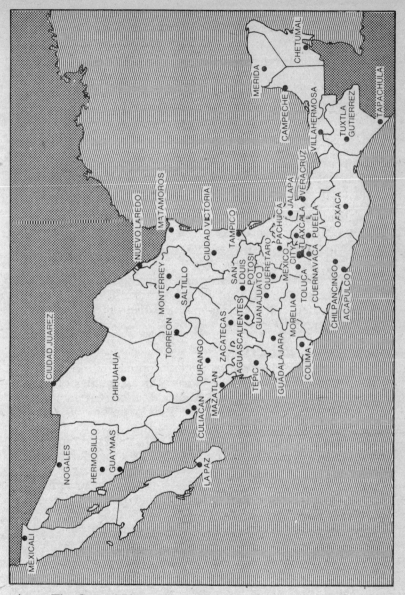

winter. The Central Plateau, on which lies Mexico City (altitude 7350 feet), enjoys a pleasant, springlike climate. It is warm and sunny throughout the year, although regular afternoon showers or storms can be expected from June to October—the Rainy Season.

In the deserts of northern Mexico and throughout Baja California temperatures of over 100°F are to be expected during the summer months. It is similarly hot on the coast, although the sea breezes are cooling. But in the lush tropical jungle lands to the south of the Tropic of Cancer, humidity is high and the annual rainfall is nearly as great as anywhere else in the world. On the northern side of the Isthmus of Tehuantepec, rainfall reaches a staggering 10 feet a year. The large numbers of rivers and the frequency with which they become rushing, swollen torrents, make the land impassable by permanent rail or road systems.

WHAT TO WEAR
Light clothing made of natural fibres (cotton, etc) are recommended. Bring a jacket or something warmer for Mexico City and the Central Plateau's cool evenings, plus raingear for the rainy season.

TIME ZONES
Virtually all of Mexico, from the Yucatan to the Pacific due west of Mexico City, falls within the zone corresponding to Central Standard Time in the US. The west coast from Tepic up to the border, and including the southern half of Baja California, is an hour earlier, while the northern half of Baja is an hour earlier still and corresponds to Pacific Standard Time in the US.

THE MEXICAN SITUATION
Modern Mexico is the product of three distinct historical phases: pre-Columbian (or pre-Cortez) Indian, three centuries of Spanish colonial rule, and, since 1821, independent Mexican government. The chief landmark of the last phase, the Revolution of 1910, followed years of instability, violence and oppression, but this revolution which began as a massive popular uprising against a corrupt aristocracy subsequently petered out into misery and despair for millions of poor Mexicans.

Starting around 1940, things began to improve in some quarters with significant strides in industrialisation and, especially, in agricultural production consequent upon a doubling of the harvest area in what is by nature an often arid country. But this has been accompanied by a more than trebling of the population which is now approaching 70 million, and a surge of urbanisation which has seen Mexico City leap from a population of 1.5 million in 1940 to nearly ten million at present. The overall standard of living has increased, but the lion's share has gone to the haves, while the have-nots additionally suffer from chronic inflation (about 50 percent a year in 1982, over 30 percent in prior years) and loss of traditional incomes. The housing situation has actually deteriorated for the majority of the population, unemployment and living standards would be far worse than they are were it not for the large numbers of Mexicans who, legally or illegally, cross over the border to work in the United States, and the country is desperately dependent on the tourist trade and foreign investment (both predominantly American).

More than a quarter of able-bodied Mexicans are permanently un-employed or seriously under-employed, and always underpaid. The poor live, frequently without water, light or drainage, in over-crow-ded slums where illiteracy is common and malnutrition rampant.

The role of the peasants in the 1910 Revolution, typified by the brilliant guerrilla leadership of Emiliano Zapata, was crucial, but though the Revolution eliminated the traditional power structure, it did not give full participation and benefit to the peasants. Instead it was the middle sector of farmers who gained and have acted as instru-ments of an 'internal colonialism' directed by the Institutional Revo-lutionary Party (PRI) which has held office since 1929. In spite of the considerable economic progress of Mexico and the large-scale land distribution that has taken place over the last fifty years, there are at present a higher percentage of landless peasants than when the Revo-lution began.

Meanwhile, the government, with full executive power vested in the president, remains firmly in the hands of the PRI, whose nominee is invariably elected president, which has a large majority in Con-gress, a strong hold on the administrative machinery, control of the trade unions and the support of big business. Massive oil discoveries in the 1970s made it appear as though Mexico was on the verge of prosperity and stability; this was illusory, however. Today the country is reeling under the biggest economic crisis in its history: a world oil glut, falling crude prices, a sharp decline in tourism and a horrendous national debt and high interest rates all conspired to produce three peso devaluations in 1982, nationalisation of the banks, and a chaotic situation of 50 percent inflation and fluctuating prices.

CULTURE
Mexico is a fascinating and colourful country, physically and cultur-ally, bridging the gap between America North and South. It is a feast of art and history, with more than 11,000 archaeological sites, temples, pyramids and palaces of bygone civilisations, and many museums which are generally regarded as being among the best in the world. Although Mexico City and resort towns like Acapulco have their share of tall buildings, expensive hotels and general North American glitter, rural Mexico is something else again and the whole pace of life visibly alters the moment you cross the border from the United States.

Three centuries of Spanish rule have left their mark not only on the lifestyle of the country but also on its appearance. The fusion of

Spanish baroque with the intricate decorative style of the Indians produced the distinctive and dramatic style called Mexican Colonial. A number of towns rich in Mexican Colonial buildings are preserved as national monuments and new building is forbidden. The most important colonial towns are: Guadalajara, Leon, Guanajuato, San Miguel de Allende, Morelia, Taxco, Cholula, Puebla and Merida.

Despite its Spanish architectural and linguistic overtones, Mexico has a distinctly Indian soul: fatalistic, taciturn, reflective and strong on tradition and folklore. You will notice this most sharply in the villages, where it is easy to misinterpret the dignified shyness of the villagers as coldness. Various towns stand out as being Indian in character: Queretaro (where the Mexican constitution was drafted in 1917), Patzcuaro, Oaxaca, Tehuantepec and San Cristobal de las Casas. Not to be missed are Indian market days and festivals. Toluca, an hour's drive from Mexico City, has an outstanding Indian market.

There were six major pre-Columbian cultures in Mexico: the Olmec, Mixtec, Maya, Zapotec, Toltec and Aztec. Among the most important archaeological sites are the following. In the Mexico city area: Pyramid of Cuicuilco, Teotihuacan, Tepoztlan near Cuernavaca, Tula, Pyramid of Tenayuca, and Tzintzuntzan on Lake Patzcuaro. Near Zacatecas in central Mexico: La Quemada. Near Oaxaca south of Mexico City: Mitla and Monte Alban. On the Yucatan peninsula in southeast Mexico: Palenque, Chichen Itza, Uxmal and Tulum. Admission to most archaeological sites is about 30 pesos.

MONEY
Mexico uses the peso which is divided into 100 centavos. The sign denoting peso is $, the same as the US dollar sign. Important note: all peso prices in this section are written as _____pesos. All US dollar prices are given as US $_____.

The peso devalued three times in 1982 and as we go to press is somewhat 'stabilised' at an official rate of 95 to the US dollar. However, pesos at anywhere up to 150 to the dollar can currently be purchased outside Mexico, eg at banks in San Francisco and other large California cities. At present, you are allowed to bring in and take out a maximum of 5000 pesos. Once inside Mexico, you will do much better by paying in pesos instead of dollars. 'If you pay in pesos, it's very cheap; in dollars, just cheap.'

Inflation has been running 30 percent a year but in 1982 leaped to over 50 percent, so the 'bargain' prices may not remain so for very long. The devaluation was undertaken mainly to make tourism more appealing, so it is probable that hotel and restaurant prices will hold true the longest.

Please note: the monetary situation is extremely volatile, so please check with a travel agency and other sources just prior to your trip for an update.

Tipping. Where there is tipping, 10–15 percent is standard, but 'we found that tips were neither given nor expected in cheaper restaurants—in fact they'd be most surprised if you gave them anything'.

Banks. Banking hours are usually 9am–1pm Monday to Friday. 'Banamex is the best bet for changing money. Others often refuse, and one actually told me they had no money!'

ACCOMMODATION

The range of hotel accommodation in Mexico is wide, from ultra-modern marble skyscrapers, and US-style motels along the major highways, to colonial inns and haciendas to modest guesthouses, called pensiones or casas de huespedes. There is also a marked difference between north and south Mexico. In the north of the country hotels tend to be older, often none too clean with bad plumbing, and large noisy ceiling fans to hum you to sleep. In southern Mexico hotels 'are a joy'. They are rarely full and often offer a high standard of comfort and cleanliness at low rates. It is fairly common to find hotels which are converted old aristocratic residences built around a central courtyard. Hoteliers will probably offer you their most expensive room first. A useful phrase in the circumstances is: *Quisiera algo mas barato, por favor* (I'd like something cheaper, please). Ask to see the room first: *Quiero ver el cuarto, por favor*. Of course a double room always works out cheaper per person than two singles, but also one double bed—*cama matrimonial*—is cheaper than two beds in a room. On the other hand, cheaper hotels often don't mind how many people take a room. 'Travelling in a group of four, considerable savings are possible. Most hotel beds are big enough for two people; therefore a double-bedded room can accommodate four.' Prices are fixed, and should be prominently displayed by law; penalties for breaking the rules are severe.

Hotel rates may vary between high and low season. High season extends from mid-December to Easter or the beginning of May, the remaining months being low season. Seasonal variations will be more marked at coastal resorts. *As most travellers using this Guide tour North America, including Mexico, in the summer months, low season rates have been quoted.*

'We notice that cockroaches are mentioned by people assessing places to stay. Even the best hotels are full of them—they are part of the scene and should not be regarded as unusual.'

'As it is rare indeed for Mexican wash basins to have plugs, I would recommend travellers to be equipped with this useful item.'

Mexico also has a bed and breakfast programme, called Posado Mexico, Apartado 21-C, Cuernavaca, Morelos; phone 731-2-1367 or 731-2-6419. It has B&Bs in Cuernavaca, Guadalajara, Guanajuato, Jalapa, Merida, Mexico City, Oaxaca, Taxco and Veracruz. About US $30 double, possibly less since the 1982 devaluations.

The Mexican Youth Hostel programme (whose acronym is CREA) has over 20 hostels in such places as Mexico City, Cancun, La Paz, San Luis Potosi, Veracruz, Mexicali, Durango, Oaxtepec, Acapulco and Zihuatanejo. They cost roughly 150–250 pesos for lodging, 350 to 600 pesos for room and three meals. Consult an International Handbook or contact Agencia Nacional de Turismo Juvenil, Garieta del Metro Insurgentes, Local C-11, Mexico 6 DF.

FOOD AND DRINK

Because high altitude slows digestion, it's customary to eat a large, late, lingering lunch and a light supper. (You may be wise to eat less than usual until your stomach adjusts.) Do not eat unpeeled fruit and avoid drinking tap water, unprocessed milk products and ice cubes.

Stick to bottled mineral water, bottled juices, soft drinks or the excellent Mexican beer. Mexican milkshakes or *licuados* are made with various fruits and are delicious; probably best to avoid *licuados con leche* (those made with milk). 'The most important thing is to eat plenty of limes, garlic and onions—all "natural disinfectants"— we didn't have any stomach troubles.'

The Mexican menu revolves around ground maize (first discovered by the Mayas), cheese, tomatoes, beans, rice and a handful of flavourings: garlic, onion, cumin and chiles of varying temperatures. Using this limited palette, the Mexicans have devised a delightful and delicious cuisine. The ground maize flour is made into pancake-shaped *tortillas*, which appear in a variety of dishes and also on their own to be eaten like bread. *Tortillas* are also made with wheat flour: restaurants will customarily ask, '*De maiz o de harina?*' (Do you want corn or flour tortillas?) Enchiladas are tortillas rolled and filled with cheese, beef, etc, baked and lightly sauced. *Tacos, tostadas, flautas* and *chalupas* all use fried tortillas, which are either stacked or filled with cheese, beans, meat, chicken, sauce, etc. *Tamales* use softer corn dough, filled with spicy meat and sauce and wrapped in corn husks to steam through. Other dishes to sample: *pollo con mole* (chicken in a sauce containing chocolate, garlic and other spices), fresh shrimp and fish (often served Vera Cruz style with green peppers, tomatoes, etc). Beans and rice accompany every meal, even breakfast. A good breakfast dish is *huevos rancheros*, eggs in a spicy tomato-based sauce.

breakfast: *desayuno*
coffee and a roll: *cafe con panes*
lunch: *almuerzo* (lighter) or *comida*
dinner/supper: *cena*
fixed-price meal: *menu corrida*
eggs: *huevos*
fish: *pescado*
meat: *carne*
salad: *ensalada*
fruit: *fruta*
beer: *cerveza*
I want something not too spicy, please: *Quiero algo no muy picante, por favor*.

Mexico is noted for its pastries, honey and chocolate also. The best-known hard liquor is tequila, a potent clear liquid made from the maguey cactus plant and tasting 'similar to kerosene'. Margarita cocktails made with tequila are popular on both sides of the border but macho Mexicans prefer to take their tequila neat with a little salt and lime juice on the back of the hand. Cheaper still than tequila are *mescal* and *pulque*, both maguey derivatives. Mexico produces decent wines but is famous for its beer; don't pass up Dos Equis dark.

TRAVEL

Now for your basic Spanish travel vocabulary: bus—*autobus*; train—*tren* or *ferrocarril*; plane—*avion*; auto—*carro*; ticket—*boleto*; second class—*segunda clase*; first class—*primera clase*; first class reserved seat (on trains)—*primera especial*; sleeping car—*coche dormitorio*; which platform?—*cual anden?* which departure door/gate?—*cual puerta?* What time?—*que hora?* And inevitably: How many hours late are we?—*Cuantas horas de retraso tenemos?* Street—*calle*; arrival—*llegada*; departure—*salida*; detour—*desviacion*; north—*norte*; south—*sur*; east—*este* or *oriente* (and abbreviated Ote); west—*oeste* or *poniente* (abbreviated Pte). Junction—*enpalme*; indicates a route where one must change buses/trains; avoid *enpalmes* at all costs.

Bus. Bus travel is the most popular means of transportation for Mexicans. Buses cost a bit more than trains, but will cut travelling times by anything from a quarter to a half and in any case are absurdly inexpensive by American or European standards: Tijuana to Mexico City (1871 miles/2995 kms) costs about US $40. All seats are reserved on first class (*primera*) buses, but 'beware of boarding a bus where there are no seats left—you may be standing for several hours for first class fare'. Sometimes it's advisable to book for second class also although in southern Mexico a reader advises, 'Normally there are no standby passengers on first class and you get a reserved seat; on second class buses this is rarely the case'. Standards of comfort, speed, newness of buses, etc, vary more between bus lines than between first and second class, although second class will invariably be slower (sometimes days slower with attendant expenses) and cheaper on longer runs. Travellers generally recommend first class buses: 'By far the best—quite exciting, cheap, fast'. Most towns have separate terminals for first and second class buses. Always take along food, a sweater (for over-air-conditioned vehicle) and toilet paper.

When making reservations you are always allotted a particular seat on a particular bus so if you want a front seat book a couple of days ahead. No refunds are made if you miss the bus; and be careful of buying a ticket for a bus which is just pulling out of the bus station! No single carrier covers the whole country and in some areas as many as 20 companies may be in competition, and while this doesn't mean much variation in fares, it can mean a big difference in service. The Ameripass is not valid in Mexico, though by waving a student card you can sometimes get a substantial discount—though really this is only for Mexican students during vacations.

Though you shouldn't have too much faith in the precision of its contents, ask for *un horario*—a timetable—showing all bus lines and issued free.

Rail. The principal company is the Mexican National Railways although some lines have remained separate from this central organisation. Though Mexican trains are a good deal slower than buses, they are also cheaper, the food served on board is inexpensive, and the scenery always magnificent. Students can sometimes get a discount (see under buses). As with buses, we recommend first class travel. First class trains are very good for sleeping, with reclining seats and at extra cost, berths. When booking, ask for *primera especial*, that is, a first-class reserved seat. To get a berth, you must buy a *primera dormitorio* (first class sleeping car) ticket plus a ticket for *cama alta* (upper berth) or whatever. 'Apart from the price, the only differences are that first-class seats are better, windows larger, class of people wealthier. Toilets are still dreadful and every 20 minutes at night peddlars plod through, shining torches in your face.' 'Always take food, several bottles of water for drinking and washing faces.' 'If possible choose a carriage far from the station entrance and get a seat in the middle of the carriage, away from the loos and women with screaming babies.' 'Despite discomforts, second-class was great fun—marketplace for parakeets, avocados, tequila, lugubrious serenades by buskers at 2am for which the Mexicans—incredibly—gave money.' 'Very useful rail timetable for all of Mexico from Mexican Tourist Office in New Orleans.' NB: The only fast train in Mexico is the *Aztec*

Eagle from Nuevo Laredo to Mexico City: same fare as other trains, offers comfort, air conditioning and speed—journey is two days, one night. Book well ahead.

'You dismiss second class rail travel, but huge savings can be made this way for starvation budget travellers who are prepared to rough it. And rough it is the word. You are not guranteed a seat (they are terribly uncomfortable), toilet facilities are awful, and nighttime finds people bedding down on the floors. My journey from Mexicali to Mexico City took three nights and two days (24 hours longer than by bus) with a five-hour stop-over at Guadalajara. But you become totally immersed in Mexican life. The train stops about every 10 miles and this brings all the villagers to the trackside to sell cooked food, fruit and juices. The further you travel southwards the more people board the train to sell their wares.'

Particularly recommended routes are: through the northern desert between Monterrey and San Luis Potosi (10 hours); and from Chihuahua through the spectacular Tarahumara (or Copper) Canyon (four times wider than the Grand Canyon) and down to the west coast at Los Mochis. Enroute the train passes through 89 tunnels, crosses over 30 bridges, crosses the Continental Divide three times, and climbs to 8071 feet at the track's highest point. The Canyon is the home of the primitive Tarahumara Indians. Stop off at Creel if you want to visit them.

Air. AeroMexico and Mexicana service all major cities and resorts within the country and many smaller airlines also reach more out of the way places. Although they may not hold true for long, fares are now about five US cents per mile, eg Mexico City to Merida (937 miles) for US $54 or 3795 pesos. See earlier comments under Getting There and Money.

Enquire about discounts as well: now semi-nationalised, Aeromexico and Mexicana offer a 25 percent domestic air fare discount called Visit Mexico. It has numerous conditions: passengers must have round-trip regular or charter tickets from outside Mexico, and must land and leave from either Guadalajara, Mexico City or Acapulco. Good for 45 days.

Car. When you enter Mexico you will have to produce a valid driving licence and car registration certificate. If you don't own the car you will need a notarised authorisation from the owner. You must have Mexican auto insurance which you can get either in advance from a US insurance broker or at the border. The cost is around $75 per month for the average car, but collision coverage (and you need it) is quite a bit extra.

The principal highways lead from Nogales, Ciudad Juarez, Piedras

Negras, Nuevo Laredo, Reynosa and Matamoros, all on the border, to Mexico City. The Mexicans are proud of their highway system, claiming it to be the best in Latin America. All main roads are patrolled by the Green Angels (Angeles Verdes) fleet, radio co-ordinated patrol cars manned by English-speaking two-man crews. They are equipped to handle minor repairs, give first aid and supply information. A raised hood on a parked car will convey to them your need for assistance.

Garage repairs are reported as 'often incredibly cheap, particularly if you avoid 'authorised dealers''; if you go to an authorised dealer, expect to pay through the nose. Always get a price quote first!

Be on the alert for cattle, donkeys, hens, or people on the roads and if you see branches or rocks strewn about the highway, stop. They are there as an indication that there is a hazard ahead. Potholes, bumps and narrow bridges (*puente angosto*) are other hazards to watch for.

Some signs: *Alto*—Stop; *No se estacione*—no parking; *bajada frene con motor*—steep hill, use low gear; *vado a 70 metros*—ford 70 metres; *cruce de peatones*—pedestrian crossing; *peligro*—danger; *codo*—sharp curve; *camino sinuoso*—winding road.

Gasoline in Mexico is nationalised under the name Pemex. 'Don't buy cheap gas. Pemex Nova caused our car to shudder and stall. A mixture of Nova and Extra (the better quality) was a vast improvement.' It is sold by the litre. Never let the gas level go low and fill up at every opportunity. Gas stations are few and far between in remoter areas. 'Extra is almost impossible to come by in southern Mexico.'

'Drivers should be warned that after entering the country there is a "free zone" of about 100 miles in which three to four customs stations may be found along the road. You may be stoped at any or all of these and you will have to bribe at least one official in order not to have your car ripped apart.'

'Also, you are considered fair game for police along the road, who will stop and fine you for "speeding". Haggle with them, they always come down to 5–10 dollars. After you get out of the "free zone", you will have no more problems with customs and hardly see any police.'

'When crossing the border you may be asked by the Mexican customs and immigration officials for "tips". They actually hold out their hands and ask for "tips". If you don't give them money, you could be in for a difficult time. One man was asleep in his car in Nuevo Laredo when the Mexican police arrested him for speeding—although the car was parked at the time. Only on payment of a bribe was the poor man released. Nuevo Laredo is a corrupt dump, and an insult to Mexico.'

Most scenic road in Mexico is the well-maintained 150-D which sweeps through the Puebla Valley past the volcanic peaks of Popocatepetl and Orizaba, climbs into lush rain forests and down through foothills covered with flowers and coffee plantations, to end up in the flat sugarcane country around Veracruz.

Hitching. Can be hazardous with long waits (not just for a lift but for a car to come along) in high temperatures. However . . . 'found hitching pretty easy in northern Mexico. If you don't speak Spanish at all (like me) show a sign saying *estudiante* and giving your destination. Plan your trip with a map and accept rides only to places you know, unless the driver can make it clear to you in any other language.' 'Water in the desert, I never realised how important it was. Anyone hitching should take a water canteen.' *Not* recommended for women.

SHOPPING
'The cheapest market by far for sarapes, ponchos and embroidery is Mitla, near Oaxaca. Knock them down to one-third the asking price, and make rapid decisions because the price is higher if you return having thought about it. The best place for leather is San Cristobal. Best for hammocks is Merida.'

COMMUNICATIONS
Mail. Do not have mail sent Lista de Correos (Poste Restante) unless you are sure of being able to collect it within 10 days. After that time it is likely to be 'lost'. Letters or postcards to North America are 4 pesos; to Europe, 7 pesos; to Australia and New Zealand, 9 pesos. Cables can be sent through Western Union and are cheapest 7pm to 7am. 'Domestic cables are very cheap and a good way to communicate with other travellers.'

Telephones. Public phone booths are to be found only in the major cities. Elsewhere make use of telephones in stores, tobacco stands, hotels, etc. The Mexico City telephone directory has a green-page section in English for tourists. Long distance calls are cheapest between 7pm and 4.30am.

ELECTRICITY
125V and 220V, 50 cycles AC, except in Mexico City and Acapulco where it is 60 cycles.

HEALTH
Medical services are good, and in Mexico City it's easy to find an English-speaking doctor. Fees are reasonable compared to the US, and some hospitals will examine you and give prescriptions free. Nevertheless, where a fee is likely you should ask for a quote beforehand, and insurance is advisable.

'If you travel in the US before Mexico, you'll hear many ghastly tales of internal infections and uncontrollable bacteria. It's not true. Almost everywhere the water is so chlorinated that you're more likely to kill off your own bacteria than find any new ones.' But if in doubt, especially outside the cities, use purifying tablets. All *farmacias* sell Lomotil, an excellent antidote for '*turista*'.

Anti-malarial drugs are advisable in tropical and southern coastal areas—but as Mexico denies (perhaps rightly) that it has malaria, it's difficult to get any drugs for it there, so bring them with you. Well before arriving, travellers should get a smallpox vaccination and it wouldn't hurt to have inoculations against yellow fever, cholera, typhoid and polio.

'It helps to warn people—but hopefully they won't be frightened off.'

LANGUAGE
The more alert among you will have guessed by now that it's Spanish. The point is, you should know some, especially the words for numbers, food and directions. 'Well worth learning some Spanish if you can: don't expect too many Mexicans to know English.'

THE METRIC SYSTEM
Mexico is metric. See Appendix.

6. MEXICO

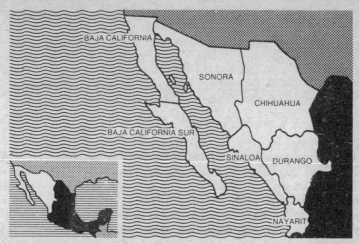

NORTHWEST MEXICO

This vast arid region of stark desert, sharp mountains, deep valleys and canyons contains the states of Baja California, Sonora, Chihuahua, Durango, Nayarit and Sinaloa.

The nearness of Mexico to the US is deceptive once you learn that one way or another, you must cross many miles of thinly populated and largely boring terrain in this northern sector.

The coastline offers some relief, especially from Hermosillo southward as it gradually becomes greener, until you reach the lush and humid jungle around Tepic and San Blas.

Baja California has its own peninsula to the west; poorest of Mexican states, beautiful in a bare-bones sort of way, especially on its eastern coast on the warm Sea of Cortez (also called the Gulf of California).

BAJA CALIFORNIA. To most visitors, Baja is nothing more than **Tijuana**, 12 miles south of San Diego, and **Ensenada**, 60 miles further down on the coast. Neither is typical of mainland Mexico, but may satisfy your lurking urges for cheap handicrafts, cheap tequila, cheap prostitutes, and also bull-fighting, jai-alai and squalor. You will do Mexico an injustice if you judge the country primarily by these and other border towns which cater to the day-tripper. Dollars are readily accepted, but try to deal in pesos for the best deals (see elsewhere).

From Mexicali you can take a good paved 125-mile road to **San Felipe**, a two-hour drive through desert and beautifully harsh mountains. A likeable, ramshackle fishing village on a photogenic

447

headland overlooking the Sea of Cortez, San Felipe has miles of white sand beaches, superb fishing (and fresh shrimp off the boats) and warm paddling in the calm Sea of Cortez.

The main Baja highway is narrow but paved **Mexico 1**, about 1700 kilometres from Tijuana to Cabo San Lucas in the south. 'Throughout its central section, this is a dusty, rutted, oil-pan gouging road just like the old one.' A four-wheel drive would be useful, especially if you plan to explore terrain off Highway 1. The highway is pretty dull until it meanders eastward to San Ignacio and then traces the eastern coastline from Rosalia to Mulege and Loreto. **San Ignacio** is a delightful oasis village which makes its own wine.

Ferries run between **Santa Rosalia** and Guaymas; **La Paz** and both Los Mochis and Mazatlan; and **Cabo San Lucas** and Puerto Vallarta.

See San Diego, California section for bus service to Tijuana; three Tijuana-based bus services go to Ensenada (about 105 pesos with air conditioning), Mexicali, Los Mochis (22 hours, 600 pesos) and other points. 'When going to Ensenada via Tijuana, get Trailways rather than Greyhound so you end up at the main bus station. Otherwise a hot wait to catch local bus.' 'Drive to Ensenada along the coast is beautiful—well worth crossing the border just to experience the complete change of environment.'

CHIHUAHUA. The first major town on the route down from El Paso, Chihuahua is a prosperous industrial and cattle-shipping centre, once famous for breeding tiny, hairless and bad-tempered dogs of the same name. The city is of interest primarily as the inland terminus for the dramatic *Al Pacifico* train ride from Los Mochis on the coast through the Barranca del Cobre (Copper Canyon).

ACCOMMODATION
Hotel del Cobre, 10th and Progreso, 5-16-60. Nr Central Camionera bus depot. From US $6 single, $9 double.
Hotel San Juan, Calle Victoria 832, 2-84-91. Off the Plaza Principal. From US $10 single, $14 double. 'Clean and friendly.' 'Lovely patio.'

OF INTEREST
A crumbling **Cathedral** in Colonial style overlooks the Plaza Principal.
The Palacio de Gobierno, where Migual Hidalgo, the 'Father of Mexico', was executed at 7am, 30 July, 1811, is decorated with 'lovely lurid murals'.
The Museum of Pancho Villa is a fortresslike 50-rm mansion, Villa's home and hideout. At Calle 10, number 3014; take bus from Plaza Principal to Parque Lerdo. Calle 10 (unmarked so ask for Calle Diez) is opposite the park, running SE of Paseo Bolivar. Open (approximately) Mon–Sat 10am–2pm and 4pm–6pm. A relative will take you through for a small *propina* so you can see the revolutionary's weapons, bullet-riddled death car (he was ambushed in 1923) and other artefacts.

TRAVEL
The 13-hr *Al Pacifico* train to Los Mochis passes through Copper Canyon, 1500 ft deeper and 4 times wider than the Grand Canyon. At Divisadero Barrancas it stops

to allow passengers to see and photograph the spectacular view on foot. 'I'd recommend the night train; the day train invariably runs late, and you just get past the canyon before it gets dark.'

The Tarahumara Indians who live in the canyon can be seen enroute; despite the tourism the train brings, they live in largely traditional ways. You can break your journey in **Creel**, 30 miles beyond Divisadero, staying at the Hotel Nuevo for about US $15 per person with 3 meals. Camping also possible but bring a tent (summer is rainy season).

Three services: Autovia daily except Wed, Sun, departing 8am and taking 12½ hrs; Vista Domes on Mon, Thur, Sat, departing 8.20am and taking 12 hrs; overnight trains Tue, Fri, departing 9.50pm and taking 16 hrs. Night train is the cheapest and arrives at Divisadero at 5.57am. 'Leaves the fabulous canyon and mountains for early morning but check sunrise times beforehand.' Fares begin around US $10 for night trains, 2nd class, up to $20 for 1st class Vista Dome. Buy tickets at the station of Ferrocarril de Chihuahua al Pacifico, near intersection of Paseo Bolivar and Blvd Diaz Ordaz, call 2-22-84 or 2-38-67. Also ask at the Tourism Office of major hotels. Buy your ticket at least an hour before departure; 'for 1st class, I recommend reserving the day before'. 'Breath-taking journey—2nd class was quite comfortable and the people inside the train were just as interesting as the scenery outside.' See Los Mochis for return journey.

LOS MOCHIS. A dull agricultural city of interest only as the southern terminus for the *Al Pacifico* rail journey and its ferry connections with La Paz in nearby Topolobampo. 'Filthy hotels, town and unfriendly people.'

ACCOMMODATION
Hotel Beltran, Hidalgo and Zaragoza, 2-00-92. Central. About US $10 single, $15 double with showers, toilet and air conditioning. 'Clean.'
Hotel Lorena, Av Obregon, 2 blocks from bus station. Singles or doubles about US $10 with shower, AC. 'Clean; what a relief after a long bus trip.'

TRAVEL
All *Al Pacifico* trains (see under Chihuahua) leave Los Mochis at 7am. Travellers recommend beginning trip at Los Mochis in order to appreciate the best views; get right-hand seats. Buy tickets at the station only. Taxis to and from the train station are costly—'It took us ages to haggle him down from 500 to 150 pesos'; 'Charged 50 pesos a person, 6 to a cab'. Take the municipal bus instead; train station is 3 miles from town. 'If travellers come by train from north or south, they can change to the *Al Pacifico* at Sufragio station.'
Ferries for La Paz sail from Topolobampo 3 times a week, but tickets are often sold out 24 hrs in advance. Cost is about US $5. Los Mochis-Topolobampo bus, US $1. If you have to wait for the ferry, 'a night under the stars at Topolobampo is fun. Fishermen cook freshly caught fish and shrimp over wood fires and invite people to partake. If you're there for awhile, they may invite you out fishing too. But don't count on Topolobampo for food for the ferry—few shops, buying even basics is difficult.'

MAZATLAN. Big-city, boisterous, a major gringo tourist town and quite un-Mexican, Mazatlan is noted for superb game fishing and that's about it. Piedra Isla, a tiny island just offshore, has good beaches, diving and camping possibilities. Get there via tourist boat;

after the last boat leaves at 4.30pm, it can be very congenial. Free camping on Piedra Isla.

ACCOMMODATION
Hotel del Centro, Canizales Pte 18, 1-26-73. At town centre, near intersection with Juarez. US $8 single, $10 up double, more with AC. 'Spotless.'
Hotel Olas Altas, 1-31-92. Walk south along coastline to point where Osuna and Miguel Aleman join Olas Altas road. Single US $10, double $12. 'Quiet, overlooking bay, cool, clean.'
Fiesta Hotel, opposite bus station. US $12 double with bath. 'Clean. Nothing to do in Mazatlan.'

TRAVEL
Local bus 'Zaragoza', 25 pesos, from bus station into town.
A deep-sea ferry crosses the Gulf of California 3 times weekly to La Paz, about 16 hrs.
'The route (Mexico 40) from Mazatlan to Durango is absolutely breath-taking. Although it's just over 300 miles, it took us a long time to cover as the road twists and turns up to 10,000 ft where it crosses the Continental Divide. A part of Mexico that should not be missed.'

SAN BLAS. An hour's drive off the highway just north of Tepic takes you through increasingly lush tropical country to San Blas, once a sleepy seaside village, but no longer. 'Signs advertising granola and yogurt, expensive hotels and food, dirty beaches and medium surfing.' 'Very hippified but nice with a good swimming beach.'

ACCOMMODATION
Casa Maria, 'mosquito-proofed rooms, showers, clean for US $10'.
Hotel Bucanero, Juarez 75, near plaza. Doubles about US $14. 'Clean, popular with young people.'
Hotel Los Flamingos, down the road from Bucanero. About US $12 for doubles, 'clean, shabby, cell-like rooms, twin beds with shower'.

FOOD
Try the little cafes along the beach for inexpensive fish, oyster meals. Also check to see if the pool in the bar of the Torino restaurant still has 4 crocodile residents.

INFORMATION/TRAVEL
Tourist Info, opposite plaza, has useful booklet with maps, lodgings, etc.
Buses from Tepic to San Blas fairly regularly. 'Interesting jungle scenery enroute.'

NORTHEAST MEXICO

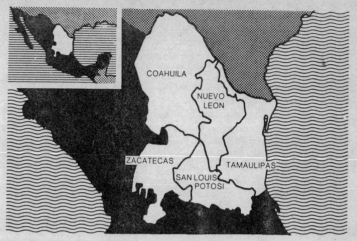

Even more than their western counterparts, the northeast states of Coahuila, Nuevo Leon, Zacatecas, San Luis Potosi and Tamaulipa offer little that is special. **Monterrey**, on the route down from Nuevo Laredo, is Mexico's principal industrial city, hot, sprawling and expensive, due to its proximity to the US border. Give it and **Torreon** a miss if you can. If you are driving, Mexico 85 (the Pan-American Highway) is the most scenic and is also a fairly fast road, some 1220 kilometres from Nuevo Laredo to Mexico City.

451

CENTRAL MEXICO

Mexico seems to save itself scenically, culturally and every other way in order to burst upon you in central Mexico, in a rich outpouring of volcanic mountains, pre-Columbian monuments, luxuriant flowers, exuberant people and picturesque architecture. This is the region where the Mexican love of colour manifests itself and the air is cool and fresh on the high Central Pleateau. Be prepared for mugginess on either coast around Acapulco and Veracruz, however.

Mexico City lies in the centre of this region, surrounded by a dozen tiny states from Tlaxcala to Guanajuato. Northwest of Mexico City is the orbit of Guadalajara, second largest city and home to the largest colony of American expatriates. That fact makes its outlying satellite towns of Tlaquepaque, Chapala, Ajijic and so on quite expensive.

PUERTO VALLARTA. Now pushing 90,000 residents, PV has lots its small-village charm in the traffic and the singles bars but its emerald green setting on a perfect crescent of beach still pleases the eye if not the pocketbook. Come here to enjoy the tremendous breakers and the carefully non-maintained cobblestone streets, to dance and drink margaritas and eat Gulf shrimp and oysters. (The big ones from Guaymas are called *zapatos*—'shoes'—for their strapping size.)

ACCOMMODATION
Hotel Central, Calle Juarez 70. Single US $7, doubles $10. 'Very plain, decent, probably cheapest on north side of river.'
Apartamentos La Pena, PO Box 177, 2-12-13, near the Dolphin Hotel, 1½ blocks from beach. 'A 5-bed suite with bath, kitchen, patio cost us US $15 total. The owner Ramon is a great guy.' NB: PV rates usually 25% lower May through mid-Dec.

El Oceano, 31 de Mayo and Galeana, downtown on ocean. 2-13-22. US $11 single, $15 double.

Puesta del Sol Hotel, Calzada Camaron Sabalo, near El Cid on hotel row NW of city and on beach. Singles from US $13, doubles from $15. Pool, bar, clean beach, own boat to nearby island.

The Rio Cuale divides Puerto Vallarta into north and south. Cheapest lodging on the south side, especially along Basilio Vadillo with its numerous *pensiones* or *casas de huespedes*.

FOOD/ENTERTAINMENT
La Hacienda, '*The* restaurant in PV. We had oysters, octopus, wine and dessert for US $10 each. Service out of this world. The best!'

Try El Ostion Feliz on Calle Libertad for good *ceviche* (marinated fish) and oysters. Impromptu music and dancing on the beach at night. Lots of Europeans, Yanks and Canadians, all trying to score.

TRAVEL
Several buses a day from Tepic (3 hrs) and Guadalajara (7 hrs).
Flights from Guadalajara and Mexico City.

ACAPULCO. A thin rind of elegance round a beautiful palm-fringed bay, Acapulco's phalanx of tall hotels gives way four blocks back to some of Mexico's worst slums. This extraordinary mix of haves and have-nots means that thievery and every sort of scam are endemic, so watch your wallet.

The summers get very hot and humid, occasionally enlivened by summer rainstorms in June, September and October, but these factors are balanced by the fall in hotel prices and the deliciousness of the water.

ACCOMMODATION
Note: rates fall considerably in summer; always check to see if you're being quoted *precios de verano* (summer prices).

Hotel Mariscal, Quebrada, 35. 2-00-15. Near where divers leap. Singles US $12 and up, doubles $18 and up. 'Very basic, clean.'

Hotel California, La Paz 12 near Zocalo. 2-28-93. US $11 and up for singles, $16 up for doubles. 'Very clean, spacious rooms, shower, fan.'

Hostel, Ardillas 121, 6 kms from corner of Carretera Pie de la Cuesta. About US $3 per night including breakfast, with ISIC or AYH card. May have meals also.

Aloha Playa, Gran Via Tropical 155, 2-12-00. 3 miles from downtown with view of bay. Singles US $12, doubles under $20.

Bali-Hai Motel, Ave Costera Miguel Aleman, 1 block from beach. 4-11-11. Costs US $11 up for single, $17 up for doubles.

FOOD
Cheapest restaurants for both Mexican and American food are found around the Zocalo.

OF INTEREST
The famous **high-dive act** takes place nightly off the rocks at the far end of La Quebrada: 9.30pm, 10.30pm, 11.30pm and 12.30am. The torch-lit drop is 130 ft and the diver hits the water at about 60 miles an hr. You can either sit in the lounge of the Mirador Hotel to watch, in which case you'll have to buy an (expensive) drink, or you can go down the steps from the hotel to a public platform overlooking the cliff, paying a modest 'contribution'.

Beaches: Playas Caleta and Caletilla are known as 'morning beaches', Playas Hornos and Hornitos are 'afternoon' ones, because of the movement of the sun and tides. Lots of other less crowded beaches to try, though, such as Playa Guitarron on the east bay. For the rest, there's fishing, boating, water skiing and underwater diving. If you're good enough, you can explore sunken wrecks and the underwater shrine of Our Lady of Guadalupe off La Roqueta Island.

ENTERTAINMENT
Generally sky-high; the only sure way to hold onto your pesos is to grab a table around the Zocalo and watch the goings-on: organ players, gigolos, chewing-gum salesmen, old ladies flogging flowers—they're all selling it.

INFORMATION
Dept of Tourism, Miguel Aleman and Rio de Camaron. Phone 2-21-70. They suggest contacting them if you need help finding lodgings; you should not accept 'guidance' from bus station and taxi driver hustlers who may tell you (sometimes by pretending to phone) that your hotel is full and that you should go where they suggest.

TRAVEL
Buses to Acapulco from Mexico City leave from Terminal Central de Autobuses de Sur, near the Metro Taxquena; trip is 7 hrs.
Numerous flights from Mexico City; this is one of the 3 gateway cities for the 'Visit Mexico' discount fares.

MEXICO CITY. National capital and located in its own Federal District (Distrito Federal—abbreviated DF and pronounced 'day effay' in Spanish) is Mexico City, massive at nearly ten million people in its core, 14 million in its greater metropolitan area. It is set in a lofty valley a mile and a half above sea level but the weight of all those people and multistoried buildings is causing Mexico City to sink.

Mexico City was founded on a swamp in 1325 by the Aztecs, who built the city they called Tenochtitlan where they saw an eagle alight on a cactus to devour a snake, a symbol you'll see on the Mexican flag, currency and elsewhere. The Aztec city grew to 300,000 or more before its conquest in 1519 by the Spaniards. The surrounding area of high plateau is heavily populated, making Mexico City also the economic and transportation hub of the nation.

The city assaults your senses with its smog, incessant din and more pleasantly with its striking architecture from Aztec through Spanish Colonial to modern, from pyramids to enamelled skyscrapers, from modern subways to archaeological finds preserved *in situ* at Metro stops. Great wealth and poverty exist side by side but residents at all economic levels tend to be the most hospitable of Mexicans, making visitors welcome indeed. 'North America is incomplete without a visit to this vast, fascinating city.'

ACCOMMODATION
Hotel Atlanta, B Dominguez 31 at Allende, 518-12-00. US $8 up single, $12 up double with bath. Nr Zocalo, close to sights in old town. 'Clean, comfortable.'
Hotel Conde, Revillagigedo and Pescaditos, near Alameda Park, 583-23-88. Doubles US $7 and up; 'extremely good value'. Phone, TV, shower. 'Best value and friendly.'

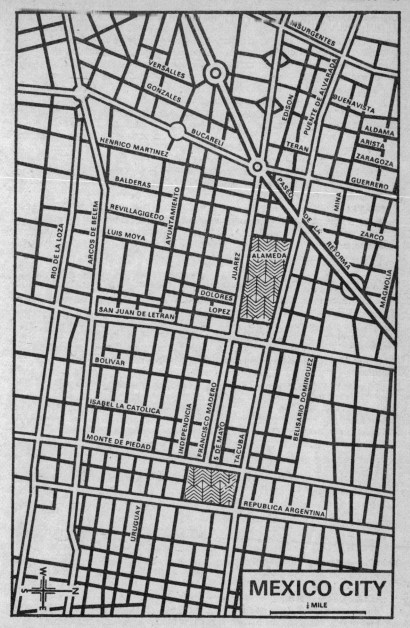

MEXICO CITY

¼ MILE

Hotel Monte Carlo, Uruguay 69. 585-12-22. Single without bath US $5, 'clean and friendly'. Doubles with bath about US $10. Built in 1772 as an Augustine monastery, D H Lawrence later lived here.

Hotel Panuco, Ayuntamiento 148 at Enrique Martinez, 585-13-55. US $5 for one person, double bed with sink, bath, toilet. 'Drinking water supplied, very clean, central and helpful.'

Revillagigedo Street, Alameda Park area, has loads of cheapies, including Fleming at 35, Guadalupe at 36. These are both modern, no-frills but comfortable.

Casa de Mexico, youth hostel at Cozumel 57. US $2.50 with breakfast, 'excellent value'. From Terminal del Norte take bus marked Insurgentes to last stop, then walk remainder. Takes YH/ISIC, though sometimes Mexican student card (another $2) required—can join on the spot. Closes at midnight. 'Strongly recommended; used almost exclusively by European backpackers.'

Motel Bristol, Nelaxa Plaza, 200 yards from British Embassy. 'Single room US $5 and upwards; 1½ miles from Chapultepec Park.'

Outside Mexico City:

Tlamacas Youth Hostel at Popocatepetl. 'Near snow line, US $2.50, brand new, clean, with magnificent views (dorms). Food available but not that cheap so bring with you.' Bus from Mexico City (San Lazaro Metro) to Amecameca, 50 pesos, then taxi up to Tlamacas for US $5–$7. 'Well worth the trip!'

FOOD

Mexico City is a good place to taste frothy Mexican hot chocolate, a drink once so prized that only the Aztec and Mayan nobility drank it, to the tune of 50 tiny cups a day. A dish invented locally and now popular all over Mexico is *carne asada a la tampiqueña* (grilled beef Tampico style).

Due to reports of rude waiters and rapacious mariachis, Plaza Garibaldi is no longer recommended as 'best and cheapest'. 'Good cheap eating at small restaurants around Glorieta Insurgentes situated where Insurgentes crosses Paseo de la Reforma. Fewer mariachis than Garibaldi but you can sit in greater comfort to hear them.'

Fleming (formerly Romfel) Hotel Restaurant, 35 Revillagigedo. 'Small, colonial style', 'good food at reasonable prices', 150 pesos and up.

Las Cazuelas, Av San Antonio 143E, open 8am–midnight daily. Savoury home cooking, lots of choice: try their *chiles rellenos* or *pollo en pipian* (chicken in pumpkin-seed sauce). Mariachi-filled but non-touristy.

The House of Tiles, Av Madero 4. 400-year-old courtyard with fountain and lush blue-and-white Puebla tiles. 'A relaxing cup of coffee in an old, elaborate restaurant.'

Restaurante Bolivar, Bolivar 74B. Meals under 140 pesos. 'Many delicious Chinese chicken recipes.'

OF INTEREST

Anahuacalli, Calle Tecuila 150, near Division del Norte. Diego Rivera-designed black lava building housing his large collection of Aztec, pre-Columbian artefacts. Open Tue-Sun.

Hotel de Mexico, tallest building in the city, but get a gander at its lobby: its *March of Humanity*' mural by David Siqueiros is indescribably wonderful—like being inside an opium dream.

University City. 11 miles south, reached by CU58 bus from Av Juarez, or by cable bus from San Juan de Letran. Famous for its modern design and colourful murals, mosaics and bas-reliefs by Rivera, Juan O'Gorman, Siqueiros and others.

Torre Latino Americano, corner of San Juan de Letran and Madero. A miniature Empire State building that floats, with a magnificent view (smog and weather permitting) from its 44th floor. 50 pesos. Open 10am–12pm.

Palace of Fine Arts, S Juan de Letran and Juarez. This heavy white opera house contains Mexico's finest art collection. Upstairs are some of the best murals by Orozco, Siqueiros, Rivera and Tamayo. 50 pesos. 'Worth every centavo.'

Hotel del Prado, Juarez 70. Expensive hotel whose lobby contains the famous Rivera mural, *Sunday Afternoon in Alameda Park*. Painted in 1947, it is 50 ft by 23 ft; free lectures at 10pm and some mornings at 10am in the lobby.

Floating Gardens of Xochimilco, 15 miles south. Cheapest to catch bus from corner of Pino Suarez and Mesones (if you get on after that, you almost certainly won't get a seat). Very crowded weekends, boats take you around lake, other boats sell food, drink. 'A complete waste of time—muddy canals and gardens.' 'Smelly canals full of refuse.' Boat prices: 'Take one-third off first price quoted.'

Basilica de Guadalupe. Take 44 bus, destination La Villa, on Reforma. Holiest of Mexican shrines, especially to those of Indian blood, the basilica leans in all directions because of subsoil instability. Visitors often show their devotion by walking on knees across the vast, hot courtyard. Behind the Basilica, marvellous views of the Valley of Mexico, the city, the volcanoes.

Tepotzotlan, 25 miles north by *auto-pista* (freeway). Has a magnificent 18th-C **church**, possibly Mexico's finest, with a monastery and an interesting art collection.

Old Mexico City. This is the area north and east of the Zocalo or main square and includes many cheap markets. Worth an afternoon's exploration.

The Cathedral at the Zocalo is the oldest church edifice on the North American continent (1573–1667) and was built on the ruins of the Aztec temple. On the east side of the Zocalo is the **National Palace**, begun in 1692, interesting on its own and for its enormous murals by Diego Rivera.

The Pyramids of Teotihuacan and **Temple of Quetzalcoatl.** Take Metro to Indios Verdes (last station on north end of line 3), then take bus (50 pesos) marked 'Pyramids'. (NB: no backpackers on Metro). $1\frac{1}{2}$ hrs each way. The temples are part of the ruins of the once-great city built even before the Aztecs. The Pyramid to the Sun is 216 ft high (248 steps to the top where the sacrifices were made) and the Pyramid to the Moon, $\frac{1}{4}$ mile away, although less vast, is just as impressive. The Temple of Quetzalcoatl is about $\frac{1}{2}$-mile from the pyramids and has some superb Toltec carvings. Open 9am–5pm, entrance 50 pesos, 40 on Sunday. 'When climbing pyramids, take care—they're very steep. Traders everywhere—even at the top of the pyramids.'

Chapultepec Park. Most of the city's important **museums** are in the Park, but it is also an attraction in its own right, especially on Sun when all the families in the city seem to parade there. 'Should be a compulsory visit—very colourful.' Free **zoo** contains 'Cancun', the first captive panda to be born outside China.

Anthropological Museum. The claim that this is the finest museum in the world is well-founded; contains Mexico past and present. 'Deserves every accolade thrown at it. Worth going here *before* you visit the pyramids at Teotihuacan.' Cameras but no tripods allowed, so bring fast film or flash. 'Worth taking your own photos, since postcards of exhibits are very poor and few (as in all Mexican museums I've visited).' Open Tue-Sat 9am–7pm, Sun 10am–6pm. Closed Mon. Fee 50 pesos, 40 on Sun. Take Metro to Chapultepec.

Gallery of Mexican History, a cleverly designed building just below Chapultepec Castle, with a first-rate presentation of Mexican history since 1500. Open 10am–5pm daily.

Museum of Modern Art, Mexico's more recent masterpieces. 'Excellent collection, not only of Orozco, Rivera, etc, but some charming primitive paintings.' Be sure to see *La Revolucion* by Lozano. Open 11am–7pm daily except Mon. Fee 50 pesos, 25 with student card. The above 3 museums are all in Chapultepec Park.

Chapultepec Castle, old castle with original furnishings and objets d'art. Found fame in 1848 when young Mexican cadets fought off invading Americans here. Rather than surrender, the final 6 wrapped themselves in Mexican flags and jumped from the parapets to their death. Nothing exciting now, but a good view from the top.

National Museum, Calle Moneda, off Zocalo. Notable for Aztec sacrifical and calendar stones. Open 9am–6pm daily. Free Sun, otherwise 5 pesos.

Two museums in the southern suburb of Coyoacan. Take buses 9 or 87 south along Reforma and Insurgentes, or 48 south along Burcareli—they should be marked 'Coyoacan' or 'Col del Valle' and the journey takes an hour. Both museums open 10am–6pm daily except Monday.

Museo Frida Kahlo, corner of Allende and Londres. Frida was Diego Rivera's wife and this, their house, is filled with their effects and many of Frida's works.

House and Museum of Leon Trotsky, Viena 45, 2 blocks north, 4 west of Frida's house. Ring door buzzer to be let in. This is where Trotsky was pickaxed to death in 1940; his tomb is in the garden.

The **volcanoes of Popocatepetl and Iztaccihuatl** can be seen on a clear day in the east, although 'for good views take bus to Amecameca from ADO Terminal'. The peaks are some 3000 ft higher than Mts Rainier or Whitney in the USA. 'Mind-blowing view when sitting on the right-hand side of bus from Mexico City to Puebla.'

Mexican **Independence Day celebrations**, 15 Sept at 11.10am. President gives traditional cry of liberty to crowd in the Zocalo amid churchbells ringing, fireworks firing, confetti floating, much rejoicing. **Military parade** 16 Sept down the Reforma.

ENTERTAINMENT

Jai alai, the fastest game in the world, nightly at 6pm except Mon and Fri at Fronton Mexico, on Plaza de la Republica. Fee. Jacket preferred. Complex betting system; stick to the pre-game parimutual.

Bullfight season runs Nov to March; other times of year, you can see *novilladas* (younger bullfighters, younger bulls) which are cheaper and may please you just as well if you know nothing of bullfighting. Fights Sun at 4pm; booking in advance recommended. Cheaper seats at Plaza Monumental than at El Toreo; both outside town. Monumental (also known as Plaza Mexico) is at 50,000 seats the biggest in the world; buy '*sol*' seats in *barrera* or *tendido* sections to see anything.

Ballet Folklorico at the Palace of Fine Arts, Sun at 9.30am, 5pm and 8pm; Wed at 6pm and 9pm. Book in advance. 'A real must—not classical ballet but a series of short dances representing Spanish, Indian and Mexican cultures.' Incredible costumes! From 350 pesos.

Casa del Canto, Plaza Insurgentes. Music from all over Latin America, cover charge about 140 pesos. 'Terrific.'

Plaza de Garibaldi. Nightly after 9am, mariachi music, sometimes free, sometimes not.

SHOPPING

Many good markets including the Saturday Market at San Angel; Merced Market (pottery) at Fray Servando and Av Anillo de Circunvalacion; Lagunilla (also known as Thieves' Market) at Allende and Ecuador. Just south of Plaza Garibaldi is an evening Artisans Market, 'not too expensive if you're careful'. Leather shops on Pino Suarez. Shopping also at the Central Crafts Market at Aldama 187; and the Indian Market, Paseo de la Reforma and Lerdo 13.

Books, guidebooks, American mags: American Bookstore, Madero 25.

MEDICAL SERVICES

American-British Cowdray Hospital, Observatorio and Calle Sur 136. Call 515-85-00 or in emergencies 515-83-59.

TRAVEL

Taxis: 4 types, drivers described as '99.9% cheats—best to find out roughly how much the journey should cost before taking it. Wherever possible, fight to the death!' Regular taxis have meters, and you pay 10% more at night. Jitney or 'pesero' taxis cruise the main streets; the driver's finger held aloft indicates that he has space among the other passengers, who fill the taxi like a bus. 'Taxi Metros' operate from bus stations into the city to Metro stops; agree on fare beforehand if possible. Outside hotels, etc, you'll find unmetered taxis; always agree on fare beforehand. 'Taxi meter or not, arrange price beforehand. Hard to bargain, you get overcharged all the time.'

Also streetcars, trolleys and buses; buses cost about 10 pesos. If time is short, Chapultepec Tours do a day tour: 15-52-48. 'If staying more than a day, buy a good street map—about 50 pesos (bargain).'

The Mexico City Metro, opened in 1970, is clean, fast and has 3 lines that cover all sectors of the city. Still incredibly cheap, under 2 pesos, book of 5 tickets about 10 pesos. 'The world's best transport bargain.' 'Use it whenever possible—the streets are absolutely choked with traffic.' 'Bad at rush hour.' Metro stops have artefacts uncovered during excavation of the Metro; Pino Suarez station has Aztec pyramid foundation and other objects, with more artefacts at Bellas Artes and at Zocalo, 3 models of the city—pre-Columbian, Colonial and modern.

When leaving the city, it is best to consult the Tourist Office for info.

For buses getting into or out of Mexico City: 4 terminals, each located near a Metro stop. North arrivals/departures at Terminal Central del Norte, 7 blocks from La Raza Metro station on line 3. (Also get there by bus, 'Insurgentes', to Insurgentes and Buena Vista). South: Terminal Sur, at the Taxqueña Metro stop, southern end of line 2. West: Terminal Poniente, at Observatorio Metro station, west end of line 1. East: Terminal Central del Oriente (also known as ADO), at the San Lazaro Metro station, to the east on line 1. 'At terminal it was possible to buy cheap Trailways pass.'

Airport service: take trolley bus to Metro station 'Aeropuerto', 20 pesos, and Metro to city. Takes 1 hr.

For bus and train discounts around Mexico during Mexican student vacations, get a SETEJ student card, Calle Hamburgo 273. 'Costs about 350 pesos but saves a lot.'

Central de Autobuses, Genova 2-H; a clearing-house for tickets and information on bus lines, English spoken, 5-33-04-15.

INFORMATION

Post Office on San Juan de Letran and Tacuba, has a *poste-restante* section where letters are held up to 10 days for you.

The *Excelsior* morning newspaper has an English page; the *Mexico City News* is an all-English paper with good travel section.

Mexican Government Tourist Bureau, Presidente Masaryk 172, north of Chapultepec Park—rather out of the way. Otherwise phone 250-0123 for English-language tourist information.

Tourist Police are seen along Reforma and Juarez wearing light blue uniforms with US/Canadian/British flag badges indicating that they speak English. Friendly, well-informed, they provide on-the-spot information.

GUADALAJARA. With three million population, Guadalajara is Mexico's second largest city, located 240 miles west of the capital. Once famous for its pristine skies, springlike weather and unhurried pace, its air is now sullied with smog and cacaphonious with construction and traffic. Guadalajara is still a good city for sidewalk cafe idling, especially around the Plaza de Mariachis, and for strolling. Among other goods, the city produces Mexico's *tequila*; Sauza and other distilleries offer free tours and samples if you can handle this Mexican 'white lightning'.

ACCOMMODATION

The bus and train stations are at the south end of Calzada Independencia; to reach downtown, head north past 2 roundabouts (called 'glorietas' in Spanish).

Hotel Central, 28 de Enero, opposite bus station. US $5 single, $8 double, another $3–$5 for rooms with bath. 'Not luxurious but clean and convenient.'

Hotel San Jose, 25 de Febrero 116, opposite bus station. 17-27-26. US $5 single. 'Very nice place, clean and friendly.'

Hotel Occidental, Huerto and Villa Gomez, left of C Independencia past 2nd glorieta. 13-84-06. US $5 singles. 'Excellent value, very clean, central.'

Hotel Americanos, Hidalgo between C Independencia and Teatro Degollado. About US $4.50 for single with bath. 'Clean, friendly—new. Best value in town by far. Worth the walk to get away from noisy, dirty bus station area.'

Morales Hotel, 243 Av Corona, overlooking San Francisco Park, downtown. Colonial mansion, charming patio and rooms. Singles with bath US $7.50, doubles $10-$15.

FOOD

The huge Libertad Market at Calzada Independencia and Mina is good for cheap food and indeed cheap anything: it's the biggest open market in the Western Hemisphere, more than 1000 stalls covering 4 square blocks.

Reasonably priced cafes, restaurants along both Av Vallarta and Av Juarez.

Torino's Restaurant, on Degollado nr Juarez. 'Best place we came across.' Comida corridas (daytime only) from 140 pesos.

OF INTEREST

Palacio de Gobierno, facing Plaza de Armas between Morelos and Pedro Moreno. The 17th-C palace of the governor of Jalisco has early Orozco murals including one of Hidalgo brandishing a flaming sword against the Nazis.

The cathedral at Liberation Plaza off Morelos, was built in the same century and has fine views from its twin towers.

The **painter/muralist Jose Orozco** lived in Guadalajara and the house in which he did some of his work, at Aurelio Aceves 27, is now a **museum**. Open 1pm–5pm weekdays except Mon, 10am–2pm Sun. Paintings, murals, personal effects. Orozco died in Mexico City in 1949. The street runs off Juarez at the beautiful Glorieta Minerva fountain.

Regional Museum, 1 block north of the Palacio de Gobierno. Has Spanish painter Murillo's *Assumption of the Virgin*, 10 other Murillos, plus Spanish, Mexican art. Closed Mon.

Nearby and beautiful **Lake Chapala** is famous for its fish. On its shores are dotted primitive Indian villages as well as heavily American retirement communities. Buses leave the Central Camionera every ½ hr from 7am to 9pm. Stay at the Casa de Huespedes 'Las Palmitos', Juarez 531. 'Cheap, pleasant, not far from lake shore.'

Near Guadalajara is **Tonala**, a most interesting village which is entirely given over to family arts and crafts workshops; their specialties are papier-mache, pottery and brass, of good quality, subtle workmanship. Take the 2½-peso bus from C Independencia and Juan Manuel that's marked 'Ruta 110, Section 6' to get there. Tonala is 10 miles away and the trip takes about 40 minutes.

'SE of Guadalajara and SW of Morelia is **Uruapan**. Nearby is the **Paricutin volcano** which last erupted in 1943 and destroyed a whole village except for a church. In the village of **Angahuan** you can hire a horse and ride to the church or walk (2½–3 hrs round trip) or you can go up to the crater (6–7 hrs there and back). It's a fantastic trip. Take the Los Reyes bus from Uruapan: 1½ hrs over a bumpy track, 70 pesos each way. Nowhere to stay at Angahuan: at Uruapan we stayed at the Hotel Tivoli on the plaza, US $7 double with bath. We ate in the Hotel Progreso on Calle 5 de Febrero, a good comida corrida for about 150 pesos. Hotel looked lovely with patio, fountain, bright and airy—didn't look expensive.'

Patzcuaro is 125 miles SE of Guadalajara as the *cuervo* flies and 24 miles east beyond Uruapan. About half-way between Guadalajara and Mexico City (near Morelia), and could be visited enroute. The town overlooks Lake Patzcuaro, highest in Mexico. 'An old colonial town rather than a colonial city, it's an agreeable place with interesting corners. Frequent ferries cross to Janitzio Island rising steeply from the lake with lovely views from its highest point. Indian fishermen living on the island are famous for their butterfly nets (now used for photogenic rather than practical matters).'

Wide choice of hotels in Patzcuaro; Meson del Gallo at 20 Dr Cross, has singles from US $9, doubles from $10, pool, bars, English-speaking staff. Buses from Guadalajara via Uruapan, or from Mexico City via Toluca and Morelia. Food: 'Try street stalls—excellent value.' Lake Patzcuaro is famous for its whitefish.

INFORMATION
Tourist Office, Av Juarez 638; phone 14-27-02. 9am–3pm, Mon–Fri, 9am–1pm Sat. 'Best month to visit is Oct for their festivals. Pick up details from tourist office.'

QUERETARO.
One hundred and thirty-seven miles northwest of Mexico City, Queretaro is a town with a fascinating history. Hidalgo launched Mexico's fight for independence here in 1810; the Treaty of Guadalupe Hidalgo, ending the Mexican War with the US was signed here; the Emperor Maximilian was executed here in 1866; and the present Mexican Constitution was drafted here in 1916.

Tucked away off main streets are numerous little plazas and cobblestoned by-ways, hidden pools and streams of tranquillity. Queretaro is often given a miss or visited only cursorily by tourists in a rush to get to Guanajuato or San Miguel and thereby preserves a freshness of atmosphere. 'This town is the best I've been to in Mexico. Clean, beautiful and very friendly. So nice after Mexico City. People open and spontaneous—I was dragged into a bar by the market, fervently embraced, and regaled with tequila.'

ACCOMMODATION
Hotel Hidalgo, Madero Oriente 11. Phone 2-00-81. Nr main square. About US $7 single, $11 double with bath. 'Looks a bit posh from outside but backpackers welcome. Clean and comfortable old colonial style building. Same prices as Gran Hotel nearby on the Zocalo.'
Motel Azteca, Kilometer 236, Highway 57 (need car). 2-20-60. Singles US $8 and up, doubles $10–$14.

FOOD
La Flor de Queretaro, Juarez Norte 5. A large selection of inexpensive dishes.

OF INTEREST
The **Cerro de las Campanas** (Hill of Bells) just outside town is topped by a large statue of Juarez, just below which is the spot where Maximilian, ruler of a briefly dreamed Empire of Mexico, was shot by firing squad. An Expiatory Chapel, built by the Austrian government, contains portraits of Max and Carlotta, and engravings of the execution scene.

The local museum at Corregidora 3, contains further Max-memorabilia including his coffin. Also has interesting comparative displays of Mexican and European paintings matched period for period. Open 10am–2pm, 4pm–6pm daily. 10am–3pm Sun. Closed Mon.

The Convent of Santa Rosa de Viterbo was built in the 18th C by Mexico's greatest religious architect, Eduardo Tresguerras.

Aqueduct, built 1726–35, 6 miles in length, some arches 55 ft high. It ends in the cloisters of the **Convent of Santa Cruz**. The convent and its church are open to visitors. Here in 1693 was established the first college for missionaries in the Americas. In 1863 the convent was HQ and then, briefly, the prison of Maximilian.

SAN MIGUEL DE ALLENDE. One of three Mexican towns declared a National Monument, San Miguel is a treasurehouse of art, past and present, from its Colonial palaces built by silver-rich aristocrats to its Instituto Allende, which draws art students and painters from all over the world. Its setting is one of great beauty, with steep cobblestoned streets climbing a mountainside, six hours north of Mexico City off Highway 57. Despite the high proportion of American students, writers and artists, the village maintains an engaging, slightly Bohemian air.

ACCOMMODATION
Hotel Hidalgo, Calle Hidalgo 22, under US $5 single with bath, about $8 double. 'Still clean, pleasant and cheap.'
Hotel Quinto Loreto, Calle Loreto. Doubles about US $10. 'Really excellent place. Beautiful garden, swimming pool. It's paradise.'
Hotel Sautto, Hernandez Macias 59. 2-00-52. About US $8 double with shower. 'Clean, quaint—rooms open out onto courtyard with gardens and parrots in cages.'
Posada de las Monjas, Canal 37. 2 blocks from centre. 2-01-71. Singles from US $6, doubles from $11. Atmospheric, a former convent of *monjas* (nuns).

FOOD/OF INTEREST
Cafe Colon, San Francisco 21. 'Good food, reasonable prices, quick, friendly service.'
The Parroquia, unique among Mexican churches for being designed by an untutored Indian architect in French Gothic style.
Instituto Allende, founded in 1938, has become a well-known arts and crafts school, which also draws many foreigners (especially Americans) to its writing classes and Spanish language studies. The number of students in town keeps long-term rents low but demand high.
Sanctuario de Atotonilco, just outside town, houses collection of popular art associated with the Revolution.
'A road from San Miguel to Guanajuato passes through **Dolores Hidalgo**, where a plaque in the parish church marks the spot where Miguel Hidalgo rang the bell to start the fight for independence.'

GUANAJUATO. Just west of San Miguel and 250 miles north of Mexico City, Guanajuato is another Spanish colonial town whose mines once supplied one-third of all the silver in the world in the 16th–18th centuries. Its picturesque site is a canyon so steep that auto traffic is confined to one street. Known for its cultural activities, especially the International Cervantes music and drama festival in April and May, Guanajuato also has the ghoulish pleasures of mummy-viewing, a collection of local citizens preserved in an extraordinary fashion by the climate.

ACCOMMODATION/FOOD

Casa Kloster, Calle de Alonzo 32, 2-00-88. US $5 per person in this bright pension. Also try the Hosteria del Fraile, 2-11-79, and Hotel San Diego, 2-1300. Information pillars along Av Juarez give prices and locations of local hotels. Avoid festival times here unless you have a booking.

The cafeteria at the University of Guanajuato on Positos is cheap and congenial.

OF INTEREST

For a great **view of the town**, walk up Calle Sopena from the Jardin de la Union, turn right up the Callejon del Calvario and up the steep winding path to the **statue of Jose Barajas**, also known as Pipila. Barajas was the young miner who on Hidalgo's order set fire to a strategically-positioned grain warehouse in which Royalists were hiding during the War of Independence. The restored warehouse, the **Alhondiga de Granaditas**, is now a museum. On Calle Canitos, it contains exhibits on Hidalgo, pre-Columbian relics and samples of local crafts, 20 pesos. Closed Mon. 'If your only day in Guanajuato is Mon, go look at least at the courtyard and the lovely colours in the stone.'

Interesting buildings include: the **Iglesia de la Compania**; the **church of San Cayetano**, called La Valenciana, after the silver mine across the street; **Teatro Juarez**, where some of the world's greatest artists once played and sang; the ruined **Teatro Principal** and **Placita de Mexiamora**, enclosing a haven of green-lawned tranquillity. **Diego Rivera** was born in the house (now museum) at Calle de Positos 47.

Mummies. Over 100 of the local citizenry are on display as *momias*, preserved by the climate. Their mummified state was first discovered when the town ran out of cemetery space and dug up those folks whose families had failed to pay maintenance costs for 5 years. Guanajuatans quickly agreed that there's nothing like a mummy for paying the bills, thus the display which costs you 20 pesos to view mummies with and without clothing, some with mouths soundlessly agape. Deliciously spooky. In basement cavern at El Panteon cemetery, 1½ kms SW of the main plaza. Daily 9am–6pm. If locked, wait around until someone shows up and lets you in.

There are many old **silver mines** around the town, some still in operation, none reachable by public transport however.

INFORMATION

Tourist Office at 5 de Mayo and Juarez. Maps showing places of interest. 'English not always spoken and maps have no street names! Rather more useful are the 40 guides employed by the bureau who will show you the town free provided you bump into one. Try looking lost at the bus station.'

TOLUCA. At 8760 feet, Toluca is the highest city in Mexico. This capital of the State of Mexico lies about an hour's drive west of Mexico City with magnificent scenery in-between.

The main attraction is the Friday market, the stall-keepers mostly Indians, the regional specialties straw goods, papier mache figures and sweaters. The last might come in handy as summers are mild and winters often downright chilly. Before risking the shirt off your back in bargaining, go to the Museum of Popular Arts and Crafts where an adjoining Government store sells many of the goodies you'll see at the market at very reasonable prices. If you can't knock the stall-keepers lower than the Government, you'll know you're being screwed.

Three miles north of town on the Queretaro road is the Calixtlahuaca archaeological zone where digging is still in progress.

OF INTEREST

Museum of Popular Arts and Crafts, ¼ mile east of bus station. Contains regional crafts, replicas of Mexican kitchens, a cool airy place to take a breather. Open 9am–2.30pm weekdays, 10am–1pm, 4pm–6pm Sun. Closed Sat.

Calixtlahuaca is best reached by taxi; the most interesting structure unearthed is the circular pyramid.

TRAVEL

In Mexico City: take Metro line 1 to Observatorio station, then take bus from Observatorio to Toluca, about 1 hr, 70 pesos.

TAXCO. Beyond Cuernavaca and about 130 miles from Mexico City, Taxco sits high in the Sierra Madres and is Mexico's silver centre. Views in any direction are marvellous, and the town itself charmingly enbalmed in the colonial period by order of the Government, which in making it a National Monument has prevented the construction of modern buildings.

The narrow streets are roughly cobbled, the roofs tiled red, the twin-spired ornate Santa Prisca church illuminated at night. 'One of the prettiest towns in Mexico, set in magnificent countryside. Be sure to climb up to the top of the town for the view below.'

ACCOMMODATION

Hotel Agua Escondida, on Spratling by the Zocalo. 2-01-70. About US $7 single, $11 double with bath. 'Very comfortable, nice situation, good views.'

Posada del Jardin, Celso Munoz 2. 2-00-27. Along the street on the left flank of the Santa Prisca. US $7 and up single with bath. 'Clean, peaceful with wonderful mountain views from balcony patio.'

Santa Prisca Hotel, 1 Cena Oscuras, 2 blocks off plaza. Small rooms giving onto patio, good location, unpretentious and very Mexican. From US $20 per person with 2 meals included.

OF INTEREST

There are at least 300 **silver shops** in town, many of them fascinating one-man design factories. No bargains, however; even Mexico City sells silver jewellery cheaper.

TRAVEL

From Mexico City: take Metro to Taxqueña and Terminal Sur, where you catch the bus. Enroute, it may be worth stopping at **Cuernavaca**, a sleek summer resort once favoured by Aztec emperors, Cortez, Maximilian and Carlotta and most recently and briefly the Shah of Iran.

PUEBLA. Eighty miles east of Mexico City, Puebla is approached over a route recommended for its varied, sometimes wild and mountainous scenery. As you draw nearer, the volcanoes of Popocatapetl (dormant) and Iztaccihuatl (extinct) rise snow-capped into view.

Nine miles west of Puebla, just off the main road, is **Cholula**, a pre-Columbian religious centre second only in importance to Teotihuacan with over 400 shrines and temples. The Spaniards destroyed most of them and built Christian edifices on their ruins. The Pyramid of Tepanapa here is the largest in Mexico; a Spanish shrine and marvellous view are met at the top. 'In the nearby villages of Tonantzintla and Acatepec are churches with beautifully tiled walls and richly decorated interiors.'

Puebla itself is renowned for its ceramics, which decorate fountains, houses and patios, and for its 60 churches, the more noteworthy of which have their facades or domes completely covered with locally made polychrome faience. Puebla is also the home of a succulent dish called *mole* (that's *mo*-lay), made of turkey, chocolate, chilis and other puzzling but delicious things.

ACCOMMODATION
Hotel Colonial, 4 Sur 105, 42-49-50. 1 block from bus station. From US $7 single, $15 double. 'Full of character.'
Hotel Latino, 6 Norte 8. 41-23-25. On same block as bus station. US $8 single or double, with bath.

OF INTEREST
The Cathedral. 'Second only to St Peters in Rome. Magnificent Mexican baroque carvings and numerous beautiful chapels.' Begun in 1562 at the command of Spain's Phillip II and completed just over 100 years later.
Santa Monica Convent, 18 Poniente 103. Mexican law once prohibited convents, but this one operated secretly from 1857 to 1935, when it was discovered by government officials. Kept as found, it's now a museum, open daily 10am–5pm.
In the vicinity of Santa Monica is the **onyx workshop area**.
The best **market** is along Av 8 Poniente, from Calle 7 Norte to Calle 5 de mayo.
On the hill NE of Puebla, about 2 miles from the Zocalo, is **Ft Loreto**. Here on 5 May, 1862, 2000 Mexican troops defeated a French force of 6000 (part of Maximilian's attempt to establish an empire in Mexico), a date recalled with great national pride and responsible for all the '5 de Mayo' streets in Mexico. Entry 10 pesos.

INFORMATION
Tourist Office, Av 5 Oriente 5. 46-12-85.

VERACRUZ. Ever since Cortez put ashore on Good Friday 1519, the Rich City of the True Cross has been the main point of invasion and principal port of Mexico. The Spanish shipped most of their gold and silver out of here, an activity that did not escape the attention of pirates. These, as well as the regular forces of France and the United States, invaded and sometimes ransacked the port on half a dozen occasions. A producer of fine cigars and sugarcane, Veracruz shows echoes of Havana in the old days, a humid, sometimes rough and raucous city with a strong Mardi Gras tradition.

ACCOMMODATION

Hotel Central, Av Diaz Miron 1612, next to Central Camionera bus station. 3-22-22. Doubles from US $11; add a dollar for AC. Not at all central as the bus station is south of downtown, but perhaps convenient for the weary.

Hotel Santillana, Landero y Coss 209, at Dehesa. 2-31-16. US $5 single, $7 double with shower. In the market area.

There's a CREA Youth Hostel in Veracruz; enquire at the Tourism Office. Rates are about US $6 for rm and meals.

OF INTEREST

El Tajin. The ruins of this Totonac holy city surround the 7-storey Pyramid of the Niches, whose name derives from the 366 niches believed to be linked to the Toltec calendar. The Veracruz Indians were obsessed with ball games and from this area came the rubber to make the balls. Engravings at El Tajin clearly show that games were no light matter; some of the losers were ritually decapitated (just as at Mayan and other sites).

Beaches: The best are Mocambo and Boca del Rio, both reached by bus which runs along the sea front. Somewhat muddy, beaches here have shark-infested waters. Wise to enquire *Hay tiburon?* before plunging in.

ENTERTAINMENT

Mardi Gras in Veracruz could well be the best in the hemisphere. 'Friendlier than New Orleans.'

INFORMATION

Tourism Office, Palacio Municipal (city hall), Plaza de Armas, downtown. 2-16-13.

TRAVEL

Frequent buses to and from Mexico City, twice daily to Oaxaca, 3 times daily to Merida.

Train station is downtown on the harbour; direct trains to Guatemala but difficult connections to Merida, requiring a train change in the middle of the night.

OAXACA. Located about 330 winding miles south of Mexico City, the principal city in south Mexico lies in a semitropical valley surrounded by beautiful jagged peaks. For over 2000 years, this region has been the domain of the Zapotec Indians, who in 1806 produced Benito Juárez, Mexico's Abraham Lincoln. The city is noted for a variety of crafts from leather goods to cottons to hand-carved knives, all of which you can see at the Saturday market in the southwest corner of Oaxaca. But five miles from the city is the greatest attraction: the Zapotec religious centre and necropolis of **Monte Alban**, towering 1300 feet above Oaxaca.

A beautiful, narrow mountain road zigzags up to Monte Alban, suddenly opening out onto the great square of this religious acropolis. The summit of the mountain was levelled to provide a platform for pyramids, sanctuaries, observatories and palaces. The magnificent perspectives along the north–south axis are broken only by Building J, looking curiously like the prow of a ship and in fact a great astral observatory used to work out the Zapotec calendar.

Mitla, at a further distance from Oaxaca, was the centre of the

Mixtec world. Between AD 900 and 1200, the Mixtecs moved in on Zapotec territory, consolidating their conquest by diplomatic inter-marriage with the Zapotec. Consummate artists, the Mixtecs had no peer in ceramics, turquoise mosaics and goldwork. When the conquistadores came this way, Mixtec princes were living in numer-ous palaces, although only one remains well-preserved today. Each facade is decorated with tiny mosaics forming diamond, coil and key-like patterns symbolising, in highly stylised form, the Plumed Serpent.

Many of the treasures of both Mitla and Monte Alban are on view in the Oaxaca Regional Museum in town. Be sure to see the treasure of Tomb Seven, an immense quantity of gold and turquoise jewellery, quartz and pottery found in the grave of a prince and rivalling in splendour the Tutankhamun find.

ACCOMMODATION
Lots of cheap hotels in the market area (Aldama and 20 de Noviembre).
Hotel Pasaje, Calle Mina, 1 block south of Aldama, US $5 double. 'Friendly, clean with a talking parrot named Lorenzo.'
Hotel Rex, 308 Calle Las Casas Colon, nr market. US $6 single, $9 double with shower. 'Good value, popular with foreigners.'
Hotel Veracruz, next door to 1st class bus station; turn left out of station. US $7 single, $11 double. 'Excellent value.'

FOOD
'In the market (mercado) are hot food stalls where dishes are prepared before your eyes. Similar to Plaza Garibaldi.'
'The Restaurant Colonial, nr Zocalo, can be recommended.'

OF INTEREST
Oaxaca Regional Museum, Calle de Manilico Alvarado, next to Santo Domingo Church. Open 9am–1pm, 4pm–6pm, Tue–Sat; 9am–1pm, Sun/holidays. 40 pesos entrance, 10am on Sun. Students 10 pesos anytime.
Rufino Tamayo Museum of Pre-Hispanic Art, Av Morelos 503, nr Zocalo. Open 10am–2pm, 4pm–7pm daily, closed Tue. 10 pesos, students 5. 'Well displayed col-lection of exceptional and striking pre-Columbian art. Much more impressive than the archaeological exhibits at the Oaxaca Museum as it is primarily artistic in intent.'
Monte Alban, 5 miles out of town. Parts of the city date to 500 BC. Excavations are still underway. Entrance 40 pesos, 15 on Sun. No student discount. Buses at 10.30am, 1.30pm, 4pm, 40 pesos return, from Trujano 607. 'Best site in SW Mexico.' You can also take the 1-hr walk back to town.
Mitla. To the southeast, only partly excavated. Buses (2nd class) from terminal at the end of Calle Trujano, take 1 hr, cost 35 pesos each way. 'Mitla is not very impressive, but you can stop along the way at the Tree of Tula, 2500 years old with a 43-yard girth, and at the crossroad to Yagul (1½ mile walk), a lately discovered ruin in magnificent surroundings with long, beautiful views.'

ENTERTAINMENT
'Oaxaca is deservedly popular with tourists, especially at Christmastime. The Feast of the Radishes on 23 Dec and Christmas Eve festivities provide 2 successive evenings of great interest in the Zocalo.'
Free band concerts in Zocalo most evenings.

SHOPPING

'There's a small market by the cathedral where you can see Indians weaving things you'll see done nowhere else.' In villages around Oaxaca you can buy wares directly from the Indians cheaper than at the market, eg serapes at Teotitlan del Valle, left off the road enroute to Mitla; dresses and blouses at San Antonio Ocotlan, south of Oaxaca. The whole area is renowned for weaving.

INFORMATION

Tourism Office, nr cathedral at Independencia and G Vigil.

TRAVEL

The train from Mexico City runs overnight: 'Sleeping cars are old British Pullmans, very aristocratic.' Departs 5.30pm, arrives (in theory) at 8am. 'Usually much later.' The bus allows you to do it by day, 9 hrs, 'nice scenery'.

Both train and bus stations are outside the downtown area; easiest to take a taxi, about 50 pesos to the Zocalo. Otherwise, catch buses marked 'Col America' or 'Col Reforma' left out of the bus station, to get to the centre. From the train station, take the bus marked 'Estacion', which runs along Av Hidalgo to the Zocalo, or 'Centro', which runs along Aldama.

From Oaxaca (altitude 5070 ft) on, the road to the isthmus and southeast Mexico is downhill, lower altitudes meaning greater heat and humidity.

SOUTHEAST MEXICO

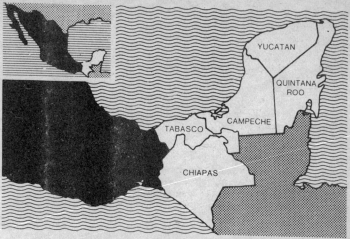

The five states making up southeast Mexico contain some of the most beautiful, varied and untouched territory in all of Mexico: lush orchid jungles, cool mountain highlands, arcing waterfalls, bone-white beaches, delta river country, tiny offshore islands. But the great Mayan ruins and the artistry and colour of their present-day descendants are the chief draws of the region.

From the isthumus, you can either make the coast-run down into Guatemala via Highway 200, or choose the superlative uplands route that takes you through bustling oil city Tuxtla Gutierrez and picturesque San Cristobal de las Casas on Highway 190 (the Pan-American Highway).

Not all of the enormous region is worth exploring, however; the Tabasco coastline, Villahermosa and environs are full of oil fields. Further south, large portions of the Yucatan peninsula have little to interst the eye, a monochromatic sameness of low tropical brushland.

SAN CRISTOBAL DE LAS CASAS. Spanish colonial in appearance, San Cristobal's position in the lovely green Jovel Valley has made it a major trading centre for numerous Indian tribes of the Chiapas. Every day is market day here and you'll see Tenejapas in black serapes, Chamulas in white wool tunics, Zincantan Indians in red-striped gowns, together with some of the finest crafts and the most luscious produce to be found anywhere. A very fine spot, even with Instamatics snapping away.

ACCOMMODATION
Posada del Abuelito, Tapachula 18, US $4 single, $2 for dorm. 'Pleasant, visitors made welcome but on opposite side of town from bus station.'

Casa de Huespedes Pola, Calle Insurgentes, opposite Hotel Capri. US $3 per person.
Casa de Huespedes Santa Lucia, opposite 2nd-class bus station. US $3 single, $6 double. 'Clean.'

FOOD
La Olla Podrida in Diego Mazariegos, off the south side of Zocalo. Variety and good quality, including 'magnificent vegetable soup which is a meal in itself'.

INFORMATION
If you take a fancy to the area, go to the Libreria El Recoveco bookshop on the Zocalo and get the guidebook to San Cristobal, which contains much useful info and is written by an Englishman. Incidentally: 'This is the best bookstore between Mexico City and Guatemala.'

TRAVEL
The bus terminal is 5 minutes outside town. Buses to Palenque leave at 7am, 1.15pm, take about 7½ hrs, cost 140 pesos, from 2nd-class depot. 'The road is mostly unpaved through superb and lush mountains.' 'The road via San Cristobal is the nicest way to go to Guatemala.'

VILLAHERMOSA.
The area around Villahermosa marked the westernmost limits of the Maya Empire. Today the Gulf Highway (180) running from Mexico City out to the Yucatan passes through here. Located inland by a river, the city is nearly at sea level and consequently quite hot in summer. The local oil boom has made this a busy, increasingly sprawling and expensive place where budget accommodation is now hard to come by. A pause but not a stay is recommended.

ACCOMMODATION
Casa de Huespedes Mary, Calle Juarez 225, nr the market. US $6 single, $8 double. 'A friendly place.'

OF INTEREST
La Venta, 84 miles west, was the home of the Olmecs, generally considered the originators of pre-Columbian civilisation in Mexico. In the 1950s, the archaeological finds at the site were transferred *in toto* to escape destruction from oil drilling. The colossal Olmec heads of basalt can now be seen at the archaeological museum in Mexico City, at the Tabasco Museum in Villahermosa, and at Parque Museo La Venta, on Rt 180 nr the airport. Apart from the 3 heads, the site has stelae, altars, mosaics and a model of the original site. Self-guiding tour map, 2 pesos; entrance 10 pesos, free Thur. Open 8.30am–5pm daily.
Tabasco Museum, Allende and Guerrero off the Zocalo. After the Archaeological Museum in Mexico City, perhaps the best in the country with carvings, murals, ceramics and artefacts of Mayan, Mixtec, Olmec, Zapotec, Aztec and other Indian cultures. Open 10am–1pm, 5.30pm–8.30pm daily. 30 pesos.

PALENQUE.
About 80 miles inland from Villahermosa are the jungle ruins of the Classic Mayan sacred city of Palenque, which flourished AD 300–700. Built on the first spurs of the Usumacinta Mountains, the gleaming white palaces, temples and pyramids rise from the high

virgin jungle. Its visually compelling site, its compact size (the excavated portion is about three-quarters of a mile by half a mile, out of the 20-square-mile extent of the city) and its dramatic burial chamber make Palenque, to many minds, more outstanding than Chichen Itza. The 1950 discovery of an ornate crypt containing fantastically jade-bedecked remains of a Mayan priest-king revised archaeologists' theories about Mayan pyramids, which were earlier believed to be mere supports for the temples on top. Although it's a hot, steep and slippery journey, you should climb the Temple of the Inscriptions, descend the 80 feet into its crypt to view the bas-reliefs: chilling and wonderful. NB: here you'll see the relief of *Chariot of the Gods* notoriety. Tomb contents are in Mexico City museum, however.

ACCOMMODATION
Posada Alicia, outside centre, 10 minutes' walk from bus. 'Reasonable rates for room and board which in Palenque is rare. The cognoscenti stay at Alicia's.'
Hotel Misol-Ha, Juarez nr plaza in front of church. 5-00-92. US $6 single, $9 double. 'Comfortable, well-run, everything in working order. Best value encountered in Mexico.'

OF INTEREST
The ruins—'most spectacular we saw in Mexico'—are served by local bus, 20 pesos, leaving from main street several times daily.

TRAVEL
Train station is about 3 miles outside town; take local bus, 20 pesos. There are 2 trains to Merida: 2nd-class cheapo taking 20 hrs and a 'rapido', with both 1st and 2nd class, taking 14 hrs. Delays common. The 2nd-class bus leaves at 5pm and takes about 8 hrs.
Air connections: daily flights from both Mexico City and Merida to Villahermosa.

MERIDA. Called the 'white city', partly for its tidiness, more so for the striking regional dress worn by both men and women, Merida is the Yucatan capital and bustles at 300,000. Built upon the remains of Tiho, a Mayan settlement, Merida looks Spanish colonial (lots of fine churches and homes) but still sounds and tastes Mayan. Don't fail to sample Yucateco cooking: *sopa de lima* (chicken with lime soup), *huachinango* (red snapper fish), *panuchos* (Yucatan version of a taco) and Carta Clara beer.

A delightful city for strolling, which will enable you to see details such as the clay animal sculptures sometimes placed at street corners in lieu of signposts. Local crafts include all items made from sisal fibre—hammocks, shoes, baskets and panama hats (here, not Panama, is where they come from). Merida makes a good base for exploring the Yucatan peninsula, most especially the ruins of Uxmal and Chichen Itza.

ACCOMMODATION
NB: Merida is laid out on a grid system. All streets are numbered *calles*, whether north–south or east–west; the N–S ones are even-numbered, the E–W ones, odd.

Hotel America, Calle 67, 500. 1-51-33. US $4 single, $6 double with shower. 4 blocks from ADO terminal. 'Central, clean and very friendly.'

Casa de Huespedes, Calle 62, nr Hotel Oviedo which is 515 on Calle 62. US $6 double.

Hotel Chac-Mool, Calle 54, 474 at Calle 55. US $6 single, $8 double, with pool. 'Marvellous after the train journey from Palenque.'

Gran Hotel, Calle 60, 496. 1-76-20. US $7 single, $12 double with bath. 'Impressive but fading grandeur.'

Sevilla Hotel, Calle 62, 511. 1-52-58. AC rooms, US $10 single, $12 double, $13 triple. Central.

Hotel Caribe, Calle 59, 500. 1-92-32. Single US $10. 'Clean, friendly, helpful. Central, with pool.'

FOOD
Los Almendros, Calle 59, 434 (between Calles 50 and 52). 'Try this for inexpensive Yucatan specialties—excellent!'

Hotel Flamingo Restaurant, Calle 57, 485. Tasty 4-course meals under 150 pesos.

Café Alameda, Calle 56, 518. 'Very inexpensive Lebanese.' Closes around 7.30pm.

OF INTEREST
Casa de Montejo, main plaza on Calle 63. Built in 1546 by Don Francisco de Montejo, Merida's founder, and occupied until recently by his descendants. Open 10am–noon, 4pm–6pm. Closed Sun. 35 pesos. The plateresque doors are its best feature.

Merida Market, juncture of Calles 60 and 65, sells embroidered shirts, blouses, leather goods, hammocks, etc. 'Knock them down to at least half their asking price.' 'Good market, very friendly people.'

Free outdoor concerts Sun eves at Parque de las Americas and Thur eves at Parque Santa Lucia on Calle 60.

INFORMATION/TRAVEL
Yucatan Weekly Bulletin, English info on local events, customs, sights; available free in hotels.

Flights from Mexico City and from Miami and elsewhere in the US.

To and from Mexico City, there are trains (30 hrs) and buses (22 hrs).

UXMAL and CHICHEN ITZA. Along with Palenque, Uxmal was one of the chief Mayan cities and the showpiece of that civilisation's finest architectural accomplishments. Chichen Itza, on the other hand, was first a Mayan city and later occupied and built on by the belligerent Toltecs, becoming in the process the most stupendous city in the Yucatan.

Fifty miles of good road lead from Merida to **Uxmal**, where the clean, open lines of the ancient city create an impression of serenity and brilliant organisation on a par with the greatest cities of either Eastern or Western civilisation at that time. As white as marble and gilded by the sunshine, the limestone complex of the Nunnery Quadrangle, the Palace of the Governor and the Pyramid of the Soothsayer has a fascinating and almost modern beauty. The friezes of the palaces are decorated with stone mosaics in intricate geometric designs.

In the 10th century the peaceful Maya world was disturbed by the warlike Toltecs, who came down from their northern plateau capital of Tula to conquer the Yucatan cities and make **Chichen Itza** their southern capital. The monumental constructions you see are both Mayan (eg El Caracol, the circular observatory) and Toltec (eg the Court of a Thousand Columns). The city is dominated by the Great Pyramid with its stairways of 91 steps on each of four sides, making a total of 364. That figure plus one step round the top totals the days in the year.

ACCOMMODATION
You'll probably make Merida your overnight base, but there are a few cheap digs at Chichen and Valladolid as well.
Posada Novello, at Piste, 1 mile from Chichen going toward Puerto Juarez on the main road. US $4 per person.
'Plenty of cheap accommodation in Valladolid'—see also Travel.

INFORMATION/TRAVEL
35 pesos for each site. English-language books on sale.
Buses to Uxmal, Chichen Itza leave from Merida depot at Calles 68 and 69. Several buses, both 1st and 2nd class, starting from 8am, go to Chichen and/or Uxmal, some of them tours taking in other sites in the area as well. If you have to choose between Chichen and Uxmal, go to Uxmal.
'It's possible to get an early bus from Campeche, spend several hours at Uxmal, continue to Merida on a bus leaving the ruins at about 2.30pm.'
'The main road from Merida to the east coast of the Yucatan passes right through the Chichen ruins. Beyond the ruins is Valladolid with plenty of cheap digs, frequent buses.'

ISLA MUJERES. Off the northeast corner of the Yucatan peninsula, this 'island of women' got its name when the first Spaniards found a large number of female idols here. The beaches are excellent, the foliage semi-tropical, the island beautiful, the pace relaxed and informal. Don't expect an undiscovered paradise, however. Granted, the big bucks go to Cancun and Cozumel, but Isla Mujeres is getting the overflow and the purple prose in US travel mags, with attendant hotel-building and price-climbing.

ACCOMMODATION
Hotel Caracol, Av Matamoros 5, off Av Madero. US $7 single, $11 double. 'Spartan.' 'Inexpensive restaurant in lobby.'
Poc-Na Hotel, 70 pesos per person for dorm. 'Beautiful place, clean and safe.'
Roca Mar Hotel, Av Nicolas Bravoy, Zona Maritima. 2-01-01. On cliff. Singles US $12, doubles $16 up.
Camping: on North Beach. 'Take your own tent and hammock—cheaper. Or rent hammock on spot.'

FOOD/OF INTEREST
Be sure to sample *caracol* (conch meat), either grilled or made into marinated *ceviche*; turtle steak: barbequed barracuda; and good local beer—León Negro is a full-bodied ale.
Fishing, swimming and snorkeling are the things to do; you can rent equipment locally. Snorkeling is magnificent.

On the other side of the island are a few **Mayan ruins**, a 3-hr walk there and back, but a pleasant excursion—just you and the iguanas.

TRAVEL
For Isla Mujeres, take the bus from Merida to Puerto Juarez, where it connects with a ferry costing 60 pesos. (Usually a wait).

If you do decide to go to Cozumel, make sure you get the bus for Playa de Carmen, not Ciudad de Carmen. 'Don't get on the bus going the wrong way from Merida like I did.'

From Isla Mujeres there are boats to Cancun, where you can take a boat to Cuba or fly to Mexico City or Miami. Trendy and artificial Cancun does have an excellent Youth Hostel on the beach; 250 pesos for dorm bunks, up to 590 for dorm with 3 meals. No curfew, has bar, disco, pool, tennis courts, 15-day stay limit.

'For anyone wishing to cross from Yucatan into Belize, the bus leaves the border town of Chetumal at 10am on Tue, Thur and Sat, arriving Belize City about 4pm.' But otherwise, 'Stay away from Chetumal. Lousy people, even more lousy town. If desperate, stay at the Hotel San Jorge, US $6 double, clean, with fan and shower.'

APPENDIX I

TABLE OF WEIGHTS AND MEASURES: conversion to and from the metric system

Mexico employs the metric system. **Canada** is adopting it piecemeal and the **United States** as yet uses it only within its National Parks.

Temperature

Fahrenheit into Centigrade/Celsius: subtract 32 from Fahrenheit temperature, then multiply by 5, then divide by 9. *Centigrade/Celsius into Fahrenheit:* multiply Centrigrade/Celsius by 9, then divide by 5 then add 32.

Linear Measure

0.3937 inches	1 centimetre
1 inch	2.54 centimetres
1 foot (12 in)	0.3048 metres
1 yard (3 ft)	0.9144 metres
39.37 inches	1 metre
0.621 miles	1 kilometre
1 mile (5280 ft)	1.6093 kilometres
3 miles	4.8 kilometres
10 miles	16 kilometres
60 miles	98.6 kilometres
100 miles	160.9 kilometres

Weight

0.0353 ounces	1 gram
1 ounce	28.3495 grams
1 pound (16 oz)	453.59 grams
2.2046 pounds	1 kilogram
1 ton (2000 lbs)	907.18 kilograms

Liquid Measure

1 US fluid ounce	0.0296 litres
1 US pint (16 US fluid oz)	0.4732 litres
1 US quart (2 US pints)	0.9464 litres
1.0567 US quarts	1 litre
1 US gallon (4 US quarts)	3.7854 litres
3 US gallons	11.3 litres
4 US gallons	15.1 litres
10 US gallons	37.8 litres
15 US gallons	56.8 litres

The British imperial gallon (used in Canada) has 20 fluid ounces and 4 imperial quarts and is equal to 4.546 litres.

APPENDIX II

CHEAP BUDGET MOTEL CHAINS IN THE US

Regal 8 Inn, PO Box 1268, Mt Vernon IL 62864. 800-851-8888.

Red Roof Inns, 4355 Davidson Road, Amlin OH 43002. (614) 876-9961.

L–K Motels, 1125 Ellen Kay Drive, Marion OH 43302. 800-848-5767.

Budget Host Inns, 2601 Jacksboro Highway, Suite 202, Ft Worth TX 76114. (817) 626-7064.

Knights Inn, 6561 E Livingston Avenue, Reynoldsburg OH 43068. (614) 866-1569.

Interstate Inns, PO Box 760, Kimball NE 69145. (308) 235-4616.

Econ-O-Inn, Box 2603, Fargo ND 58108. (701) 235-3141.

Thrifty Scot Motels, 1 Sunwood Drive, St Cloud MN 56302. 800-228-3222.

Exel Inns, 4706 E Washington Avenue, Madison WI 53704. 800-356-8013.

Econo-Travel, PO Box 12188, Norfolk VA 23502. 800-446-6900.

Days Inn, 2751 Buford Highway NE, Atlanta GA 30324. (404) 325-4000.

Friendship Inns, 739 South 4th West, Salt Lake City UT 84101. (801) 532-1800.

E–Z 8 Motels, 2484 Hotel Circle Place, San Diego CA 92108. (714) 291-4824.

California/Western 6 Motels, 1156 S 7th Avenue, Hacienda Heights CA 91746. (213) 961-1681.

Sixpence Inns, 1751 E Garry Avenue, Santa Ana CA 92705. (714) 540-0985.

Imperial 400 Inns, 1830 N Nash Street, Arlington VA 22209. 800-531-5300.

Chalet Susse International, 2 Progress Avenue, Nashua NH 03060. 800-258-1980.

Save Inns, 100 South Trail, Suite 305, Sarasota FL 33577. 800-323-1776.

Scottish Inns of America, 104 Bridgewater Road, Knoxville TN 37919. 800-251-9513.

Super 8 Motels, PO Box 1456, Aberdeen SD 57401. 800-843-1991.

Motel 6, 51 Hitchcock Way, Santa Barbara CA 93105.

Write to any of the above for their directories of motels, containing full information on rates, facilities, locations and often small maps pinpointing each motel.

INDEX

CORRECTIONS AND ADDITIONS

The detail, accuracy and usefulness of future editions of this Guide depend greatly on your help. Share the benefit of your experiences with other travellers by sending us as much information on accommodation, eating places, entertainment, events, travel, etc, as you can.

These printed forms are supplied to get you started. Additional information should be sent on separate sheets of paper. *Please do not write on the back of these forms, nor on the back of your own sheets.* When making remarks, bear in mind that a comment on a hotel like 'Quite good' or 'OK' conveys little to anyone—be as descriptive and as quotable as you can, though also be concise. *Free copies of the next edition of this Guide will be sent to those readers who have contributed most to its updating.*

Completed slips should be sent to: the General Editor, The Moneywise Guide to North America, Travelaid Publishing, PO Box 369, London NW3 4ER, England *or* Presidio Press, 31 Pamaron Way, Novato, CA 94947, USA.

EXAMPLE

Place: LONE PINE, CALIFORNIA   Date: 4 July

Subject: ACCOMMODATION

~~Correction~~/Addition	Remarks
Redwood Hotel, 123 Spruce Ave. (209) 976-5432 $20 single, $22 with bath. $25 double, $27 with bath.	Clean, bright, though simply furnished. Vibrating water bed. Friendly and helpful. Turn left out of bus station and walk two blocks.

Place: Date:

Subject:

Correction/Addition	Remarks

- -

Place: Date:

Subject:

Correction/Addition	Remarks

- -

Place: Date:

Subject:

Correction/Addition	Remarks

Place: _____ Date: _____

Subject: _____

Correction/Addition	Remarks

- -

Place: _____ Date: _____

Subject: _____

Correction/Addition	Remarks

- -

Place: _____ Date: _____

Subject: _____

Correction/Addition	Remarks

Place: Date:

Subject:

    Correction/Addition   Remarks

- -

Place: Date:

Subject:

    Correction/Addition   Remarks

- -

Place: Date:

Subject:

    Correction/Addition   Remarks

Place: Date:

Subject:

Correction/Addition   Remarks

Place: Date:

Subject:

Correction/Addition   Remarks

Place: Date:

Subject:

Correction/Addition   Remarks

Place: Date:

Subject:

Correction/Addition   Remarks

- -

Place: Date:

Subject:

Correction/Addition   Remarks

- -

Place: Date:

Subject:

Correction/Addition   Remarks

Place: Date:

Subject:

Correction/Addition	Remarks

- -

Place: Date:

Subject:

Correction/Addition	Remarks

- -

Place: Date:

Subject:

Correction/Addition	Remarks

Place: Date:

Subject:

Correction/Addition   Remarks

Place: Date:

Subject:

Correction/Addition   Remarks

Place: Date:

Subject:

Correction/Addition   Remarks

Place: Date:

Subject:

Correction/Addition	Remarks

Place: Date:

Subject:

Correction/Addition	Remarks

Place: Date:

Subject:

Correction/Addition	Remarks

Place: _____ Date: _____

Subject: _____

Correction/Addition | Remarks
_____ | _____

- -

Place: _____ Date: _____

Subject: _____

Correction/Addition | Remarks
_____ | _____

- -

Place: _____ Date: _____

Subject: _____

Correction/Addition | Remarks
_____ | _____